RESPONSE TO MODERNITY

STUDIES IN JEWISH HISTORY
General Editor: Jehuda Reinharz

OTHER VOLUMES ARE IN PREPARATION

RESPONSE
TO MODERNITY

A History of the Reform
Movement in Judaism

MICHAEL A. MEYER

OXFORD UNIVERSITY PRESS
New York   Oxford

Oxford University Press

Oxford   New York   Toronto
Delhi   Bombay   Calcutta   Madras   Karachi
Petaling Jaya   Singapore   Hong Kong   Tokyo
Nairobi   Dar es Salaam   Cape Town
Melbourne   Auckland

and associated companies in
Berlin   Ibadan

Copyright © 1988 by Oxford University Press, Inc.

First published in 1988 by Oxford University Press, Inc.,
200 Madison Avenue, New York, New York 10016

First issued as an Oxford University Press paperback, 1990

Oxford is a registered trademark of Oxford University Press

Library of Congress Cataloging-in-Publication Data
Meyer, Michael A.
Response to modernity.
(Studies in Jewish history)
Bibliography: p.   Includes index.
1. Reform Judaism—History.   I. Title.   II. Series.
BM197.M48   1988   296.8'346'09   87-29354
ISBN 0-19-505167-X
ISBN 0-19-506342-2 (pbk)

Illustrations are from the following sources: Mendelssohn, Frankel, Geiger. I. M. Wise, Einhorn, Wise Temple, Kohler, E. G. Hirsch, CCAR. HUC, Freehof, Silver, S. S. Wise. Mattuck-Montagu-Baeck, Emanu-El, UAHC, Eisendrath, Glueeck—courtesy of American Jewish Archives, Cincinnati; Jacobson, S. R. Hirsch, Sulzer, Synod—courtesy of Leo Baeck Institute Archives, New York (originals of Jacobson in Österreichische Nationalbibliothek, of Sulzer in HUC-JIR Library, New York); Yahel—courtesy of UAHC Archives, New York; Gamoran—courtesy of Rabbi Hillel Gamoran; Seesen Temple—*Bau-und Kunstdenkmäler des Herzogtums Branschweig,* 1910; Holdheim—*Liberal Judaism,* Fed. 1946; Berlin Reform Congregation Board—Arthur Galliner, *Sigismund Ster;* Mannheimer—*Leo Baeck Institute Year Book,* 1961 (original in Österreichische Nationalbibliothek); Vienna Synagogue—*Menorah,* 1926, p. 133; Montefiore—*CCAR Year Book,* 1938; Yom Kippur Worship—*American Jewess,* Oct. 1895.

2   4   6   8   10   9   7   5   3   1

Printed in the United States of America

To Margie the Rabbi,
Daniel in Israel,
Jonathan and Rebecca

Preface: Considerations
of Historiography

Well over a million Jews in the world today identify themselves religiously as Reform, Liberal, or Progressive. Although the vast majority live in the United States, some can be found in almost every major Diaspora community and also in the state of Israel. They represent that branch of Judaism which has been most hospitable to the modern critical temper while still endeavoring to maintain continuity of faith and practice with Jewish religious tradition.

A great Jewish historian of the nineteenth century, Heinrich Graetz, early in his career pointed out that Judaism could not be understood by philosophical analysis of its beliefs, but only by the study of its history. And indeed, Judaism has repeatedly lent itself to divergent, even contradictory intellectual systems; in modern times it has also been subject to a variety of definitions, sometimes straining, though seldom rupturing its sense of continuity. Similarly, Reform Judaism can scarcely be comprehended by reference only to its current spectrum of beliefs and practices. As a movement within Judaism which has prided itself on openness to the challenges that historical change poses for tradition, it especially requires the specific skills of the historian. In the space of two centuries the social and intellectual contours of Reform Judaism have been altered radically. In its present situation it embraces contradictory tendencies, and its very ideology of integrating tradition with a changing modern life posits that its character in the future will evolve in unforeseen ways.

Surprisingly, no full-scale history of Reform Judaism has been published since the first decade of this century. Those studies that we possess are woefully outdated, biased, and polemical, or—in the case of more recent works—deal only with a segment or an aspect of the subject. The prolonged reluctance to attempt an encompassing history is perhaps best explained by the formidable methodological problems discussed below. But an additional significant factor is the relative paucity of more narrowly focused studies on which a broad synthesis might be built. The historian of Reform Judaism soon discovers that in most instances there is little secondary literature on which to rely, no choice but to grapple with a sometimes overwhelming mass of printed and archival primary sources. It may well be that Jewish scholars of the next generation will be better equipped to undertake the broader task of synthesis. Yet neither Jewish history nor Reform Judaism is well served by having to rely on the general works currently at hand. The synthesis attempted here is scarcely definitive, but it does, I believe, advance our present state of knowledge and conception.

The methodological difficulties that confront the historian of Reform Judaism begin with the name itself. "Reform Judaism" designates a particular position on the contemporary Jewish religious spectrum represented by a broad consensus of beliefs and practices and a set of integrated institutions. While suited to the present, the term tends to limit and obscure its subject when it is employed historically. Not all Jews who advocated significant religious reforms during the last two centuries identified their position as Reform Judaism. In Germany the radicals took possession of the term as a self-designation; in England it identifies the more conservative movement. Initially, religious reformers aimed at effecting changes that would eventually be acceptable to all Jews, and only in the course of time did they make peace with the realization that they spoke for a mere segment of the community. Only gradually did a denominational entity emerge out of a larger, less crystallized religious movement.

Clearly another term than "Reform Judaism" is therefore preferable, one which broadly encompasses the modern effort to bring about Jewish religious reform and is not limited by self-designation or institutional boundaries. To go to the other extreme, however, and deal generically with all religious reforms in modern Jewry is to ignore the coherence of effort that did exist, the growing sense of common identity, and the gradual self-exclusion and separate institutionalization of more conservative positions. It therefore seems most adequate to speak of a "Reform movement," which eventually produced Reform Judaism. The capital "R" in this case does not at the beginning represent institutional identity, but simply a unity of purpose.

To designate the subject of this history as a movement is, of course, to associate it with other movements both outside and inside Judaism. Generally, movements set clear goals, which they either achieve or fail to reach. In American history, the Abolitionist movement and the Woman's Suffrage movement attained their objectives. Their development can be traced relatively easily and reaches a distinct climax with the passage of constitutional amendments. But other movements are less clearly focused, less consistent internally, and undergo basic changes in self-definition. The Zionist movement achieved only a portion of its original aims: it established a Jewish state but was unable to gather in most of the Diaspora. Throughout its history, adherents of Zionism have differed with regard to ultimate objectives, some setting socialism or theocracy alongside the national goal. Though occasionally still calling itself a movement, world Zionism in the past generation changed fundamentally; outside of Israel those who consider themselves Zionists mostly define that identification merely as being friends and supporters of the Jewish state.

The term movement is used less frequently in the religious than in the sociopolitical sphere, perhaps because the goals here are more diffuse. Yet religious movements do possess a sense of direction and, at least initially, a dynamism which makes "movement" more appropriate than any other designation. Protestantism was in its beginnings clearly a movement, setting itself apart from prevailing Christianity and seeking the restoration of an earlier, purer form. Later, as it became internally fragmented by denominationalism and unable to impose its views on Christendom as a whole, Protestantism was transformed into a branch of Christianity bent primarily on perpetuating itself within the basic framework laid down by the Reformation. This pattern seems to fit the Jewish Reform movement fairly well. It too intended initially to bring about changes that would affect all of Jewry within its sphere: it hoped to reform Judaism as a whole, to tear down much of the old and create a distinctly modified structure. Like Zionism and Protestantism, it succeeded only partially, giving up—or relegating to empty oratory—its ambition to win over all Jews. Yet, like Conservative Judaism (though not Orthodoxy), it has continued to use the term "movement" to convey a sense of dynamism. I have called it a movement in *Judaism,* rather than in Jewry, to emphasize its essentially religious character. However, this indicates no intent to neglect its social foundations. It was not merely a movement for doctrinal or liturgical reform unrelated to the realities of Jewish existence, and therefore its history cannot be adequately studied using only the tools of the history of ideas or the history of religions. It was a movement among Jews whose individual and collective motivations transcended the purely religious, even though they cannot be explained by simple reference to a fixed class orientation or to an overriding political purpose. It is only by attention to the interplay of idea and social situation that the Reform movement becomes fully comprehensible.

It is not possible to isolate a doctrinal essence of the Reform movement. While certain teachings, such as the historical nature of Judaism, progressive revelation, and universalized messianism, take firm hold once they appear, only the last is present from the start. Some tenets prominent at an early stage lose their significance or are even rejected in the course of time. The negative attitude toward the national component of Jewish identity is the best example. At times, especially among the laity, the rejection of Jewish national identity seems to have been the principal distinguishing feature of Reform or Liberal Judaism. But the turnabout on this issue in recent years has not significantly disturbed the continuity of the movement. One is thus required to trace the separate strands which at different times are woven into the movement, some of them eventually to change their hue or to be excised altogether. One cannot presuppose even a relatively uniform complexion for the entire history of the movement.

Instead of seeking its essence, it is perhaps more helpful to understand the movement in terms of dynamic tensions created by specific sets of polarities. Any list of such polarities is necessarily arbitrary and incomplete. Yet some of them are obvious. Perhaps the most basic set for the Reform movement involves its self-definition: Is the movement wholly continuous with Jewish tradition, a mere variant of earlier forms, or does it constitute a sharp break with the past, a radically new configuration? For it to stress only the elements of continuity has meant running the risk of losing separate identity, whereas strongly emphasizing the breaks has meant to flirt with sectarianism. A second set of polarities counterpoises authority (represented by revelation, tradition, and the institutions of the movement) with freedom of individual conscience. While a dialectical shift to the side of authority brings the Reform movement closer to orthodox religion, a powerful thrust in the opposite direction approaches anarchy. There have also been the ongoing tensions between universalism and particularism. Again each pole possesses its dangers, here complete loss of specific Jewish identity in the case of universalism and chauvinism when particularism reaches an extreme. It is characteristic of the Reform movement that it has shifted its ground repeatedly and dialectically along the axes represented by these and other polarities, seldom settling for long into any fixed position.

The origins of the movement are as difficult to determine as its essence. There is no decisive event or individual by which one can mark its onset, no sharp break with the past that leads forward to all that follows. As we shall see, Moses Mendelssohn favored a reform in current practice with regard to burial of the dead and believed the Jewish religion had to be purged of the dross that dulled its glory, but in general he pressed only for educational and cultural reforms while rejecting any conception of religious progress. Israel Jacobson instituted specific synagogal reforms, but he too lacked the typically nineteenth-century conception of religious evolution which was to characterize the rabbinical leadership among Reformers of the next generation. The beginnings of the movement are therefore best traced in the gradual rise of sentiment favoring proposals for doctrinal or practical religious reform prompted by increasing exposure to the world outside the ghetto whose values and demands, gradually accepted and internalized, were perceived to conflict with the inherited tradition. In time, various harmonizing and adaptive elements which later compose the movement coalesced and were transformed from individual opinion into collective statements, from proposals into institutions.

Scholarship on the Reform movement has tended to concentrate on focal events: controversies with the Orthodox, the establishment of new Reform institutions, rabbinical conferences, the adoption of guidelines and platforms. These attracted the attention of contemporaries and left behind compact nodules of literature. However, it is questionable whether in themselves they represent the most significant developments in the history of the movement. They merely convey to the public arena deep-seated and ongoing religious, social, and psychological shifts until then not collectively articulated. The public events present the results of what has less obviously occurred preceding them; they bring to awareness or seek to implement ideas that have been gestating in individual consciousness. Our historical image of the movement requires some adjustment of its contours, especially an elaboration of the processes underlying the focal events.

Attention must be given to two kinds of time: chronological and generational. The former is continuous and nonrepetitive. Actuated by external influences and its own inner dynamics, the Reform movement underwent continual change, so that its overall configuration was never the same. Yet it was also affected by the rhythmic and repetitive pattern of generational time. Again and again children grew up in Orthodox homes, rebelled or drifted away, some reaching the point where they cast their lot with efforts to reform Judaism in general or tried to find an already existing non-Orthodox religious expression of Jewish identity that addressed their own religious situation. Ongoing in one sense, the movement also continually experienced its rebirth, so that the literature is replete with the renewed expression of ideas that are patently old, yet put forward repeatedly with the fresh energy of newcomers who have ventured upon them in the course of personal odyssey.

There have been few fanatics in the Reform movement, few who made the reform of Judaism their life's passion. By its very nature, the Reform movement legitimated a reduced role for specifically Jewish activities in the life of individual Jews in order to make room for non-Jewish ones. One must therefore ask: How significant has the Reform movement been for its adherents? How deep have their commitments been to it? The answers seem to vary with time. At points of innovation and controversy the salience of Reform identification stands at a very high level, while in those periods when neither novelty nor agitation bring it to public attention a routinized and very segmental allegiance seems the norm for the vast majority. An accurate appraisal of the real historical and personal impact of the movement requires repeated consideration of its importance for Reform Jews.

Given the impossibility of fixing upon any one self-designation or religious idea in order to decide definitively what falls within and what outside the Reform movement, its boundaries must necessarily remain indistinct, and practical decisions about what to include and what to exclude in the history of the movement remain arbitrary. Most broadly conceived, the Reform movement might be understood to embrace efforts to establish any Judaism that differs from inherited forms and beliefs as a result of encounter with the modern non-Jewish world. Thus the Neo-Orthodoxy of Samson Raphael Hirsch would have to be given its place since it accepted modernity, although it disavowed most of the beliefs and practices associated with the Reform movement. Even more, the Positive–Historical trend of Zacharias Frankel in Germany and the Conservative movement of American Jewry would have to be included because they sought a reform of traditional Judaism, however much limited by ongoing loyalty to Jewish law. Yet the modern Othodox and the Conservatives each developed their own separate religious and organizational identities. They became rivals of the organized Reform movement even as they shared some of its principles. Thus, while the more traditional movements of Jewish religious modernization, especially their intellectual origins, cannot be wholly absent from a history of the Reform movement, they appear here principally to provide contrast. Like the secularists at the other end of the spectrum, they represent alternative, related responses to a common set of historical challenges.

Eastern European Jewry has generally been regarded as wholly outside the range of the Reform movement, although historians have traced the spread of the Jewish Enlightenment, the Haskalah, from Prussia on to Galicia and to Russia. Hungary has usually been set as the outpost on the eastern boundary. Yet not only were modernized services on the central European pattern instituted in several of the larger communities of the Tsarist Empire, but Russian Jewish thinkers and writers were animated by sentiments which in some respects closely paralleled those of reformers in the West, even as they differed in others. Although religious reform was far less decisive for Russian Jewry than for central European Jews, its limited penetration eastward and its failure to attract larger numbers there require careful explanation.

The conceptualization which thus emerges for our study may be summed up in this way: the Reform movement came into being gradually out of a coalescence of elements; it was subject to a complex dynamic of external and internal interactions and was renewed by recurrent generational breaks with tradition. It varied in relative salience among its adherents both at any one point of time and over time, extended from radical rejections of tradition to very mild ones, and eventually touched virtually all of Western Jewry. It coheres as a historical entity more on account of a perceptible center of gravity created by the overlap and abundance of significant elements than on account of fixed definitions or boundaries. Reconciled to this amorphousness of the subject, the historian can do no better than to keep sight of that center of gravity, subject it continually to analysis, and trace the shifting periphery of its influence.

In this study, I have chosen to focus on origins. Although the American Reform movement soon greatly surpassed its European antecedent, it was its heir in ideology and forms. The fundamental issues were first raised in Europe, especially in Germany; the first practical innovations occurred there. By the second half of the nineteenth century, when Reform began to emerge strongly in the United States, it had already disputed with its opponents over most of the important questions. Consequently, I give particular attention to the early European developments, thereafter—for both Europe and America—focusing only on significant new challenges, countertrends, and organizational developments. Frequently I try to show how the environment and particular situation of Jews in the various countries to which the Reform movement spread directly affected its local character and its chances of success, at the same time also examining the links that made it an international entity. I also give special attention to key personalities, for a movement cannot be understood apart from the character and quality of its leadership. However, for lack of sufficient perspective, I avoid evaluation of those individuals who still play a major role in Reform Judaism. Hence the last chapter is necessarily more impersonal than those that precede it.

This book ends with the mid-seventies of the twentieth century. At that point the dominant American movement had just adopted a new prayerbook and platform. It had elected new presidents of its seminary and its union of congregations. The succeeding, most recent period of Reform's history is not yet ripe for interpretation.

In place of a conventional bibliography I have appended a brief bibliographical essay tracing the general historiography of the Reform movement. References to more detailed studies, as well as to primary sources, occur in the notes. Where appropriate, I have given the notes a bibliographical character.

I wish to express my gratitude to colleagues, students, and friends who have aided me in various ways during the dozen years that this study was in preparation. Their stimulation and suggestions have been invaluable. Lest I forget one of them, I shall not attempt to mention all their names. However, I am especially indebted to four colleagues who read all or major sections of the manuscript. Professors Jakob J. Petuchowski and Barry Kogan critically analyzed the entire study; Professors Jonathan Sarna and Benny Kraut did the same for the chapters dealing with the United States. The title for the volume was a suggestion made to me by Professor Ismar Schorsch during a conversation in 1984.

My thanks are due, as well, to the research institutions whose obliging and extraordinarily helpful staffs made archival and rare materials readily available to me: the Jewish National and University Library and the Central Archives for the History of the Jewish People in Jerusalem, the Leo Baeck Institute in New York, and the American Jewish Archives and HUC-JIR Library in Cincinnati. I am grateful also to Donna Swillinger and Debra Poulter for their care and devotion in typing the manuscript.

A portion of this study was carried out under a grant from the American Council of Learned Societies, which made possible a semester free of teaching responsibilities. Most of the first two sections of chapter 2 appeared in slightly different form in *The*

Jewish Response to German Culture, whose editors, Professors Jehuda Reinharz and Walter Schatzberg, kindly agreed to republication.

I should also like to thank Professor Jehuda Reinharz for suggesting that my study appear in his series and for his editorial comments. It has been a pleasure to work with members of the staff and associates of Oxford University Press.

My debt to my wife, Margie, is beyond acknowledgment. To her and to our children this book is dedicated.

Cincinnati, Ohio   M. A. M.
August 1987

Contents

RESPONSE TO MODERNITY

Prologue: The Question of Precedents

It is a characteristic of reforming movements that they seek precedents. Unlike revolutions, they tend to stress continuity, links with the past rather than radical departure from it. From its beginnings, the Reform movement in modern Judaism was accused of sectarianism, of removing itself from the chain of tradition. Not surprisingly, its exponents were therefore perpetually concerned to show that they were merely elaborating elements found within Jewish history. They argued that religious reform had been indigenous to Judaism from earliest times and that they were simply giving new energy to currents that had dried up, mostly through persecution and isolation. Classical Judaism, they maintained, had been hospitable to reform. It was only with the authoritative codification of Jewish law in Joseph Caro's *Shulḥan Arukh* (The Set Table) in the sixteenth century that it had become stagnant.

In making their case, some of the Reformers were not averse to setting forth a one-sided, distorted view of Jewish history. In 1854 Rabbi Samuel Holdheim, the most prominent among the radicals in Germany, devoted two sermons to Johanan ben Zakkai, the first-century rabbi who witnessed the destruction of the Second Temple in the year 70 C.E.[1] In Holdheim's eyes, Johanan was a reformer because he recognized in the apparent catastrophe the working of God's providence and the need to reshape Judaism to fit the new circumstances of Jewish existence. Prayer and good deeds would now take the place of animal sacrifices; the new center at Yavneh, where the ram's horn would be blown even on the Sabbath (as it had been hitherto only in the Jerusalem Temple itself), would elevate Judaism to a higher level. In drawing the consequences from a divine act, Johanan was providing a model for nineteenth-century

European Jewry. As ancient Judaism once required radical adaptation to the new situation of the loss of its sacrificial altar, so did contemporary Judaism now require an equally radical response to unprecedented cultural and social integration. Holdheim's purpose was not to understand the ancient rabbi in terms of his own worldview—he ignored Johanan's hope that the Temple would be speedily rebuilt. Holdheim was trying to create a "usable past," which would justify his own program of reform.

A half century later, in a 1910 address to the Central Conference of American Rabbis, the American Reform rabbinical association, Rabbi Jacob Raisin argued that the term "reform" could properly be applied to many stages within the tradition itself.[2] He did not hesitate to assert that the book of Deuteronomy "was the first textbook of Reform Judaism." And so too, in Raisin's eyes, every attempt at adjustment or innovation was a reform qualitatively similar to the Reform movement of modern times. He swept nearly all the ancient "heros" into the fold: the biblical Prophets, Ezra, the Alexandrian philosopher Philo, and the Palestinian teacher Hillel. For him the Talmud was replete with reforms, as were the teachings and legal decisions of prominent figures in medieval Jewry. The nineteenth-century Reformer Abraham Geiger could thus be seen as someone who did not impose foreign values upon Judaism, but was merely a link in the chain of reform, "the new Hillel."

The historian—as opposed to the ideologist—is tempted simply to dismiss such self-serving attempts as essentially mythic in character and to begin discussion of the Reform movement with the challenges posed by modernity. To deal at all with earlier periods is to run the risk not only of superficiality but also of falling victim to unconscious prejudice. The degree to which Jewish tradition in premodern times was open to change remains a much disputed issue among thinkers of the various denominations in contemporary Judaism.[3] Yet it seems necessary for an understanding of the modern Reform movement to attempt at least a brief assessment of the extent to which it was in fact precedented.

What needs to be emphasized at the outset is that premodern Judaism was, of course, not Reform Judaism, and that biblical, talmudic, or medieval Jewish authorities were not religious reformers in the modern sense. The Reform movement was a particular response to a new set of historical circumstances that gradually emerged beginning in the late eighteenth century. It was the product of modes of thinking that did not exist earlier and cannot be read back into previous periods of Jewish history. Its origins do not lie in a rediscovery of forgotten elements in traditional Judaism. Such elements were sought, elaborated, and sometimes wrenched out of context when the need arose to find examples of reform in the past. But the indications of change were not inventions. Principles and practices which were later incorporated by the Reform movement can be documented in earlier phases of Jewish history. The configuration of Reform is surely new, but many of its components are not. They constitute a prehistory, a prelude that we must consider in order to measure the extent to which the Reform movement represents a novum in Jewish history.

In a sense, Jews in premodern times regarded their religion as eternal and unchanging. The revelation of the Written and Oral Law to Moses on Mount Sinai was complete, and in theory no Jewish leader was permitted to add to it or to subtract from it. All subsequent creativity in legal matters was conceived as an elaboration of the one-time revelation, which already contained, at least implicitly, a response to every novel situation. This viewpoint was most concisely stated in a well-known passage from the

Palestinian Talmud: "Even what a veteran student will one day set forth before his teacher was already said to Moses at Sinai."[4] Traditional Judaism did not weigh the claims of the law against the claims of the age. It could not consciously allow new external values to supersede those contained within. An important thrust of halakhic activity was to conserve tradition and to protect it from violation. The law was absolute and demanded complete allegiance; it could not in theory be compromised. Human beings had no right to tamper with it. It was, in the language of the Sages, "from heaven."

And yet if Jewish law was to be applied, it needed to adjust to changing historical circumstances. Thus it became necessary to uphold its immutable character while at the same time devising instruments for extending and appropriating it to deal with new situations. The early legists, the Tannaim (first and second centuries C.E.), developed hermeneutical rules by which the Written Torah could be elaborated from within its own text; they created a literature of interpretation, Midrash, which enormously broadened the scope of the Written Torah; and they resorted as well to legislation, Mishnah, not directly connected to the text of the Torah, in order to extend the application of the law yet further. In engaging in these forms of legal creativity, the Sages firmly believed that by their commentaries, enactments, and regulations they were only bringing to actuality what was contained potentially in the Sinaitic revelation. They were themselves links in a chain of tradition through which the Mosaic authority flowed from generation to generation.[5]

Complete identification with the spirit of the Torah made it possible for the early Rabbis in some instances to alter what seems to have been the plain meaning of Scripture or to enact legislation lacking any scriptural source.[6] Like the later Reformers, they were aware of the demands made by changing historical circumstances and found general sanction for their regulations in such biblical verses as: "It is a time to act for the Lord, for they have violated your teaching" (Psalms 119:126). They issued decrees for the sake of *tikun ha-olam* (the general good) or *darkhe shalom* (preserving peace among individuals).[7] A number of the early enactments and reinterpretations seem in retrospect quite radical. Well known is the sage Hillel's creation of a legal device, the *prozbul,* to make possible lending activity despite the biblical law (Deut. 15:2) which cancels all debts in the sabbatical year.[8] Certain biblical laws, which the Sages must have viewed as cruel, and hence in their plain meaning not the real intent of the Torah, were reinterpreted: the law of an eye for an eye and a tooth for a tooth became material compensation instead; the law requiring capital punishment for the rebellious son (Deut. 21:18–21) was so hedged about by restrictions as to be deemed, according to at least one of the sages, merely a stimulus to interpretation, not a law to be actually carried out.[9] The Talmud itself recognizes the tangible development of the law in a legend where Moses visits the academy of the second-century sage Akiba and is perturbed at his inability to understand the discussion that is taking place. He is calmed only when Akiba declares that the law in question originates in an explicit revelation to Moses at Sinai.[10] The Rabbis even allowed that contradictory positions, such as those taken on particular issues by the School of Hillel and the School of Shammai, could equally be "words of the Living God."[11] They insisted that legal decisions could be made only on the basis of majority decision of the Sages, not by producing a sudden theophany or miracle.[12]

Later authorities continued to broaden and extend the law, promulgating *takanot* (edicts) for their communities, which in some instances were observed widely and for long periods of time. Responsa were issued to deal with specific questions raised by unprecedented situations and sent to leading rabbis for resolution. Veneration for the dicta of earlier scholars was balanced by recognition that the legal process needed to be carried forward if Jewish law was to avoid atrophy.[13]

The Reform movement therefore did not confront a legal tradition which had been insulated from history, although its flexibility in practice had decreased in recent times, especially since the definitive codification of Jewish law in the sixteenth century. It could and sometimes did attach itself to certain tendencies within the Halakhah itself, although its opponents questioned the Reformers' good faith. However, Jewish law, while open to history, had developed basically out of an inner dynamic conceived as a process of unfolding, rather than out of a recognized dialectical relationship with its environment. When some of the advocates of modern Reform began to oppose its prevalent conservatism, to question the unity of Written and Oral Law as equal components of revelation, or to historicize the entire process of halakhic development, they created a real break with the Jewish legal tradition. To the extent that they attributed theological status to the spirit of the new age or to the conscience of the individual, they undermined the exclusive claims of Jewish revelation and created a form of Judaism that was radically new.

Not only with respect to its attitude toward Jewish law did the Reform movement combine elements from earlier contexts of Jewish history into a new configuration. A variety of themes, including the legitimate appropriation of religious ideas and practices from the non-Jewish environment, certain proposals regarding prayer, and a more positive assessment of the Diaspora, were present before the Reform movement adopted them.

Modern biblical scholarship has dwelt extensively on the high degree of cultural adaptation that characterized the society of ancient Israel within its Near Eastern context. Similarly, scholars dealing with the intertestamental and early talmudic periods have pointed to the influences of Persian, Greek, and Roman concepts in religion, law, and social custom. The degree to which foreign practices could legitimately be absorbed into the faith of Israel was a perennial issue between Kings and Prophets, Hellenists and Zealots, Sadducees and Pharisees. As Rabbinic Judaism became increasingly fixed and normative in the early centuries of the Common Era, variety diminished, but Judaism did not become monolithic, nor did it by intention or in effect ever insulate itself completely from its environment. Of course, the degree to which it remained open to ideas from beyond its own sphere varied greatly from one part of the Jewish Diaspora to another and in different periods of Jewish history. Generally, Judaism was more hospitable to external influence in those times and places where Jews were relatively less excluded from Gentile society, where social and sometimes intellectual relationships were possible despite the barrier of religion. Not surprisingly, those members of Jewish communities possessing the most contact with the outside world were the more likely to incorporate its values.

In medieval times the principal distinction among Jews was between those living in Franco-German lands, who in the later Middle Ages migrated eastward to Poland (the Ashkenazim), and the Jews of Spain (the Sephardim), who following their expulsion in 1492 scattered throughout the Mediterranean world and into other parts of Europe. Whereas the Ashkenazim lived within a Christian context, the Sephardim existed for long periods within a predominantly Muslim environment. It is among the latter that we encounter the greatest openness to the surrounding intellectual world. Medieval Jewish philosophy, culminating, though not ending, with Moses Maimonides in the twelfth century, developed within Spanish Jewry, as did Jewish mysticism. Both drew upon the heritage of the Classical world as well as contemporary currents within the religious environment.

Certain Jewish intellectuals in Spanish Jewry maintained a philosophical stance with regard to Jewish religion even after Spain became almost entirely Christian. They regarded observance of Jewish ritual law as merely instrumental, serving to sustain the bodily health which was necessary in order to engage in philosophy. They denied that divine providence extended to individuals and believed that prayer was useful only to "purify thought." Some did not wear the traditional phylacteries *(tefilin)* since they regarded them as mere external reminders of God's commandments and thought that the act of recollection could be better accomplished by words than by symbolic acts. For them regular public prayer became dispensable.[14]

Although the influence of philosophy remained limited to a particular stratum of Sephardi Jewry, Islamic customs affected the institutions of the entire community and sometimes influenced normative religious practice. Synagogues in Muslim Spain were built in the style of mosques, with an abundance of wall inscriptions and with women more strictly segregated from men than was true among Jews in the medieval Christian world.[15] In nearly all Islamic lands Jews washed their feet, as well as their hands and face, before prayer in the manner of the Muslims, a nontalmudic custom entirely strange to their Ashkenazi contemporaries. Maimonides' son, Abraham, went so far as to declare that the biblical dictum "You shall not follow their customs" (Lev. 18:3) did not apply to Muslims and that a Jew who imitated them did not violate this prohibition. Maimonides himself was concerned that Jewish religious practices should not evoke scorn in Muslim eyes. When it became common for worshipers not to pay attention when the silent petitional prayer *(tefilah)* was repeated aloud by the leader of the service, he ordained, in opposition to the Talmud, that the petition be said only once and in unison. Not only had the repetition become a prayer virtually said in vain; it had led Muslims to believe that Jews did not take prayer seriously.[16]

In the sixteenth and seventeenth centuries Sephardi Jewish communities received an influx of Marranos, Jews who had maintained a vestige of their religion secretly when forced to adopt Christianity and who now sought, when possible, to return to Judaism. Cut off for generations from specifically Jewish traditions, they were well acquainted only with the Bible and sometimes assumed that it alone represented the true Judaism.[17] Their influence in European Sephardi communities created a current of Biblicism which continued into the eighteenth century and was absorbed by certain of the Reformers, especially in England.[18]

Because Sephardi Jewry was generally more open to its cultural environment, because its decisions in matters of ritual law were for the most part less rigorous than those of the Ashkenazim, and because it was centered less upon the Talmud, the Sephardim frequently served the early Reform movement as a model. As we shall see, the first modern reformers adopted the Sephardi pronunciation of Hebrew, some of their prayer formulations, and the decorum of their services.

Yet the Ashkenazim too were influenced by, and borrowed from their environment, though perhaps to a lesser extent.[19] The edict forbidding polygamy attributed to the medieval authority Gershom of Mainz was most likely a reaction to the Christian milieu and was not recognized by Jews in the Muslim world. Similarly, it was the

Ashkenazim who adopted from Christianity the practice of lighting a *Yahrzeit* candle on the anniversary of a family member's death.[20] Numerous superstitions and cere- monies related to life-cycle events were taken over from the local population.[21] As synagogues in the Muslim world copied the style of mosques, those in Christian Europe were modeled on local churches, resembling them so closely that synagogue structures shed light on contemporary church architecture.[22] It is even likely that the Eternal Light—today standard in all synagogues, but first mentioned only in the sev- enteenth century—was taken over from similar lamps which hung in Catholic churches.[23] Long before the Reform movement, a synagogue in the city of Prague had installed an organ, which was played regularly on Friday evenings to welcome the Sabbath.[24]

Italian Jewry, a composite of Sephardi and Ashkenazi communities, was particu- larly sensitive and open to its cultural and religious environment. Despite ghetto walls, Italian Jews during the Renaissance maintained extensive contact with Chris- tians. Leon Modena's sermons, delivered in Italian, were attended by non-Jews, while he in turn went to hear the best known Christian preachers of Venice. Synagogue music was composed by the outstanding musician Salomone de' Rossi according to the most cultivated taste of the period. On the major festivals a trained choir sang in multipart harmony. The Italian Jews held that rejoicing with song was appropriate even after the destruction of the Temple and despite the Exile, as long as it served a religious purpose. Aesthetically pleasing song was a tribute to God. On the other hand, to "bellow like a dog or screech like a crow" was to disgrace the Jew in Gentile eyes.[25]

Among Italian Jews we also find the beginnings of the historical perspective that would later characterize the Reform movement. Leon Modena argued in a responsum that the dicta of the ancient Rabbis must be understood with regard to "the place, the time, and the person." According to Modena, the passage of time and the extension of the Diaspora necessarily rendered many of their prohibitions invalid. What was appropriate in one set of circumstances might be inappropriate in another.[26] The extraordinary Renaissance scholar Azariah de' Rossi went even further. While rec- ognizing that in matters of revelation the earlier the scholar the more authoritative his interpretations, he believed that in matters requiring speculative thought and prac- tical experience knowledge was cumulative, with those who came later building upon the achievements of their predecessors.[27]

By the seventeenth century, proposals and themes that become characteristic of the Reform movement appear frequently in the popular Jewish literature of central Europe. Moral treatises dwell upon the need for decorum during the worship service. They stress the validity of meaningful prayer in the vernacular for Jews who do not know the Hebrew language. An often reprinted Yiddish work of the seventeenth cen- tury, *Lev Tov* (A Good Heart), suggests to its readers: "Whoever does not understand the Holy Tongue should pray in whatever language he understands well. . . . Better— indeed, a thousand times better—is a very small amount of prayer which he under- stands, and therefore prays that little bit with concentration *(kavanah)*, than praying a great deal without understanding."[28] In fact, translations of the prayerbook into Judeo-German were commonly used by Hebraically ignorant German Jews in the pre- modern period, especially but not exclusively by women.[29] It was only when the Reformers introduced modern High German into the public presentation of the prayers and added newly composed hymns in that language that they broke sharply with tradition.

Similarly precedented in pre-Reform Jewry is a weakened sense of exile due to a more positive attitude toward the states in which Jews lived. Occasionally there were even extreme expressions. A prominent Jewish banker of Renaissance Italy protested: "I have no desire for Jerusalem; I have no desire or affection except for my native city of Siena."[30] The Sephardi community in Amsterdam early in the eighteenth century supposedly held that Amsterdam was its Jerusalem.[31] More representative is the position of the eighteenth-century German rabbi Jacob Emden. In commenting on the verse of the Passover Haggadah, which expresses the hope that although Jews today are slaves, next year in the land of Israel they will be free, he notes that the current exile is not similar to that in ancient Egypt when the Hebrews were in fact slaves. He adds: "It is a sign of God's providence that [the nations] allow us to dwell in their lands by God's mercy to us. Therefore, this cannot be considered slavery."[32] Emden did not, however, give up his hope for the return of Israel to Zion. It was only with the new prospect of political emancipation, which emerged after his death, that exile for some began to seem a totally inappropriate concept, one which should be removed from the liturgy.

These parallels from various periods of Jewish history—and the number of examples could easily be multiplied—indicate that the Reform movement was in large measure composed of elements that had appeared earlier in various premodern contexts. Thus it could and did find precedents for its proposals when it sought to present itself as continuous with the Judaism of the past. Yet the Reform movement was not an internal Jewish development. It came into existence out of confrontation with a changed political and cultural environment. Only after it began to elaborate its response to the new status of Jewry and attempt to reconcile the Jewish heritage with shifting religious sensibilities and values internalized from the modern world did the Reform movement set out to legitimate its novelty in terms of venerated tradition.

1

Adapting Judaism
to the Modern World

The Historical Background

The self-aware movement for religious reform, which emerged in the nineteenth century, appeared only after profound changes had taken place in the external situation of the Jews and in their understanding of themselves. It arose in response to historical trends that gained momentum during preceding generations, their combined impetus eventually producing a concerted effort to create new modes of religious thought and practice. While the most significant forces were those impinging on Jewish life from the outside, some of the groundwork for the Reform movement was laid by internal events, and even when external factors predominated, they effected change only gradually as their impact was carefully assessed by reflective individuals and accepted or rejected with less awareness by others. The significant stages and elements in this preparatory process provide essential historical background.

Scholars have attempted to trace the chain of causes producing the Reform movement as far back as the seventeenth century. The great scholar of Jewish mysticism, Gershom Scholem, persistently sought to show that the origins of both the Jewish enlightenment (Haskalah) and the Reform movement lay in Sabbatianism, the messianic movement which began with the turbulent career of Shabbetai Zevi (1626–1676).[1] Scholem searched for points of contact between Sabbatians and Reformers stretching down to the nineteenth century. It seems, however, that direct influence was most limited.[2] Early as well as later Reformers prided themselves on their rationalism; they could accept neither the idea of a miraculously appearing messiah nor the mystical doctrines that were used to justify his authenticity. Least of all were they able to muster enthusiasm for an imminent return to Zion, which would be led by the messiah. For the Reformers, messianism of the Sabbatian variety was more an embarrassment than a legacy. They did not see themselves as its continuers.

Yet the Sabbatian movement certainly played a role in preparing the ground for Reform. As Scholem pointed out, Sabbatianism divided the Jewish world for generations. Virulent polemics between Sabbatians and anti-Sabbatians rent Jewish communities into warring factions. In Germany a protracted dispute between two leading rabbinical authorities, Jacob Emden (1697–1776) and Jonathan Eybeschütz (1690/95–1764), over the latter's suspected covert Sabbatian sentiments created extreme bitterness and revulsion. Writs of excommunication were hurled back and forth. A community so divided was less able to oppose new ideas in its midst or to project the image of unified authority that might have suppressed emergent centrifugal forces. As a result of the Sabbatian controversies traditional Judaism lost respect in both Jewish and Gentile eyes. Beyond this, Sabbatianism presented an example of religious antinomianism. The Sabbatians subordinated observance of Jewish law to the word of the alleged messiah and to mystical interpretations. The later excrescence of Sabbatianism in the circles of the adventurer Jacob Frank (1726–1791) brought this antinomian tendency into certain central as well as east European communities. While Reformers had nothing but contempt for Frankism, and initially at least sought to enact their reforms within the framework of the Halakhah, Jewish law was no longer unchallenged as the bond uniting all Jews. It was therefore more vulnerable to a program of reform.

More significant than Sabbatianism as background for the rise of the Reform movement was the gradual penetration of European cultural elements into certain strata of central and west European Jewry, a process made possible by expanded social contacts with non-Jews. In the seventeenth and eighteenth centuries such contacts were most evident on the lowest and highest economic levels. Jewish beggars, vagrants, and other rootless elements, long known for their religious laxity, now appeared in large numbers, posing a severe problem for Jewish philanthropic institutions. Finding themselves with no source of charitable support, some joined criminal bands together with non-Jews. It was not unusual for them to be converted several times—without conviction—in return for material reward. A few dressed like Christians, wore no beards, spoke the local German dialect, and violated Jewish dietary laws.[3]

A similar process of acculturation was at work on the uppermost rungs of the Jewish economic ladder. Each of the numerous absolutist states which emerged in Germany following the Thirty Years War sought to strengthen its economic position and extend its political influence. For the sake of amassing wealth, rulers of both large and small states were increasingly willing to rely on capable Jews to perform a variety of financial and commercial functions. Drawn into the spheres of power and influence, these Court Jews to varying degrees adopted the mores of the non-Jewish circles in which they moved. They dressed stylishly, invited the aristocracy to their lavish homes, and employed Christian tutors to teach their children. Some remained scrupulously observant, others did not. One of the best known, the extraordinarily powerful Joseph Süss Oppenheimer of Württemberg (1698/99–1738), neither kept the dietary laws nor attended synagogue, even on the Day of Atonement.[4] But it would be an error to designate the Court Jews as precursors of the Reform movement, though some of its early leaders and participants were drawn from their ranks. They were rather, as Selma Stern described them, individuals caught between the Baroque culture of their court surroundings and the traditional life of the Jewish communities. They were often torn personalities in an age that lacked synthesis. Their two worlds remained incompatible; no universalistic ideology as yet established a common ground.

While the social extremes of German Jewry drifted furthest from the constraints of tradition, religious laxity was becoming more common also along the center of the spectrum.[5] Contact between Jews and Gentiles outside of business hours was becoming ever more common as was a more positive attitude toward the study of secular disciplines. In the course of the eighteenth century, the attraction of non-Jewish culture was increasingly felt. Some parents began to send their children to non-Jewish schools. A few Jewish students were studying disciplines other than the customary one of medicine at German universities. For a growing percentage of German Jewry secular interests, whether material or intellectual, were pushing aside religious ones. At the same time, Jewish institutions were becoming ever weaker. Higher Jewish education virtually ceased in Germany; rabbis as well as teachers soon came almost exclusively from Poland and the gap in worldview between them and the German Jews whom they instructed widened more and more. Boys often received only a minimal Jewish education, girls almost none. As early as 1785 one concerned Jew expressed severe distress at the lack of systematic religious instruction. "Why have we Jews," he asked, "been unable to match the other nations in the education of our children, to impress their hearts with the fundamentals of faith and imbue them with love and awe of God, so that they might know whom they bless as well as the foundations and principles of worshiping God and keeping His commandments?"[6]

When after the death of Frederick the Great in 1786 new opportunities for political and social integration seemed to lie open, there was no lack of Jewish intellectuals and businessmen in Prussia pressing forward to attain the removal of disabilities and full social acceptance. Their ambitions led them to see their Jewish origins as a misfortune. Since they found nothing of value in Judaism and everything worthwhile in the world outside it, being Jewish became a burden. Some of them converted during the next decades; others resentfully endured or cast off bit by bit a demanding religious regimen to which they lacked emotional and intellectual commitment. For a few, the ideas of the French Enlightenment became a substitute faith replacing belief in the revelation at Sinai. One such Jewish Voltairean felt that being a Jew meant being "cast into chains" by a religious system to which he did not subscribe.[7]

The authority of that system, represented by the rabbis, was becoming weaker as Jewish juridical autonomy was more severely circumscribed and the right to excommunicate either taken away or made practically meaningless. A 1792 Prussian rescript reflects the long apparent tendency of the absolutistic state to eliminate internal religious controls within the Jewish community, thereby hastening fragmentation. The decree required specifically that all coercion in matters of religious practice cease and that it be left to each individual head of a family to decide on matters of ritual observance.[8] The result was soon chaos. By the first decades of the nineteenth century religious harmony among some city Jews had ceased to exist even within individual families; children no longer shared the values of their parents. Varying degrees of observance without apparent rhyme or reason became characteristic in certain circles. While it soon became a common phenomenon in modern Jewry, such individual choice in religious matters was unprecedented in earlier times and seemed bizarre to contemporaries. One Berlin Jew observed that some of his coreligionists went to synagogue only once a year, others three times; they observed certain insignificant customs with great fervor while neglecting biblical prohibitions; parents sometimes refused to eat in the homes of their children or surreptitiously whispered grace over nonkosher meals.[9]

Thus the first religious reformers in central Europe did not confront a Jewish community which was united in its Judaism. On the contrary, many of its members were severely disoriented. While most Jews, especially in the smaller towns, remained more or less steadfast in their traditional faith and practice, the intensity of Jewish life in the larger cities had been much diminished and the communities factionalized. The impact of two complementary forces, both external, had become increasingly evident. The first was the policy of governments to reduce the sphere of Jewish autonomy and the effectiveness of Jewish community control. Thus dissent could no longer be suppressed, the walls of separation from the outside world no longer maintained intact. The second force was the more hospitable attitude toward Jews on the part of enlightened elements in Christian society.[10] It was the latter, based on universal, inclusive conceptions of humanity, which drew Jews into broader cultural identifications and soon made traditional Judaism seem excessively particularistic and inappropriate in the modern world. The role of Judaism in a socially, culturally, and (they hoped) soon also politically integrated Jewry became an ever more agitated issue requiring theoretical and practical attention. In Germany, during the last three decades of the eighteenth century, thoughtful Jews began to grapple with the religious issues.

Enlightenment and First Thoughts of Reform

Moses Mendelssohn (1729–1786), the first Jew to participate prominently in modern European culture, was a reformer of Jewish life, but—with slight exception—not a reformer of Judaism. By the example of his own life and through the circle of admirers who gathered about him in Berlin he advanced the intellectual integration of fellow Jews into their cultural milieu. Through his Pentateuch translation he encouraged the displacement of the Judeo-German dialect by High German, opening up new vistas in science and literature and breaking down the linguistic barriers between Jew and Gentile. Despite the persistence of anti-Jewish prejudice, Mendelssohn believed that the common ground of natural religion, accessible to all rational human beings, would eventually unify cultured humanity on the deepest level. He encouraged his disciples to modernize Jewish education and to expand the scope of secular studies. Unlike contemporary rabbis, he did not fear that philosophy would undermine Jewish faith. Judaism, to his mind, was wholly compatible with reason. It possessed no dogmas that ran counter to it; it promised salvation to the morally upright of all nations. What set it apart was the revelation at Sinai, where a particular law was given to Israel, binding the Jews to God in a lasting covenant.

Unlike some of his younger contemporaries, Mendelssohn remained steadfast in both faith and observance. He did not believe that Judaism required fundamental reforms in order to remain viable outside the spiritual ghetto. On the contrary, if it was properly interpreted, with due emphasis on its rational character and its universalistic elements, the Jewish religion could be shown to be more compatible with modern thought than most contemporary forms of Christianity. It was only in the practice

Moses Mendelssohn.

of their ceremonial laws that Jews were different and would always remain so. As an observant Jew, who was culturally, and to some extent socially, integrated into his environment, Mendelssohn came to serve as a model for the modern orthodox Judaism which developed in Germany two generations after his death. He was not, however, even a forerunner of the Reform movement. Mendelssohn lacked a notion of religious development. For him Judaism was static because it was eternal. Its truths had always been accessible to reason; its laws were revealed for all time. They stood above the vicissitudes of historical change. Appropriate for one age, they were—with perhaps slight modification—no less fitting and worthy of observance in another. Mendelssohn believed that Jews could not in good conscience free themselves from the obligation to keep the entirety of the law. Speculation on its significance was permitted but observance was required. Only God, through a new revelation, could alter what He had commanded at Sinai.[11] The radically changed situation of Jewry in Germany did not for Mendelssohn, as it would for others, possess the equivalent force of such a new revelation. It must be remembered too that Mendelssohn grew to intellectual maturity in an age before historical conceptions permeated philosophical thought and when the impact of modernity on Jewish life was only beginning to be felt.

Beyond this, Mendelssohn was a man of conservative temper, not given to radicalism in thought or action. He preferred, if at all possible, to avoid acrimonious controversy either with Gentiles or with fellow Jews. It was only when he was drawn into a dispute in spite of himself that he reluctantly took a position. On at least one occasion this occurred with regard to a matter of Jewish practice. The incident serves well as a measure of the limited degree to which Mendelssohn did favor reform. Moreover, the issue that it raised became the first touchstone, which for a generation separated champions of a rigid status quo from advocates of at least some degree of religious reform.[12]

According to Jewish law, it is prohibited, except under special circumstances, to delay burial of the dead beyond the day of death.[13] In Mendelssohn's time this proscription came under attack by Gentiles, who claimed that the fact of death could not be rapidly ascertained and that there was a real possibility the person might still be alive at the time of interment. When in 1772 the Jews of Mecklenburg–Schwerin were presented with a ducal edict requiring them to wait three days before burying their dead, they turned to Rabbi Jacob Emden and to Mendelssohn, requesting them to produce a memorandum for the government supporting the traditional position. The community saw in the edict an unprecedented interference in internal Jewish affairs and an attempt to force Jews to accept the Christian custom.[14] Emden's view, like that of the Schwerin community rabbi, Mordecai Jaffe, was clear cut: the existing custom must be preserved. Emden held that there could be no justification for even the slightest variation. If there were a danger to life in early burial, surely the Sages themselves would have recognized it. In matters of Jewish law, moreover, one did not take medical opinion into account lest "the very foundations [of the Halakhah] be weakened and its pillars tremble." Despite the fact that he possessed greater appreciation for most secular disciplines than did his contemporary colleagues, Emden believed that Jewish law could survive in the modern world only if it were kept wholly intact, removed from any confrontation with external knowledge or external values.

For all of his conservatism, Mendelssohn here differed with the Altona scholar, whom in general he respected highly. Although he acceded to the Schwerin community's request for a memorandum (in German) favorable to the traditional position, he also addressed a Hebrew letter to its leaders in which he took a quite different position. Mendelssohn did not believe that the duke's edict represented a serious threat to Judaism or that it imposed any violation of Jewish law. His letter began with halakhic arguments resting on authoritative sources, and in particular on the principle of preserving life *(pikuah nefesh)*. It went on to contrast the current custom with the ancient one of watching the body of a dead person for three days before final burial in order to determine if there were any renewed signs of life. The letter also drew on current medical opinion. In the end, Mendelssohn proposed a variant of the ancient custom—temporary interment above ground at the cemetery. He was calling for a return to the practice of a previous age, not for an unprecedented innovation. Yet even this mild proposal aroused suspicion. Acceptance of prevailing practice as normative in all matters was the hallmark of contemporary Judaism. Even a seemingly peripheral custom, such as making noise at the mention of the villain Haman during the reading of the Scroll of Esther on Purim, was not to be violated. Rabbi Moses Isserles, the great sixteenth-century Ashkenazi codifier, had noted in his glosses on the *Shulhan Arukh* with regard to this very matter: "One is not permitted to abrogate or to treat lightly any customs whatever, for not without some purpose were they instituted."[15] How much the more was this true of a matter like early burial of the dead, which, it was recognized, maintained its hold on the Jewish masses because of the kabbalistic belief that between death and burial the body was subject to attack by demons.[16] Mendelssohn was too much of a rationalist to accept such superstitions and too much a part of the modern world to declare medical knowledge irrelevant and potentially injurious for Jewish practice. Indeed, he earlier admitted having "detected human additions and abuses in my religion which, sadly, all too much dim its luster."[17] He believed strongly that the human mind must not be constrained by ecclesiastical coercion and thus urged the abolition of excommunication among all religious groups. While religious offenses had indeed been punished in ancient Israel, the Mosaic constitution—the Torah as a binding political document—was in existence no longer. Jews should now be forced to obey only the laws of the states in which they lived. Religion was left to individual conscience. Not only did Mendelssohn's views thus encourage the free expression of heterodox religious beliefs, they soon led to the conclusion—not accepted by Mendelssohn himself—that the Diaspora was a new stage in Jewish history for which the Mosaic law was never intended at all.[18] This was the position which had been taken by Spinoza a century earlier.[19] While Mendelssohn rejected it outright, some of his disciples did not.

Mendelssohn lived in a milieu that was not tolerant of the idea that a Jew might wholly participate in the social and intellectual life of non-Jews and still remain unchanged. Some, like the Swiss clergyman Johann Caspar Lavater, with whom Mendelssohn carried on a bitter controversy, held that full emergence from the ghetto necessitated inner and outer conversion to Christianity. More liberal spirits believed that, at the very least, the Jews would have to "improve" if they were to enjoy equal status with Christians. The term "reform" in this period was used in a broad sense to include all aspects of this transformation. The Jewish Enlightenment (the Haskalah) in Germany, which followed Mendelssohn's example, was undivided in advocating that the Jews undergo basic changes in their economic lives and their culture.[20] The maskilim, as they were called, favored broadening the Jewish occupational spectrum, encouraging Jews to take up crafts and agriculture and thereby eliminating the vices that often went along with petty trade or vagrancy. Jewish education too required reform. Mendelssohn's friend and associate, Naphtali Herz Wessely, made an eloquent plea for the introduction of secular studies into the Jewish curriculum following the Toleration Edict of Emperor Joseph II of Austria in 1781. New Jewish schools, incorporating secular education, were established in Berlin and elsewhere; the Hebrew periodical *Ha-Measef* was founded by disciples of Mendelssohn in part to broaden Jewish cultural horizons. The maskilim hoped that such changes would encourage governments to eliminate the economic and political disabilities under which Jews continued to suffer. Religious innovation was initially part of this larger Haskalah program. However, it soon became a specific and separate point of contention between moderates and radicals: Did the religion of the Jew likewise require "improvement"? In the generation after Mendelssohn a spectrum of opinion developed on this question, ranging from an undeviating adherence to Mendelssohn's own position to a call for fundamental change.

The notion that Jewish integration required a new look at the Jewish religion was raised among other issues and in a very friendly spirit by a non-Jew, Christian Wilhelm Dohm, in a famous tract favoring Jewish equality, *Concerning the Amelioration of the Civil Status of the Jews,* first published in 1781. A deist by belief and a practical statesman, Dohm had little regard for the historical differences among religions and hoped that good government and prosperity would weaken the influence of divisive religious principles. He was ready to admit that a Jew could strictly obey all of the ceremonial laws and still be a dutiful citizen, and he was even willing to allow Jews the legal autonomy which they had earlier enjoyed. But Dohm also assumed that once wider horizons were opened to them, they would of their own accord abandon many of their religious practices. "They will then reform their religious laws and regulations according to the demands of society. They will go back to the freer and nobler ancient Mosaic Law, will explain it according to changed times and conditions, and will find authorization to do so in their Talmud."[21] Dohm's book was widely read by the maskilim and some of them soon shared his expectations. Other Christian writers saw the reform of Judaism not as a by-product of their emancipation, but as its prerequisite. The outstanding philosopher of the age, Immanuel Kant, held that Jews and Christians could become brothers only if the Jews would purify their religious ideas and cast aside their outdated ritual.[22] After all, Christianity too was undergoing change.[23] This was a theme that continued to be sounded well into the nineteenth century. Jews became aware of the political significance of religious reform, and it entered into their thinking. It is after the death of Frederick the Great in 1786, when prospects for the improvement of Jewish status in Prussia seemed greatly enhanced, that Jewish proposals for their own reform, including the religious sphere, begin to appear. Yet on the whole, over the course of a long and wearisome struggle for complete emancipation in Germany, Jews refused to allow political considerations, however important to them, to dominate their religious thinking.[24] If they began from the mid-1780s to call increasingly for varying degrees of religious change, it was mainly because they had begun to internalize new religious and cultural values, which conflicted with elements of their heritage.

The Haskalah nestled within the orbit of the German Enlightenment. Unlike its French prototype, the *Aufklärung* was not antireligious.[25] It appreciated organized religion, provided that it maintained due respect for reason and individual autonomy. The enlightened churchmen in Germany, the "Neologists," gave little weight to inherited dogma, stressing instead the elementary rational truths of natural religion. The universalism of their faith, which stood in sharp contrast to earlier Orthodoxy and Pietism, seemed a model for Jews in the larger cities where Neology was most widespread. Young Jews absorbed a disdain for superstitious beliefs and the practices based on them and they became hospitable to a conception of religion that stressed virtue as its chief aim and associated ceremonialism with primitive faith. Even the most unprejudiced of the German enlighteners, Gotthold Ephraim Lessing, had connected historical Judaism with an earlier stage in the religious development of the human race, one which humanity had left behind.[26] The exponents of religious reform were influenced by Lessing's thinking. They too came to believe that Judaism in its inherited form did not belong to the modern age. What set them apart from Lessing was that, instead of consigning Judaism to the past, they sought to bring it into line with what they thought and felt were the essentials of religion for the modern human being.

The reconceptualization of Judaism which appears in Germany in the late eighteenth century follows a pattern evident earlier in Christianity. For Martin Luther, religion meant absolute obedience to God's will, the fulfillment of a supreme duty. Its purpose was service to God, not enhancement of personal life. During the next two centuries, however, the center of gravity in Protestantism shifted increasingly from an objective God-centered faith to one which focused on the individual's subjective religious conscience and quest for salvation.[27] By the eighteenth century religion was widely believed to further the achievement of a broad sense of spiritual contentment or happiness called *Glückseligkeit*. Judaism in Germany, like early Lutheranism, had paid little attention to the subjective religious state of the individual. Centering upon fulfillment of the traditional 613 commandments, it regarded observance as an end in itself, not the means to any other. That conception gradually changed in the last decades of the eighteenth century, as individual Jews began to ask themselves a novel question: Did the practice of their religion indeed provide spiritual fulfillment? Before the first practical reforms in the worship service were undertaken, a religious mentality emerged which made it requisite to measure traditions against a new standard located in the subjective consciousness of the individual. Repeatedly, as we shall see, the claims of tradition would be weighed against a religious goal called in German *Erbauung,* "edification." Customs and ceremonies that did not serve to uplift religious sentiments, the reformers would declare, must give way to innovations which through their aesthetic appeal and instructive value were capable of transforming the inner life of the individual.

Long before such considerations affected the worship service they had begun to influence the enlightened Jews' attitude toward traditional sources. The talmudic literature—the basis of Jewish law—was neglected by the maskilim in favor of the Bible. In part this trend was due, of course, to the Bible's status as the common heritage of Jew and Christian and also to its place as the "classical" text of Judaism in a time when classicism enjoyed intellectual vogue. But the contributors to the Hebrew journal *Ha-Measef,* who lavished their interest on biblical studies and sought to imitate biblical poetry, found the Bible as well a source of spiritual inspiration. Like the German philosopher and aesthete Johann Gottfried Herder, they perceived in its pages "the most ancient, innocent and perhaps heartfelt poetry on earth."[28] Initially they did not criticize the Talmud, but their preoccupation with the Bible, not as a legal document but as the spiritual treasure of Judaism, shifted the focus away from the normative authority of Jewish classical texts to their literary qualities and their value for religious exaltation. The newly gained aesthetic sense, first applied to the Bible, would later be focused on the worship service of the synagogue.

As religious and aesthetic values derived from the environment were increasingly internalized, contemporary Judaism was subjected to ever sharper critique.[29] Not only superstitious practices but the entire traditional Jewish life, lived with painstaking attention to every detail of the law, was stigmatized by extreme maskilim as grossly inappropriate to the present age. More moderate writers hoped that the duly constituted religious authorities might be persuaded to abolish at least some of the prohibitions that hindered Jews from full participation in society and were no longer regarded with reverence. One maskil, as early as 1790, proposed that instead of allowing events to take their course, fragmenting the Jewish community, the rabbis should "meet together and speak words of love to the people, easing the burden of superfluous [restrictions]."[30]

During the last decades of the eighteenth century, barely perceptible shifts of thought began to take place even among Jews who in most respects remained traditional. Later their ideas could be carried further by others, who felt less constrained. Mordecai Gumpel Schnaber (d. 1797), a physician born in Berlin who spent time in England and in Sweden before settling in Hamburg, provides a good example of such transitional thought. He developed no theory of reform nor did he urge any changes in religious practice; he drew heavily on authoritative figures from the past—especially Maimonides. Yet, while following Mendelssohn in recognizing the continuing validity and binding force of all the commandments, Schnaber gave extraordinary attention to the role of the Oral Law in adapting God's written word to changing historical circumstances. He distinguished between belief in the existence of God, which represents "the foundation of the Torah," and all the other mitzvot. And he added: "All the remaining commandments may change according to time for they are only matters of belief, but this foundation will not even for an hour cease to be true."[31] In good traditional fashion Schnaber concluded that the observance of one commandment was as important as that of any other. But he opened the way for more audacious thinkers to conclude that only what Mendelssohn had called the Eternal Truths, those attainable by reason, required adherence, whereas ceremonial observances were subject to reevaluation by Jewish scholars—if not indeed by every man.

As dissatisfaction with contemporary normative Judaism spread, it reached even to persons who were so closely connected with the rabbinical establishment, or dependent on the good will of traditional Jews, that their critical opinions had to be expressed in disguised form. Their views appeared in satirical writings published anonymously, ascribed to nonexistent individuals, or fictitiously attributed to historical figures. Only men of independent means, or unusual audacity, who could scorn community opprobrium, felt free to express their ideas openly and in their own names. Saul Berlin (1740–1794) was not one of the latter.[32] The scion of a leading rabbinical family and the son of Hirschel Lewin, rabbi of Berlin, he received a thorough traditional education and for a time held the rabbinate in Frankfurt-on-the-Oder. However, while in the Prussian capital, he gravitated into the Haskalah circle, and increasingly he was torn by doubt and ambivalence. In a satire defending the maskil Naphtali Herz Wessely and ridiculing the traditional educators (the *melamdim*), Berlin asked in mock horror: "Did he [Wessely], God forfend, trample upon such good and pleasant customs as swinging a chicken around one's head on the eve of the Day of Atonement, striking the floor with a stick at the mention of Haman on Purim, or eating the head of a sheep, cabbage, dates and green vegetables on the New Year?" If Wessely had violated such significant injunctions, Berlin tells his readers tongue in cheek, then certainly the attack on him would have been justified.[33] For years, Berlin's satire circulated in manuscript among those who sympathized with its tone and attitude; it could appear in print only after his death. Berlin did, however, publish a much larger and more ambitious work in 1793, which he claimed consisted of hitherto unknown but genuine medieval responsa, especially from the pen of Asher ben Yehiel (c. 1250–1327). In fact it was for the most part, or entirely, his own work. Realizing he could not win acceptance for his views if they were stated in his own name, Berlin resorted to the devious stratagem of pseudepigraphy. Perhaps because these responsa could be credible only if the tone were moderate (and later legal authorities did quote from Berlin), they were not only presented within the familiar medium of halakhic discourse, but they put forward deviant points of view only sporadically and sometimes hesitantly, hedging them about with conditions or contrary opinions. Nonetheless, Berlin did make his medieval authorities appear far more lenient than the contemporary Ashkenazi rabbinate. For example, the responsa allow Jews to shave their beards, if the shaving is done by a Gentile, and under special circumstances to ride on the Sabbath. They deem it as no matter of great concern if the worshiper omits some of the prayers, provided he says the remainder with proper devotion. They leave it to the individual to give up all those later customs which seem repugnant and contrary to the Talmud. Perhaps most remarkably, one of the responsa poses a possibility which could but refer to Berlin's own time: "If, God forfend, it

would be possible to imagine that an age would come when the laws and commandments of the Torah would bring evil upon our nation . . . or even when the individual
would in no way achieve happiness through them, we would have to remove their
yoke from our necks."[34] Berlin thus raised the frightening possibility that perhaps Jewish law as a whole no longer served its divinely appointed end. Quite explicitly he
made it subject to the goal of all religion, which, as we have seen, in eighteenth-century
Germany was conceived as personal spiritual fulfillment. Berlin was surely a tragic
figure who, like others to follow, was unable to overcome the emotional distress of his
break with the conventional Jewish thought and practice in which he had been raised.
In time he must have come to regard himself as beyond the bounds. Exiled to London,
he requested that he not be buried in a Jewish cemetery.

The mathematician and educator Lazarus Bendavid (1762–1832), another stu-

Another figure who eventually had to regard himself outside the Jewish pale was
Solomon Maimon (c. 1753–1800). A talented and original philosopher within the
Kantian tradition, this Polish Jew quickly left behind the world of east European
Jewry and gained access to Mendelssohn's circle in Berlin. As a rationalist who
believed that style of life must follow from philosophical position, Maimon did not
hesitate to draw out the practical consequences for himself and for others. Upon his
own reflection, he had eventually accepted Mendelssohn's position that the basic laws
of Judaism are those of the ancient state transplanted to the communities of the Diaspora. There they continued to be binding for all those who considered themselves
members of the theocratic Jewish polity and desired to enjoy its benefits. Unlike Mendelssohn, however, Maimon believed that excommunication for violation of the ceremonial laws was wholly justified since every polity possesses juridical rights. Maimon took a stance of either–or: there could be only one Judaism, to which faithful
Jews must wholly submit. He declared improper the behavior of those individuals
who for reasons of family attachment or personal interest continued to regard themselves as Jews and violated some of the ritual laws. To his mind, the only alternative
to complete religious obedience was to leave the polity entirely, either by joining
another or by remaining apart from them all. A rebellion against traditional Judaism
was justified only when it was total—when, for example, it led to the adoption of a
rival worldview such as paganism or the religion of philosophy. The latter, consisting
simply of pure natural religion—rationally founded belief in God, human perfectibil-
ity, and immortality—was in fact Maimon's own position.[35] He was not a reformer of
Judaism. In fact, his arguments for excluding a third possibility between orthodoxy
and apostasy would later be used by the opponents of the Reform movement.

The mathematician and educator Lazarus Bendavid (1762–1832), another student of Kant, did not accept Maimon's absolute dichotomy. Instead he tried to root
natural religion in biblical Judaism. It would thus become possible to give up deeply
resented ritual laws without thereby either abandoning all historical religion or converting to Christianity. Writing in 1793, he put it negatively: "Insofar as the Jews do
not intervene in the reforms which will be or have been undertaken on their behalf
by abolishing the senseless ceremonial laws, which are wholly inappropriate for present times, insofar as they do not establish among themselves a purer religion more
worthy of the Father of all—the pure teaching of Moses—they will necessarily, even
after acceptance of baptism, remain indifferentists and injurious as citizens of the
state." Bendavid believed that among the German Jews a few truly enlightened individuals had emerged who were attempting to retain a connection with the Jewish religious and moral tradition. They distinguished themselves from a larger, no less assim-

ilated group which was falling victim to the temptations of a hedonistic, unprincipled life held out to the increasingly affluent Jewish bourgeoisie. But though the former group appreciated religious values, they had given up most or all of the rituals, and Bendavid thought it was not possible to put them into the same religious category with Jews observant of all the biblical and rabbinic laws. They were, he said, "equally far removed from Judaism and from indifferentism." Like Maimon, Bendavid regarded Jewish law as indivisible; one accepted or rejected it in its totality. But the enlightened Jew, who abandoned the law, could at least remain on the periphery of the Jewish community by affirming natural religion as the foundation of Judaism, the central teaching of Moses.[36]

The main problem with Bendavid's position was its artificiality. Moses was not an early incarnation of eighteenth-century philosophy, his teaching was not equatable with natural religion. Moreover, a philosophical faith was as easily attributable to Jesus as it was to Moses. Bendavid had simply rejected what Mendelssohn had posited as the differentiating element of Judaism—its ritual laws—while giving a Jewish coloring to what Mendelssohn had determined were its universal components. The totality—universal and particular, faith and practice—remained bifurcated except that all allegiance to the latter elements was withdrawn. Thus Bendavid too did not write as a reformer of the Jewish religion, but as the spokesman for those who merely wanted to find some historical basis, albeit tenuous, for religious rationalism within the tradition of their ancestors. Later generations of Jewish intellectuals, similarly alienated, would make comparable efforts to justify their continuing identification as Jews despite modes of thought and styles of life that set them apart from their coreligionists. But like Bendavid, they also remained on the periphery, their arguments too obviously rationalizations. The road of religious reform in the eighteenth century led elsewhere: in the direction of bringing together again what Mendelssohn had sundered, forging a new totality of thought and practice out of those elements from both categories which seemed viable in the new historical context and which, while congruent with reason and universal aspirations, would separate Judaism both from philosophy and from other religions.

Though little appreciated or influential in his own day, Saul Ascher (1767–1822) deserves attention as the first theoretician of this reorganization of elements within the framework of religious reform. Ascher came from an established Berlin family but was not among the Jewish wealthy elite. He worked as a bookdealer and journalist, had many non-Jewish acquaintances, and was not actively involved in the leadership of the community. No less than his friend Maimon, he was a rationalist and dared to express unconventional views openly, in his own name.[37] In 1792 he published a treatise on religion with particular respect to Judaism called *Leviathan.*[38] Of its three sections the first dealt with religion in general, the second with Judaism, and the third specifically with Judaism's "purification." His object was in part apologetic: Judaism has been misunderstood by Christians who have failed to recognize that it is a religion of high principles, an object wholly worthy of philosophic inquiry. They have failed to grasp its essence, misled in part by Mendelssohn, who had based its particularity on the law. In Ascher's redefinition, Judaism becomes a *religion,* not a theocratic polity, and like other faiths it consists of both theoretical and practical components, together forming a unity. Its uniqueness lies in its embodying a particular variation of the spirit common to all faiths. As a religion, Judaism was intended by God to bring happiness to a portion of His creatures. It is a "higher means" by which Jews can learn their true self-interest and social responsibilities. The vicissitudes of Jewish history become for Ascher necessary elements in this process of religious education, which constitutes a special instance of Lessing's broader notion of the spiritual education of all humanity. The laws of Judaism have served as means to this end, but they are not its essence. Moreover, in the course of time they ceased to act as vessels of the faith, deteriorating into mere patterns of behavior. Means was confused with essence, leading eventually to Mendelssohn's erroneous view of Judaism as revealed legislation. For Ascher the essence of Judaism consists of its dogmas; they alone reflect its spirit and purpose. Though a rationalist, he was willing to admit that reason would forever have to appropriate a realm for faith.

Ascher agreed with Maimon that the present "constitution" of Judaism was binding upon all who called themselves Jews. He differed in believing that it could be changed by human initiative. Thus Ascher called for a "reformation" within Judaism which would transform it into a religion rather than a polity, bringing its contemporary adherents spiritual satisfaction by binding them to belief in God without restricting their autonomy of will. Ascher did not specify the details of this reformation, but he was venturesome enough to formulate what he regarded as the principal dogmatic and symbolic elements of a reconstituted Judaism. The dogmas include belief in a God of love who revealed His will to the Patriarchs and to Moses, who rewards and punishes, whose providence rules the world, and who will bring redemption through His messiah. Judaism further requires commitment to circumcision, to Sabbath and festival observance, and to penitence. Here, then, was Judaism as a religion clearly differentiable both from Christianity and from a merely philosophical faith. No longer the old, all-encompassing theocratic polity, it had been reconceived through rational reflection. Yet it remained distinctive, the particular faith of a particular people.

In truth, however, *Leviathan* is not a consistent book. At times Ascher seems very close to Bendavid in favoring, at least for the few, a rational religion unencumbered by any ceremonial acts whatever. Even in the course of listing Judaism's essentials, he felt constrained to note that while "observance of the laws was sacred to our ancestors and preserved them upon their way, we now walk upon it simply with faith in God and His prophets."[39] But at the same time, and unlike Bendavid, he did not want to isolate the enlightened Jews as a separate sect. However crudely and inconsistently executed, Ascher's effort was directed toward laying out a common ground which might be acceptable to the broadest possible spectrum. Also—and more important— he was trying to retain for Judaism those who believed their ancestral faith to be hopelessly outmoded and that the Jewish people had come to the end of its historical path. Beyond all theorizing, Ascher was concerned for Jewish continuity, which could be preserved only if reformation replaced rebellion. In an extraordinarily emotional outburst toward the end of his work, Ascher pleaded with those Jews who had despaired of continuing within the fold:

> But no! Remain, children of Israel, upon the path of your parents. Our religion is for all human beings, for all ages. Demonstrate that your religion can make you fully human and that it can educate you to become citizens. Only the constitution of the religion must be reformed, the religion itself can never lose any of its essence. If you are able to do this resolutely, we will be a people worthy of the Divine in all places and among all people; we will always remain such and be able to continue thus undisturbed.[40]

Ascher's hopes for a comprehensive reformation were disappointed. The rabbinate remained loyal to the old "constitution" even if it was increasingly unable to enforce adherence to its provisions. For the time being, governments likewise were uninterested in forcing or even initiating such a transformation. Although they wanted to weaken and narrowly circumscribe Jewish religious authority, they did not want to invalidate some of their best arguments against removing the Jews' disabilities. Thus Ascher's ideas were not followed up by a reformation setting Judaism as a whole upon a "purified" foundation of dogma and symbol. Disaffection with ritual observance simply spread to wider circles, though the majority of German Jewry—especially those in the countryside and of the lower middle class—continued to be observant for another half century. But if circumstances disallowed any all-encompassing reformation, they did not exclude the possibility of specific reforms. The latter did not necessarily require a central authority and each proposal could be judged on its own merits. The suggestions for reform soon left aside matters of individual observance, such as dietary laws, and concentrated on two institutions: the school and the synagogue.

Proponents of Jewish educational reform in the last decades of the eighteenth century were interested in more than just expanding the conventional curriculum. They not only wanted Jewish studies to make room for secular ones; they also desired that the Jewish heritage be conveyed in a manner very different from the traditional one. Instead of the customary immediate immersion in sacred texts, the maskilim suggested that Judaism be taught like other religions, by means of a catechism, so that the Jewish child would know what it was that Jews believed. This more orderly study of Judaism, some thought, would necessarily affect the way the next generation regarded its heritage. The children would learn to distinguish between the essence of their faith and those customs which were as inappropriate as "a garment from a different time and place."[41] The maskilim devoted their attention to establishing modern Jewish schools not least because they would thereby create a generation prepared to mediate between the Jewish religion and the values of modern culture. Unlike their parents, they would have the perspective of both secular and Jewish education and thus be able to deal rationally, and not arbitrarily, with those areas in which they seemed to clash. Even though reformers came to concentrate their efforts increasingly on the synagogue, religious education remained always within their purview as preparation for a Jewish life whose ceremonial aspects were to be centered upon the house of worship.

Influenced by the popular thought of their day, the maskilim began to see the synagogue in a new light. It was not simply a place where the Jew fulfilled the commandment of daily prayer, but where prayer could affect the spirit of the worshiper. For Isaac Euchel (1756–1804), one of the editors of *Ha-Measef,* the religious "service of God" *(Gottesdienst, avodah)* was an appropriate designation for the sacrificial cult in the ancient temple, but not for modern prayer. "God does not desire our service," Euchel wrote, "instead He permits us to make use of outward acts in order thereby to reach the great goal of our own improvement and perfection." Prayer is "the engagement of our soul *(Gemüth)* with God," and it requires purity of heart and trust in providence. God answers prayer by transforming the disposition. One leaves the synagogue purified, freed of guilt and with a consoled heart; one now treats acquaintances with greater love as the impetus of the worship experience is felt in the moral dimension of daily life. In Euchel's view, it is thus not the recitation of the prayers that matters, but their ability to serve as the vehicle for a communion with God which transforms the subjective state of the worshiper.[42] It is this new understanding of Jewish prayer which provides the theoretical basis for the earliest proposals for synagogue reform.

In the late eighteenth century, such suggestions appear with increasing frequency. If Judaism in the modern world was to be a religion like other religions, then the synagogue would have to be for the Jews what the church was for Christians: the focus of religious life. But synagogue attendance was declining in the larger German cities where secular pursuits increasingly replaced daily and even Sabbath public worship. Some Jews visited churches and found the service, with its aesthetically pleasing music and edifying sermon, to be more uplifting than the singsong of the traditional synagogue cantor and his two musical assistants. They were especially impressed by the decorum and the apparent rapt attention of the congregation, while in the synagogue, by contrast, discussion of business matters often provided relief from a tedious liturgy understood in its totality by few of the worshipers.

The first object chosen for attack was also the most vulnerable. Like many leading rabbinic authorities before them,[43] the maskilim criticized the late, often incomprehensible liturgical poems called *piyutim,* and argued they should be eliminated from the liturgy. They contributed nothing to the subjective state of the worshiper. In 1786 Isaac Euchel went so far as to suggest that no sensible Jew could approve of the *piyutim* and that undertaking a reformation in this instance would be a most meritorious enterprise. Not surprisingly, he was severely attacked for so bold a suggestion and was forced to defend his position.[44] About the same time, the Italian rabbi Elijah Morpurgo published a series of proposals for educational reform in *Ha-Measef.* Among them was the suggestion that if Jewish children could be taught music in school it would, in the course of time, lead to more harmonious singing in the synagogue—as was already the case among the Sephardim.[45] Here and there too the wish was already expressed for Jewish preachers who would deliver moral addresses in the manner of the Protestant sermon.[46] However, such proposals were not acted upon in Germany until the first decades of the nineteenth century.

Only one significant step was taken very early: the translation of the liturgy into modern German. Rendering the traditional prayers into the vernacular was not itself a novelty. Translations into Judeo-German had long been available in central Europe, intended especially for women. But now some of the younger women were more at home in High German than in the Jewish dialect. And the earlier translations had left much to be desired with regard to accuracy and literary appeal. Moreover, ignorance of Hebrew had spread as well to many men, so that one maskil could claim that the majority of Jews did not know enough of the sacred tongue to "consider in their hearts what their mouths were jabbering."[47] In response to this situation, two modern German translations of the liturgy appeared, both in 1786. One was in Hebrew characters, the other in Gothic.[48] These translations, done respectively by David Friedländer and Isaac Euchel, were characterized by the lack of any significant reforming tendency either in the prefaces or in the way the prayers were rendered into German.[49] Only here and there did Friedländer, the later radical, make an effort to avoid an anthropomorphism or to tone down an unpalatable reference. Thus in the prayer directed against the *malshinim,* he uses the abstract noun "slander" rather than "slanderers" to designate the target of opposition. Both translators retain the prayers for the return to Zion and the reestablishment of the sacrificial cult. In his commentary Euchel even goes out of his way to justify the blessing in which the Jewish man thanks God for not having made him a woman. Euchel believes that it expresses proper gratitude for not having to undergo the travails of menstruation and childbirth.[50] Neither of the translators intended his work for formal presentation by the prayer leader in the synagogue. Euchel called his translation a "book of devotions" *(Andachtsbuch);* he wanted it to be used in the home and especially in the instruction of children. As for public worship, there he believed that the Hebrew prayerbook, a precious treasure handed down from ancient times, should be used exclusively and all present "praise God together in the holy tongue." In the synagogue, Euchel favored only the abolition of unspecified "abuses" *(Missbräuche),* which had crept into the service in recent times.[51] He was probably referring to elements that disrupted decorum.

These translations must have filled a need. Seven hundred and fifty individuals presubscribed to Friedländer's version; close to three hundred copies of Euchel's were sold in advance. They also aroused some opposition. Rabbi Elazar Fleckeles of Prague declared that nothing less than the biblical plague of leprosy befell those who translated Hebrew into other languages.[52] He feared, of course, as had opponents of Mendelssohn's Pentateuch translation, that the availability of sacred texts in German would further reduce direct knowledge of the original. What Fleckeles did not contemplate was that modern translations would be the first step toward the introduction of vernacular prayers into the religious service itself. But in Germany that would not occur for another generation.

The French Impetus

A program of practical reforms within the synagogue itself was first instituted in Holland. In 1795 French forces had conquered Holland, displacing the rule of the house of Orange and enabling local sympathizers to create the Batavian Republic. Almost immediately the new democratic state followed the example of France in promulgating its own "Declaration of the Rights of Man and Citizen." After about a year and a half, on September 2, 1796, the Dutch granted emancipation to the Jews of Holland, even as the French National Assembly had earlier given full equality to the Jews of France—at first to the Sephardim in 1790 and then to the Ashkenazim in 1791. The Dutch Jewish community at the time numbered about 50,000, nearly half of them living in Amsterdam—which thus had a larger Jewish population than any other city in Europe. All but about 3,000 were Ashkenazim whose principal language was Judeo-German (Western Yiddish). Though some Jews participated in Dutch international trade, most were poor, and many were dependent on charity. The upper class, which controlled Jewish affairs, had enjoyed special economic privileges under the old order and was mistrustful of the new republic. In Amsterdam the Ashkenazi community was governed by a council of seven administrators *(parnasim)* chosen from among the wealthiest taxpayers and absolute in its rule.

Very soon after the French conquest, the *parnasim* found themselves in opposition to a faction whose leadership consisted largely of younger Jewish intellectuals imbued with the ideals of the French Revolution and dissatisfied with the existing community structure. These maskilim banded together with a few non-Jews to form a pro-French patriotic society called Felix Libertate. When its Jewish members failed in an attempt to bring about changes from within, twenty-one of them created a rival community, Adath Jeschurun, which provided its adherents with their own rabbi, synagogue, slaughtering house for kosher meat, and ritual bath. They also acquired their own cemetery, in which the dead were buried only after forty-eight hours had elapsed following death. The leaders of the "new community," as it was soon called, were able to act with impunity since the separation of church and state, instituted in 1796, made the *parnasim* powerless to prevent their act of secession. Membership grew to one hundred families, mostly of limited means. During the course of a lively polemic, carried on in Judeo-German, the members of Adath Jeschurun accused their opponents of oppressing the poor while unfairly favoring the rich with honors in the synagogue. Though the "old community" in turn accused them of a variety of doctrinal and ritual offenses, and even prohibited intermarriage with them, the secessionists maintained that they were entirely loyal to "our holy faith."[53]

The rabbi of Adath Jeschurun was Izak Graanboom, a Swedish convert to Judaism, who had earlier served as a teacher in the old community and performed rabbinical functions for it.[54] Now he became the spiritual leader *(moreh tsedek)* of the new community and the chief singer *(ha-zamar ha-rishon)* in its synagogue. The festive dedication of their house of worship, which took place on June 23, 1797, was celebrated with a choir chanting original liturgical poems in Hebrew, for which rhymed Dutch equivalents had also been composed. Those attending prayed that their persecutors in the old community would seek rapprochement. In the spirit of the dedication of Solomon's Temple, they also extended their prayers to include non-Jews, petitioned for peace among the nations, and expressed a universal messianic hope to speed the day when all peoples would be unified in the service of God.[55]

Adath Jeschurun used a traditional prayerbook, but Graanboom did introduce a number of synagogal reforms which reflect a new orientation.[56] In order that the prayers would be said more slowly and with greater devotion, insignificant accretions were omitted from the service. The hymns were sung musically with each word carefully enunciated. Every Sabbath a sermon was delivered that stressed moral virtues and to which the congregation listened silently, not raising points of controversy as was customary in response to the traditional halakhic discourse. In contrast to prevalent practice, the honor of reading from the Torah was not auctioned off to the highest bidders. In general, the tendency of the congregation was to remove disruptive and secular elements from the synagogue, transforming atmosphere more than substance. The aesthetic thrust was probably influenced by the more decorous service of Amsterdam's Sephardim, though none of the latter were members and the Hebrew pronunciation remained Ashkenazi. With equality of civil rights already a fact, the members felt no externally motivated need to remove or alter any of the particularistic passages in the liturgy, nor apparently were they greatly bothered by them on any other grounds. Only one change seems to have been ideologically motivated: the omission of the *av ha-rahamim* (God of mercy) prayer that originated during the Crusader persecutions and called upon God to "avenge the spilled blood of His servants."[57] Graanboom's son wrote in defense of all their changes that they were simply in matters of custom, not Jewish law, and that varying liturgical traditions had existed side by side in more than one community. He sought to justify the innovations by reference to the Halakhah. Nonetheless, Adath Jeschurun was sufficiently different that a contemporary Christian observer could refer to the group as "the remarkable men of the reformed Jewish community in Holland."[58]

The separatists survived for less than a dozen years. In 1808, Louis Bonaparte, who in becoming King of Holland had put an end to the Batavian Republic, decreed reunion of the two communities in a single consistory system for all of Holland of the type ordained by his brother for the Jews of France that very year. Although some of Adath Jeschurun's leadership was absorbed into the structure of the centralized community, the separate services ceased shortly thereafter and the momentum of religious reform in Holland was lost.[59] Graanboom had died in 1807 and the old Jewish community leadership entrenched itself anew, especially after the defeat of the French and the restoration of the House of Orange.

The pro-French sympathies of the Dutch maskilim had led them to send three representatives of Adath Jeschurun to Paris in 1807 as official visitors at the Sanhedrin called by Napoleon.[60] The old community had refused to send any. But for Dutch Jewry the impact of that French gathering was not at all toward religious change, only toward loss of the reformers' institutional identity in a consistorial system based on the French model and dominated by the earlier leadership.

At the time of its emancipation French Jewry, consisting of about 40,000 souls, was culturally and religiously divided. The Sephardi Jews of the southwest were far more Frenchmen than their Ashkenazi brethren living in Alsace, and many of them had become notably lax in religious observance. Their rabbis lacked independence and authority. They were a wealthy, privileged elite of Marrano ancestry which had long neglected talmudic literature, teaching their children instead a Judaism based mainly on the Bible. A number of them came under the influence of Voltairean ideas, drifting away from religious belief and practice or, in the fervor of the Revolution, embracing a radical rationalism and decrying the influence of all religion.[61] By contrast, the Ashkenazim by and large remained intense in their Jewishness with a strong religious leadership that was wary of the consequences of emancipation.

In their quest for equal rights, a few French Jews went out of their way to state publicly that their religion did not conflict with the duties of citizenship. They minimized the practical significance of the messianic return to Palestine, declaring in a petition to the National Assembly that Jews believed only the dogmas of natural religion and practiced only three principal rites: circumcision, Sabbath, and festivals.[62] As in Germany, some French Jews preferred to think of their faith as simply the "religion of Moses." The years following the Revolution were religiously devastating for the newly emancipated Jews of France. During the Terror and the Thermidorian reaction a virulent campaign directed against all religions made it difficult or even dangerous for Jews to attend synagogue, keep the Sabbath, and provide themselves with kosher meat.[63] A few became fervent advocates of the revolutionary "cult of reason" and for the first time there were mixed marriages. Napoleon's restoration of the Catholic Church, through a concordat with the pope in 1801, therefore came as welcome relief to the faithful. Jews were grateful to Bonaparte for reestablishing religion in France.[64] But the subservient position now assigned to Catholicism, and even more to Protestantism, within the centralized absolutistic Napoleonic state was bound to lead sooner or later to a similar subjugation of Jewish institutions.

It was in response to complaints from Alsatian peasants about Jewish "usury" that Napoleon finally acted with regard to the Jews. In 1806 he called to Paris an assembly of over one hundred Jewish notables and had his commissioners put before it a list of twelve questions, intended not to elicit information, but to evoke formal acknowledgment of the state's supremacy over the Jewish religion.[65] The delegates obliged, citing the traditional halakhic principle that "the law of the state is law." They declared that the Jews are no longer a separate people—attempting to refute the widespread notion, expressed also by Napoleon, that they were in fact "a nation within a nation." The majority could not, however, accede to Napoleon's desire that the Jews of the Empire encourage their own disappearance by advocating mixed marriages. In response to the crucial third question, they insisted that the rabbinical members of the assembly would be no more inclined to bless the union of Jews and Christians than would Catholic priests. At the beginning of 1807, a "Great Sanhedrin" of seventy members, composed mostly of rabbis, gave solemn religious sanction to the responses of the assembly.

There was little specific talk of religious reforms at these two gatherings. One of the rabbis, quoting Mendelssohn, said that he considered it his duty to reveal those accretions, based on superstition, which he thought degraded the faith.[66] But since the delegates did not set their own agenda, the subject could be discussed no further. The French officials who stage-managed the proceedings were not interested in reform but in conformity. Strictly religious matters—without political consequences—were of little interest to them or to Napoleon. In fact, the Great Sanhedrin was wholly unlike its ancient prototype, which had been for Jews the highest legal authority, constituted for the purpose of developing the Halakhah and adjudicating cases in accordance with it. The French Jews did not themselves initiate this latter-day version; it was an instrument forced on them, whose pernicious intent escaped many of its members in their enthusiasm for France and its emperor. Indeed, the Reformers' rabbinical conferences held in Germany in the 1840s were in some respects more like the ancient institution than was the Parisian Sanhedrin, which sought to imitate it in form. For the development of the Reform movement, however, the Sanhedrin did provide an important precedent. Later reformers pointed in particular to its official recognition of religious and political obligations as two separate realms which should not be allowed to conflict.[67] Thereafter, it became an ongoing task, which continued throughout the nineteenth century, to resolve those points where friction persisted nonetheless.

In France itself the two assemblies did not generate a profound rethinking of Judaism or an impetus to principled cultic reform. In 1808, a decree establishing a consistory system organized all of French Jewry under the watchful eye of the government. The new centralized hierarchy, composed of rabbis and laymen, proved to be conservative in religious matters except where citizenship was directly involved.

However, a similar structure could also be used to institute and supervise a coherent program of reform. And this indeed became a principal aim of the consistory which was established that same year for the Jews living in the French-controlled Kingdom of Westphalia.

The Royal Westphalian Consistory of the Israelites

During the first decade of the nineteenth century a popular and relatively coherent ideology of religious reform appeared in the writings of the German maskilim. Preceding and parallel with the Westphalian consistory, it was sufficiently developed and widespread to serve as its intellectual basis. The principal vehicle for this new thinking about Judaism was the journal *Sulamith,* which began to appear in 1806 and after

1808 became the literary voice of the consistory. Its editors were David Fränkel (1779–1865) and Joseph Wolf (1762–1826), both of them teachers of Judaism in Dessau.

Fränkel and Wolf believed they were continuing the work of Moses Mendelssohn, extending and deepening enlightenment, culture, and universal sympathies among their fellow Jews. As educators, they were committed to creating personalities in which the Jewish heritage and modern values achieved harmonious integration. Frequently they and other writers in their periodical discussed religion in general without immediate reference to Judaism or Christianity, as if to stress that being religious in a universal sense was what mattered most, not the divisions imposed by a particularizing history and conflicting traditions. One of them put the goal of religious education this way: the child should come to realize on his own "that there is only one true religion as there is only one humanity and one God, and that all religions are but forms of it."[68] Kantian in character, this universal religion was dominated by its moral component. Indeed for some of the writers morality—innate conscience—became the criterion by which specific religions should be judged. Man is created in the image of God, one of them wrote, not by virtue either of his limited grasp of the supernatural or his inadequate reason, but because of his moral sense. Judaism, they believed, possessed the highest degree of morality. But it was lacking in other respects.

In the very first issue of *Sulamith,* Wolf stressed the task of instilling a Judaism that could be deeply felt, one that was neither a variation of cold deism nor composed of mere externals. The ceremonies of Judaism had to be understood instrumentally, as possessing the capacity to create solemnity and devotion. They were not the essence of religion, but a vehicle, the more necessary for those who required sensual aids to glimpse the divine. Regrettably, contemporary Jews lacked the ability to distinguish genuine religion from ceremony, which was properly only its companion or handmaiden. What was required therefore was an effort to separate the two, and to differentiate within the category of ceremony the religiously meaningful symbols from those practices which for many Jews were empty of content. The metaphor that recurs in almost every discussion of the subject at this time—and later—is "the separation of the wheat from the chaff" *(den Kern von der Schale).* The problem of how to divide the two became an ongoing, central issue, and *Sulamith* was unable to give a definite answer. It is of interest, however, that one writer as early as 1809 suggested that the distinction between divine teachings and human laws would have to be drawn on the basis of scholarship. Only after there were rabbis and Jewish teachers trained in theology and other disciplines could a proper reformation be set in motion. Meanwhile *Sulamith* was content to ridicule certain peripheral customs such as the monetary transactions preceding weddings and the boisterous behavior at the celebration of circumcisions. It refrained from frontal attacks on Jewish law. One of the writers even held up the talmudic rabbis as models for the adaption of the Halakhah to the prevailing *Zeitgeist.*[69] Sometimes radical in thought, the journal drew no far-reaching practical conclusions. Its principal purpose was mediation, not aggravation of differences.

Along with integrating Judaism among the religions, *Sulamith* sought to integrate the Jews among the Germans. Fränkel called upon his readers to remove the barriers that separated them from "sensitive human beings" who were non-Jews and attempt "to keep pace with the spirit of the times." Jews should adopt prevalent modes of behavior "so that the Jewish citizen will not stand out too much from the Christian."

Often these maskilim still referred to the Jewish "nation," using the term in its eighteenth-century sense devoid of political connotations.[70] However, increasingly it is replaced by a strictly religious terminology which identifies Jews as adherents of a particular faith. It is in this period that the self-designations "Israelite" and "Mosaist" become common substitutions for the term "Jew." *Sulamith* itself was originally identified on its title page as a periodical propagating culture and humanity "among the Jewish nation." Beginning in 1810, however, it was doing the same "among the Israelites." The rationale was that "Jew" was a term of late origin and national in character, whereas the other designations were more specifically religious and were based on the Pentateuch. Interestingly, this change in terminology was from the first not limited to religious reformers. In fact, some strictly traditional communities began, as in Hamburg, to call themselves "Israelite" following the model of the Napoleonic *Assemblée des Israélites.* Later in the century, the reformer Gabriel Riesser would be exceptional when he resisted the trend by calling his periodical defiantly *Der Jude.* To be an Israelite in Germany, as in France, required gratitude to the state by the expression of willingness to accept the obligations of citizenship along with its privileges. For Fränkel—as for many who would later express themselves similarly—it also meant a transfer of loyalties: "Wherever you are treated humanely," he wrote, "wherever you prosper, there also is your Palestine, your fatherland, which in accordance with your [*i.e.,* Jewish] laws you must love and defend."[71]

Fränkel was disappointed that the Parisian Sanhedrin had not undertaken a genuine reformation but had contented itself instead merely to restate indisputable principles.[72] He hoped for the creation of a more permanent body, a synod, deriving its authority from the throne, which could successfully make his "Israelite coreligionists aware of their *true* religious and political duties and encourage their fulfillment."[73] Not long afterward, Israel Jacobson selected Fränkel to be one of the two lay members of the Westphalian consistory and therefore an active participant in carrying out just such a program.

If *Sulamith* represented the ideological freight carried by the new consistory, Israel Jacobson (1768–1828) was surely its moving force.[74] In fact, he is often considered the first of the practical reformers or even "the founder of the Reform movement." Certainly his personality and his deeds left their impress on the religious development of German Jewry. Jacobson was not an original thinker and lacked formal secular education; his religious ideals were simply those of the later maskilim. But his wealth, his unflagging energy, and for a time the authority granted him by the Westphalian state enabled him to implant these values in new and existing institutions.

Although Jacobson was born into an affluent family, the extraordinary wealth he possessed by middle age was mostly obtained through his own acumen. Originally destined for the rabbinate, he received a thorough Jewish education but soon gravitated to those enterprises in finance and industry which were characteristic of the Jewish upper class. He was a latter-day Court Jew, who served the Duke of Brunswick and had financial dealings with other German rulers as well. In return he received a variety of business concessions and distinctions, not the least of them an honorary degree from the small university of Helmstedt. Yet like some, but not all of the Court Jews, he felt a deep and persistent sense of *noblesse oblige.* He generously supported a variety of charitable enterprises, mainly but not exclusively Jewish ones. His persistent efforts contributed to the abolition of the demeaning "body tax" imposed on Jews

Israel Jacobson.

in a number of German states. Despite his repeated calls for rapprochement with the Christian world, he remained an observant Jew who enjoyed nothing more than to lead the worship service, and later also to deliver sermons. His irrepressible fervor, imagination, and good-naturedness invariably moved those who heard him. When the consistory implemented certain controversial reforms, acquaintances of Jacobson's youth believed that others must have led their friend astray.[75] Contemporary observers stress that Jacobson was also vain, that he loved to be in the spotlight, and that, like the *parnasim* who governed traditional communities, he could be imperious in his demands. But they could not deny that both his devotion to universal Mendelssohnian principles and his attachment to fellow Jews were genuine and sincere.[76] Aside from his business activities, Jacobson's efforts were bent to improving the situation of the Jews politically and economically while gaining respect for the Jewish religion among non-Jews. The reforms of the consistory which he headed were above all intended to make the Judaism which he professed more attractive to a generation of Jewish "citizens" by embellishing it with the accoutrements of a modern religion.

When his father-in-law Hertz Samson died in 1795, Jacobson inherited both his title as District Rabbi for the Weser region and his position as Cameral Agent for Duke Charles Ferdinand of Brunswick. In 1804 he was granted naturalization for himself and his family, henceforth enjoying rights entirely equal to those of non-Jews. Jacobson served the duke faithfully, but bristled at the disabilities, especially economic ones, which his fellow Jews continued to suffer. He complained to the duke that the personal example of moral virtue which he (like Mendelssohn before him) was trying to set had been without effect. It convinced neither ruler nor people that Jews who chose to worship God in their own way could be useful citizens. At the same time the emancipation of the Jews in France impressed him deeply and he hoped that the French influence would extend equality to Germany.[77] In 1806 he wrote a letter to Napoleon calling upon him to act for the benefit of German Jewry.[78] He proposed the establishment of a "Supreme Council" with its seat in France which would govern religious matters for Jews all over western and central Europe. Jacobson wanted Jews to bring order into their own affairs, which would be possible only through the creation of a Jewish central authority. The alternative which was shortly thereafter chosen in Frankfurt—subjugation of the Jewish religious life to Gentile authorities—was distasteful to him in the extreme. In an 1807 ordinance intended to "improve the Jews," Frankfurt's archduke, the Prince Primate of the Rhine Confederation, had made selection of rabbis dependent upon approval by the Christian consistory. The successful candidates were divested of all authority, special permission for circumcisions had to be obtained from the government, and Jewish schools were to be placed under the Christian school commission, which would decide the curriculum. In a letter to the Prince Primate, Jacobson deplored these provisions and expressed the Mendelssohnian view that in religious matters there could be no coercion.[79] It was the task of the enlightened state to emancipate the Jews, and it could well leave cultural and spiritual enlightenment to their own initiatives. Emancipation, Jacobson believed, must precede reform. And that, in fact, was the sequence of events in Westphalia, the first state in Germany to grant full equality to the Jews.

On July 7, 1807, with the signing of the treaty of Tilsit, Napoleon reached the height of his imperial success. On that same day he appointed his youngest brother Jerome as the ruler of a Kingdom of Westphalia to be constructed out of various states and territories that had fallen to the French. Jerome Bonaparte was neither as brilliant nor as imposing as his older brother; he had a reputation for being uncultivated, lazy, and licentious. But he was also more tolerant, especially in matters of religion, to which he was personally indifferent. Once he told a Protestant theologian plainly: "In every religion one can be a good man."[80] According to the constitution which Jerome promulgated on November 15, 1807, all subjects received equality before the law, and the various confessions were free to practice their religions as they wished. Three months later came a decree relating specifically to the Jews, which removed all disabilities. Unlike their coreligionists in France, whose status had deteriorated when Napoleon subjected them to new exceptional legislation, the 15,000 Westphalian Jews thus gained—at least on paper, if not always in practice—the fulfillment of their emancipatory hopes.

Not surprisingly, Jacobson was drawn to Cassel, the new Westphalian capital, as were other officials of the now defunct Duchy of Brunswick. Very early he gained the new king's favor by a substantial loan to fill the empty state coffers. Like his brother, Jerome thought it proper to call an assembly of Jews from his domains in order to obtain promises of loyalty. However, unlike him, and to Napoleon's distress, Jerome received the deputies personally and with ceremony. Jacobson had been entrusted with choosing the twenty-two representatives from the eight departments of the kingdom and he was elected to preside over their assembly. Only two of them were rabbis; six were local community officers. The instructions given to the deputies by the Minister of Justice and Interior reflect the concerns of the government: to obtain an exact census of the Jews, to require them to keep careful records and to take family names, to pay community debts, and to limit the jurisdiction of the rabbis to ritual matters in accordance with the Code Napoléon. The state simply wanted easy and efficient centralized control over a maximally integrated Jewish population. Neither Jerome nor his officials were interested in imposing religious reforms. The latter was purely an aim of Jacobson and the deputies; the government's role was only to give them authority. To this end, it ordered the establishment of a consistory which would regulate Jewish life and to which all of the rabbis in Westphalia would be subject.[81]

In their report to the Minister, the deputies entrusted ongoing functions to the Jewish consistory whose structure they had laid out. Among them was "the task of bringing a number of customs, which have crept into Judaism, more into line with changed circumstances and the spirit of the times, and to take the steps necessary for this purpose." Perhaps sensing that the government might not approve of all their actions, they promised that the consistory would render it regular reports. The deputies decided that Jacobson should be president of the consistory and that he should select its members. Before doing so, however, he consulted with a number of advisers whom he brought to Cassel or with whom he exchanged letters. Among them were radicals like Aaron Wolfssohn, who had earlier expressed his desire for a government-sponsored comprehensive program of religious reform, and relative conservatives like Lazarus Jacob Riesser of Hamburg. In making his appointments to the consistory, Jacobson decided to pass over the radicals, including his own close associate, the Seesen educator Bendet Schottlaender.[82] He needed a broad consensus to help him obtain his principal objective: a kind of *aggiornamento,* a bringing of Judaism up to date.

Aside from Jacobson, who was considered a representative of both rabbinate and laity, the consistory's structure provided for three rabbis and two laymen. Senior among the rabbis Jacobson chose was Löb Mayer Berlin (1738–1814), the chief rabbi of Cassel, an author of talmudic works and a man favorable to moderate religious innovation.[83] Serving with him as "spiritual councilors" were Simeon Isaac Kalkar (1754–1812), who had held a rabbinical post in Stockholm, and the chief rabbi of Hildesheim, Menahem Mendel Steinhardt (1768–1825). The last was the youngest, but also the most gifted of the three. The lay representatives were to serve also as educators and to supervise the Jewish schools. For these positions Jacobson selected two young maskilim: Jeremiah Heinemann (1778–1855), who served as his personal secretary, and David Fränkel (1779–1855), the Dessau educator and editor of *Sulamith.* It is difficult to judge the extent to which the five members of the consistory were free of subservience to their president. However, we hear of no conflict within the consistory, and a number of significant orders were issued in Jacobson's absence.

At the opening session Jacobson told his colleagues that, unlike the consistories of their Christian brethren, this one could not be satisfied with sustaining what already exists and merely tinkering with a minor problem here and there. He spoke of "improvements" (not reforms) which thoughtful Israelites had long proposed but, until now, in vain. At last a body had been constituted which would understand how "to separate the wheat from the chaff and to modify inessential customs and practices to the extent that reason presents them as useless or injurious." Jacobson outlined no plan for a theological reformation; his interest was in externals.

In some respects the consistory played a role parallel to the Westphalian government itself. Like Jerome and his officials, the members of the consistory attempted to bring order, uniformity, and central control where local traditions had earlier prevailed. The consistory gathered into its hands all significant decision-making authority. In imperious language it demanded complete obedience to its decrees. All over Westphalia religious services were now to begin at exactly the same hour, one standardized curriculum was to be introduced into the schools, and matters of ritual would be decided for all of Westphalian Jewry by the consistory or its three rabbis. Quite apart from their religious thrust, the decisions of the consistory were therefore bound to evoke resentment, if only because they necessitated breaking with local traditions and giving up longstanding prerogatives.[84]

The consistory appointed chief rabbis, rabbis, and rabbinical adjuncts for all of the departments and districts of Westphalia, in general employing those already serving in the vicinity. Each of them had to send regular reports to Cassel; their salaries were paid centrally by the consistory according to rank from taxes levied on the communities. In a sense, rabbinical status was raised, since all recognized rabbis now became state officials, as were their counterparts among the Christian clergy. They even had the right to send official mail free of postage. But they were expected to toe the line. The first significant order of the consistory, dated March 15, 1809, was entitled "Duties of the Rabbis."[85] A large portion of the twenty-one obligations which it imposes deals with administrative matters or Westphalian patriotism, but a few paragraphs are significant as they represent the first authoritative attempt to redefine the rabbinical role. The rabbi is told at the very start that he is to set an example of moral conduct for his community. It is thus not the scrupulousness of his religious observance (which is not even mentioned) that matters most, but his human relations. Like Christian clergy, the rabbi is expected to comfort the ill and the bereaved, thus exercising a pastoral function which in Judaism had not heretofore been specially assigned to him. He is also to prevent disturbances in the synagogue and to prepare the youth for a confirmation ceremony, which as yet remained undefined.

High on the list of rabbinical duties was the presentation of edifying sermons and talks for special occasions, "if possible in the German language."[86] At least twice a year a text had to be sent to the consistory for its approval.

Sermons in the non-Jewish vernacular were not without precedent in Judaism, even in recent years. Among Italian and Sephardi Jews they were common, and they had just been ordered for the Jews of France. Moses Mendelssohn himself had written German sermons for Prussian patriotic occasions, which were delivered by the rabbis of Berlin. The first German sermons to be presented by their authors were given in the two largest Breslau synagogues on December 3, 1797. Each of them memorialized the recently deceased King of Prussia, Frederick William II. They were delivered by two prominent maskilim, Joel Loewe, who had been a member of Mendelssohn's circle in Berlin, and Mendel Bresselau, one of the founders of *Ha-Measef*.[87] A special-occasion sermon in German was likewise given by Israel Jacobson in the Cassel synagogue, in February 1808, during a ceremony of gratitude for the recently granted emancipation.[88] A few months later, Shalom Cohen, soon to become the last editor of *Ha-Measef*, delivered there on Shavuot, the Feast of Weeks, the first German sermon not written for a political occasion. Entitled "On the True Spirit of the Mosaic Legislation" and delivered to a large congregation, it took as its text Deuteronomy 30:11–14, which was interpreted to mean that God's law was not in the heavens—and therefore external—but in the human heart. Interestingly, Cohen's lengthy sermon was not simply shallow moralizing. It included exegesis of the Ten Commandments, much attention to biblical history, and quotations from the Talmud and later authorities. The speaker's concern was not to belittle ceremonial laws, but to argue that ritual acts must not be performed out of habit; rather they should always point the soul to God.[89] Cohen was only a visitor in Cassel and so did not preach there regularly. Once the consistorial school was established, however, members of the consistory alternated in giving sermons in its synagogue every Sabbath for the students and their parents. Outside of Westphalia regular German sermons were given during this period only in Dessau, where Joseph Wolf preached on holidays and occasional Sabbaths from a small portable pulpit covered with red velvet, which was placed directly in front of the holy ark each time that he spoke.[90] Even within the kingdom, German sermons in most places remained rare, despite their inclusion among the rabbinical duties. As late as August 1811, Jacobson was still trying to persuade the rabbis he had appointed to give appropriate brief sermons (he doesn't specify in German) during the approaching holidays.[91]

Rabbis in Westphalia were also expected to conduct all weddings and could delegate this task to others only under special circumstances. The consistory worked out a model form for the marriage contract, which could be adjusted to the particular situation of the two families and then registered with the civil authorities. The religious ceremony that followed was to take place under a canopy *(hupah)* in a chandelier-lit synagogue immediately in front of the holy ark. Under no circumstances might the wedding, in accordance with traditional practice, be held out of doors where its solemnity could be spoiled by boisterous, undignified behavior. The rabbi was to open the ceremony with a short German talk, intended to make the couple aware of their duties to one another. He alone was to chant the traditional seven blessings and to read a brief wedding certificate *(Trauungs-Brief)* in the German language, which replaced the traditional Aramaic *ketubah.* Under no circumstances was the rabbi to tolerate such disruptive and superstitious customs as breaking a glass for good luck or throwing grains of wheat on the couple for fertility. In short, wedding ceremonies were to be serious and sober occasions, wholly respectable to every eye. Since Jews were participating in the Westphalian army, it was decided to alter the legal prescriptions of certain marriage contracts. Rabbi Berlin instituted the provision that where brothers of the groom were subject to the draft, the bride would not have to postpone or forgo remarriage should her husband die and the conscripted brothers not be able to perform the ceremony of *halitsah,* which excuses them from the obligation of levirate marriage.[92]

The desire for dignity and decorum which motivated the wedding regulations was shortly thereafter directed to the ritual of the synagogue. On September 24, 1810, the consistory issued a set of regulations *(Synagogenordnung)* for all the synagogues of Westphalia, which became the prototype for similar documents throughout the nineteenth century.[93] The consistory sought to fulfill the mandate it had been given by the deputies "to take definite measures to avoid all disorder during the service, to create the necessary solemnity, and to separate the essential elements from the inappropriate ones."[94] In forty-four paragraphs these regulations attempted to transform the synagogue into a sanctuary, a sacred place where reverence was undisturbed by disorder or intrusions from the profane world outside. Of course, the provisions therefore made the Jewish service more like the Christian. But there is no reason to doubt that the members of the consistory—and with them at least a portion of Westphalian Jewry—seriously believed that such a transformation represented no violation of Jewish law (which it did not) and that it was in keeping with their own religious aspirations. Moreover, as they pointed out in the introduction, the consistorial councilors hoped that thereby attendance at the services "would not further diminish."

The regulations tend to minimize active congregational participation, assigning nearly all liturgical functions to the regularly appointed cantor. Thus, for example, no boy celebrating his Bar Mitzvah was permitted to read from the Torah. Its authors were convinced that true devotion is peaceful, calm, and reverent. They were uncomfortable with physical rituals, like the procession carrying palm fronds *(lulavim)* during Sukkot, the Feast of Tabernacles, or the beating of willow branches on Hoshana Rabba, the seventh day of Sukkot, and so they wanted to limit these as much as possible. The number of those called to recite blessings at the reading from the Torah scroll and to carry it around the synagogue on Simḥat Torah, the Feast of Rejoicing in the Law, was to be greatly diminished. They sought to eliminate entirely the flagellation *(malkut)* in the synagogue on the day before Yom Kippur as well as the raucous noisemaking at the mention of the villain Haman's name on Purim. In their quest for decorum members of the consistory—perhaps unintentionally—thus created a greater distinction between officiating clergy and largely passive congregants than was customary in Jewish worship. It was a gap that would become wider in the course of time.

In deference to the government, the regulations ordered that only individuals who had acquired family names could be called up to the Torah (using these new names), while a newly composed prayer for Jerome, which thanked him "for benevolently removing the millennial yoke from our bowed necks," was to be recited in German, though a Hebrew version was also composed. The idea of equality was transplanted into the synagogues by eliminating special privileges belonging permanently to particular members.

Most of the changes to be introduced into the liturgy itself were either for the sake of brevity or to avoid medieval compositions, which breathed a spirit of oppression and suffering. The number of *piyutim* was severely limited; as in the case of Adath Jeschurun, the vindictive *av ha-raḥamim* prayer was excised. The standard prayers remained intact and no new prayerbook was issued. Nor did the regulations require that any of the liturgy—excepting only the prayer for the king—be rendered in the vernacular. Nonetheless, although they were generally accepted, the regulations aroused resentment and discontent in some circles. Despite explicit prohibition of public worship anywhere but in the regulated synagogues, small prayer groups *(minyanim)* continued or sprang up in various places, their members conducting the services as they saw fit. In response, the consistory found it necessary to obtain a royal decree forbidding all such gatherings and imposing a stiff penalty for its violation; but it too was evaded in one way or another.[95]

The synagogue regulations were not, however, the most controversial act of the Westphalian consistory. Among the functions given it by the deputies was the granting of dispensations from prohibitions imposed by Jewish law or custom. On this basis, it issued an official letter to Westphalian rabbis on January 18, 1810, relating to Passover, the Feast of Unleavened Bread. It was signed by all six members of the consistory. After brief discussion of differing opinions among traditional authorities and reference to Sephardi custom as precedent, the letter ceremoniously declared that "in accordance with religious law, every Israelite is allowed, and may therefore with good conscience be permitted, to consume on Passover such legumes as peas, beans and lentils, as well as rice and millet." The recipients were ordered not only to inform their communities of this concession, but also to set a good example by their own actions, lest the consistory consider them unworthy of its trust. Although the order was justified by reference to inquiries received from Jewish soldiers who would be unable to obtain sufficient quantities of unleavened bread, the alleviation was not limited to Jews serving in the army. Baking *matzot* in large quantities, the consistory pointed out, would render their purity less certain and the poor would, in any case, be unable to purchase enough to serve as the staple of their Passover diet.[96]

The outcry against this permission to violate a prevalent Ashkenazi prohibition mentioned specifically in Moses Isserles' glosses to the *Shulḥan Arukh* was unexpectedly loud. How could the members of the consistory arrogate to themselves the right to contravene the dicta of notable halakhic authorities and set aside prohibitions that were observed for centuries by Ashkenazi Jews all over Europe? The three Parisian rabbis of the French Central Consistory sent Jacobson an angry letter disputing the right of the Westphalians to make such decisions and expressing astonishment that, although they had been consulted in other relatively minor matters, on this occasion their advice had not been sought. The French rabbis requested to see further justification for this precipitous act.[97] In response to all of the opposition—to the Passover concession and to the synagogue regulations—Menahem Mendel Steinhardt, the junior rabbinical member of the Westphalian consistory, published a brief work written in the manner of halakhic responsa. Entitled *Divre igeret* (Words of a Letter), it is the first attempt to provide extensive legal and other justification for a program of modern reforms, and therefore deserves special attention.

Steinhardt enjoyed an excellent reputation among traditional Jews, no less than among maskilim and Gentiles. The historian Heinrich Graetz, no friend of the Reform movement, called him "a knowledgeable and clear-headed talmudist."[98] As early as 1804 Steinhardt had published a book of responsa in which he sought to reconcile the legal opinions of the earlier authorities and to choose among various views of the later ones. As yet, however, he was unwilling to do more than raise some doubts about current practice. "With regard to tea," he wrote then, "I know of no reason to fear that the leaves will ferment. However, since everyone is accustomed to refraining from them [on Passover], they fall into the category of those things which, though apparently permissible, others have prohibited and one is not free to permit them, thus negating views to the contrary."[99] Eight years later Steinhardt published his *Divre igeret* with the approval of Wolf Heidenheim, an editor of widely used, strictly traditional prayerbooks, who added a few comments. More than half of the thin volume is concerned with the consistory's decision permitting consumption of legumes on Passover. The author tells us that the decision was unanimous and without misgivings among all three of the consistory's rabbis to whom Jacobson had entrusted it. Quoting extensively from halakhic sources, Steinhardt asks his readers to consider that the Talmud and the early decisors did not prohibit legumes. He complains bitterly of those contemporary authorities who govern themselves wholly according to abbreviated versions of the *Shulḥan Arukh,* as if these handy compendia were given at Sinai. But why had no Ashkenazi authority of previous generations instituted this concession? Why were they the first to do it? Steinhardt's answer to this general question—which recurs frequently with regard to reform proposals hereafter—is twofold. First there is a general point: our ancestors left us an opportunity to show our own abilities.[100] Second, earlier authorities were fearful that their rivals would mock them. "But we, the members of the consistory," he concludes, "because of the cry of the poor and of the Jewish soldiers, are not concerned on account of the scoffers and gossip mongers among our people."[101]

Most of the remaining nine responsa concern reforms in the worship service, either those stipulated in the synagogue regulations or additional ones instituted at the synagogue of the consistorial school in Cassel. Side by side with halakhic arguments Steinhardt here relates his own experiences. He tells us, for example, that during the parade of palm fronds around the synagogue, he witnessed several times that one man would stick another with his *lulav* or insist on walking in front of him causing a loud and bitter altercation. The result was that "instead of the memory of Jerusalem our holy city and our Temple (may it be speedily rebuilt) being called to mind, no one is concerned for Zion—and therefore for the sake of Zion I cannot be silent and must raise my voice like a ram's horn. Shall this be called a house of God and this the gate of heaven?"[102] For Steinhardt it was not just a matter of decorum, but of the synagogue's sanctity. As for the liturgical omissions, he justified these for the sake of greater concentration in prayer, because of the desire to eliminate distinctly kabbalistic references, or because certain of the prayers directly—and now inappropriately—reflected an earlier time of persecution.[103] He believed that to recite such lamentations would be gross ingratitude, not merely to Jerome, but to the King of Kings, who had inclined the nations to treat the Jews with greater favor.

In one of his responsa, Steinhardt referred to a reform that had been instituted in only two Westphalian synagogues: the singing of German hymns by a boys' choir. These two synagogues—that of the consistory school in Cassel and the temple of the school founded by Jacobson in Seesen—represented the leading edge of religious reform in Westphalia.

Even more than improvements in religious life, the consistory sought to reshape and modernize Jewish education. In Cassel it established and supported a "consistorial school" intended to serve as a model for similar elementary institutions elsewhere in Westphalia. The Cassel school opened in 1809 and shortly thereafter had 76 students divided into three classes. Many of the boys were from poor families and received free board and tuition. Particular attention was given to instruction in religion, which was intended more to convey the principles and obligations of Judaism than to concentrate on texts. Every Sabbath a vesper service was held in the synagogue of the school where a member of the consistory spoke to the children and their parents on matters of religion and morality. The services themselves were abbreviated and conducted alternately in Hebrew and in German. Fränkel reported that the children "understand what they are praying, and for this reason exemplary quiet and holy devotion reign in this synagogue. One of the teachers leads the service, pronouncing the words clearly and distinctly, while the children pray along silently with him." Only a few prayers were said aloud by all, and the main petitional prayer *(shemoneh esreh)* was recited only once. The Bible was read—not chanted—by someone designated for the task. Following the blessing after the scriptural readings, one of the students ascended the platform *(Katheder)* and read the equivalent passages in Mendelssohn's German translation. None of the regular prayers was chanted, but upon completion of their recitation an "inspiring" concluding hymn in Hebrew or in German was regularly sung by all.[104]

Although the consistory did not ordain the use of the German language in public prayer, readings, and song for all synagogues in Westphalia, its appearance in Cassel was sufficient to evoke negative response. Samuel Levi Eger [Egers], the rabbi of Brunswick, wrote a letter to his old friend Jacobson expressing two concerns that would recur frequently thereafter. While Eger realized there was no halakhic objection to liturgical use of the vernacular, he feared that if Hebrew were not used exclusively in the synagogue, the principal motive for learning it would be removed and it would gradually disappear from Jewish education. In addition, Hebrew was a bond that tied Jews everywhere to one another. "If we now pray in German here and the Jews of France in French, those in Italy in Italian—the bundle will come apart."[105]

The consistory was not, however, interested in the disintegration either of the Jewish community or of Judaism. Along with the consistorial school it also established a seminary in Cassel for the training of "genuinely religious" rabbis and teachers. It opened in 1810 with five students. Steinhardt gave classes in Talmud and in Maimonides' legal code, the *Mishneh Torah*. The curriculum for rabbis, as the consistory envisaged it, was to consist of a thorough secular education along with the traditional rabbinic disciplines. The student was also to learn homiletics and gain the ability to present his ideas clearly in writing. He would be considered eligible for a rabbinical position only if he possessed moral qualities to match his academic achievements. The candidate was also expected to observe the ceremonial laws strictly and take the well-being and moral improvement of his community to heart. Little more is known about the origins or development of the seminary; the Westphalian kingdom collapsed before it could produce any graduates. However, it possesses historical significance as the first attempt to create a modern institution for the training of rabbis. In Germany there would not be another for more than forty years.[106]

Both educational and religious goals were to be served by the confirmation ceremony, which is first mentioned officially in Westphalia among the duties of the rabbis in 1809. Clearly this was an institution adopted from Christianity where it represented the culmination of a course of study intended to prepare the young person for adult status in the church. Jewish confirmation was not, however, an original idea of the consistory. The ceremony apparently goes back as far as 1803 when it was instituted by the newly created modern school in Dessau.[107] From there it spread to Wolfenbüttel where the later founder of modern Jewish scholarship, Leopold Zunz, was confirmed in 1807. Initially, the ceremony was held in the home or the school, individually, and for boys only. That was the pattern during the first years in Dessau and also in Wolfenbüttel. Zunz's confirmation began with the teacher asking the thirteen-year-old to give well-rehearsed answers to questions about his belief in God and its sources in nature and scriptural revelation. The confirmand then recited Maimonides' Thirteen Articles of Faith in response to a question asking what he was required to believe. Finally, the teacher gave him a paternal admonition and the young Zunz recited an original Hebrew prayer of thanksgiving.[108]

The method of instruction for confirmation was the question-and-answer technique of the catechism.[109] As early as 1595, Abraham Jagel, an Italian Jewish educator, had published his *Lekah tov* (A Good Doctrine), which attempted to present the teachings of Judaism through a dialogue between a rabbi and his student. Though influenced by Christian models, it was often reprinted and translated into various languages. It seems not, however, to have been used regularly in Jewish schools. In the early nineteenth century an abundance of Jewish catechisms in Hebrew, German, and other languages made their appearance, including one by Jeremiah Heinemann, a member of the consistory. In most instances their stress was on universal principles and obligations rather than on particular Jewish ones. If in the traditional Bar Mitzvah ceremony the young man was to show his capacity to read from the Torah and often also to give a rabbinic discourse, in the confirmation ceremony he was to demonstrate that he had learned the principles and duties of Judaism as a religion.

From the first, this borrowed custom aroused misgivings, even in Haskalah circles. One writer noted that while the recitation of articles of faith was essential to Christian confirmation, Jews did not become Jews by learning religious doctrines. Another preferred a different designation—"religious festival" *(Religions-Fest)*—and regarded the ceremony more as a *rite de passage* than as a confession of faith.[110] Still, it was widely felt that the Bar Mitzvah ceremony had in many instances become an empty shell, that it was deficient in that it did not extend to girls, and that in an era when powerful centrifugal forces were eroding Jewish identity there was an urgent need for some ceremony in which the Jewish child would solemnly declare his or her commitments.

Although the Westphalian consistorial councilors intended that confirmation be undertaken everywhere in Westphalia, the ceremony seems to have struck root in only three or four cities. In Cassel the first confirmation was held in the school's synagogue in 1810, where the confirmand was blessed by Rabbi Berlin after making his declaration of faith and obligations. Two years later a similar ceremony was held in the larger community synagogue.[111] Although girls were supposed to be confirmed in Westphalia (at age twelve) along with boys (at age thirteen), there is no evidence that any girl did in fact participate.[112] Only in 1813 did the consistory more energetically attempt to extend the ceremony, suggesting that for a boy elements of the Bar Mitzvah, such as being called up to the Torah, could be combined with a solemn acceptance of the teachings of the Jewish religion and the promise to make them the guide of his life.[113] But there was not time to carry out the intent before the consistory's demise.

It is of interest that the consistory would not tolerate a confirmation ceremony whose character was too obviously Christian. On Shavuot in 1810, the director of the Jewish school in Seesen, Bendet Schottlaender, conducted the ceremony for several boys using questions and answers on which he gained the advice—and possibly also the co-authorship—of an Evangelical pastor. The consistory concluded that Schottlaender's catechetization was fine for Christians, but not for Jews. It required him to submit all future questions and answers for its approval and until he received it to refrain from holding any further confirmations. The members of the consistory mistrusted Schottlaender sufficiently that they forced him to send in the notebooks that students kept in religion class, and on one occasion two of them arrived unannounced at the school to examine the pupils.[114]

Yet it was precisely in Seesen that Jacobson hoped to realize his fondest hopes. As early as 1801 he had established a trade and agricultural school for poor Jewish boys in the tiny town, which then belonged to the Duchy of Brunswick. Two years later the institution admitted a few Christian students as well—in itself an extraordinary innovation. Attached to the school was a prayer room where services were held not only for the Jewish pupils but also for the half-dozen families who made up Seesen's Jewish community. As school and community grew, Jacobson decided—as early as 1803—to build a larger sanctuary for both constituencies. The original plan called for a domed octagonal structure with a bell and clock tower rising 70 to 80 feet into the sky. However, the Brunswick authorities considered such an impressive synagogue, resembling both a church and contemporary conceptions of the ancient temple in Jerusalem, to be inappropriate for Jewish worship. The construction plan that was

The Seesen Temple, completed in 1810.

carried out from 1805 to 1810 was therefore considerably more modest. In its final form the building was a rectangular structure with a curved roof containing clock faces on all four sides. It was topped by a belvedere from which a short bell tower—really a louver—extended upward an additional few yards. The bells, so obviously Christian that they are to be found in only one later German synagogue, were a point of great controversy, raising objections from both Jews and Gentiles.

The most radical innovations were the interior arrangements. The reader's platform *(bimah, almemar)* was moved from its traditional position in the center of the room closer to the ark, where a raised pulpit was erected for the delivery of sermons. Latin inscriptions adorned the building along with Hebrew ones. Jacobson also installed an organ, an innovation precedented only in a Prague synagogue during the previous century. The instrument was built by a local craftsman under the supervision of the cantor from a neighboring town. Only in perpetuating complete separation of the sexes did the interior remain traditional. Women sat in the balcony extending along three of the walls behind an apparently opaque barrier.[115] Taken as a whole, the structure made a social statement: Jews worship as do Christians; they are their equals in religion as in civil life. No longer an Oriental, foreign faith transplanted to Europe, Judaism—like Christianity—is homeborn in the accoutrements of its worship no less than in its loyalty to the state.

Jacobson called his synagogue a "temple." In this he was not original. A century earlier synagogues were occasionally referred to as temples.[116] More recently the Society of Brothers in Breslau had used the term for the new synagogue it dedicated in 1802.[117] By 1810 it had become common in Germany due to its frequent use in France as a universal designation for a house of prayer, especially for those of non-Catholics. During the period of French occupation and influence in Germany, its use spread to strictly traditional Jewish communities. Moreover, it could refer to a rented room as well as to a structure.[118] Jacobson's choice of the term, however, did have ideological ramifications. Not only was this new building given a name which was not exclusively used for Jewish houses of worship (like "synagogue") and which pointed to its distinctiveness from earlier structures, it would also recall—however distantly—the ancient temple in Jerusalem. Jacobson urged everyone to "see here a small, weak imitation of what Solomon's temple was for our entire people."[119] However, Jacobson drew the analogy only for the sake of expanding upon Solomon's universal hopes for his temple (I Kings 8:41–43). Later reformers would see in the modern temple a place where prayer and edification had become permanent and welcome substitutes for the ancient sacrificial service.[120]

The dedication ceremony for Jacobson's temple was memorable.[121] Notable Jews and Christians from all over Westphalia were invited to Seesen for the occasion. Among them were rabbis, pastors, and priests, government officials, and businessmen. The festivities began at nine o'clock on the morning of July 17, 1810 with a procession into the new building announced by the pealing of its bells. Teachers and students led the way followed by Jacobson, who was accompanied by the consistorial councilors and the attending rabbis, all wearing clerical apparel. Other guests brought up the rear. Once inside, they heard an original nondenominational cantata composed by the assistant music director of the University of Göttingen and performed by sixty to seventy musicians and singers. There were also the customary Hebrew prayers and rituals, including seven processions around the synagogue bearing the Torah scrolls. Several passages from the Pentateuch were read in Hebrew and then translated into German. Later came a chorale in Hebrew and in German as well as German hymns that were sung by all. Jacobson led the prayers, assisted by the attending rabbis, and he gave the principal speech, which was the highlight of the celebration.

Jacobson addressed himself sequentially to his fellow Jews, to the Christians present, and to God. He assured his coreligionists that he was a faithful and observant Jew who did not desire that Judaism should disappear or be merged into a universal religion of reason. Yet he urged them to accept Westphalia as their fatherland and to help the consistory purge those elements from Jewish ritual which were "rightfully offensive to reason and to our Christian friends." From Christians he asked that they accept the Jews into their midst without prejudice, and he thanked God for having created man as a rational, autonomous being. The overall thrust of Jacobson's speech was this: the time has come for a rapprochement between Judaism and Christianity, a common recognition of the fundamental similarity of the two faiths, separated for the most part merely by formal differences. For Jacobson there was high symbolic significance in the fact that so many Christians were attending a Jewish religious ceremony. Perhaps he was aware that during the Middle Ages Jews had been forced to enter churches to hear conversionary sermons. Now Judaism was no longer a pariah faith. The celebration in Seesen was evidence that it belonged within the family of modern religions. The occasion was perhaps the first example of the interfaith brotherhood activity which would later become so important a component of Reform Judaism.

Organ music, choral song, German prayers, and sermons all continued in the Seesen temple after its dedication, along with confirmations. But the new house of worship did not create momentum for similar innovations elsewhere in Westphalia. The orders of the consistory encountered passive resistance, which was difficult to overcome. In March 1812 it complained to the Minister of the Interior, but to no avail. Jerome himself publicly displayed to Jacobson his displeasure that the consistory was apparently creating sectarianism. It became evident that the communities were unwilling to bear the heavy collective taxes that supported the consistory and its institutions, though the Jewish population of Westphalia was growing. As a result, there were difficulties in paying the rabbis their salaries. Financial problems no less than ideological ones motivated opposition, which hamstrung the consistory many months before its collapse.[122] The end came with the demise of the Kingdom of Westphalia in September 1813. Its leadership soon scattered. Of the rabbis, we know that Steinhardt continued to work for moderate reforms from his position in Paderborn, as did some other Westphalian rabbis, like Samuel Eger of Brunswick, who had supported the consistory up to a point.[123] Jacobson himself resettled in Berlin, where he was soon again to play an active role in the institution of liturgical reforms.

The consistory had been a valiant but mostly vain attempt to foist changes from above upon an entire Jewish population. A few were ready to accept the whole program; most were probably willing to go partway; some opposed it in principle. Perhaps had the consistory lasted longer, some of its constructive achievements, especially in education, would have borne fruit. Beginning in 1815, however, those interested in religious change set out upon a new path. If it was not possible—and perhaps not even desirable—to reform an entire Jewish community at once, at least the like-minded could band together and create a religious service that was meaningful to them.

Frustration in Berlin

During the first two decades of the nineteenth century about 3,500 Jews lived in the Prussian capital. They possessed a single community synagogue, which had been completed in 1714. Although additional private services were prohibited, about a dozen small *minyanim* met regularly. Secularization and disaffection with inherited ritual had made severe inroads among Berlin Jews, so that the old, and now inadequate synagogue was rarely filled. Many left behind the unstable combination of traditional practice with cultural integration espoused by Mendelssohn for partial or utter neglect of the former as feelings of belonging to modern Europe and a culturally emergent Germany replaced inherited Jewish values.

At first enticed into more universal identifications by the sympathy shown them by enlightened Christians, Berlin Jews were dumbfounded when a profound change in intellectual climate, characterized by a narrow chauvinistic Romanticism, replaced the broad, encompassing ideas of the *Aufklärung*. In 1812 they had been heartened by an edict that granted Prussian Jewry outside of Posen equal rights with non-Jews, excepting only access to state offices (including educational positions). But the defeat of Napoleon ushered in a reaction that led to the continued exclusion of Jews from all positions of honor and trust. Prussian Jewry remained "emancipated," but it was generally deemed unworthy of true equality.

A number of Berlin Jews during these years converted to Christianity, mostly for opportunistic reasons. Those few who were themselves attracted by the Romantic movement, especially the Jewish hostesses of the famous Berlin literary salons, found in Christianity the only faith which they believed expressed genuine depth of feeling.[124] Judaism in their eyes was either a crass legalism or—in its modern guise—an arid rationalism. At the other end of the spectrum were the Berlin Jews who remained fully observant of Jewish traditions and saw no need for any religious reform. They constituted perhaps half of the community. But they too had begun to feel part of the larger milieu and their children often forsook the observance of their parents. Jewish education was woefully neglected. Although there were some private institutions with curricula that were either strictly traditional or integrated Jewish with secular studies, there was no community-sponsored Jewish school until 1826.

At the head of the Jewish community stood a few wealthy individuals whose religious views ranged from conservative to radical. The more traditional among them became the spokesmen for that portion of the community which contemporary sources call the believers in the old way *(die Alten);* those who favored religious modernization represented the faction of new Jews *(die Neuen).*[125] In the struggle over religious reforms in the Berlin community, which lasted for nearly nine years from 1815 to the end of 1823, the two sides became involved in a severe confrontation, due mainly to a reactionary Prussian government, which would not allow free religious development among its Jewish subjects.

The most prominent Berlin Jew, though not the wealthiest, was David Friedländer (1750–1834), an avowed disciple of Mendelssohn who had gone beyond his master in rejecting the ongoing divine authority of the ceremonial laws.[126] Friedländer had gained the gratitude of fellow Prussian Jews on account of his untiring efforts to obtain their political emancipation. However, his religious position placed him among the radicals, those who rejected conversion simply because Christianity contained dogmas which they could not accept as rational men and because they still felt a sense of attachment to Jewish family and friends. At the end of the previous century Friedländer had actually proposed his own conversion, and that of similarly minded associates, if belief in supernatural dogmas were not made a precondition. But Friedländer's "infamous" proposal to an enlightened Christian, Provost Teller, was rejected by its recipient, and he remained a lifelong Jew. Surprisingly, he continued to exercise a role of leadership in the Berlin Jewish community for another decade.

Friedländer became a proponent of the most extreme religious reform as an alternative to conversion. In 1808, Jacobson's proposals for mild liturgical changes in Westphalia struck him as absurdly inadequate. "Either–or," he wrote in a letter, "either we entrust repair of the structure to competent, daring builders, who possess authority, or we leave everything to time, allowing the building, whose pillars are crumbling and all of whose parts are decayed, to collapse into ruin."[127] Friedländer did not believe in halfway measures. He sought nothing less than a thoroughgoing reformation.

The Prussian emancipation edict of 1812 prompted Friedländer to express his views in some detail. A paragraph of that decree suggested that the advice of knowledgeable Jews should be sought in determining the "ecclesiastical status" of the Jews and the improvement of their education. In response, Friedländer published a pamphlet outlining a major transformation of Jewish life.[128] The area most urgently requiring attention was, to his mind, the worship service. He saw a need to purge the liturgy of all elements which marked the Jews as strangers or made reference to kabbalistic doctrines. Late additions to the prayerbook, less lofty than earlier customs, reflected a situation of persecution and alienation. Medieval lamentations should now give way to new songs of gratitude and joy. Moreover, the modern Jew could not with integrity pray for his return to Jerusalem, for restoration of the ancient temple and its sacrificial service. These petitions no longer reflected heartfelt desires. Friedländer saw little value in study of the Talmud—a legal document which had ceased to be relevant in a state where Jews were subject to secular jurisdiction—and he believed Hebrew should be learned only by philologists. Yet he did possess appreciation for the ancient spiritual treasures of Judaism—especially the Bible and the Jewish moral tradition—and he felt that "the shining colors of the Oriental style cast an inimitable luster" on the liturgy as a whole. He also believed that without a newly shaped religious life the Jews "would not be able to survive" as Jews or to develop their creative potential.

Friedländer's pamphlet polarized Prussian Jewry.[129] Scores of supporters in Berlin and Breslau expressed sympathy with his views. Others objected totally or found his ideas too extreme, especially with regard to the abandonment of Hebrew. He was now too controversial to exercise general community leadership and gradually withdrew himself from all Jewish activities. For a time Friedländer took an interest in the modernized services that were held in Berlin beginning in 1815. But he soon regarded them as too much of a compromise with the traditionalists. He had come to the conclusion that the times demanded nothing less than completely new prayers and a Sabbath service conducted on Sunday.[130] At the same time he also objected to the confirmation ceremony of the Christian kind because of his Mendelssohnian *idée fixe* that Jews do not possess a confession of faith, and he expressed himself as vehemently against Christianity as against Judaism.[131] Soon neither he nor his family were attending the new worship services.

For a time, during the German War of Liberation from France (1813–1814), religious matters were put aside as Prussian Jews made every effort to prove their patriotism on the battlefield and on the home front. But when it was over, their consideration began anew. It was, in fact, the happy conclusion of that war which occasioned the first factionalizing incident in Berlin. In 1814, the Society of Friends, a fraternal and benevolent organization of acculturated Jews, sought permission to celebrate the forthcoming peace with a religious observance in the community synagogue.[132] The ceremony was to consist of a sermon and the singing in German of appropriate psalms. Men and women would sit together and the choir would include female voices. While the community elders gave their assent, the rabbis, the synagogue wardens, and those who supported them voiced strong opposition. Rather than press the matter, the Society chose to conduct the celebration in its own meeting hall. The incident made it clear to the proponents of religious reform that the attempt to introduce changes in the community synagogue would create a severe conflict of uncertain outcome. As a result, they grasped the only alternative open to them: the creation of a modernized religious service outside the bounds of the official community, one which might serve as a model for what could only later become the norm.

The catalyst for the creation of such a service in Berlin was the arrival of Israel Jacobson in the Prussian capital toward the end of 1814. The one-time president of the Westphalian Consistory still enjoyed considerable prestige and possessed the initiative which others lacked. In the spring of 1815, when his son Naphtali reached the age of thirteen, Jacobson arranged a confirmation in a home chapel on the festival of Shavuot. The cream of Berlin Jewish society, as well as highly placed Gentiles, were present for the ceremony. The gathering left such a favorable impression that Jacobson continued to hold services in his house every Sabbath for those who desired to come. They were wholly a private venture, without community sanction, Jacobson himself giving the sermon and sometimes leading the prayers. An old, rather raucous organ, played by a non-Jew, accompanied the German hymns intoned by a choir in which initially there was some Gentile participation. The services, which lasted from eight o'clock in the morning until about ten, were conducted mostly in Hebrew, with only a weekly selection from the preliminary prayers in German. The Torah was read in Sephardi Hebrew without the musical accents, while those called up to recite the blessings received cards indicating the sequence in which they would be honored. Within a few months three young men were engaged by the congregation as preachers. When Leopold Zunz first attended the service on the Day of Atonement that year, he was deeply impressed. "People who for twenty years had no communion with Jews spent the whole day there: men who believed themselves already beyond religious emotion spilled tears of devotion; the majority of the young people fasted." When attendance grew to over 400 hundred on some Sabbaths, it was decided to transfer the gathering to roomier quarters in the home of Jacob Herz Beer.[133]

Although traditionalists in the community privately condemned these unorthodox religious services, they did not publicly raise their voice against them. Worship in the community synagogue remained as it was; reform energies were deflected away from collective institutions. It was rather the Prussian monarch who took the dimmest view of what was going on in the homes of Jacobson and Beer. Frederick William III and his officials shared the fear that the Jews might create a new "sect" which would be attractive even to Christians, and that any evidence Judaism could be modernized would weaken missionary efforts to bring about their conversion. When the king learned of the private services late in 1815, he immediately ordered them closed. The effect was to drive the reformers back to the community synagogue, the only place where Jewish worship would be tolerated. It was at this point that they collided with the traditionalists and a protracted battle began over the common domain. Only after the community elders, in their majority favorable to reform, found that the old synagogue building required extensive repairs did they succeed in getting permission for the Beer home to serve temporarily as one of three abodes for community-sponsored services until the synagogue was rebuilt.

For six years therefore, from 1817 to 1823, a service was held in the Beer house while the character of future public worship in the rebuilt synagogue remained in dispute. It was a chance for the reformers to show a broader segment of Berlin Jewry what a modern Jewish service was like. But because it was no longer a private venture, the "temple" was soon caught up in a maelstrom of differing opinions, some members urging compromise, others desiring a sharp break with tradition. Behind the ferment within loomed the unfriendly specter of the Prussian government, which continued to look upon the reform endeavors with grave suspicion. Under such circumstances, the results could not fully satisfy anyone.

The leadership of the new congregation at first lay in the hands of a few individuals and then in an elected commission. Particularly prominent were two wealthy, middle-aged men who also served as elders of the general community. Both were moderate in their desires for reform, attempting to carry as much of Berlin Jewry with them as they could. Jacob Herz Beer (1769–1825), who had established sugar refineries in Prussia and Italy, was at the time the wealthiest Jew in Berlin, his fortune having increased markedly during the war years. Three of his four sons later gained general fame, one as a composer, one as an astronomer and politician, and one as a poet and playwright. To provide his children with a Jewish education, Beer hired modern educators, who lived in his lavish home. A contemporary described the household as not orthodox, but nevertheless strictly Jewish. If against the dominant pattern among wealthy Berlin Jews, all of the sons continued to identify actively as Jews during their entire lives, this was due especially, it seems, to the influence of their mother. Beer's wife, Amalia, was an educated, cultured woman deeply attached to her faith. She knew Hebrew and was fond of quoting the Bible. In fact, it is not unlikely that she was an important influence behind the establishment of the temple in her home in 1815. Their oldest son, Giacomo Meyerbeer, composed a Halleluyah chorus for the new services that same year.[134]

Like his agemate Beer, Ruben Samuel Gumpertz (1769–1851) was an elder of the general Jewish community and a wealthy man, though his fortunes had recently declined. In addition, he was the grandson of a rabbi, a student of Mendelssohn, and a man of considerable Jewish knowledge. Though devoted to the cause of religious reform and a declared opponent of rabbinical authority, Gumpertz shared with Joseph Muhr, a fellow member of the temple commission, and undoubtedly also with many other supporters of the new services, the conviction that moderation must be maintained even at the cost of principle. The circumstances demanded it. To his young friend and distant relative, Leopold Zunz, Gumpertz wrote: "Above all we must consider the mixed, heterogeneous public . . .what one segment criticizes another loves, and it is only through incongruous and often inconsistent combinations that the totality can be sustained. Without this mixture our cause—however pious the intent of the founders—would not have reached its present stage." A younger contemporary described Gumpertz as a man who was enthusiastic but too careful, too certain that the traditionalists could be brought into the process of reform.[135]

Beer, Gumpertz, and the other wealthy community leaders who devoted funds and energies to the cause of reform in Berlin were eager to utilize the talents of a small circle of Jewish students and graduates which had gathered in the Prussian capital after the opening of the university there in 1810. These young men generally received financial support for their studies from the likes of Friedländer and Jacobson and they served as tutors in the homes of the wealthier, more acculturated families.[136] While they were grateful to their benefactors, they did not want to jeopardize their independence of thought and action. "One should not become too familiar with the rich," one of them wrote.[137] Recognizing their economic inferiority, they nonetheless felt intellectually superior to the magnates who provided their bread and butter. They were proud of possessing a structured academic education which placed them closer to current trends in German culture than were the community leaders, whose secular education had been an unsystematic, autodidactic gleaning of concepts from the German *Aufklärung*. In 1819 a group of these young, formally educated Jews created a "Society for Culture and Scientific Study of the Jews," which endeavored to give expression to Jewish consciousness in conceptions drawn from Hegelian philosophy and in scholarship that applied to Jewish sources the canons of critical historical research.[138] Aware of their debt to the acculturated community elite, they welcomed some of them into their Society, but ambivalences caused by the difference in social status and differences of worldview resulted in a very uneasy relationship.

When the new services began, some of the younger men were drawn in to serve as preachers; others participated in organizing them or simply attended. However, unlike the community leaders, they favored a more principled, consistent program of liturgical reforms. They saw little value in compromise and were intolerant of lassitude. When Leopold Zunz, after serving as one of the preachers for two years, finally became exasperated at the lack of real progress, he wrote bitterly to a friend that its leaders could find "some other toady *(shafel)* who would dissemble nicely, flatter them, and inspire the dear children." For Zunz it had come to a conflict between "community leaders *(parnasim)* and tyrannical Jews versus the Society, money versus science, hypocrisy versus true religiosity."[139] But despite Zunz's sharp criticism, the two groups for a time worked together closely and quite well, creating a worship service which enjoyed considerable appeal.

From a diagram in a contemporary letter we know that the temple or synagogue (both names are used) in the Beer home consisted of a long hall created by breaking down the walls between three rooms. In what had been the central chamber an ark was erected for the Torah scrolls, a permanent canopy for weddings, a reading desk, and a pulpit. Here too sat the wealthy community leaders and—for a time at least—the scholars. The remaining men sat to one side, in front of an organ and boys' choir, facing the center, while women sat on the opposite side, likewise facing the middle room. There is no indication that any partition impeded the women's view of the service.[140]

For many, especially those who had until then ceased attending services, the principal attraction was the German sermon, which was delivered every Saturday morning. The young men who were employed for this purpose sought to give the congregants a message that would deepen their devotion, provide spiritual exaltation, and transmit a feeling of religious "edification" to the worshipers. Unsurprisingly, the preachers drew upon Christian models. With varying degrees of success, they incorporated the techniques of the best known masters of the art. Occasionally Christian preachers in Berlin would even visit the services and give suggestions to their Jewish admirers. Some of the sermons were universal in content; they preached the human value of personal religious belief and sentiment. Others referred specifically to the situation of contemporary Jewry and to obligations owed fellow Jews. Biblical texts were quoted frequently and extensively; rabbinic sources less often. While the sermons extolled the virtues of reason, they also recognized its limitations.[141] Some of the young preachers in Berlin began to see their efforts as a vocation for life, which would provide acculturated German Jews with a leadership more adequate to their spiritual needs than the rabbis of the old style, whose activity was mostly limited to decisions of ritual law. While the delivery of regular, edifying sermons in the vernacular was an innovation in German Jewry, it was not as such objectionable to traditionalists. But the notion that young men with a secular education, whose ideas and religious practice were suspect, considered themselves and were considered by others to be the new spiritual guides, instructing the congregation of Israel—that was difficult for the traditionally inclined to accept.[142]

The context in which the sermons were given, of course, also placed their legitimacy in doubt. It was, for example, rather questionable that the Beer services should employ the Sephardi pronunciation of Hebrew, although those attending were Ashkenazim. The motive for that innovation is not entirely clear. In part it may have been identification with Sephardi Jewry, which in general had taken a more favorable attitude to non-Jewish culture than its Ashkenazi counterpart. It may also have been connected with the aversion for Yiddish and Yiddish intonation of Hebrew, which was inherent in the German Haskalah since Mendelssohn. But the decision was no doubt influenced as well by a contemporary debate in which a number of authors tried to show that the Sephardi pronunciation was historically the correct one. It had begun in 1808 when a Dutch Jew, Moses Lemans, attempted to explain by historical arguments why he, though Ashkenazi, employed Sephardi Hebrew. While Lemans himself cautioned that he was not advocating Ashkenazi Jews should therefore give up their longstanding custom, the Berlin circle apparently saw no reason to preserve a tradition which had been shown to be a distortion of the original classical form.[143]

More controversial than the pronunciation of Hebrew was the music employed in the service. The organ in Berlin served not only to enhance the ritual aesthetically, but also, as one source tells us, "to regulate the wild synagogue chanting." Its tones set a single cadence for prayer, helping to create order and unity in the service. There was also a choir of boys from one of the Berlin Jewish schools to lead the hymns and sometimes to present liturgical music, generally composed by Gentiles, in multipart harmony. The German hymns were taken from a songbook most of whose lyrics had originally been written by Jeremiah Heinemann for the Consistory synagogue in Cassel.[144]

Our sources do not provide us with complete information regarding the liturgy of the Berlin services. It seems that a prayerbook was first issued anonymously, probably in 1815, and served the congregation at least until the fall of 1817 when two of the preachers, Eduard Kley and Carl Siegfried Günsburg, began to issue a two-volume work which either served as an alternative or replaced it.[145] Both of the prayerbooks omit customary Ashkenazi *piyutim* for the holidays, as well as some secondary prayers, and use Sephardi transliterations. They indicate that the petitional prayer was said only in unison, rather than first individually.[146] Neither was intended to represent the service as it was actually conducted, since both indicated that particular sections were to be said in Hebrew, for which they merely offered a German equivalent or the names of the rubrics. Throughout the period of the Berlin services, the liturgy was mostly conducted in Hebrew and in accordance with the traditional prayer formulas.[147] There was some preference for the Sephardi rite, including the custom of elevating the scroll before, rather than after reading from it.

An ideological tendency is manifest only here and there. Both prayerbooks (though probably not the leader of the service who read it in Hebrew) altered or omitted the passage calling upon God to gather Israel from the four corners of the earth and to reestablish it in its land. In each case the word Redeemer, in reference to the messiah, was rendered by the impersonal "redemption." However, prayers referring to Zion and even to the sacrificial service were for the most part retained, as was every reference to the chosenness of Israel. Neither prayerbook contains the *kol nidre* prayer chanted on the eve of the Day of Atonement, undoubtedly because the text, annulling vows taken under duress, had frequently been the object of Gentile accusations of Jewish duplicity. It was probably as a substitution for the *kol nidre* that the Kley–Günsburg prayerbook presented an original Hebrew composition dealing with the theme of repentance. We do not know, however, whether the Aramaic chant of the *kol nidre* was, in fact, eliminated or simply not mentioned in the translations, which would be seen and read by Gentile visitors to the services.

From time to time confirmations were conducted in the Beer temple, including a ceremony for two girls in 1817.[148] The preachers performed weddings there, as well as in other places in the vicinity. On such occasions they gave the sermon but they were not allowed to conduct the ceremonial acts uniting the couple in wedlock. That task was reserved for a rabbinically trained Jew *(lamdan)* who had to be present.[149] For a time, it seemed as if the Berlin model would spread to other communities in Prussia. In January 1821 a "German service" was to begin in Breslau, but a government courier came from Berlin at the last minute with an order prohibiting it. The efforts of Berlin Jews on behalf of their brethren in Breslau and a brief presented by Zunz to the Prussian authorities were both to no avail. In Königsberg, Isaac Asher Francolm was able for a time to conduct confirmations for boys and girls and to give sermons in the community synagogue, but the service there remained unchanged, and Francolm's innovations were soon eliminated when the traditionalists protested to the government.[150]

In Berlin the pressure of Jewish opponents and the suspicion of the government prompted the Beer circle to commission a defense of their innovations which would appeal to the canons of Jewish law and custom. The man who undertook the task was a Hungarian Jew with a rabbinical education named Eliezer Liebermann. A character of apparently questionable reputation, he had been a teacher and wandering preacher when he arrived in Berlin and spent about ten months there, either in 1815 or in 1817. At first he gave traditional-style sermons in the community synagogue, then he found his way to the reformers after initially being suspicious of their enterprise. The polemical nature of the sources on Liebermann does not allow us to say what won him over to the reformers' cause. But during his stay in Berlin he did agree, or propose, to give halakhic support to their innovations by publishing two Hebrew tracts. The first was a collection of rabbinical responsa requested from authorities abroad; the second was a work in which he expressed his own opinions. They appeared together in Dessau in 1818.[151]

The collection of responsa, *Nogah ha-tsedek* (The Radiance of Justice), contained three favorable legal opinions on various innovations introduced in Berlin. Two came from Sephardi rabbis in Italy: Shem Tov Samun in Livorno (Leghorn) and Jacob Recanati in Verona; the third was composed by Aaron Chorin, a Hungarian rabbi in Arad. There was also a brief approbation by another Hungarian rabbi, Moses Kunitz from Ofen (Buda).

Shem Tov's responsum dealt exclusively with the permissibility of organ music, presenting for the first time the major arguments that would appear repeatedly as this issue became a central point of contention between reformers and traditionalists. Shem Tov insisted that copying a Gentile custom was prohibited only when imitation was the principal purpose. Moreover, since Levites had played musical instruments in the ancient temple, the Gentiles were simply doing what they had learned from the Jews. It was therefore not a matter of disobeying the injunction "You shall not follow their customs" (Lev. 18:3). On the contrary, Shem Tov insists, "It is our own custom." He added a practical reason as well: the music attracts men and women to the synagogue; though they may come at first for the wrong reason (aesthetic appreciation), soon they will attend for the right one (to pray). Recanati, who similarly concentrates on the organ question, adds further arguments, but he ends with a condition: on Sabbaths and holidays the instrument may not be played by a Jew because he might, without thinking, make a minor repair and thus violate the prohibition against working on a day of prescribed rest.

By far the longest and most comprehensive of the three responsa was written by Aaron Chorin, the early proponent of religious reform in Hungary. He addressed himself to five issues: use of the vernacular in prayer, the organ, the formation of a separate congregation, the abolition of the silent petitional prayer, and the Sephardi pronunciation. Chorin was not an opponent of Hebrew. Like most of the reformers in Berlin, he believed that the central portion of the liturgy must remain in the original and even added that its use was "a trustworthy indication of our faith in the ingathering of the exiles ... and the upbuilding of the temple where we shall express our petitions in the Hebrew tongue." However, the preliminary prayers could and should be said in the language that most people understood. Like Recanati, Chorin approved of organ accompaniment, but he insisted that the organist be a non-Jew. He did not approve in principle of omitting the silent petition, but he recognized the necessity for it since, unfortunately, few worshipers listened attentively to the cantor's repetition if they had already said the petitionary prayer individually. He saw no objection whatever to the use of Sephardi pronunciation. On one point, however, Chorin criticized the Berlin reformers: they held their services only on Sabbaths and holidays. He could not justify their giving sanction in this way to the more limited role of collective religious worship in the lives of most Berlin Jews.

To this thin collection of responsa Liebermann added his own much lengthier defense of the reformers' innovations. His *Or nogah* (Radiant Light) is both a halakhic treatise and a personal document. Of particular interest are his own convictions. Liebermann favored reciting a portion of the liturgy in German, but only because many Jews did not understand Hebrew. Where they did know the language, as in Poland, they should pray in the sacred tongue. He even went so far as to castigate German Jews for neglecting the Hebrew education of their children. They had no qualms about spending a fortune to teach their children sciences and other languages. Why could they not also educate them in their own linguistic heritage? Hebrew, after all, was the most ancient classical tongue. He also noted that at the services some people simply sat passively without a prayerbook in their hands. The congregation, he implied, was thus in danger of becoming a mere audience. These criticisms aside, Liebermann praised the temple for drawing alienated Jews back to Judaism and especially for attempting to bridge the widening gulf between those who clung tenaciously to every custom and those who mocked and scorned everything the tradition had to offer. If the Jewish people did not soon awaken to the new historical reality, everything would be swept away.[152] The time had come for urgent action, and Liebermann believed that the reformers were moving in the right direction. As we shall see, *Nogah ha-tsedek* and *Or nogah* soon blew up a polemical storm which swirled around the temple in Hamburg. In Berlin, however, their influence was limited. There social and political forces were rapidly bringing the new religious venture to an unhappy conclusion.

The unstable accommodation between the established community leaders and the irrepressible young intellectuals could not last. The latter increasingly found fault with the timid and inconsistent reforms, with the lack of a guiding principle. Saul Ascher, a maverick of the older generation, argued—not surprisingly—that a new dogmatics had to precede liturgical innovation. Isaac Marcus Jost complained that the service was chaotic, and later reflected that it was not a fruit that developed upon the stem, but a graft that did not take hold. Jost was distressed that at a confirmation ceremony children could be required to swear they would observe Sabbaths and holidays in the traditional fashion—when in fact there was no such intent. Leopold Zunz described the reform activity as a patchwork; it lacked system and a firm foundation. Zunz, then in the radical stage of his changing Jewish outlook, believed that nothing of significance could be achieved "until the Talmud will be overthrown." He noted that the most enlightened Jews of Berlin dissociated themselves from the temple, apparently because it did not go far enough. After counseling with his young, like-minded friends, Zunz gave a sermon attacking the lack of resolve displayed by the temple's leadership, and very shortly thereafter resigned his position as preacher, apparently under some pressure.[153]

When he visited the Beer temple in 1821, the young Danish preacher Isaac Noah Mannheimer was similarly appalled at the incongruities. It was, he wrote, "the old routine in a new dress, and the new dress is already tattered." For him it was scarcely different from an orthodox service. "The auditorium was noisy and restless, and people yelled *kodausch* (holy) like in a typical Jews' synagogue *(Judensynagoge)*." One reason for this surprisingly indecorous atmosphere was, of course, the desire to accommodate everyone who wanted to join and to avoid conflict if at all possible. But there was another reason as well. When Mannheimer questioned the temple leaders about their compromises with principle, he received the reply that "the government is against the new temple and, therefore, under no circumstances do we dare to change anything."[154] Indeed, it was above all mounting pressure from the outside that first weakened the temple from within and finally led to its demise.

While the conservative leadership of men like Beer, Gumpertz, and Muhr dissatisfied younger intellectuals like Jost and Zunz, it did not make the services any more acceptable to the Prussian government. The belief that religious forms more similar to Christian ones would be welcomed by non-Jews was correct only with regard to a few liberals, but not in respect of Frederick William III. In 1821, the king issued an order prohibiting Christian clergy and public officials from attending Jewish ceremonies, lest such participation detract from the status of Christianity and lead to an undesired rapprochement with Judaism. Jewish religious occasions were no longer to receive coverage in the press. A year later the king gave his approval to the newly created Berlin "Society for the Propagation of Christianity among the Jews."[155] His Minister of the Interior praised its work as "the only true religious improvement of the Jews" and wrote to its president that reform of the Jewish service made Jews "even more dangerous to civil society than they were before."

In September 1823 the government closed the Beer temple. For a brief time a "devotion" *(Andacht)*, consisting of a sermon and German hymns, was allowed in the community synagogue following the customary Saturday morning service. But the traditionalists objected strenuously to these extraordinarily well-attended exercises, apparently concerned that most congregants were coming to the synagogue only after conclusion of the regular service. They wrote to the sympathetic monarch whose well-known order of December 9, 1823 echoed the traditionalists' own language: the services in the community synagogue were the only ones authorized and they would be held "without the slightest innovation in language, ceremonies, prayers or hymns, wholly according to the established custom."

Frustration and despair now gripped the Berlin reformers. There was nothing further they could do. For all of their shortcomings, the Beer services had provided a meaningful Jewish religious experience for many Berlin Jews who previously had none. A few of them now returned to the community synagogue; most felt stifled. Some turned to Christianity, while others simply became indifferent to all religious expression. Throughout the reign of Frederick William III Prussian Jews were consistently deprived of the freedom to shape their religion as they wished. Gabriel Riesser, a partisan of the reformers, put it most strongly: "An entire generation was robbed of its religious devotion, the budding youth were robbed of the living love of their religion, and many thousands of souls were robbed of the only true and sincere expression of their piety and reverence for God."[156] If religious reform was to have any immediate future in Germany, it could only be outside the boundaries of the Prussian state.

Hamburg, Where Religious Reform Struck Roots

The free city of Hamburg, at the mouth of the Elbe River, had long been a thriving commercial center. Its Jewish community, once consisting mainly of Marrano descendants, by the nineteenth century was predominantly Ashkenazi, and with over 6,000 souls was the largest in Germany. Although a number of Jewish families had gained great wealth as bankers and merchants, Hamburg Jews continued to suffer political disabilities for more than a generation following a short-lived emancipation during the French occupation from 1810 to 1814. In August 1819 there were popular riots against the Jews, which welled up from a reservoir of ongoing animosity. However, in Hamburg the motivation was primarily economic and social, rather than religious. The Hamburg Senate was less concerned than the Prussian monarch about how the Jews chose to practice their Judaism. It was therefore possible for the Jewish reformers to establish themselves institutionally here without fear that the non-Jewish authorities would be biased against them.[157]

By the second decade of the nineteenth century, a portion of Hamburg Jewry had become highly secularized. The wealthy found in their material goods a security that substituted for the faith of earlier generations. Rifts opened up within the community: "Brother separated himself from brother and parents had to avoid eating at the tables of their children."[158] Business concerns increasingly drove out piety, so that regular attendance at religious services shrank to an ever smaller proportion of Hamburg Jewry. Religious institutions were exceedingly weak; the communal school was, by general agreement, in a sorry state. In 1799 Raphael Kohen had resigned his post as rabbi of the combined communities of Altona, Hamburg, and Wandsbeck because the government had withdrawn his right to excommunicate Jews who violated the ceremonial law.[159] Since then religious matters lay in the hands of three superannuated rabbinical judges *(dayanim),* whose authority was widely ignored and who were unable to make Judaism attractive to the younger generation.

With the expulsion of the French and the restoration of local sovereignty in Hamburg, the acculturated segment of the community found itself in an environment where prerevolutionary values were once again given prominence. In Hamburg, as in the rest of Germany, religion enjoyed an unexpected revival after 1815 and swept away the philosophical skepticism of the preceding thirty years. It became clear that the European culture of the nineteenth century would not, after all, be postreligious.

As Gentiles once again became more Christian, Jews who had strayed from their faith also began to look back more positively upon what they had left behind.[160] But a return to the existing institutions was not possible; they had become too much a part of the world outside Judaism to cast its deeply internalized values aside. They were equally unwilling to accept the self-segregation which once more adopting traditional Jewish practice would require. What scores of Hamburg Jews were now seeking was a means to express religious feelings within an acceptable setting that would reestablish their Jewish roots while compromising neither their aesthetic and moral sensibilities nor their social relationships with non-Jews. Some also hoped that religious forms more similar to those of Christians would speed the process of emancipation.[161]

As early as the fall of 1815 the first efforts were made to establish a temple in Hamburg on the model of Jacobson's in Berlin, but the project gained momentum only after Eduard Kley, a preacher at the Berlin services, arrived in Hamburg to take over the privately financed Jewish free school two years later. Kley began to conduct a class in religion at the school, open to the public, every Sunday morning. It included a sermon based on a passage from Kley's catechism, impromptu prayers, and hymns sung in Hebrew and German to the accompaniment of a small organ. Parents of the children, as well as an increasing number of other Hamburg Jews, attended these devotional exercises—often more than 150 persons. Meanwhile, plans were laid for the creation of a temple like the one in Berlin. This temple, however, would be a collective project from the very beginning, with an elected leadership and a rented sanctuary not located in a private home.[162]

On December 11, 1817 a meeting was held at Kley's initiative where sixty-five members of the Hamburg community signed the statutes of the "New Israelite Temple Association in Hamburg." The statutes proclaimed the intention of restoring dignity and meaning to Jewish worship and thus reviving interest in the ancestral religion. The signatories hoped to achieve this goal by the recitation of some prayers in the vernacular, by a German sermon, and by choral song with organ accompaniment. As a religious community, the congregation would also provide ceremonies for the occasions of the Jewish life cycle, including confirmation. It would enable its young people to receive "an enlightened Jewish education" and create a firm Jewish norm for those who until now had been irresolute in their views and commitments. The charter members elected a directorate of four members and a deputation of five to govern the association. Soon others joined, so that within three years membership exceeded one hundred families—a sizable congregation, though still less than ten percent of Hamburg Jewry.[163] Interestingly, most of the truly wealthy Jews in Hamburg were not among the founders of the temple. Those who chose to join the new association at its beginning were predominantly at the middle of the economic spectrum, with a disproportionate percentage of merchants. It appears that most of the established wealth of the city, concentrated in the older generation, remained distant from the new enterprise while younger men, more acculturated and possessing more commercial and social contacts with non-Jews, chose to affiliate with the association.[164]

Two members of the directorate, Seckel Isaac Fränkel (1765–1835) and Meyer Israel Bresselau (1785–1839), devoted themselves to the cause of the new association with particular intensity. These personal friends were excellent Hebraists, and though autodidacts in their general education, they had gained a broad cultural perspective. Both were members of the Hamburg branch of the Society for Culture and Scientific Study of the Jews in Berlin. Although Fränkel, the older of the two men, had begun his career as a teacher, his business acumen soon enabled him to gain financial success first as an accountant and then independently as a merchant banker. He possessed a remarkable knowledge of ancient and modern languages and published two Hebrew poems. Throughout his life he maintained an interest in Jewish scholarship, producing a translation of the Apocrypha from Greek into Hebrew, which was reprinted many times and was still regarded as a worthy model in the twentieth century.[165] Bresselau, who earned his living as a notary, was likewise an extraordinary linguist, with a special penchant for Semitic languages, Hebrew grammar, and medieval Hebrew poetry. Possessing a legal mind, well versed in talmudic as well as contemporary jurisprudence, Bresselau was, like Fränkel, interested in the immediately postbiblical literature. He composed a translation of the book of Ben Sira from Syriac into Hebrew—which, however, remained unpublished.[166] Together these two men undertook to edit a prayerbook for the new temple, and shortly thereafter each of them wrote a tract in its defense.

The new temple was dedicated on October 18, 1818 in rented quarters which provided 142 seats for men on the ground floor and 107 for women in the balcony. Although the reading desk remained in the center, as in a traditional synagogue, the unique character of the temple was apparent from the special balcony erected at the rear for an organ and choir and by the lack of a partition in front of the women's seats. The congregation drew to its ranks Hamburg Jews who had not visited a synagogue for fifteen years, and on special occasions, such as confirmations, it attracted large numbers of nonmembers as well. Mannheimer, who was highly critical of the services in Berlin, was favorably impressed by the Hamburg temple and by the commitment and Jewish knowledge of its leadership.[167]

While it is difficult to determine the extent to which the services in Hamburg were a response to the particular desire of Jewish women, Zunz tells us that "the inclination for a reform of the worship service was stirred among many, especially among the female sex." Aaron Chorin claimed that "the barbaric days are gone when the stronger half of humanity sought to lord it over the nobler half, when it was regarded as sinful to place the woman on the same level as the man." He concluded that therefore the Jewish service could not be for the men alone; it had to appeal to both sexes. And indeed the Hamburg temple drew a far higher percentage of women than did the traditional services. Very few women, either older or younger, knew a significant amount of Hebrew, and hence the need for German prayer was often justified with particular reference to them. It seems, also, that women were especially appreciative of the sermons that were delivered each Saturday morning.[168]

The Temple Association had hired two young men, Eduard Kley (1789–1867)—already mentioned—and Gotthold Salomon (1784–1862), to be the preachers *(Prediger)* of the congregation. Their title indicated that their role was principally homiletical. The designation "rabbi" was specifically avoided—even though Salomon, at least, possessed ordination from Menahem Mendel Steinhardt—both to avoid conflict with the Hamburg community's *dayanim* and to indicate that the role did not call for decisions on dietary laws and the like. Born into poverty, Kley had managed to get a doctorate from the University of Berlin while supporting himself as a tutor in the home of Jacob Herz Beer. His particular interest in Jewish religious education was expressed through a popular catechism which he wrote and through his service for many years as head of the Free School in Hamburg simultaneously with his duties as preacher at the temple. He was regarded as a man of firm principle, though also a bit of a pedant. While his sermons were exemplary in form and content, they lacked imagination and metaphor. His homiletics spoke to the congregation's mind, not to its heart.[169] Quite the opposite was true of his colleague, who was a far more skilled orator. Salomon too had begun as a teacher, in his case in Dessau. Unlike Kley, he never attended a university, but he had sufficient self-confidence in his own scholarship to undertake a complete Bible translation later in his career. Salomon's sermons were popular, his delivery passionate, his use of images and parables effective. He was the favorite preacher of the women, who managed to ignore his apparent vanity. Salomon was also among the first preachers to make extensive use of rabbinic literature in his sermons, moving away from the Christian models with which he began toward a more specifically Jewish, modern homiletics.[170] He continued to be one of the respected personalities in the Reform movement throughout the first half of the nineteenth century, although his views were soon considered dated or superficial by the more penetrating intellectual leadership of the next generation.

The Hamburg temple prayerbook was the first comprehensive Reform liturgy. Above a horizontal line on each page it placed the Hebrew and German texts that were publicly recited, below the line a translation into German—and in some cases a Sephardi transliteration—of those prayers that were said in Hebrew.[171] Only the German hymns, gathered in a separate volume, were excluded.[172] Title pages appeared in both languages and the volume untraditionally opened from left to right. The liturgy was in most respects similar to that of Berlin, but it departed further from the customary formulas of the prayers. Theological conception, which might have been expected to cause intellectual difficulties, were apparently of little concern to Fränkel and Bresselau. They retained intact, both in Hebrew and German, the references to the resurrection of the dead and even passages referring to the angelic hosts. They were more disturbed by the prayers for the reinstitution of the sacrifices. While the prayerbook did not exclude them completely, in the festival service the Hebrew text was changed to read: "May it be Your will, O Lord our God and God of our fathers, to receive in mercy and favor the expression of our lips in place of the obligatory sacrifices." The desire to eliminate or alter passages that dealt with the return to Zion was carried out partly by choosing less troublesome Sephardi formulas and partly by omissions and original substitutions. Yet the editors left unchanged the petition: "May our eyes see Your return to Zion in mercy. Blessed are You who restores His presence to Zion." The Hamburg reformers had not lost their love of Zion, nor did they fail to recognize its significant role in Jewish history. But they did not hope or desire to return there themselves or to rebuild the ancient temple.

The Hamburg service followed or exceeded its Berlin model in a few other respects. It retained the highly particularistic adoration *(alenu)* only on the High Holidays; the weekly reading from the Prophets was eliminated to allow more time for the sermon; and the Torah readings were reduced in length by the introduction of a triennial cycle instead of the customary annual one. The abbreviated service was conducted by a Sephardi Jew from Amsterdam, David Meldola, who presented a recitative of the Hebrew prayers in the Spanish–Portuguese manner and led the reading of the German passages.[173]

Music for the service was a problem. Traditional synagogues employed a cantor assisted by a bass and a boy soprano. The trio generally lacked any formal musical training and used melodies that were often adopted from popular secular songs; they made a cacophonous sound. Jews exposed to contemporary music or familiar with the role of hymns in the church found the situation aesthetically insufferable. But there was as yet nowhere to turn for a more acceptable Jewish music. The lyrics for the German hymns sung in the Hamburg temple were composed by Jewish writers, including Kley and Fränkel, some of them based on traditional Hebrew hymns like *Adon Olam*, others on psalms or—in most cases—on general religious themes. However, the music was mostly commissioned from Gentile composers. Although the choir was composed of Jewish school boys, the organist was a Gentile—in part perhaps on account of the halakhic problem of a Jew playing an instrument on the Sabbath, but also for lack of qualified Jewish musicians. The result was a strange combination of Sephardi modes in the Hebrew together with the contemporary style of church music in the German hymns. Only in succeeding decades would a modern Jewish liturgical music develop, after the appearance of talented synagogue composers like Solomon Sulzer in Vienna and Louis Lewandowski in Berlin.[174]

In the fall of 1820 a service similar to that in Hamburg was instituted in the Saxon city of Leipzig for those times, twice a year, when Jews from all over Europe gathered there for the fairs. It took place in an academic lecture hall donated by the local university and drew an attendance of 250 for the dedicatory sermon. Jews from as far away as Brody, Bucharest, Vienna, Cracow, and Amsterdam participated in the worship. These services continued for a number of years until a permanent synagogue was established in the city.[175] A year earlier a temple association on the Berlin and Hamburg model had been established in Karlsruhe in Baden. It held services in its own house of worship from 1820 until 1823, when its members rejoined the traditional majority, which had agreed to adopt the inclusion of a sermon, some German prayers, decorum, and a confirmation ceremony. At least some elements of the new style of worship spread to other cities as well.[176]

In Hamburg the Temple Association and its liturgy immediately aroused controversy.[177] It seemed that it would be easy enough to obtain the required approval from the community's board of elected officials *(Vorsteherkollegium)* since no less than four of them, half their number, had signed the statutes of the temple. But strong opposition emerged from two of the remaining board members and from the three rabbinical judges. Fearing a serious rift, the community board as a whole began to cast about for a compromise. But they soon found they were unable to persuade either the reformers to give up their new prayerbook or the traditionalists to tolerate the temple. The leaders of the temple held that their association was a private one, financed by its members, who nevertheless continued to pay their taxes to the general community. Therefore neither the community's elected officials nor its rabbinical judges possessed any jurisdiction over it. The traditionalists, on the other hand, saw the temple as simply another communal house of worship, and hence subject to central control. In between stood the majority of the community board, which was less interested in religious issues than in maintaining unity and the steady inflow of voluntary donations to charitable institutions.

The Hamburg Senate was now besieged with petitions and declarations from all three parties. Its solution was to impose a compromise. On September 17, 1819, it issued an edict which scrupulously avoided using language partial to either side. It held that the association had created neither a synagogue nor a temple, but "a place for public edification." Its spiritual leaders were neither rabbis nor preachers, but merely "teachers." Thus the new association was made to seem supplemental to existing community institutions rather than in rivalry with them. The secularly minded city authorities really cared little what the Jews did with their religion, as long as they avoided a split in the community, which could create problems in supporting the Jewish poor. From the point of view of the government, the new institution could organize its liturgy and ritual as it wished.

The traditionalists in the community, however, were not so tolerant. Although their efforts to persuade the government failed, they hoped for greater success in a propaganda venture to so blacken the new institution in Jewish eyes that its members would be regarded as outcasts. The three rabbinical judges issued a proclamation that declared it strictly forbidden to alter liturgical formulas in the slightest, to pray in any language other than Hebrew, or to have a musical instrument played in the synagogue on Sabbaths or holidays—even by a Gentile. The judges noted that as long as only individuals had strayed from the path of traditional practice they had been content to grieve in silence. But now an institution had been created which, as it were, granted legitimacy to a heterodox expression of Judaism. Vigorous condemnation had therefore become a necessity. To their dismay, they had found that, unlike in the past, their authority was challenged, their collective voice not obeyed. Thus they were turning directly to all members of the community, warning that it was prohibited to pray from the new prayerbook and urging parents to keep their children away from the temple lest they fall victim to it. They called upon the temple members to repent of their evil ways and to return to the fold.

Placed on the defensive both by the new temple in their midst and by Liebermann's two tracts—which seemed to justify the Hamburg reformers no less than those in Berlin—the judges sent letters out to rabbinical authorities in central Europe calling on them to strengthen their hand and prove to Jew and Gentile alike that the work of the "innovators" stood outside the pale of Judaism. They succeeded in gathering no less than twenty-two opinions signed by forty rabbis, which they published in Altona in 1819 as *Eleh divre ha-berit* (These Are the Words of the Covenant), along with German excerpts in both Hebrew and Gothic characters.

For the most part, the rabbis confined themselves to quoting authoritative texts against the innovations of the temple and pronouncing them forbidden. Their halakhic grounds were stronger in some instances, such as the wording of the prayers, weaker in others, like use of the vernacular. Basically, they were all opposed to any alteration of existing practice, in accordance with the dictum that "the custom of Israel is Torah." With varying degrees of vehemence they condemned the reformers as "evil men" who were destroying Judaism in order to find favor in Gentile eyes. Like all sinners these deviants from established practice and flouters of rabbinical authority were deserving of divine punishment. Or, one rabbi suggests, perhaps it would be best if the champions of tradition were to take practical steps, making entreaties to the government so that "the house of the wicked will be demolished" (Prov. 14:11), "and the arms of the wicked be broken" (Psalms 37:17). The respondents sought to invalidate *Nogah ha-tsedek* and *Or nogah* not only by refuting the arguments they contained but also by inducing Aaron Chorin to recant (at least for the moment) and impugning the character of Eliezer Liebermann. Only one of the respondents, Rabbi Eliezer of Triesch in Moravia, in his second opinion recognized the need for any reform at all. He condemned the disorder and frequent quarrels in traditional synagogues and proposed the introduction of regular edifying sermons.

Instead of seeking government support for coercive measures, as he had recommended earlier, Eliezer now recommended peaceful persuasion.[178]

Other Hebrew tracts appeared attacking the reformers. Nachman Berlin, a repentant maskil of Lissa in Posen, favored using every available means against the enemy. He not only suggested burning Liebermann's work but noted also that the reformers could easily be pictured as rebels, first against religion and then against constituted political authority. Thus it would not be difficult to bring external pressure to bear on them.[179] The most extensive polemic against religious reform came from the pen of Abraham Löwenstamm, a rabbi in Emden, not far from Hamburg.[180] Of particular interest is the last of nine sections into which Löwenstamm divided his book. Bearing the title *Kets ha-yamin* (The End of Days), it deals with a subject that the Hamburg prayerbook had forced into the foreground and which was addressed by most of its opponents: the traditional conception of the messianic redemption.

Without question the omission and alteration of certain liturgical passages dealing with the messianic return to Zion was the most audacious innovation of the Hamburg reformers.[181] It cast doubt on a central principle of Jewish faith firmly grounded in all layers of Jewish tradition. To deny hope of Israel's reconstitution as a nation on its own soil and the rebuilding of the temple, it was felt, amounted to a denial of Judaism itself. Yet messianism was a touchy issue because it could be interpreted to imply lack of complete loyalty to the rulers under whom Jews lived. Moreover, it was an exclusive doctrine which posited an age when God would exalt Israel above the other nations of the earth. Once hope of emancipation in Europe had undermined, or at least come to rival, the desire for return to Palestine, Jews were faced with the problem of rejecting messianism completely, in some way reconciling the two, or reinterpreting the older belief to fit their new situation. Neither reformers nor traditionalists took the first course. Judaism without some future hope, nearly all recognized, would be devoid of energizing force. Some traditionalists chose to point out that the promised return to Zion in no way conflicted with their loyalty and love for the rulers whose good will toward them they appreciated greatly. Others, including Löwenstamm, began also to stress the universal elements in the Jewish vision. The messiah would bring peace to the nations; his coming would be a boon to all humankind. Their interpretation further stressed that Jews were not permitted to initiate the redemption. It could only come by God's will and in God's own time. Consequently, messianic hope demanded political quietism, certainly not disloyalty to established institutions or any attempt to overthrow them.

What severely disturbed the traditionalists about the Hamburg reformers was that they had not merely reinterpreted messianism to tone down its particularism and reconcile it with patriotism. They had transferred their messianic hopes entirely to Europe and had given that shift expression in the prayerbook itself. Their worship service in Hamburg was for them a permanent substitution for the sacrificial cult in Jerusalem. They preserved memories of Zion, but their hopes lay elsewhere. For the champions of tradition this was no mere heresy, it was a step beyond the pale. Löwenstamm went even further. He argued that a Jew who ceased to believe in the coming of the messiah was not even a civilized human being, since Christians and Muslims no less than Jews were messianists, though in their case the messiah had already come.

The united voice of rabbinical authority against the Hamburg temple now put the reformers on the defensive. Fränkel came out with a German tract justifying the changes contained in the new prayerbook; Bresselau brought together in a brief German work all the rabbinic passages he could muster supporting prayer in the vernacular.[182] The latter also published a brief, largely satirical, and stylistically remarkable work in Hebrew, *Ḥerev nokemet nekam berit* (The Sword Which Avenges the Covenant), in which he held the opinions of the rabbinical authorities in *Eleh divre ha-berit* up to ridicule.[183] The German pamphlets add little that is novel to the debate. They combine halakhic argument with personal sentiment, attempting to show both the legitimacy and the desirability of combining Hebrew and German, traditional and innovative elements, as had been done in the service of the temple. Bresselau's Hebrew tract, however, is of more than passing interest. Cleverly playing upon biblical phrases, its author was able to exploit his literary skill as a Hebraist to paint two contrasting portraits. One was of the traditional community whose shepherds, the three *dayanim,* had allowed their flock to stray from Judaism until "our sons and daughters were lost to another people." Although in its synagogues attendance had decreased drastically, insistence upon existing customs remained undiminished. Like the Israelites addressed by Jeremiah (7:4), they had put their trust in the illusion that God's house would always stand fast. Inside the synagogue was noise and disharmonious song so that it was not possible to concentrate on prayer; few understood the liturgy or the obscure sermons. It was a picture of decay and imminent ruin through self-destruction. The temple, by contrast, Bresselau portrayed as a happy place attended by a large congregation, children as well as adults, who came away uplifted and edified. It was stemming the tide of assimilation. The youth, unlike their parents, would not be "a rebellious generation."[184]

In the midst of such vituperative polemics, such black and white images, there were few voices of moderation. An exception was Lazarus Jacob Riesser, the widely respected son-in-law of the uncompromising Rabbi Raphael Kohen. Though not a member of the Hamburg temple, Riesser recognized that secularism was eroding traditional belief and practice, that it was creating a severe rift in the community. He welcomed the temple as a valiant effort to bring alienated Jews back to their faith and to their people. Traditionalists should not condemn the new services, he believed, but perceive them as a bridge leading back to more complete observance.[185]

Since Riesser recognized that the temple spoke to a genuine need but could not personally endorse all of its liturgical innovation, he soon became involved in a project which, by appropriating some of the temple's attractive elements, had the effect of reducing its appeal and even relegating it to the periphery. Within days after the temple held its first service, the initial suggestion was made to the community board that the time had come to hire a new rabbi for the entire community.[186] Soon there were 117 signatures on a petition requesting a spiritual leader who would replace the aged *dayanim,* introduce a modernized ritual, fully in keeping with the Halakhah, into the community synagogues, and improve Jewish education. The project was frequently discussed by the board during the next two years. Not surprisingly, it aroused the opposition of some members of the Temple Association, who wanted to avoid additional community taxes when they also had to pay the salaries of the temple's preachers. But their opposition did not prevail. Riesser was delegated to work out arrangements with the most promising candidate, Isaac Bernays (1792–1849), a young rabbi with a university education who was committed to acculturation and halakhically permissible modernization in religious externals, but also to the preservation of inherited customs and ceremonies. He thus could present a model for the youth:

modernity within the framework of tradition. Once appointed, Bernays did not hesitate to don the garb of Christian clergy (like the preachers of the temple) and to give regular German sermons in a community synagogue. Since he conducted life-cycle ceremonies in a decorous, dignified manner, there was now less reason to become associated with the temple—and to pay its additional dues. Bernays' appointment in 1821 in effect marked the end of the dispute over the Hamburg temple. The new *hakham* (the Sephardi designation which Bernays preferred to that of rabbi) was specifically enjoined by his contract from interfering with, or even condemning the activities of the Temple Association. For the time being at least, a situation of religious pluralism and mutual toleration was created within the Ashkenazi Jewish community of Hamburg. Neither faction had been able to displace the other; each in its own way was now responding to the challenge of modernity.

The Hamburg temple controversy thus concludes the first stage in the development of the Reform movement. Basic religious issues had been raised, the first successful institutionalization completed. Rabbinism of the old type, which could only condemn modernity, was being forced to give way to varying degrees of accommodation. The reformers, for their part, had shown that, despite the views of some, Judaism was not "a mummy that crumbles into dust when it is touched by a free atmosphere."[187] But they had also been forced to recognize that in the immediate future they could hope to exercise influence over only a fraction of the community and that governments were not necessarily disposed in their favor. Most important, they had not yet created a real sense of being a movement with clearly defined goals and an ideology on which to build institutions. By their own admission, they had confined themselves to immediate objectives. As Bresselau put it: "We sought to improve the worship service and this we have done; I do not consider myself called to be a reformer."[188] In Hamburg the movement struck its first lasting roots. But if it was to survive and grow, it needed to deepen those roots and send out branches.

2

Ideological Ferment

The Intellectual Context

Most of those who associated themselves with the temples in Berlin and Hamburg did so for personal and social reasons. They found the services comprehensible, edifying, and religiously meaningful, and at the same time less strange to the Christian milieu that was increasingly becoming their own. Few gave much attention to the more philosophical aspects of Judaism's viability in the modern age. Only after a generation did the realization dawn that unless Judaism could be made intellectually—and not just aesthetically and socially—respectable, the formal accomplishments would rest on a foundation of sand; worship would be the modernized but merely ephemeral expression of a vestigial inherited identity. For Judaism itself to survive in its new environment Jews, and preferably also Gentiles, would have to recognize that the older faith was not only compatible in form with modern (Christian) modes of religious expression but also that as a historical entity and system of belief it was sufficiently alive and flexible to meet the onslaught of hostile currents of thought. The early temples created a milieu in which the acculturating Jewish worshiper could feel at home. It was left to a new generation of Jewish religious intellectuals to rethink the Jewish faith in a way that would justify its persistence alongside Christianity.

As far back as the middle of the eighteenth century it was widely assumed that Judaism could not possibly continue to appeal to Jews who had absorbed the culture of the Enlightenment. Thus the Swiss theologian Johann Caspar Lavater had believed that the unfanatical and philosophically inclined Moses Mendelssohn would surely be persuaded of the truth of Christianity. Later representatives of Christian and academic thought in Germany were no less certain that Judaism was inherently incompatible with modernity. They set forth influential religious and philosophical systems which consistently assigned it a limited role in history, and one inferior to Christianity. Since the Reform movement was predicated upon harmonizing Judaism with modernity, its intellectual leadership was eager to relate Jewish doctrine to prevalent philosophies. At the same time its commitment to a revitalization of Judaism forced a confrontation with the elements in those philosophies that made Jewish survival in the modern age seem anachronistic and efforts to modernize Judaism appear misguided or vain. The theologies developed by Jewish thinkers in Germany thus emerged out of a tension between the desire to incorporate contemporary modes of thought and the equally strong desire to preserve continuity with the Jewish past while refuting those judgments upon Judaism which in one way or another denied it a future.

It is ironic that the earliest and most fundamental modern challenge to Judaism should have arisen from its own midst. A product of the Sephardi community in Amsterdam, Baruch Spinoza (1632–1677) moved rapidly beyond the traditional Jewish teachings upon which he was raised until he eventually developed a philosophical system that contradicted the most basic doctrines of Judaism. Excommunicated for the expression of his views, he bequeathed to subsequent generations a disagreeable but highly influential conception of his ancestral faith. Although for the most part modern Jewish thinkers took issue with Spinoza's ideas, whether or not they mentioned his name, there were certain elements in his thought that appealed to some of them.[1]

Spinoza's major work, the *Ethics,* undermined the foundations of Judaism and of Christianity alike. The transcendent creator God of the Bible was replaced by the purely immanent God equivalent to nature. In a deterministic system, free will—the basis of moral responsibility—no longer had its place and personal immortality became an illusion. Mendelssohn had already recognized the incompatibility of Spinozism with Judaism and felt compelled to deny the accusation that his friend Lessing had been converted to it. Similarly, even the most radical Reformers of the following century rejected Spinoza's ontology. In his *Theologico-Political Treatise,* Spinoza made Judaism out to be religiously superfluous. Reason was sufficient to determine the goodness and eternal divinity of God, and therefrom to deduce a morality. The Bible was necessary for the masses, but not at all for the philosopher. Nor were the Prophets a unique treasure. Spinoza relativized their message: prophets, he noted, appear also in other nations; the prophetic gift was not peculiar to the Jews. No less problematic was the preference Spinoza expressed for Christianity over Judaism. Although he never converted, Spinoza assigned to Jesus a role in revelation far more elevated than that of the Hebrew prophets: "If Moses spoke with God face to face as a man speaks with his friend (*i.e.,* by means of their two bodies), Christ communed with God mind to mind." At another point he says: "Christ was not so much a prophet as the mouthpiece of God." In Spinoza's clearly jaundiced view, Judaism was exclusivist and predominantly concerned with material needs; Christianity alone was universalistic and spiritual. In fact, Judaism was actually a deleterious influence which, Spinoza suggested, may well have emasculated the minds of its adherents. If the Jews had nonetheless persisted to modern times, their survival was not on account of any innate virtues in their religion but because they had separated themselves from other nations, attracting universal hatred not only by their outward rites, which conflicted with those of other nations, but also by the sign of circumcision which they scrupulously observed.[2]

These were views no Jewish religious thinker could allow. Yet other elements of Spinoza's biblical criticism were to a greater or lesser extent absorbed by those Jewish writers for whom the commitment to historical analysis did not stop short even at the text of the Pentateuch. Spinoza had cast serious doubt on the Mosaic authorship of the Torah; increasingly so did the Reformers, especially after the higher biblical criticism became more widely accepted in the second half of the nineteenth century. But Spinoza's most divisive legacy was his limitation of the Mosaic law's validity to the period when Jews possessed their own state and temple; it was, he argued, the constitution of their polity and had lost all binding force once the Jews went into exile.[3] Mendelssohn and most Jewish thinkers who followed him rejected this idea, but prominent radical Reformers, beginning with Samuel Holdheim, adopted it to justify abrogation of ceremonial observance.

In Germany, Spinoza's thought enjoyed considerable popularity beginning with the last decades of the eighteenth century. His view of Judaism corresponded easily with Christian prejudices and even influenced those who were favorably disposed toward individual Jews. Spinoza had written that "religion was imparted to the early Hebrews as a law written down, because they were at that time in the condition of children, but afterwards Moses and Jeremiah predicted a time coming when the Lord should write His law on their hearts."[4] This notion, that Judaism represented the faith of people who were spiritually children, was echoed by Gotthold Ephraim Lessing (1729–1781) in his influential essay *The Education of Humanity*.[5] Lessing clothed the established Christian idea of the supersession of the older faith by the younger in a new, historical garment. Revelation and reason, in reciprocal relation, led upward as the human spirit progressed from stage to stage. For centuries religious progress characterized ancient Israel, but during the Second Commonwealth Judaism reached the end of its capacity for internal religious development. While its rabbis misguidedly and in vain sought to read more advanced ideas into the elementary textbook of the Hebrew Bible, a better pedagogue, Jesus, appeared and enabled humanity to advance further upon its path. Lessing thus made contemporary Judaism an anachronism. Jewish writers were forced to reject his relegation of Judaism to a primitive stage in a process which had gone beyond it. But ironically the thrust of Lessing's approach soon became essential for the theological enterprise of the Reformers. While Mendelssohn had insisted on an unchanging Judaism whose eternal truths could never be supplanted or even substantively refined, Reform ideologists adopted Lessing's notion of religious advance during the course of history. For them, too, revelation became progressive as succeeding ages built upon the past. But they parted company with Lessing in their insistence that Judaism was still capable of progress. Far from being merely a stage in a universal process of religious development, it was itself the bearer of ever richer insights into the nature of the Divine and God's will for all humanity.

Among German philosophers Immanuel Kant (1724–1804) had by far the most widespread and lasting influence on modern Jewish thinkers. His rejection of Christian dogma, especially the innate corruption of man, together with his insistence that religious faith begins with action rather than atonement, made Kant's thought highly attractive to a Judaism that stressed divine commandment rather than the salvation wrought by faith. Like Lessing, Kant presented a wholly unacceptable conception of Judaism.[6] But he also outlined the possibility of a rationally viable faith, challenging Jewish writers to reinterpret Judaism to fit his definition of an intellectually and morally respectable religion.

Eight years after Lessing's *The Education of Humanity,* in 1793, Kant published his *Religion within the Limits of Reason Alone.* Under the influence of Spinoza and Mendelssohn, but probably also of longstanding Christian tradition, Kant here defined Judaism in its original form as "a collection of mere statutory laws upon which was established a political organization." In fact, Judaism was "really not a religion at all" since it made no claims upon conscience. Insofar as it possessed genuinely religious characteristics, these were foreign imports derived from Greek wisdom. Biblical Judaism stressed only external acts and outward observances, lacked belief in a future life, and excluded all but ancient Israel from its communion. Its God was a political autocrat, who merely desired obedience to commands and mechanical worship, not the moral Being required by religion. Christianity, since it was utterly different in all these respects, could not have arisen out of Judaism; it was rather the suddenly created product of a revolution which for the first time produced a genuine religious faith.[7] Much as Kant's conception of biblical Judaism represented a severe distortion, its articulation by the most highly regarded of all German philosophers made it easier for Jews personally inclined to reject their heritage to justify the step of conversion. Moreover, Kant's influential idea that beyond all historical religions there was "a single, unchanging, pure religious faith"[8] dwelling in the human conscience— in essence the religion of the future—made indifference to all specific elements of Judaism religiously respectable. For if God required nothing more than steadfast diligence in leading a morally good life, in fulfilling one's duties to fellow human beings, then all ceremonial and symbolic expressions were ultimately superfluous.

Rejection of the Kantian misconception became the task of all who sought to rescue Judaism's reputation. What singles out the Reformers' relation to Kant is their adoption of so much that the Königsberg philosopher pointed to as being not Jewish and stressing its centrality within their own Jewish self-definition. The idea that pure religious faith is essentially moral rapidly became the theoretical basis and the practical operative principle of the Reform movement. Its influence dominates the writings of Reform Jewish thinkers. No less is the primacy of morality reflected in the prominent role given to the sermons that were delivered in the new congregations— sermons which focused not on points of ceremonial law, but on virtuous conduct in business or family relationships. Kant had declared that ceremonies to please God were morally indifferent and historically representative of paganism. A house of God was properly a "meeting place for the instruction and quickening of moral dispositions."[9] Thus, instead of being the religion of no morality—as Kant defined it—the Reformers sought to present Judaism as the religion most exclusively concerned with morality, and hence most worthy of the future. The Kantian idea of individual autonomy in religion likewise assumed centrality among the Reformers, where it was used to undermine the authority of tradition, forced consideration of how God could both command and allow for human moral responsibility, and militated against the Reformers' own sporadic attempts to impose varying degrees of religious conformity.

Kant recognized, moreover, that historical faiths were bound to sacred texts which did not necessarily reflect the highest morality. Where text and conscience were in conflict, Kant left no doubt as to which should be forced to yield. He agreed with Spinoza that the highest purpose of scriptural study was moral improvement. Consequently it sometimes became necessary—and wholly justifiable in his eyes—to utilize forced rather than literal interpretations when the latter might work against moral incentives. In opposition to more conservative spirits, Kant held that the Bible had to be expounded according to moral conceptions, not moral conceptions adjusted to the word of the Bible.[10] His insistence upon rational and moral criteria external to the text by which the religious value of individual passages should be judged was adopted by the Jewish Reformers as it was by liberal Christians. Jewish thinkers all across the religious spectrum engaged in forced interpretation of morally problematic passages, but only the Reformers were willing to suggest that their reinterpretations were grounded in a morality which had transcended that of the Bible itself. Ultimately Kant's rational religion was supposed to free itself of all texts and traditions. Kant believed that when humanity entered its adolescence, statutes and traditions, which were once helpful, turned into fetters. Thus all historical religions were destined to give way before the one universal rational and moral faith.[11] Reflecting upon Kant, Reform ideologists felt that what they had to do was to demonstrate that Judaism, once properly reinterpreted and purified of ceremonialism, would be far from the statutory pseudoreligion which Kant had called it; on the contrary, it could become just that faith which Kant ascribed to the future.

Although the Kantian challenge and its influence on the Reform movement remained strong well into the twentieth century, Enlightenment thought (which in Germany climaxed with Kant) was soon overshadowed by the radically different worldview of Romanticism. Its outstanding theological representative, Friedrich Schleiermacher (1768–1834), presented no more positive a view of Judaism than did earlier writers. However, his sharply contrasting understanding of religion in general helped to lead modern Jewish thought, too, in a new direction. Like Kant, Schleiermacher believed that Judaism had no future in the modern world. In 1799 he had written that "Judaism is long since dead. Those who yet wear its livery but sit lamenting beside the imperishable mummy, bewailing its departure and its sad legacy."[12] Again like Kant, he deplored Judaism's lack of universalism and tended to minimize the historical connection between Judaism and Christianity; and like Spinoza and Lessing he, too, described it as childlike compared to its successor faith. In his very influential dogmatics, *The Christian Faith,* first published in 1821–1822, Schleiermacher placed Judaism, along with Islam and Christianity, on the highest level of monotheistic faith, but Christianity, because both universal and freed of all sensualism, represented its purest and most perfect form. Only a sick soul, he noted, would abandon it for one of its rivals.[13]

Schleiermacher was determined to restore respect for Christianity by insisting that religion was animated by feeling, not rational postulates. Intuition, not logical argument, established its most basic certainties. Since religions did not exist apart from "pious communities," natural religion, which had never served as the faith of any historical entity, was nothing more than the result of abstracting common elements with the tools of reason. In contrast to the Enlightenment, Schleiermacher did not believe that Christianity would be absorbed into a purely rational faith. It was forever bound by its scripture, which placed at its center a Redeemer of humanity, not merely a teacher of moral truths.[14] The effect of Schleiermacher's thought for Judaism was to remove it much further from Christianity than had been true during the Enlightenment. Mendelssohn had been able to make his religion appear modern by stressing that it fully embraced natural religion, adding to it only revealed legislation. Schleiermacher cut Christianity loose from Judaism in two respects: not only did Christianity lack historical continuity with Judaism, it was also not joined to it by an underlying bond of natural religion. In fact he declared it a separate species. But thereby—at least implicitly—he also created a rationale for its persistence. For if Judaism was the unique faith of a historical community that possessed its own individuality and was shaped by its own revelation and experience, if it could not be compartmentalized into universal natural religion and particular observance, then neglect of the ceremonial law did not mean the end of Jewish particularity. By reviving respect for positive, historical religion, Schleiermacher's thought became one of the influences which turned the Reformers to examining Judaism in terms of its particular development and not alone its conformity with reason.

If Schleiermacher's reevaluation of individuality among religions unintendedly gave Judaism a rationale for separated, ongoing existence, Hegel's conception of Judaism within the scheme of historical religions left it once again consigned to the past. For Georg Wilhelm Friedrich Hegel (1770–1831), as for Lessing, Judaism represented but a single stage of human development. While for Lessing that stage was a level of religious education, in Hegel's thought it became a thrust in the dialectical progress of the World Spirit. Thus Hegel's mature writings presented Judaism as the "religion of sublimity," one-sidedly emphasizing a transcendent God toward whom the worshiper assumed an attitude of fear.[15] Christianity corrected this imbalance through the Incarnation, which brought God directly into history. Because Hegel's philosophical thought was predicated upon pantheism, Christianity with its doctrinal immanentism was far more conducive to it than Judaism. Moreover, Hegel's veneration for the state as the highest embodiment of the World Spirit created an atmosphere of political quietism which stifled prophetic morality. For about a generation before midcentury, Hegel's influence in Germany was enormous. Jewish thinkers could not help but be affected by his grand system and its cherished goal of freedom. Yet like Spinoza, Hegel left no room in his thought for significant individual responsibility. And that was essential to any conception of Judaism, especially for the Reformers, who dwelt on Judaism's moral imperative. Although thoughtful Jews had to grapple with Hegel's philosophy, ultimately they all rejected some of its most basic elements.

It is within this intellectual context that the early theological enterprise of the Reform movement must be understood: an environment in which no major thinker believed that Judaism was the equal of Christianity or that it could meet the challenge of modernity. Yet Jewish thinkers could not ignore the Christian philosophers and theologians, for their views represented the very modernity which Judaism had to confront if it was not to retreat into intellectual isolation. We shall first briefly consider the most philosophical spirits among the Jewish writers. Their abstruse systematic writings, to be sure, had little influence on the average Jew, but it was they who confronted the theoretical challenge most directly. Then we shall dwell upon the new critical scholarship, which presented both a challenge and an instrument to the Reformers. Finally, we shall deal at greater length with the practical ideologists, those who sought to develop central concepts and purposes by which to define and give direction to a modernizing Judaism.

New Conceptions of Judaism

Three important systematic thinkers appeared within German Jewry in the first half of the nineteenth century. One of them, Solomon Ludwig Steinheim (1789–1866), was a physician who remained distant from day-to-day religious controversies and spent the last twenty years of his life mostly in Rome. The other two, Solomon Formstecher (1808–1889) and Samuel Hirsch (1815–1889), were both rabbis who participated actively in the Reform movement. None of the three was principally concerned with the traditional Jewish preoccupation of the law. For each of them—as increasingly for the Reform movement—significant Jewish intellectual endeavor lay rather in the sphere of theology.[16]

It is generally agreed that of the three Steinheim was both the most original and the least influential.[17] He was a man of unusually broad learning and creativity, a writer on medical subjects as well as a poet and theologian. He played an active role in the Jewish community of Altona and wrote on behalf of Jewish emancipation, but his knowledge of Jewish sources seems to have been limited mainly to the Bible and a few of the medieval writers. When in his early forties, Steinheim began to interest himself seriously in theology and in 1835 published the first of four volumes entitled *Revelation According to the Doctrine of the Synagogue*.[18] Apparently he was agitated by the urging of friends that he convert to Christianity, and like Mendelssohn before him and Franz Rosenzweig much after him, he felt challenged to justify his persistence in Judaism. He was also concerned that the centrifugal force of assimilation was dissipating Jewish consciousness. Whereas in Christianity, following the Enlightenment, religion had been reunited with culture, the same was not, he believed, true for Judaism.

Steinheim therefore set out to defend Judaism philosophically, attempting to shore it up against the erosion that was undermining its foundations. He did so by raising Judaism high above history where the ravages of time could do it no damage. In a sense he was following in the footsteps of Mendelssohn, who had also believed Judaism eternal, stressing its adherence to the rational truths of natural religion and its legislation revealed to the Jewish people for all historical time. However, Steinheim rejected both of the pillars of Mendelssohn's faith. Natural religion in his eyes was a new paganism devised by the Enlightenment; the biblical legislation was national, local, and temporary. What made Judaism eternal was something quite different: a foundation of doctrinal revelation as unchanging as the principles of mathematics. This revelation allowed for neither internal development nor growth. Since it was given by God, it was perfect from the first. The history of religion was thus not a history of revelation itself, as Lessing had held, but only a history of its acceptance or rejection. For Steinheim the true revelation, which God had transmitted to ancient Israel, consisted essentially of the doctrines of God's transcendence and uniqueness, divine and human freedom, and God's creation of the world out of nothing. Human reason, Steinheim argued, could not have arrived at these ideas; in fact they contradict the whole tradition of philosophical thought from pagan antiquity to modern times. Yet once revealed, they force rational assent even against preexisting inclination. Revelation does not simply reinforce what is latent in the human spirit; it demands a complete transformation of the inner person, "a spiritual rebirth." Whether or not ancient Israel was a primitive people did not really matter for Steinheim, since the revelation stood above its bearers.[19]

According to Steinheim, revelation stands in the sharpest opposition to paganism, with which it engages in perpetual combat. The Jewish people has been and still is the "trustee" of this revelation, whereas philosophy champions the naturalism of the pagans. Between the two lies Christianity, a mixture of both, which has sought in vain to reconcile what is irreconcilable ever since it carried biblical revelation to the heathen. Judaism alone preserved the revelation in the "pure, unadulterated, pristine form" in which it was destined eventually to win the struggle with paganism. Steinheim's understanding of revelation clearly placed his own religion above Christianity; Judaism not only preceded Christianity; it was also destined in the course of time to succeed it.[20] He thus provided a personal reason for remaining Jewish and at the same time a reply to all those conceptions of Judaism which made it an anachronism.

Although Steinheim was deeply rooted in the modern European intellectual milieu, his views stand in sharpest contrast to it. Not surprisingly, he utterly rejected Spinozism, which he regarded as a classic example of the pagan tradition, calling Spinoza himself "the great denier of God in the covenanted people." But no less did his views contrast with Hegel's equally deterministic system. While Steinheim shares with Schleiermacher the rejection of natural religion, he specifically objects to the Christian theologian's insistence that the religious consciousness requires no external communication of God's nature, will, or plan for humanity.[21] It is generally thought that, especially in his later writings, Steinheim was closest to Kant.[22] Indeed, among the moderns, it was Kant who first recognized the limitation of human reason, stressed human freedom, sharply separated the "is" from the "ought," and outlined a religion far removed from what Steinheim termed paganism. But Kant was not a believer in supernatural revelation, and Steinheim was.

Among Jewish thinkers as well, Steinheim stood alone. His theology was a revolt against the Mendelssohnian compartmentalization of Judaism into universal philosophy and particular observance. On one occasion he epitomized this lack of inner unity by calling Mendelssohn "a heathen in his brain and a Jew in his body." Steinheim was no less severe a critic of contemporary Jewish orthodoxy, which he accused of rote ceremonialism and gross mystification. He did not believe that revelation extended to the institutions of ancient Israel—explicitly not to animal sacrifices—and he thought that the prayerbook had unfortunately incorporated pagan elements. He was thus a proponent of ritual reform and welcomed the Hamburg Temple. He was also a universalist who stressed that the Jewish religion, including its messianic teaching, was free of particularism. Difference with regard to religious forms was justifiable in Judaism only "as long as philosophical paganism is still wandering alive among us." For the present, if the forms of Judaism too closely resembled those of Christianity, its fundamental inner distinctiveness would be overlooked and thereby its mission—to propagate the pure revelation—remain unattained. But if Steinheim sympathized with ritual reform, in his later writings he decried the theology of other Reformers. They had been ashamed to speak publicly of revelation to their congregations; some of them, he believed, had in their theoretical writings mistakenly identified the revealed doctrines of Judaism with modern pantheism or idealism.[23]

Steinheim consistently paid little attention to postbiblical Judaism, and in this he differed not only from the Orthodox but also from a Reform movement that was becoming increasingly conscious of history. While the Reformers stressed religious development, Steinheim denied it; while the Reformers linked their enterprise to the rationalist tradition of Jewish philosophy, Steinheim was unfamiliar with much of that tradition and rejected what he knew. Those Jews who believed in the supernatural revelation of doctrine believed no less in the divine origins of the Halakhah, but Steinheim did not; those Jews who rejected or limited the authority of the ceremonial law were usually also rationalists unwilling to admit a fully supernaturalist conception of revelation. It is not surprising, therefore, that Steinheim remained an isolated, if fascinating, figure.

Had there been professors of Jewish theology at German universities, Solomon Formstecher tells us in the preface to his *The Religion of the Spirit* (1841), practical men like himself would not have had to occupy themselves with writing on the subject in their leisure hours. But at that time and all through the nineteenth century no German university was prepared to establish a chair of Judaica even when funds were offered by the Jews themselves. Thus Formstecher, who throughout his career remained a preacher in the Jewish community of Offenbach, took it upon himself at the age of thirty-three to publish a comprehensive theoretical and historical description of Judaism which would place it into relation with the reigning philosophy of absolute idealism, especially as expounded by Friedrich Schelling, and also with Christianity and Islam. He remembered from his own university years in Giessen that what was taught in the lecture hall about Judaism was derisive, emotionally biased toward Christianity, and grossly in contradiction with his own conception and first-hand experience of his faith. He had come to the conclusion that only a Jew could write impartially of Judaism. Formstecher therefore attempted both to raise Judaism to intellectual respectability by applying to it the terminology of academic thought and to set it above the rival faiths, especially Christianity, which claimed to succeed it. He was aware that he could not simply present Judaism within the context of one of the idealist philosophies or theologies, since to do so would necessarily produce a totally unacceptable conception. He could only utilize selectively some of the terms and ideas of the intellectual environment, remaining always conscious of the ramifications for Judaism.[24] The result is that while one can trace the influence on his thought of Schelling, and perhaps also of Fichte and Hegel, Formstecher remained eclectic in his approach, more determined to be a vindicator of Judaism against idealistic philosophy than a Jewish philosophical idealist.

The principal thrust of Formstecher's work was to relate the development of Judaism intimately to the development of humankind. He wanted to show that despite the prevalent tendency to regard it as alien, Judaism had played, and was still playing, an absolutely essential role, that in its further evolution it would become the universal religion of civilized humanity. Like Steinheim, Formstecher raised Judaism above the possibility of historical obsolescence, except that in his case the eternity of Judaism was not determined by a clear, doctrinal revelation communicated to the Jews at the beginning of their history. Rather the historically given revelation had to evolve within the people until the Jews, and indirectly through them the rest of humanity, reached full awareness of the prehistorical, absolute revelation implanted by God in every human spirit. Also unlike his predecessor, Formstecher insisted that every truth of religion must likewise be a truth of reason and that the content of revelation consisted of the absolute good.[25] In this rationalism and ethicism he was much closer to the dominant mood of the Reform movement.

Formstecher distingushed between Judaism as an idea and as a historical phenomenon. While the former was pure, the latter could absorb foreign elements, which served it as a protective shell. Jews who despaired of their religion's viability in the modern world had failed to understand either the unchanging idea within or the historical phenomenon's capacity for further development. Formstecher juxtaposes Judaism with paganism, not dialectically but as polar ideal types. Paganism is the religion of nature, which represents God as the world-soul; Judaism is the religion of spirit, which represents God as a purely ethical being who transcends the universe He created. Although pagan religion played an indispensable role in the development of the human spirit, it was destined to oblivion since it could never encompass spirit, while Judaism, the religion of spirit, could eventually encompass nature.[26]

In Formstecher's view, the development of Judaism reflects a "progressive revelation" stretching back to biblical prophets who, far in advance of their time, were first enabled by God to bring to awareness the unconscious content of their spirit. Scripture and tradition preserved and refined the prophetic revelation. The further history of Judaism, with all its vicissitudes, could be described as a perpetual striving to realize the spiritual ideal.[27] Its history was therefore coincident with the spiritual history of all humanity. Far from being a mere stage in that history, Formstecher's Judaism became parallel with its entirety. Judaism continues to exercise its influence on the universal spiritual development of humanity through Christianity and Islam, which are here represented as missionary faiths that Judaism has sent into the pagan world. They do not succeed Judaism; they are its agents. And because the success of their task requires the adoption of pagan elements, they—but not Judaism—are "transitory phenomena," which will cease to exist as separate entities once they have purified humanity of its paganism.[28]

Not only does Formstecher thus ascribe to Judaism a very different role in the religious history of Western Civilization; he also removes philosophy from its venerated position at the leading edge of human spiritual development, declaring it merely the product of a futureless paganism. Without mentioning their authors by name, Formstecher condemns the philosophies of Fichte, Schelling, and Hegel. He then states unequivocally: "Modern philosophy manifests a subjective paganism which negates itself and therefore, in its incapacity to become the consciousness of humanity, will once again disappear as an ephemeral phenomenon." He singles out Hegel and Schleiermacher as guilty of the gnostic pretension to know God's inner essence and hence unable to appreciate the antignostic, essentially ethical character of Judaism. Formstecher suggests that only a second Kant, who would act positively to supplant metaphysics with ethics, could appreciate the truth of Judaism.[29] But such a philosopher would already have transcended philosophy.

Not surprisingly, Formstecher was no more favorably inclined to Jewish philosophers. He believed there could be no Jewish philosophy, only a Jewish ethics. To his mind, Philo as an Alexandrine mystic and Maimonides as an Aristotelian were both pagan, while Spinoza on account of his pervasive "pagan pantheism" could be neither Jew nor Christian. Mendelssohn, by contrast, had not adopted pagan elements. Aside from medieval Jewish philosophy, Judaism, as a historical phenomenon, had interacted with its environment in other ways as well. The Kabbalah—to which Formstecher was not unremittingly hostile—was another product of pagan influence; so too were certain Jewish ceremonies. Like his fellow Reformers, Formstecher believed that religious customs had played a positive role in insulating Judaism from detrimental influences. However, despite all his criticism of contemporary philosophy and Christian theology, Formstecher—quite inconsistently—did believe that German Jewry lived in an environment where paganism represented a declining threat. Jewish separation was therefore no longer appropriate intellectually and it would cease to be appropriate politically once German Jewry had achieved full emancipation. In short, Formstecher ultimately looked beyond Judaism to a completely universal faith—just as he looked beyond the state to a supranational spiritual theocracy. Formstecher's messianism thus transcended historical Judaism, though not the universal ideal which he believed had characterized its essence from the first.[30]

Unlike Formstecher, Samuel Hirsch did not make his entire career in a single community. A product of village Jewry in Rhenish Prussia, he attended yeshivot in Metz and Mainz before embarking on studies at the universities of Bonn and Berlin. The breadth of knowledge which he gained both in Jewish and in general philosophical and historical literature was matched by few Jews in early nineteenth-century Germany. Ordained by Samuel Holdheim, he served as rabbi first in Dessau, then Luxembourg, and finally in Philadelphia. Over the years his views became progressively more radical, reflecting shifts in the social context as well as the trajectory of his own independent spiritual development.[31] For about half a century, in both Europe and America, he played a guiding and active role in the Reform movement. Already in Dessau, where he preached and taught from 1839 to 1841, he was so mistrusted by some members of the Jewish community that appeal was made to the Prussian order of 1823 prohibiting all religious innovations. During these years he was also working on a book which, as he wrote to his older friend Leopold Zunz in Berlin, was to be a "philosophical exposition of the system of Jewish theology," its purpose "to draw sharply the boundaries between Judaism, Christianity and paganism."[32]

Hirsch's *The Religious Philosophy of the Jews,* which appeared in 1842, a year after Formstecher's book, was his largest and most systematic work.[33] And although its author soon went beyond a number of his own conclusions, it continued to be influential as theory in the Reform movement.[34] This is the more remarkable as Hirsch, no less than Steinheim and Formstecher, presents a conception of Judaism that yields very little to its intellectual milieu. The propositions put forth in Hirsch's book are grounded in the Bible, as well as in Talmud, Midrash, and traditional commentaries, the latter quoted extensively in Hebrew or Aramaic as well as in German translation.[35] Throughout it seems apparent that Hirsch was not seeking to cut and shape Judaism to fit the dominant philosophy of the day.[36] Quite the contrary, in terms of the reigning Hegelianism he was determined to show that Judaism as a whole, based on its own sources, could be understood as the hub of a systematic religious philosophy which drew upon Hegel but rejected his most basic assumptions.

At the beginning of his book Hirsch places his project into the context of contemporary Jewish history. With Mendelssohn there began a period in which German Jews were determined to acquire the culture *(Bildung)* of their age. Echoing Goethe, Hirsch calls this time the years of apprenticeship *(Lehrjahre).* In the process Jews had given up their peculiar characteristics. But now the time had come to reverse the thrust. "Today the concern is precisely to understand the peculiarity, the positive worldview of the Jewish religion, and to understand in their absolute necessity the forms which it has given itself in order to keep the worldview always before it, namely its ceremonies and customs, and to raise them again in the heart to the status of living deeds—to build rather than tear down, preserve rather than abandon."[37] In short, Hirsch felt that the time had come for a reassertion of Jewish particularity. But to be respectable that reassertion had to be made within the context of contemporary philosophical thought.

Hirsch's critique of Hegel has received considerable attention and can be briefly summarized.[38] Against Hegel, Hirsch raises religious knowledge to the level of philosophical thought so that philosophy can no longer be seen as absorbing religion's content while superseding it in form. According to Hirsch himself, the major point at which he departs from Hegelian philosophy is in his rejection of the necessity of evil as means to the good. Hegel held that man began in a state of nature but then sinfully set himself into opposition with it. Only when this negation was itself negated could the higher unity of virtue appear. Hirsch refuses to accept the necessity of a dialectical process in which sin, meaning the alienation of man from nature, plays a necessary role. For him sin is not a determined stage in human development, and certainly not to be equated with man's separation from nature. Sin is neither necessary nor consigned to the past. It is a permanent option and always the result of individual free choice. Herewith Hirsch rejects not only Hegelian pantheism but also the closely parallel Christian doctrine of original sin overcome by the Incarnation, which Hegel had incorporated into his own philosophical construction. Thus while Hegel's system is congenial to Christianity, it is distinctly inhospitable to Judaism, which is predicated on free moral choice. There can be a Hegelian Christianity, but not a Hegelian Judaism. Hegelianism, Hirsch tells us, is "the most sublimated paganism." For him as for Steinheim and Formstecher, a direct line runs from the ancient world to modern philosophy. Hirsch makes a detailed examination of paganism to support his view that it represents a passive religiosity which, in moving from fetishism to the anthropomorphic representations of Greece and Rome, negates itself dialectically. Necessarily it emerges with nothing because it was based on the false proposition that human beings must subordinate themselves to nature. Judaism, by contrast, represents an active religiosity, based on human decisions choosing either sin or virtue. It is not a further development of paganism; it is essentially different.[39]

For Hirsch, Judaism begins with Abraham, who was the first to recognize that human beings are free and without sin except insofar as they bring it upon themselves. Passing through trial after trial, Abraham emerges as the victor over paganism and becomes the model for true religion. Unlike Steinheim, Hirsch believes that Abraham required no supernatural revelation to achieve his realization of human freedom, but God was active in educating Abraham, as God actively educates, or is the source of religious self-education (Hirsch wavers on this point), for ancient Israel and for all humanity. Here again is Lessing's theme of revelation as divine education, except that Abraham has already achieved its highest level. Here too is a rejection of the Hegelian notion that the Jewish God—unlike the Christian—is not directly involved in human history. On the contrary, Hirsch notes, Judaism requires the mediation neither of a church, as in Catholicism, nor of Scripture, as in Protestantism.[40]

On the whole, Hirsch is more favorably inclined to Christianity than either Steinheim or Formstecher. Jesus stands within Judaism and, like Abraham, he represents an ideal for humanity. Although Paulinian Christianity, by promulgating the idea of original sin, left Judaism behind, it was only through this concession to paganism that Christianity was able to perform the "extensive" role vis-à-vis the pagan world, which an essentially "intensive," pure Judaism could not enact. For Hirsch, Christianity will not be superseded by Judaism, but together with Judaism it will constitute the absolute religiosity of the future. By contrast, modern philosophy will not endure, for it merely recapitulates on a deeper level the stages of its ancient pagan predecessor. Thus, for example, the skeptical Kant becomes in Hirsch's view the equivalent of Socrates, while Fichte, in building a new system, performs a task equivalent to that of Plato. With Hegel philosophy seeks to encompass all, but Hegel's own disciples, especially those on the left like David Friedrich Strauss, have already undermined his system. Modern philosophy, like ancient paganism before it, lies in shambles.[41]

The way therefore lies open to what Hirsch calls "the philosophy of revelation," which is reflected in the growing awareness of human freedom. For Hirsch the biblical God created miracles and prophecy in order to demonstrate divine sovereignty over nature and to call ancient Israel to its vocation of recognizing the possibility of moral choice. Sinai was the capstone of this revelation since it united miracle with prophecy. But revelation continued providentially until Israel, learning to imitate God as the model of freedom, had become fully aware of its destiny.[42] Although that destiny brought the Jews untold suffering, their sorrows were to be understood either as divine chastisements on account of those Jews who failed in their vocation to show the world that one need not sin or, in the case of pious men and women, as demonstrations that virtuous conduct even under duress was possible without supernatural grace. Hirsch was not an optimist about the future. He believed that hatred of the Jews lay dormant and he pointed to its recrudescence in the Hep-Hep riots of 1819 and the Damascus blood libel of 1840. At the same time he deplored the fact that Jews had not stood the test of remaining loyal to their vocation despite the temptations of assimilation. Mistakenly they considered themselves a denomination *(Confession)*, when in fact they were a "spiritual nationality." Hence the messianic age remained distant. But when it would come, Israel and the other nations would be united in a single religion of human freedom. Sin would remain a possibility, but no one would choose it. The nations of the world would then bring Israel to Jerusalem, not to establish a state but to found there the "ritual of all rituals, the Jewish national ritual," symbolizing the Jewish national vocation. United with humanity in word and deed, Judaism would remain particular in its mode of religious practice.[43]

Looking back upon all three thinkers, we can appreciate their independence of the milieu in which they wrote. To be sure, their philosophies of religion were prompted by the reigning systems of thought that they encountered in the lecture halls of the universities they attended and in their own reading. Their writings attest to the shared conviction that the deghettoization of the Jewish community must be accompanied by a deghettoization of Judaism. The old faith could not be expected to survive among cultured Jews unless, reconceptualized, it could be shown to be still intellectually viable. Such a proof required confrontation with the prevalent philosophical and theological systems of the day.

What seems most striking about the Jewish theological response, however, is that, for all its variety, it evidences so little concession on basic issues. The German milieu presented a series of intellectual and religious challenges to which the reply was characterized less by submission than by reinterpretation and reassertion. Each of the three thinkers recognized clearly the danger to Judaism posed by determinism, whether in Spinozistic or in Hegelian form; necessarily each rejected the milieu's prevailing conceptions of Judaism that, for one reason or another, limited it to the past. Like the Reformers after them, they assigned their own faith—more so than Christianity—to the future. Steinheim, Formstecher, and Hirsch were men concerned both with translating Judaism into the philosophical languages of Europe and with reaffirming what each regarded as its essentials. Later Reform thinkers would react similarly to new intellectual challenges.

Wissenschaft des Judentums

The formulation of theological systems in which a reconceptualized Judaism was assigned a central and ongoing role in Western civilization represented an effort to make continued adherence to Judaism defensible for modern, philosophically inclined Jews. However, the impulse to create a Judaism at home in the modern world did not come only from philosophy. It came also from the empirical study of history. In an age when precise analysis of the past stood high on the intellectual agenda, Judaism could not be considered modern unless it too had rendered itself a historical account. For the Reformers, historical study came to assume special importance since knowledge of the past could help to determine the perimeters and direction of religious change. By pointing to general and specific precedents from earlier ages, it could both hold in check arbitrary reforms motivated by assimilatory pressures and lessen resistance to more carefully considered innovations. Moreover, scholarship of a modern kind could serve the Reform rabbinate as a new form of legitimation, replacing the traditional authority which rabbis had gained through their nonhistorical training in Jewish law. Although new conceptions of Judaism within philosophical frameworks continued to appear in the Reform movement with varying degrees of impact, the grounding of Judaism in the flux of history provided a more direct support for the Reform enterprise. Christian scholars claimed that for contemporary Jews to enact significant reforms in belief and practice meant nothing less than ceasing to be Jews.[44] Jewish traditionalists too equated prevalent norms with an eternal faith. Refuting this view by showing that variety and change were characteristic of Jewish tradition assumed the highest priority for the Reformers. While relatively few among the intellectual leaders of the Reform rabbinate became systematic theologians or philosophers, many tried their hand at historical scholarship.

Wissenschaft des Judentums, the scholarly study of the Jewish religion and people, is not a traditional Jewish discipline.[45] It emerged in the second decade of the nineteenth century among young Jewish intellectuals who had been exposed to the ideal of an impartial, scholarly, and developmental approach to the past during their studies in German universities. They had come from traditional Jewish homes and education and they had been jarred not only by the contrasts between contemporary Jewish medievalism and the society into which they sought to acculturate, but by the profound difference between the talmudic, legally oriented, and essentially nonhistorical content of their Jewish knowledge as opposed to the historical and critical approach applied to religious and cultural institutions in the university. For some these contrasts seemed too great to overcome, and they eventually chose conversion from Judaism or indifference to it. Even those who were determined to cast their lot for the preservation and renewal of Judaism at times despaired of the possibility of harmonization. *Wissenschaft des Judentums* created a bridge. Like the earlier and contemporaneous experiments with liturgical reforms, the incipient scholarly movement gave new shape to the inherited content of Judaism. In the former aesthetic considerations prevailed, in the latter scholarly ones. If in the temples Jewish worship was to some extent made to fit the model of the church, in the new scholarship Jewish literature was studied according to the model of university disciplines.

The origins of *Wissenschaft des Judentums* lie within the small circle of mostly young men who founded the "Society for Culture and Scientific Study of the Jews" in Berlin in 1819. We have seen that one of its leading members, Leopold Zunz, was also active for a time as a preacher at the Beer Temple. However, Zunz, who became the most universally respected modern Jewish scholar of the nineteenth century, gradually distanced himself from the cause of religious reform. From the first he had been ambivalent about the future of Judaism in the modern world. As a young man he had fleetingly considered conversion, had hoped that the rule of the Talmud could be overthrown, and was convinced that the age of Hebraic creativity had come to a close. In later years he looked with disdain upon attempts to grapple with the practical problems of religious life. Unlike most of his contemporaries in the field of Jewish *Wissenschaft,* he did not serve as a congregational rabbi. Yet Zunz was no mere antiquarian. His motto—"true scholarship produces deeds"—attests to his belief that the kind of meticulous, detailed study of which he was the master could become the essential basis for modern Jewish religion. Moreover, despite his break with the Beer Temple, Zunz ten years later continued to advocate religious reforms in his first larger work, *The Sermons of the Jews* (1832). Here he wrote that religious reform was the present impulse of Judaism, that its task was to create religious forms and institutions in keeping with both the new political status of the Jews and the fruits of scholarly research.[46] The whole point of Zunz's book was to show that sermons were well precedented in Jewish religious life and to argue for their reintroduction. However, the future direction of Zunz's spiritual concerns is already present here as well. "Reform does not consist of externals," he wrote, "but of the divine spirit of piety and knowledge."[47] As the Reform movement came to deal more and more with practical, mostly "external" reforms, Zunz applied his immense knowledge to explaining the traditional world of Jewish piety, especially as it had manifested itself in the poetic literature of the synagogue. He distanced himself from theology, which he believed was too ready to appropriate the fruits of scholarship for its own purposes; increasingly he did not want the scholarly enterprise yoked to any ulterior purpose. His younger contemporary, Moritz Steinschneider (1816–1907), went even beyond Zunz in this regard. An incredibly prolific bibliographer, Steinschneider wanted to remove Jewish scholarship as far as possible from contamination by theological considerations. He deprecated rabbinical seminaries as inherently incapable of producing objectivity. For Steinschneider, more clearly than for any other leading figure, *Wissenschaft des Judentums* was an end in itself.

Ironically, it was Leopold Zunz, the later opponent of Reform institutions, who as a young man set down most clearly the role of scholarly study in the Reform movement. In an article published in the first scholarly Jewish periodical, which he edited, Zunz noted that once Jewish historiography was able to elucidate the inner life and striving of the Jews, their inherited and acquired ideas, and their persistence down to the present—"then we will rediscover the great laws of history and nature, of permanence and change, in every paragraph of Jewish history, and we will understand how to separate the divine from the mundane."[48]

Zunz's early confidence in the capacity of *Wissenschaft des Judentums* to provide objective criteria for reform proved illusory. The task of distinguishing the divine from the mundane in Jewish tradition turned out to be beyond the capacities of scholarship. In fact, it was disagreement over the extent of the sacred which soon distributed the religious leadership along a spectrum from Neo-Orthodox to radical Reform.

Modern scholarship was respected by the entire new generation of university-trained rabbis. But its claims had to be related to those of revelation and tradition on the one hand and the demands of daily life on the other. Some feared that scholarship would relentlessly secularize and relativize the entire Jewish heritage, resulting in a historicism that left no room for absolutes. Others were so overwhelmed with the perceived demands of the *Zeitgeist* that they became impatient with historical interpretation and its tendency to seek continuities from age to age. By looking closely at the thinking of four pivotal figures in German Jewry of the early nineteenth century the principal positions on the ideological spectrum should emerge clearly. We shall begin with the extremes and then move toward the center.

The Poles of Modernization: Samson Raphael Hirsch and Samuel Holdheim

Samson Raphael Hirsch (1808–1888) surely has no place in a strictly institutional history of the Reform movement. He is known as the founder of a countermovement, Neo-Orthodoxy, which sought to shore up traditional Judaism against the attacks of Reform.[49] Yet Hirsch was not a medieval Jew. Like the Reformers, he sought to make peace with modernity, attempting to establish the fully observant Jewish life within it. In the process he too "reformed" Judaism, although his principles were very different from those who identified themselves with the Reform movement. To be sure, Hirsch's position stands at the boundary of our subject, but only if the boundaries are clearly seen does it become possible to map out the territory within.

Hirsch's modern orthodoxy is put into perspective when we note that his affirmation of secular culture was not shared by the leading champions of traditional Judaism in the early nineteenth century. Not only in eastern Europe and Hungary did there continue to be strong opposition to the Haskalah, but in Germany too there were still those who opposed the Mendelssohnian model of European cultural identity combined with a fully observant Jewish life. As late as 1840, Rabbi Solomon Tiktin of Breslau held that anyone who had studied at a university was not fit to become a rabbi.[50] Hirsch, however, was born into a family which followed in Mendelssohn's footsteps, and Hirsch himself became the best example of the Mendelssohnian ideal carried forward into the nineteenth century. He received a traditional Jewish education but he also studied in a secular high school and spent a year at the University of Bonn. He developed a lifelong attachment to German classical writers, especially Friedrich Schiller. When he assumed his first rabbinate, in Oldenburg, neither his appearance nor his actions conformed to the image and role of the traditional rabbi.[51] On the pulpit he wore a black robe with white collar bands, he had no proper beard, and one contemporary engraving even shows him without a head covering. In the synagogue, he introduced a regular German sermon patterned on Christian prototypes, a male choir, and proper decorum. His most radical innovation was omission of the *kol nidre* prayer on the eve of Yom Kippur, as its formula for the renunciation of vows might be misunderstood by Gentiles. Hirsch's inclination to consider the norms of the milieu made him especially unpopular in his second rabbinate, in Moravia, where modernization of any kind was still viewed with great mistrust. He evoked consternation when he performed wedding ceremonies within the synagogue, instead of in its courtyard, allowing the bride's mother to stand at the canopy and addressing a short message to the couple. With respect to such externals, he held that there was nothing wrong with imitating the Gentiles. Hirsch was not a traditionalist by principle. He did not believe that customary practice, however venerable, was binding in the new age simply on account of its antiquity. Far more sharply than the orthodoxy which preceded his own, Hirsch distinguished between custom (minhag) and divine commandment (mitzvah).[52]

In another respect also Hirsch broke with the past. While in traditional Jewish education study of the Talmud assumed pride of place, in Hirsch's writings the rabbinic literature, though retaining its theological status, becomes pedagogically secondary. The Bible, especially the Pentateuch and the Psalms, are given priority in Jewish study, along with the prayerbook. Hirsch wrote commentaries on these more popular and accessible texts, and he wrote them in German.[53] Unlike the older generation of rabbis, he had little regard for talmudic dialectics; he ignored Jewish mysticism; and he scorned the secularly uneducated Polish *melamdim* (elementary teachers). His ideal was the harmonious relationship of modern humanistic learning with commitment to Jewish observance. It would be embodied in what he called the *Mensch–Jissroel*—the integration of human being and Jew.

Like the Reformers, Hirsch thought of Judaism in universal terms. In his seminal *Nineteen Letters on Judaism* (1836), he wrote: "Land and soil were never [Israel's] bond of union, but rather the common task set by Torah."[54] He even went so far as to say that "from where the Torah emanates, there is my Zion."[55] International Jewish concerns, whether acts of antisemitism or welfare campaigns, barely stirred him to activity.[56] Israel's unity, he believed, was spiritual, not political. Its return to Zion lay in God's hands and Jews were prohibited from accelerating its advent. While Hirsch certainly did not approve of removing prayers for the messianic return from the prayerbook, in his eyes they represented only a distant hope, not an immediate concern. For the foreseeable future it was the Jews' task to disseminate "pure humanity" among the nations. That, Hirsch insisted repeatedly, was the "mission of Israel," for which it had been exiled from its land.[57] Jews in the new Europe were to direct their spiritual energies outward as well as inward, to share in the cultural and political life of the countries in which they lived, to become like non-Jews in most externals. They would differ only in their undiminished adherence to the Halakhah.

It is indeed Hirsch's belief in the divinity of the entire scope of Jewish law that sets his Neo-Orthodoxy apart from the wide range of Reform thought and determines as well his rejection of *Wissenschaft des Judentums*. Like Mendelssohn, Hirsch believed that all 613 commandments contained in the Pentateuch, plus the Oral Law of the Rabbis, were literally revealed by God to Moses at Sinai. In his writings Hirsch undertook to explain the law, to point out its symbolic meanings and its moral usefulness, in short to spiritualize it and make it appear relevant to the times. However, in the last analysis the law was binding because of its source, not its humanly derivable content. The Jew was called upon to obey. Unlike the Reformers, Hirsch refused to differentiate among the commandments. The Oral Law was no less worthy of observance than the Written; ceremonial laws were no less divine than moral ones; there could be no distinction between kernel and shell. It was wholly illegitimate to subject Torah to any criterion outside itself: to historical criticism or to the practical demands of the *Zeitgeist*. Never were observances to be treated as merely means to humanly determined religious ends. Torah was eternal, sealed and complete from the start, a revelation that stood above history and was therefore never subject to development. The Jews were its bearers but in no sense its creators. If Judaism stood in conflict with the age, it could only be that the age was at fault. "Only then, when the times will conform with God, will Judaism also conform with the times."[58]

Like Mendelssohn, and unlike the Reformers, Hirsch insisted that it was law, and not belief, that constituted the specific character of Judaism. He deplored the excessive concern with theology and with prayers which narrowed the scope of Jewish religion to the school and synagogue. The law applied much more broadly, to most aspects of daily life. Hirsch attacked the Reformers for giving legitimacy to a truncated Judaism, for wiping out the guilt which he hoped would eventually bring some wayward Jews back to the fully observant life.[59] The law in its totality thus became for Hirsch the inviolate bastion of Judaism. European literature, art, and manners did not represent a threat to it. These allowed Judaism to reinterpret itself from within, to spiritualize the law with the hermeneutics of symbolic meaning. However, in the shape of historical criticism, modern culture could too easily breach the fortress walls. It was therefore of the utmost importance for Hirsch to launch a counterattack on *Wissenschaft des Judentums*.

Hirsch's conception of Judaism required shielding the totality of the traditional revelation from all historical investigation lest any portion of it be shown not to originate as God's word spoken on Mount Sinai. If one had to choose, Hirsch admitted, "better to be a Jew without *Wissenschaft* than to have *Wissenschaft* without Judaism." The only Jewish scholarship he could allow was of the traditional kind: study of the texts and their interpretation in order to better carry out God's commandments. On the other hand, to approach Judaism with the tools of criticism was nothing less than to "crucify" it. Like religious reform, *Wissenschaft des Judentums* was to Hirsch's mind an unjustifiable concession to the *Zeitgeist*. It too legitimated nonobservance and alleviated guilt.[60]

Hirsch fought against historical criticism on two levels. Theologically he simply ruled it out by asserting that the Torah is unique as God its source is unique, and hence it cannot be measured by any external standard. Against moderate scholars, who allowed only that the Oral Law possessed a human component, Hirsch declared that it was precisely the Oral Law which represented the complete revelation. It had been given before the Written Law, which was nothing more than an abbreviated version of it. But Hirsch recognized that he also had to fight the critics on their own grounds, and so attempted in a number of writings to show that their arguments for change and novelty in Jewish law rested on a biased misinterpretation of the texts.[61]

Increasingly, Hirsch came to see himself as the lone defender of tradition against religious reform and historical criticism.[62] Beginning in 1851 he was the rabbi of a small religious society in Frankfurt whose members all shared his orientation. Although in his earlier years Hirsch had boasted that the mass of German Jewry was on his side, during the second half of the century his position became that of a diminishing minority. It was now his goal to set the faithful Jews apart through independent religious institutions and, after 1876, a legally separate community. As an Orthodox Jew, Hirsch did not believe in a religiously pluralistic Judaism and he had come to realize that his program would not win over most Jews. Consequently, he retreated to his circle of the like-minded where uniformity of belief and practice might be expected to reign among a saving remnant.

Samson Raphael Hirsch.

Samuel Holdheim.

Unlike Samson Raphael Hirsch, Samuel Holdheim (1806–1860) had no hesitancy about calling himself a Reformer and participating in the rabbinical conferences of the Reform movement. Yet his position too marks a boundary. Although Holdheim became a model for radical Reform Judaism in nineteenth-century America, within his German historical context he represented the pole of religious modernization opposite that of Hirsch. And despite the profound differences between the two men, there were underlying similarities between them.

Holdheim's life began in the premodern closed world of Polish Jewry and ended within the circle of highly assimilated Jews in Berlin.[63] His intellectual development described a trajectory from all-embracing talmudism to the utmost acceptance of modernity's demands. It was not an easy journey. The increasing alienation from tradition, like that of others of his and later generations, was fitful and uneven, creating a constant struggle to justify each new departure, to overcome inner conflicts, and to achieve a consistent, harmonious position. Holdheim did not quite succeed.

He was born in Kempen, a town in the eastern Prussian province of Posen, which had been part of Poland until 1793. His family, unlike that of Samson Raphael Hirsch, had remained untouched by the Haskalah. Their son grew up with an exclusively talmudic education, in which he excelled so remarkably that he was soon respected as a prodigy in the dialectical exposition of rabbinic texts. Not until he was in his late twenties did he attend university lectures in Prague and Berlin. Those who knew him claimed that something of the pilpulist always clung to Holdheim. He seemed to possess more acuity than depth; he was a talented, formidable polemicist whose enthusiasm for his opinions never waned, even when the opinions themselves changed.[64] Lacking pretension—and some thought the dignity appropriate to his pastoral office— Holdheim saw himself above all as a teacher and a truth-seeker.[65] Unlike the more moderate reformers, he had little tolerance for compromises in theory or practice. Hence the inner turbulence, the occasional combativeness, the willingness to cast his lot outside the mass. His opponents branded him an enemy of Judaism,[66] yet in his own mind he was certain that radical reform of Judaism was but its necessary purification.

During his first rabbinate, in Frankfurt-on-the-Oder from 1836 to 1840, Holdheim remained committed in word and deed to traditional Jewish thought and life. Like Samson Raphael Hirsch, he favored order in the synagogue and in his sermons expounded the spiritual content of the ceremonial laws. But his ideas were changing and gradually he felt less at home in the Frankfurt environment. He later claimed that it was in particular his reading of Zunz's *The Sermons of the Jews* that directed him to the path of consistent religious reform.[67] During the following seven years, while he served as chief rabbi in the Grand Duchy of Mecklenburg–Schwerin, Holdheim's rapidly altering views found expression in an outpouring of articles, pamphlets, sermons, and speeches at rabbinical conferences. By 1847 he had become the leading champion of radical reform.

The progress of Holdheim's thinking is best understood as the protracted quest for an acceptable religious authority. The process was one of gradual restriction that led finally to a basic transfer. As a youth Holdheim had accepted the entirety of the rabbinic tradition as normative; later he assumed the right to disagree with the more recent sages; and then he began to distinguish what was divine tradition within the Talmud, specifically the hermeneutical rules of biblical interpretation, from the conclusions reached on the basis of those rules. The next step was to deny all authority to the Talmud, going around it in order to reach back to the Bible itself, and it alone. For a time Holdheim believed that all of Scripture was divine revelation, though he insisted that with the destruction of the ancient commonwealth, God had made known His will that the civil and ritual laws were no longer to be in force; only the religious and moral teachings still remained.[68] Yet even this severest restriction of the textual basis of authority ultimately seemed inadequate. Holdheim's final position was that Scripture represented but the human reflection of divine illumination.[69] Thus modern Jewry, or more precisely its religious leadership, became the final authority, the judge of tradition. Authority lay not in the texts at all, but in reason and conscience.[70]

Yet Holdheim could not easily persuade his reform-minded colleagues to abandon the Talmud. In seeking continuity with the past, they brushed aside those laws and expressions of opinion which seemed most out of keeping with contemporary sensibility and emphasized those they could most readily accept. They read their own views into the text or, without admitting it, were highly selective in their references. To Holdheim all this seemed dishonest. In the area of marriage and divorce, the contrast was especially apparent. The woman was scarcely treated as an equal in Jewish law; the statutes were primitive by modern standards. To be sure, there were passages in the Talmud that spoke of marriage in the most exalted religious language, but the law had remained unchanged—and as authoritative tradition was in principle unchangeable.[71] The only forthright solution was to take a position outside the legal tradition, to assign the entire realm of law, including matters of personal status, to the state. The task of religion would then be solely to lend sanctity to a marriage, not to provide its legal basis.

Separating out the legal from the religious elements in marriage was part of the thoroughgoing division which Holdheim sought to impose between the political or national aspects of Judaism and its character as a religion.[72] For Holdheim, law was not a properly religious category, at least not in the present. The Talmud had mistakenly and artificially preserved the legal system of ancient Israel in the Diaspora—to the extent that the demise of institutions governed by it, such as the ancient Temple, did not make it inapplicable. Yet even those laws that could not presently be carried out were regarded by the Rabbis as merely suspended, not abrogated. Holdheim's view was the opposite: to reinstitute the sacrificial service would be the worst example of religious retrogression, the return to an outgrown primitive form of worship. God's dispersion of Israel had been a revelation which abrogated the law no less decisively than the theophany at Sinai had brought about its institution. Only those elements of the law which enhanced religious consciousness might still be preserved, not as law but as religious custom. However, to maintain the ceremonial law as law in the present age meant nothing less than to delay the messianic epoch, while to give it up was to set a universalist example.[73] Holdheim tried to show on the basis of rabbinic texts that the tradition itself was not of one mind regarding the observance of ritual law in messianic times. But, more important, he argued that modern Jewry was already far enough along the road to the messianic age that it no longer required the crutch of ceremonies. Proper religion, Holdheim averred, was not a matter of ritual deeds at all, but of beliefs, sentiments, and moral commitments. Repeatedly he stressed that what mattered was "inwardness," not externals—an emphasis which brought Judaism close to the basic orientation of Protestantism.[74]

In fact for Holdheim the differences between an undogmatic Christianity and a Judaism purified of its legal components became almost inconsequential, at least to the point that, after civil marriage became permissible, he was willing to lend rabbinical sanction to wedding ceremonies of Jew with Gentile. He justified this position by arguing that the ancient prohibition of outmarriages referred to foreign peoples, not religions, and, more important, that it was basic in Reform to substitute "the holy God and Father of humanity for the holy God of Israel, the holy human race for the holy people, the covenant between God and humankind for the covenant between God and Israel." Nonetheless, recognizing the need to justify an act spurned by his Reform colleagues, Holdheim told one couple that as a rabbi he was speaking to them "in the name of the religion of the purest human love, in the name of Judaism, as it lives in my spirit and in that of so many of my coreligionists."[75]

In these words to a mixed couple, Holdheim displays an interpretation of Judaism that has reached the furthest point of subjectivization: what is Jewish is what has passed into the religious consciousness of the individual Jew. Consequently, tradition takes on a very different form. For Holdheim it can no longer be described as a chain whose links must occasionally be polished or reforged to assure continuity with the past. Instead it has become a treasure-trove of religious ideas to stimulate and exalt.

On the pulpit the preacher dips into this wealth of spirit, selects the most precious jewels, and sets them into a sermon addressed to his congregation. Robbed of their authority, the words of the ancient Rabbis can indeed be esteemed as a truly valuable treasure. "There is so much that is precious in the Talmud," Holdheim writes, "that the use of it for the religious life of Judaism will never—even in the Messianic Kingdom—be dispensable."[76] He even wrote a textbook on the Mishnah, which included some legal texts as well as the better known moral sayings. As a selectively used source of insight, the entire tradition could be enthusiastically affirmed.

If tradition has thus changed its shape from chain to treasure-trove, ritual expression seems to have lost its shape altogether. It is not the Jewish holidays as such which are to be celebrated but the "idea of the holiday," the content poured out from its vessel.[77] Thus it was possible for Holdheim to argue that the Sabbath could be celebrated on Sunday without a major loss to the basic values represented by it. Similarly, one did not require such externals as the *lulav* on Sukkot or the *shofar* on the New Year. Hebrew was dispensable as merely a mode of expression, easily separable from the content of the prayers expressed by it.

Holdheim had little patience for "romantics" who used forms like the Hebrew language to conceal the abyss between contemporary reality and the past. For him the gulf created by the Jews' new political and social position and by their new understanding of religion could not be filled in. One had either to leap across or remain on the other side.[78] His insistence that only the present stage of religious awareness, as represented by those Jews who have most fully internalized it, can be determinative on practical issues separated him not only from conservatives but also from Reformers who were not as willing to urge revolutionary change.[79]

Ironically, at his most extreme, Holdheim in some ways comes to resemble his polar opposite, Samson Raphael Hirsch. For Holdheim, as for Hirsch, historical development was ultimately not of religious importance. Just as for Hirsch Judaism was fixed once and for all by the revelation at Sinai, so for Holdheim its ideal content, as monotheism and morality, was present from the beginning, though it was given normative form and substance by the religious consciousness of the present age.[80] Neither man was required to show a gradual development, to display a thread of historical continuity despite all change. Consequently, *Wissenschaft des Judentums* was no more crucial for Holdheim than for Hirsch. Although he occasionally did so, Holdheim did not need to seek historical precedents. The new age had produced a new Judaism, not simply continued a process. Like Hirsch, too, Holdheim soon found himself outside of the mainstream, seeking refuge in a circle of the like-minded. In 1847, he became rabbi and preacher of the newly created Reform Society in Berlin, a homogeneous separatist congregation like Hirsch's in Frankfurt-on-the-Main, intended to embody the purer doctrine for which the united communities were not yet ready. Each in his own way, Hirsch and Holdheim were equally uncompromising. Both forsook the mass for the elite—in the one case for those who would most completely preserve the tradition alongside modernity, in the other for those who would absorb it the most selectively into their modern lives.

Yet despite his hopes and best efforts, Holdheim was not entirely able to ignore history or to affirm the present unconditionally. Well known is his remark that one should say of rabbinic tradition: "The Talmud speaks out of the consciousness of its age and for that time it *was* right; I speak out of the higher consciousness of my age and for this age I *am* right."[81] But to affirm "the consciousness of the age" was not to accept all of its manifestations uncritically. While Holdheim repeatedly argued that Jewish law must in every instance give way before the laws of the state, the same was not true for Jewish religion. "Religion may under no circumstances yield to the needs of the age," he wrote, "since otherwise the needs of the age . . . are raised to the level of religion. Religion ceases to be religion when it lowers itself to become the handmaid of the age and its needs." The Jewish religion, as prophetic ideal, stood above current realities.[82]

Holdheim's own age was characterized by the messianic enthusiasm of the turbulent 1840s followed by political reaction after 1848. The state that Holdheim venerated, and that he believed it a holy duty to serve as soldier and civil servant, was a state still to be fully created: it was the universal human state of the future, not the discriminatory German Christian state of the present.[83] Even as he expected Judaism to give up its connection with talmudic law, so he expected Christianity to sever its relationship with the state. As the fifties gave little evidence of progress in overcoming official prejudice, Holdheim's messianic enthusiasm began to cool and discordant notes appear in his universalist rhapsodies. At the end of the decade he wrote a scholarly work on Jewish personal status, and surprisingly wrote it in Hebrew, which he here called "our language."[84] In his last speech at the yearly public examination of the students in his religious school, a few months before his death, Holdheim said:

> The light of [Judaism's] history shall burn eternally, the fire of its past never to be extinguished. Whoever in swearing allegiance to the religion of reason quenches the fire of history on the altar of Judaism, he sins against God who along with light also created warmth; and he who has become indifferent as to whether the fire is extinguished in himself or his descendants sins no less. Israel must never cease to be a historical people, Judaism a historical religion.[85]

Holdheim never did become a consistent universalist. History proved inescapable even for him. Still more was it important for those who sought to remain within the community.

A Historical Judaism: Zacharias Frankel and Abraham Geiger

If Samson Raphael Hirsch and Samuel Holdheim marked the opposing boundaries of Jewish religious modernization, Zacharias Frankel (1801–1875) and Abraham Geiger (1810–1874) established the two most significant trends within those limits. While Hirsch and Holdheim were at one in drawing a moment of time—Sinai or the contemporary *Zeitgeist*—out of the flux of history and making it determinative, Frankel and Geiger both sought to draw a line of continuity through history from the ancient revelation that made Israel a people down to its present situation. Yet the essence of the continuity—whether it consisted of law or of theology—differed for the two men, as did the relative significance they ascribed to the perpetuation of tradition as opposed to the implications of modernity for theory and practice. Their thought made it apparent that even within a Judaism that recognized and affirmed historical change and development, there could be such deep-seated differences as to prompt bitter debate and lead ineluctably to separate religious identities and independent institutions.

Zacharias Frankel, the ideological father of present-day Conservative Judaism, seems never to have experienced a crisis of Jewish identity, never to have despaired of Judaism's continued viability. As if organically, he grew out of the traditional world of his upbringing into the role of a modern German rabbi, well versed in the scholarship and culture of his day. Without apparent ambivalence or inner conflict, he reached a position advocating moderate religious reform and a delicate compromise between textual authority and historical criticism. During more than forty years of public activity, his position remained essentially the same: he was always a man of the golden mean.

Frankel was born in Prague, an ancient center of Jewish learning that had produced both notable expositors of the law and men with unusual secular learning. His family was among the most prominent of the community, his ancestry studded with famous rabbis. Not until he was well into his twenties did Frankel go to Budapest in order to supplement his religious studies at a secular high school and then at the local university. His doctoral degree, achieved by examination in 1831, made him the candidate most acceptable to the Bohemian authorities for the position of rabbi of the Leitmeritz district. Indeed, he was the first rabbi in Bohemia to possess a university education. In Teplitz, where he took up residence, Frankel introduced no radical reforms and made it clear from the beginning that he would tolerate no lay initiatives to change existing religious practice. Yet he did introduce regular German sermons—for the first time in Bohemia—as well as order and decorum. In 1836 Frankel moved to Dresden as chief rabbi for Saxony, one of the German states which granted Jews the fewest civic rights. His early writing there was dedicated to improving the political situation, especially doing away with the demeaning oath still required of Jews. Though soon offered the rabbinate of Berlin, Frankel chose to remain in Dresden for eighteen years, until he assumed the founding directorship of the Jewish Theological Seminary in Breslau in 1854.[86]

It was during his Saxon rabbinate that Frankel established himself as the champion of a moderate religious reform that was to emerge gradually, quietly from within. Very shortly after his arrival in Dresden, Frankel wrote to an inquiring colleague indicating his support for religious change. "But," he added, "the salutary purpose must always be kept in mind, properly grasped, and worked for in such a way as to achieve it. The means must be grasped with such care, thought through with such discretion, created always with such awareness of the moment in time, that the goal will be reached unnoticed, that the forward progress will seem inconsequential to the average eye."[87] Only a few should be able to envisage the final result in its incipient stages. Never should a frighteningly different portrait of the future be held up to disturb and to divide. From the first, Frankel placed Jewish unity above reform. He wanted to begin with the inherited corpus of traditional belief and practice, altering, chipping away, or adding elements—but always retaining the foundation. Consistency, though he advocated it, was ultimately much less important for Frankel than continuity.

Although Frankel's interpretation of Judaism has been invariably described by his own designation as "positive–historical," his outlook is not fully understood unless one stresses the absolutely decisive role which he ascribes, not to Jewish law *per se* or to *Wissenschaft,* but to faith *(Glaube).*[88] No less than for Samson Raphael Hirsch, faith was for Frankel the ultimate determinant of truth. Repeatedly he placed it before and above both critical inquiry and systematic philosophy. It was the "center of gravity" which alone could withstand the corrosive effects of secular culture. Faith was eternal, beyond history, yet it was also "inward, to be apprehended with warmth." Whatever had removed itself from the circle of faith, he believed, had ceased to be Judaism.

Those Jews who had substituted modern culture for belief in God had ceased to be part of the people of revelation.[89] Of his own position he wrote openly to a more radical reformer: "I take my stand on faith and I still possess a great hope that in the future modernity will eventually embrace it."[90] What set Frankel apart from Orthodoxy in this respect was his endeavor to draw *Wissenschaft* into the circle of faith where it could serve as fructifying influence. But he would not allow it to become the master. Though he wrote of a "thinking faith," Frankel set clear bounds to historical inquiry: like Mendelssohn, he believed the Pentateuch contained "revealed laws" communicated to Moses at Sinai, and he resisted *a priori* all scholarship directed at showing historical divisions within its text.[91]

As head of a modern Jewish seminary, Frankel sought to raise a generation of rabbis well acquainted with modern *Wissenschaft* but also "suffused by faith." Though the Breslau students attended university as well as seminary classes, Frankel favored the cloistered atmosphere of his modern yeshivah for the faithful transmission of the tradition. Jewish learning, he believed, had to be passed on "from shepherd to shepherd, from teacher to teacher." In the seminary's classrooms its director could wed scholarship with faith.[92]

For Frankel, faith belonged in the category of what he called the "positive" aspect of Judaism, which for the first time he linked closely with its "historical" aspect in 1843.[93] The later hyphenated connection between the two ("positive–historical") in fact symbolized Frankel's mediating position between Orthodoxy and radical Reform. The positive basis of Judaism was what raised it above history, what had to be accepted by faith. It consisted of the Sinaitic revelation, which could not be abrogated by considerations of historical vicissitude. "A positive religion," he wrote, "can acknowledge progress only to a certain point; it indicates by its very designation that it possesses something which is fixed, indissoluble, that must be preserved; it is revelation and not *Wissenschaft*."[94] It was this positive element which set definite limits to reform and prevented Judaism from dissolving into the stream of history. More radical reformers than Frankel also required such a positive element—and indeed Holdheim had already written in favor of a "historical–religious positive Judaism"[95]—but they tended to limit it to the realm of theology and morality. For Frankel the positive component of Judaism likewise embraced Jewish law, the equivalent for Jews of what dogmas were for Christianity.[96] The introduction of the historical element, in turn, separated Frankel from the Orthodox. Whereas the Pentateuch was outside of history, the tradition was not. Though guided by divine Providence, it had come into existence through human creativity over a period of many generations.[97] The Written Law of Moses, supernaturally revealed, had been supplemented and reinterpreted in the Oral Law of the Rabbis so as to meet the exigencies of changed historical circumstances. Positive–historical Judaism therefore held in tension faith and scholarship, eternity and temporality, revelation and tradition.

Frankel devoted his important scholarly efforts to the study of that portion of the heritage which was rooted in human history.[98] He wanted to show that rabbinic law had not always been stagnant, as it was in his time, that especially in its early stages it had been responsive to the needs of the community. His ultimate purpose was to write a history of the Halakhah which would illustrate its dynamic development. At the least he meant to show how the early Rabbis were able to cope with profound historical change without leaving the framework of Jewish law, without losing a sense of continuity. The Mishnaic authors had not intended "a rigid, frozen formation," which would result in unnecessary hardships of observance. Only the necessity of committing the law to writing to prevent its disappearance in uncertain times had brought about progressive stagnation. But that process could be reversed. In an age of new spiritual freedom the law no longer needed to be seen as a completed given. With all due reverence for its antiquity, one could hope to make it fluid and responsive once again.

The principles upon which Frankel's scholarship was based—that the Rabbis did in fact innovate, that the tradition came into existence over time, that laws ascribed to an oral tradition extending back to Sinai could in fact be later creations—were sufficiently radical to draw down upon him the severest condemnation of the Orthodox. Samson Raphael Hirsch castigated Frankel because in his principal work, *Darkhe ha-mishnah,* which was used as a textbook for the seminary students, he had made the rabbinic law into the intellectual creativity of its teachers. In Hirsch's eyes he had thereby left orthodox Jewish faith behind. Yet the very attention Frankel lavished on Jewish law was at the same time an implicit renunciation of radical Reform. In his historical writing Frankel hinted broadly at a parallel between the Jews of ancient Alexandria and contemporary efforts to cast aside ritual observance. Of the first-century Jews who had dissolved the Halakhah into Hellenistic allegories he wrote:

> They went from error to error, foolishly neglecting the ritual commandments, and in the course of time they strayed as well from the covenant of the Lord their God. Their memory is lost and no longer are they a part of the House of Israel. We owe thanks to our Sages that all of their concern was with the essence of the commandments and with the foundation and purpose of the religious deed. It was they who bequeathed us the Torah as an eternal heritage.[99]

Reestablishing a flexible Halakhah was one way in which Jewish religious life could be sustained. Another was proper regard for the collective will of the people. The extraordinary status which Frankel ascribes to the ingrained beliefs and practices of the community is probably the most original element in his thought. The living religious consciousness of the community, Frankel audaciously claimed, contained a revelation that deserved no less recognition than that transmitted directly by God. As such, its validity was immune to attack by would-be reformers. Only the people's representatives, gathered collectively in a synod—not the theologians alone—could decide on reforms. Frankel entertained the possibility that one day the people might demand radical change; in that case even the traditional Hebrew worship service would have to give way to something quite different, despite the very early legal traditions establishing the present order. But he perceived the mass of Jews in his day to be essentially conservative. They had internalized new modes of thought and desired certain reforms for the sake of their children, but they were still emotionally tied to the ceremonial life of Judaism. Reforms should never be allowed to violate the sanctity of their religious practice, even where halakhic considerations did not stand in the way.[100]

Genuine religious reformers thus would have to not only base themselves on the Halakhah but also possess a lively sense of the people's will. They could not represent cultural standards external to the community; they would have to help the community reach out to modernity from within. This was a task that required emotional qualities of heart and mind *(Gemüt)* no less than intellect. The people would have to regard its leaders as truly representing them. A leadership deeply rooted in the sentiments of the people would advocate only "moderate reform," for the masses by and large were still faithful to tradition. However, where individual lay leaders were themselves no longer firmly anchored in ancestral thought and practice, Frankel favored the strongest rabbinical opposition to them, reinforced, if necessary, by government authority.[101]

Frankel's appreciation for the emotional ties binding the Jewish community did not make him into a precursor of Jewish nationalism. Unlike the Hamburg Temple Association, Frankel did indeed favor retention of all the liturgical passages expressing hope of return to Zion. He felt that the idea of a future renewal of Jewish ethnicity under conditions of political independence lent Jews dignity and self-respect. Why abandon the notion that God has a great future in store for Israel? But for the present, Jews were a "religious community like every other denomination living in the state." In 1842 Frankel strongly opposed Frederick William IV's plan to reimpose corporate status on Prussian Jewry, which would have meant the reintroduction of Jewish courts operating according to rabbinic law and the penalty of excommunication. Frankel clearly did not want the German Jews reghettoized. He believed that wherever Jews received civic equality, wherever they could feel a sense of belonging, there they quite properly gave up their particular Jewish nationality. Only in lands of persecution was a separate nationality still "forced on them from the outside." It was for the east European and Asian Jews, not for the German Jews, that the messianic hope of return was directly relevant. From his Dresden pulpit Frankel spoke in universalistic tones of the concord reigning between Jew and Christian and of the common fatherland they shared.[102]

Though Frankel explicitly recognized that he was living in a period transitional between a stable past and a yet to be shaped future, he did not seek to give the historical passage from the one to the other decisive guidance. He could make fun of hyperorthodoxy and deplore religious fanaticism among Hungarian Jews,[103] but in Germany he sought mainly restraint, not innovation. His writings bear few examples of concrete proposals for reform. The scant evidence indicates that he favored elimination of some of the late liturgical poetry (the *piyutim*), permission to eat legumes on Passover, modifying some of the ceremonies associated with mourning and circumcision, and perhaps eliminating the second days of certain holidays. He was not opposed to organ accompaniment of the worship service on Sabbaths and holidays, but he supported it only if the musician was a non-Jew and if the congregation did not regard the organ as a symbol inextricably associated with the church.[104] In deciding for or against liturgical reforms, Frankel was as much motivated by subjective factors of emotional attachment as by the norms of Jewish law or the historical study of the development of customs.[105] Especially was this true for his insistence that Hebrew be preserved as the language of Jewish liturgy despite the halakhic permissibility of the vernacular and the precedent of Aramaic prayers in ancient times. When a slight majority of his colleagues at the rabbinical conference of 1845 failed to agree with him, Frankel walked out of the meeting and thereafter no longer participated in the collective efforts of the Reformers. He parted company in order to continue independently on his own path: the path of cautious, hesitant, conservative reform.

In retrospect, it is not surprising that Frankel should have won widespread admiration within German Jewry. His harmonious personality, his knowledgeable respect for tradition combined with worldly culture, and his ability to integrate critical scholarship into Judaism without serious compromise of faith—these evoked a sense of reassurance and confidence that modernity's challenges could be met without radical, unsettling change. Although the mass of German Jewry soon ceased to represent a collective will rooted in tradition, Frankel's outlook, propagated through his students, continued to be influential in Germany, and later in America as well. Yet its separate institutionalization as Positive–Historical, or Conservative, Judaism draws it out of our narrative except insofar as it continued to influence the development of the Reform movement.[106] Initially, Zacharias Frankel's position represented the right wing of Reform's historically oriented center. But differences in theory and practice proved too great to sustain organizationally a single, variegated nonorthodox Jewish faith. The crucial doctrines of the Reform movement were developed within the more turbulent personality and brilliant intellect of Abraham Geiger.

To Geiger, if to anyone, belongs the title "founding father of the Reform movement." Although Reform ideas and liturgical innovations did not begin with him, it was he, a figure of the second generation, who more than anyone drew together the strands and wove them into an ideology for the movement. Geiger's intellectual and scholarly eminence were recognized even by those who differed with his religious views; his gifts as an orator were immense. In voluminous writings, regularly delivered sermons, and occasional lectures he gave Reform a rationale and a sense of purpose. Geiger did not lead alone, but he was clearly first among his peers. Thoughtful and introspective, he was unable to easily transcend the conflicts between modernity and Jewish tradition. Within him, as not within Frankel, they collided with devastating force. Geiger could set no limits to *Wissenschaft;* scientific truth, not faith, remained his ultimate standard. His personal life and career became an ongoing struggle to achieve integration. His dilemmas were shared by others in his generation and thereafter; his resolutions set a permanent seal on the movement.[107]

Geiger spent the first years of his life in a traditional ambience. His fully observant family provided him with an early intensive education in Jewish sources and destined him for the rabbinate. Yet the Jewry of his native Frankfurt had not remained untouched by the Enlightenment and the young Geiger was soon allowed to supplement talmudic studies with privately arranged secular ones. In 1829, at the age of nineteen, he began to study Classical and Oriental languages at the University of Heidelberg. But while he became a fine Orientalist, philology did not become for him the scholarly ideal that it was for Leopold Zunz. It soon seemed too specific; it could not answer the pressing larger questions which increasingly troubled his mind. After Geiger moved to the University of Bonn only a few months later, his interest shifted rapidly to philosophy and history. He now wanted to understand human spiritual development in its broadest dimensions and to relate Judaism to it. Despite his philosophical turn, he nonetheless eschewed adherence to Hegel's comprehensive system, as he would reject all philosophies, deeming them bound by their age. He was drawn instead to Johann Gottfried Herder's philosophically informed historical studies of human spiritual development. It was Herder, the scholar of broad perspective, the historian of culture, and the admiring student of biblical poetry, who early became Geiger's favorite writer and ideal. Herder's works, and also Lessing's critical theological writings, influenced him deeply at a crucial time. Yet Geiger found in them, as in all of his reading, more stimuli for his own thought than models to be slavishly followed. The question he seems to have asked himself about all that impressed him favorably at the university was: How can these ideas be applied to Judaism? And beyond that: How can Judaism absorb them?[108]

Zacharias Frankel.

Abraham Geiger.

When he assumed his first pulpit, in the small Rhineland community of Wiesbaden in 1832, Geiger had by no means answered such questions. On the contrary, he was severely torn between the ideology of free inquiry, which he had internalized in Bonn, and the realities of the practical rabbinate. How could he serve congregants whom modernity had touched only in the external aspects of their lives, to whom philosophy and historical criticism remained strange and irrelevant? Even before he came to Wiesbaden, Geiger had toyed with the idea of avoiding the problem by inducing a schism: establishing separate communities, on a state-wide scale, for those Jews who no longer felt an attachment to the Talmud. That, he believed, might alone prevent the greater schism of conversion. At moments of frustration in his congregational rabbinate, Geiger returned to the same idea. But unlike Holdheim, he ultimately rejected it in favor of seeking reforms within a united Jewish community, however slow that process might be.[109]

At first Geiger looked enviously across at Christianity. He believed that its dogmatic structure would collapse, but a new faith compatible with modern philosophy and criticism would emerge from the ruins. Christian theology was keeping pace with *Wissenschaft,* while its Jewish counterpart was prematurely engaged in systematization before the necessary spadework of historical criticism had been done. At a time when Christianity was reshaping itself to become the religion of modern society, Judaism was looking ever more antiquated; Christianity was at the forefront, Judaism crept behind.[110] The result, Geiger realized with regret, was that university-educated Jews were beginning to treat Judaism as a relic to be avoided or scorned rather than as a living faith.

While at the university, Geiger still felt, as Frankel did later, that the reformer's task was simply to confirm the abandonment of those ideas and practices which the community itself had already set aside. But he was too much of an activist to be long satisfied with reaction alone. The role he soon envisaged for Jewish leadership was to become nothing less than organs of history, slowing or speeding the wheel of time, directing its course. Yet this somewhat pretentious ambition was offset by recurring self-doubt. His self-declared "stormy soul" was filled with conflicting feelings: a deep-seated attachment to Judaism on the one hand, an equally profound alienation from its present forms on the other. At times of despondency, he saw his work as a useless thrashing about, a hopeless effort to bring together opposites. His proposals could be radical: demolition would have to precede construction, the divine authority of the classical texts broken by historical criticism. "The Talmud must go, the Bible, that collection of mostly so beautiful and exalted—perhaps the most exalted—*human* books, as a divine work must also go." But bringing the sacred texts into human history did not mean rejecting them. On the contrary, it made possible a closer identification. The young Geiger could also write: "I feel an attachment of love to the whole spiritual development of Judaism from its earliest beginnings down to most recent times as well as to various parts of its present structure; in a way they are a part of my personality."[111]

These two feelings—the need to destroy an antiquated Judaism so that a new one could arise from its ruins and the desire to preserve an inner emotional connection with the Jewish legacy—came to be represented in the two spheres of Geiger's activity: as scholarly critic and as rabbi. Carefully he sought to define for himself and others the respective role of each. The critic was to seek only the complete and unvarnished truth, to speak and write it regardless of the consequences. His place was ideally in the university, where no practical considerations would inhibit the free expression of his conclusions. He was "the priest of the true *Wissenschaft,*" the disturber of the peace. The rabbi, by contrast, was the trusted shepherd of his flock. He must be a man of compromise who begins with the given and seeks to purify it to the extent circumstances allow. The rabbi must deprive himself of his own inner peace in order to bring about the slow advance of those who follow him. His task is to renew the venerable edifice in which earlier generations have lived.[112]

Geiger would have preferred to become a university professor rather than to be split, internally and externally, between the conflicting feelings and roles of the writer of critical essays that could only undermine accepted beliefs and practices and the practicing rabbi who spoke of preservation and unity in his weekly sermons and apologetic writings.[113] He argued for the establishment of a Jewish theological faculty at a leading university. But in the anti-Jewish atmosphere of nineteenth-century Germany, his efforts and those of others met no success.[114] Thus in spite of himself, Geiger was forced to integrate the two roles, though the tension between them, like his own ambivalence, was never completely resolved. Fortunately for the Reform movement, the result was a twofold contribution: the scholarly one, both critical and constructive, leading to a new comprehensive understanding of Judaism; and the practical one, conserving and immediate, addressing the specific issues of the community. In each of these two roles Geiger was a religious reformer.

Wherever his rabbinical vocation would take him—to pulpits in Wiesbaden, Breslau, Frankfurt, and Berlin—Geiger always found time to write. He edited and was the chief contributor to two journals, one in his youth, the other in the last years of his life. His books, essays, and reviews range from very specific points of philology to studies of periods and personalities, to reflections on the state of contemporary Judaism. Few of his writings can be termed pure *Wissenschaft*, in the sense of bearing no relationship to the present. Though he felt bound as a scholar not to distort the past, he studied it mainly in order to hold it up to the present. Historical knowledge, Geiger's work tried to show, was the essential prerequisite for reform. It liberated the present from the shackles of a timeless tradition even as it created the basis for a new sense of continuity with the past.

As Geiger saw it, contemporary Judaism was bereft of historical consciousness. It lived in a "long present," which had not so much grown out of the past as fully absorbed it.[115] The inner history of Israel was commonly seen to be essentially uniform; later texts interpreted and supplemented earlier ones, but supposedly never misunderstood or took issue with them. As Judaism was unchanging in the past, so could it be true to itself only if it remained so in the present—despite all the unprecedented challenges of modern life. But if the opposite could be shown, if Judaism had in fact displayed extraordinary variety, if its texts reflected historical vicissitude, then reform in the present would represent not an arbitrary break with the past but its logical continuation. The sharp hoe of historical criticism would loosen the soil, so that new seeds could be planted in it.

As a historical critic Geiger was deeply influenced by David Friedrich Strauss, the "most notorious" of nineteenth-century Christian theologians. His *Life of Jesus,* published in 1835/36, openly repudiated the veracity of the Gospels, reduced them to myths, and thus destroyed the historical foundations of orthodox Christianity. Geiger was impressed by Strauss's audacity; he must also have felt an empathy with the Christian scholar and theologian's effort to build religion on the moral and spiritual values inherent even in nonhistorical biblical tales. But what may have influenced Geiger most in Strauss's work was its thesis that the New Testament myths were created to make Old Testament prophecies apply to Jesus. According to Strauss, that unity was a forced one, and he proceeded to tear the testaments apart. While Geiger later attacked Strauss for ignoring the continuity of the New Testament with Judaism, he early applied the Christian scholar's critical method to rabbinic texts. They too clung to earlier strata, denying novelty; and Geiger set out to expose the forced connections.[116]

He began with the two components of the Talmud, the earlier Palestinian Mishnah and the later Babylonian Gemara. Already in his teenage years, Geiger had begun a Hebrew commentary on the Mishnah, whose purpose it was to explain the earlier text independently of the meanings given to it in the Gemara.[117] Later, in 1845, he published a textbook and reader for the Mishnah, which behind its philological exterior clearly conveyed the historicity of Jewish law.[118] Mishnah and Gemara reflected different cultural milieus; the later text did not merely expand and interpret the earlier one; it introduced its own points of view. Thus the Talmud could not be a single unit, the product of an unchanging divine will. It was the reflection of an ongoing human legal creativity ever responsive to its environment. Even more radically, Geiger separated the Mishnah, in turn, from the still earlier stratum of the Bible. The Rabbis of the talmudic period, the Tannaim and Amoraim, had been influenced by the development of Judaism since biblical times. But they could not admit that influence without doing violence to their concept of revelation. Hence they tended to force their views into the text of the Bible.[119] Especially was this evident in the Midrash, the collections of halakhic and homiletical commentaries on the Torah.

Twelve years later, in his epoch-making magnum opus on the original text and early translations of the Bible, Geiger proceeded to historicize and relativize the most sacred text of all.[120] Behind the received version, he claimed to detect transitions and transformations, a process of inner development reflected in textual alterations that were suggested by the variant readings of translations. He was led to posit an earlier pre-Mishnaic Halakhah, which he attributed to the Sadducees and which lost out to the Pharisaic one only after the defeat of the Bar Kokhba revolt in 135 C.E. Most important, his book made the Bible, no less than the Talmud, dependent on the changing historical context that conditioned its final form.

What Geiger did not discuss in his volume was pre-exilic biblical history. This was clearly the most ticklish subject of all—"too hot to handle," he believed at first. It was one thing to suggest variant versions of the received text, quite another to take an unorthodox position on its origins. Yet he wondered privately how long rabbis could continue deceitfully to tell Bible stories from the pulpit as if they represented actual historical events. The Bible, no less than the Talmud, had to be understood as a product of its time. Geiger had early and carefully studied Spinoza's biblical criticism and he kept up with what Christian scholars were writing. He noted that Wilhelm Vatke was applying to the Old Testament the same tools with which Strauss had analyzed the New. And during the last decades of his life Geiger did publish his own critical studies of pre-exilic Israelite history, though not in the form of a comprehensive work.[121] He openly expressed his view that Deuteronomy represented a separate source from the rest of the Pentateuch. While he did not distinguish other longer documents in the text, he regarded the remainder, the *Grundschrift,* to be essentially Ephraimitic in origin with the notable exception of the Decalogue, which he believed may have antedated Joshua's conquest.[122]

The cumulative effect of Geiger's critical work was thus to historicize and therefore to relativize every sacred text of Judaism, biblical no less than rabbinic. Each reflected its age of origin, none stood above its historical milieu, none could serve as unassailable norm. Whatever history had produced, the ongoing history represented by present and future could alter or even abolish. But recognizing historical relativity did not necessitate rejection. Every element of tradition could claim *relative* validity as a revelation of the religious consciousness within the community of Israel at a particular point in its development. If it still possessed viability in the present, then it was worthy of reaffirmation.[123]

Thus demolition made way for construction; the broken chain of continuity could be reforged with new links. Texts that could not be understood as timeless norms for belief and practice could be seen as *sources* for the spirit of Judaism. This spirit, expressing itself anew in every age, progressing in religious and moral awareness, became for Geiger the cement which bound one age of Jewish history to another and made the modern period, as well, but another link in the chain. Not a timeless or even a developing Halakhah was the basis of Judaism's continuity, but its inner creative spirit, which produced not alone the specifics of law, but also religious principles and moral ideals. That spirit rested within the Jewish collectivity and characterized it whether, as at the beginning of their history, the Jews constituted a nation, or whether, as in the present, they were best defined as a religious community.[124]

This new conception of Judaism made it possible for Geiger to transcend arbitrary rejection of some Jewish texts in favor of others. Unlike radical lay reformers of the earlier generation and of his own time, he was never a "Mosaist," who spurned rabbinic Judaism. On the contrary, in the manner of the German historian Leopold Ranke, he sought to understand and appreciate each age of Jewish history in its own terms. In time he spoke of his own "inner attachment to Judaism's *entire* rich course of development, to *all* the creations of the various centuries. . . . Every age in the evolution of Judaism constitutes an impulse in its history, and the present can no more detach itself completely from the past without suffering damage than a single limb can be torn without harm to itself from the entire body of Judaism."[125] Moreover, precedents and models were to be found in many periods. The Talmud too was an expression of Judaism's spiritual evolution, of its "healthy creative drive":

> In [our contemporary] strivings we shall indeed listen to the voices of the ancients, seek to discover genuine Jewish spirit in the Talmud as a document in the great and lengthy history of Judaism. With an analytic and probing eye we shall take as our model the admirable way in which the talmudic teachers, especially the earlier ones, inquired of their age in establishing and altering institutions—even if they feebly sought support in biblical verses and their own views were in turn misunderstood by those who followed. Like them we should be concerned not for the letter, but for the spirit.[126]

Geiger was especially drawn to the earliest creators of rabbinic Judaism, the Pharisees. Rejecting out of hand the hostile conception prevalent in Christian scholarly circles, which saw the Pharisees much as the New Testament pictured them, Geiger drew a very different portrait. Politically, the Pharisees were the democrats, the party of the people; religiously, they brought Judaism to a higher stage of development.[127]

The breadth of Geiger's scholarly *oeuvre* is astounding. With the exception of the mystics and the later codifiers, who represented to his mind a weakening of Jewish spiritual vitality induced by political oppression, Geiger studied virtually every phase of Jewish religious and cultural history and wrote extensively on many of the major figures. He was interested, for example, in medieval Jews who had defended their faith in polemics with Christianity.[128] In the biblical commentaries written by the rabbis of Northern France, beginning with Rashi in the eleventh century, Geiger found an admirable desire to understand the text simply, soberly, and without bias; in the case of Rabbi Joseph Kara of the twelfth century he found a critical bent as well. In fact the medieval Ashkenazi Jews, Geiger believed, were considerably more impartial in determining the original meaning of the biblical text than their Sephardi contemporaries, whose views were influenced by philosophical prejudices and by their need to polemicize against the schismatic Karaites.[129] Yet for Geiger there was no finer expression of Jewish spiritual creativity than the legacy of the Spanish and Italian Jews. Aiming at empathetic understanding, Geiger set himself the task "to delve lovingly into the soul" of the writer he was studying in order to comprehend his work fully and judge him fairly. He was careful not to make medieval figures more modern than they were in fact and to convey an appreciation for sentiments which he himself did not share. He wrote movingly of the Spanish Hebrew poets and translated samples of their work into German; among the Italians he found neglected figures who, though still lacking historical consciousness, in other respects possessed a modern temperament.[130] Thus Geiger the historical critic was increasingly balanced by Geiger the empathetic historian of Jewish spiritual creativity. Here, too, was the elusive bridge from scholar to rabbi.

Abraham Geiger was a man aware of his talents. Though in his youth he felt occasional self-doubt and despair, he became ever more determined to play a decisive role in the Jewish life of his day. In 1837, when only twenty-seven years of age, he succeeded in drawing fourteen rabbis to the little town of Wiesbaden for the first Reform-oriented rabbinical conference. In his relations with others he was perceived as dominant; he could love his fiancee only because she fully submerged her identity in his. In polemics he was vehement and unrelenting—to yield was a sign of weakness. With almost no interest in nature and surprisingly little in such diversions as art, music, and drama, Geiger concentrated his immense energy on the Jewish tasks before him.[131] He became a highly controversial figure, who had both intensely loyal partisans and bitter enemies. With his shaven face, his long, straight hair tucked behind his ears, and looking out pensively but confidently through narrow wire-rimmed glasses, Geiger must have appeared to his congregants as a modern intellectual who was also somehow their rabbi—distant, perhaps a bit cold, but a man who had something to say.

Neither historical criticism nor agitation for ritual reforms was the substance of Geiger's sermons. On the pulpit his purpose was to inspire his listeners and deepen their conviction that Judaism represented ideals not antiquated by contemporary thought and culture. He wanted to instill Jewish self-respect and loyalty by pointing to Judaism's universal values and hopes while at the same time implanting those same values among his congregants by pointing out their Jewish basis.[132] As preacher, Geiger was willing to be consciously ahistorical, in the manner of Midrash to read contemporary wisdom into the ancient texts, suspending his principle of development:

> Even as in other areas I demand that life accept the fruits of scholarship, so, too, being myself directly involved in life, I recognize the duty to render fruitful the impulses and opinions which prevail within it. And so, to the extent that I can, I try to link my sermons to their earlier form in the synagogue. By drawing on appropriate excerpts from Talmud and Midrash, and by agadic expansion of the meaning of biblical verses in the manner of the ancients, I endeavor to show that the new idea is but the fruit of older shoots, rooted and visible in the earlier sources of Judaism. Though *Wissenschaft* may sometimes rage, life peacefully unites past and present.[133]

What Geiger preached from the pulpit and attempted to draw from all of its classical texts was what he called "Prophetic Judaism." The message of Israel's ancient Prophets, universalized beyond its original context, became for Geiger, as for the Reform movement, the most viable and important component of Judaism. The Prophets' concern for the poor and downtrodden, their contempt for ritual acts unaccompanied by social morality, and their vision of peace for all humanity—these made Amos, Isaiah, Micah, and the others both timeless and contemporary. Their ideals and the faith in the one God as their source, Geiger argued in his first Breslau sermon, were the eternal elements in Judaism. The vicissitudes of modern life could not shatter them. Customs and ceremonies would change; Israel itself in its external form would change. But the divine imperative to sanctify life would remain—and so too, therefore, as a community of faith, would Israel.[134]

On the role of ritual in Judaism Geiger's views did not differ appreciably from earlier Reformers. Like them he saw it as instrumental. Where personal observances were devoid of spirit, where they did not elevate the soul, he found no reason to argue for their continuance. They were not, to his mind, eternally binding divine commandments. Although throughout his life he personally observed the dietary laws, it was apparently more because his rabbinical position required it than because he felt any inner sense of obligation. Well known is his private reference to circumcision as a "barbaric, bloody act, which fills the father with fear."[135] Yet where traditional ritual could be made meaningful, Geiger valued its capacity to enhance religious life. Personally significant ceremonies, he came to believe, were not merely a shell that could be cast away but a tangible representation of the spirit, and hence, though changing in form, were its ongoing mode of expression.[136] Geiger was a severe critic of Romanticism, which he accused of thoughtlessly venerating whatever was ancient. But he was not on that account a "cold rationalist." Bitterly he deplored the lack of poetry in contemporary holiday observance. It had been forced out, he believed, by the prose of just obeying the law, of doing the ritual just the right way. In the celebration of festivals free expression of emotion had been stifled by attention to form. Enthusiasm and spontaneity were sadly lacking: "Fragrance, blossom, colorful splendor has vanished from the realm where poetry should reign. A trampled, dirtied paper flower remains. Who will pick it up?"[137] The worship service was, for Geiger, the "purest expression of the religious community's collective consciousness, the witness of its solidarity, and the spiritual bond which most closely unites its members." Hence no liturgical reforms should be undertaken which could seriously undermine that unity. And, in fact, Geiger was moderate in the changes that he introduced into the prayerbook which he edited for the liberal sector of the Breslau community in 1854. To be sure, he would not compromise on points of principle: his prayerbook reflected abandonment of the desire to return to Zion and reestablish the sacrificial service. Positively it gave voice to Israel's universal hopes and spiritual role within modern history. But Geiger left the structure of the service intact and retained almost all of the classical prayers. Having chosen to be the rabbi of a broadly based community, and not of a separatist congregation, he bowed with little regret to the sentiments of the majority. He was trying, he said, to achieve "collective progress." As a liturgist, no less than as a historian, Geiger sought to gain an inner understanding of his subject, in this case by attempting to reenact the religious sentiments of the original writers of the prayers. His German translations were attempts to transpose those feelings which remained transferable into contemporary idiom.[138]

In the synagogues where Geiger was the rabbi, the service was conducted almost entirely in Hebrew. Though most congregants scarcely knew the literal meaning of the prayers, they preferred the familiar sounds and cadences. Geiger's own attitude to the Hebrew language was highly ambivalent. At one time he declared it "a foreign dead language" and he believed it an inadequate vehicle for serious historical criticism.[139]

But he was himself an elegant Hebrew stylist, who wrote a number of scholarly articles for Hebrew periodicals. He regarded Hebrew as the universal language of Jewish scholarship and wrote of his "love for the Hebrew tongue." Though German Jews thought and felt in German, which was therefore the appropriate language for private prayer, Geiger recognized the value of Hebrew in public worship, for it still possessed deep historical associations. At least for the immediate future, he wanted its use in the synagogue to continue.[140]

Geiger did not think of Hebrew as a *national* bond, for he did not regard contemporary Jews as a people. In 1840, when the Damascus Affair, with its blood murder calumny, aroused Jewish anger, Geiger remained surprisingly unperturbed, far more concerned for the cultured Jews of Germany than for the backward ones living in the Near East. As a Jew, he was interested in his fellow Jews' spiritual and intellectual development; their physical welfare concerned him only as a human being.[141] Geiger's position in this instance was extreme among his Reform colleagues, and he himself eventually modified his views. When Romanian Jewry suffered persecution in the late 1860s, Geiger sought to gain Prussian intervention on their behalf. "We feel fully German," he wrote at that time, "but our heart does not cease to beat warmly for our Jewish coreligionists in all lands."[142]

Geiger did not believe in Jewish survival for its own sake. But he did affirm the reluctance of Jews, as representatives of a minority religion, to encourage mixed marriages and so favored the alternative of easier conversion for the Gentile partner. What irritated him greatly was Jewish religious indifference or, in the worst instance, opportunistic apostasy. These were the two forms of withdrawal which implied that Judaism had failed the test, that it had nothing significant to say in the modern world. For Geiger, those who had torn their ties to Judaism had been "made deaf by the thunder of the age." It was the rabbi's task to persuade them that what was best in contemporary religious thought was already present in the spirit of Judaism.[143]

Geiger believed strongly in maintaining Jewish honor. Much as he desired full emancipation for German Jewry, he categorically rejected religious reform motivated by the quest for civic equality. Jews had to retain their "religious autonomy." Emancipation would come about when political liberalism triumphed in Germany, almost irrespective of how the Jews themselves behaved. It was not that emancipation required religiously reformed Jews, but that religious reform required politically emancipated persons who would be able to make religious decisions in their lives without regard for external factors. The same attitude led Geiger to scorn reforms which were patent imitations of Christian customs and ceremonies. In this regard there was little difference between Geiger and Frankel: both recognized that genuine religious development could come only from within.[144]

The Judaism of his day, Geiger believed, had become estranged from its own inmost self. Concentrating on externals, it had lost access to its essence: "the free development of the inner moral force." Throughout his life Geiger argued for an "inner regeneration" of Judaism, the revival of its spirit. More important than specific reforms was the inward renewal without which all changes in synagogue ritual were scarcely more than useless.[145]

During his forty-year rabbinical career Geiger was forced to weather controversy and disappointment. His selection for the Breslau rabbinate in 1838 resulted in a prolonged and nasty dispute with the Orthodox rabbi of the community, Solomon Tiktin, and then with Tiktin's son Gedaliah. Geiger's failure to gain the ardently desired first directorship of the modern seminary in Breslau was a devastating blow, which more than anything else led to his leaving the city for a rabbinate in his hometown of Frankfurt in 1863. Finally, in the last years of his life, he moved to Berlin, attracted especially by the opportunity to teach at the liberal seminary opened there in 1872. Though Geiger's restless spirit seems never to have found lasting tranquillity, the dichotomy which characterized his youth gradually lost its severity. He came to recognize that historical change was a slow process, that revolution more easily brought destruction than new growth. The last decades of Geiger's life reveal both a greater ethnocentrism and a firmer faith in God.

While as a young man Geiger had feared that Judaism would quickly be overwhelmed by modernity, in time he came to appreciate its staying power. He also became more critical of the *Zeitgeist,* seeing the modern age as part of a long process of decomposition not yet complete. After midcentury the idealism to which Geiger had sworn lasting allegiance in his youth fell into disrepute. Interest in material and technological progress displaced it. *Wissenschaft* went its own way, oblivious of theology. Christian scholarship, which had once served Geiger as a model, was mired in a recrudescent orthodoxy. In his later writings Geiger became a virulent critic of Christianity, declaring it the enemy of modern culture and questioning its survival as a spiritual factor in world history. At the end of his life Geiger also became less enthusiastic in his Prussian patriotism; he was dismayed by the effects of Bismarck's "blood-and-iron" theory manifest in the Franco-Prussian War of 1870.[146] The message of Judaism, by contrast, now seemed the more important and enduring:

> Judaism is not a transitory phenomenon, it is a primal possession of mankind which reached its full significance within a particularly gifted tribe. It bears staying power within itself and must strive for its dissemination throughout all humanity. . . . Let us not draw hasty conclusions about what great convulsions of history may one day produce, but until then we will *not* give up the much maligned name "Jew," to which the purest knowledge of God, the noblest freedom of spirit and moral purity are attached. . . . It is precisely to Judaism that all the great religious transformations, which determine cultural perspectives, attach themselves. Christianity and Islam have issued forth from it, been nurtured by it, and it is within Judaism therefore that the new religious transformation must take place.[147]

It was likewise in his last years that Geiger reached the position on revelation which has become associated with his name. From early on his faith hovered between the traditional conception of a transcendent, commanding God, which seemed to allow little room for human autonomy, and the immanentist Hegelian pantheism which made God into an impersonal Absolute Spirit. All along Geiger sought to affirm a personal God beyond the grasp of human reason, yet whose will was reflected in— and could never contradict—the highest aspiration of the human mind and heart.[148] Yet only in the last decade of his life did he extensively formulate his understanding of the role of revelation in Jewish history. The people of Israel, Geiger now argued, possessed an ethnic "genius" for religion, even as the Greeks possessed a similar genius for the arts. Its prophets were able to achieve unprecedented insights into the relationship between the Divine Spirit and its human counterpart. But Geiger went further: its insights were vouchsafed to Israel by acts of divine enlightenment which could not be explained by reference to natural development alone. God touched Israel and gave it not specific laws and commandments, but sudden understanding. It became "the people of revelation" and henceforth bore the message of the one eternal and moral God. Israel's task in the world was to preserve and propagate that message whose basic content remained unchanging, though its elaboration evolved from age to age. The message was sustained by the ongoing working of God's spirit in and through Israel. It was that spirit, divine in origin but human in expression, Geiger argued, which assured the continuity of Judaism even as it destined it ultimately to become the religion of humanity.[149] For a long time, and to some extent still, these views remained the common coin of the Reform movement.

The men here discussed all belonged to a single generation of German Jewry. As individuals they explored the options—systematic, scholarly, theological—which lay before a modernizing, fragmenting Jewish community. They established ideological positions and justifications for differing attitudes to religious practice. Against the background of their thought emerges the collective institutional history of the Reform movement in this same period: the conferences and controversies, the large and small issues, the practical successes and failures.

3

Growth and Conflict
on German Soil

A New Generation of Rabbis

Abraham Geiger was one among a few dozen young men who in the 1830s and 1840s offered a new kind of spiritual leadership to Jewish communities in the various German states. In their training, their views of the world and of Judaism, and their conception of the rabbinical task these men were set apart from their predecessors of the old school.[1] Although their religious positions fell along a broad spectrum, they soon gained a sense of common purpose. At a time when the traditional role of the rabbi seemed to many hopelessly irrelevant, they sought to redefine their vocation in order to give the rabbinate continued significance.

Initially the Reform movement had sought to circumvent the rabbinate, considering its representatives simply incorrigible. Very few rabbis at the beginning of the nineteenth century were as flexible as Menahem Mendel Steinhardt of the Westphalian consistory or the respondents (all of them from outside Germany) who approved the services instituted by Jacobson in Berlin. When he was asked to supply information orally to a Prussian official for the benefit of the Saxon government in 1820, one of the leaders of the Berlin temple, Ruben Gumpertz, had declared that the rabbi was in fact nothing more than a *Kauscherwächter,* a supervisor of dietary laws without spiritual authority, and that his role was unlike that of Christian clergy.[2] The Berlin and Hamburg reformers had looked for edification instead to young men of very different orientation, whom they designated as "preachers" and who did not perform the ritual tasks of the traditional rabbinate. Well into the nineteenth century, the title "preacher" (frequently combined with "teacher") continued to be used for religious officials whose principal task was to give German sermons and oversee Jewish education. This was true both in larger cities, where the rabbinate remained in the hands of traditionalists, and in small towns, where the new men served as the principal spiritual leaders but lacked rabbinical stature.[3] Yet gradually dissatisfaction emerged with being merely a preacher. The principal spiritual leader in Judaism, after all, had since ancient times borne the title of rabbi, and "preacher" was clearly a Christian term. Representatives of the new generation thus sought recognition as rabbis even though they understood the role very differently. As these men gradually assumed positions in small and large communities, they often created conflict, but they also renewed the viability of rabbinical leadership.

The first extensive program for a modernized rabbinate appeared in a Hebrew work published in 1820—the very year that Gumpertz presented his derogatory view—by the Posen maskil and educator David Caro.[4] The rabbis of the present, Caro argued, neither lived up to the standards of classical times nor were qualified to meet contemporary challenges. The ancient sages knew the languages of the countries in which they lived, they were well versed in secular disciplines, and they were willing to alter Jewish law when the times demanded it. Not so the rabbis of the present. Many were grossly ignorant not only of the world around them but of Jewish tradition as well. They tended to be withdrawn, arrogant, pietistic, and excessively stringent. They placed undue emphasis on the peripherals of religion while neglecting its essentials. To Caro, they represented the pitiful degeneration of a once noble profession. But unlike Gumpertz, Caro was not ready to relegate the contemporary rabbinical office to insignificance. He envisaged a new, distinctly modern rabbinical role and sought to spell it out in some detail. According to Caro, the nineteenth-century rabbi should be chosen for his moral conduct (a traditional consideration to be sure), his clear knowledge not just of Talmud but of all aspects of the Jewish religion, his attainments in secular studies, his ability to teach with enthusiasm, and his capacity to judge religious matters knowledgeably and fairly. Among his foremost tasks was to present Judaism in a way that would make it appealing in its new historical context. Aside from the classroom, the new rabbi would fulfill his task most effectively from the pulpit. In carefully crafted and appealing German sermons he would interpret Scripture, urge fulfillment of God's commandments, inspire considerateness in personal relations, and imbue love of country and of humanity as a whole. Above all, the rabbi was to be a *mofet,* a model for the modern Jew—and that, Caro noted, was worth a thousand sermons. In short, he believed that the rabbinate could be radically transformed: old–new rabbis, combining traditional functions with modern ones, could become effective spiritual, moral, and practical guides. Far from wanting to limit rabbinical influence, Caro argued for its expansion. In his person and his role the new kind of rabbi would demonstrate the possibility of harmony between Jewish religion and modern culture.

In 1820 Caro's vision seemed excessively optimistic. Almost all German states had virtually eliminated the once extensive juridical powers of the rabbinate; talmudic academies in Germany had declined for lack of students; rabbinical positions were filled by Polish immigrants or not at all. The incumbent rabbis were unwilling, and mostly also unable, to assume a new role. Raised without secular education, determined to preserve every element of what they believed to be a wholly sacrosanct tradition, they resisted even minor changes in ritual and practice. Yet Jewish communities, which worried about increasing religious indifference among the younger generation, as well as some German governments, desirous of having secularly educated men in the rabbinates of their states, began to await eagerly the rise of a new generation of rabbis attuned to the altered status of the German Jew. And indeed during the following decades such men appeared, combining the traditional education gained in youth with years spent in a German university. As they emerged from their studies, they were often unsure how to combine the two worlds. There was, they often lamented, no Jewish theological faculty at any German university or as yet a modern seminary that could bring the secular and Jewish realms together. They had no choice but to undertake the lonely and difficult task of attempting a synthesis themselves.[5] Yet during the thirties and forties, in one community after another, in both large and small towns, the new rabbis replaced the old. While in 1832 Zunz could think of only six rabbis in Germany who possessed a university degree, by the time of the rabbinical conferences of the 1840s, twenty-two (more than half) of the participants were men who had received the doctorate.[6]

The transformation of the German rabbinate did not always mean the acrimonious substitution of a secularly trained, reform-minded younger man for an older rabbi of the premodern type. While reforms did sometimes begin only with a change of rabbi, this was not always the case. Some quite traditional rabbis lent their support to modernization as long as it did not involve outright violation of Jewish law. Rabbi Samson Wolf Rosenfeld (1780–1862), for example, had studied at the yeshivah in Fürth and managed to get a German high school education, but he never attended a university.[7] He was fully committed to Jewish law but also to modernizing reforms which would not violate it. As early as the second decade of the nineteenth century, in the Bavarian town of Markt Uhlfeld, he began giving regular edifying sermons in the German language. In fact, he was the first ordained and recognized rabbi to give such sermons in Bavaria, and possibly the first anywhere in Germany. For two years, from 1835 through 1836, he edited a German-language weekly Jewish newspaper called *Das Füllhorn* (The Horn of Plenty), which included sermons, poetry on Jewish themes, popular theology, and news reports of Jewish interest from all over Europe. Though short-lived, his paper created a model for many similar publications to follow. As early as 1819, Rosenfeld had argued that "the spirit of the age" demands more decorum, harmony, and dignity in the religious service.[8] After obtaining the rabbinate of Bamberg in 1826, he introduced a variety of reforms including regular sermons, confirmation, and the abolition of *piyutim*. Yet he opposed more substantial changes, such as elimination of the *kol nidre* chant. While in the twenties he was regarded as an innovator, in the more radical forties he was deemed conservative.

Rabbi Samuel Levi Eger [Egers] (1769–1842) presents a second example of flexibility among the older generation of rabbis.[9] A learned and highly respected talmudist from one of the leading rabbinical families, who had criticized Jacobson, he was a traditionalist reluctant to tamper with customs hallowed by many generations of practice. Yet like Rosenfeld, he too considered it permissible and desirable to make the religious service more attractive through increased solemnity and heightened aesthetic appeal. With less traditional men he shared the desire to impress the fundamental teachings of Judaism upon children in the most effective manner. As chief rabbi of Brunswick, he began in 1831 to conduct confirmations of boys and girls and he gave occasional edifying sermons in German along with more traditional exegetical ones in western Yiddish. In his last years he acquiesced to a set of synagogue regulations which he believed did not violate Jewish law, though they included the introduction of some German elements into the liturgy. As his associate and successor he designated one of his students, Levi Herzfeld, who was a university-educated rabbi clearly of the new type and who carried reform considerably further. Thus in Brunswick the transition from old to new occurred gradually and smoothly, without violent conflict or bitterness.

While in Prussia official policy persistently sought to encourage conversion by depriving Jewish religious leadership of respect and status, other German states, especially in the southwest, set out along precisely the opposite path. They began to support the development of a modern rabbinate on the model of the Christian clergy. Here too conversionist motives were not lacking, but they mingled with an apparently genuine desire to improve the condition of the Jewish community and integrate it among the other religions of the state. Thus in the southern German state of Baden, which had about 17,000 Jews, a government official as early as 1823 argued that rabbis must change the nature of their profession. Instead of concentrating their attention principally on deciding matters of dietary law, they should be raising the spiritual level of their flock, visiting the sick, and presiding over a purified ritual in the synagogue. Future rabbis should be men who had studied in a German gymnasium, were well versed not only in Bible and rabbinic texts but also in practical rabbinics, and had undergone an internship with a functioning rabbi. In return, rabbis would be recognized as equal to their Christian counterparts. In Baden rabbis did indeed receive such status. In Heidelberg and Mannheim, for example, local rabbis served on the school board along with clerical representatives of the Catholics and Protestants.[10] In a number of states rabbis began to wear a prescribed *Amtstracht,* apparel peculiar to their office which visibly designated their station. In Württemberg the garb consisted of white collar bands (called "Moses Tablets"), a robe, and a black velvet skullcap.[11] In the course of time official documents were prepared outlining in detail the duties of the rabbinical office in a manner which made them parallel to those of Christian clergy. A number of the states were willing to recognize their rabbis as public officials and legitimate representatives of the Jewish faith whose views were authoritative; in a few places, such as Württemberg and Bernburg, they even received financial support from state funds. Thus outside of Prussia the rabbinate was emerging with enhanced dignity and some sense of its own power.[12]

The extent to which German rabbis were free to guide their communities in the directions of moderate or radical reform depended very much on the policies of the particular state in which they served. In Germany of this period organized religion of whatever faith was considered properly subject to state control even if efforts were usually made to avoid violations of conscience. The representatives of religion were to be loyal servants of the state.[13] In those places where the rabbi was elevated to the position of Christian clergy, he was expected to advance public morality, preach law-abiding religiosity, and generally serve the state's interests. Jewish spiritual leaders were especially exhorted to encourage occupational integration and cultural Germanization, to help "raise" the level of fellow Jews to where they might be worthy of civil equality. With the exception of the most orthodox, who remained ambivalent about emancipation and its concomitant religious and cultural integration, German rabbis and laity enthusiastically supported this process of "betterment" and its hoped-for rewards. Yet remarkably, virtually all refused to regard specifically religious reforms as a price to be paid for civil equality. Religion, they insisted, must be left to Jewish religious considerations alone.[14]

In regulating Jewish religious life, states generally relied on the rabbinical and lay leadership of the Jewish communities to put forward reformist programs which seemed broadly acceptable in the Jewish community and were satisfied simply to provide the stamp of governmental authority. Thus most of the largely cosmetic reforms instituted in the twenties and thirties encountered only sporadic and limited opposition. One notable exception was the Grand Duchy of Saxe–Weimar. If Prussian policy represented the extreme of encouraging the dissolution of Judaism through inner decay, in Saxe–Weimar it was deemed best to break the bonds of tradition forcibly in order to speed up the process of amalgamation. In 1823 the government prepared a regulation which among its provisions forced the Jewish communities to conduct their entire religious service in the German language. Only the Torah could be read in Hebrew if followed immediately by a translation. So great was the opposition that the government backed down until 1837 when it finally sought to fully enforce the regulation. By that time Mendel Hess (1807–1871), one of the most radical of the Reform rabbis, was serving as the state's chief rabbi, and though he did protest at least some aspects of the regulation (which originated five years before he obtained his position), his acquiescence as a state official to its enforcement, including even required attendance, subjected him to criticism all along the German rabbinical spectrum. The state did not relent until midcentury when the 1,400 newly emancipated Jews of Saxe–Weimar were finally again free to pray as they saw fit.[15]

In Catholic Bavaria, whose more than 50,000 Jews made up the second largest Jewish population of any state in Germany after Prussia, the government for most of the nineteenth century severely and cruelly restricted Jewish settlement and propagation.[16] But while its demographic policy remained consistent, it sharply reversed itself on the question of Jewish religious reform. In the late 1830s, factors not directly related to the Jews themselves turned encouragement into opposition. The earlier view is well represented in a lengthy treatise written in 1828 especially for the government by J. B. Graser, a knowledgeable Bavarian official, pedagogue, and theologian.[17] While respecting the Jews' right to be free of coercion in their religious affairs, Graser urges official initiative to transform both the Jews and their religious practices. Deeply ambivalent about his subject, he wavers between a manifest aversion to things Jewish and what seems a genuine desire to integrate the Jews, as Jews, into the Bavarian state. After making far-reaching proposals for the reform of Jewish education, but favoring study of Hebrew, and—in contrast to Saxe–Weimar—its use in the service, he points to the need for enabling "young rabbis" to meet the challenge of reconciling Judaism with modern culture. Accordingly, he proposes nothing less than the establishment of a Jewish theological faculty at a Bavarian university, to which not only the Jews but also the state would lend financial support. By this means alone, he believes, Judaism can achieve truly equivalent intellectual status with the Christian denominations. Graser is willing to reward the Jews with a high degree of religious equality provided they will reshape at least the externals of their faith to differ minimally from the Christian model. While the state must not interfere in strictly religious matters, Graser argues, it has the duty to forbid cultic forms which militate against "moral improvement." Though Jewish reaction to Graser's treatise was sharply divided, leading its author to accuse his opponents of ingratitude, some Bavarian Jews were well satisfied with it.[18] And government policy was working in the same direction.

As late as 1837 the most clear-cut Reformer among the Bavarian rabbis, Joseph Aub of Bayreuth (1805–1880), was able, upon his return from the Wiesbaden rabbinical conference, to win government agreement and support for a wide-ranging program of religious reforms. But only a few months later a new ultramontane government came into office which was determined to lower, not raise, the status of Jews as well as Protestants. It frowned upon notions of religious development and issued a rescript that newly appointed rabbis in the state must be strict adherents of "all genuine Mosaic doctrines and ceremonies and discountenance all destructive neology." It forbade the ceremony of confirmation and the attendance of Bavarian rabbis at the rabbinical conferences of the 1840s.[19] In this changed atmosphere Aub tried to persuade the regime that neither his own views nor those of any modern rabbi in Bavaria could properly be termed "neology," for that term implied a lack of positive, revelation-based religion. But he *did* believe in Mosaic revelation, though he thought that it became better understood in the course of Jewish spiritual development. The Oral Torah, as he understood it, was an ongoing interpretive instrument which continually redefined Jewish law and made it newly applicable. While he honored the Rabbis' accomplishment in this regard, he could not consider it completed. Thus, Aub argued weakly, surely the rescript was directed only against reform of revealed Mosaism, not of a necessarily developing Judaism.[20] But Aub might have saved his ink. Theological arguments could not persuade a regime which henceforth and until after 1848, like Prussia in the two preceding decades, regarded religious innovation of any kind as a threat to the legitimacy of the status quo.

In a number of German states reforms were incorporated as official policy in *Synagogenordnungen* (synagogue regulations), usually worked out by the chief rabbis, sometimes together with lay leaders, and then submitted to the government for its authoritative stamp of approval. We have already examined the first such regulation promulgated by the Westphalian consistory in 1810. Its pattern was followed by the numerous later versions which appeared in succeeding decades.[21] In general, the regulations stressed maintenance of dignity and decorum, prohibition of boisterous or uncouth folk customs in the synagogue, and the introduction of a regular German sermon. Most of the later regulations also provided for a few liturgical changes, especially with regard to prayers expressing suffering and the desire for revenge, and eliminated some of the medieval *piyutim*. Children's choirs and confirmations were also commonly introduced and unmarried girls were permitted and encouraged to come to the synagogue. Only where a wide gap existed between the sensibilities of the authors and the pious traditional attachments of the communities did the synagogue regulations arouse broad resentment. Usually they were accepted readily after a short transition, though sometimes individual provisions were ignored by some of the communities.[22]

Although publication of the regulations tended to make for uniformity as each new effort was guided by its predecessors, there remained room for innovation and individual rabbinical initiative. For example, we possess two detailed and most enthusiastic accounts of the ritual reforms introduced by Zacharias Frankel shortly after a new community synagogue was dedicated in the quite traditional Jewish community of Dresden.[23] Written by Bernhard Beer, a scholarly lay leader and close friend of both

Frankel and Geiger, they illustrate the religious reforms that characterize this period. On the holiday of Shavuot (The Feast of Weeks) in 1840, we learn, a choir of twenty to thirty men and boys was positioned high up in the second gallery, where it responded harmoniously to the chants of the cantor, who led the service from a table located directly in front of the ark. The congregation recited its prayers silently or in unison. Many of the *piyutim* had been excised, but for the sake of the most traditional worshipers, singing of the *akdamut* (a special lengthy Aramaic poem for the holiday) was retained. During the Torah chant no one was permitted to sing along out loud. Following the scriptural reading, Chief Rabbi Dr. Frankel ascended the pulpit and spoke on the religious significance of the holiday, applying the verse "You shall be to Me a kingdom of priests and a holy nation" (Ex. 19:6) to the mission of Israel: its task to pass on the word of God through the generations until it becomes the common treasure of all humanity. After the sermon Frankel went on to conduct a confirmation, as he did every year on Shavuot. This time there were two boys and five girls. He asked them questions regarding the most essential points of Jewish belief and practice, then spoke to each of them in turn on his or her plans for the future and gave them his blessing. A German chorale followed in which some of the Christians present also joined. But the most impressive innovation was yet to come. When the time arrived for the priests to bless the congregation, the folding doors in the side hall opened and with measured step fourteen *kohanim* entered, dressed alike in black clothing, white robes, and skull caps. In precise and pleasing unison this "choir of priests" intoned their blessing of the congregation in alternation with the cantor and choir. "Tears of the most heartfelt emotion streamed from most every eye. The numerous non-Jews of every station who were present were taken aback; they had not anticipated anything like it." How very different it was from the customary dissonance! The liturgy for the second day of the holiday resembled that for the first except that the sermon was replaced by a short German prayer followed by a memorial service.

Later that year, observance of the Ninth of Av, the fast day which commemorates the destruction of the first and second temples, was similarly transformed. The rituals of Tish'ah Be-av had been the subject of the severest critique, not only by radicals who saw no reason for mourning the demise of the ancient sacrificial service and bewailing the Diaspora, but also by moderates who were repelled by its cruder customs and therefore tended to stay away from the public service. But in Dresden this year the worship was not as it had been. Once again we have Beer's account. As congregants arrived on the eve of the fast day, those who chose to remove their shoes as a sign of mourning were required to do so in the entrance hall outside the sanctuary and to put on a presentable foot covering in their place. No one was permitted to bring low benches or to sit on the floor. When they entered, worshipers found the synagogue draped in black and dimly lighted so that the pulpit area remained shrouded in darkness. Only a pale shimmer of light, reflected from a silver Shield of David hanging above the ark, somewhat illuminated its surroundings—as if to symbolize the lone ray of Israel's hope. Instead of the cacophonous wailings which characterize the traditional service on this day, the lamentations were rendered by cantor, choir, and congregation in a restrained but sincere manner. The next morning Frankel gave a sermon in which he alluded to the persecution just then being suffered by Jews in Damascus as a result of the ritual murder accusation leveled against them there. The singing by cantor and choir of the medieval poet Judah Halevi's famous Ode to Zion concluded the observance. Even the most venerable elders in the congregation, Beer concludes, had to concede that this year—even though they had not sat on the ground—they had for the first time experienced truly heartfelt mourning at the grievous loss of the ancient sanctuary.

Such transformations of the atmosphere of worship occurred in many German communities, especially when a new synagogue was erected or a new rabbi assumed his position. They did not violate Halakhah and they left the liturgy mostly intact, merely excising some of the late and secondary accretions. Generally they were called simply "improvements" *(Verbesserungen)* rather than reforms, and they were clearly responses to the altered religious sensibility evoked by acculturation. However, there were some passages in the basic liturgy itself that became ethically and politically problematic for even moderate reformers. Frankel, for example, in 1843 changed a number of ancient prayers, including the daily *ve-la-malshinim,* which vividly petitions for the destruction of slanderers and of God's enemies.[24] A comparison of the texts indicates the radicality of Frankel's alteration. The traditional formula reads: "And for the slanderers let there be no hope; let all evildoers perish swiftly and all your enemies be speedily cut off. Uproot, crush, cast down and humble the arrogant speedily in our days. Blessed are You O Lord who breaks enemies and humbles the arrogant." Frankel's version reads: "And for the slanderers let there be no hope; let evil perish swiftly, and speedily humble the arrogant so that they might return to You. Blessed are You O Lord who breaks evil and humbles the arrogant." Similar alterations of this prayer—or its omission—became common elsewhere.[25]

Another candidate for change or elimination was a passage in the twice-weekly prayer *ve-hu raḥum,* which in the traditional text reads: "They [Israel's enemies] have detested us like the impurity of a menstruant woman. How long will your strength remain captive and your glory in the hand of the foe? Arouse your might and zeal against your enemies, that they be put to shame and shattered in their might." Frankel and others simply skipped over this passage, which to them was both morally offensive and politically provocative. Similar passages in other prayers, were likewise emended or omitted. Thus even in moderately traditional circles, alongside the aesthetic improvements, limited liturgical reforms began to spread from community to community. The prayerbook which congregants held in their hands, however, as yet remained unchanged. And the major conflict over the limits of religious reforms was just beginning.

Until the mid-1830s there was little sense of a self-conscious and focused Reform movement in German Jewry. To be sure, a number of synagogue regulations had already been promulgated; sermons, confirmations, and decorous religious services were becoming more common. But it was not until the second third of the century that distinct but interrelated developments coalesced to create a feeling of unity, direction, and quickened pace. In the preceding chapter we discussed the systematic theologies that now began to appear, the increasing application of *Wissenschaft* to the Reform enterprise, and the laying down of fundamental ideological positions. Without these there could have been neither depth nor self-understanding. The theoretical elements were in turn sustained by the growth of an acculturated, secularly educated rabbinate, which, supported by a new generation of lay leadership increasingly favorable to at least moderate reforms, was beginning to apply its new attitudes to Jewish religious life. Yet beyond theory, leadership, and practical efforts, if there was to be a concerted movement, then a sense was needed that its various elements and manifestations constituted parts of a larger whole. In the 1840s, such a collective consciousness did emerge, though its boundaries were almost immediately called into question. Along with rabbinical conferences and common struggles against the Orthodox came severe inner tensions and conflicts.

If the Reform movement was able to achieve and retain a sense of unity through all the controversy which lay before it, the credit lies largely with one man who was determined above all that the center would hold.[26] Ludwig Philippson (1811–1889), preacher and then rabbi in Magdeburg, was not a scholar–intellectual like Abraham Geiger or a radical like Samuel Holdheim. Neither was he a proponent of the very slow pace of religious reform favored by Zacharias Frankel. Early in his career he declared a commitment to "progress which respects what exists but strives for its ennoblement."[27] Philippson believed in Mosaic revelation and in the value of post-biblical Jewish tradition, yet he thought that tradition should remain flexible. He was a moderate Reformer who hoped for a religious regeneration that would eventually spread to all Jewry. While other Reformers envisaged a wholly transformed Judaism of the future, Philippson focused his attention on the possibilities of the present. Pragmatic considerations weighed as heavily with him as matters of principle; he was not a lover of conflict. In 1837 he founded the *Allgemeine Zeitung des Judentums,* a Jewish newspaper which addressed itself to every Jewish interest. For more than fifty years he remained its editor, seeing it achieve considerable influence and outlast all its early competitors. For Jewish history in general the *Allgemeine Zeitung* possesses major significance as a force for sustaining the sense of a worldwide Jewish peoplehood despite assimilatory pressures. For the Reform movement it was of even greater importance. Geiger's periodical was directed only to the most scholarly and thoughtful Jews. It lacked—and did not seek—mass appeal. But Philippson's newspaper chose to discuss religious matters in less learned language and in direct relation to practical concerns. Regularly it printed reports of synagogue reforms undertaken in this or that state or community; it gave readers a sense of widespread, if not concerted, religious progress. It also put religious reform into a larger context. Because the *Allgemeine Zeitung* did not limit its attention to religious matters—because its interests were far more broadly Jewish—it did not become the newspaper of one particular religious orientation. Reports of religious developments competed with news of the struggle for Jewish emancipation in Germany and elsewhere, with refutations of antisemitic slander, and with bits of information about Jews all over the world. Reform, as Philippson conceived and propagated it through his newspaper, was thus portrayed as a movement within Jewry as a whole, not as a divisive sectarian trend. When in the 1840s the Reform movement in Germany achieved its height of activity and controversy, Philippson's newspaper was there to serve as the chief sounding board for conflicting views and to raise the profile of the movement, giving it the salience it had previously lacked. Himself an active participant in much of the reforming activity and swirling controversies of the decade after he founded his newspaper, Philippson as a talented publicist, man of the center, and inveterate optimist sought to restrain and direct the powerful forces which now came to the fore. Yet, as we shall see, the 1840s produced a turbulence which neither one man nor one newspaper could entirely hold in check.

Controversy in Breslau and Hamburg

While the other German states were encouraging and lending sanction to religious change, Prussia stood firmly opposed to any modernization of the religious service or elevation of rabbinical status. Its policy dictated that Judaism continue to appear alien and visibly disfavored. This despite the high degree of civic equality that most of the nearly 180,000 Prussian Jews themselves had enjoyed ever since the Emancipation Edict of 1812.[28] In Prussia, Judaism was defined as nothing more than a tolerated private religious association. The state did not recognize rabbis as religious officials, the way it did ministers and priests; it felt no obligation to support or regulate Jewish religious life. Yet through its various departments, it exercised a police power over the Jewish communities whose sole purpose was to prevent any action that might be injurious to political interests.[29] Ever since Frederick William III's edict of 1823 putting an end to the Beer Temple in Berlin, those interests were defined to exclude all "innovations" in Jewish worship, since "sectarianism" of any kind was believed to constitute a danger to political stability.

For about a dozen years, during a period of general political reaction, Prussia held stringently to its policy. It set no qualifications for rabbis except that they be able to read German or Polish and be morally without blemish. It would not allow rabbis to dress like Christian clergy or to use the title of preacher. In places where confirmations had been held, they were now prohibited; the attempt to give a German eulogy at a funeral could produce police interference. In Königsberg, German Sabbath sermons were declared illegal, as were any changes in the wedding ritual, or even a short wedding talk (except where the couple explicitly requested it).[30] Reforms were tolerated only in the Jewish schools, which as a result became for some Jews a surrogate for the synagogue. In Berlin, for example, the community school held Sabbath services attended by large numbers of adults as well as children. Although the prayers remained unchanged, one of the teachers gave a German sermon and a choir of boys sang Hebrew psalms in four-part harmony. But government and traditionalists joined to make sure that in the community synagogue all would remain almost exactly as it had always been. Still in the 1830s auctions were held for synagogue honors and any attempt to introduce decorum was held to be a prohibited innovation. Even as late as 1842 the only noticeable reform was a men's choir wearing uniform velvet skull caps.[31]

By the middle thirties, however, some local Prussian officials were willing to ignore Jewish religious reforms in those places where there was no active traditionalist opposition. Thus Magdeburg in 1833 became the first Jewish community in Prussia to succeed in once again employing a preacher (Ludwig Philippson), introducing regular sermons, confirmations, and choir. The Orthodox rabbi did not object and the local authorities, favorably inclined, managed to evade or counter ministerial inquiries. Other Prussian communities followed the lead of Magdeburg and official opposition grew ever more sporadic.[32] By 1841, following the ascension to the throne of Frederick William IV, Rabbi Joseph Maier in Württemberg even looked to the "enlightened government" of Prussia to set an example of encouraging religious progress.[33]

Just where the Prussian government stood on religious reform by the late thirties was tested in perhaps the most significant controversy of the early Reform movement. It took place in Breslau, within a sharply divided, relatively affluent community of some 5,000 to 6,000 Jews. Ever since the Prussian government had aborted a reform effort there in 1821, religious life had run in its accustomed channels. The gap felt among young people between education received in Christian schools and the very different, to them alien atmosphere of the synagogue, as well as the incursion of secular pursuits and values among the adults—these bred indifference on the part of many and left religious life securely in the hands of the most traditional elements.[34] Solomon Abraham Tiktin (1791–1843), the chief rabbi of the community, was a firm adherent of the old ways, who had purposefully evaded a community statute requiring him to preach on religious and moral subjects once a month. In 1838, acting in response to a petition by 120 members, the community officers decided to engage a new assistant rabbi, who in addition to serving as a member of the *bet din,* the rabbinical court, would also deliver weekly edifying sermons in the largest synagogue.[35] The community board, at this time firmly in the hands of modernists, had given up all hope that Tiktin would change his views. They wanted a counterforce in the community, a man with the capacity, "if necessary, to defeat Tiktin on his own turf."[36] They also hoped to set Breslau in the forefront of religious progress. Although at first Abraham Geiger was considered too radical for the position, after he had given a stirring sermon in Breslau that summer, a panel of fifty-seven electors chose him as assistant rabbi, with only one opposing vote. Clearly the majority of the Breslau community (or at least of its voting members), which proceeded to elect Geiger-supporting councils at two-year intervals thereafter, was by now in favor of religious change. Yet the Orthodox segment of the community decided immediately that it would not acquiesce; it would fight the election with every available weapon.

The prolonged clash which followed assumed symbolic proportions.[37] Tiktin came to be seen as the champion of stable traditionalism, the venerable representative of the old ways, committed to stemming the tide of modernization at all costs. Geiger came to symbolize both contemporary historical criticism at its most radical and the persistent impulse for practical reforms in Jewish liturgy and law. If Breslau fell to Geiger, the traditionalists feared, all they held sacred would be swept away, nonorthodoxy would gain legitimacy, and the Reform movement would for the first time have captured a large Jewish community.[38] On the other hand, if Geiger could be discredited—on account of his views, his intentions, or his conduct—then Orthodoxy would, at least for the present, remain secure, able to adapt to modernity in its own limited fashion.

Orthodox opposition to the Geiger election was immediate. Believing the Prussian government still to be on the side of religious stability, the traditionalists began expensive and prolonged proceedings intended to show why the Wiesbaden rabbi should not be granted the Prussian citizenship he required to settle in Breslau. Playing upon the theme of dangerous innovations and sectarianism which Geiger would foster and casting aspersions on his religious observance, they succeeded in delaying the appointment for a year and a half. Further protests followed even after Geiger was finally able to assume his position in January 1840. But all were to no avail. The Prussian government was no longer interested in banning German sermons or in opposing minor aesthetic reforms in the synagogue. Although it was not yet ready to allow Jewish services to resemble Christian ones or to give clerical status to the rabbinate, it was willing to let the Jews themselves, through their elected officers, decide the putative orthodoxy of their religious leaders.

Unable to remove the new rabbi from office, the Orthodox faction sought to limit his growing influence. Geiger's well-crafted and eloquently delivered sermons were regularly packing the largest synagogue while Tiktin's authority was waning more and more.[39] The older rabbi began to feel—with some justification—that he was being pushed out by this younger man of such different religious orientation. To protect his own honor and that of the tradition he represented, Tiktin refused to give any indication that he acknowledged Geiger's status as a rabbi in the community. He would not co-officiate with him at weddings; he chose to pray in a different synagogue. Most important, he would not serve together with him on the community rabbinical court, which dealt with matters of divorce and absolution from levirate marriage *(halitsah)*. Geiger might be the preacher, but that was as far as Tiktin was willing to compromise. It was a suggestion Geiger could not accept. To have done so would have meant to cut himself, and therefore also the movement for reform, off from the traditional source of Jewish authority represented by the rabbinate. Geiger therefore insisted on all the rabbinical prerogatives. For two years, from 1840 to 1842, there was a standoff. The court did not meet and community members needing its services simply betook themselves to a neighboring community. Matters were about to come to a head when an incident occurred that brought simmering passions to the point of violence. At the funeral of a prominent member of the community both Tiktin and Geiger had been asked to speak. Following the senior rabbi's address, which made veiled derogatory allusions to his colleague, the "second rabbi" (as Geiger was then called) attempted to give his eulogy. Suddenly the cemetery exploded with shouts by Tiktin's supporters deriding Geiger, immediately answered in kind by the other side. Caught in the midst of mutual verbal abuse—and soon thereafter fisticuffs broken up by the police— Geiger wisely chose to cut short his address.[40] The community board now had an excuse to act. The next day it suspended Tiktin on longstanding grounds of not performing his statutory duties. Despite a wave of public sympathy for the older rabbi, whom the council now accused of being concerned only for his own autocratic rule, the suspension was not revoked until the government finally overturned it as illegal a few months later. Shortly thereafter, Tiktin died and Geiger became the senior rabbi of the community.

The final outcome of the dispute was a division of Breslau Jewry into two separate religious societies. The strength of feeling on each side permitted nothing less. Where Orthodoxy and Reform were each represented by principled and unyielding points of view, and where the Prussian government now refused to intimidate either side, there could be no other solution. Thus Reform in Breslau would not be separatist as it was in Hamburg, but neither would it be institutionalized for the entire community as in the synagogue regulations of various German states. In 1846, Solomon Tiktin's son, Gedaliah, became the rabbi of Breslau's Orthodox faction and ten years later a new community constitution was promulgated whereby Geiger and Gedaliah Tiktin enjoyed equal status as rabbis of the entire community, though each served the needs of his own party.[41] Breslau thus set a precedent for the larger German Jewish communities which, while remaining unified for purposes of social welfare, would increasingly attempt to serve differentially the religious needs of the liberal and traditional factions. The Reform movement, which had sought to reform all of Jewry, was thus gradually being transformed into a denomination: Reform, Liberal, or Progressive Judaism—a particular philosophy and mode of practice shared by one segment of the community. Though liberals and traditionalists continued to struggle over control of community boards, a modus vivendi was emerging. Intracommunity disputes over religion would diminish as the principle of mutual toleration within the larger community gained widening acceptance. Only the most radical at each end of the spectrum would find it necessary to take separatist paths.

As the Geiger–Tiktin conflict resulted in establishing intracommunal institutional lines between Reform and Orthodox, so did it lead to a clarification of the theoretical differences between the two factions. In the first volumes of his scholarly periodical Geiger had begun to lay down the philosophy of Judaism that was discussed earlier. The Breslau controversy brought that incipient conception prominently into public view. It was attacked by the champions of tradition and defended by Geiger's supporters. Out of the polemics arose a clearer awareness of who the Reformers were and what they stood for, of the image of Judaism they shared.

The main issue of principle, as it emerged from the controversy, was whether an individual who possessed views such as Geiger had expressed in writing could legitimately serve as the rabbi of a Jewish community. The traditionalists set forth a very clear definition: the rabbi's principal role—in the present as in the past—was to be an interpreter of the law and a religious judge. He must be intellectually and emotionally committed to the absolute value and validity of the law, to the Oral as well as the Written Law, to the minutiae not less than to the general principles. Never could he allow external circumstances to diminish that commitment.[42] As two of Tiktin's chief supporters put it: "The rabbi is an official of the existing rabbinic Judaism. As such he may not create any new doctrine. Rather in assuming his office he explicitly accepts the obligation of preserving that which is already given, *i.e.,* the fundamental teachings of Judaism as it exists, and of conscientiously disseminating them by word and deed."[43] If a rabbi were unwilling to adopt that role, he would have to lay down his office.

Clearly Geiger did not share these beliefs and commitments, and Tiktin's defenders had little difficulty finding passages in his articles which cast grave doubt on his orthodoxy. Geiger did not believe that the Rabbis had invariably interpreted the biblical text correctly or that their hermeneutics possessed the force of divine revelation. His opponents accused him of being, like the Sadducees and Karaites, a denigrator of the Oral Law. He was apparently also a deprecator of Jewish customs for he had severely castigated *Formglaube,* the belief that religious forms in Judaism possessed intrinsic and absolute value. Geiger thus seemed wholly unfit for the rabbinate: "If he likes, let him call himself doctor, or scholar, even preacher. Who can object to that? But with what right rabbi?"[44] In turn, Geiger and his supporters were forced to argue that the young theologian's principles, however seemingly unorthodox, did not run counter to what was basic in Judaism and that a modern Jewish scholar, who freely applied *Wissenschaft* to the sources of Jewish religion, could still be a legitimate and acceptable rabbi.

Geiger himself responded by pointing out that he did not oppose forms as such; he only deplored the deleterious effect they produced when divested of the fluidity which could relate them always anew to essential spiritual values. He distinguished sharply, as he had earlier in his journal, between the critical scholar, who must see all phenomena in terms of their historical origins and development, and the rabbi of a community, who was obligated to observe community regulations and to treat with respect and veneration every custom held dear by religious sentiment. Thus as community rabbi he would willingly oversee the *ḥalitsah* ritual, even though as a scholar he was persuaded that its social function had long ceased to exist and as a private individual he believed it should be abolished, since where the brother-in-law was unwilling to forgo his prerogative or could not be located, the widow—cruelly—would be unable to remarry. More theoretically, Geiger utterly denied any affinity for Sadducees or Karaites. On the contrary, he was a Pharisee and a Rabbinite in holding to the principle of tradition. But for him that principle did not consist in a given divine revelation, rather in continuing and timely development. The Bible was canonized but not the Talmud. Just as the talmudic ordinances were not fixed for all times, neither could the Judaism of the present be regarded as an unchangeable given; it was the ongoing task of oral teaching to regenerate the written word.[45] Geiger thus made clear his position, but his definitions and distinctions could only further unsettle and antagonize the traditionalists.

Feeling that the case for their new rabbi before the governmental authorities required outside support, the Breslau community board turned to those European rabbis who might be expected to take a stand favorable to Geiger. During the latter months of 1842 it collected, and then published in two volumes, responsa from seventeen of them.[46] Nearly all of these rabbis were younger men; most possessed a doctorate and were serving communities in the south and west of Germany.[47] They were asked to address the following questions based on accusations already made: Is progress at all allowed in Judaism? May the large number of individuals who have different views from earlier generations with regard to the value and validity of talmudic regulations still properly be called Jews? Can Jewish theology bear scholarly treatment and free inquiry? And finally, is a man who has adopted and striven to disseminate a freer, more scholarly theological conviction entitled to claim the rabbinical office?

Though differing on specific points, the responsa reveal a remarkable consensus. These rabbis, like Geiger, distinguished Mosaic revelation from the total corpus of the Oral Law. They used historical arguments and presented extensive proof texts to show that Judaism had indeed developed through the ages. Since earlier institutions had been modified or replaced by later ones, advocacy of further changes could not be regarded as counter to its spirit. While particular statements in the Talmud itself would seem to exclude from salvation anyone who denies the revelatory status of so much as a single point of Jewish law, such utterances could be understood in terms of contemporary polemics or counterbalanced by less extreme dicta both in the Talmud itself and in later traditional writers.[48] The more radical respondents went so far as to suggest that talmudic morality did not always conform with present-day conscience, that the Rabbis had been children of their time, and that the spirit of God did not always speak through them. Contemporary Jews could not abandon their own moral sensitivities as they sifted through the Talmud's contents. If, then, there were conflicts between elements in the sources and present-day religious feelings, not only should the contemporary rabbi be free to inquire into the history of Judaism; he was obligated to do so in order to attempt a separation of "the truly divine in the Oral Tradition from the mass of undeniably human elements in the Talmud." And therefore Geiger, in whom, as one of them said, "we honor the first representative of scholarly theology in Judaism," could not be faulted for his critical studies. Moreover, since he restricted his views to the realm of theory, he did not represent a threat to communal unity.

The publication of the responsa, which came only a few months after the appearance of a similar collection in support of liturgical reform in Hamburg, displayed publicly the emergence, strength, and apparent unity of the Reformers within the new rabbinical generation.[49] The common objective which they set for themselves was strikingly illustrated by a simile that Rabbi Leopold Stein of Burgkundstadt included in his responsum. The Orthodox rabbis, he believed, were like a man who observes a driverless wagon moving slowly by him. Instead of jumping into the empty driver's seat and subduing the horses, he calls out: "Halt! Halt!" But to no avail. His shouts simply make the horses realize they have no master and they gallop away faster and faster until they cannot hear the cries at all. Stein and his colleagues claimed that they too saw the wagon moving by, but they believed it their duty to master the horses before it was too late.

Simultaneously with the later stages of the Geiger–Tiktin dispute a second controversy drew renewed attention to the Reform movement. It took place in Hamburg, where Reform had established its first lasting institution two decades earlier. Here alone during the twenties and thirties there had been a clearly nonorthodox Jewish religious service with its own unique prayerbook, organ accompaniment, and freedom from the need to compromise for the sake of communal unity. Over the years, the Hamburg Temple had become an established landmark at the border, if not within the city's Jewish community.

That community, which had been augmented by recent migration from the neighboring states, numbered close to 10,000 souls by the 1840s. Although Hamburg Jews still lacked the civil rights their coreligionists enjoyed in Breslau and Berlin, and were even prohibited from living in certain parts of the city, they had nonetheless grown very attached to Hamburg, perhaps because of the sense of personal freedom—especially freedom of expression—for which the city was known. Gradually they integrated occupationally and the wealthy among them continued to profit from Hamburg's commercial status. Most, perhaps two-thirds, could still be described as orthodox in the early forties, though secularization was making rapid inroads. Socially, as well as religiously, traditionalists and modernists kept their distance. Adherents of the synagogue avoided marriages with temple families and even refused to bury their dead in the community cemetery.[50]

Private neglect of Jewish rituals was increasing, and at one community event in 1841 came prominently into public view. The occasion was a twenty-fifth anniversary dinner given by friends of the *Freischule,* the free school for impoverished Jewish boys headed by the recently retired Hamburg Temple preacher, Eduard Kley. Some 200 men and women, mostly of the Jewish elite, had gathered in a local hotel banquet room. Only a few, it seems, were scandalized when the menu of the evening included "crabs, oysters, and pig's head."[51] Although not all guests partook of these courses, and the next day the students themselves were served a festive kosher meal, the fact that utter disregard for Jewish dietary laws was possible at a public Jewish celebration represented a novelty. It also indicated that for a growing number of Hamburg and other German Jews, Jewish identity no longer meant observance of Jewish law, but only Jewish philanthropy—as represented by the *Freischule*—and religious worship in a Jewish house of God.

The synagogues of Hamburg had changed very little since the first Hamburg Temple dispute. To be sure, Ḥakham Isaac Bernays gave sermons, but for the most part they proved recondite and obscure, failing to fulfill the expectations of those who had hoped for inspiration within a traditional setting. Despite some cosmetic change, the

service itself lacked most of the "improvements" which had become common elsewhere. Attendance was low, especially among women and young people. The subjective attitude to religion, discussed earlier, was becoming ever more widespread: Jews
would not come to a service unless they felt it uplifted them spiritually. It was that
need, rather than the felt duty to pray in a congregation, which increasingly determined whether they would go to a synagogue. Those who attended regularly still did
so out of a sense of commandment or tradition; the others went as the spirit moved
them: on occasional Sabbaths or only on holidays.[52] Necessarily this individualistic
approach to religion was the more common among those who belonged to the temple.

The Hamburg Temple's somewhat over 200 member families ranged from the very
rich to those of most limited income, from highly observant Jews to religious minimalists. Not a few kept the dietary laws strictly and said their traditional daily prayers
at home wearing *talit* (prayer shawl) and *tefilin* (phylacteries) but—in some instances
because of their wives and children—preferred to attend services at the temple. Others
had completely abandoned personal observance and their only obeisance to Jewish
religion came at the High Holidays, when the 250-seat capacity of the temple's rented
quarters proved wholly inadequate to contain the crowd.[53] During two decades the
temple had made a conscious effort to become an accepted part of the Hamburg Jewish community. Its members continued to pay their community taxes and to contribute to its charities.

The temple's greatest failure had been its inability to serve as a model for would-
be reformers in other communities. Everyone agreed that it stood "isolated," a beacon
whose light no one seemed eager to welcome. Its preachers could claim that all communities which instituted even limited reforms had to some extent been influenced
by the Hamburg Temple. But they had adopted only limited, mostly formal aspects
of its service, not the ideology, the prayerbook, or the organ. Only at the fairs in Leipzig, where its affiliated branch continued to function during the holidays, did it spread
its unique ritual and philosophy abroad. The Hamburg Temple was vaguely familiar
to virtually everyone. As the symbol of thoroughgoing reform, it was admired by some
and castigated by others; but it was not copied.[54] As the Temple Association
approached its twenty-fifth anniversary in 1842, it sought to break out of this isolation
and gain the influence its leadership believed it had long deserved. Coming after
nearly a generation of mutual toleration, the effort precipitated a new Hamburg controversy, scarcely less significant than the first one at its birth or the contemporary one
in Breslau. Like the Geiger–Tiktin dispute, this one between temple and synagogue
illustrated the growing strength and self-consciousness of the Reform movement; but
it also laid bare its inner division.

The immediate cause of the conflict was the Hamburg Temple's move to enter the
community itself and gain dominant influence within it. In the winter of 1840 the
temple's directors and about eighty members sent a long petition to the community
board in which they recounted the temple's contributions to Hamburg Jewry and their
wish to strengthen even more their bonds with the larger community. Then they asked
that about a quarter of the temple's budget henceforth be paid from community funds.
As they put it: "We therefore desire, and consider ourselves entitled, to be regarded
also in the most sacred matters, in religious respects, as a homogeneous constituent
of the community and to be put on an equal footing with every other segment that
has its particular house of worship."[55] The directors also mentioned a longstanding
intention to build their own building so that the poorer Jews who visited the services

would be able to purchase seats inexpensively. Not only was this petition refused by the community board, whose composition at this time—unlike both the earlier and the later period—was distinctly unfriendly to the temple, but it sounded the first warning signal to the Orthodox that Reform in Hamburg was taking on new aggressiveness. It was embarking on an expansionist course by making a bid for those Hamburg Jews who for financial or religious reasons had so far refrained from joining.[56] Here then was a renewed threat to the champions of tradition.

Within a short time the Temple Association raised sufficient funds for an elaborate sanctuary that would contain no less than 800 seats—and this at a time when the two synagogues of the Ashkenazi community were inadequate and quite old. Traditionalists began to complain to their spiritual leader, Isaac Bernays, that such a structure would make the temple seem like the "main Jewish house of worship, to the deep mortification of all believing souls."[57] Bound by the contractual limitations of his authority, Bernays at first remained passive. But when the Hamburg Senate, in deliberating on whether to grant construction rights, requested an opinion from both the community board and Bernays, he wrote a lengthy memorandum in which he accused the temple of sowing religious indifference, not combating it as it claimed to do. For, as Bernays saw it, the fight against indifference did not involve what a Jew did to fulfill present religious needs, such as spiritual exaltation, but rather his relation to the past, as represented by observance of divinely ordained law, and to the future, as represented by affirmation of Israel's national aspirations.[58] Neither of the latter had the temple strengthened. In other words, the temple had stressed only a subjective Judaism, not the more significant objective one. Therefore, any expansion of the temple would serve to increase indifference and gradually lead to "the demise of religious life in our community." The new structure should certainly be prohibited and the activity of the temple restricted. It should be allowed to call itself only an "edification association," not a temple, not a house of God.[59] Nonetheless, despite the opposition of both the community board and Bernays, the Senate granted the Temple Association's request in September 1841.

Construction of a new edifice, however, was but one prong of the Temple Association's thrust for increased influence.[60] The second was publication of a new edition of its prayerbook. To be sure, the old one had run out and in any case no longer reflected accurately the actual conduct of the service. But there was also a second reason for the new version. The editors hoped that the new prayerbook would satisfy not only their own needs but also "all those Jewish communities in whose midst the spirit of intellectual understanding and striving for progress reign alongside genuine fear of God."[61] Although the main title indicated that the liturgy within conformed to "the custom of the New Israelite Temple," the facing page called it simply "Prayerbook for the Public and Private Worship of Israelites." Clearly the new edition was motivated in part by the desire that it be adopted elsewhere as well as Hamburg.[62] It was for this reason, not because of any novelty, that it further stirred up the furor already raised by the Temple Association's construction plans.

The 1841 prayerbook was, on the whole, no more radical than its 1819 predecessor. It reintroduced in Hebrew the *pesuke dezimra,* the psalmodic passages which had been omitted earlier; it added daily services and a grace after meals. There were no significant ideological changes.[63] Yet the new edition called fresh attention to what had been present in the old one all along. And that was sufficient cause for a new round of vituperation. With the tacit consent of the community board, Bernays issued a *moda'ah,* a public notice, which was read in the Hamburg synagogues and sent abroad to other communities. In it he not only declared that a Jew could no more recite his obligatory prayers from this new edition than from the earlier prohibited old one; he also cast aspersions on the motivations of its editors, using such terms as "frivolous" and "mischievous" to describe their work. The Temple Association's directors responded, in turn, with an equally nasty counterdeclaration. It was not until the Hamburg Senate intervened that the Bernays *moda'ah* was transformed into a much abbreviated *azharah,* a simple warning to Orthodox Jews regarding the nonefficacy of prayer from the temple prayerbook, and the Association was persuaded to remove its posted reply.[64]

In his public notice Bernays did not charge that the second edition represented anything new. He simply used the occasion for a very brief attack, publicly for the first time, on what he regarded as the temple's ongoing violation of three cardinal doctrines: redemption, messiah, and resurrection. That seemed sufficient. He did not write a halakhic treatise or a responsum to reinforce his views as had the supporters of the Hamburg *dayanim* in 1819. Nor did he explicitly question the temple's use of German for some of its prayers. Only Rabbi Jacob Ettlinger (1798–1871), in neighboring Altona, a militant opponent of religious reform, raised the language issue in the single public rabbinical statement agreeing with Bernays' condemnation.[65]

Because the question of the new prayerbook's permissibility had come to the attention of the Hamburg Senate, the Reformers deemed it wise to strengthen their hand by seeking rabbinical opinions from presumed partisans—as the Orthodox had done in the first round, but did not do this time. The idea of collecting such responsa seems to have come from Gabriel Riesser (1806–1863), the much admired champion of Jewish emancipation, whose visible leadership role in the Temple Association at this time was undoubtedly an important factor in providing the temple with newfound energy and prestige.[66] A dozen opinions were printed together, all of them deploring Bernays' condemnation of the prayerbook and declaring that an observant Jew could indeed fulfill his religious obligations from it. The collection demonstrated that, beyond the Hamburg Temple, there was a broadly based movement favoring liturgical reform among the younger rabbinical generation. The respondents found no difficulty in showing that despite Bernays' accusations, the temple prayerbook fully preserved the traditional conception of resurrection, that it spoke specifically of a *go'el,* a redeeming messiah, and in a number of passages retained references to the hoped-for restoration of Zion. Only with regard to the desire for personal return to the Land of Israel and for the reinstitution of the sacrificial service—evident especially in the *musaf,* the additional prayer on Sabbaths and holidays—was there a notable and distinct ideological variation from the traditional liturgy.[67]

However, the longer-term significance of this dispute over a but slightly changed version of a twenty-two-year-old prayerbook lay not in the controversy between Bernays and those who thought his virtual excommunication sadly inappropriate to the new age. It lay rather in the difference of views which it elicited among the defenders themselves.[68] Three opinions, all of them appearing outside the volume of responsa, are of particular interest. Zacharias Frankel, like his colleagues, deplored Bernays' *moda'ah:* the Ḥakham, he thought, should have resorted to persuasion, not condemnation. Moreover, from a halakhic point of view the prayerbook was quite acceptable. But Frankel also used the occasion of his responsum to subject the temple's liturgy to severe criticism from his own modernist but conservative position. To his mind, it failed on three grounds: *Wissenschaft,* seriousness, and appeal to religious sentiment. Frankel dwelled on the prayerbook's obvious inconsistencies; it abounded in contradictions. Lacking a distinct unifying principle, it had fallen into eclecticism. Moreover, the editors' choices of what to retain, what to omit, and what to alter were in many cases not those Frankel himself would have made. They seemed to him both capricious and oblivious to the religious sentiments of the larger Jewish community. In terms of neither the objectivity and consistency demanded by *Wissenschaft* nor the subjective reality of religious feelings did the prayerbook measure up. His own (no less subjective) liturgical preferences would have produced a considerably more conservative prayerbook.[69]

Abraham Geiger's critique was in its structure remarkably similar to Frankel's, though its conclusions were entirely contrary.[70] Like Frankel, Geiger noted the prayerbook's lack of consistency, its halfheartedness, its compromises for lack of principle. He believed that the temple, unbound by the constraints of having to serve a diverse community, should have become the leading edge of religious reform, representing the sentiments and feelings of that advanced segment of the community which had already emancipated itself intellectually and emotionally from outdated doctrines. It should, in other words, have represented the spirit and sentiments of the future. Referring to criteria similar to Frankel's, *Wissenschaft* and subjective appeal, Geiger declared the prayerbook had not gone far enough—whereas Frankel thought it went too far. Their divergence of views not only presaged the conflict within the Reform movement that would soon manifest itself so sharply and bitterly, but also marked the inability of competent scholarship to lay out a broadly acceptable path for liturgical reform, even among modernists.[71]

Both Geiger and Frankel had also failed to appreciate the editors' own liturgical purpose. Each held up his own ideal and measured the Hamburg prayerbook by it. The actual intent of the editors had not included consistent adherence to principle. What they wanted above all was to serve more adequately the specific religious needs of a congregation which had been in existence for more than two decades. Their position was best stated by Moses Haarbleicher (1797–1869), a lay member of the editorial committee. Although, he tells us, the two preachers among the editors could easily have made the prayerbook consistent, the laity, including himself, had been opposed. They recognized that the constituency of the temple included families of diverse orientation, some of them modernists to be sure, but persons who did not want to move too far away from the larger community. Average temple members, he believed, wanted first of all to identify themselves simply as Jews, not as a separate denomination. Personally he urged that "all of us progressives must not appear to the world as anything other than Jews, without secondary designation—not to our brothers, whom we ardently love, even less to Christians." Most of the members were quite attached to tradition, whatever their practice at home. The men could never agree to uncover their heads in the synagogue or to a service that was not fundamentally in Hebrew. While they were universalists, Haarbleicher had personally noted that "those sermons and hymns possess the greatest appeal which speak of the collective destiny of Israel in suffering and in joy."[72]

Though, as we have seen, they did harbor broader aspirations, Haarbleicher and his associates were concerned primarily to produce a slightly revised prayerbook for a particular congregation of Jews which was attached to its own moderately divergent customs. Their liturgy was intended to reflect the diverse membership of the temple and to carry on an established tradition. Necessarily, the editors could satisfy neither Frankel's nor Geiger's principles, but only the practical reality of their own congregational life.

The evident inner diversity among Reformers, however, held together within the Hamburg Temple by the compromises of its prayerbook, was even then about to break into fragments. Not all laymen shared Haarbleicher's desire for Jewish unity. In other cities the most extreme among them now sought to break free from association with virtually all other Jews. In place of traditional doctrines and practices which they utterly rejected they planned to substitute their own.

The Revolt of the Radical Laity

Like Hamburg, Frankfurt-on-the-Main was an independent city state which in the early nineteenth century continued to discriminate against its Jewish residents. Marriages were restricted in an attempt to keep down numbers; certain branches of trade remained closed to Jews. Though by the forties a few Jews participated with Gentiles in the scientific, artistic, and cultural societies of the city, social spheres remained mostly separate. While the Orthodox segment of the community included the established wealth of affluent financiers, especially the Rothschild family, most upwardly mobile Frankfurt Jews were rapidly leaving Jewish tradition behind. Unlike Hamburg, in which traditionalists remained the majority, in Frankfurt Jews who had given up orthodox belief and practice represented as much as two-thirds of the 4,000-member community.[73]

Although the Frankfurt community board had early come into the hands of nonorthodox Jews, it repeatedly postponed synagogue reforms, so that until the forties the service retained its traditional cast. This lack of impetus was due especially to the existence of a community school for both sexes, originally called the Jewish Philanthropin, which drew students from affluent as well as poorer families. Beginning 1814, the school held a Saturday morning devotional exercise *(Andachtstunde),* which consisted of German hymns accompanied by an organ and an inspirational sermon. It was held after the regular service in the synagogue; there were no Hebrew prayers, very little that was specifically Jewish, and the only book used was a hymnal prepared by one of the teachers. Particularly after a special large room was furnished for the devotions in 1828, they became for some Frankfurt Jews a substitute for the synagogue. Confirmations and holiday devotions were held there; guest preachers augmented the school's staff in presenting sermons. Downstairs in the "devotional hall" students, teachers, dignitaries, and guests mingled with community members who had paid for their assigned seats. Nonpaying participants sat in a gallery upstairs. Men did not wear hats and, while the sexes sat separately in the balcony, they were mixed down below. The majority of the nonstudents who attended regularly were women.[74] Since the devotional hour did not constitute a religious service, it failed to arouse the ire of the Orthodox. As in the case of the services which had begun about the same time in private homes in Berlin, they deflected the reforming drive from the central religious institutions.

Among the teachers of the school, one individual deserves special attention. Michael Creizenach (1789–1842) was a mathematician and natural scientist with a university degree, whose extraordinary talents—in Germany of the 1820s—could secure him no more appropriate a position than as an instructor of children. He did have a sincere interest in Jewish religion, however, and outside the fifty weekly hours he spent in the classroom sought to apply his considerable intellectual energies to the issues of its progress.[75] Unlike his contemporaries, and perhaps because he was not a modern rabbi, Creizenach emphasized that practical reform could not be simply a matter of modernizing the synagogue service and providing an edifying sermon. Public worship was, after all, only one element of Judaism, and traditionally not the most significant. The real question, he thought, was how to reconcile teaching *(Lehre)* with life *(Leben)*—and that meant mostly dealing with Jewish practices outside the synagogue. Too long had such issues as Sabbath observance and dietary laws been swept under the rug. "The view that one must ignore rituals so they will silently decay is reprehensible and frivolous," he insisted.[76] But what precisely were the religious duties that remained incumbent on the modern Jew? In 1833, Creizenach published the first of four volumes which he called collectively *Shulḥan Arukh* (The Set Table), echoing the title of Joseph Caro's sixteenth-century guide to Jewish practice.[77] It was, however, a far cry from that earlier work.

Creizenach began by listing the 613 Mosaic commandments which medieval writers had enumerated, together with a few early rabbinic ordinances such as the festivals of Hanukah and Purim. He thereby immediately laid down a boundary: the 613 commandments were divine and hence binding; practices not deriving directly from them had a purely human origin and were subject to change or abolition. But he still had to deal with the talmudic interpretation of the biblical laws. Despite clear and increasing ambivalence, Creizenach was not ready to abandon the Talmud entirely since he believed, as did Geiger, that a stage of Judaism's history could not be ignored without doing violence to the whole. His solution was as simple as it was problematic: he would show his readers that the Rabbis had not only expanded the biblical laws and made them more severe; they had also created numerous alleviations *(Erleichterungen)* of the laws' rigor. In his second volume he stressed the latter and tried also to show how and why various customs and usages arose. Then each reader, who presumably had known only the existing Jewish practice of the home in which he grew up, would be able to judge for himself. He could identify with the talmud by following its less stringent prescriptions while rejecting whatever made sense in an earlier context but conflicted with life in the present. Had the early Rabbis lived today, Creizenach argued in the third volume, they would have made every effort to reconcile the law with the demands of modernity. Creizenach's concern was clearly for those who believed that in abandoning Jewish rituals they were necessarily forsaking Judaism— or at the least sinning grievously against its precepts. By pointing out that the Talmud itself was not rigid, that much of what it prescribed could still be adopted even by Jewish men and women who sought the fullest political, cultural, and social integration, he tried to persuade them that they were still faithful Jews. He did not want alienated Jews to separate from the community by celebrating the Sabbath on Sunday or in some other way cutting their ties with coreligionists. And that meant—at least for the present—that the Talmud had to serve as a guide, if not an authority.[78]

Creizenach possessed an unstable, contradictory mind and personality. He was a religious man who deplored the atheistic spirit of French literature then popular in Frankfurt; he loved the Hebrew language, even founded and edited a Hebrew periodical called *Tsiyon* (Zion) to perpetuate and glorify it; and he believed strongly in preserving a united Jewry grounded in its historical sources.[79] Angrily he lashed out at those who in the thirties were speaking of "repudiating the Talmud" and who felt ill at ease practicing any rituals in the home.[80] He deplored their separatist leanings, since cutting the ties would leave the larger community without the ferment it required for religious progress. But in the course of time Creizenach himself lost confidence in the enterprise of reform on a talmudic basis, and his later volumes reflected it. The futility of his endeavor became evident: the traditionalists would not be selective among the talmudic prescriptions and the modernists did not seek talmudic authority. Moreover, in his personal life, Creizenach strayed away from traditional observance. For a number of years he presided over a mainly Jewish masonic lodge at whose public functions dietary laws were not observed.[81] Creizenach failed to find a clear middle path for himself and therefore could not easily pass his message on to the next generation, not even his own children. Soon after Michael Creizenach died in 1842, his son Theodor helped to found precisely the separatist, antitalmudic sect which his father had repeatedly warned against and tried to prevent.

By the 1840s there had arisen at the edge of German Jewry a generation so fully Germanized and Europeanized that non-Jewish identity all but crowded out ancestral loyalties. These men (for they, not the women, were the actors upon the larger stage) were, to be sure, a small minority of German Jewry, their numbers ever eroded by those who stepped across the boundary into Christianity. But they were no longer, as in the earlier generation, isolated individuals. Some grew up in homes where parents had already partially or completely made the break from traditional observance. They went to Christian schools or to Jewish schools that stressed secular disciplines. Most had attended a university where they encountered the dominant philosophical currents of the day. As they returned home from their studies or settled in a new city, they could find little in common with most Jews, whose Europeanization was less advanced, who continued in the traditional Jewish occupations, and whose beliefs and observances seemed to them quite foreign. Within the Jewish communities these individuals constituted a radical fringe, tenuously attached to the whole. They felt great ambivalence toward their Jewish origins. On the one hand, they were influenced by the anti-Jewish and antireligious currents they encountered in philosophical literature and in the conversation of Gentiles. In many instances they harbored resentment that their Jewish origins prevented them from achieving the personal career goals for which they were clearly qualified. With ill-concealed anger, they derided Jewish exclusiveness, especially as manifest in talmudic doctrine and prescription. They felt a strong desire to tell the world that they themselves were not talmudic Jews, to openly declare their dissociation from all those elements of the tradition that they had irrevocably given up. Yet at the same time many felt a profound sense of attachment to fellow Jews, an ethnic identification—though in the German political context they could not call it that. Moreover, as men of integrity, they believed it a duty to stick by their fellow Jews, just and especially because Jews still suffered discrimination. The sentiments of these intellectuals are well expressed in the words of one of them:

> If I ask what obligates me to work for Judaism and its betterment, I must say to myself that it in no way lies in a bond of religious kinship with the great mass of its adherents. For a long time I have surely been as far removed from it as from Christianity. . . . What binds me to Judaism, what sets its adherents closer to me than other people are, is the pure obligatory sense of filial piety.[82]

Alienated from Christian society because they were Jews, and from the Jewish community on account of their religious nonconformity, they sought mutual support by banding together. In Frankfurt the two Jewish masonic lodges no doubt served such a purpose, though not all of the lodges' members were that far removed from Judaism.[83] But social communion was only an incomplete solution to these men's problems of identity. Their specifically religious concerns needed addressing as well, and it was for this purpose that a group of them joined together in the fall of 1842 to create an association called *Reformfreunde,* Friends of Reform.[84]

The Frankfurt *Reformfreunde* never attracted large numbers. No more than forty-five men associated themselves with the group, and the active membership seems to have been less than half that. But its importance for the history of the Reform movement exceeds its small size. Here for the first time a truly radical lay element claimed for itself the vanguard of the movement. Pointedly excluding rabbis from its ranks, it sought to set a faster pace for religious progress than could be adopted by the professional spiritual leaders who were bound by commitments to communal unity and to an organic process of historical development. The Friends' ideas reverberated in the Jewish and general press. Even as they aroused the most vehement opposition among Reform rabbis, they also stirred the rabbis to their own more aggressive and collective activity. Though their association soon disappeared from the stage, its influence prompted similarly inclined laity in other cities to present similarly radical views.

The *Reformfreunde* principles in their final version consisted of only three points:

1. We recognize in Mosaism the possibility of an unlimited further development.
2. The collection called the Talmud, as well as all the rabbinic writings and statutes which rest upon it, possess no binding force for us either in dogma or in practice.
3. We neither expect nor desire a messiah who is to lead the Israelites back to the land of Palestine; we recognize no fatherland other than that to which we belong by birth or civil status.

Of these statements the third enjoyed the widest support within the Reform movement. We have seen that the Hamburg prayerbook embodied it in the liturgy and most of the rabbinical responsa gathered in support of the second edition did not find fault on that score. Indeed, even more traditional German Jews stressed that Germany was surely their *Vaterland.* The second statement was more problematic because of its utter negativity. To repudiate the Rabbis meant to renounce most of Jewish religious tradition. Moreover, it represented a clear dissociation, as if to say, especially to Gentiles: "Don't hold us responsible for what the Talmud (then, as so often, under attack in press and literature) says or requires." But the most problematic element to critics of the Friends lay in the belief that Mosaism was subject to "unlimited development." For that meant there were no boundaries delimiting Judaism at all. Either the Bible was not revelation but only humanly produced literature, or biblical revelation was intended only for a particular period in Judaism's history. In either case the statement left a Judaism that was no longer a "positive" religion, no longer one based on the still inviolable word of God in a sacred text.

Within the Reform camp only the most extreme among the rabbis, Mendel Hess of Saxe–Weimar, supported the *Reformfreunde* position; most leading Reformers attacked it severely. The rabbis found that the Frankfurt platform came close to substantiating the often repeated charge of Reform sectarianism.[85] Though they might agree with some elements, they could not as a whole find it constructive. No more widely acceptable than the principles was the Friends' position on circumcision. Though a statement declaring it "not binding as a religious act or symbol" had, along with a similar one disavowing dietary laws, been eliminated from the publicized version of the principles, the members were known to regard circumcision as a pre-Mosaic, perhaps physically dangerous, and always intrinsically particularizing ritual. They commissioned one of the teachers at the community school, Joseph Johlson, to publish a pamphlet in which he argued that a properly constituted Jewish authority would be entitled to substitute another ceremony in its place. Johlson even outlined a brief ritual for what he called "The Sanctification of the Eighth Day," the first equivalent ceremony for both male and female infants.[86] On this issue, as on the principles, moderate reformers joined traditionalists in attacking the views of the Friends of Reform, contributing their responsa upholding the indispensability of circumcision alongside those of Orthodox colleagues.[87]

The lack of positive content, so readily apparent in the *Reformfreunde* principles, betrayed a general lack of commitment to Judaism. The Friends were unable—perhaps because not fully willing—to create any concrete institutional forms. They held some meetings; they appointed a committee to explore the possibility of Sunday services. But after about three years the society died a natural death. The members were too conflicted, too ambivalent, too uncertain in their loyalties and beliefs to establish anything permanent. For a brief time they appeared at the periphery of the Reform movement in Germany, but they were ill suited to become its leading edge.

Aside from their internal problems, there were external reasons for the Friends' lack of success. The longstanding *Andachtstunde* at the community school still attracted many who sought a highly universalized Judaism. And in 1843 the community board finally moved ahead with the selection of a second rabbi from the younger, reform-minded generation, a man capable of changing the image at the center from one of stagnation to one of progress. Leopold Stein (1810–1882), who was chosen for the position, was a moderate reformer, far more conservative than the *Reformfreunde,* but still too radical to win approval from the elderly traditional rabbi Solomon Trier or from the Rothschild family. In the first months after his arrival, he introduced various liturgical reforms, including omission of the daily prayer in which the Jewish man gives thanks for not having been created a woman. His well-delivered sermons aroused great enthusiasm, drawing back to the synagogue some who had hitherto attended the *Andachtstunde.* One generally critical contemporary thought he combined outstanding oratorical talent with admirable qualities of mind.[88] With Stein's appearance in Frankfurt, the radicals lost potential new supporters and their isolation increased even more. Since few could reidentify with communal religious institutions, they drifted aimlessly, at the edge of Jewish loyalty.

Of greater long-term significance was an equally radical yet far more numerous, better led, and more positively oriented Reform circle in Berlin.

In the early 1840s the Prussian capital had a Jewish population of about 7,000, easily double what it had been a generation earlier. On the whole, the community was well-to-do, with established families augmented by economically successful or ambitious immigrants from smaller towns. Few lived on charity. The overwhelming majority was involved in commercial enterprises ranging from banking and manufacturing at the top to dealing in old clothes at the bottom. A few were artisans and there was a thin layer of intellectuals and professionals, the former frequently book dealers, the latter generally physicians. The Berlin University, like the various agencies of government, employed no Jews, but its faculty did have a number of prominent converts, to whom their one-time coreligionists reacted with mingled pride and pain. In Berlin, unlike Frankfurt, few but the poor attended a Jewish school. More than two-thirds of Berlin's 1,000 school-age Jewish children went to non-Jewish institutions, receiving little or no religious instruction. The governing board of the community, still elected according to a law of 1750 which favored the wealthiest, consisted of men who were interested above all in preserving communal harmony. Themselves only partially or not at all observant, they were content to leave religious mattters in the hands of Orthodox Jews, who cared about them passionately. The community synagogue, with a capacity of about 1,000, drew only small numbers. It was not unusual for village Jews to leave religious observance behind when they entered the gates of Berlin.[89]

In the late thirties a portion of the traditionalists who frequented the synagogue succeeded—though not without opposition—in introducing a modicum of decorum into the worship. Honors were no longer auctioned off and those honored could no longer demand that an endless number of relatives and acquaintances receive a public blessing *(mi sheberakh)* on their account. Once the Prussian government had demonstrated its willingness to tolerate innovation by approving Abraham Geiger's naturalization request so he could serve Breslau, the Berlin community board began to look actively for a modern rabbi of its own. After Zacharias Frankel declined their offer because the government refused to grant him official status, they turned to Michael Sachs (1808–1864), who accepted the position of assistant rabbi and preacher in 1844. Sachs was a master of the German language and a scholar in the new *Wissenschaft* tradition, but also a religious conservative with an intense, indeed romantic veneration for Jewish custom and ceremony. His attempts to introduce minor reforms, such as a larger choir, a few German prayers and hymns, and elimination of some *piyutim,* aroused vehement opposition on the part of the most orthodox elements, who succeeded for a time in blocking them. But these same traditionalists appreciated Sachs's well-attended, eloquent sermons, for in them he preached adherence to Jewish law and condemned ideological reform. Indeed, it was disappointment with the selection of Michael Sachs that helped instigate a religious rebellion among a portion of Berlin's Jewish laity. Over 200 community members protested the process by which he had been selected. Apparently they had hoped for a clear-cut reformer like Geiger, not a pronounced conservative like Sachs.[90]

The Sachs appointment seemed especially galling to those who compared it unfavorably with contemporary developments in German Christianity. During the early forties, movements that sought to overturn established dogmas and traditions appeared simultaneously in both Protestantism and Catholicism. Among the Protestants, a group soon known as Protestant Friends, or Friends of Light *(Lichtfreunde),* declared itself for a radical individualism which placed religion firmly within the spirit of the believer, not in texts or church doctrines. Within Catholicism a similar movement, whose members called themselves German Catholics *(Deutschkatholiken),* or Christian Catholics, rejected the widespread veneration of relics, stressed their non-subservience to the papacy, and prepared to call a general synod. Each group harbored a democratic, antihierarchical thrust, which not only indicated displaced political dissatisfaction, but also raised the status of the laity as against the clergy. Though relatively small, these two movements received much attention in the contemporary press and were greatly on the minds of the educated. Their notoriety redirected interest to

religion and testified to the possibility of breaking out of confining religious frameworks and creating new religious initiatives outside the established order. While the
Jewish lay radicals seldom admitted the direct influence of *Lichtfreunde* and *Deutschkatholiken,* their opponents were not mistaken in linking them with their Gentile
counterparts.[91] Still, what made the Berlin movement into something more than a
mere flash in the pan—and hence unlike Frankfurt—was that it went beyond negative
reaction to the new rabbi and response to external stimuli, that it created its own
ideology and established a permanent institution. It is with regard to this internal
dynamism that we must here consider rather carefully the crucial contributions of two
remarkable, but fundamentally very different lay intellectuals.

Sigismund Stern (1812–1867) came to Berlin from a small town in Posen and
became a student of philosophy and philology at its outstanding university. Upon
completing his studies and crowned with a doctorate from Halle, he became the director of a small Berlin school for Jewish boys. But pedagogical work exhausted neither
his talents nor his energies. Stern was an intellectual, schooled in Hegelian philosophy,
influenced by Schleiermacher's lectures at the university, and determined to bring
Judaism fully into the stream of contemporary culture. He was a serious, seemingly
self-confident man, clear if not excessively original in his thought, his public speech
rich and rhythmic in its cadences. Optimistic and certain of his goals, he was a unified,
harmonious personality, a man who could influence others.[92] In 1843, in his early
thirties, he began to set out his ideas in articles, and then, during the winter and spring
of 1845, he expanded them into a series of lectures that drew ever larger crowds.[93]
What made Stern's ideas attractive to the men and women who flocked to hear him
was a fascinating, paradoxical combination of Jewish self-assertion and self-diminu-
tion. Deeply under the spell of Hegelian philosophy, Stern attempted—like some of
the thinkers discussed in Chapter 2—to argue against the Hegelians that Judaism need
not be regarded as the mummylike remnant of a former age. Believing that the state
was a moral organism, he held that while Judaism no longer possessed a political foundation of its own, it was capable of becoming a living limb of the Prussian state. In
ancient times Jews had possessed their own history; in the Middle Ages they had been
consigned to history's margins. But now, not only could individual Jews reenter history as citizens of the states in which they lived, but Judaism as well—if it were properly reconceived—could attain "world historical existence." Alongside Christianity,
not superseded by it, Judaism would have its honored (if slightly inferior) place in the
body of the state and its valued role in the spiritual development of humanity. That
meant Jews who wanted to enter the political and cultural circle of the current age
would not have to leave Judaism behind at the periphery. Not they alone, but also
their ancestral heritage, could be at the center. Such integration would also constitute
modernity's crucial test for Judaism: "If it is able in this form to maintain the strength
to preserve itself as an independent entity and to develop, then it will have indisputably documented its right to historical existence."

Stern's stimulating ideas were, however, problematic in two respects. Only a few
years earlier, in 1840, the new monarch Frederick William IV had brought a converted
Jew, Friedrich Julius Stahl, to succeed another convert, Eduard Gans, as professor of
law at the University of Berlin. In his lectures and writings Stahl elaborated the reigning doctrine of a Christian state in which Lutheranism alone could represent the moral
basis of government: Judasim would have to remain on the outside. Thus if Prussian
officials were now more tolerant of religious change within the Jewish community, it

was not because they desired Judaism to progress, but only because what outsiders believed really did not matter. As one of them wrote privately: "The Christian state has no interest whatever in whether Judaism sooner or later disintegrates into different sects."[94]

As few Christians could accept the idea of Judaism playing an active role within the state, so even moderately traditional Jews could not accept the shape which Stern assigned to this new Judaism in order to fit it to its role. He had argued that Judaism would have to change rapidly in order to prove capable of participating in the larger collective development. It would have to accept fully the supremacy of the state into whose life it entered and which it hoped to influence. It would become a "German-Jewish church," which meant on the one hand demanding assertively the same public recognition as Protestantism, but which also meant diminishing Judaism by excluding all those elements that extended beyond the universal message of ethical monotheism—the ceremonies and national customs separating Jew from Gentile. Stern recognized that neither the rabbinate nor the community leadership of Berlin Jewry was ready to support so radical a transformation. But he believed that a vanguard could bring enlightenment to the whole. He called on fellow Jews who agreed with the thrust of his thought to band together—not for purposes of dissociation from the past, as in Frankfurt—but to explore for everyone the path ahead. Not surprisingly, when a like-minded group did form during the very course of Stern's lectures, they selected him to lead their movement.

Aron Bernstein (1812–1884), Stern's agemate and the other significant figure among Berlin's radical Jewish laity, shared his associate's belief that Judaism would be able to survive meaningfully only if it underwent a fundamental transformation. But his similar conclusion flows from a very different set of concerns and a strikingly contrasting personality.[95] Bernstein, who in his early writings used the pseudonym Rebenstein, was a riven man. Born in Danzig, he received a formal rabbinical education but was purely an autodidact in secular studies. In the early thirties he moved to Berlin where he lived in humble circumstances as a bookdealer, journalist, and popular writer on scientific subjects. In the Revolution of 1848 he fought on the barricades and during the reactionary fifties he spent time in prison for publishing his liberal political views. No less intrepid about expressing his ideas in the field of religion, he accepted the most radical biblical criticism and later in life published a short work revising the prevailing documentary hypothesis with regard to the patriarchal narratives in Genesis.[96] His break with orthodoxy was sharp but apparently not bitter. He cherished pleasant memories of his youth and later wove them into nostalgic, humorous tales of traditional Jewish life. Unlike the ideological, self-assured Stern, Bernstein was a poetic, ironic personality—a man who in an unsentimental age was not afraid to express feelings. In Bernstein's writing on contemporary Judaism one image above all stands out: the tragic separation of three generations, with his own in the center: "The fathers *cannot* understand us," he laments, "and the children *will not* understand us."[97] In a speech delivered to those who could share his feelings, Bernstein expressed a personal motivation for favoring radical reform:

> With sacred, deep earnestness we received our religion from our ancestors in these venerable forms. And yet they have already disappeared from our lives, which have succumbed to a younger and mightier force, the force of time, and the recognition of our present. How shall we face our children who were born into the bright present for the sake of a bright future, who have not seen the earnest martyrdom, who

have no notion of the feelings with which that earlier generation daily struck their breasts with their fists and fell on their faces to confess their sins before a merciful and gracious God? They grew up without the reverence which we were still able to conjure up artificially. . . . How can we, with strife in our hearts, persuade them to pass on a hypocrisy . . . ? Set down as we are between the graves of our fathers and the cradles of our children, the age admonishes us with sacred earnestness, first of all to rescue ourselves from the great abyss which reason, custom, and life have torn open between two generations, the one before and the one after us. Then we shall become the *last* generation of a great heritage, the one which, while appreciating its external appearance, is able only to take it up, no longer to bear and transmit it. But then we shall also become the *first* generation which with unflinching courage, with ardent fellowship, and through word and deed lays the foundation stone for the generations which follow us.[98]

The progressive rabbis, Bernstein believed, had failed to perceive the severity of this crisis. Patiently they waited for Judaism to enter a new stage in its historical development. But meanwhile time was passing: "Small matter! When Judaism reaches that higher stage—if it really does—it won't find any more Jews." Hence the need for laymen to act without waiting for the rabbis, whose attachment to the past, to communal unity, and to their jobs, spawned intellectual dishonesty and precluded their taking the radical measures necessary to prevent massive defection in the next generation.[99] Bernstein, himself a father, sounded a resonant note.

Just as the emotional tie with earlier generations had snapped, so, Bernstein believed, had the intellectual one. Here too it was he who put the matter most candidly: Easily enough could one declare the Talmud a human document, the product of its own history, but what of the Bible? Historical criticism could not stop with the rabbinic literature. In radical Protestant circles the claim was being made just at that time that Scripture does not convey verbal revelation; it merely expresses the spiritual content of its day.[100] Bernstein writes similarly: "The Pentateuch is *not* a revelation; it is a *testimony of the revelation* of a God consciousness to our ancestors."[101] This denial of supernatural status to any sacred text was Bernstein's chief intellectual contribution to the radical movement in which he now joined Stern.

On March 10, 1845, spurred by Stern's lectures, about thirty individuals gathered in the meeting room of Berlin's Jewish culture society, to which some of them belonged, in order to discuss "important matters related to Judaism" and to select a working committee. These men scarcely represented a cross section of Berlin Jewry. In a community where only about seventy had completed university studies, no less than eleven of those who agreed to be present—more than a third—had a "Dr." before their name. And of those who did not possess the degree, like Bernstein, for example, nearly all had received some formal or informal higher education. A portion had been raised in orthodoxy and remembered something of the traditional Judaism from which they had made their break; others knew little of their religious heritage and were involving themselves in Jewish matters for the first time. Preponderantly they were not native Berliners. Among the eight members of the chosen committee, seven had been born outside the Prussian capital; of fifteen deputies later elected, thirteen were migrants to the city. Even in a rapidly growing community where perhaps the majority of members were not natives, such disproportion requires explanation. It suggests the group was mainly composed of men who, because they lacked roots in the Berlin community, were less reluctant to create their own organization at its periphery. Moreover, as one contemporary critic suggested, their views could at least partly be explained by distance from childhood memories and the pious homes in which some of them grew up.[102] Given the opportunity, they sought the fellowship of men with similar experience. Together they aired their dissatisfactions with Judaism as presently constituted and sought to discover how and whether progress was possible.

At the beginning of April a slightly altered group, now twenty-eight in number, signed an "Appeal to Our German Coreligionists," which was published in the local and Jewish press.[103] Based on a draft by Stern, Bernstein, and Moses Simion, it spoke of the inner conflict *(Zerrissenheit)* produced by a transformed religious consciousness at odds with the established forms of rabbinic Judaism. It declared the need to determine which elements of the tradition could be brought into harmony with their own spiritual development and which they would need to reject. They were not prepared to make those decisions themselves but projected a synod which would give form and substance to their new Judaism. Then came the words soon to assume the character of a motto or a watchword: "We want faith; we want positive religion; we want Judaism." Apparent in this threefold affirmation was the desire not to cut ties, but to reestablish them. Yet their interpretation of the individual elements bordered on negation. Following Bernstein, the Appeal expressed belief in a God who only "enlightened the spirit of our ancestors," but did not directly reveal the biblical words. Hence Judaism could not be faith in a sacred text whose prescriptions remained binding for all times. Rather it was a fluid faith, contained and developed in the individual and collective spirit. Hence practices and beliefs would always change. They could no longer pray for an earthly messianic kingdom in Palestine or practice laws intended for an earlier age. While they did not want to dissociate themselves from fellow Jews who disagreed with them, their purpose was to gather the like-minded and through the synod "renew and establish Judaism in that form in which it will be capable and worthy of living on in us and in our children."

The Appeal marks a departure in the history of the Reform movement. Here for the first time a collective statement affirms a Judaism determined almost entirely by contemporary religious consciousness, not by texts, traditions, or historical evolution. The final criterion for viability lies within the Reform Jew. Hence neither law nor historical research is required for what has become a fully subjective faith, one which moves beyond individual arbitrariness only by the device of collective expression, first in a common statement and finally through the synod. Stern put the point decisively in his commentary to the Appeal: "It is my personal, my current need, which my religion must satisfy." And then: "The essence and significance of our movement, I say, is to be sought in the fact that it is not theological, not *wissenschaftlich,* but religious, i.e., that it has proceeded from the religious thought and feeling of the collectivity."[104] This is a position not only far removed from orthodoxy but also self-consciously detached from the moorings of history so much stressed by progressive rabbis across the spectrum from Frankel to Geiger.

The Appeal called on sympathizers to join together for the purpose of laying down the principles for that new faith which, as Stern and others believed, would give Judaism a permanent place not only in their own lives but in the public life of Prussia and the other German states. It said nothing about so specific and concrete a matter as creating their own mode of religious worship. However, it soon turned out that most of the nearly 300 local men who had added their signatures to the Appeal were not willing to wait for a synod. With the approach of summer, they insisted that the new group, now under Stern's presidency and officially called the Association for Reform in Judaism, prepare its own High Holiday services—even if that meant laymen would have to decide immediately, albeit only provisionally and locally, what form their worship should take.[105] The lay committee selected to prepare the services did not hesitate to make the most radical decisions. For the first time it created a liturgy with the subjective criterion as the paramount, almost exclusive determinant. Their principal task, as they saw it, was to engage the minds and hearts of Jews greatly alienated from tradition but nonetheless seeking a religious bond with fellow Jews, a form of communal worship at the holiday season.

From contemporary sources we can easily reconstruct those first services held for the Jewish New Year in 1845.[106] The number of worshipers was unexpectedly large, rising to about 600, with many turned away for lack of space. Some of those who came had not attended any service for decades, others had spent holidays in the community synagogue. Both men and women sat on the main floor, equal but separate, in the manner of German churches.[107] Most of the men were bareheaded, though a few wore the black skullcaps specifically permitted in the announcement sent out in advance.[108] Only the guest preacher for the holidays—surprisingly the otherwise moderate Ludwig Philippson—wore a prayer shawl in addition to a head covering. The choir, which included both sexes, consisted of volunteers from families in the Association. An organ accompanied their song. Early in the evening service Stern gave an introductory address, and it was he who served as reader. The liturgy lay before the congregation in the form of a special prayerbook unlike any European predecessor. Hitherto liturgical reform had consisted, in conservative instances, of pruning a few superfluous or particularly unsuitable elements, or more radically—as in the case of the Hamburg Temple—of ideologically transforming the messianic conception. But here the traditional liturgy served only as a very loose framework. Although the most basic rubrics were retained, prayers were rendered in the freest paraphrase and with utmost abbreviation. Original compositions filled some of the lacunae; the central feature of the service became the sermon.[109] The evening service and separate morning services for each of the two days of the holiday together made up a book of only forty-eight pages, opening from left to right and containing in Hebrew only the single lines of the *shema* and the *barukh shem,* the three responses of the *kedushah,* and the priestly benediction. In the mornings the *shofar* blast was not heard since its use was encrusted with kabbalistic notions and its raucous, primitive sound was believed more likely to disturb devotion than to stimulate it. The Torah was read in Hebrew, followed by a German translation, but the portions read were not the usual ones assigned to the New Year festival. The first day's selection was apparently the opening verses of Genesis. No one was called up to the Torah and no Additional Service followed its reading. The priestly benediction was not spoken by *kohanim,* but by the reader, whose rendition alternated with choir response and congregational amen. The service for the Day of Atonement had only slightly more Hebrew. On that day members were not expected to fast and could go home during an afternoon break while those who chose to remain listened to selections from Scripture and later Jewish literature. Yet for all their radicality, the services retained some theologically traditional elements: divine judgment at the High Holiday season, the election of Israel, the Sinaitic revelation, reward and punishment, even resurrection. There were historical references to the *people* of Israel, arousing the objections of some. In retrospect, Philippson pronounced the worship "Jewish through and through."

Sigismund Stern (center) at a meeting of the Berlin Reform Congregation Board, 1855.

The enthusiasm which these services generated created a broadly felt desire to hold a reformed service every week. The question was only whether to do so on Saturday or Sunday. Both positions had fervent supporters, with the result that a compromise was reached at the end of lengthy debate. Identical services would be held on each day, so that those who desired, and whose occupational circumstances permitted, could attend on the historical Sabbath, while others would be able to come on the common German day of rest. Although the Association's members stressed that the Sunday service was not an imitation of Christianity, but only an accommodation to life's realities, they thereby broke as sharply with the Jewish calendar, and hence with the Jewish collectivity, as they had already broken liturgically with traditional Jewish worship. A few years later, as anticipated, the Saturday services died for want of par-ticipants, and the Association became the first and only European congregation to conduct its weekly service exclusively on Sunday.[110]

In the months following its initial holiday services the Association grew in num-bers, swelling to 327 member families in Berlin and another 426 supporters elsewhere. Its function was now twofold. First, it served as a congregation for its adherents in Berlin, conducting radically revised services weekly and on holidays and soon estab-lishing a three to four hour per week religious school which taught Bible, Jewish his-tory, ethics, and a bit of Hebrew.[111] Second, it continued to pursue its plans for a synod which would give sanction to the practical endeavors and lay down principles for the new Judaism. The latter project required spreading the Association's message to other German communities. The organizers had been heartened when their initial appeal produced numerous letters of support and stirred up the laity in various places. In Königsberg, for example, a similarly inclined group was prompted to issue its own statement, no less radical than the Berlin appeal.[112] In Breslau a circle likewise emerged, in this instance simultaneously and apparently independent of the Berlin Association. It too issued a statement in 1845, and the following year it succeeded in winning clear support from the community rabbi, Abraham Geiger. In Geiger the local radicals possessed a rabbinical reformer within the established framework, a man who, unlike Sachs, preached for, not against their views from the synagogue pulpit.[113] The Breslau group therefore accepted Geiger's advice to act as a force for more rapid reform within the existing religious structure rather than to create its own. As a result the Breslau circle did not achieve the institutional permanence of the Association in Berlin.

In Berlin, by contrast, the Association's relationship with the Jewish community remained distant. To be sure, there were no complaints about their services to the government. But that would in any case have been useless since official approval had been secured in advance. The community board was content to let the Association exist as long as its members continued to pay their regular community taxes, thus in effect supporting both their own organization and the religious institutions of the community. However, it refused to grant the Association any token of communal acceptance. When it sought a more equitable arrangement, whereby the Association would form a separate synagogue union within the community, open conflict ensued. It resulted for a while in Association members not paying their community dues, but in the end the government forced submission. In general, the Prussian authorities did not favor the Association. They tolerated its existence but, despite repeated requests, would not grant it independent legal status.[114]

Meanwhile, efforts to create the synod of rabbis, scholars, and laymen met with disappointing results. A preparatory organizational meeting held in Berlin drew only seven participants from outside the city.[115] A second gathering in 1847 passed a set of principles that would govern the creation of a common prayerbook, but matters went no further. Even a monthly newspaper, which Bernstein edited for the Association, generated little interest and collapsed after a year.[116] More and more it had become apparent that this highest aspiration of the Association was unrealistic. With the exception of the historian Isaac Marcus Jost, Jewish scholars remained cold to the idea.[117] Nor did average Reform laymen share deeply the intellectuals' desire to set Judaism on a new foundation. They were content if tangible improvements could be instituted within the community synagogue or—in Berlin—if their needs were met by a ritual of their own. The election of Samuel Holdheim as rabbi and preacher for the Berlin membership of the Association sealed the fate of the project.[118] Not only did Holdheim oppose the synod, but his authority supplied on a local level the sanction which the synod was intended to provide more broadly. In 1850 the Association for Reform in Judaism, a national organization, became the "Jewish Reform Congregation of Berlin."[119] As such it continued, giving birth to no progeny in Germany, neither growing in size nor diminishing, but serving in each generation those Jews at the periphery who sought to remain at least slightly inside. Holdheim tells us that during the first twelve years of its existence only one member converted to Christianity. It could be called, he said, "an alliance against apostasy."[120]

Rabbinical Reassertion

The radical laity's impatience with the progressive rabbinate was not unjustified. While the laymen sought to adapt Judaism to the reality of their daily lives, most of the rabbis were concerned with anchoring religious life in Judaism. This is not to sug-

gest they were uninterested in developing Judaism forward, but only that they were
far more determined not to allow the historical tie to snap. Unlike the earlier generation of lay reformers in the second decade of the century, the younger rabbis who
favored reforms, even radical ones, wanted especially to stress their Jewish historical
basis—though not alone or necessarily the halakhic one. They were particularly sensitive to the criticism that their reforms were mere imitations of Christian practice
and hence un-Jewish. During the thirties they went out of their way to prove otherwise, or to give their reforms a more specifically Jewish character. Thus, for example,
they increasingly delivered sermons based more on the interpretive mode of the traditional *derashah* than the model of the Christian homily. Philippson wrote: "We
must present *Jewish* sermons, breathing the spirit of our *revelation,* referring to the
history of the nation, drawing upon the prevailing form of Judaism, and stepping forward against public and private attacks upon our religion."[121] Catechisms began to
stress particular Jewish elements, not just universal ones, and confirmation became a
ceremony less imitative of its Christian counterpart.[122] All but the most radical
Reform rabbis felt that it was their special task as spiritual leaders to represent historical doctrine and tradition. The laymen could represent life.

The laity proved troublesome to the progressive rabbinate because they clustered
well away from it in both directions. The lay traditionalists regarded all customs and
ceremonies of equal authority simply because they represented the Judaism in which
they were raised; the lay radicals—in the extreme instance the Frankfurt Friends of
Reform—were ready to cast virtually every distinctive characteristic of Judaism aside.
Despite efforts to assert authority in their own communities, the rabbis failed to exercise much influence on their own against lay boards that were concerned above all
with preventing communal strife and which viewed the rabbi very much as a paid
employee.[123] By the early forties the course of reform seemed chaotic. In some communities there had been considerable change, at least in synagogue atmosphere; in
others very little. There was no central authority to lay down criteria and provide links
between theoretical conceptions of Judaism, the results of scholarly research, and
practical reforms. As individuals, rabbis were unable effectively to give sanction and
direction. It was Geiger who first took the initiative to deal with this situation. In 1837
he called together a group of fourteen progressive rabbis in Wiesbaden so they could
get acquainted and share concerns. But the gathering was not a structured deliberative
body.[124] It took another seven years until, at Philippson's urging, the first formal
assembly convened. Against the backdrop of the Frankfurt radicals' revolt, the rabbis
now sought consensus for the middle path they favored.[125]

Three rabbinical assemblies were held in Germany during the 1840s: the first in
Brunswick in 1844, the second in Frankfurt-on-the-Main in 1845, and the third in
Breslau in 1846.[126] Most of the participants were young men in their thirties, born in
Germany, who had taken over their current positions within the last decade. They
were rabbis or preachers in larger Jewish communities like Frankfurt, Hamburg, and
Breslau, as well as in smaller towns with populations of only a few hundred or less.[127]
Some had made a name for themselves through the publication of books and articles,
other were little known beyond their own community. Of the participants in one or
more of the conferences those with the widest reputations were Jospeh Maier, rabbi
of Württemberg, who served as president of the first conference; Samuel Holdheim,
the most articulate radical among the participants, then rabbi in Mecklenburg-

Schwerin; Gotthold Salomon, one of the oldest participants, who had been preacher of the Hamburg Temple since 1818; Ludwig Philippson, rabbi in Magdeburg and editor of the *Allgemeine Zeitung des Judentums;* Abraham Geiger, who served as president of the third conference; Zacharias Frankel, then chief rabbi of Dresden, the leading conservative; and Leopold Stein, newly appointed rabbi in Frankfurt, spokesman of moderation, and president of the second conference.

Not all those who announced their attendance for a particular conference actually came. In some instances they changed their minds when it became clear that the complexion of the group would be more radical than originally anticipated. In the case of the rabbis from Bavaria, they did not succeed in gaining permission from their government, as the authorities were apparently convinced the conferences represented a destabilizing institution. Only in the instance of the rabbi of Marburg did his local government actually require him to attend. Most German governments remained neutral.[128]

The assemblies were planned to consist only of rabbis and preachers regularly employed in Jewish communities. Though Isaac Marcus Jost participated actively in the second conference, it was not on account of his reputation as a historian, but because he served as a preacher at the devotions of the Frankfurt community school. Leopold Zunz did receive a special invitation "to visit" the third conference, but he did not attend.[129] Not surprisingly, the decision to limit participation to practicing rabbis and preachers called forth protests of hierarchical pretension. These came from both right and left, arguing either the lack of a significant distinction between clergy and laity in Judaism or the democratic spirit of the age. It was true that the participants did have a sense of their special calling as "theologians," trained in both Judaism and general religious philosophy, and as *Geistliche,* "spiritual leaders," in their communities. However, the decision to limit participation to men regularly employed by a Jewish community was also determined by the need to provide relatively objective criteria for admission. Otherwise, they would have had to decide *ad hominem* on the intellectual qualifications of each applicant. Moreover, only the rabbi within a community would be in a position to work for implementation of the assemblies' decisions.

The invitation to the first conference did not stipulate a favorable attitude to reform.[130] It would theoretically have been possible for a large number of very traditional rabbis to have come and given the conferences a distinctly conservative character. However, no strictly orthodox rabbis came, probably because they could not be sure a sufficient number of like-minded men would join them and they therefore feared being associated with a group that would make unacceptable decisions. Moreover, in most instances the orthodox rabbis, who later protested the first conference, represented the older generation which had not received university training and lacked a common language with their younger colleagues.

Thus the right of the spectrum at the conferences consisted of a few individuals who believed in the authority of both Bible and Talmud but were willing to make minor changes, largely of a formal nature, on the basis of Jewish law. They were readily visible in that they wore skullcaps during the deliberations.[131] Almost invariably they were outvoted unless they had support from the much larger but very diverse centrist group, which was concerned with historical continuity while at the same time being willing to make some sharp departures from tradition. Philippson and Stein represented the most conservative members of this faction, Geiger its radical wing. At the far left was again a small group, represented especially by Holdheim, which sought a thoroughgoing reform of Judaism on the basis of the spirit and circumstances of the new age, with little regard for historical precedent.

The first conference, which took place in the centrally and conveniently located city of Brunswick, lasted for eight days, from June 12 to June 19, 1844. There were twenty-five participants. At the very beginning two important decisions of procedure were made. The first was to use parliamentary form: the assembly decided to adopt statutes, select officers, keep official protocols, and reach decisions by majority vote. The impression was thus immediately reinforced that this assembly intended to go beyond a mere informal exchange of views. It began to appear more like a legislature that had given itself the right to determine religious laws for German Jewry. Under-standably, this impression contributed greatly to the ferocity of the attacks upon the assemblies. The second significant procedural step was to make the deliberations pub-lic. This resulted in far greater general interest by both Jews and non-Jews and it removed suspicions of hidden intent, but it also made for more rhetorical, lengthy speeches directed to a visitors' gallery of guests and reporters. An additional prelimi-nary matter was to determine whether resolutions of the assembly would be binding on its members. It soon became apparent that the rabbis were not at all eager to abdi-cate their own autonomy, choosing to declare only that the decisions of the conference would be "morally binding" for those members who voted with the majority and that, insofar as it was within their power, they would endeavor to put such resolutions into effect in their communities.

A great deal of time was taken up by members using the discussion of particular issues as a springboard for setting forth their general principles of reform. Thus the initial discussions consisted largely of each member indicating the stance which would determine his attitude to the various questions expected to arise. Few issues of sub-stance were actually voted on at Brunswick. Most of the proposals that came to the assembly from its members and from individuals and communities outside of it were referred to the commissions selected during the conference. Two significant issues on which votes were taken were the *kol nidre* prayer on the eve of the Day of Atonement and the Jewish oath. The former was regarded as an embarrassment since it had often been used by antisemites as evidence that the promises of Jews could not be trusted. Even so staunch a champion of modern orthodoxy as Samson Raphael Hirsch had removed it from the liturgy in his community of Oldenburg five years earlier. Not surprisingly, the assembly, with apparent unanimity, declared that the *kol nidre* was inessential and asked that members work for its removal from the service in their communities even as early as the next Yom Kippur. The assembly's decision on the Jewish oath was more a matter of Jewish dignity than religious reform. In various German states Jews were still required to utilize medieval demeaning forms when giving testimony. The assembly decided unanimously that they should be required only to swear a simple oath in the name of God. In Brunswick itself the decision apparently influenced a local change in the oath's wording.

Without question the most controversial decision of the Brunswick conference concerned the matter of mixed marriages. Ludwig Philippson had proposed that the assembly endorse the twelve answers given to Napoleon by the French Sanhedrin in 1807. His intention was to remove suspicion regarding Jewish loyalty to the state and thus remove any grounds for state interference in Jewish religious life. As in the case of the Parisian Sanhedrin, it was the third question, on the permissibility of mixed marriages, which stirred the most debate and later aroused the most controversy. Ironically, Philippson's intent was not to stress the issue of mixed marriage, which he certainly did not favor. But once the resolutions of the Sanhedrin as a whole were put forward, the assembly had to face the question: Does Jewish law allow Jews only to marry among themselves? Discussion of the issue enabled one radical, Mendel Hess, to express himself generally in favor of mixed marriages. But it also forced the vast majority to take a position which, while not contradicting the answer of the Sanhedrin declaring mixed marriages valid, nonetheless expressed a lack of sympathy for them. Most of the participants were caught between their reluctance to give the impression that Christians were unworthy of marriage with Jews and their realization that the multiplication of such marriages would decimate the Jewish community. In the end, they did not give their blessing to such unions or even simply repeat the answer of the Sanhedrin. On Samuel Adler's urging a most important qualification was added, so that the resolution adopted by the majority read: "The marriage of a Jew with a Christian, marriage with adherents of monotheistic religions generally, is not prohibited, provided that the laws of the state permit parents to raise the children of such a union also in the Jewish faith."[132] In this manner the conference made clear its concern for the continuance of Judaism. Moreover, its qualification effectively eliminated any immediate practical effect of the decision. For there were in fact no states in Germany at the time that allowed for a mixed marriage in which the children could be raised as Jews. The same was true in Denmark, where mixed marriages between Jews and Christians were more common than in Germany, but where the law specified that children had to be raised in the Christian faith.[133]

Despite the relative paucity of actual decisions, the Brunswick assembly stirred up widespread and lasting opposition. While its participants regarded themselves as preservers and continuators of Judaism, opponents saw them as usurpers of authority and destroyers of the Jewish faith. Picking out statements of individuals, they were able to make the conference appear more radical than it was in fact. Seventy-seven, and later 116 Orthodox rabbis, mostly from Germany and Hungary, signed a protest against the conference.[134] In Holland, Zevi Hirsch Lehren and Abraham Prins gathered and published thirty-seven letters of opposition by rabbinical authorities in Europe, and later five more from Palestinian rabbis. The authors hurled a variety of accusations against the participants. They charged them with being "shepherds who err and make others likewise to go astray," with being base men whose only goal was "to purchase temporal and political contentment." One of the contributors, Samson Raphael Hirsch, went so far as to read them entirely out of Judaism, exclaiming: "Are not the members of this assembly by their own words members of another faith?" Yet unlike most of his colleagues, Hirsch indicated that he did favor German sermons, a choir, and such formal changes as would make it possible to worship God in the most suitable and aesthetically pleasing manner.[135]

The Orthodox opponents of the conference were joined in their opposition by Christian missionaries to the Jews, who regarded religious reform as dangerous to their cause, and by at least one Jewish convert to Christianity. Both noted that only an orthodox Jew was likely to become an orthodox Christian. They objected to any modification of Jewish law since it would make less likely the total renunciation of the law, which was prerequisite to the acceptance of Christianity. Moreover, the notion of a developing Judaism ran directly counter to their theological position that Judaism was inherently incapable of change without thereby destroying itself.[136]

However, the Reformers did not expect support from such circles. More discouraging were the attacks by two individuals who, while more traditional than most members of the conference, were respected for their contributions to modern Jewish scholarship. Solomon Judah Rapoport (1790–1867), who had been the chief rabbi of Prague since 1840, addressed himself directly to the assembly when it met a year later in Frankfurt. After making excuses for not attending, he proceeded to call into question its right to take almost any actions whatever. His objections were grounded in a well-known rabbinic saying: "A court of Jewish law may not invalidate the decisions of another unless it be greater in wisdom and in size." Since the Brunswick rabbis could not easily make such a claim, they had acted sinfully and must turn from their evil ways. To those who urged them to act they should have simply replied that it was the sole task of the rabbinate to teach the people all that had been transmitted from former generations. Such change as was permissible would occur without their intervention. In Rapoport's words: "Should there be among our customs and laws some matter which requires reform or renewal, it is the passage of time which will bring about the reform or renewal." Thus if there was to be any religious change at all, it could only be the unguided forces of history, not a rabbinical conference, which would be its agents.[137]

The closest in spirit to the members of the conference among its critics was Zacharias Frankel. When the assembly was first proposed, he had favored the meeting provided it would consist only of a private exchange of views, leaving decisions to the convention of a synod which would include laity as well as rabbis. However, once the protocols of the Brunswick conference appeared, Frankel had no difficulty in finding fault. The conference had indeed passed formal resolutions and had conducted its sessions in public. Moreover, it had reached conclusions which Frankel believed ran counter to popular Jewish sentiment. Without mentioning names and in a much more restrained tone than the other opponents, he took issue especially with the most radical speakers, often finding fault with their logic or with the historical bases for their arguments. His conclusion was devastating: the Brunswick conference had contributed nothing to the preservation of Judaism and had fostered new errors.[138] Nonetheless, he was sufficiently ambivalent about the institution of rabbinical assemblies that he decided to attend the second one himself.

The Frankfurt conference attracted thirty-one members, six more than the previous year, and lasted for fourteen days instead of eight. In some respects it was the most significant of the three assemblies, not least because it marked the final break between the very moderate reform represented by Frankel and the more thoroughgoing commitment of most attending the conference. Frankel's presence was intended to determine whether he and his colleagues stood on common ground. While on the theoretical level no clear division became apparent, on the practical one the disparity was soon obvious.

Already at the Brunswick conference Solomon Formstecher, whose theology was discussed in Chapter 2, had argued that the assembly required a principle or norm by which to act, lest debates focus simply on the citation of conflicting proof texts. In the general discussion others had in fact set forth criteria ranging from continuity with the Talmud to the standpoint of the modern age. Frankel had articulated his own principle in the prospectus for his journal two years earlier. There he had said that the further development of Judaism was to proceed on a "positive historical" foundation.[139] At Frankfurt he insisted on acceptance of some general principle, and he proposed his own. Perhaps to his surprise, the assembly's chairman, Leopold Stein, immediately indicated to him that the conference's position was likewise that of positive historical Judaism. Thus if Frankel had planned to make the matter of principle a test case, he failed in his intent. The difference between him and the others lay rather in the variety of interpretations that could be given to "positive historical" and the practical conclusions to be derived from it. This became immediately apparent from the remarks made on the specific issue which had called forth the discussion of principle in the first place: the use of Hebrew in the religious service.

Frankel could not disagree that the Talmud explicitly allows prayer in any language. But he regarded Hebrew as intertwined with the beliefs of Judaism and part of its essence. He further held that it still lived in the emotions of the people, even if knowledge of it was declining. This was not Frankel's view alone. Philippson and most other members of the assembly shared his feeling that Hebrew was important for Jewish survival as an integrated minority.[140] Jacob Auerbach and Leopold Stein made eloquent pleas for continuing to teach it to the children. But Geiger and a number of others held that they and most other German Jews were more affected by German prayers than by Hebrew ones. When it came to a vote, the assembly was nearly unanimous in declaring that there was no *objective legal necessity* for retaining Hebrew in the service; yet at the same time it was fully unanimous in holding that retention of Hebrew was *subjectively* necessary. A major difference of opinion arose only on the question of whether it was objectively necessary for reasons other than legal ones. Here the vote was very close: fifteen to thirteen in the negative. Of those voting against the proposition only about half a dozen wanted to see Hebrew eventually eliminated from the service entirely. Most of the participants favored a balance between Hebrew and German. Nonetheless, Frankel took the vote as evidence that the majority did not share his sentiments on a basic issue. Although for the moment he remained in the conference, by the next day he had decided to cut his ties with it.[141] He sent the assembly a message justifying his action and publicized it widely. Soon thereafter he received letters of thanks for his departure from numerous individuals and Jewish communities.[142] Opponents of the conference, who feared Frankel had gone over to the other side, now felt reassured of his loyalty.

Frankel's departure did not, however, greatly disrupt the conference. The assembly proceeded on to the discussion of a basic issue of belief: the coming of the messiah and the return to Zion. Although varying points of view were expressed, the general sentiment was that the messianic idea was part of the essence of Judaism, differentiating it from Christianity, but that its political side could no longer be meaningful under circumstances of integration. Only its universal aspect remained relevant. Specifically, the majority decided: "The messianic idea deserves a significant role in our prayers, but the petitions for our return to the land of our fathers and the establishment of a Jewish state should be eliminated from them."[143]

By the time of the rabbinical conferences an allied conception had begun to reshape the messianic hope. Though going back at least to Mendelssohn and repeatedly voiced as well by traditionalists like Samson Raphael Hirsch, it soon became the special currency of Reform. This was the idea of the "mission of Israel."[144] Philippson had said in Brunswick: "Every people has its mission in history. The Jews too have their mission: they are the people of religion." And David Einhorn said in Frankfurt:

> The collapse of Israel's political independence was once regarded as a misfortune, but it really represented progress, not atrophy but an elevation of religion. Henceforth Israel came closer to its destiny. Holy devotion replaced sacrifices. Israel was to bear the word of God to all the corners of the earth.[145]

This mission concept was in essence a radical reinterpretation of the chosen people idea and a direct rejection of the Christian claim to supersession. The Germans too believed they possessed a civilizing mission, often, as in the case of Schleiermacher, closely linked to that of Christianity.[146] In substituting the mission of Israel for the messianic return, the Frankfurt rabbis thus not only universalized messianism and made more room for the human role in historical progress; they also asserted that the special vocation of Judaism—to be a priest people among the nations—could be set aside neither by the daughter faith nor by the national culture with which they themselves identified.

Most of the rest of the conference was devoted to specific points of liturgy and ritual practice. It was decided unanimously to eliminate prayers for the restoration of the sacrificial cult, though most wanted to retain mention of the sacrifices as a historical memory. The rabbis voted in favor of a three-year cycle for reading the Torah and that the Haftarah be read in German. They decided almost unanimously that it was permissible for the organ to be played during Sabbath services even by a Jew. Aware of the argument that use of the organ represented an ostensible imitation of the Gentiles and a violation of the prohibition "You shall not walk in their ways," they chose to base their preference for it not on the Christian model but on its similarity to the *magrefah,* a musical instrument used in the ancient temple in Jerusalem.

One of the most interesting practical decisions made by the conference came in response to a question sent it by the community of Bingen. It seems that the communal ritual bath there was not used by most of the women mainly on account of its filth. The questioners asked the assembly whether it was permissible for a new facility, using drawn water, to replace it. In their response permitting *mayim she'uvim,* the rabbis, while going more directly against talmudic law than on any other decision, at the same time affirmed their support for the use of a *mikveh,* an institution peculiar to Judaism and one which was rapidly losing support in the younger generation. The conference also turned down a suggestion sent in by a physician that circumcision either be abandoned or the ritual fundamentally altered. Clearly, even after Frankel's departure, the conference had not abandoned all attachment to Jewish particularity.

Ironically, the third conference, held in Geiger's community of Breslau and over which he presided, turned out to be in some respects the most moderate. This was so despite the fact that none of its twenty-six participants could be called truly conservative.

The major subject dominating the twelve days of that last meeting was the Sabbath. Geiger had headed a committee to deal with Sabbath observance, which completed its report before the Frankfurt conference, but there had not been time to discuss it. The report called for enhancing celebration of the Sabbath but also for making accommodations, especially where a conflict existed between Sabbath observance and obligations to the state. It quoted the Midrash: "The Sabbath is given to you, not you to the Sabbath." Discussion of the report in Breslau ranged from attempts to define the concept to specific exemptions which should be granted Jewish soldiers and civil servants. Of all the speeches, that of the radical Samuel Holdheim was the most interesting. He developed a philosophical concept of the Sabbath according to which it was one of the essentials of Judaism, but its meaning had changed in the course of time. While in the biblical period rest made up its substance, expressing symbolically God's existence beyond time, there later arose the additional notion of the Sabbath as sanctification in a religious and moral sense. It was in the latter understanding that he found its true contemporary significance. But a worthy sanctification of the Sabbath was no longer possible on the seventh day as Jews lived within a Gentile society. He therefore made the radical suggestion that in order to preserve the Sabbath for those who could not celebrate it properly on its historical day it would have to be moved to Sunday.

Holdheim's extreme conclusion was not echoed by his colleagues. Leopold Stein argued pithily that to transfer the Sabbath to Sunday would be to bury Judaism on Friday in order to resurrect it as another religion on Sunday! The conference did not even bring the Sunday possibility to a vote. It adopted a declaration which began with the need to restore "a worthy celebration of the Sabbath as a day of rest and consecration" and to heighten consciousness of its sanctity through communal worship and home observance. However, to preserve the Sabbath on Saturday under conditions of economic integration meant to face an intractible problem which the assembly could not decisively resolve. They were willing neither simply to permit Jewish work generally on the Sabbath nor to prohibit it entirely, especially since such a proscription would likely not have had much effect. At length they chose a middle course, stressing the sanctity of the Sabbath rather than the obligation to rest, and making concessions especially for service to the state. Some saw a justification in the latter since they could regard the state as a moral, if not actually a religious force. Others rejected this prevalent view, except perhaps as an ideal, and refused to attribute religious significance to state service. Finally, in order to take some practical positive action and not restrict itself to alleviations, the conference recommended the institution of local societies to help create and sustain a meaningful observance of the Sabbath.

Decisions were also reached on three other topics: holidays, circumcision, and laws of mourning. In the case of holidays, the rabbis gave sanction to the actual situation wherein second days were little observed except for the second New Year's day. The question of circumcision had been brought before the assembly by a father, himself a physician, whose first son had been permanently weakened and his second son bled to death following the operation, apparently because of hemophilia. The father wanted to know whether he should have a third son circumcised as well. The conference responded that even where only one son had died the second should not be circumcised until a physician thinks it safe to do so. It thus eased the talmudic law which stipulates the death of two sons before circumcision may be suspended. The assembly also decided upon a series of regulations that would make the rite safer and more hygienic. Finally, the conference approved some alleviations with regard to mourning practices and expressed itself against those physical expressions of grief (like tearing one's clothing) which it regarded as inappropriate in the present age.

Some other subjects were not discussed for lack of time, even though preliminary work had been done on them. Of these the most interesting, in retrospect, was the status of women. Since only men were required to pray regularly, women tended to stay away from the synagogue and were sometimes not even permitted to attend until married.[147] The Jewish education provided girls amounted to little or nothing beyond instruction by example, from mother to daughter, on the duties incumbent upon women in the home. The Reform movement had early begun to change this situation through combined religious instruction, a common ceremony of confirmation, and the introduction of sermons which could appeal to both sexes. In an 1837 article Geiger had gone further, suggesting abolition of those legalities, such as *halitsah* and the status of the *agunah* (whose husband had disappeared but was not provably dead), which imposed indignity or cruelty on Jewish women, and proposing that women and men should be entirely equal in religion except where differentiation flowed from natural distinctions between the sexes. In a Hebrew treatise prepared for the Frankfurt conference, Rabbi Samuel Adler argued for the religious emancipation of women based on an extensive consideration of the talmudic sources. At Breslau, a specially appointed commission presented its report on which discussion had to be postponed for lack of time, but which seems to have had wide support among the participants. Its most significant provisions obligated women to time-related duties considered still binding, such as prayer, made them countable members of the worship quorum *(minyan)*, and declared that women's vows could not be abrogated by husbands or fathers.[148] One other important matter which was not taken up at all, but was scheduled for the next conference, was the dietary laws, which, as strictly a matter of personal practice, had not been given priority.

If the first conference particularly stirred up opposition in the camp of Orthodoxy, the second and third resulted in the clear disaffection of the radicals. In the hope of establishing a relationship with the assembly, the Association for Reform in Judaism had sent its leaders from Berlin to Frankfurt in order to read a declaration of support. However, the reply formulated by the conference was less than enthusiastic. Unlike the members of the Association, the rabbis continued to favor reform within the community structure, not outside of it, even if that meant a slower pace and more compromise with the traditionalists. At the third conference the members of the Association did not again appear, sending instead a letter which indicated a parting of the ways. In a curt reply, the Breslau assembly stated that its decisions regarding the Sabbath should leave no doubt that the conference's position diverges considerably from that of the Association. After the Breslau conference ended, some lay radicals found it necessary to declare publicly that it did not speak for them. Two protests against it circulated in Frankfurt. The signers had hoped the assembly would remove all points of collision between Judaism and daily life. When it failed to do so, their expectations were disappointed.[149]

If the conservatives were less vocal in their opposition to the work of the third conference, it was due in part to their own plans to create a similar but slightly different body which they hoped would supplant it. Even before the Breslau conference, Zacharias Frankel had issued the call for a gathering of "Jewish theologians," which would include scholars as well as practicing rabbis. The participants were required to be men of faith devoted to both the preservation and the progress of Judaism. The first meeting was scheduled for the fall of 1846, and by the summer about forty individuals had indicated their intention to take part. Among those planning to come were Solomon Rapoport of Prague, Michael Sachs of Berlin, and the young historian Heinrich Graetz. However, faced with unexpectedly strong Orthodox opposition, Frankel found it necessary to postpone the conference repeatedly and eventually to abandon the idea entirely.[150]

Although it had been scheduled for Mannheim the following summer and documents had been prepared for it, the fourth rabbinical conference likewise did not take place. At first there was some difficulty in securing local government permission. By the time it was received and a new date set for July 1848, the revolution of that year had made such an assembly impossible to convene. Moreover, a gathering of rabbis now seemed out of keeping with the democratic spirit of the moment. Only a synod to include laity as well as rabbis would be appropriate. But the revolutionary political atmosphere soon drew attention away from religion entirely, leaving little more interest in synods than in rabbinical assemblies. For nearly a generation in Germany neither the one nor the other would take place.[151]

In retrospect it is clear that the rabbinical conferences faced formidable problems. They were intended to create a collective authority, yet the participants were themselves divided on whether their mandate to deal with "the needs of the hour" was based on a continuation of the ongoing, albeit slowed process of rabbinic interpretation or on individual awareness produced by cultural level and contemporary values. Moreover, in most cases they were not empowered to vote on behalf of their communities and were themselves reluctant to accept the authority of those majority decisions in which they did not concur. The conference decisions could claim no more than "moral authority." In fact few of the concrete resolutions were immediately and widely implemented, though many gradually made their way into the communities during the following decades. The conferences also had an "image problem." Because they sought to bring about the acceptance of change, they appeared as essentially destructive, more visibly lopping off leaves and branches than stimulating growth. Whatever enthusiasm the participating rabbis displayed for Judaism in weekly sermons and in articles defending it in the press, here they were perceived as acting negatively, even if they themselves saw their task as "tearing down for the sake of building up." Finally, the conference members had difficulty in deciding whether their assignment was simply to sanction changes and omissions already current or to influence the course reform would henceforth take. They were caught between conflicting desires not to offend traditionalists at home by supporting radical new proposals and their wish to play some role in shaping the Judaism of the future.

Although the rabbinical conferences ended after only three years, they set in motion or spurred projects and developments which were later to reach fruition. The outline for a new prayerbook which they formulated influenced the Reform prayerbooks composed by individual rabbis and adopted by German Jewish communities— or at least their liberal segments—during the following decades. The plan for a Jewish theological faculty, given prominence at the conferences, was not realized due to government opposition, but it did spur the creation of the Jewish Theological Seminary in Breslau in 1854.

During their time the conferences attracted much attention among Jews all over Europe and within the general public in Germany. The former could no longer ignore the pronounced tendency to religious reform which had manifested itself in Germany. The latter was impressed primarily by the character of the emerging, university-trained Jewish religious leadership, which could conduct serious deliberations in proper parliamentary fashion and with impressive dignity. Despite their difficulties, the rabbis did not fail entirely in reasserting their importance.

Above all, the conferences had made it apparent that the liturgical pattern set by the Hamburg Temple almost thirty years earlier and the ideology formulated in the succeeding decades enjoyed widespread support among a significant portion of the German rabbis. German Jewry as a whole was now approaching the point where its majority would be considered non-Orthodox.[152] Many more Jews than a generation earlier were open to the conception of Judaism offered by the Reform movement. But the determined reforming thrust of the heady forties would not return. During the next decades the movement in Germany would proceed quietly, without the éclat of loud controversies, much publicized lay appeals, and rabbinical assemblies. Meanwhile, it was also gaining a foothold outside of Germany.

4

European Diffusion

There is no single answer to the question of why it was especially Germany in which the Reform movement flourished during the first half of the nineteenth century. A combination of factors seems to have been at work. Demographically, German Jewry was of sufficient size—about 400,000 souls in the various states by midcentury—to support diversity. Reformers were not isolated individuals in the larger communities. There were enough of them to create their own institutions, as in Hamburg or Berlin, even when they remained a minority. Absorbed in a process of acculturation that accelerated after Mendelssohn, German Jews soon felt an incongruity between the world of their origins and the modern German and European world with which they identified and in which they longed to participate. In northern Germany that world was distinctly Protestant. It celebrated the Lutheran Reformation in which it perceived the decisive break from medievalism; it defined religion as a private matter between God and the individual, unmediated by a clerical hierarchy. During the eighteenth century, German Protestantism absorbed much of the rationalism and universalism of the Enlightenment, setting aside particular tenets that separated it from other faiths. Although under the influence of Schleiermacher and others, Christian exclusivity, and even orthodoxy, regained prominence in the nineteenth century, the Protestant environment gave a crucial impetus to Reform. It provided a model for theological, not merely formal reformation, for the rejection of an old hierarchy, and for liturgy in the vernacular. Protestantism placed the sermon at the center of the service; it focused on words spoken and sung, not physical ritual acts; and as a religion which had itself revolted and developed further, it raised the hope that, in its liberal formulations, it would go far toward meeting Judaism on common religious ground. Catholic environments were not nearly as conducive.

That Jews in Germany were neither wholly denied civil rights nor granted them completely must also be seen as an important stimulus to religious reforms, especially those that removed national elements from the liturgy. Had German Jews been totally without hope of full acceptance, as in eastern Europe, or already achieved it entirely, as in France, they would not have felt as self-conscious about the prayers for return to the Land of Israel. They would have been more inclined to leave them alone, although for many their recital had become an empty exercise. Finally, we must add the rise of the new religious leadership described in Chapter 3. Young men who had received thorough education in Jewish sources went on to German universities where they learned critical scholarship. Without the hope of academic employment, they became rabbis in Jewish communities, all the while struggling—as did Geiger—both within themselves and within their spheres of influence between conflicting intellectual and communal commitments. This sizable cadre of a secularly trained rabbinical leadership, ranging in orientation from the radicalism of Samuel Holdheim to the extreme conservatism of Samson Raphael Hirsch, was unique to Germany.

Yet we have seen that at the very beginning it was French influence which triggered the first religious reforms in Holland and Westphalia. And even thereafter the Reform movement did not develop solely as a German phenomenon. The periphery of its influence soon stretched to other places in central and western Europe. We must now trace this process of diffusion.

To Copenhagen and Vienna

When Moses Mendelssohn published the first installment of his Pentateuch translation in 1780, no less than fifty-seven subscribers were Danish Jews. Two leading figures of the German Haskalah, Naphtali Herz Wessely and Isaac Euchel, had grown up in Copenhagen, which soon possessed a sizable stratum of acculturated Jews. As the European Enlightenment spread within Danish Jewry, the same pattern of educational, followed by religious reforms occurred there as it did in Germany. First, in 1805, came a modern boys' school patterned after the *Freischule* in Berlin, then an equivalent school for girls five years later. Delayed burial started in 1811. As in Germany, it was emancipation that triggered ritual innovation. A royal decree of March 29, 1814 gave Denmark's approximately 2,000 Jews civil equality.[1] One provision, however, required that children of both sexes pass a public examination in the Jewish religion before assuming their roles in society. The textbook approved for the examination was a specially prepared Danish version of a catechism by Shalom Cohen, abbreviated to eliminate most specifically Jewish observances and beliefs. This universalist thrust was in keeping with the sentiments of those men who at the time controlled Jewish affairs in Copenhagen. The leading figure among the proponents of educational and ritual reform was the prosperous businessman, and later prominent editor and economist, Mendel Levin Nathanson (1780–1868). It was Nathanson who had pressed the case for Jewish equality most vigorously and it was through his efforts that a highly talented young man, Isaac Noah Mannheimer (1793–1865), the son of a local cantor who had studied Talmud with the enlightened head of the Jewish boys' school and completed his secular education at the University of Copenhagen, was appointed first as teacher at the two schools and then, in 1816, received a government appointment as royal catechist. In the latter capacity, it was Mannheimer's special task to prepare students for the required public examination, which was soon referred to as confirmation.[2]

The first such ceremony in Copenhagen took place on May 19, 1817 in a spacious room that had once served as a concert hall. An organ had been placed on the east wall, a table bearing two candles stood on the west in front of a plaque displaying the Ten Commandments. A large crowd gathered to hear Mannheimer conduct the examination and deliver a Danish sermon on the text from Job: "Wisdom, where shall it be found?" Some psalms were sung in the vernacular to musical accompaniment. The ceremony apparently made such a favorable impression on many Jews, and also on Gentiles present, that it prompted the community leadership to initiate regular devotional exercises in the same hall. They were held, beginning that summer, once a month on Wednesday afternoons after the close of the stock market. Men did not cover their heads at the devotions, but there is no evidence that the sexes sat together.[3]

Although the exercises were not intended to replace the regular worship, for some Jews they must have begun to do just that. Thus, although the royally sanctioned confirmation ceremony was tolerated by the community's traditionalists, the regular Wednesday devotions provoked active opposition. A vicious intracommunal struggle erupted comparable to those just then taking place in Berlin and Hamburg. Here too each side sought to win the government to its position—with devastating results. Families split; deep animosities emerged in a community already fragmented religiously into a dozen prayer groups ever since the community synagogue had burned down in 1795. Each side was led by a few rich and influential men who drew others into the dispute. Neither the traditional community rabbi nor Mannheimer was in a position to influence the course of events; they were simply tools in the hands of rival factions. Among the disputants, Mannheimer later noted, were not a few whose zealousness for Judaism concealed factual nonobservance. Among the reformers were highly assimilated families, including that of Nathanson, whose hold on Judaism was so weak that it could not prevent apostasy in the next generation.[4]

The battle lasted for more than three years. Some parents refused to let Mannheimer teach their children. He was branded a rash young man and even an atheist who propounded a form of natural religion. In turn, Mannheimer vehemently attacked a number of Jewish customs in a letter sent to the government chancellery.[5] But the government refrained from deciding for either side. Gradually, radicalization gave way to apathy; antisemitic outbreaks in 1818 and 1819 cooled the ardor for internal polemic. After a time the devotions ceased, perhaps because the novelty wore off or perhaps because the proponents became weary of dispute. Only the confirmations continued. Yet the Copenhagen community remained divided between unbending traditionalists and Jewish minimalists. Only with the appointment of the secularly educated Abraham Alexander Wolff (1801–1891) as its rabbi in 1828 did Copenhagen Jewry finally draw itself together, build a new community synagogue, dedicated in 1833, and unite in a religious service that was mostly traditional, but also decorous, somewhat abbreviated, and included a choir and regular edifying sermons. These reforms, it was noted, were intended simply "to remove the rust." Steering clear of what he called "enlightenment gone insane" no less than "false attachment to every element of tradition," Wolff succeeded, during a rabbinate of more than sixty years, in bringing the badly fractured community together on common middle ground.[6]

For Mannheimer, however, the role of royal catechist had brought little but frustration. In 1821 he received a leave of absence from the "dry bones" community, as he later called it. He traveled to Hamburg and Berlin, where he observed and participated in the services of both temples. While in Berlin, he heard that an inquiry had come from Vienna to the leaders of the Beer temple. A group of Viennese reformers was looking for someone to advise them on their own plans and perhaps become their spiritual leader. Israel Jacobson suggested to Mannheimer that he go there. The Copenhagen venture, he believed, was damaged beyond repair, but in Vienna "you will surely be hired—I guarantee it."[7]

When Mannheimer arrived in the Austrian capital to give three sermons and counsel with the reformers in the summer of 1821, he found a Jewish community which was ready to modernize its religious life but uncertain about the course it should take. Viennese Jews were both better and worse off than their coreligionists in German cities to the north and west. In 1820 there were only 135 tolerated families, plus their employees and temporary residents; the Jewish elite mingled freely with highly placed Gentiles. Some had attained fabulous wealth serving the financial interests of the Hapsburg Empire, and more than a tenth of the tolerated families, in 1809, could boast patents of nobility. But the status of the Jews in the capital remained insecure and their lives hedged about with special burdens and restrictions. There had been no emancipation of the Jews in Austria and would be none until after the Revolution of 1848. The bigoted Maria Theresa, the enlightened Joseph II, and the reactionary Francis I all pursued a policy of keeping Jewish numbers as low as possible while maximally exploiting Jewish wealth and financial skills. Most Jews remained observant at least to some degree and there was a small circle of maskilim who came to work for the non-Jewish Hebrew publishing house of Anton Schmid. But conversion became an ever more popular escape, especially in court circles where social integration, the abandonment of Jewish ceremonials, and belief in a nondenominational religion of universal love made the transition easy and almost painless. Fanny von Arnstein, who introduced to Viennese Christians the custom of the Christmas tree from her native Prussia, could easily encourage her only daughter to go one step further and leave Judaism entirely. Vienna of this period produced no Jewish religious figures of consequence. And Jewish identity was eroding rapidly.[8]

The wretched state of Jewish religious life stood in sharp contrast to the glitter of the Hapsburg court. The toleration patent of Joseph II specifically denied Viennese Jews a public synagogue and refused them recognition as a religious community. They were permitted a rabbi only under the designation of "supervisor of kosher meat." Since the wealthy had their children tutored at home, the one Jewish school became an institution for the poor alone. There was a common house of worship, but its atmosphere was deeply depressing. A contemporary wrote of it: "One can scarcely enter this gloomy and dank subterranean chamber without horror and disgust. It resembles a dungeon more than a house of God." Only in 1811 were the Viennese Jews able to get permission for a communal building to house their prayer service, school, and ritual bath. In the following years Jewish neglect of their own institutions and government opposition to a visible Jewish presence at last began to give way.[9]

Before the end of the decade a sizable group of some fifty among the tolerated Jews expressed their wish for religious renewal through worship reform of the kind which some had themselves witnessed in Berlin, Hamburg, and at the special services conducted by the Hamburg Temple during the Leipzig fairs. They desired it, they said, only for those similarly inclined, and they were willing to pay the costs by voluntary subscription. Only a few months after the reformers set out their plan, and apparently independent of it, Francis I, on January 22, 1820, issued a personal decree which included the provision that all Jewish services must eventually be conducted in the vernacular. The aims of the reformers and the monarchy thus seemed to coincide. Negotiations were conducted with government officials; a prayerbook and songbook, probably those of the Hamburg Temple, were prepared for inspection. It was just at this time that Mannheimer came to Vienna and left a lasting favorable impression on nearly everyone. However, it soon became apparent that the government was not at all eager for substantive Jewish reform. The Austrian regime dreaded religious innovation no less than the Prussian. The desire to assimilate the Jews, expressed in the (soon forgotten) provision regarding the vernacular, melted away quickly before the possibility that Jewish reformers might introduce heterodox religious doctrines. Moreover, as an agent reported to Count Sedlnitzky, the proposed Jewish services just might be more attractive than those of the Christian churches, causing Catholics to waver in their faith. The count himself derogated the reformers' intentions to the king, describing the initiative as nothing more than the plaything of nouveau riche Jews who wanted to avoid praying together with their poorer coreligionists. Not long thereafter, negotiations failed and plans for a separate congregation had to be abandoned.[10]

But then a new possibility arose. The building that housed the existing Jewish institutions was declared unsafe and needed to be torn down. Permission was obtained for a new structure to be built in its place. Of course the façade could not front the street— that would be too obvious a concession to Judaism's acceptability—but the opportunity was presented to build a modern house of worship, not only for a few reformers, but for the whole community. The moving force behind these developments was an affluent financier and entrepreneur of the second rank, Michael Lazar Biedermann (1769–1843). He speedily recognized that Jewish religious life in Vienna would be transformed if three elements could come together at once: an attractive new building, a modern spiritual leader, and a cantor whose singing could hold its own in musically rich Vienna. By the time the new temple was completed, Biedermann had succeeded in bringing Mannheimer to the Hapsburg capital as director of the Jewish school (officially Jews could have no preacher) and the remarkably talented young Solomon Sulzer to chant prayers and direct a choir.

The dedication ceremony, on April 9, 1826, symbolized a new status for Judaism in Vienna. Designed by a fashionable architect of the day, the building which the participants entered was a marvellous example of the reigning Empire style. Its oval interior was surrounded by Ionic columns and surmounted by a small dome that let in copious daylight. It resembled a tasteful theater more than a contemporary synagogue. Ladies were seated in the galleries behind a gracefully executed latticework. Men sat below or in part of the second gallery, all with heads duly covered. A special section was reserved for the three highest ranking Jewish notables, the Freiherrn von Arnstein, von Eskeles, and von Rothschild. Those present that Sunday evening, including many Gentiles, heard specially commissioned instrumental music, including Davidic psalms performed on the harp. Although the compositions were by a non-Jew, the thirty-voice choir and the musicians, except for the drummer, were all Jews. A torchlight procession brought in the scrolls of the law. Mannheimer spoke impressively and with great enthusiasm; Sulzer's singing was both musically correct and passionate. The liturgy, essentially unchanged, was all in Hebrew with the sole exception of the prayer

Isaac Noah Mannheimer.

Solomon Sulzer.

Interior of Vienna Synagogue, dedicated in 1826.

for the emperor. The new building and its service proclaimed to all that Judaism in Vienna had at last achieved a dignified public presence. Viennese Jews now had a showpiece to which they could point with pride, a house of worship no longer incongruent with the cultural world in which they lived. And it was all achieved without splitting the community. That no ideological changes had been introduced into the liturgy mattered to few. In the multinational Hapsburg Empire, where Jews had no reason to feel the patriotic attachment of a citizen, the return to Zion was no embarrassment. In a Catholic ambience, pomp and ceremony were much more important than theological considerations. Jews, too, cared more about the form than the content. Moreover, in the oppressive and reactionary political atmosphere of Metternich's Austria, which was unconducive to innovations of any sort, no more radical reform would have been permissible. Indeed, it was only after the intervention of Solomon Rothschild that the government finally agreed to confirm Mannheimer in his position. He was, after all, known as a man who in Denmark had expressed patently reformist views. Permission to exercise his functions was finally granted only if he would refrain from propagating "any innovation or deviation whatever from the . . . sanctioned forms and manner of the Jewish religious service." In the Vienna of that day reformation was more safely referred to as "restoration."[11]

It took a short while to curb Mannheimer's reforming zeal. At first he was unhappy with imposed compromises and pressed unsuccessfully for thoroughgoing liturgical change. To Leopold Zunz, his friend from Berlin days, he wrote with disappointment: "I accommodate myself to the intellectual environment and do what my vocation demands." But within a few years Mannheimer had made his peace with reality, and when the statutes of the temple were presented for ratification by all the tolerated Jews in 1829, he was content merely to preserve through them the progress that had already been made. He did press for the introduction of some German songs so the congregation could participate more fully, but increasingly he began to feel that further reforms could serve no constructive purpose. They would only alienate those who came regularly to the temple while the youth would be attracted only briefly—until the new had also become old. Although he maintained friendly relations with the two preachers of the Hamburg Temple and wrote on behalf of their revised prayerbook in 1842, Mannheimer was not in sympathy with what he regarded as the essentially destructive work of the rabbinical conferences, and he refused Geiger's special invitation to come to the third one in Breslau. The only substantive reforms Mannheimer instituted in Vienna were reduction in the number of *piyutim,* confirmation, and, in the forties, elimination of the *kol nidre.* More and more Mannheimer's Judaism came to resemble that of Zacharias Frankel. It too weighed pious Jewish sentiments more heavily than questions of principle or even halakhic permissibility. The tones of the organ, he conceded already in 1830, no longer addressed his feelings; they were too obviously identified with another faith.[12]

Unlike most of his contemporaries in office, Mannheimer was not a rabbi either in title or function. Although he presided over life-cycle events, he did not render halakhic decisions and frequently told his friends: "I am not a *rav.*" Nor was he a scholar. He was the first to admit that his talmudic knowledge was limited and that he could aspire to no prominence in *Wissenschaft des Judentums.* He was certainly a fine preacher, whose regular discourses of hour-long duration drew a large attendance. His passionate sermons, flowing over with unrestrained gesticulation, were deeply felt, often personal, and not any less effective because they were formally imperfect.[13] But the role Mannheimer aspired to above all during his nearly forty years in Vienna was none of these. His goal more than any other was to be a devoted *Seelsorger,* a pastor. "I regard the so called pastorate," he wrote early in his career, "as the most sacred calling, hold it in higher respect than either teaching or preaching." And later in life he prided himself especially on what he had accomplished in this particular area. The community, he said, had become his extended family. He had stood at the cradles of their children, confirmed and married them, accompanied their earthly remains to burial, and comforted the mourners. He had dunned the rich to support charitable endeavors and commiserated with the poor. Among the important leaders of modern Judaism in nineteenth-century Europe, Mannheimer was perhaps the most beloved by his flock.[14]

Not only did he thus pioneer the Jewishly nontraditional role of pastor, but Mannheimer was also among the first modern Jewish religious leaders to speak out openly for social justice. Few nineteenth-century Jewish sermons in Europe treated social issues. They dwelt rather on personal faith and dealt only very generally with individual moral conduct. Carefully they avoided politics. But Mannheimer refused to separate burning social and political concerns from his religious office. When the year 1847 brought widespread crop failures and resultant famine, not a few Viennese—probably also including Jews—got rich at the expense of the poor. Mannheimer, who esteemed the Prophets of Israel highly, responded with a Passover sermon that minced no words:

> Here in this holy place and at this sacred hour I call down a curse upon everyone who misuses the distress and inflation in order to enrich himself from the marrow

of the land and the misery of the poor; the curse of God upon everyone who gains
the profits of usury from the wretchedness of the hungry. . . . But let there be blessing upon his head who generously and mercifully dispenses his bounty, breaks his
bread and shares it with the poor, who to the extent that God has made it possible
for him, puts an end to the misery.[15]

When political revolution came to Austria in 1848, Mannheimer and Sulzer were
active participants. Dressed in their clerical vestments, they joined Catholic priests in
publicly mourning the victims of the March revolt—two of them Jewish. Elected to
the constituent assembly as a representative of the largely Jewish city of Brody,
Mannheimer argued successfully for the elimination of the Jews' tax. To the dismay
of the lay leadership, which feared the consequences, he sat on the "left" in the Reichstag itself and spoke out freely. His principal speech there was an eloquent plea for the
elimination of capital punishment in every instance except treason in war and mutiny.
Despite his liturgical conservatism, Mannheimer here gave evidence of a clear belief
in religious progress. To be sure, he noted, the Bible provides amply for capital punishment, but some of its legislation represents an "older, lower, and inferior stage of
culture." Proudly he pointed out to his colleagues those talmudic passages which
expressed the Rabbis' reluctance to impose the death penalty. It was now time, he
added, to turn Austrian prisons into correctional institutions. The spirit of the times,
Mannheimer felt, was moving rapidly and it was his Jewish responsibility to participate in that progress. Even during the reactionary years that followed the defeat of the
revolution he continued to express idealistic political views at least obliquely in his
sermons—with the result that he aroused displeasure on the community board, which
on one occasion briefly suspended him from office.[16]

Yet it was not so much Mannheimer's activity as pastor and moral activist which
directly and immediately became models for the Reform movement elsewhere. It was
rather the religious service that had been instituted in the new temple and which
remained mostly unchanged through the years. Its ritual became known as the *Wiener
Minhag,* the Viennese rite. Part of that Minhag, of course, was the large role given to
sermons, on which Mannheimer lavished many hours of preparation, drawing upon
midrashim and commentaries to derive contemporary lessons. But even more impressive for Jewish visitors to the Austrian capital was Sulzer's music. It was both professional and passionate. Sulzer, who was a friend of Schubert and well regarded in Viennese musical circles, brought the highest standards of contemporary musicology into
the synagogue. His taste was impeccable, his rich voice scarcely equalled anywhere in
Vienna. With publication of the first volume of his *Schir Zion* in 1840, his musical
compositions spread to hundreds of congregations. Since Sulzer and his all-male choir
sang a cappella, their music, though different from contemporary cantorial practice,
could easily find its way into the liturgy of even very traditional synagogues. Only
relatively late in life did Sulzer become an outspoken proponent of the organ, which
by the seventies was used in Vienna for weddings and similar occasions.[17]

In its attention to decorum, aesthetics, and socially relevant preaching, the Minhag
of Vienna clearly represented a reform of previous practice and values. Precisely
because it did not go further, spurning the ideological path of the Hamburg Temple
and the rabbinical conferences, it was also a reform far better able to serve as the focal
point for a community whose numbers, especially after midcentury, were augmented
by an influx of traditional Jews from the east. Likewise it could more easily become
a model for synagogues elsewhere in the Austrian Empire.

Along the Austrian Periphery

Although, as we shall see, religious reform in Bohemia and Galicia, as in Vienna, was characterized by considerable moderation, it has an ideological prehistory which is nothing less than radical. Beginning at the end of the eighteenth century, two Bohemian Jews, Herz Homberg (1749–1841) and Peter Beer (1758–1838), sought to utterly transform traditional Judaism, especially its structure of authority and the content of religious instruction. Both were men with almost no regard for historical continuity and very high respect for what they believed the state desired. Reformation of the Jewish religion in their eyes was not an end in itself but a way to make over the traditional Jew in an entirely new image.

Herz Homberg began his career by transforming himself.[18] A precocious student of the great Rabbi Ezekiel Landau in Prague, he learned the German alphabet only in his eighteenth year, and soon, like other maskilim thereafter, found himself persecuted for engaging in secular studies. He fled to the more hospitable Berlin, where he lived in Mendelssohn's house as a tutor of his children and an associate on his Pentateuch commentary. By the time he returned to the Hapsburg Empire, Homberg was far more radical than Mendelssohn. In 1787 the emperor named him supervisor of the German Jewish schools in Galicia, a region which Austria had only recently acquired in the partitions of Poland, and which remained a bastion of traditionalism. Here, where hasidic enthusiasts battled with their more intellectualist opponents, the mitnagdim, both parties soon joined forces against the intruding maskil. Garbed in modern European dress topped by a powdered wig and speaking pure German, Homberg seemed to come from another world. He was rapidly ostracized, frustrated, and soon very angry. The only way to modernize the Jews, he determined, was to uproot all those institutions which stood in the way of complete assimilation. In memoranda and in conferences with government officials, he proposed censorship—or even burning—of certain Jewish books and the replacement of an incorrigible rabbinate by a cadre of modern Jewish teachers able to completely reeducate the backward Jews, even if it be against their will. Of Judaism there would remain only its original, biblical version, without the ceremonial laws, which Homberg believed no longer applicable, and which he personally did not observe. As an educator, Homberg published textbooks on Judaism, one of which, *Bne-Zion* (1812), became the basis for an examination Hapsburg Jews had to pass before they were allowed to marry.[19] The Judaism which he preached in his writings was a rational faith that urged love of neighbor and loyalty to constituted political authority, a universal religious morality grounded in biblical texts. Through his writings and pedagogical activities, Homberg sought to destroy that Jewish "esprit-de-corps," which was based on talmudic study, rabbinical authority, Yiddish language, and distinctive garb. "Teachers" could then remold the Mosaic remainder into a guide for model subjects of the state.

Few Jews sympathized with Homberg's views. In Galicia he was widely despised; later in Prague he remained an outsider, not active among the religious reformers. Homberg's odyssey took him to the boundary of Judaism, beyond reform to abdication and self-hate. In a petition to the government he was proud to note that four sons had already converted to Christianity; five other children were "still Jews."

Peter Beer's career is almost a carbon copy of Homberg's.[20] He too was born in a Bohemian village, studied with Landau, acquired general education initially on his own, and was inspired by Mendelssohn. And he too went beyond Mendelssohn—as well as the later evolution-oriented German reformers—in espousing a pure Mosaism, cleansed of talmudic accretions. Rabbinic laws, he wrote, had to be seen as "arbitrary and unsanctioned human additions to the true and divine religion of Moses and the Prophets." Beer even went so far as to sympathize with the antirabbinic Karaites, projecting that medieval sect all the way back to the Second Temple.[21] Yet Beer was a degree or two less radical than Homberg, for example in valuing some Jewish ritual.[22] Unlike Homberg, moreover, he took an ongoing interest in liturgical reform.[23] Two decades after he came to Prague in 1811 as a teacher in the Jewish state school, Beer was among the chief initiators there of a moderately reformed religious service.

In 1830 close to 10,000 of the 67,000 Bohemian Jews lived in the provincial capital of Prague. Its Jewish community was one of the largest in Europe, boasting nine public synagogues and many smaller prayer quorums; its rabbis had been among the most notable scholars and mystics. Prague Jewry had also been more open to its environment than communities elsewhere, harboring an active circle of moderate maskilim from the last decades of the eighteenth century. An earlier Jewish traveler's description, of about 1720, relates how on Friday evenings, before the entry of the Sabbath, a group of instrumentalists would play for an hour or so on organ pipes, cembali, and violins, accompanying the cantor and other singers in the *lekhah dodi* hymn and also performing a number of "delightful pieces." With Joseph II's patent of toleration for Bohemia, issued in 1781, new economic opportunities were opened for enterprising Jews and its encouragement of secular education stimulated a process of rapid acculturation.[24]

Authority in religious matters remained vested in the three rabbis composing the Prague rabbinical court. At their head in the 1820s was Samuel Landau, a staunch traditionalist, whose influence with the government proved sufficient to bury any and all proposals for religious reform. But then, in 1832, an anonymous article, appearing in a local newspaper, publicly suggested the establishment of an ordered service on the Vienna model and the engagement of an appropriate preacher. It quoted the imperial decrees of 1820 and 1821, which clearly indicated official support for more decorous worship, thus disarming opposition.[25] The author, who had disguised himself as "a noble lady" ready to contribute generously of her own funds for the project, turned out to be Ludwig Pollak, an energetic young industrialist. It was he who immediately became the driving force behind the realization of his plan. Within a few days more than fifty men gathered to found an "Association for the Improvement of Jewish Worship."[26] The supporters included members of the community board, the wealthiest Jewish merchants and industrialists, intellectuals like Peter Beer, and also a considerable portion of the Jewish middle class. Before long, the Association received government approval to use one of the community synagogues, the *Altschule,* for a "regulated" service and to remodel the building appropriately. Not surprisingly, Landau immediately condemned the plan, dragging out all the old arguments and also insisting that to alter the synagogue structure would violate Jewish law. When the government turned a deaf ear, he tried to persuade seatholders in the *Altschule* not to exchange their ancestral accommodations for equivalents in other synagogues. Landau's opposition held the project up for many months. It was only after "the last of the Mohicans," as Pollak called Landau, died in 1834 that the project could move forward with the acquiescence of Landau's young and uninfluential successor. On February 12, 1835 the Prague-born Zacharias Frankel, a man respected by both parties, gave the address as the old synagogue was festively turned over to the Association. The building would remain the property of the community, but its reconstruction, which now began, was to be paid for by voluntary contributions. The 280 Association members would worship separately from other Jews, though remaining within the community. Prague Jewry was simply too large and too divided to create a single modern religious institution for all, as had been possible in Vienna.

The success of the new society depended very much on finding an appropriate German preacher who could serve as its focal point. Beer and Pollak turned to Leopold Zunz, whose scholarly reputation was unmatched, who had served as a preacher in the Jacobson-inspired temple in Berlin, and who was looking for suitable employment. The major problem standing in the way of any reformer coming to Prague was the government's insistence that the preacher must be subservient to the three members of the rabbinical court. Despite the Association's repeated petitions to grant its spiritual leader complete independence, the Bohemian authorities remained convinced that if they allowed such freedom, the Orthodox would wage an unending battle against the Association, produce a split in the community, and likely drive the group to dangerous radicalism. Thus Pollak raised vain hopes when he wrote to Zunz that the Association's preacher would speedily become the religious authority for all the Jews of Prague, indeed for all Bohemia; that his position would carry more influence than Mannheimer's in Vienna; and that since the government was clearly behind the project, the Association would be able to go further than the Vienna temple—for example to the introduction of German prayers, which Mannheimer had been unable to achieve. Soon, he suggested, the Association's model would spread to the eight other synagogues of the large community and then out to the towns and villages. Prague, not Vienna, would become the exemplar. Thus Zunz arrived in Bohemia with high expectations—and was grievously disappointed. The remodeling was then just beginning. Most of his time was taken up with preparing a set of synagogue regulations, and he preached only four times during his brief nine months in Prague. Zunz quit so soon after his arrival in part because the Association's efforts to free him from subservience to the rabbinical court failed, but also because he felt intellectually exiled in Prague and because, like fourteen years earlier in Berlin, he could not bear the Jewish lay "aristocracy" of wealth.[27] By the time the building was ready, Zunz had long since retreated to Berlin.

It was Michael Sachs who, in April 1837, conducted the first service in the newly remodeled Moorish structure with seats for some 400. Sachs, who, as we saw earlier, was a most moderate reformer, presided over a service that included German sermons, a few German prayers and songs, a choir, and organ accompaniment, though in the Prague tradition the instrument was not played on the Sabbath itself. He also introduced confirmation and was able to achieve elevated personal status for both himself and the Association when, in 1839, the government finally agreed to make its preacher the fourth rabbi of the community, alongside the three members of the rabbinical court. That court's new senior member after 1840 was Solomon Judah Rapoport. Himself a maskil and modern scholar, Rapoport established a warm relationship with Sachs and his successor.[28]

Some other communities in Bohemia, and even in the more traditional Moravia, followed the model of Prague (and Vienna), so that moderate synagogue reform became widespread in the hereditary Hapsburg lands.[29] Yet the Reform movement in Bohemia was unable to strengthen greatly the religious identity of nonorthodox Jews, chiefly because it did not direct itself with sufficient vigor to modern Jewish education. Jewish children of enlightened families in Prague attended the government school where only secular disciplines were taught. Parents left the Jewish subjects to the old *ḥadarim* or to tutors—or they gave their children no Jewish education at all. The result was a silent but steady process of assimilation.[30]

Compared with the Jews of Prague, Galician Jewry in the early nineteenth century was less acculturated. Its masses were partly hasidic, its orientation inward; it viewed the non-Jewish world as foreign, not as an object of identification. Very few among the 350,000, mostly impoverished Galician Jews could be called "enlightened." One reason was that the immediate intellectual environment remained barren of stimuli: Jewish Torah study was much above the intellectual level of their Gentile neighbors. When non-Jews derided Jewish customs, their mockery was not ascribed to a higher level of culture but to ancient prejudice. Yet even this more self-enclosed community produced both thinkers and practical men who belong to the history of the Reform movement.

Within Galician Jewry arose a remarkably creative individual whose philosophical reflections in a number of respects parallel those of the thinkers discussed in Chapter 2. Like them, Nachman Krochmal (1785–1840) sought to mediate. An observant Jew, he nonetheless exposed himself fully to the critical philosophical and historical conceptions which books and newspapers brought across from Germany to Galicia. Soon he was wrestling with the same issues that beset the Reformers further to the west. He too confronted the challenge of German idealist philosophy, especially in its Hegelian form. And he too felt compelled to alter traditional conceptions. For Krochmal, God became the "Absolute Spirit" and "the source of all spiritual being in its totality." Such a God was neither personal nor fully supernatural; in fact Krochmal preferred the adjective "divine" for describing the spiritual aspect of living things over the noun standing for a separate entity. Israel's awareness of divinity, he believed, was not complete at Sinai. Only in the course of history did the Jewish people progressively free itself from externals and attain higher levels of spirituality. Yet Krochmal never drew the conclusion that the mitzvot therefore became superfluous. They still helped to keep Israel separate, and that separation, determined by a special relation to the Absolute Spirit, preserved the Jewish people and its message. Like the German Reformers, Krochmal argued in the face of non-Jewish religious and philosophical thought that the Jews could not be relegated to an earlier stage of spiritual development. Israel had been preserved while others had perished "so that it might become a Kingdom of Priests, i.e., teachers of the revealed absolute faith to the human race." Unlike Samson Raphael Hirsch, but like most of the Reformers, Krochmal sought to meet the challenge of historicism by acknowledging that Jews and Judaism were indeed subject to the forces of history, while also arguing vigorously that Israel's relationship to God placed it in advance of modern civilization and made it imperishable to the end of time.[31]

If Krochmal was the most significant intellectual figure of the Galician Haskalah, Joseph Perl (1773–1839) was its most effective practical advocate. Like Krochmal he was an avowed enemy of contemporary Hasidism, whose superstitions he castigated in biting satire. Perl was also a devoted pedagogue who in 1813 established in Tarnopol the first modern Jewish school in Galicia, one in which traditional Jewish subjects were integrated with secular ones. Like Israel Jacobson in Seesen, Perl decided to provide a religious service for his students and their families which would be in harmony with the atmosphere of the school. Thus at his own expense he established a "Temple for Regulated Worship," connected with the school, in which the service was more decorous, a boys' choir sang, and Perl himself in later years gave occasional edifying sermons. Though school and temple both met opposition, they were able to persist, serving as examples of educational and religious reform for other Galician towns.[32]

It was in the large Jewish community of Lemberg (Lwow) that the most violent confrontation in the history of the Reform movement anywhere occurred. Here the vast majority of Jews were antimodern Orthodox, some of them hasidim. Not only had they despised Herz Homberg, but in 1816 their leaders had cast a ban on moderate maskilim in the city, including Solomon Judah Rapoport. Yet acculturation went forward among a small but growing minority. The latter was distinguished by their west European contemporary dress, as opposed to the old-fashioned Polish long coats and fur hats of the traditionalists. With the factions thus visibly set apart, defections from Orthodoxy to the camp of the "Germans" were immediately apparent and party allegiance obvious to all. The local Austrian authorities, who had not involved themselves in community affairs, in 1842 tilted toward the maskilim when they appointed a number of them to the governing board of the community. It now seemed possible for the modernist faction in Lemberg to obtain those institutions which already existed elsewhere in the Austrian Empire and which they had long hoped to establish for themselves: a modern Jewish school and a reformed worship service.

Already in the early years of the century there had been a Lemberg synagogue just outside the city itself whose customs differed: the worshipers there did not kneel during the *alenu* prayer on the High Holidays, they did not perform the ceremony of *tashlikh* (casting their sins into the river), nor did their bridegrooms break a glass at the wedding ceremony. Apparently the maskilim gravitated to this synagogue, but they also hoped for an institution of their own.[33] In 1840 two influential lawyers and a physician called together some fifteen doctors, lawyers, bankers, and merchants from the Jewish intelligentsia of the city to discuss the establishment of a progressive synagogue.[34] What distinguished the thinking of these religious reformers from their counterparts in Germany was a clear commitment to *national* Jewish identity. "We should not be ashamed of our nationality among different peoples or nations," one of the founders, Jacob Rapoport, said to a circle of supporters, "similarly we should not be ashamed of our own worship service, neither from the point of view of language nor of ritual."[35] All present fervently agreed that the Hebrew language and the basic prayers would be retained. The new "German-Jewish House of Worship" would differ only in its decorum, its music, the elimination of *piyutim,* and the introduction of German sermons. Lemberg, they decided, would follow the model of Vienna and Prague.

Using their influence on the community board, the reformers advanced plans for the temple with considerable success. Contributions were raised and a structure similar to the one in Vienna began to rise. For their preacher, the group selected Abraham Kohn (1807–1848), who had been recommended by Solomon Sulzer and was known to be observant and moderate. As a trained educator, he could also serve as director of the Jewish school established in 1844.

Abraham Kohn was not a shallow rationalist or extremist like Homberg, who had aroused so much enmity in Lemberg half a century earlier. After he came to Lemberg from the Tyrolean town of Hohenems in 1844, he made a genuine effort to understand Galician Jewry, to appreciate its virtues no less than to condemn what he regarded as its shortcomings. Rare among enlightened Jews was his high regard for the religiosity of the hasidim. To be sure, he believed them superstitious and backward, but their innocent faith and genuine sense of community aroused his admiration. Hasidism, Kohn suggested in a series of "Letters from Galicia," was "itself a popular reform that paved the way for more rational reform. In particular, it has brought more freedom into synagogue ritual and in the course of time permitted itself significant changes." While a hasidic service might be aesthetically unattractive to a cultivated sensibility, it had the virtue of being lively and vigorous, magically drawing in the mass of worshipers. Kohn hoped to retain for enlightened Jews the hasidic elements of heart and spirit.[36] But Kohn was also a reformer. He condemned *tashlikh* and the ceremony of transferring guilt to a chicken twirled around one's head *(kaparot)*. The Orthodox could not forgive him for quoting the Bible in German during his sermons, wanting to impose German clothing, and arguing that married women should leave their hair unshorn. In the new house of worship, which he dedicated in 1846, Kohn eliminated the medieval prayers for vengeance and instituted a confirmation ceremony that his opponents believed was a step toward apostasy. Nonetheless, even in Galicia such a mild reformer would probably have been grudgingly accepted by the Orthodox had Kohn remained, as he was initially, merely the "religious instructor and preacher" for those who accepted his authority.

The forces that led to Kohn's tragic demise were set in motion only when his supporters secured for their preacher the coveted position of District Rabbi. This was a post that had lain vacant since the death in 1839 of Jacob Meshullam Ornstein, a noted halakhic scholar. That a "German" with relatively little talmudic knowledge should be Ornstein's successor and "their" rabbi was more than the Orthodox could bear.[37] Especially bitter, of course, were those descendants of Lemberg rabbinical families who themselves desired the honor. Kohn was soon made the object of false accusations to the government and repeated attempts to remove him from office. The animus directed against him swelled to a crescendo when he became the champion of an extended effort to abolish onerous taxes on kosher meat and on the candles Jews lit on Sabbaths and holidays. The collectors of those taxes were two wealthy leaders of the Orthodox party who now saw the intruding rabbi not only as a spiritual foe but also as a dangerous underminer of their fortunes. By 1848, the year of political turmoil and sometimes near anarchy in the Austrian Empire, verbal opposition gave way to physical violence. Kohn was knocked to the ground in front of his school; rocks shattered the windows of his house. Then a rumor was spread that his family had been infected by the prevalent cholera. Finally, one day a poor Jewish goldsmith, hired for the task, entered the Kohn kitchen; unobserved, he managed to drop a large dose of arsenic into the family soup kettle.[38] A few days later, the forty-one-year-old Kohn and his youngest child were dead. However unscrupulously, the effort to keep the reformers from extending their influence had succeeded. Shortly thereafter the Lemberg community split, Kohn's successors serving as spiritual leaders only for the growing circle of Germanized maskilim.

In Hungary, too, Orthodoxy retained its strength. Most Hungarian Jews lived in the countryside, where they remained untouched by the Haskalah. The leading religious figure, Moses Sofer (1762–1839), drew hundreds of students to his yeshivah in

Pressburg, where he preached uncompromising rejection of modern culture as the only way in which Judaism could survive. Even moderate religious innovation was anathema to this staunch advocate of unbending and militant orthodoxy. For generations, the influence of Sofer, his descendants, and his disciples made Hungary into a bastion of resistance to modernity.

Yet Hungarian Jewry was growing rapidly both from within and by immigration from other portions of the Hapsburg Empire. From 75,000 in 1785, the Jewish population swelled to more than a quarter million by the 1840s. In the cities, population influx and commercial development prevented insularity. Pest, on the eastern bank of the Danube, which did not even have a Jewish community until 1784, could boast of over 10,000 Jews by midcentury, its immigrant Jewish population keeping up with the growth of the city itself, which during the nineteenth century came to overshadow Buda, the once more important town across the river.[39] Soon some among the new urban Jews expressed a desire for religious modernization. Initially, Reform was an isolated phenomenon in Hungary, limited almost entirely to a single rabbi and his community; then it spread to other cities in the moderate form that characterized the movement in the Hapsburg Empire. Finally, in Pest during the 1848 Revolution, it assumed a radicalism comparable only to the Association for Reform in Judaism of Berlin.

We have already encountered Aaron Chorin (1766–1844) as one of the four rabbis to sanction the reforms of the Beer Temple in 1818.[40] He was likewise a supporter of Geiger in the Breslau dispute and of the Hamburg Temple in its second controversy with the Orthodox. Indeed, for a quarter of a century Chorin served as a valued authority for the German Reformers: a venerable talmudic scholar from another land who supported their efforts. In fact, Chorin was one of the movement's pioneers. In 1789 he had come to the central Hungarian town of Arad, where he became the first rabbi of a small and new community. For a while he played the traditional role, establishing a yeshivah and presenting well-received talmudic discourses to his flock. But soon he began to deviate from the norm. First he adopted and defended the controversial view that sturgeon was a kosher fish; then he started to read philosophical rationalism into the Talmud. He condemned the practical kabbalah as worthless and insisted repeatedly (even tediously) that Jews were required to treat Christians as "brothers" no less than fellow Jews. In the Arad religious service he instituted such reforms as prohibiting spitting at the mention of Gentiles during the *alenu* prayer and pounding the floor during the mention of Haman's name at Purim. He also banished amulets, abolished *kaparot,* and later excised the *kol nidre* chant. The lay leadership of the Arad community supported Chorin, but his published writings aroused some opposition at home and especially angered other Hungarian rabbis. More than once they coerced him to recant what he had written.[41] Yet in each instance he returned to his reformist views, bouncing back as soon as the pressure was relieved, and quickly becoming even bolder.

Chorin was a reformer on the basis of Halakhah, not historical development. In this respect he resembled the educator Michael Creizenach of Frankfurt (discussed earlier) more than he did Abraham Geiger. Persistently he sought to show that talmudic Judaism was far more flexible than contemporary Orthodoxy and that progress was possible on the basis of Jewish law, if only one were ready to be as innovative as the early Rabbis. Far removed from setting up either a pretalmudic biblical Judaism or the spirit of the contemporary age as his exclusive criterion, Chorin insisted that "it is precisely and only the Talmud, rabbinism, . . . which can bring about a significant reformation of religious practice."[42] Not alone in Germany, but increasingly also in Hungary, individuals were tearing themselves away from observance simply on the basis of personal and arbitrary decision. What was needed to stem the tide, Chorin believed, was an authoritative body which would make decisions alleviating the severest restrictions and accommodating Jewish practice to contemporary values and circumstances. He urged the establishment of a sanhedrin, or at least of synods in each country, composed of unprejudiced Jewish scholars who also possessed knowledge of contemporary literature. The Hungarian synod's members would be appointed, not elected, since the masses could not be expected to vote for progress. Its reforms would be carried out by a consistory, not unlike the one which Israel Jacobson had established in Westphalia.[43] When the German rabbis met in Brunswick in 1844, Chorin welcomed the gathering as constituting the kind of centralized authority which he had advocated. In Hungary, by contrast, when the rabbis gathered that same year in Bacs, it was only to uphold the status quo.

While maintaining his halakhic approach to reform, Chorin became progressively more daring in his views and actions. As early as 1826, he advocated—without practical success in Arad—that Jews should pray with uncovered heads since that was the way one paid homage in the West. "May it be God's will," he wrote, "that the fear of heaven be upon the worshiper, like the awe experienced before a king of flesh and blood to whom one makes petition."[44] If it was proper to take one's hat off as a sign of respect before such an earthly monarch, how much the more so before the King of Kings! While in 1818 Chorin had still believed in the return to Zion, by the early forties he held that the Jews were no longer a nationality.[45] He did insist that the Sabbath be kept on the seventh day, but toward the end of his life he wrote legal opinions which gave permission to travel on a train and for a Jew to play the organ in a synagogue on that day.[46] In 1842, when an organ was introduced in Arad, the elderly, long-bearded rabbi expressed his hope that the services there would soon emulate fully the worship in the Hamburg Temple.[47]

If for Chorin the German Reform movement served as principal inspiration, for less thoroughgoing religious reformers in Hungary it was the temple in Vienna which became their model. The Viennese rite came first to Pest, shortly after the strictly Orthodox chief rabbi there died in 1826. A young, energetic lay leader had visited the temple in the empire's capital and returned with the enthusiastic desire to introduce its ritual into his private prayer group, called Chesed Neurim or Jungen-Schul. A local teacher, hired to be the preacher, was sent to Vienna to learn his craft from Mannheimer; the cantor chosen, appropriately enough, was dispatched for a quick course with Sulzer. As its name suggests, the group was composed of young people, apparently more open to change than their elders. Most had only recently moved from Altofen (O-Buda) to Pest across the river. They were not affluent, but probably upwardly mobile. The new services, which began in 1827, were so attractive that within a few years a large temple was built and given the status of "community synagogue" alongside the Large Synagogue, which continued to follow traditional ritual. Although this official recognition caused some opposition, Pest Jewry soon accepted the existence of two formally divergent rites, both of them within the community structure. The sense of unity received further expression when the secularly educated, moderate reformer Löw Schwab, from Prossnitz in Moravia, became rabbi of the community in 1836, alternately giving modern sermons in the temple and old-style *derashot* in the synagogue.[48]

As Vienna influenced Pest, so did Pest in turn become the model for smaller communities in Hungary. Trade fairs brought Jewish merchants regularly to Hungary's principal city, where they visited the orderly service in the temple and were impressed by the appealing music and edifying sermon. Moderate reforms on the Pest model soon took root in Kanischa and in Pressburg. In Kanischa, a relatively important commercial center, some among its 900-member community created their own Temple Association within five years after Pest. So did a few Jews in Pressburg, which—though the very heart of Orthodoxy—had seen the establishment of a modern school some years earlier.[49] During the 1840s the pace and spread of religious reform in Hungary increased, as they did in Germany. In 1846, when it built a new synagogue, the Kanischa community decided to go further, installing the second organ in a Hungarian synagogue, four years after Arad. Eperies in the north and Lugos in the south instituted confirmation. More common were vernacular sermons, now heard in at least half a dozen communities. The preachers were mostly young rabbis, the communities sometimes new, the reforms mainly choir and decorum. In Papa, a sizable community of about 5,000 Jews, the construction of a new synagogue prompted leaders of the "progressive party" to seek rabbinical opinions on proposed reforms. The twenty-one respondents included the entire spectrum of modern German rabbis from Holdheim to Frankel, as well as four Hungarians. All agreed that it was permitted to place the pulpit near the ark, have choral music, perform weddings inside the synagogue, and allow community board members to attend business sessions without a head covering. They split only on whether leather shoes were forbidden on the Day of Atonement since the latter was a prohibition grounded in the Talmud. For many of the respondents these questions had been settled long ago in favor of the nontraditional position. Still, some of them felt constrained to supply brief arguments based on halakhic or historical precedent, realizing that in Hungary such considerations still mattered a great deal.[50]

Among the reformers active in Hungary during the 1840s one stands out as a radical scholar and thinker. Born in Moravia, having studied in Prague and traveled to Germany, Moses Brück (1812–1849) eventually came to the south Hungarian town of Nagy–Becskerek where he joined a local circle of religious reformers.[51] As early as 1837 Brück had argued for the necessity of restoring the pristine, prerabbinic Mosaic Judaism. With considerable knowledge and acumen he had shown in specific detail how numerous individual rituals and customs were late creations that disfigured the earlier faith, encrusting it with superstitions and creating religiously unjustified burdensome restrictions. He had appealed to history, the "universal judge," to distinguish the ancient and venerable from the medieval and inessential. In 1847, now in Hungary, he went so far as to argue that most talmudic explanations of Mosaic law could be shown to contravene the intentions of the lawgiver.

A year later Brück drew radical conclusions. In one hundred anonymously published theses for the reform of Judaism he proposed a service with all prayers in the vernacular, where men do not cover their heads and a mixed choir sings, where the Torah is not read from a scroll and no ram's horn is sounded; a congregation which celebrates the Sabbath on Sunday and observes no dietary regulations at all except that matzot—along with leavened bread—would be eaten on Passover. His last thesis summed it all up: "All rabbinic institutions, usages, and customs which contravene the spirit of Mosaism or the duties of the citizen are no longer binding." What set Brück's final work apart from the writings of other Jewish radicals of the time was his extraordinary use of comparative history. Repeatedly, he pointed to parallels between Jewish practices and those of other ancient peoples. Thus, he noted, the Egyptians, Indians, and Greeks had their dietary laws too, similar in some respects to those of the ancient Israelites and also intended in their case to prevent close social contact with foreigners. As for the phylacteries, the Persians likewise wore talismans on their foreheads and left arms. Thus Brück sought to discredit distinctive Jewish practices, one by one, finding them either characteristic of other primitive peoples, based on faulty science, or standing in the way of Jewish social progress. In his hands religious reform became demolition, leaving behind only the blandest "spirit" of Judaism, divested of almost all ceremony and sense of separate destiny.[52]

Brück composed his theses at the beginning of the Hungarian rebellion against Hapsburg rule. For him the promise of emancipation it held out meant nothing less than *"Israel is redeemed."*[53] He was ready and willing to accept the political leaders' condition that Jewish equality required prior radical reform, and his theses were intended to show just how far he felt it necessary and proper to go. Although in thus fully subordinating religion to a political goal, Brück was nearly alone among the Jewish religious leaders in Hungary, he was not isolated in his religious radicalism. At that time similar views were being heard from a new Reform circle in Pest.

Since its beginnings in 1827, the service of the Pest Choir-Temple, as it was now called, had changed very little. Among the new generation of young, unmarried men who had completed gymnasium or university studies, the question of reform, which had emerged twenty years earlier, now appeared once again. In 1846 a small group of young people established a Vienna-style service in Ofen (Buda) with a local teacher sometimes giving his own sermons, sometimes reading from those of Ludwig Philippson. The moderate rabbi of Pest, Löw Schwab, lent the group his support and even gave an occasional sermon for them. A year later, the small circle elected Ignaz Einhorn (1825–1875), a brilliant rabbinical candidate, to act as preacher in their "Religious Society of Ofen Jewish Youth."[54] A Hungarian by birth, Einhorn had devoted himself to philosophy, Jewish theology, and classical studies; he was fluent in both German and Hungarian and showed promising talent as a journalist. As soon as the new interest in reform traveled across the river to Pest—where it assumed a far more radical form—Einhorn went along with it.

In Pest a circle of students and intellectuals had gathered in order to carry reform considerably further. Initially they hoped that their endeavor could come under community auspices, as the Choir-Temple had been able to do two decades earlier. But Rabbi Schwab opposed this group as going too far, and they were forced to strike out on their own. In July 1848 they formed the Central Association of Hungarian Israelites, published a statement explicitly calling themselves "radical," and decided that they would take their cue from the radicals in Germany. Like the Berlin Reform Association, they sought at first to create a league of such associations in Hungary, but, also like the Berlin group, they failed in the venture, becoming merely the local Pest Israelite Reform Association. Drawing in wealthier members, the group was able to arrange for a suitable building and hold its first services for the High Holidays in 1848. They chose Einhorn as their "rabbi and preacher" and not long thereafter sent him off to the Prussian capital to learn Reform directly from Holdheim.[55]

All of this organization took place against the backdrop of the Hungarian national revolt. Jews in Hungary, as elsewhere in the Hapsburg Empire, had not enjoyed equal rights and, in addition, had suffered the severe hostility of economic competitors in the cities. With the coming of the revolution, the acculturated among them hoped to gain the emancipation which Austria had denied. Although Jewish intellectuals remained tied to German-speaking Jewry (Philippson's *Allegemeine Zeitung* was as widely read in Hungary as anywhere),[56] Magyarization took hold during the forties. Soon there were sermons in Hungarian as well as German. Yet the Hungarians proved to be a bitter disappointment. Their national revolution unleashed pogroms in various cities while their leaders for a time banned Jews from service in the military. Emancipation was postponed until July 1849, just before the rebellion was put down by the Austrians and Russians. Nonetheless, moderate reformers, like Löw Schwab of Pest and Leopold Löw of Papa, supported and participated in the abortive revolt no less than radicals like Brück and Einhorn. Even the Pressburg yeshivah sent a contingent of volunteers. When it was suppressed, some Jewish participants were imprisoned and all of Hungarian Jewry was required to pay a large penalty.[57]

There can be no doubt that these emancipatory hopes stimulated interest in the Pest Reform Association, which grew rapidly during the revolution. As early as 1844, Louis Kossuth, the Hungarian leader, had written that the Jews must prove through proper reform and a solemn ecclesiastical proclamation "that the social institutions of the Mosaic laws do not constitute an essential part of the Jewish religion."[58] Yet unlike Brück, the Pest Association explicitly rejected such conditions. In August 1848 they issued a protest which put it most strongly: "We would be unworthy of freedom," they said, "if we had to haggle *(erschachern)* for it in this way. We would be unworthy of the name Jew—martyr for faith and freedom—if we let the reform, which is demanded of us by our most sacred *religious* consciousness, be reduced to a means for attaining *political* rights."[59] They would reject emancipation, they insisted, unless it were given without differentiation to all Hungarian Jews. But even though the Association was thus unwilling to accept the Magyars' conditions, its members did find the revolution a fresh breeze that could sweep away all outworn institutions, leaving Christian and Jew to live in closer social and cultural contact. It was this hope, as much as religious and intellectual considerations, which determined the principles that Einhorn formulated for the Association.

Freshly returned from Berlin, the Association's rabbi put forward a program based neither on halakhic reform nor on "Mosaic" Judaism—in fact not on a reform of historical Judaism at all, but on an alternative *kind* of Judaism called "Reform." Though Einhorn said little which had not already been expressed by Holdheim, nowhere previously had the principles and program of a radical Reform Judaism been formulated as clearly. For Einhorn, Judaism consisted of two elements: spirit and matter—faith and morality on the one hand, ceremony on the other. The time had come to abolish the latter almost completely because advanced religion itself demanded it. But the higher Judaism called also for a reform of religious and moral conceptions: only the barest essentials—the belief in the one providential God and in the principle of morality—remained eternally valid. It was this abstract message which Israel was chosen to disseminate in the world. For centuries the task had required commands and prohibitions, but that was no longer the case. Israel had finally reached the level of spiritual maturity where its religion could exist without the crutch of ceremony. Very much like Zacharias Frankel, Einhorn found his authority in what he called "the religious consciousness of the people," except that here the people *(Volk)* consisted of the most acculturated among the Jews, those most rooted in the present.[60] Coming down to specifics, Einhorn proposed the permissibility of mixed marriages with monotheists, the replacement of circumcision by spiritual consecration, and Sabbath services on Sunday for those whose work prevented their attending worship on Saturday. Indeed, the true Jew, Einhorn concluded, sounding a note that would be heard often thereafter in American Reform Judaism, was recognized simply by his idea of God and the moral dicta on which he acts.

The Sunday worship in the Pest Reform Association embodied these principles. There were few tangible symbols. Following Holdheim's services in Berlin, men wore no hats, the prayers were said almost entirely in the vernacular; an organ and choir provided music. The prayerbook was that of the Berlin Reform Congregation. Einhorn preached alternately in German and Hungarian. There is reason to believe that partners in mixed marriages were accepted as members.[61] After Einhorn was forced to leave Hungary following the revolution's failure, his position was held for a short time by David Einhorn (not a relative), the talented radical who would later become a leading figure in American Reform. Similar independent congregations had sprung up in other Hungarian towns. Then, in 1852, the Austrian government closed down the Association's temple. In a period of resurgent conservatism, the message came across clearly: Jews were expected to return to their own traditions.

Along the southern periphery of the Hapsburg Empire, in northern Italy, no significant movement for the reform of Judaism came into being. Perhaps the most basic reason for this absence is that in its moderate form such a movement would have been superfluous, in radical guise quite foreign. Italian Jewry was not insular like the communities to the north and east. Although they had lived in ghettos for centuries, Italian Jews spoke the common language and participated freely in Italian culture. Their children received secular as well as Jewish educations. Their religious services were decorous, the music appealing, the vernacular sermon a commonplace, and the organ was not regarded as an exclusively Christian instrument. Thus, as we saw in Chapter 1, two Italian rabbis, Shem Tov Samun in Livorno and Jacob Recanati in Verona, could be among the respondents who gave their approval to worship with an organ in the Beer Temple in Berlin. It was also understandable that Italian Jews should show the least resistance to the expansion of secular studies and be the first to create a modern rabbinical seminary, at Padua in 1829.[62] It seemed unnecessary and undesirable to go any further.

The leading intellectual figure of nineteenth-century Italian Jewry, Samuel David Luzzatto (1800–1865), combined a remarkably productive career in Jewish scholarship with strictly orthodox belief and practice. His close association by correspondence with German Reformers, like Abraham Geiger, did not prevent him from deploring their use of *Wissenschaft* to undermine the foundations of traditional Judaism.[63] Similarly, although Italian rabbis were open to the world around them, they were nevertheless staunch opponents of every proposal to alter fundamentally, or even moderately, the character of Judaism or its practices. Throughout the century, with rare exceptions, they remained enlightened representatives of the status quo.[64]

Few Italian Jews would have had it otherwise. Italian Catholicism lacked models of liturgical reform; no newfound patriotism clashed with Jewish national hopes. To be sure, secularization affected Italian Jews as much as it did their coreligionists anywhere in the West, but they felt it unnecessary to justify their lack of practice or to create a Reform Judaism whose mandates they could more easily fulfill. In ever-increasing numbers, they simply drifted away from observance and from the synagogue. Like secularized Catholics, they participated minimally in religious life, choosing simply to remove themselves personally from existing institutions rather than undertake the arduous task of creating new ones. Thus Judaism in Italy remained, one is tempted to say, "classical" in its impermeability to change, esteemed and venerated by most, but practiced fully by very few.[65]

In Catholic France

In 1840, the poet Henrich Heine, then an exile in Paris, wrote of French Jews:

> Many of them still practice their ancient ceremonials, the external rites; they do it all mechanically, from ingrained habit and without knowing why. As for inward conviction, there remains not a trace, because in the synagogue as well as in the Christian church the spiritual corrosive of Voltairean critique has exercised its dissolving influence.[66]

Observing the French scene from Breslau, Abraham Geiger agreed. Unlike the German Jews, he noted, their coreligionists across the Rhine had failed to develop a modern faith. Following their Catholic fellow citizens, they had rejected religious progress and reform, choosing either to continue with the old forms or to leave Jewish practices aside entirely. Criticism, the vital essence of historical religion in Geiger's eyes, was virtually unknown. And without serious Jewish scholarship there could be no religious progress, only petrifaction on the one hand and religious indifference on the other.[67]

Certainly France did not offer a hospitable climate for the Reform movement. Its Enlightenment, unlike the German *Aufklärung,* had been distinctly hostile to religious belief and practice; its eighteenth-century heritage of anticlericalism long remained pervasive in educated circles. The restored Catholic church of the nineteenth century presented no model for reform. Nor could its mostly ill-educated priests serve as examples of an enlightened, vigorous clergy. Catholicism simply did not play the same significant intellectual role in France that Protestantism did in Germany. The French were Catholic to be sure, but for the educated that identity had become peripheral. The "lukewarmness" which characterized religion generally in France, one French Jew complained, had quietly penetrated Jewish life as well.[68] The political emancipation gained by French Jewry during the Revolution, and the separation of religious loyalty from political allegiance affirmed by the Napoleonic Sanhedrin of 1807, had removed issues over which reformers and traditionalists in Germany struggled, both together against various state governments and with one another. In nineteenth-century France, Judaism could be easily relegated to the private sphere, where it became subject to neglect.

Neither the Sephardi Jews of the southwest nor the Ashkenazim in the east seemed likely to espouse religious reform. The former, like the Italian Jews, already possessed a decorous and dignified service, the latter, despite emancipation, remained in the mass insufficiently acculturated to be disturbed by incongruities between their traditional religious life and the French civilization with which they were only beginning to become acquainted. Indeed, Jewish insularity remained common in France for half a century after the Revolution.

Since 1808, Jewish life was controlled by a hierarchical system of consistories, whose members at first saw their task as principally the furtherance of political and economic integration. When the central consistory did deal with religion, as in rejecting a catechism proposed by the German Jewish educator Joseph Johlson in 1813, it hewed to a strict traditionalism, urging modification of contemporary practice only with regard to regular sermons, since these could instill desirable qualities of character. Especially after 1831, when the Jewish religion in France joined its Christian counterparts in receiving state subsidies, the consistorial system became so powerful that it could easily stifle independent reform of the kind that succeeded in Hamburg and later in Berlin.[69] Throughout the nineteenth century no such separatist movement came into being. Only gradually did the consistory leadership itself become more hospitable to moderate reforms, especially after its lay faction gained greater relative influence.

Geiger was right that in France *Wissenschaft des Judentums* was lacking. In fact until the end of the century French Jewry produced very little Jewish scholarship of a critical nature. Absent too, for the most part, was the philosophical basis for seeing Judaism as an evolving faith. French Jewish writers tended rather to the eighteenth-century notion of eternal verities, allowing only that customs and practices were subject to historical development. Yet despite all these obstacles and lacks, French Judaism by the last third of the century, in its own way, had incorporated a number of the significant ideological doctrines and ritual innovations that characterized German Reform.[70] In fact, in the absence of the need to struggle for emancipation, religious reform became a more central topic of discussion in the Jewish periodical literature of France than it was east of the Rhine.

The first outstanding proponent of Jewish religious reform in France was also the most radical. Olry Terquem (1782–1862) was born into an esteemed and economically comfortable family in Metz.[71] Having received a good education in Jewish sources, he was able to complement it with extensive secular studies, especially in mathematics. By 1815 he was living in Paris where he became a librarian and professor at the royal academy for artillery and an expert in mathematical applications to French weaponry. He published a scholarly journal and wrote extensively in his field. He also intermarried, raised his children as Catholics, and soon ceased to participate in Jewish rituals. Yet for many years this French Jew, who was so fully assimilated professionally, socially, and religiously, continued to act—almost obsessively—as the severest critic of French Judaism, forcing moderates and traditionalists alike to take his strictures seriously. In a series of twenty-seven, often caustic letters, most of them signed Tsarphati (*i.e.,* "Frenchman" in Hebrew), and then in frequent articles appearing in the *Archives Israélites,* Terquem challenged not only individual observances, but the most important sources of Judaism.[72] He also made forays against the consistories from his secure position as an intellectual outside the system.

Beginning with the first of his letters in 1821, Terquem's main theme as Tsarphati was the Sabbath. Initially, he urged only that an auxiliary service be established on Sunday for those French Jews—especially workers, civil servants, and children in state schools—who were unable to observe a day of rest and worship on Saturday. Terquem saw little hope of reforming the existing service, nor the necessity for doing so if an alternative were available. Moreover, the Sunday devotions could begin afresh—with French sermons and a new French liturgy "that would create itself." Later, however, he argued more generally that the Sabbath day should be changed for all Jewry. In a vein reminiscent of Holdheim, he maintained in 1845 that the *day* of the Sabbath did not matter; it was the *idea* of the Sabbath that needed to be protected. The common view, alas, amounted simply to "Long live Saturday, and let the Sabbath perish!" Throughout his Jewish writings Terquem expressed particular solicitude for the Jewish workers. Saturday Sabbaths and the large number of holidays on the Jewish calendar made it difficult, if not impossible, for them to gain proper employment and still remain acceptably observant Jews. As a result, Terquem pointed out, they were mired in poverty and became easy prey for generous Christian missionaries.[73]

In arguing for consideration of the religious needs of the poor, Terquem also directly attacked the wealthy. These members of a new "moneyed aristocracy" were given the best places in the synagogue while the workers were pushed into a corner. Worse, they rarely occupied those seats, since most of them—including some lay consistory members—were themselves nonobservant. Yet the consistory leadership championed the status quo and refused to take steps that would make Judaism more accessible to those who wished to practice it within the limits set by occupational commitment. This, to Terquem's mind, represented intolerable hypocrisy, and he was determined to expose it ruthlessly. His object was to shame the leaders into promoting a thoroughly reformed Judaism in which all would share fully, in which there would no longer be lip service to beliefs and practices that had long been abandoned in fact. To his mind, French Jewry, though emancipated politically, still lacked an "interior emancipation," which could come about only by its own efforts. For Terquem that meant liberating Judaism from all of its "Asiatic forms and formulas" so that it could truly become part of "the great French family." Individual reforms were but halfway measures. On one occasion Terquem tellingly used the French word *refonte* to describe what was necessary: nothing less than a melting down and "recasting" of the contents of Judaism into a new mold could meet the contemporary challenge. The Jewish metal itself, however, was still malleable, he believed, and it would remain different from the Christian one. Judaism, he said, was the religion of the "God–God and not the Man–God." That, to his mind, was enough to keep it separate for the present; and in the long run even this separation would cease. A recast Judaism and a Christianity without incarnation and trinity could eventually become one.[74]

Radical as these ideas were, in themselves they would not have made Terquem the object of such widespread controversy. What provoked the severest criticism from a broad spectrum of liberals and traditionalists was Terquem's self-appointed role as the *enfant terrible* of French Judaism. Driven by a compulsion to expose and hold up to ridicule venerated but potentially embarrassing points of Jewish doctrine and practice, he became a threat to all those who prided themselves on what they believed to be Judaism's conformity with such contemporary values as rationality, equality, and tolerance. Terquem, to their horror, unabashedly chose "to wash the dirty laundry in public," and nothing was spared. In his pamphlets, and then in a general newspaper appearing in Metz, he dwelled on such subjects as the dangers of circumcision, the unemancipated Jewish woman, and the alleged scientific absurdities of the Jewish calendar. Not only did he poke fun at talmudic quibbling and prick contemporary rabbinical pretensions by quoting Jesus against the ancient Rabbis, he would not stop even at the Hebrew Bible. In truly Voltairean fashion he held up to scorn such unedifying episodes as the wholesale slaughter of the Shechemites and Amnon's rape of his half-sister Tamar. On one occasion he chose to dwell on those portions of the Passover Haggadah which call upon God to pour out His wrath upon the nations that had not known Him and declare that the Jews still consider themselves slaves in their exile. Still not enough, Terquem proclaimed that, in view of such Passover traditions, perhaps it was at least partly the Jews' own fault if they were accused of hating Christians—and this at precisely the time of the Damascus blood murder libel in 1840. Not surprisingly, his opponents argued that by denigrating Judaism, Terquem was serving its enemies.[75]

In a most basic respect Terquem was the French equivalent of Samuel Holdheim. Like the German radical rabbi, he utterly refused to prettify Jewish tradition. He would not allow it to be forcibly reinterpreted or selectively quoted so that the result would appear to be in perfect harmony with French enlightenment. Like Holdheim, who so strenuously rejected the attempt to create what he believed was a false historical continuity by ignoring the gulf between talmudic and contemporary mentality, so too Terquem would not have the differences papered over. He was, we may say, an antiapologist, and it was precisely that basic thrust of his writing which, more than anything else, made him an outsider among his fellow Jews. While they were at pains to show how much Judaism was in harmony with the values of post-Revolutionary France, Terquem had set out to show just the opposite.[76] He soon became a loner, a "leader without an army," as a later writer put it.[77] Yet in the tolerant atmosphere that prevailed within French Jewry, Terquem was never placed beyond the pale. Moderates as well as traditionalists polemicized against him, but even after he had written the most mordant and sarcastic of his articles he continued to be a valued contributor to the *Archives Israélites,* whose editor eulogized him as one of those elite intellects which Providence provides so sparingly.[78] The French idea of tolerance, which Jews had internalized so well, made them less prone to the invective hurled back and forth by factions among their coreligionists across the Rhine.

Yet the more moderate religious reformers in France did explicitly reject Terquem's tone and most of his substance. This was "a serious century," one of them wrote, not a time for resurrecting Voltaire.[79] Unlike Terquem, their intent was to proceed with caution; they did not want to replace the old structure, but merely to repair it. Their goal was to restore its one-time beauty while embellishing it with some new adornments that would make it look better on the French street where it now stood. The moderates' spokesmen were mostly men associated with the consistorial system, and they believed reform should come about through the hierarchy. Their task, as they saw it, was to make the lay leadership and the rabbinate more amenable to their suggestions.

The most persistent of the moderate religious reformers in France was Samuel Cahen (1796–1862), a teacher in the consistorial school in Paris, translator of the Bible into French, and editor of the long-lived *Archives Israélites,* the periodical which became the chief sounding board for reform proposals in France. Unlike Terquem, Cahen believed that the cause of reform was best served by calm deliberation and gradual progress. He saw himself as a man of the center, between the *stationnaires,* the stand-patters who countenanced no changes, on the one side, and those *réformistes* who sought far-reaching change instead of modification and amelioration, on the other. The Jews felt at home in France ever since the Revolution, he noted, but their faith still remained strange to its milieu. Hence the need for reforms. French synagogues, he argued, should have organs like Catholic churches, and he invoked the proreform literature of the first Hamburg Temple controversy in his support. The intolerant *ve-la-malshinim* prayer, incompatible with "the charitable sentiment at the base of our religion," would have to go. He criticized also the narrow curriculum of the rabbinical seminary in Metz and urged its removal to Paris where broader influences could be brought to bear on budding rabbis. Cahen's theoretical position was that of the more traditional German reformers. Like them, he believed in linking reforms to the Halakhah, in reviving the dormant process of reinterpretation.[80]

Prominent French Jews actively shared Cahen's fundamental concerns. Among them were Solomon Munk (1803–1867), the leading Jewish scholar in France, and the Orientalist Albert Cohn (1814–1877), who was in charge of the French Rothschilds' philanthropies. Although both Munk and Cohn attacked Terquem, neither could be counted among the *stationnaires*. Like Cahen, they favored moderate ritual changes. Indeed, even Simon Bloch (1810–1879), the most articulate of the French Orthodox, was a proponent of the confirmation ceremony and, at one point early in his career, wrote that he agreed with Terquem on the need for an organ, prayers in French, and regular sermons.[81]

Repeatedly the French reformers called attention to the progress of the Reform movement in Germany. Already in the first volume of the *Archives Israélites* Cahen wrote that the works of Chorin, Creizenach, Jost, and Geiger were justly attracting the attention of all educated Jews, and added: "It is for us to follow in their footsteps." Cahen's newspaper announced and helped distribute Formstecher's theological work, printed excerpts from two sermons by Abraham Geiger, and kept its readers well informed of contemporary German developments. Generally, as in the Geiger–Tiktin dispute, Cahen took the side of Reform. He expressed envy of the liveliness with which the religious debate was conducted in Germany and the active role which the German rabbinate played in advocating reforms. He deeply regretted that France had remained unrepresented at the Frankfurt rabbinical conference of 1845. Readers of the *Archives Israélites* were made to feel that French reform efforts were part of a larger movement whose center of gravity lay to the east.[82] Yet French moderates also felt some ambivalence about German Reform. Few could identify with its most radical manifestations; there was no pleasure in the admission that French Jewry, mired in indifference, had to seek stimulation from Germany. But what seems to have given the greatest pause was the schism which the religious disputes of the 1840s were introducing into German Jewry. French Jews admired the vigor of the argumentation, but they also sought to prevent similar divisions at home.

Given this feeling, as well as the powerful position and pervasive influence of the consistories, it is not surprising that independent reform initiatives met with little or no success. Beginning in 1818 there had been special Sabbath devotions in the auditorium of the Jewish school in Metz. Resembling their counterparts in the schools of Frankfurt and Berlin, they consisted simply of reciting the *shema* in Hebrew and French, plus an invocation, sermon, and a prayer for the king—all in French. Adults as well as children attended in large numbers. But, for reasons that are not clear, this early attempt at religious edification outside the synagogue ceased in 1824.[83] Twelve years later the moderates, Cahen, Munk, and Cohn, sought permission from the Paris consistory to hold modified High Holiday services for more enlightened Jews. They hoped to use a small synagogue adjoining the main temple. However, the consistory refused their request, and they did not make good on a threat to seek quarters elsewhere.[84]

The most carefully elaborated initiative to create an alternative service was undertaken in Metz in 1841. Gerson Lévy (1784–1864), a local bookdealer and teacher, attempted to establish an association whose members would worship in a specially arranged chapel on Sabbaths and holidays. As he conceived it, the liturgy would be conducted in a dignified manner and pruned of its less obligatory elements. Men and women would sit separately but on the same floor. A decorous Hebrew service, early in the morning, would be followed by one in French accompanied by a French sermon. Individuals would decide which service to attend. In this way Gerson Lévy hoped to attract a wide range of alienated Jews who had ceased to attend the consistorial synagogue. But he did not get very far. Meetings were held, thirty-three signatures obtained on an open letter to the Metz consistory, but sufficient support did not develop to launch the project. Admitting failure, he explained that the plan had been too radical for the older generation and insufficiently so for the younger.[85]

Certainly one reason why independent reform did not succeed in France was the absence of rabbinical leadership. The French rabbinate did not remain uniformly orthodox throughout the nineteenth century, but it was always dependent on the consistory system. Rabbis were trained in the consistorial seminary in Metz and then employed by the consistories either at the rank of *grand rabbin* or the lower one of communal rabbi. Rabbinical students tended to come from impoverished, unacculturated families in the eastern departments. At the Metz seminary, where the language of instruction for a time remained German, the chief preoccupation was traditional study of Halakhah—and this not on the level of yeshivot in eastern Europe. Few graduates obtained any advanced secular education beyond the courses offered by the seminary itself. Thus French rabbis possessed neither the professional nor the intellectual independence to act apart from the desires of the consistories' lay leaders. Interestingly, it was reformers like Cahen who urged the rabbis to assert their religious authority more forcefully, welcoming every sign of religious liberalism in their ranks.[86]

Until the 1840s the French rabbinate remained decidedly conservative. It neither instituted change nor was forced to respond to pressure from the laity. But then, as specific reform proposals gained increasing attention, clear factions began to develop, so that in rabbinical elections the candidates' positions on issues came to play as much of a role in their success as did personal qualifications. Thus in 1846, for example, candidates for the position of grand rabbi of the central consistory were asked to state their views with regard to a number of proposed reforms. These included a more dignified service, fusion of the Ashkenazi and Sephardi rites, limited excisions from the liturgy, introduction of an organ, and acceptance as a Jew of anyone who was born either of a Jewish father or a Jewish mother and claimed to be a Jew. The extant replies indicate widespread support among French rabbis for more decorum, a single rite, and the elimination of *piyutim*. The organ, however, had become a point of division; and so was the question of who is a Jew, with some rabbis willing to accept anyone who declared his or her Jewish identity. Finally, in 1856, Solomon Ulmann, the liberal who had become grand rabbi of the central consistory three years earlier, undertook the first and only significant rabbinical initiative on behalf of reform. He called a rabbinical conference for the purpose of collectively considering certain ritual changes and innovations. The eight consistorial grand rabbis who gathered with

Ulmann in Paris decided by majority vote such matters as permitting—but not necessarily urging—the playing of an organ at Sabbath and holiday services by a non-Jew, reducing the number of *piyutim,* and eliminating the vengeful *av ha-raḥamim* prayer. Ulmann stressed that the conference was but an "intimate discussion," not a sanhedrin or synod; its decisions were not binding on any consistory. Yet the 1856 gathering gave clear indication of rabbinical willingness to contemplate, and even advocate, moderate reforms.[87]

In fact, by the time of the conference, French Judaism had already, quietly and without official pronouncement, undergone profound change in both principle and practice. It is true that passages which called for the return to Zion and the reinstitution of sacrifices were not expunged from the liturgy. But what French Jews wrote and spoke on the subject of their status in France and their hopes for the future emptied such prayers of any real significance. Like their German counterparts, French Jews—even the more conservative among them—denied they were in exile and evidenced little longing for Jerusalem. In a High Holiday sermon delivered in the Paris consistorial temple in 1843, Lazare Wogue, one of the most influential of the French rabbis, declared baldly: "We are not a *people;* we are a *religion.*" Laymen went further. "Jerusalem," said Gerson Lévy, "is but a historical memory." And Samuel Cahen was yet more emphatic: "Jerusalem is no longer for us anything but a *memory;* it need no longer be a *hope.*" The Jewish messianic expectation was put forward as the longing for an age of fulfillment for all nations, not for a special destiny of Israel.[88] The messianic idea among the Jews, wrote Joseph Salvador, French Jewry's most prolific religious writer, was "the personification of an epoch and a new condition, of a universal dispensation bestowed upon the human race."[89] Like their counterparts to the east, French Jews also believed in the mission of Israel in the Diaspora. In propagating a purer faith, they were convinced, Jews helped bring nearer the messianic goal.

In practice, French Judaism in mid-nineteenth century underwent a thoroughgoing assimilation to Catholicism. It adapted at least as fully to its particular religious environment as German Judaism had to its Protestant milieu. That the Catholic mass remained in Latin best explains why there was no successful effort to introduce Jewish vernacular prayer. Hebrew, after all, was also a venerable classical language. That an edifying French sermon was a staple of the Catholic service explains its general acceptability among French Jews once they and their rabbis had properly learned the language. Many eagerly awaited the emergence of talented preachers. During the forties and fifties services in the consistorial temples became increasingly decorous, resembling the worshipful atmosphere of the church. Rabbis, cantors, and beadles dressed like their Catholic counterparts. The auction of synagogue honors—still carried on "in poor German" in the Paris synagogue as late as 1843—disappeared almost everywhere as soon as alternatives were found for the revenues which it raised. The confirmation ceremony gained rapid and widespread acceptance. A correspondent of the *Archives Israélites* in Bordeaux, describing how both public demand and rabbinical support had brought about its introduction there in 1841, noted proudly that the ceremony much resembled "what is elsewhere called first communion." In Paris, where it began the same year, girls wore the white dress customary at such a "religious initiation." Similarly adopted under Christian influence was the custom of bringing newborns into the synagogue for a blessing, a rite that recalled baptism.[90] In accordance with Catholic practice, Jewish weddings in the Paris temple varied from highly elaborate, with music and full illumination, to plain and simple, depending on the amount that the wedding party was able to pay. Burial practices similarly became more like their Catholic equivalents. Organ music was heard in a number of French synagogues already in the 1840s. In Marseilles the local grand rabbi defended use of the instrument in his Yom Kippur sermon in 1841. Arguing both on the basis of Halakhah and present Jewish circumstance, he pointed out that Jews in France were no longer strangers like the ancient Israelites in Babylon who had hung up their harps in sad recollection of Jerusalem.[91] All in all, French Judaism at midcentury was blending rapidly into its religious environment. It was a trend which particularly struck visitors from Germany and caused one French Jew to complain that what his coreligionists desired above all was for Gentile visitors at their service to exclaim with satisfaction: "Why it's like our own!"[92]

French Jews also resembled their Catholic counterparts in one other relevant respect: the decreasing attention they gave to religion as their educational, social, and economic status rose. Generally they remained proud of their Jewish identity and gave it occasional symbolic expression, but ever more of them relegated it to the periphery, as educated French Catholics did with their faith. A single consistorial synagogue with no more than 500 seats served the 8,000 Jews of Paris (about one-tenth of French Jewry in 1840)—and it was usually empty. Although there were also about twenty small prayer gatherings, especially for recent arrivals from Alsace and Lorraine, non-observance was not only widespread but, as Terquem was fond of pointing out, represented no disqualification for consistorial leadership. Samuel Cahen was troubled by what he perceived as an ongoing process of estrangement from Judaism. "Will liberty effect what persecution has been unable to do?" he asked with concern. But he and his fellow reformers believed that if only the exterior forms of Judaism could be made more attractive and native to their milieu, and if Judaism could be presented as a religion that from ancient times had affirmed the liberal values of post-Revolutionary France, then French Judaism would survive and flourish. Its eternal verities would then withstand the test of modernity.[93]

Thus Judaism in France was indeed transformed—after much debate, but without schism. In gaining the adoption of so much of their program, the reformers in France were remarkably successful. By the last decades of the century official French Judaism was fully reshaped to fit its religious environment. "Consistorial Judaism" had adopted moderate reform.[94] Yet Judaism in France remained unable to overcome the *tiedeur*, the characteristic lukewarmness to religious concerns, which spread ever more widely.[95] Clearly religious practice was still, as Heine had noted in 1840, without much inner conviction. Perhaps that was so, at least in part, because the reform issues had been so easily—and superficially—resolved.

In Anglican England

The Reform movement in England, in contrast to France, was born in schism. Unlike their French counterparts, the English advocates of religious reform struck out on a path of their own. Against the opposition of constituted religious authority, they established a Reform synagogue, the representative of an organizationally independent denomination.[96]

The English community had been reborn in the middle of the seventeenth century when Jews were once more officially tolerated in the country for the first time since their expulsion in 1290. Though initially the community was composed mainly of Sephardim, Ashkenazim immigrated increasingly, soon overshadowing, in numbers if not in wealth or influence, their coreligionists of Spanish and Portuguese origin. Never subject to the severe disabilities suffered by Jews elsewhere, English Jewry by the 1840s lacked only the privileges of holding certain public offices and of attending the universities in Oxford and Cambridge. It was a relatively small community of some 25,000 in 1815, reaching 35,000 in 1851, with two-thirds concentrated in London. At the top of the social scale was an aristocracy of wealth, both Sephardi and Ashkenazi, beneath them a rising middle class, and on the bottom the poor, consisting especially of recent immigrants. Few English Jews of any class possessed an advanced education either in Jewish or secular subjects.

Religious life reflected its counterpart among Christians. Like other Englishmen, an increasing number of Jews had grown apathetic to religion, departing more and more from personal observance even as they continued to show reverence for inherited forms. Already in the early eighteenth century, some were showing a degree of religious laxity unparalleled elsewhere in Europe at the time. Consumption of kosher meat fell, as did observance of the Sabbath. Secularization spread as a reversal of priorities, the pursuit of business success and temporal pleasure becoming more important than religious ritual. As in France, neither most community leaders nor most average Jews attended synagogue regularly. A census taken in 1850 showed that total Jewish participation on a particular Saturday morning amounted to only about 10 percent of English Jewry. Nevertheless, even marginally observant Jews could still consider themselves Orthodox simply because they espoused no alternative. In gentlemanly fashion, their laxity was tolerated, if not excused, by more scrupulous coreligionists.[97]

Few voices called for a fundamental revision of Judaism. Exceptional was an anonymously published radical volume by Isaac D'Israeli, a Sephardi Jew and the father of Benjamin Disraeli, who was later to become British Prime Minister. D'Israeli argued in 1833 that all the laws of Judaism, both biblical and rabbinic, were human in origin and hence were subject to repeal and amendment as the times demanded. He called upon English Jews "to educate their youth as the youth of Europe, and not of Palestine; let their Talmud be removed to an elevated shelf, to be consulted as a curiosity of antiquity, and not as a manual of education. . . . Let [Christians and Jews] only separate to hasten to the Church and to the Synagogue."[98] What remained immutable in Judaism, D'Israeli thought, was only its "genius," its philosophical foundation. And even that, apparently, was insufficiently positive to prevent him from baptizing his sons.

Less extreme were those English Jews who called for complete adherence to biblical Judaism but felt free to reject the Oral Law of the Rabbis. The former alone they believed to be divine. In elevating the Bible while derogating the Talmud, these "scripturalists" were likely responding to pervasive Gentile opinion. From Reformation times, Bible rather than Pope had been the chief authority for the Anglicans, a centrality the more firmly established during the Puritan epoch. Though eclipsed in the eighteenth century, the fundamentalist veneration of Scripture reemerged powerfully with the evangelical revival in early Victorian England. For nineteenth-century Jews to question biblical law, therefore, would have meant to challenge dominant British belief.[99] At the same time, rabbinic Judaism was coming under persistent external attack. The London Society for Promoting Christianity among the Jews, which had earlier used talmudic passages as proof texts for conversion, now disparaged rabbinism as indicative of Judaism's inferiority. "There is but one way to meet [these accusations]," responded a Jewish biblicist, to "rest our hopes and form our observances upon the Laws of God alone."[100]

Such biblicism was to distinguish the early Reform movement in England, setting it apart, at least by degree, from the continent. But it was not the only element that went into its formation. As elsewhere, the character of the religious service became a principal bone of contention. In England, too, disorder reigned in the synagogue with as much time devoted to discussing business as to concentrating on prayer. Honors were auctioned off to the highest bidder; women rarely attended; the officiant singers were satisfied to make "unharmonized noise" into "noise harmonized."[101] There were no regular sermons in the vernacular. The Ashkenazi chief rabbi, Solomon Hirschel (1762–1842), never learned English properly and was satisfied to live out his long tenure quietly among his books, oblivious to religious crisis and unsympathetic to pressures for change.

These pressures began to appear in London during the 1820s among both Ashkenazim and Sephardim. In the Great Synagogue (Ashkenazi) efforts to achieve minor reforms, such as reduction in the number of *mi sheberakh* blessings, met with only limited success. At Bevis Marks, the Spanish and Portuguese synagogue, moderate suggestions made by a Committee for Promotion and Improvement of Religious Worship likewise aroused resistance. Here it was principally more recent immigrants from the Mediterranean region who rejected Anglicization. In each synagogue, the most determined among the progressives felt frustrated at their inability to bring about decisive change.[102] As early as 1831, Isaac Lyon Goldsmid, in part out of dissatisfaction with what he regarded as the overly timid political leadership of British Jewry, threatened to withdraw from the Great Synagogue and establish an independent house of worship with the assistance of like-minded younger men. The projected synagogue, he noted, would follow the liturgy of the Hamburg Temple.[103] Remarkably similar was a request laid before the Sephardi elders in 1836 calling for "such alterations and modifications as were on the line of the changes introduced in the reform Synagogue in Hamburg and in other places."[104] Although this agitation resulted in some steps to introduce greater order and solemnity in Bevis Marks, opposition to substantive change remained overwhelming in both congregations. By the end of the decade, factional lines were drawn, and the most determined of the reformers found it increasingly difficult to remain within.

Still, the founding of an independent Reform synagogue would likely have been avoided at that time had it not been for demographic trends which brought an increasing number of the more affluent and established Jewish families to the West End of London, separating them by a considerable distance from the synagogues in which they grew up. Since neither the Great Synagogue nor Bevis Marks was at the time ready to erect branches in the area, the felt need for a local house of worship spurred the creation of a new institution that would also incorporate the sought-after reforms. That Sephardi and Ashkenazi families came together in its foundation was likewise due to nonreligious factors. The Mocattas on the Sephardi side and the Goldsmids on the Ashkenazi, who between them represented fully half of the founding members and all of the original officers, were associated by ties of business and marriage. It is hence understandable that they should want a synagogue which bridged the longstanding liturgical division and would enable them to pray together. It was to create such a bridge, not to stress political loyalty, that the new congregation was called "West London Synagogue of *British* Jews."[105]

The prehistory of this Reform synagogue begins in 1840. In that year a kind of "Reform Club" had been established in which Horatio Montefiore, brother of Sir Moses Montefiore, was prominent on the Sephardi side, and Isaac Lyon Goldsmid on the Ashkenazi. In April this group, now composed of nineteen Sephardim and five Ashkenazim, issued a declaration deploring the distance of the existing synagogues from their homes, "the length and imperfections in the order of services," the inconvenient hours, and the lack of religious instruction. Consequently, they had decided to establish their own congregation in the western section of the metropolis.[106] Shortly thereafter they informed the Frankfurt Jewish educator and historian Isaac Marcus Jost of their intentions and commissioned him to announce their desire to employ a spiritual leader who possessed requisite theological knowledge, classical education, and practical skills as an orator, preferably a man who had studied at one of the German universities.[107] At the same time they turned to David Woolf Marks (1811–1909), a young man without formal theological training, but English-born and experienced as a lecturer and reader of the Torah in Liverpool. When Marks showed interest and Jost could find no suitable German candidate, he was selected to be minister of the new congregation. His religious and political views coincided well with those of the founders. Like some of them he was a biblicist, who had caused a stir in Liverpool when he refused to read from the Torah on the second day of festivals. In his political views he favored the activism of the Goldsmids.[108]

Marks's first task was to create a new prayerbook for the congregation. Aided, among others, by Hyman Hurwitz, Professor of Hebrew at University College in London, a fellow scripturalist but also a defender of the Talmud,[109] he produced a liturgy with full English translation that did not stray far from tradition. What changes it did incorporate, Marks noted in the introduction, were justified by the fact that, as Zunz had shown, the contemporary liturgy was itself the product of historical vicissitude. *Seder Ha-Tefilot—Forms of Prayer* appeared from 1841 to 1843 in five volumes for daily, Sabbath, festival, and High Holiday worship. Like the Hamburg Temple prayerbook, it blended the Sephardi with the Ashkenazi rite, though accentuating the former; unlike Hamburg, it opened from right to left. Mainly the prayerbook curtailed repetitions and reduced the number of psalms and *piyutim,* thus abbreviating Sabbath and festival services to no more than two and a half hours including the English sermon. Some passages were omitted on account of objectionable content; for example, those referring to angels or demons, the daily malediction of slanderers, and the *kol nidre* on the eve of Yom Kippur. The most unusual alteration was the omission of the blessing preceding recitation of the Hallel (Psalms 113–118) and the reading of the Scroll of Esther, and of the first blessing for the Hanukah candles. Since the Hallel, the reading of Esther, and the lighting of candles at Hanukah had no scriptural bases, declaring of these rites that God "has commanded us" regarding them ran counter to the belief that only the Written Law was divinely revealed.[110]

The services themselves, held in a rented chapel dedicated in January 1842, did not give the impression of radical reform. Men and women sat separately; men's heads were covered; no organ accompanied the liturgy. Melodies were mostly taken from the Spanish and Portuguese tradition and sung by a male choir. Decorum was better than elsewhere: since the services started later in the morning, members tended to arrive before they began instead of straggling in later; prayers were read aloud by the minister alone; no one was called up to the Torah. Unusual was the solemn recitation of the Ten Commandments as the scroll was removed from the ark, an ancient custom but one rejected by the Rabbis. Annually, on the New Year after the *shofar* was sounded, a confirmation ceremony was held for boys and girls who had reached the age of thirteen. The liturgy was recited in Sephardi pronunciation with even Aramaic portions, like the Kaddish, translated "into the sacred Hebrew (the language of the law), a knoweldge of which we trust it will be the pride, as it is the bounden duty, of every Israelite to attain."[111]

In sharp contrast to Reformers on the continent, the West London Synagogue during its early years in no way rejected or even neutralized Israel's hope of restoration to its land. Not only was the liturgy on this subject left fully intact, even including reestablishment of the sacrifices, but Marks repeatedly preached on the simultaneous return to Zion and the coming of the Messiah. In a religious sense, he noted on one occasion, Jews still remained "a nation within a nation."[112] In another sermon, he called for mourning and fasting on the Ninth of Av, the date of the two ancient temples' destruction. He then added:

> O let it not be said, my hearers, that the tie which bound us to Zion is eternally severed; or that we have abandoned the hope of seeing her restored to her pristine grandeur. It is much to be deplored, that there should be any body of Israelites so degenerated in Jewish spirit, as to renounce publicly their belief in the advent of the Messiah, and restoration of the House of Jacob to the land of the patriarchs. . . . Whatever be the views which others may entertain, let it not be said, my hearers, that we forget Zion and her destinies. *Im eshkaḥekh yerushalayim tishkaḥ yemini*—"If we forget Jerusalem, may our right hand forget its cunning."[113]

Of course Marks hastened to add that this undiminished hope did not reduce the Jews' attachment to England and that such restoration would have to be initiated by God. But the biblical prophecy was not to be denied. Moreover, within a British religious milieu that accorded fundamentalist regard to Scripture, the Jews could scarcely be faulted for taking the sacred words seriously.

The most radical reform instituted by the West London Synagogue was the abolition of worship on the second days of holidays. Predominantly this was due to the biblicism of Marks and others among the founders. The second days, after all, were a rabbinic innovation, and as Marks put it most strongly in his dedication sermon: "For Israelites, there is but One immutable Law—the sacred volume of the Scriptures, commanded by God to be written down for the unerring guidance of his people until the end of time."[114] Double celebrations were understandable as long as the calendar had not been determined astronomically. But once that was done, to observe festivals on a day other than that prescribed meant to violate explicit scriptural command. In addition, it was felt that repetition of the festival liturgy reduced its subjective impact; and for some there was also the consideration that less celebration of holidays would make Jews more likely to attain those positions of public responsibility which precluded frequent absence.[115] More than any liturgical change, it was this blatant break with tradition which persuaded Orthodox opponents that the Reformers, although they had never declared it collectively, were indeed deniers of the Oral Law, and hence heretics.

Concerted opposition first appeared in the form of a brief "Declaration" drawn up in the late summer of 1841 at a meeting chaired by Moses Montefiore, the most prominent and inveterate opponent of the Reformers. Apparently with some reluctance, it was signed by the Ashkenazi Chief Rabbi Solomon Hirschel and then concurred in by the Sephardi religious authorities. The following January it was read from synagogue pulpits. The Declaration asserted that "any person or persons publicly declaring that he or they reject and do not believe in the authority of the Oral Law, cannot be permitted to have any communion with us Israelites in any religious rite or sacred act." In the three-month interval between the formulation of the general anathema and its promulgation, there appeared a more specific "Caution," warning against use of the West London prayerbook and declaring that anyone who did so would be accounted sinful.[116] The practical consequences of these two documents were not long in coming. The London Committee of the Board of Deputies of British Jews, chaired by Montefiore, refused to recognize the Reformers as consituting a legitimate synagogue, and hence would not certify Marks, as its official secretary, to register marriages. Couples were forced to go before a public registrar and then have their religious ceremony in the synagogue. Mixed marriages between Orthodox and Reform partners became an issue when Herschel's successor as chief rabbi, Nathan Marcus Adler, refused to sanction one such a union without a promise that the Reform partner would break her tie with the West London Synagogue and conform to Orthodoxy. Only in 1857, when Parliament passed a "Dissenters' Chapels Bill," was what their opponents contemptuously called the "Burton Street Place of Worship" explicitly recognized for purposes of registration. Similar was the refusal to provide a proper burial, or any at all, for West London members in the cemeteries belonging to Bevis Marks and the Great Synagogue, an attitude which resulted in the Reformers' early purchase of their own cemetery.[117] Yet many British Jews deplored such actions. Some synagogues had refused to read the ban; the one in Plymouth had burned it. Moreover, social and family ties between Reformers and Orthodox were not easily severed. Thus, though much bitter feeling remained, in the course of time the Reform synagogue became a familiar, if not entirely welcome feature of London's Jewish landscape.

The founding members of the West London Synagogue seem to have been mostly, but not exclusively men of early middle age, dominantly from the Sephardi community. They represented a portion of those established, wealthy families who could trace their ancestry in England for generations. Yet soon there were also less affluent congregants, and the synagogue prided itself on making no distinctions between rich and poor.[118] Among the founders were some traditional Jews, like Abraham Mocatta, who never rode on the Sabbath and was most reluctant to cut his ties with Bevis Marks; also Francis Henry Goldsmid, whose obituary mentions his "strict adherence to all Mosaic rites and ceremonies."[119] Such conservatives, prominent also in the second generation, used their influence to restrain the West London Synagogue from radicalism, resisting efforts to widen the distance from Orthodoxy. During succeeding decades the congregation grew modestly in size, moving to larger quarters first in 1849, when it numbered about 150 families, and then again in 1870. Marks gained independent prestige when he succeeded Hurwitz first as teacher, and then as professor of Hebrew at University College. A second minister was soon appointed, and then a third to assist him; a Jewish school was established under the auspices of the congregation. In the course of time the synagogue instituted a few further reforms: an organ in 1859, a mixed choir, removal of the petition for restoration of the sacrificial offerings, and a few prayers in English. Otherwise the pattern established at the beginning remained unchanged.[120]

Its particular identity made the West London Synagogue something other than simply an extension of the German Reform movement. It was more a response to the specific circumstances of Anglo-Jewry than to the ideology of a Geiger or Holdheim. Yet despite the unusual qualities which set it apart from the continent, British Reform was by no means isolated from its counterparts elsewhere, nor so completely different from them. We know that Benjamin Goldsmid, Isaac Lyon's uncle, had early established close ties with David Friedländer, Lazarus Bendavid, and Israel Jacobson.[121] In 1839 Anna Maria Goldsmid, Francis' sister, translated into English twelve sermons by Gotthold Salomon, preacher of the Hamburg Temple, noting admiringly in the preface that Germany was the "land of profound Hebrew historians, scholars, and theologians."[122] British Reformers expressed awareness of the ritual changes undertaken in various German communities.[123] Even the biblicism of the English Reformers was not so far removed from similar expressions in Germany. After all, the debate there too was over the divinity of the Oral Law, over whether it could, in fact, be traced back to Sinai. To be sure, the English biblicists put the distinction more sharply and drew more radical conclusions, but they did not call themselves "Neo-Karaites." In his dedicatory sermon Marks stressed that only the Written Law was divine, but he also praised the rabbinic writings as "a valuable aid for the elucidation of many passages in Scripture," and added that "we feel proud of them as a monument of the zeal and mental activity of our ancestors." Moreover, as one of the leading Reformers pointed out, since the West London liturgy retained the basic prayers considered obligatory by the Talmud, its ritual, at least, did not amount to a rejection of the Oral Law; the modifications made were "in perfect harmony with the mind of the Talmud and of the later casuists." Even the abolition of the second days of festivals had been proposed by German Reform rabbis well before it was undertaken in the West London Synagogue.[124]

In Manchester, where a Reform congregation was established in 1856, the German influence was more obvious and direct.[125] This relatively large provincial community by midcentury embraced a substantial number of immigrants from central Europe. As early as 1838 it had introduced regular sermons, and at the time of the Reform agitation in London it had undertaken various measures to impose decorum. But Tobias Theodores (1808–1886), an intellectual of sorts who had grown up in Berlin during the period of the Beer Temple and come to Manchester in 1826, desired to go further. As a scripturalist, he opposed attributing divine authority to the Talmud and its practical consequences, though like the German Reformers, he wanted to accord the rabbinic literature a place of honor in Jewish history. Beginning in the 1840s, he pressed for more decisive religious reforms of the sort that had been instituted in Germany. After a while his views began to enjoy considerable support among recently immigrated German Jewish merchants, though their commitment was less ideological than his. By 1856 Theodores was prominent within a newly established Reform Association consisting of forty-six members of whom twenty-nine were born in Germany. The group declared for the establishment of their own house of worship, adopted the prayerbook and ritual of the West London Synagogue, but differed in that conservatives among them succeeded in retaining the second days of holidays. The building, which was dedicated by David Woolf Marks in 1858, separated the sexes, but included an organ. With room for 400 men and 250 women, it was about as large as the new synagogue built by the Orthodox at the same time. Their first rabbi was the Hungarian-born Dr. Solomon Schiller-Szinessy. Although once a student of Aaron Chorin, he was a religious conservative, whose sympathies were never wholly with the group. When, in 1860, the majority decided to abolish the second days of holidays, he chose to resign. His successor was the more radical Gustav Gottheil, later to become the rabbi of Temple Emanu-El in New York.

Aside from Manchester, Reform in England spread only to a small group in Hull (during the 1850s), and in 1873 to Bradford, which also had a considerable number of central European immigrants.[126] The West London Synagogue itself did not grow rapidly in the second generation and failed to develop daughter congregations elsewhere in the city. It was soon apparent that Orthodoxy in England would remain dominant, with Reform but grudgingly tolerated.

Reform's failure to gain greater influence in Britain requires explanation. One apparent reason was that, as in France, and to some extent in Germany, the synagogues which called themselves Orthodox in England soon met the Reform challenge by adopting much of its program. One Orthodox Jew exulted over the "wholesome agitation" that was destroying the prevalent religious apathy. Even as the Reformers were seceding from Orthodox congregations, the Western Synagogue, most independent of the traditional houses of worship in London, was itself considering a variety of ritual reforms. Nathan Marcus Adler, who was elected Ashkenazi chief rabbi in 1844, soon formulated a series of regulations which, like the German *Synagogenordnungen,* brought order and solemnity to the service. Such measures enjoyed the support of a substantial body of "progressives" who chose to remain within Orthodoxy.[127] Not only were branches of traditional synagogues established in the West End of London during the 1850s, but ritual modifications in form, if not in content, now became widespread. Choirs were introduced, as were English sermons; the auction of honors was abolished. Within a few years changes that seemed revolutionary in the thirties and early forties had become commonplace almost everywhere. Orthodoxy seemed no less native to its environment than Reform. A visitor to the Great Synagogue after its redecoration in 1852 could describe it as "on the whole recalling a handsome English Protestant Church." The communal vocabulary, too, was distinctly British, employing terms such as "vestry," "wardens," and "Guardians." Clerical gowns and canonicals had long been *de rigueur* for the chief rabbi and for synagogue officiants.[128]

Increasingly, Orthodoxy could believably claim to be the Jewish counterpart of the Church of England, with its chief rabbi the rough equivalent of the Archbishop of Canterbury, its values in complete harmony with the religious milieu. The British, too, venerated tradition and constituted authority; they too had little love for revolutionary change. Englishmen regarded the Book of Common Prayer as sacrosanct, to be transmitted through the generations "in its pristine simplicity, glory and excellence." Alterations in liturgy, English Christians believed together with Orthodox Jews, could take place only with permission of the highest ecclesiastical authority. The Jewish Reformers, by contrast, could be condemned as usurpers of such authority: they were "not qualified to innovate," wrote a would-be conciliator.[129] Worse, they were "sectarians" or "schismatics," terms whose negative connotations in England the Orthodox were easily able to exploit. Unlike the United States, nineteenth-century England did not regard itself as religiously pluralistic. Spiritually bolstered by the established Anglican faith, it tolerated other Christian denominations, but clearly stigmatized them as outside the inner circle. The Jewish Reformers, too, could be made to appear as less than fully legitimate and were in fact branded "the Secession Congregation." With little success the West London Synagogue tried to shake off the analogy, claiming that they did not see themselves as dissenters, however much they might be characterized as such by others. The notion of secession, they pleaded, was odious to their feelings as well.[130]

For a generation, Orthodox spiritual and lay leaders kept the Reformers outside the established structure. Not until 1874 was the West London Synagogue granted representation on the Board of Deputies of British Jews, and then only by a majority vote of three. Persistent opposition came from two powerful men: the chief rabbi, Nathan Marcus Adler (1803–1890), and the titular lay head of British Jewry, Moses Montefiore (1784–1885). Adler held his position for forty-five years; Montefiore remained president of the Board of Deputies from 1838 to 1874. Already in his native Germany Adler had been a vociferous opponent of Reform. Once in England, he rapidly established his authority in all religious matters. Not only was he the chief rabbi— Adler was the *only* recognized rabbi in England. Officiants at synagogues were termed merely "ministers," a designation similarly applied to Marks, who indeed lacked rabbinical training and could certainly claim no equivalent religious authority. Since the West London Synagogue remained beyond Adler's authority, he used his position to stigmatize it as a pariah of English Jewry and refused to enter its premises even on ceremonial occasions.[131]

Still more devastating for the Reformers was having Moses Montefiore as their sworn enemy. Just at the time they were contemplating an independent synagogue, Montefiore was gaining new prestige in England and among Jews everywhere. In 1840, already knighted by Queen Victoria, he set off on his celebrated journey to the Orient on behalf of the libeled Damascus Jews. Upon his return, the successful intervention in Syria earned him the privilege of adding supporters to his coat-of-arms, a token of royal approval and regard. Though not fully observant in his youth, Montefiore had become a strict Orthodox Jew by the 1830s and spurned any diminution in the obligations imposed by the Oral Law no less than by the Written. At the beginning, he did his best to stifle the infant Reform congregation, even though his younger brother was prominent among the founders. When that failed, he simply made every effort to assure that the schismatics would remain outside the umbrella of institutional legitimacy.[132] Yet even had Montefiore been less inveterate an enemy of Reform, his symbolic presence alone, as a strictly Orthodox Jew who enjoyed the highest esteem of the Queen and of world Jewry, would have been sufficient to banish any notion that the Reformers might be better Englishmen. Wealth and social status, recognized authority and political influence, remained within the camp of Orthodoxy. Even lax observance could find toleration within its ranks without apparent stigma. Those who nevertheless chose to join the Reform congregation must have done so mainly for religious reasons.

However, the West London Synagogue was also itself partly responsible for the failure to gain wider support. In attempting to disarm critics, it became apologetic, stressing that the changes instituted at the beginning were final, that it would go no further.[133] In this regard the British Reformers did indeed differ from their German contemporaries. Absent from their intellectual world were the idea of religious evolution, so central to the ideology of continental Reform, and its supporting discipline of *Wissenschaft des Judentums*.[134] Moreover, the fixed commitment to scripturalism soon proved a practical liability as historical criticism undermined the revelatory status not only of Talmud but also of Torah. In succeeding decades the West London

Synagogue appeared ever more a creature of the years which gave it birth, not an institution developing with the times.

The European Reform Movement at Midcentury

By the second half of the nineteenth century, the Reform movement had spread well beyond Germany. Its impact was pervasive; the sense that Judaism needed to adapt to its modern context, whether only in externals or in fundamental outlook, was denied by few Jews in western or most of central Europe. Differences concerned the extent of religious change and were the result of varying political, social, and intellectual contexts. In some places the movement was embodied in independent institutions, in others it merely influenced existing ones.

At the same time profound differences had arisen among reformers (in the generic sense), leading increasingly to a sense of denominational, or at least factional, allegiance. As the Reform movement crystallized both intellectually and institutionally, it also narrowed from a broad stream that embraced all opponents of the premodern status quo to a narrower, more clearly marked current which rejected not only the religious mentality of the ghetto, but also the modernist Orthodoxy which altered form but not substance. The name "Reform" became associated with particular institutions: the Hamburg Temple, the Reform Community in Berlin, the West London Synagogue. Or it represented a permanent faction in the community. Thus by midcentury a vaguely defined movement for religious modernization was becoming a denominational stance, either outside or within the institutional structure, separating itself from the relatively more traditional positions which had become its competitors. In succeeding decades, Reform—or Liberal—Jews in Europe set about consolidating their particular form of Jewish identity.

5

Consolidation and Further Advance

Reform Within the German Communities

The twenty years following the 1848 Revolution in Germany were not a propitious time for religious liberalism. Democratic idealism, which had fueled the abortive uprising, had been dissipated by disunity and crushed by military force. In succeeding years the conception of the state as Christian regained influence and the church reasserted itself as the chief ideological support of autocracy. Religious liberalism was seen as partly responsible for what was now regarded as a sinful revolt against constituted authority. In the fifties, Protestant theologians who espoused orthodoxy held sway in universities while their lesser colleagues implanted traditional doctrines in the schools. Catholicism experienced a religious revival, successfully instilling stricter morality among its faithful and a piety which rejected enlightenment and rationalist religion. Earlier liberalizing Catholic demands for reform in ritual and even the introduction of a German-language mass were forgotten as a new ultramontanism linked German Catholics more closely with Rome. Over all, religion ceased to be a progressive influence in German society.

In this age of political and religious reaction progress was channeled into the economic sphere where it could strengthen state power. Germany began a process of rapid industrialization, which had its intellectual counterpart in the emergence of philosophical materialism. The earlier systems of idealist philosophers from Kant to Hegel, which had sought to mediate between reason and religion, went into eclipse, displaced by an outlook closely related to the rapidly developing natural sciences and distinctly hostile to metaphysical concerns. Schopenhauer, the philosopher of individual will and denier of social progress, became the favored German thinker. While philosophers were detaching their discipline from theology, many average people began thinking in frankly materialistic terms that were starkly at odds with the rediscovered pietism of the churches. Thus conflicting trends beset Germany in this period, setting against each other the academy and the church, the secular ambitions of the rising bourgeoisie and the unyielding dogmatism of the clergy.[1] Such a climate was hostile to mediation within Judaism as well.

All of German Jewry suffered from the newly repressive political atmosphere. German states which had granted the Jew equality in 1848 and 1849 withdrew or restricted it during the following decade. Their hopes disappointed, some German Jews chose to emigrate to the United States, which offered both political freedom and economic opportunity. Among them were rabbis like David Einhorn and Samuel Adler, who had played important roles in the European Reform movement. Others directed their energies to the economic sphere, participating productively in the industrial expansion. Fewer German Jews converted to Christianity in the years 1848–1878 than either before or after, probably because of diminished antisemitism in this period along with expanding economic opportunities. But religious indifference grew.[2] Increasing numbers of German Jews adopted an openly secularist posture. They identified minimally as Jews, participating only very occasionally in synagogue services as a symbolic, pious, or nostalgic gesture. Since Christianity was no longer perceived as advancing with modern culture, it ceased to serve as a model for the role of progressive religion in society. Abraham Geiger became its severe and persistent critic. Protestantism had lost its spirit of free inquiry, he now claimed, while Catholicism had reverted to the worst dogmatism.[3] Indeed, if Christian society offered any model at all, it was for the Orthodox and the indifferent. For the former, the church demonstrated how religion could uphold traditional doctrines and values; for the latter, the new philosophy justified materialism, self-interest, and religious neglect. What remained of liberal idealism among Jews rapidly became secular, setting itself against religion as irrelevant or reactionary. In such circumstances, any message of religious progress that Reform might seek to trumpet would be perceived by some as politically subversive and by many as religiously out of tune. Its leaders had no choice but to reconcile themselves to working quietly. Each in his own community tried to move forward gradually: winning greater local support, institutionalizing principles enunciated earlier, accepting compromises, and preparing for better times.

During the first years of the political reaction, Reform suffered palpable setbacks. As in the twenties and thirties, some German governments once again regarded religious change among Jews with suspicion and displeasure. In Berlin, police carefully watched the Sunday services of the Reform Congregation; in Bavaria state authorities encouraged a resurgence of Orthodoxy. The most heavy-handed attempt to reverse religious reforms occurred in Mecklenburg–Schwerin. There the successive rabbinates of Samuel Holdheim and David Einhorn had produced a wide variety of modifications in the service, which made the Schwerin synagogue one of the most reformed in Germany. The government, which had hitherto looked favorably on these changes, reversed itself in the early fifties, joining withdrawal of newly gained citizenship with removal of religious autonomy. After Einhorn was forced to leave in 1852, the archduke took over personal control of the community, himself appointing a new lay leadership and a rabbi who was rigidly orthodox. The "baneful excrescences of the reform tendency" would thus be excised. New regulations brought about a speedy reversal.

All synagogues in the duchy, they stipulated, would again have a lattice in front of the women's section, the reading desk in the center, recitation of the full Torah portion each week, and a complete Hebrew service "without any abbreviation, change, or innovation." Religion teachers who gave sermons in the smaller communities would henceforth first submit their manuscripts for approval to the chief rabbi. Although in the earlier period traditionalists had been allowed to have their own separate service, modernists now found the government unresponsive to their own similar requests.[4]

Yet Mecklenburg–Schwerin was an extreme instance. In most places the process of reform was slowed but not forcibly reversed. In the small towns, where most German Jews continued to live until the last decades of the century, as well as in the larger cities, various degrees of synagogue reform were gradually adopted. As their acculturation advanced and their economic status improved, German Jews from the countryside, too, wanted their synagogue to provide the same edification and dignified worship to be found in the cities. Only with the massive migration of less traditional, upwardly mobile Jews to the cities after 1871 did some of the rural communities, especially in southern and western Germany, revert to Orthodoxy.[5] Though initially thrown on the defensive in the early fifties, the Reform movement throughout Germany gradually regained some of its earlier momentum. By the sixties and seventies it became apparent that not Reform, but strict Orthodoxy, as a shrinking minority, would have to struggle for survival.

In one German community after another liberals reasserted or gained control of the community board and moved ahead with plans for moderate reform.[6] Unwilling to impose change on the traditionalists, the Reformers either compromised, as in the smaller communities, or, in the larger ones, offered differing religious services for each group. Often it was the construction of a new synagogue which provided the occasion for undertaking reforms. The rising economic status of German Jewry during this period created the means for building impressive and elegant structures in the larger Jewish communities. In Prussia alone, between the end of the fifties and the mid-sixties, more than forty new synagogues were built.[7] The prevalent style of this new sacral architecture, commissioned mainly by liberal community boards, reflected a regained historical consciousness. From about 1850 to 1880 that style was dominantly Moorish, a striking outward expression of the Jews' Oriental heritage. These were the years in which German Jewry moved ahead to the full political emancipation that was finally confirmed in 1871. By building synagogues in the Moorish style of Islamic Spain, it was in effect declaring that political and cultural integration did not require abdication of origins; the synagogue did not have to resemble the church. To be sure, there was no Jewish nationalism in this, but there was a greater willingness to let historical difference stand out for all to see. Not to be denied, the Oriental heritage of the Jews was now to be transplanted onto German soil. Thus the Württemberg rabbi, Joseph Maier, could say at the dedication of a new synagogue in the Moorish style, "Yes, we wish you well beloved Stuttgart, our Jerusalem," by which he did not mean to deny the historical significance of Jerusalem, but to affirm that Jews and their particular religion, visibly expressed in Oriental architecture, were now fully at home in a German city.[8]

The most magnificent example of the new architecture was the massive, opulent synagogue which the Berlin community, now numbering about 20,000, dedicated in the heart of the city in 1866. Contemporaries described it as a "modern Alhambra." Built not in a courtyard but directly on the street, it proclaimed Jewish equality in

Germany. Unlike the synagogue of the Reform Congregation, completed in the Classical style in 1854, it also bespoke the desire to preserve visible difference. This "New Synagogue" became the house of worship for the liberal Jews in Berlin while the Old Synagogue, remodeled in 1856, was now to serve the traditionalists. The community board gave much attention to developing a revised order of service for the New Synagogue, which would keep Hebrew for the basic rubrics but add German prayers and hymns.[9] It chose Joseph Aub, a moderate reformer serving as rabbi in Mainz, to be the regular preacher.

As the Moorish style of the structure asserted an independent historical tradition, so did the music of the New Synagogue avoid Christian models. Solomon Sulzer of Vienna, then still the most prominent liturgical composer, had borrowed generously from Catholic church music. In Berlin, Louis Lewandowski (1821–1894), who was chief choir master, resisted the incorporation of Protestant elements, though he did incorporate some melodies from German folk tunes. In the foreword to his second collection of compositions he said that he had sought "to hold on to the character and peculiarity of the *old melodic modes* and to ennoble them by harmonization." The ornate, romantic style which Lewandowski developed complemented well the rich adornments of the New Synagogue. Since he composed for congregational song as well as multivoice choir, for synagogues with an organ and for those without, Lewandowski's compositions soon became the standard in Germany and spread rapidly to German immigrant synagogues in America as well.[10]

To various degrees the new houses of Jewish worship throughout Germany introduced Reform-inspired structural modifications. Most common was the transfer of the reading desk from the center to the area in front of the ark, the construction of a choir loft, and the removal of the lattice in front of the women's gallery. Initially less common, and consistently controversial, was the installation of an organ. As scholars have noted, it was the organ that became the "shibboleth" dividing Orthodox from Reform. In Berlin, the community board collected responsa, for and against, before deciding in favor of installing an organ in the New Synagogue.[11] A large group of community members had petitioned for its introduction along with other reforms. While opponents of the organ throughout Germany continued to argue against it on halakhic grounds and as an imitation of the Gentiles, it was now less often perceived as either forbidden, necessarily foreign, or inextricably linked with radical Reform. Geiger argued that the organ was not a Christian invention at all but an Israelite one, recalling the *magrefah* played in the Jerusalem Temple. The time had finally come to reclaim "our ancient heirloom" from the Christians, grateful that they had perfected the instrument.[12] Even moderates increasingly agreed.

Except for a very few earlier instances, the introduction of the organ into community synagogues began in the early 1850s, especially in the Rhine valley, and then spread rapidly thereafter as new structures made provisions for the instrument. By the early twentieth century there were 130 "organ synagogues" *(Orgelsynagogen),* at least one in every major Jewish community except Hannover. It was the organ to which the Orthodox now pointed as the most visible trademark of Reform, their rejection of it serving as an important element of their own specific identity and self-definition.[13]

Judging by the rapid spread of cathedral-like synagogues, choral music, organs, and lengthy stylized sermons, most German Jews must have derived religious satisfaction—or at least pride—from the formal, dignified, even awesome atmosphere in which their worship was now conducted. Apparently they were content mostly to listen to words spoken and sung by professionals. While common at later times, criticism of this trend during its growth is rare. Exceptional, therefore, but noteworthy is an anonymous article published in Philippson's *Allgemeine Zeitung des Judentums* as early as 1849.[14] The author complained that reformed services tended to be stiff and pedantically formal, as if attempting to imitate the etiquette of court ceremonial; sermons were depressingly predictable in form and in content. No longer was the congregation composed of individual worshipers who were given occasional special roles, like being called up to the Torah on account of a personal event; it was an undifferentiated mass. More generally, he pointed out what Orthodox critics had said repeatedly: religious reforms exercised an initial attraction on account of their novelty, but as soon as curiosity wore off, the surge of enthusiasm dissipated and indifference returned. Further reform simply repeated the pattern. Yet though he made suggestions for greater congregational participation, including discussion of the sermon, this sympathetic critic saw little hope that Judaism in whatever form could fully overcome the pervasive secularizing tendencies of the age. "Modern man has too little need for a religious service," he wrote, "the old obligation to participate in worship, which our ancestors felt, is no longer present."

Nonetheless, the process of religious reform went forward in the apparent hope of making meaningful at least those few occasions when the average German Jew would attend the synagogue. Perhaps the most significant achievement of the German Reformers during the quarter century after 1848 was the creation of modified prayerbooks and their introduction for use by liberal factions in the larger communities.[15] Until the fifties only the independent Hamburg Temple and the Berlin Reform Congregation possessed Reform prayerbooks. Some German communities had abbreviated the service by skipping over pieces regarded as irrelevant, incomprehensible, or offensive to Gentiles. Modification of the Hebrew text in the malediction of "slanderers," to now read "slander," became widespread. But everywhere the *sidur* used in the community synagogues remained the traditional one.

In 1848 Rabbi Joseph Maier of Stuttgart presented an interim solution to the increasing discrepancy between what he believed many worshipers wanted to express and what the prayerbook and public service offered. As a purely personal venture, he published a book of prayers and devotions, mostly in German, which could be used by individuals in the synagogue during the public worship—though it would not match it. In Maier's prayerbook ideologically problematic Hebrew prayers were either simply omitted, replaced by a German substitute, or fundamentally altered in the German paraphrase. Since the prayerbook was not intended for adoption by Württemberg Jewry, Maier felt free to address himself to what he regarded as the altered religious sensibility of those worshipers who derived no edification from the traditional prayerbook. For the present they would have to make do with reading Maier's prayers silently during the traditional public service. But clearly it was the rabbi's hope that some day his prayerbook, or one like it, would be used by entire congregations.[16]

The following stage of liturgical reform was to bring the German paraphrases into the community prayerbook while still leaving the Hebrew text virtually unchanged. This was Rabbi Joseph Aub's intent in the Mainz community prayerbook which he edited in 1853. Such strategy was predicated on the editor's belief that the traditionalists among the worshipers, those who maintained belief in the return to Zion and restoration of animal sacrifices, would be the ones praying in Hebrew, while the modernists, who abjured those beliefs, would feel comfortable with silent recitation of the modified German text. Aub's prayerbook was the first of many such attempts to solve the problem of community division through liturgical bifurcation according to language. Prayerbooks where vernacular renditions differed from the Hebrew originals were to characterize much of Jewish liturgy in Germany and elsewhere thereafter.

The prayerbook which Abraham Geiger prepared for the liberal sector of the Breslau community in 1854 followed this same pattern in that it was more radical in its German paraphrases than its Hebrew text. Thus, for example, the German version alone transformed resurrection into the vaguer "renewal of life." Yet Geiger went further. He introduced some ideological changes in the Hebrew as well, bringing the liturgy rather closely into line with that of the Hamburg Temple. Specifically, the Hebrew text omitted the words "from among all the nations" in the blessing referring to the chosenness of Israel before the reading of the Torah, and it was altered for prayers dealing with sacrifices (including the uncompleted command to sacrifice Isaac) and the restoration to Zion. But unlike Hamburg, the Breslau service, except for a few congregational hymns, was conducted almost entirely in Hebrew, the prayerbook opened from right to left, and the service lasted longer—even though here too the weekly reading from the Torah was spread out over three years instead of one. Judging by views on liturgy he expressed earlier, Geiger would have preferred more thoroughgoing change and considerably more German in the public service.[17] But he was definitely not interested in producing a merely private prayerbook. The collective acceptance of his liturgy, he apparently realized, was far more important than ideological consistency. And in fact his was the first thoroughly modified prayerbook to be accepted by a major community for its liberal synagogue. It soon gained entry into other German communities as well.

Elsewhere similar reformed prayerbooks, composed by local rabbis, were adopted about the same time and thereafter. When efforts by Rabbi Leopold Stein of Frankfurt to create a common reformed liturgy, at least for southwestern Germany, failed, Stein himself published a prayerbook especially for the new synagogue built by the Frankfurt community in 1860.[18] Stein's liturgy introduced a new technique, which would likewise be used later. Not only did the Hebrew and German texts of his prayerbook offer ideologically variant alternatives, but even within the Hebrew itself, where necessary, it printed the "older form" in smaller letters alongside or beneath the revised one.[19] Thus the intrusion of Reform even into the Hebrew text did not have to bind those who rejected it.

With Aub's call to the Berlin rabbinate in 1866 and the completion of its massive New Synagogue, Germany's largest Jewish community was also ready for a revised prayerbook. Aub's three-volume *sidur* followed the Reform trend on basic ideological points, but it was more conservative than Geiger's liturgy, for example refusing to compromise the election of Israel. Four years later Geiger himself published a second edition of his prayerbook, in which remaining references to animal sacrifices and to the longing to reestablish the ancient Jerusalem Temple were removed.[20] But while Geiger as liturgist was moving in the direction of a more consistent reflection of Reform ideology, his own former community in Breslau was taking a step in the opposite direction, back toward tradition. The Breslau leadership intended that the new community synagogue, then under construction, should serve the entire community. It therefore required a prayerbook more widely acceptable than Geiger's, which had been used only in the community's Reform service. The lay leadership thus charged Geiger's successor in Breslau, Manuel Joël, to come up with an acceptable compromise between the traditional prayerbook and Geiger's.[21] Joël, who was a follower of Zacharias Frankel's school, agreed to use Geiger's first edition as the basis, retaining the fundamental ideological tendency with which he sympathized. But he modified it somewhat in a traditional direction and, as Stein had done, provided the traditional texts as well, in smaller characters, whenever there were modifications in the Hebrew. Thus in Breslau conservatives could quietly read the old formulas while the cantor intoned the new, just as in other places congregants glanced into a book of German paraphrases while listening to the Hebrew words of the traditional service. Through such devices the main, or the liberal, synagogue in each community could accommodate the broadest possible spectrum, though of course unbending traditionalists continued to have their own services while the religiously indifferent or agnostics simply stayed away.

It was not until the late sixties that German Reformers felt the time ripe for a new collective enterprise. During two decades the institutionalization of Reform principles in community synagogues and the composition of prayerbooks had gone forward despite the unfavorable environment. With no choice but to compromise, even the more radical Reformers had learned to accept the slow pace of local efforts. But it was less than they had hoped for. Geiger complained of "carefree security" and "indolent lassitude." With the battle for emancipation nearing successful conclusion, Jews no longer felt any external stimulus to defend their Jewishness and they had lost interest in Judaism as a religion. Jewish equality had ceased to be a political cause, Jewish faith and practice were no longer a personal need. In the Jewish community, he noted, "deadly silence reigns." While the Jews themselves had progressed, Judaism had not; religion had failed to become a spiritual force in the lives of its modern adherents.[22] To be sure, Jewish *Wissenschaft* had made progress. Indeed, Geiger's own most important studies date from this period. But scholarship had too much withdrawn itself from contemporary concerns. In a letter to his friend, the great Jewish bibliographer Moritz Steinschneider, Geiger scoffed bitterly at the *Wissenschaft* that was "cold as marble," which attempted to rid itself of all presuppositions and was content to leave Judaism unchanged by its efforts.[23]

Some of the old Reform issues no longer mattered as much. Those who had once fought to remove hats at worship, Geiger now noted, "have since grown gray and bald and cover their heads gladly; their youthful ardor has cooled."[24] Most liturgical issues had been resolved by the new prayerbooks and orders of service. But the lack of uniformity was troublesome. Rabbis and lay progressives felt the need for broader sanction of the reforms they had introduced already and those they were still planning. Of continuing major concern were certain questions of Jewish law. Halakhic forms still prevailed with regard to exemption from levirate marriage. Women whose husbands had disappeared were, in accordance with Jewish law, still left in the status of *agunot,* straw widows unable to remarry. Few rabbis felt free to violate Halakhah in order to marry a Jew of priestly lineage to a divorced woman.[25] There was discontent, as well, with the wedding ceremony since it gave no independent voice to the bride. Such practical matters, it was now increasingly felt, warranted a new national gathering of all who were interested in talking about these issues and perhaps taking a unified stand.[26]

But it was not alone the persistence of halakhic problems that renewed the desire for collective counsel. By the mid-sixties, the spiritual atmosphere in Germany was once again turning a bit more favorable to liberal religion. A newly formed "Protestant Association" called for a religious renewal that would harmonize Christianity with modern European culture. Its leaders urged far-reaching reforms within the church in order to make that rapprochement possible. They also recognized that progress was likely only if clergy were joined by intellectuals and laity in a common effort. Every year or two, beginning in 1865, they held conferences chaired by J. C. Bluntschli, a professor of law at Heidelberg. Among Jewish reformers, too, as early as the time of the 1848 Revolution, there had been considerable sentiment that laymen and scholars should be included, along with rabbis, in any collective forum. However, all efforts at that time to create a broadly based synod failed and the project remained in limbo for twenty years. Only with the newly provided Protestant example did the concept again win active support. As one layman put it, "Only in the most recent period, with everyone again becoming more and more aware that the religious question is, after all, the essence of all life and striving, has the Reform movement, on Jewish soil, again gained greater impetus."[27] Thus when Ludwig Philippson began to propagandize actively in his newspaper for a synod, he found encouraging support.

A rabbinical conference, attended by twenty-four German rabbis in Cassel in 1868, adopted a number of resolutions on the liturgy, but basically became the preliminary assembly to prepare a synod to take place the following year in Leipzig.[28] Although it was understood that the synod would be liberal in character, its organizers did not mention religious reform among its purposes. The stated goal was rather to overcome religious disunity and to promote the preservation of Judaism. Eighty-three rabbis, scholars, and lay leaders from sixty communities in Germany and elsewhere participated in the synod. Among them were conservatives like Rabbi Manuel Joël of Breslau as well as radical rationalists. The majority, however, was moderately progressive. Since the participants did not possess the right to act for their communities, the synod's authority depended entirely upon the respect that the Jewish public would freely grant it. Its opponents necessarily claimed that the institution possessed no authority whatever, since halakhic scholars alone, not a popular assembly, were entitled to decide religious issues. But even the participants themselves refused to feel bound by votes in which they did not concur or which seemed unworkable in their own communities.

Thus the Leipzig synod tried to avoid extreme positions that would narrow the base of support among its own members and on the outside. Its resolutions often simply affirmed practices that were already widespread in the larger communities, disappointing men like Geiger who wanted it to move ahead. Every radical suggestion was defeated, or simply sent to a committee, while more conservative measures found approval. The synod decided, for example, that Bible instruction of Jewish children should not take historical criticism into account. The Hebrew language, source of so much bitter dispute at the Frankfurt rabbinical conference a generation earlier, here received affirmation as an essential component of Jewish education. Hebrew was important, the resolution said, not only as the language of Scripture and the language in which Judaism's unique religious idea had been expressed through the ages, but it "had also been and should remain the firm and spiritual bond among all members of the Jewish collectivity." The synod did take a Reform position in giving its imprimatur to organ music in the synagogue, in urging the elaboration of universal themes of the liturgy, and in recommending that the weekly prophetic portion, the Haftarah, be read in the vernacular. But on a close vote it opted for a one-year cycle of Torah reading instead of the triennial one, and it defeated Geiger's suggestion that certain irrelevant or offensive special Torah portions (*Parah* and *Zakhor*) be eliminated. One initially skeptical participant was in the end forced to admit that the synod had been essentially constructive, that it had not departed from the "positive viewpoint."

In general, a festive atmosphere prevailed in Leipzig. Despite its lack of formal authority, the synod enjoyed the status of an international gathering, with representation from Belgium, England, Austria–Hungary, and the United States. It could claim the achievement of finally bringing together for religious purposes the various strands of Jewish leadership. They were all represented in its presidium. Its elected president was the noted ethnologist and knowledgeable Jew, Professor Moritz Lazarus, symbolizing Jewish achievement in general culture; one of the vice presidents was the most significant Jewish theologian and scholar present, Abraham Geiger; and the

Officers of the Leipzig Synod:
Joseph von Wertheimer, Moritz Lazarus, and Abraham Geiger.

second vice president, Joseph von Wertheimer, retired head of the Vienna community, symbolized lay leadership, philanthropy, and worldly attainment. Though they regretted that attendance was not larger, the members felt exhilaration at the demonstrated strength of liberal Judaism across central Europe and believed they were acting for unity and progress. Lazarus' closing speech roused them to the larger fight for idealism and religiosity, the struggle against the materialism of the age. He made his listeners feel that Judaism, in progressive form, not only was still alive but still had a crucial role to play in Europe.

Had it not been for the Franco–Prussian War, which necessitated postponement of the synod's second meeting to 1871, the momentum generated at Leipzig might have made the new institution into a genuine focal point for progressive Judaism. However, when the synod met in Augsburg after an interval of two years, the earlier festive atmosphere had dissipated. Attendance, instead of increasing as hoped, had declined. Under the spell of newly strident German patriotism, the second synod lacked the cosmopolitan aura of the first gathering. In addition, significant conservatives were missing this time among the fifty-two registered members. Philippson's failure to publicize the synod and his own absence because of personal pique at not having been elected to the presidium in Leipzig did not help matters either. As Lazarus, who was again elected president, recognized in his opening remarks, this gathering, unlike the first, could not justify itself merely as a symbolic gesture and as a beginning; it would have to produce tangible results. And, in fact, some resolutions of substance did win approval at Augsburg, especially in the area of marital law and custom. The synod gave its support to the double-ring ceremony, then already widely in practice, and urged that bride as well as groom be permitted to speak a wedding vow. By a large majority the members agreed that where a dead person had been identified by non-Jewish judicial authorities or a missing person was presumed dead, the widow should be free to remarry. And there was near unanimous consent for a resolution which declared that the *halitsah* ritual, being inappropriate to the present age, should not be a barrier to a widow's remarriage. With an increasing number of female converts to Judaism, especially in Vienna, the synod voted unanimously that women should be accepted as witnesses at the required ritual bath. While the synod recognized the "highly important significance" of circumcision, it declared unanimously that children born of Jewish mothers, even if uncircumcized, must be accepted by Jews. There was also a resolution on the Sabbath, which allowed riding on that day, especially to get to the synagogue, but also for charitable, educational, and recreational purposes. And, in unspoken recognition of widespread Christmas observance among German Jews, the synod unanimously recommended that the festival of Hanukah receive an enhanced celebration.

Despite this harvest of resolutions, which was later discussed by the community leadership in Berlin and elsewhere, no further synods were held. There were problems of finance as well as conflicts of opinion and personality, but mainly there was a lack of sufficient drive. German Jewry in the seventies was content with its newly achieved emancipation, with its active participation in the economic, cultural, and now also political life of the new Reich which Bismarck had so ingeniously put together. At Augsburg there was little talk of "the Jewish mission." In the flush of complete emancipation, it was apparently felt—for the moment—that the Jews had already made their contribution to Western civilization. Now the new Germany, of which its Jews were full citizens, was the bearer of spirit and culture. In those years, too, religious liberalism ebbed once more in Christian circles. The old bifurcation between Orthodoxy and religious indifference took firm hold again.

It was apparent that the Reformers had failed to produce a new generation of rabbinical leadership capable of reorientation and renewal. The rabbis present at the synods were mostly older men, largely the same ones who had been youthfully enthusiastic at the conferences of the forties, but who now lacked the old fire. And the spectrum had grown narrower. Ever since the establishment of the Jewish Theological Seminary in Breslau under Zacharias Frankel in 1854, the conservatives had their own institution whose loyal alumni almost all withheld their support from the synods as a rival institution, and one not in conformity with their outlook.

The Reform impulse in succeeding decades was stifled as well by the successful efforts of the most orthodox Jews in Germany to form independent congregations. As early as 1851 Samson Raphael Hirsch had been called to serve such a separatist community in Frankfurt, and a similar one was formed in Berlin in 1869. It was Hirsch who prevailed upon the Jewish parliamentarian Eduard Lasker to propose a bill granting members of such congregations freedom from payment of community taxes. When Lasker's proposal became law in 1876, the threat that similar *Austrittsgemeinden* would be formed in other communities became very real. The result was that perspicacious lay leaders, whatever their own progressive inclinations, leaned to the side of conservatism. They sought to avoid provoking the formation of such a separatist group in their own community or, if there already was one, to discourage its growth.[29]

One significant progressive institution, however, came into being largely because of its promotion by the Leipzig synod: a rabbinical seminary and institute of advanced Jewish studies which, unlike the Breslau seminary, would be fully hospitable to critical scholarship and guarantee complete academic freedom. Such a center of learning had been advocated for some years by various liberal rabbis. Geiger had caustically attacked what he regarded as the medieval atmosphere prevalent in Breslau; Joseph Aub had deplored to his listeners in Berlin that there was still no seminary which could send the German rabbinate young men "equipped and prepared for progress and ongoing development."[30] But it was only at the first synod, and especially once Lazarus himself took the matter firmly in hand, that efforts were concentrated and funds successfully gathered for a Hochschule für die Wissenschaft des Judentums (College for Jewish Studies) in Berlin. Founded in 1870, it opened its doors two years later. Geiger was invited to be a member of its faculty along with more traditional colleagues; Lazarus became the head of its board of trustees. For seventy years, until the Nazis closed it in 1942, the Hochschule served as an intellectual focus for Liberal Jews. Its faculty produced works of significant scholarship, its students filled progressive pulpits throughout Germany. The Hochschule was the first central institution of permanence which the Reform movement had created anywhere.

The Eastward Thrust Continues

The 1850s were no more propitious for liberal religion in Austria than they were in Germany. The Austrian Concordat signed with the Vatican in 1855 gave the Catholic Church increased influence in the public sphere; a pervasive spirit of intolerance choked intellectual life. Given the right to organize an official community for the first time in 1849, the Vienna Jewish leadership soon found that the government regarded it as dangerously "Reform." The size and composition of Viennese Jewry were changing too. With newly acquired freedom of residence in the capital, it grew rapidly from an aggregate of relatively few "tolerated" Jews into a massive community whose numbers by 1855 had reached at least 20,000 and were more than double that fifteen years later. The new Jewish residents were largely traditionalists, especially from Hungary and Galicia, who expressed dissatisfaction with the established temple ritual. In the late fifties they attempted to break off and form their own community. Although that effort failed, the support it enjoyed and the official suspicion of all religious liberalization inhibited any significant movement from the status quo that had been achieved thirty years earlier.[31]

Yet within these constraints, the community board did seek to push further. To provide for the expanding Jewish population, it built a second temple in the Leopold-stadt district with a capacity nearly triple that of the first. Dedicated in 1858, the magnificent structure resembled contemporary German synagogues in its use of Oriental models, in this instance ancient Assyrian as well as Moorish.[32] While the temple's ritual was to duplicate precisely that established by Mannheimer and Sulzer, the new preacher who was selected for its pulpit was a man more open to reforms than his senior colleague. Unlike Mannheimer, Adolf Jellinek (1823–1893) was a proponent of organ music for the new temple. Like some German Reformers, he did not read the *ketubah,* the Aramaic contract formula, as part of the wedding ceremonies, nor did he insist on the biblical *halitsah* or require that only a convert to Judaism who had been submerged in the waters of the *mikveh* could be married as a Jew. In Leipzig, where he had earlier served as preacher, as in Vienna, he often spoke out against Jews who stubbornly refused to adjust to modernity. Contemporaries noticed that he was not fully scrupulous in his personal observance of ritual laws.[32] All in all, Jellinek represented another step in the direction of Reform and was consequently disquieting to the Orthodox.

Yet the new preacher was scarcely a Reform ideologue. He was a scholar of Midrash and Kabbalah, a gatherer and editor of little known texts who did not use his studies to make polemical points. At heart he was above all a public speaker—indeed widely believed to be the finest exemplar of Jewish homiletics in the nineteenth century. In contrast to the early style of Reform preaching, Jellinek did not dwell on general moral truths but on the specific teachings of Judaism. His elegantly crafted sermons were lavishly embellished with appropriate texts from Midrash and Talmud. Their dominant purpose, it seems, was to make his listeners proud of their particular Jewish heritage, to make them "feel good" about being Jewish. With his flair for dramatic images, Jellinek on one occasion pictured the hero of the Song of Songs, representing the Jewish people, bravely carrying the banner of God through history. He celebrated contemporary Jewry, as well, stressing its accomplishments and confirming his listeners in their existing attitudes and beliefs. Though he could hardly be called a Jewish nationalist, his sermons passionately evoked the memory of Zion and Jerusalem. The ancient sites possessed significance also for the future, he pointed out, for they served as universal messianic symbols that would make Jews strive harder for self-improvement and social betterment. Thus, paradoxically, longing for Zion could make Jews more valuable Austrian citizens. Jellinek also preached repeatedly in favor of cultivating the Hebrew language as the bond among all Jews and underlined the importance of teaching it to children. To the Viennese Jewish leadership he must have seemed just the right man for their Jewish milieu: a religious leader who did not create ideological division, an accomplished preacher who provided his listeners with memorable artistic experiences, and a man who expressed their own feelings, reconfirming both Jewish loyalties and universal convictions.[34]

Jellinek was not one to disturb the peace. It was rather members of the community's lay leadership who in the late sixties pressed for further synagogue reforms. As happened so often, the attainment of full equality, gained by Austrian Jewry in 1868, prompted the effort. Proponents of more ideologically oriented reform sought to follow the German example by removing from the Vienna prayerbook all those passages that dealt with sacrifices and return to Zion; and they also wanted to introduce the organ into regular services at both community temples. To gain wider authority the community board sent representatives to the synods of Leipzig and Augsburg and afterwards heard reports on the proceedings. Predictably, however, the new thrust gave fresh impetus to Orthodox separationists. Some 300 now threatened to leave the community; 400 rabbis were enlisted to condemn the proposed reforms. The result was a compromise: organ music was indefinitely postponed while the main petitional prayers, which mentioned the return to Zion and the sacrifices, were henceforth recited only silently, leaving worshipers free to formulate them individually in accordance with their own convictions. The agreement, reached in 1872, was carefully termed a "modification" of the service, not a reform.[35]

Thus it remained characteristic of Viennese Jewry to place communal unity above ideology, to avoid labeling its official practice as anything other than the "Vienna rite." The Orthodox, who rejected that rite, worshiped in various synagogues around the city, each with its particular customs; of the many religiously indifferent Jews, some attended the special High Holiday services advertised by placards and held in temporary locations; others did not attend at all. When Mannheimer died, he was replaced by Moritz Güdemann, a conservative whose appointment represented a concession to the traditionalists, as Jellinek's had pleased the liberals.[36]

The same spirit of compromise which reigned in Vienna characterized other Austrian communities as well. In Prague the "ordered service" of its temple, complete with organ music, was taken over by other synagogues in the city without producing a serious rift. By the last decades of the nineteenth century most of the Bohemian and Moravian Jews had ceased to be Orthodox. They felt at home with the local version of the Vienna rite, which was adopted in the great majority of their synagogues.[37]

In Hungary, by contrast, communal unity could not be upheld. For although secularization and the desire for moderate religious assimilation did spread rapidly in the larger cities, modernists, here alone in central Europe, faced a militant and unyielding Orthodoxy which rejected not only religious reform but political and cultural integration as well. Orthodox leaders feared the consequences of emancipation and set themselves firmly against the study of secular disciplines. Even as integrationist ranks swelled, so did those of a self-ghettoizing Orthodoxy, which was particularly strong in the northeastern region. Traditional rabbinical leadership remained influential in Hungary and Hasidism flourished. By the last third of the nineteenth century the modernist and traditionalist factions were of about equal size.[38]

Ever since Aaron Chorin had given it impetus at the beginning of the century, religious reform had spread in Hungary. However, with the exception of the brief episode of the Pest Reform Association during the revolutionary late forties, it assumed a more moderate form here than in Germany. In fact the burning "Reform" issues in Hungary of the 1860s concerned innovations that had long ceased to provoke much controversy in Germany where they had been widely adopted by the modernist Orthodoxy which represented traditionalism there. Most—though not all—Hungarian rabbis of the old type still prohibited the vernacular sermon, regarding it as a breach in the linguistic barrier, which for centuries had helped preserve Judaism. Yet since the German sermon soon spread very widely, enjoying support among the laity even in otherwise traditional synagogues, some rabbis, while still opposing the practice, began to see its prohibition as "a decree which the community cannot bear." A second subject of controversy was the question of whether the *bimah,* the reader's desk, could be moved from the center of the synagogue to the area in front of the ark. In the town of Debrecen a decision to place the *bimah* at the front in a newly constructed synagogue fractured the congregation and provoked the question whether this reform alone was sufficient to place a synagogue that regarded itself as Orthodox into the camp of "reformed choir temples." Another cause for dispute was the nature of the *meḥitsah* that separated the women's gallery. A number of synagogues, while retaining the barrier, had constructed it in such a way that the sexes could easily see each other—a severe deviation from the Orthodox point of view.[39]

These and other innovations were deemed characteristic of the execrable choir temples, some of them with organs, which had appeared in the larger Hungarian cities, and as far south as Zagreb in Croatia.[40] For the Orthodox they represented an intolerable threat. To pray in them, some rabbis determined, was a worse offense than eating pork; worse even, declared one responsum, than the practice of idolatry. In order to lend weight to this opposition, seventy-seven Orthodox rabbis signed the condemnatory decree issued by a rabbinical meeting in Michalovce in 1865. It forbade vernacular sermons, praying in a synagogue where the *bimah* was not in the center, constructing a tower on a synagogue building, clerical vestments for cantors and singers, transparent partitions in front of the women's gallery, listening to a synagogue choir, so much as entering a choir temple, and weddings held inside the synagogue building. The conclusion was uncompromising: "It is prohibited to alter any Jewish custom or synagogue usage from what was accepted by our ancestors."[41] With this collective prohibition the Orthodox sought to hold back the gradual slippage of traditional congregations into the ranks of the Progressives, or Neologists, as the advocates of cultural integration and religious reform were called in Hungary. The Michalovce decree made clear where the boundaries of true Orthodoxy lay.

The formal organizational split of Hungarian Jewry followed shortly thereafter, ironically deriving from a failed attempt at centralization and unification. As in Austria, it was the achievement of complete emancipation, gained by Hungarian Jews in 1867, that stimulated a new thrust for religious and cultural integration. Already in 1848, as we have seen, enthusiasm for the Magyar cause had suffused the radical reform propagated by Ignaz Einhorn. Now, as Hungary began to enjoy autonomy in conducting its internal affairs following the Compromise with Austria in 1867, Magyar leaders welcomed Jewish participation in the task of nation-building. They hoped that Jewish cooptation would swell their influence over the other national groups in Hungary, which the Magyars, who fell slightly short of being fully a majority, sought to dominate. While Orthodox Jews had felt their interests well protected by the conservative Hapsburg regime, Progressives enthusiastically supported the Magyar ascendancy, which seemed to favor their orientation.[42] Some now felt that the time had come for an ideological transformation of the Jewish religion similar to that which characterized contemporary progressive Judaism in Germany. One layman urged that, with the breaking of the political chains, it was time to break the spiritual chains as well, to go beyond the existing synagogue reforms of the choir temples. He advocated abolition of prayers for return to Jerusalem and the reinstitution of the sacrifices, as well as those for dew and rain, which could apply only to Palestine. If the rabbis were too timid to act, their community leaders should take the initiative.[43] While such views remained isolated in Hungary, a more widely shared desire in progressive circles—and one which aroused greater Orthodox apprehension—was for a modern rabbinical seminary like that in Breslau. The project had gained government approval in 1864; if realized, its graduates could alter the character of Hungary's rabbinical leadership.[44] Thus in the late sixties Orthodoxy felt itself severely set upon by a new thrust directed against the religious status quo—and this just as it was asked to join itself structurally with the Progressives.

The congress of Hungarian Jewry which met at the end of 1868 was initiated by lay leaders from the Pest community, generally recognized as the stronghold of integrationism.[45] With the support of Joseph Eötvös, the liberal Hungarian Minister of Religion and Education, it had been decided to hold a broadly based election. Two contending parties immediately emerged: the Progressives, representing Neology, and the Guardians of the Faith, who championed Orthodoxy. Although the results may not have reflected Orthodox strength fully, they indicated the growing power of the Progressives, who achieved 57.5 percent of the vote and 126 seats, while the Orthodox gained only 42.5 percent and 94 seats. The purpose of the congress was twofold: the establishment of a centralized system of communal organization and regulation of the Jewish schools. In general, the Progressive lay leaders, who dominated the congress, tried to avoid alienating the Orthodox, promising that specifically religious issues would be excluded from the agenda and being especially careful not to mention German Reformers. Yet at one point the Progressive rabbi of Arad was open enough to admit that the Neologist goals under the new structure would indeed include reform of the worship service. This candor and the refusal of the majority to declare that the unified communities would conduct their affairs entirely on the basis of the *Shulḥan Arukh* provoked a large portion of the Orthodox faction to walk out of the congress. They feared being part of a centralized structure, somewhat like the French consistory system, that would be directed by Neologists, which they would be unable to influence, and which would likely institute unacceptable reforms. But even more fundamentally, as Rabbi Moses Schick put it after the Congress, the Orthodox could not envisage themselves as "one congregation" in each city with "lovers of novelties" who had introduced choir and organ.[46] Just as unpalatable to the Orthodox was the measure passed by the congress creating a modern rabbinical seminary. Since its students would engage in critical studies, the graduates would surely be rank heretics, as experience, presumably with rabbis trained at the Breslau seminary, had already demonstrated. Although they failed in the congress, the Guardians of the Faith were ultimately successful in preventing implementation of the unitary structure by pleading freedom of conscience to the Hungarian Parliament. They received permission to form their own national organization parallel to that instituted by the congress. In succeeding decades the numerical strength of Orthodoxy declined in Hungary while Neology, or "Congress Judaism," as it was now also called, established its seminary and numerically dominated Hungarian Jewry.[47] In the mid-nineteenth century the

Neologists could also claim at least one rabbi of stature, the prolific Leopold Löw (1811–1875) of Szeged, who was an active participant in both the Leipzig and Augsburg synods. But for the most part, the Hungarian version of Reform was simply characterized by the externals of the choir temple; and by the last decades of the century, it lacked ideological commitment and spiritual vigor.[48]

A more daring and scholarly critique of tradition emerges at this time from neighboring Galicia. Joshua Heschel Schorr (1818–1895) ranks among the very radical theoretical reformers and is noteworthy as the first to propagate such critical radicalism widely in the Hebrew language.[49] A lifelong resident of Brody, he took it upon himself to champion the cause of Haskalah against Hasidism, and against Galician Orthodoxy generally, wielding an agile pen that could as easily drip venomous sarcasm as produce sharply argued and eruditely documented historical criticism. Like Abraham Geiger, with whom he maintained regular contact, Schorr refused to cordon off any bastion of tradition from the damaging forays of *Wissenschaft*. Men of the middle, like Zacharias Frankel and Solomon Rapoport, who sought to be critical scholars only up to a point, became objects of his blistering satire. Unhampered by the practical considerations of a rabbinate which led even Geiger to compromises in practice, Schorr— in his later years a virtual recluse—strove for unbending honesty. Adamantly, he refused to shy away from conclusions which seemed the more radical when written in Hebrew. At first he contributed his ideas to the German Jewish journals. Later his own periodical, *He-Ḥaluts,* appearing irregularly for a generation between 1852 and 1889, made Schorr the very symbol of religious heresy or, as one contemporary said, "the Galician Voltaire."

What he regarded as the stultifying influence of the Orthodox rabbinate, Schorr believed, rested on its popular acceptance as representing divinely revealed law. The yoke of rabbinism could be broken, and Jewish religion allowed to develop freely, only if the divine sanction which served as its basis were undermined by critical study. Schorr thus set out to show why the Talmud must be seen as nothing more than a human document and hence lacking absolute authority for the present. Though he was hardly the first Reformer to humanize the Oral Law, few before him had done so with such skill and lack of reverence, with such conscious intent to render it profane. And since he was writing in Hebrew, Schorr spread the critical views, heretofore available only in German, eastward to maskilim in Galicia and Russia.

Schorr did not negate rabbinic Judaism entirely. He acknowledged that the Talmud contained precious and venerable precepts that played an important role in the spiritual history of Judaism. Like other Reformers, his respect for it simply declined progressively as later Rabbis more and more lost the daring which had characterized their forebears. The Pharisees and early Tannaim had been willing to abrogate old laws and institute new ones in accordance with their particular situation. Legislating for their age alone, they had not sought to bind the hands of succeeding generations. But with the canonization of the Mishnah at the end of the second century and thereafter, rabbinism ceased to be a free process of adaptation and became the multiplication of onerous restrictions with little concern for contemporary circumstance. Instead of advancing religious development, rabbinism had increasingly held it back. Moreover, the Rabbis had misread the Bible. Their literalism, for example, had made them find *tefilin* (phylacteries) in the text of the Torah, preventing them from realizing that the commandment "Bind [God's precepts] as a sign on your hand and let them serve as a symbol on your forehead" (Deut. 6:8) had to be understood merely as a metaphor for remembering, not as mandating a particular ritual act.

Had he been simply a foe of rabbinism, Schorr might have stopped short of Pentateuch criticism and affirmed a revealed Mosaism, as other Reformers had done. In his earliest writings he did indeed declare the Written Law to be divine. But by the time he began to edit *He-Ḥaluts,* Schorr was ready to cast the barbs of modern scholarship even into this most sacred realm. In fact, he was the first Hebrew writer to do so. Schorr dwelled on the foreign conceptions which had made their way into the Pentateuch and he did not shrink from emending the text. For him, as for the German Reformers, what remained holy was not the letter, but only, as he put it, the "spirit of God hovering over Sacred Scripture."[50]

Unlike more moderate Reformers, Schorr did not believe in modernizing the Jewish religion by building upon halakhic foundations. The talmudists, he held, were "men like us," and hence even as they had assumed the right to excise, reform, and innovate in accordance with the exigencies of their time and place, so did the sages of every generation, including the present one, possess that same prerogative. Schorr did not go on to detail a program of liturgical reforms, but his theoretical position was identical with that of Reformers to the west: the ceremonies and some of the less central beliefs of Judaism were only flexible supports for its basic principle. That principle, of course, was monotheism, the belief in God's unity, which in turn unified the people of Israel.

Yet there is a difference of nuance on the affirmative, if not on the critical side, between the German Reformers and the Galicians. Schorr and his close associate Abraham (the son of Nachman) Krochmal (ca. 1818–1888) were both staunch advocates of religious reform, of unfettered historical criticism, and in the case of Krochmal, also of the mission of Israel. Both were greatly influenced by Abraham Geiger. Yet from their Galician context they derived a broader Jewish identification than one based on the synagogue alone. While German Reform dwelled largely on liturgy, Schorr chose to single out the Sabbath (on Saturday) and circumcision as the two most important ritual elements protecting Jewish monotheism, while Krochmal argued that the religious element in Judaism could not be severed from its social base, the faith cut off from the people. Though scarcely Jewish nationalists, Schorr and Krochmal did set their radical reform more upon an ethnic than an ecclesiastical foundation. Not the assimilation of Judaism to Gentile religious practice was their goal; but ridding it of burdens that scientific criticism and contemporary circumstances could not justify.[51] In this regard they become exemplary also for thinkers even further to the east.

Synagogue reform had made its way into the Russian Empire by the mid-nineteenth century.[52] Services on the German model, incorporating decorum, a trained choir, and an edifying vernacular sermon, appeared in Odessa, Warsaw, Riga, and Vilna. The participants and their spiritual leaders mostly came from German-speaking areas, transplanting the aesthetically reformed service with which they were familiar to the Tsarist Empire. The German rabbi Max Lilienthal, later to be a leader of the Reform movement in the United States, introduced confirmation for girls in Riga in 1840, as did the Odessa synagogue (known as the "Broder Shul" since most of its founders came from Galician Brody) in 1862. Apparently only one small breakaway group from the German synagogue in Warsaw went so far as to undertake radically reformed services conducted mostly in Polish.[53] The Vilna congregation, known as Tohorat Ha-Kodesh ("the purity of holiness"), was unusual in that it was composed mainly of young maskilim, rather than the bourgeois families, which for the most part made up the other modern synagogues, and in that the language of the sermons delivered there seems to have been Hebrew. Such congregations, however, remained exceptional in Russia, simply a fringe phenomenon at the edge of its vast Jewish community.

One reason for the lack of a large-scale indigenous Reform movement in Russia was the absence of an effective progressive rabbinate. For this the heavy hand of the Russian government, persistently seeking to force assimilation, if not conversion, was largely responsible. In 1835 the government outlined an institution soon to be known as the Crown rabbinate, consisting of rabbinically trained Jews knowing Russian, who would be the only rabbis officially recognized as such. With few exceptions these men did not enjoy the respect of the communities in which they served. Public opinion differentiated between them and the "genuine rabbis," chosen informally for their knowledge and piety, but enjoying no official status vis-à-vis the government. Only here and there were Crown rabbis able to exercise real leadership. Because they had to be reelected every three years, they usually preferred to avoid antagonizing any influential segment of the community. The projects for religious reform which some of them harbored remained unarticulated for reasons of economic self-concern.

In 1847 two modern rabbinical seminaries, intended to train candidates for the Crown rabbinate, were established in Vilna and Zhitomir. They were dedicated to producing men who would be able to combine the elements that split Haskalah off from tradition: religion and empirical knowledge *(dat im da'at)*, secular wisdom and Jewish law *(hokhmah gam torah)*. As one student envisaged it, the Vilna seminary would channel the stream of modern culture into the existing riverbed, taking care that its rushing waters not damage the tender plant of religion. Continuing the horticultural image, he pictured the new rabbis playing the role of religious reformers, "with sore hands tearing out the weeds and misshapen plants from the vineyard of the Lord."

However, the seminaries proved unable to fulfill their projected goals for rabbinical training. They were beset by mistrust—if not outright opposition—on the part of traditional Jews, government interference, and a poorly motivated student body. The teaching of secular disciplines mostly by Christian teachers created a heightened awareness of separation between Jewish and general subjects rather than their integration. Few students completed the rabbinical program, and of these only a very small percentage enjoyed widespread authority. Instead of bridging the gap between Crown rabbis and the rabbis accepted as such by the masses, the seminaries only exacerbated the division. As one modern Jew in St. Petersburg put it: "Our old rabbis are obsolete and our new ones are not rabbis." Still in the 1870s, when the seminaries were transformed into teachers' colleges, Russian Jewry had been unable to produce a broadly cultured yet religiously respected rabbinate.

The absence of an effective rabbinical initiative left the propagation of religious reform to laymen drawn especially from the ranks of the maskilim. The relatively liberal reign of Tsar Alexander II, beginning in 1855, had raised hopes for political gains and created an atmosphere which some Jewish writers thought propitious for a comprehensive modernization of Russian Jewry. About 1858 Joachim Tarnopol (1810–1900), a wealthy Odessa merchant and co-editor of the short-lived first Russian-language Jewish periodical *Rassvet* (Dawn), composed a proposal for the "moderate and progressive reform" of Russian Jewry. To a greater extent than other modernist Russian Jews, Tarnopol looked to the German Jewish experience, to the writings of Ludwig Philippson, and to *Wissenschaft des Judentums*. For him—as for much of German Jewry—the worship service took on increased significance as other forms of religious observance became less common among the enlightened youth. The synagogue therefore had to be made more capable of attracting the new generation, which had received a modern education. He suggested a limited program of synagogue reforms, believing that once these had gained wider acceptance, Judaism in Russia would become both viable and respectable.

More broadly influential than Tarnopol was the prominent maskil Moses Leib Lilienblum (1843–1910), who wrote two serialized essays favoring religious reform in the Hebrew periodical *Ha-Melits* beginning in 1868. Inspired by Schorr, he stressed the liberal halakhic creativity of the early Rabbis and called upon present occupants of the rabbinical office to adopt their example, reestablishing the link between religion and life which, unlike Schorr, Lilienblum believed existed during the entire talmudic period. For him the course of German Judaism served less as exemplar than as warning: if the Orthodox rabbis in Russia did not act speedily to bridge the ever-widening gap between the law and contemporary reality, they would lose their authority, as had the traditional rabbis in Germany. Unchecked individualism would reign supreme in Russian Judaism as it already did in the West.

Among Russian advocates of religious change, Lilienblum's concerns were the furthest removed from those of German synagogue reform. For him the worship service was entirely of secondary significance. Prayer itself, he reminded his readers, was not an explicit biblical command and private prayer was not less acceptable than public. The German Jews' emphasis on the synagogue service was for Lilienblum simply an imitation of the Gentiles, for whom formal worship was the principal expression of religion. Prayer had been ordained only in place of the Temple sacrifices, and he noted that the latter were not greatly esteemed by Israel's prophets. Lilienblum was convinced that once a Jew had lost the inner motivation for prayer, synagogue reform would merely substitute an aesthetic experience for a religious one. For him the synagogue was not the symbol and center of Jewish life, as it was for Tarnopol and for Jews in the West, and therefore synagogue reform, he noted bluntly, was simply "not worth talking about."

What did matter to Lilienblum was the task of easing the burden of Jewish law and custom in order to maintain a common ground between traditional and enlightened Jews, preventing the fragmentation that had afflicted Jewry in the West. Initially, he sought only to modify those practices that had become current since the *Shulḥan Arukh,* those that had no clear talmudic basis, and those that unnecessarily set Jews apart from non-Jews or were drawn from mystical conceptions. However, Lilienblum rapidly came to challenge the authority of earlier authorities as well: first the *Shulḥan Arukh,* which he hoped to displace by a new code of Jewish law, and then the Talmud itself, declaring, as had Schorr and the German Reformers, that even in its halakhic elements it was essentially a human product subject to revision by later generations. For him, too, the Talmud remained authoritative only as a model of religious adaptation, not as a sacred text. It "was created according to [the demands of] place and time, founded principally upon the spirit of reform."

For a while Lilienblum hung on to his belief in the revealed character of the Written Law, claiming that in this respect his views differed from those of German Reformers like Samuel Holdheim. However, within a few years his exposure to biblical criticism, mediated to him especially by Abraham Krochmal, made even this last pillar of revelation collapse. Lilienblum became an outsider to religious Judaism both in belief and in practice. For a time he still argued for reforms in those areas, such as marriage and divorce, which affected all Jews regardless of their religious views or degree of observance. But he gave up hope of giving impetus to a new synthesis that would unite religion with life.

Similar disappointment with the prospect of religious reform was the lot of Judah Leib Gordon (1830–1892), the most prominent of the Haskalah poets.[54] Following in the footsteps of Lilienblum, and also influenced by Schorr and Krochmal, Gordon too had pleaded for contemporary rabbis to reconcile the commandments of the Torah with the needs of daily life by reviving the halakhic creativity of the earliest forebears. Talmudic Judaism, he noted, was itself a "reform" of the earlier Mosaic religion. In particular, Gordon stressed that Jewish modernization, and hence revitalization, was not possible without a resifting of the religious tradition, separating out what was truly essential from the plethora of trivial customs and ceremonies that only burdened its adherents and hobbled its spirit. If that did not happen soon, Gordon warned, Russian Jewry would find itself irremediably divided on religious matters. Radical solutions, like those instituted appropriately enough in their situation by the German Reformers, would unfortunately become necessary in Russia as well. Yet despite Gordon's warnings and mediating proposals, the Russian Haskalah did move on beyond Reform, in fact beyond religious faith entirely.

Perhaps the most important reasons for the failure of Reform ideas and institutions to spread more broadly in Russian Jewry lay outside the community. In the West an idealistic philosophy hospitable to religion, absorbed during the period of its prominence into Jewish thought as well as Christian, enabled theologically liberalized Judaism to withstand the blows of historical criticism. But in Russia, where Orthodox Christianity did not achieve a synthesis of religion with modern philosophy or science, the period of reform proposals coincided with the increasing popularity of an anti-metaphysical positivism which left no room for a religious faith whose authoritative texts had been shown to be the product of historical evolution. At the same time the resurgently hostile political environment was unconducive to the meliorism represented by religious reform. With hopes of integration disappointed in the last years of Alexander II, and with the reappearance of severe economic oppression and physical persecution under Alexander III (1881–1894), most of Russian Jewry either chose to remain within the psychologically protective bastion of Orthodoxy or sought its salvation by radical secular means: emigration, socialism, or Jewish nationalism. In Jewish socialist ideology there remained little room for religious expression; in Jewish nationalism loyalty to the people, not the faith, became the dominant value. Thus religious reform in Russia did not advance beyond a few peripheral institutions and some well-meaning theoretical proposals that were incapable of realization.

New Challenges, New Intellectual Vitality

The ideology of the Reform movement, as it crystallized in the first half of the nineteenth century, had been predicated on the belief that modern European society and culture would move ever closer to the universalist ideals of the Enlightenment. The Reformers were confident that a modernized Judaism could play a significant role in that messianic progress. Indeed, it was the mission of Israel, as they conceived it, to provide the example of pure monotheism and lofty moral idealism which would lend energy and direction to the forward course. Orthodox Judaism, because it was more inwardly focused and retained formidable barriers between Jew and Gentile, could not properly assume the special task cast upon Judaism. Although the mission idea was shared with Jewish traditionalists in the West, for the Reformers it assumed a greater centrality, since most of the Reform laity was alienated from the life of Halakhah, which could act as a counterweight for the Neo-Orthodox. What united Liberal Jews was, above all, a common commitment to their historical role. It gave their Jewish identity a significance transcending, though not destroying, the intrinsic value of religious faith for the individual Jew. Thus when emancipation in Germany was not followed by a greater appreciation of the Jews' past and potential contributions to modern values and culture, and when their religion continued to be the object, not of respect but of denigration or disregard by leading German thinkers and scholars, the Reform movement faced a crisis unforeseen by its founders.

German philosophy and theology, as represented by Hegel and Schleiermacher earlier in the century, had already indicated how modern thinkers could transmute the traditional conception of Christian supersession into terms acceptable to contemporary intellectuals. We have seen how Jewish thinkers like Solomon Ludwig Steinheim, Solomon Formstecher, and Samuel Hirsch attempted to reassert the ongoing validity of Judaism against such contentions. But until the last decades of the century, it was possible to believe that *political* liberalism would draw *religious* liberalism into its orbit, that Judaism no less than individual Jews would eventually be recognized as having a contribution to make toward spiritual progress. When that belief increasingly lost credibility, the Reformers were forced either into despair or into deeper self-examination. Although increased overt and subtle hostility to Jews and Judaism corroded Jewish self-respect with an intensity that Liberal Judaism was able only somewhat to diminish, the challenge it presented did, at least for a while, revive a movement which had come to suffer from apathy and fatigue.

The resurgence of political liberalism in Germany of the sixties and seventies, marked for the Jews by their formal and complete political emancipation enshrined in the constitution of the German Reich, was expected to usher in the long-awaited period of full Jewish participation in German society. And indeed, German Jews were soon playing roles as politicians in the Reichstag, as writers, and as professionals. They participated in the German economic expansion and reaped some of its benefits. Increasingly, they lived in the larger cities, especially Berlin and Frankfurt. Although certain prerogatives, such as the upper reaches of the civil service, the officer corps, and academic positions, remained difficult or impossible to attain, the Jewish presence became ever more visible. But instead of stirring appreciation, it soon occasioned anxiety.

German antisemitism, after a period of relative quiescence, reemerged in the late nineteenth century, assuming both religious and secular forms. The notion that Germany was a Christian nation, and ideally a Christian state, now achieved new popularity. The Court Preacher, Adolf Stöcker, was its most ardent representative and its chief propagandist among the masses. At the same time a new form of Jew-hatred, based on race rather than religion, emerged and gained adherents. A League of Antisemites came into existence, antisemitic political parties were formed, and anti-Jewish ideas began to percolate through broad segments of the population. An antisemitic petition, calling for fewer Jewish immigrants and less Jewish influence, drew over 250,000 signatures in 1881. Among intellectuals, as well, the new movement gained adherents. Heinrich von Treitschke, politician and popular professor of history at Berlin University, lent his prestige to the movement. To be sure, Treitschke was not an extremist: he did not believe Germany was a Christian *state,* only a Christian *nation;* he did not advocate reversal of the emancipation, only that Jews remain along the sidelines. But Treitschke was convinced that only a culture based on a single religious tradition could be integral, and that only such a culture could be productive. The Jews in Germany, public sentiment averred, were more misfortune than blessing; their proferred contribution to its culture would bring no enrichment, only mongrelization. It was, Treitschke believed, "a sin against the glory of German history to assert . . . that Judaism is just as German as Christianity." Not surprisingly, antisemites singled out the non-Orthodox Jews as most guilty of such arrogance since they were the least conspicuously Jewish, yet persisted in maintaining a purposeful religious differentiation; they clung to the intolerable idea that Judaism was a religion not simply of the past but also of the future; it was capable of further development. Even political and religious liberals, staunch advocates of Jewish equality, were less than willing to grant that Jews could make claims for the ongoing and universal significance of their faith.[55]

It was not the antisemitic attack on the Jews themselves but this treatment of their religion which most affected the Reform movement. German Reformers had from the first placed high hopes on the progress of humanistic *Wissenschaft.* Not only did they expect the scientific study of Judaism to reveal flexibility and change in Jewish tradition; they also anticipated that historical scholarship generally would divulge the broader role of the Jewish faith in the past and hence justify its continuing existence. Yet the works of biblical criticism and historical theology that appeared toward the end of the nineteenth century and at the start of the twentieth both reflected and gave scientific credence to longstanding prejudice. Written by men of *Wissenschaft* who regarded themselves as liberals emancipated from dogma, they were far more devastating than the anticipated narrowness that characterized Christian Orthodox works. If supersession in philosophy was the principal challenge to liberal Jewish thought in the first half of the century, at its end it was the maltreatment of Judaism in historically based research that appeared the greater threat.

The role of modern Judaism in German society, as the Reformers understood it, depended greatly on establishing the view that it was closely related to Christianity in religious and moral terms, though separate from Christian dogma. And that idea, in turn, was related to Christian origins. If it were acknowledged that Christianity emerged from the matrix of Judaism, then the mother faith would not only be appreciated historically, but it could not easily be cast aside in the present. What German scholarship set about to show, however, was just the opposite—and with obvious contemporary ramifications. Julius Wellhausen, the most influential Bible scholar of the age, pictured Pharisaic Judaism as being concerned exclusively with the law, to the detriment of genuine spirituality: "The law thrusts itself in everywhere; it commands and blocks up the access to heaven. . . . It takes the soul out of religion and spoils morality." His popularization of the hypothesis dividing the Pentateuch into discrete sources attributed the legal corpus to the postexilic period, making it the product of later Judaism, not of the Ancient Israel whose prophetic morality was inherited by Christianity. For Wellhausen the Gospel was not an outgrowth of Pharisaic Judaism at all but a successful protest against it, and one which put an end to Judaism's development. The Reformers' conception of a progressive Judaism was therefore built on a myth; Judaism was simply not harmonizable with modern values. Hence, Wellhausen concluded candidly, the emancipation of the Jews would have to lead to the extinction of Judaism.[56]

As German scholarship set Gospels against Pharisees, so it also set New Testament against Old. Even if Reformers had wished to deny the rabbinic heritage—as few in fact did—and dwell upon the common legacy of the Hebrew Bible, they could not have avoided the odium cast by contemporary scholarship. Comparative Semitics was revealing ever more parallels between the religion of the ancient Hebrews and the traditions of surrounding peoples. Biblical epics, laws, and observances, it could now be shown, were apparently borrowed from Mesopotamia. When the noted Assyriologist Friedrich Delitzsch popularized the accumulated findings of his discipline in two lectures entitled *Babel and Bible* presented before the German Emperor in 1902 and 1903, he simply gave added impetus to the desacralization of the Old Testament. But Delitzsch went further. The Hebrew Bible actually inspired revulsion: "The more deeply I immerse myself in the spirit of the prophetic literature of the Old Testament, the greater becomes my mistrust of Yahweh, who butchers the peoples with the sword of his insatiable anger; who has but one favorite child, while he consigns all other nations to darkness, shame, and ruin." Delitzsch much preferred to put his trust not in "Yahweh," but in the God of the New Testament alone, the God of Jesus.[57]

Three years before Delitzsch popularized the findings of Assyriology, the prominent theologian and scholar of church history Adolf Harnack delivered an equally influential series of lectures to some 600 students from all faculties at the Berlin University. Published within a year, reprinted frequently, and translated into a number of languages, Harnack's *The Essence of Christianity* made an enormous impact. Like Schleiermacher a century earlier, Harnack sought to present the cultured classes, alienated from traditional faith, with a model of Christianity they could readily embrace, a "gospel within the gospel," the kernel of Christianity within the husk. Peeling away as inessential the miracle stories, Christology, and asceticism of the New Testament, Harnack virtually reduced Christianity to love of God and man. That, however, brought it precariously close to values already expressed both in the Hebrew Bible and in Pharisaic Judaism. Anticipating the objection, Harnack drew upon what Wellhausen had once said: Yes, the Prophets had preached the same doctrine; the Pharisees had it too. But unfortunately the Pharisees "also had a great deal else besides." Thus Jesus, as Harnack pictured him, was a human figure whose message was indeed not new. What placed him far above his environment, however, was the incomparable purity and moral earnestness of his preaching. Judaism, as it emerged from Harnack's work, was not differentiated from Christianity so much by doctrine as by morality, not by what Christianity had added to it but by the legalism which Judaism had unjustifiably superimposed on the prophetic message. For Harnack, as for his more traditional predecessors, Christianity remained the *only* genuine religion. As he stressed in his speech upon becoming rector of Berlin University, there was no other religion that needed to be studied in a faculty of theology. Not that Harnack had anything vicious to say about Judaism past or present; mostly he just ignored it. With the coming of Jesus' purer morality, Judaism had lost all historical significance.[58]

The writings of Wellhausen, Delitzsch, Harnack, and many others served to justify German Jews' indifference to their religion. They also made opportunistic conversion to Christianity—which, as Harnack made clear, demanded no sacrifice of the rational intellect—so much the more palatable. In practice an ever-increasing number of Jews was drifting away from even minimal religious observance, celebrating Christian holidays, and holding only loosely to a residual Jewish identity. Yet even as political antisemitism stirred German Jewry to unprecedented collective defense efforts, so did the contemporary denigration and disregard of Judaism produce a Jewish response that gave indications of resurgent intellectual vitality. By the turn of the century significant works were beginning to appear that reasserted Judaism's moral and religious claims in the midst of this hostile intellectual climate. For liberal Jewish thinkers, to whom ethics was the heart of Judaism, it was especially important to show that the individual and social morality reflected in Jewish tradition did not fall beneath that of Christianity. In part, of course, they wanted to refute antisemitic allegations, but also they were determined to shore up their coreligionists' own respect for Judaism, to present it as a faith eminently worthy of serious religious commitment even for the Jew who practiced few of the ritual commandments.

Already during the first years of the antisemitic agitation, Jewish community leaders became convinced of the need for a comprehensive presentation of Jewish ethics. In 1883 representatives from London, Paris, Vienna, and Berlin entrusted Moritz Lazarus, the philosopher, ethnologist, and president of the Leipzig and Augsburg synods, with composing such a work. The first result was a brief, basically apologetic listing of "fifteen principles of Jewish moral doctrine," signed by 350 rabbis and Jewish teachers across the religious spectrum and published in 1885. Of much greater significance was Lazarus' *The Ethics of Judaism,* the first volume of which appeared, after much delay, in 1898.[59] The Reform movement had long been engaged in shifting the focus of Judaism from ritual acts to moral conduct. In presenting for the first time a structured, integrated conception of Jewish ethics, Lazarus delivered nothing less than a guide for Liberal Jews.

The Ethics of Judaism is not simply an anthology of moral dicta excerpted from Jewish sources.[60] It seeks to determine the particular nature of Jewish ethical doctrine, its relation to God, and the dynamics of its development. The focus of Jewish morality, according to Lazarus, is the ideal of holiness conceived as moral perfection and applied as the sanctification of life. God represents the "source and archetype of the moral idea" or even "the moral idea itself." God must also be understood (in Kantian fashion) as the creator of the moral capacity in human beings. But moral decisions remain freely chosen human ones. In fact, Jewish morality, as Lazarus understands it, is not a corpus of revelation; it is the creation of what he terms the "collective spirit" of the Jews. Hence the texts of Judaism are not intrinsically sacred. They simply reflect stages in the continuous process of Jewish moral creativity and consequently are subject to critical evaluation. The ceremonial laws derive their value as vehicles of the moral ideas, and as such they play only a mediating role in the religious life.[61] Of central significance for Lazarus is the embodiment of Jewish moral principles in charitable institutions, whether those of talmudic times or of Jewish communities in the present. Indeed, what sets the Jewish ethic apart from the Christian is its dominantly social character. It is a morality directed, for example, far more to alleviating poverty than to personal sainthood. Lazarus was thus able to present an ethics which was at the same time religious, in that it set God and sanctification of life as fountainhead and purpose; differentiably Jewish in that it drew upon traditional sources, was the historical product of the Jewish people, and was uniquely directed to social improvement; and liberal in that individual conscience, as part of the larger collectivity, was engaged in the continual process of sifting and refining the heritage transmitted from earlier generations. The *Ethics* both reflected Liberal Judaism in Germany as it had developed to the end of the nineteenth century and gave its moral impulse a more substantial foundation. In an English translation of the first volume by Henrietta Szold, it also became influential in the United States, where, as we shall see, the Reform movement had taken a similar course.[62]

Lazarus was not, however, the most important Jewish thinker in Germany at the end of the nineteenth century. That distinction belongs without question to Hermann Cohen (1842–1918), the neo-Kantian philosopher whose Jewish writings mark a transition from the domination of ethics to an independent valuation of religion.[63] Cohen had been a student at the Breslau seminary but decided to give up a rabbinical career in favor of philosophy. From 1873 to 1912 he taught at the University of Marburg, where he produced an impressive corpus of critical and creative writings. His work constituted a new philosophical system deriving from Kant's fundamental ideas but adjusting them to meet the new challenges of contemporary materialism and existentialism, as well as the expanding natural sciences. During the last years of his life, while teaching at the Liberal College for Jewish Studies in Berlin (the previously mentioned *Hochschule,* or *Lehranstalt*—the lower rank to which the government reduced it in 1883), Cohen devoted his intellectual energies to harmonizing Judaism with his neo-Kantian worldview. Through his teaching he hoped to instill philosophical depth into the religious thinking of rabbis and laity.[64]

Even during his Marburg years, Cohen had from time to time expressed himself on Jewish matters, but his position was Jewishly minimalist, along the lines of the Berlin Reform Congregation. He emphatically opposed conversion to Christianity and castigated the younger faith for denying its inheritance from Judaism. But he differentiated Judaism only according to its historical forms, not fundamental religious beliefs, and he desired that differences in practice be minimized. He favored a German liturgy, celebration of the Sabbath on Sunday, and mixed marriages. In a response to Treitschke, Cohen confessed that he was unable to discern a difference in conception of religion between Israelite monotheism and Protestant Christianity. Throughout his life Cohen remained an ardent German patriot for whom service to the state was as sacred as religious worship and for whom Palestine was merely, as he once said, "a place for a vacation trip." At this stage in his life Cohen also believed that the best way to combat the recrudescence of antisemitism was by making Jews and Christians aware of the "common religious foundation" of their two traditions. Like Mendelssohn a century earlier, he understood that common foundation to consist of rational religion. But he differed in two respects: instead of Enlightenment naturalism, the uniting faith consisted of Kantian idealism, and while for Mendelssohn there had still remained the differentiating heritage of the Halakhah, for Cohen in this period of his life no special residue of consequence was left over.[65]

Yet increasingly after 1880 Cohen moved away from his position favoring religious amalgamation. We do not know the relative significance of the various factors, some of them personal, which brought him from general philosophy to Jewish philosophy in his work and from a universal faith ultimately transcending Judaism to a reaffirmation of his ancestors' particular religion. But it seems that for Cohen, as for Lazarus, the persistent attack on Judaism was an important factor. Our enemies, he wrote in 1902, seek to destroy our individuality "which lies in our religion and must have its permanence in it."[66] In a number of shorter writings and in a large work published posthumously in 1919, *Religion of Reason out of the Sources of Judaism,* Cohen elaborated the Judaism which he now believed could and should persist as an independent entity.[67] His thought represents the culmination and representation in systematic form of the ideas which had become the common coin of the Reform movement in the nineteenth century. But in some respects it also looks forward to the reorientation the movement would undergo in the twentieth. We can here sketch only the most significant points, sacrificing its philosophical complexity.

As for the Reformers, so too for Cohen, ethical monotheism was the heart of Judaism. God is not merely one in a numerical sense *(eins)* but unique *(einzig),* apart from nature of which God constitutes ground but not substance. Most important for ethics and religion, God exists as the ground and goal of morality without which moral aspirations would be but vain illusion. Cohen's God is neither the creator of the world in a temporal sense nor supernatural revealer of specific commands at Mount Sinai. God is rather the idea and ideal which continually sustain creation and morality. The human love of God is not the love of a Person, but of a moral ideal which transcends the self. God's love and forgiveness of human beings reveal themselves in the sense of renewed moral strength. Command and law in Judaism are the self-given human response to God as archetype and prototype of human morality.[68] In Cohen's earlier Jewish writings religion itself appeared as an appendage of this religious ethics. Its specific function was only to reaffirm personal commitment to the unending moral task. Later, however, Cohen ascribed independent significance to religion as uniquely concerning itself with the relation of particular human beings to their "neighbors," while ethics concerned itself with humanity as a whole and with individuals only as its faceless representatives. Yet though he went this far, for Cohen, the lifelong rationalist, religion never took on a numinous or mystical aspect. Holiness always remained confined to the moral realm.

Like the more radical Reformers, Cohen believed in an ongoing process of revelation, humanistically understood and manifesting itself in the teachings of successive generations. Like them too, he held that Jewish ceremony derived significance only from its capacity to serve as the symbol of moral values. The Liberal Jew was to select meaningful observances from the store of Jewish tradition. Similarly instrumental, rather than absolute, in Cohen's philosophy of Judaism is the role played by the Jewish people. It exists for a moral purpose beyond itself: to preserve and propagate the monotheistic idea.[69] Though by the last years of his life Cohen did speak of the Jews as a "nationality," that nationality existed to bear a religious message of universal importance to humanity. In the disapora of Jewry Cohen saw foreshadowed the future federation of states and the universal rule of God.[70]

Cohen's religious thought points toward his messianism, his biblical faith that one day the unity of God will be complemented by the unity of humanity. He called messianism "the most significant and original product of the Jewish spirit."[71] For Cohen the focus and significance of messianism lay not in the infinitely distant goal, but in the unending task of moral improvement, in human beings responding to the divine ideal. To him that response in practical terms meant a religious socialism, symbolized by the Sabbath. In assuring the independence of religion from domination by the state, messianism made possible a religious critique of social institutions. The Kingdom of God, as Judaism conceived it, was the unattained ideal that makes all present reality pass under the rod of judgment.[72]

Like Lazarus, Cohen helped shift the focus of Liberal Judaism more toward an affirmation of self, seen eminently in moral terms, and away from the critique of Orthodoxy which in the public mind chiefly characterized it. But while Lazarus had drawn together and attempted to define Jewish morality as heritage, Cohen's messianic emphasis directed attention to Judaism's moral vocation. His increasingly deeper appreciation of the role of religion in sustaining that vocation, and in its own sphere of developing sympathy for particular human beings, were early signs of a new religious consciousness that among younger Jewish thinkers would soon transcend both humanistic morality and the unchallenged rule of reason.

Among the Jews who felt called upon to respond to Adolf Harnack's *The Essence of Christianity* was a young rabbi in Oppeln who would later, in Berlin, become the outstanding figure in European Liberal Judaism. Leo Baeck (1873–1956) had studied for the rabbinate first at the conservative seminary in Breslau and then at the more liberal one in Berlin. He soon became a man of the middle, appreciating the complementary virtues of tradition and religious progress, particularism and universalism, mysticism and rationalism. Each came to represent for him one element in a polarity, not an absolute position. Jewish creativity, he believed, emerged from the dialectical tension within such polarities. A respected scholar as well as theologian and communal activist, Baeck not only played a significant role as the undisputed leader of German Jewry during its darkest years, but also presented Liberal Judaism with a theoretical foundation that was set more broadly on Jewish historical experience.[73]

Baeck initially responded to Harnack with a lengthy review of his lectures. His criticisms of the Berlin theologican were chiefly scholarly: the apologist and polemicist in Harnack, he argued, had overwhelmed the historian. He had judged his own religion by what he subjectively found best in it, while consigning Judaism to the image of Pharisaism found in the New Testament. Harnack, of course, had the right to glorify Christianity, but not to distort the past to use it more effectively as a weapon against Judaism.[74] Yet merely to refute Harnack on historical grounds was not enough. A question remained: What, in fact, was the real Judaism which Harnack and others had misrepresented? In 1905 Baeck published his *The Essence of Judaism,* not so much any longer to counter Harnack as to set out for Jews the basic contents of their faith.

For Baeck in 1905, as for Cohen and the earlier Reformers, the essence of Judaism lay in its ethical monotheism. Like Cohen, Baeck was philosophically under the spell of Kant; the ethical commandment in Judaism, as he perceived it, was very similar to the German philosopher's categorical imperative. Like Cohen, too, Baeck read Judaism in a highly selective way, stressing the moral and universal texts, and drawing forth a rational religion. This rationality and moral emphasis, he would later stress, set Judaism sharply apart from the romanticism inherent in Pauline Christianity.[75] Yet Baeck also moved beyond philosophical idealism in that his God exists independently of human thought, and is known through revelation. God commands to all the generations of Israel; prophets and sages attempt to interpret the imperative, to respond to it, to symbolize it in ritual; Jews in every age are able to love this God as Person and address God in prayer. The election of Israel, as the people of the commandment, both sets the people apart and directs it toward a messianic task within humanity.

In the following years Baeck moved even further away from Cohen's position. In the second edition of *The Essence of Judaism* (1922) and in other works the moral and rational elements in Judaism, as well as its universal goals, are increasingly balanced by their polar counterparts, which achieve equivalent importance. However strong the moral bond between God and humans, Baeck came to believe that religion encompassed more. It was forced to acknowledge the unfathomability of the Divine, to appreciate what reason could not fully grasp. In Baeck's later writings, the concept of holiness is no longer exclusively moral as it was for Cohen. Commandment *(Gebot)* is now set into polarity with mystery *(Geheimnis)*. God "does not reveal Himself, but He reveals the commandment and the grace"; ultimate truth remains veiled: "the mystery surrounds God."[76] Baeck thus brought the numinous character of religion into Liberal Judaism, where rationalism had heretofore squeezed it out.

As Baeck's dialectical thinking sought to bring Liberal Judaism to a greater appreciation of the inscrutable transcendence of God alongside the revealed messianic imperative, so did his writings increasingly shift the emphasis from the religious message to its messenger. The Reform movement had stressed the former, subordinating Israel to the spiritual legacy it bore and to its universal task. Baeck's writings attempt to restore the balance. The Jews are neither purely a community of faith, he argued in 1917, nor simply a nation.[77] As the former they would have no real historical existence; as the latter they possess no adequate reason for remaining separate from the world. The essence of Judaism, Baeck came increasingly to believe, lies in the historical existence of the Jewish people. But that existence is meaningless without religious content; the history of Israel becomes significant only when it is understood as ongoing response to revelation. To conceive of Israel merely as a people like all others represents no less radical assimilation to Baeck's mind than to deprive it of its ethnic foundation. Here again Baeck sought out a middle path: Israel lives its historical, religious life within the polar tensions of its particular relation to God and the universal task imposed by that relation.

Behind these reflections, of course, loomed the specter of the Zionist movement, which had made religion secondary to nationhood. Indeed, it was Zionism—itself a direct response to the external attack upon Jews and Judaism—that provided a second fundamental and ongoing challenge to Liberal Judaism.

Already in *Rome and Jerusalem* (1862), the precursory work of political Zionism by Moses Hess (1812–1875), we find the Reform movement stigmatized as the wrong response to modernity. Judaism indeed consisted of kernel and husk, as the Reformers believed, but the kernel was not ethical monotheism; it was Jewish nationality. Like Geiger, Hess believed in a Jewish religious genius, but he also believed it could be revived only on native soil. Jewish ceremonies, even for the nonbeliever, possessed value as folk traditions sustaining national rebirth. In depriving the Jewish religion of its national basis, Hess argued, the Reformers had sucked the marrow out of Judaism, leaving it a dry skeleton. "Reform," he concluded, "has raised baseless negation to the rank of a principle."[78]

Generally, the Reformers tried to ignore Hess's book. Geiger, without even mentioning Hess by name, wrote only in passing of "an almost total outsider, who has gone bankrupt on socialism and all kinds of other humbug," and who was now trying to foist nationality upon the Jews. Ludwig Philippson was at first inclined to publish no review at all in the *Allgemeine Zeitung des Judentums,* but finally agreed to print a concise critical one by the Frankfurt Jewish scholar Raphael Kirchheim. Leopold Löw in Hungary did review the book at length, but he dismissed Hess's political program as "an empty phantom," based on failure to understand the real world, both Jewish and Gentile. And in an unpublished critique Samuel Hirsch pointed out Hess's particular ignorance of the Reform movement, which he mistakenly identified with its most radical manifestations.[79] Hess's work was soon forgotten and remained out of mind for a generation. The efforts at modern colonization of Palestine from eastern Europe, beginning in the 1880s, represented little threat to Western Jews, since they could claim that their own political situation, unlike that of coreligionists in pogrom-ridden Russia, warranted no such action.

It was only with the rise of an internationally organized political Zionism at the end of the century that Jews in the West generally, but especially those culturally most integrated, began to recognize that the new movement represented a frightening menace they could not ignore. Theodor Herzl (1860–1904) had argued in his *The Jewish State* (1896) that Jews were nowhere safe from antisemitism, that Jew-hatred could not be overcome by apologetics, defense organizations, and patriotic loyalty. His solution was not simply the establishment of new settlements in the land of Israel but the creation of a sovereign state. And Herzl immediately moved ahead to call a Zionist congress and to form a highly visible world movement.

The two leading German Liberal rabbis of that time now felt compelled to issue a joint statement.[80] Sigmund Maybaum (1844–1919) was an outstanding preacher in Berlin as well as a scholar who taught homiletics at the *Hochschule;* Heinemann Vogelstein (1841–1911), rabbi in Stettin, had just published a popular new Liberal prayerbook in the Geiger tradition. Together they declared that the new Zionist newspaper, *Die Welt,* was a "calamity" that must be resisted: "As long as the Zionists wrote in Hebrew, they were not dangerous, now that they write in German it is necessary to oppose them." Maybaum and Vogelstein were scandalized that the Zionist movement was planning to hold its congress in Munich, not in some east European town, and they explicitly questioned whether Jewish claims for as yet unrealized equality *de facto* could be effective if Jews declared themselves nationally separate. Of course Liberal Judaism was not alone in its opposition to Zionism. The executive board of the Association of German Rabbis, composed of Orthodox as well as Liberals, soon issued a formal protest, which was a principal factor in forcing the First Zionist Congress from Munich to Basle.[81] Across the religious spectrum German rabbis held that Zionism contradicted the messianic destiny of Judaism. They would allow only for modern colonization in Palestine, since that did not imply the establishment of a state. Only two rabbis out of more than ninety at the Association's convention in 1898 refused to confirm the protest.[82] However, it was in German Liberal Judaism that anti-Zionism became almost an article of faith and in some instances assumed extreme form. Ludwig Geiger, Abraham's son, a scholar of German Jewish history and German literature who was later editor of the *Allgemeine Zeitung des Judentums,* represented the most radical position. He perceived Zionism as the sad consequence of antisemitism and believed it would eventually disappear along with its progenitor. German Jews, he held, were clearly German in all of their cultural attributes and in their political loyalty; few would ever become Zionists. Yet Zionism was dangerous and pernicious because it drew Jewish funds away from German Jewish institutions, could lead to legal discrimination against German Jews, and was attracting talented young men whose energies were lost to the established community.[83]

Zionism was certainly unlikely to take over German Jewry. Liberals generally controlled the major Jewish communities, while the Zionist movement in Germany by 1910 had only 6,800 members. Yet the Zionists did enjoy a high degree of commitment from their membership, while Liberal Jews were mostly those who lacked both the pious devotion of the Orthodox and the infectuous enthusiasm which the new Jewish nationalism generated among the youth. Many Liberal Jews were liberals far more than they were Jews, and like political and cultural liberals in Germany generally, they treated religion with indifference or disdain. Yet antisemitism and Zionism did not allow them to forget their Jewishness entirely. If they were not to choose apostasy—as an increasing number did—they had to rally around their particular version of Judaism. The opportunity was thus created for serious-minded Liberal Jewish leaders to establish a more solid basis for their movement. This they attempted to do in the years preceding World War I through the establishment of an organizational structure and a program that would raise the Liberals' level of commitment. Indeed, it was only in this period that the German Reform movement, now well settled into denominational status as "Liberal Judaism," established ongoing national organizations and formulated its platform.

In 1898 Heinemann Vogelstein created the Union of Liberal Rabbis in Germany, which by World War I had seventy-two members. It held conferences that discussed mostly practical issues such as the permissibility of cremation, procedure for accepting proselytes, and laws of marriage and divorce. At the same time the Liberal laity was organizing as well. From local associations, created essentially to campaign in community elections, a Union for Liberal Judaism in Germany was formed in 1908, composed of both laity and rabbis, but headed by a layman.[84] Its program called for the harmonization of Jewish teaching and daily life, ample use of German in the religious service, Jewish education in harmony with the findings of science, and a larger role for women in religious life.[85] The initial conference, held that year in Berlin, drew more than 200 participants and generated considerable excitement. Liberal Judaism seemed at last to be emerging from a position of passivity and reaction to one of positive intent. In a little over a year the Union could boast over 5,000 members, representing some 200 German communities. It created a periodical, *Liberales Judentum,* edited by Rabbi Caesar Seligmann (1860–1950) of Frankfurt, which, unlike the *Allgemeine Zeitung des Judentums,* was devoted almost exclusively to religious issues. The Union and its local groups sponsored lectures on Liberal Judaism and a Liberal youth movement.

The rabbis in the Union were eager that it also produce a platform which would clearly set forth not only what Liberal Jews believed, but also what Liberal Judaism required of its adherents. After lengthy discussions by a committee of laymen and rabbis and with unanimous approval from the Liberal rabbinate, the "Guidelines toward a Program for Liberal Judaism" were presented to the third biennial conference of the Union, meeting in Posen in 1912. The proposed platform is remarkable in that it breathes a wholly positive spirit, free of any polemic against either Orthodoxy or Zionism. Of the thirteen major paragraphs, eight are concerned with theology, two with individual observance, one with religious and educational institutions, and the last two with implementation and aspirations.[86] The theological section presents the basic beliefs regarding God, moral responsibility, freedom, and personal immortality shared by all religious Jews and the aspiration that the universal principles of Judaism will one day become the religion of humanity. It is Israel's task to maintain the purity of its eternal faith and proclaim it through deed and example. Jewish observances retain their value if they bring individual Jews into closer relationship with God, remind them of moral obligations, sanctify family life, express pious sentiments toward the living and dead, strengthen the bonds of the religious community, and awaken a noble Jewish self-consciousness. The Guidelines then call for specific observances incumbent on Liberal Jews: to celebrate Sabbaths and holidays both at home and in the synagogue, suspending all working activity though not necessarily abiding by all the traditional strictures; to pray daily in the home; to circumcize and confirm children; to recite the Kaddish for the dead; and to get married—and if necessary divorced—according to religious rites modified to give women equality. The tenth paragraph then adds: "Whoever satisfies these indispensable demands is to be regarded as a religious Jew. Liberal Judaism leaves the observance of all further traditional prescriptions which affect the individual to his own religious sensibilities." Thus, for example, whether the observance of *kashrut* is of personal significance remains each member's decision. After a paragraph reaffirming the basic manner of the religious service as then practiced in Liberal synagogues and urging improvement of religious education, the Guidelines conclude with the hope that the implementation of this program will overcome widespread alienation from Judaism and secure the future of the Jewish religion.

Debate at the conference centered almost exclusively on the demands for observance in the latter part of the Guidelines. Laity pitted themselves against rabbis. While the rabbis wanted a Liberal Judaism which demanded clear religious commitments, laymen believed the draft before them represented an invasion of their freedom to decide observance or nonobservance for themselves. Agreement could be reached only after a crippling provision was introduced into the resolution of adoption. It stated: "True to the basic principles of every liberalism, the Union leaves taking a stand on the demands of the Guidelines affecting the religious life of the individual to the conscientious examination and conviction of its members." It was thus apparent that even the most committed of Liberal Jews in Germany, the leaders of the Union gathered in conference, were not ready to lend firm support to a program that would give ritual commandment a more equivalent status with moral imperative.[87] Individual freedom was an essential component of their liberalism, which they were not willing to compromise. As some put it, they did not want a new *Shulḥan Arukh*. Thus the impact of the Guidelines, adopted only with this limiting provision, and arousing more Orthodox attacks than Liberal enthusiasm, was only minimal. Though they remained the only comprehensive religious platform for Liberal Jewry in Germany until its destruction in the Holocaust, they did not produce the religious commitment for which the rabbinical leadership had hoped.

Following the 1912 conference, German Liberal Judaism gradually returned to its earlier lethargy, the promising organizational initiative weakened by the outbreak of war, the attempted positive program hobbled by a laity which continued to express Jewish identity mainly through defense against antisemitism and polemics against

Zionism. Liberal laymen, it became apparent, were in the mass irreversibly secular-ized Jews, who called themselves religious principally to escape suspicion that their Judaism might be national. They directed their energies to winning community elec-tions, lest the combined forces of Orthodox and Zionists be empowered to set a course detrimental to their candidly assimilatory ambitions.[88]

Yet simultaneously the spiritual leadership of Liberal Judaism in Germany was already moving away from the antitraditionalism, anti-Zionism, and religious ratio-nalism that still characterized the laity. We have already seen how Leo Baeck repre-sented this trend. But he was not alone. Caesar Seligmann had long spoken of a romantic "will to Judaism" as more fundamental in preserving Jewish identity than adherence to any set of religious principles; and although he personally became a Zionist only during the Hitler period, he had early welcomed the Zionist movement as bringing renewed vigor to Judaism. Max Wiener (1882–1950), one of the most thoughtful and scholarly of German Liberal rabbis, likewise appreciated the value of Zionism for Jewish renewal, and he participated in Zionist projects. Like Baeck, Wie-ner gradually abandoned the tutelage of Hermann Cohen, forsaking philosophical ide-alism in favor of the conception of a divine moral will that emerges as revelation from out of the mystery. For Wiener feelings of Jewish solidarity came to assume as much importance as Jewish thought and belief. And while he did not ascribe the same weight to ritual commandments as to moral ones, he did stress repeatedly that religious acts, not doctrines, were the basis of Judaism.[89] Thus German Liberal Judaism emerged from World War I in unresolved tension. At its center was a small inner core, mostly rabbis, which was moving toward a more traditional theology along with greater appreciation of Jewish peoplehood. On the periphery was the mass of laity, which voted Liberal in community elections and affirmed a vaguely Jewish universalism, but whose personal feelings and commitments were far more German than Jewish.

"Liberal Judaism" in England and France

During the years from 1881 until World War I a large influx of Jews from eastern Europe substantially altered the composition of English Jewry. The Russian Jewish immigrants, who settled mainly in the East End of London, differed so markedly in language, manners, and socioeconomic status from native British Jews that differences among the latter now seemed relatively minor. Established Orthodoxy, with its stiff dignity and Anglicized forms, was as strange to the newcomers as the Reform of the West London Synagogue. They remained separate from both, worshiping in their accustomed informal manner. For native British Jews, as well, religious differences among themselves now seemed less significant. To be sure, the West London Syn-agogue had had an organ since 1859, no longer prayed for the reinstitution of the sacrificial service, and after the turn of the century introduced a bit more English into the service. But men and women continued to sit apart (until after World War I), the liturgy remained only slightly heterodox, and its mixed choir had been copied by some Orthodox congregations.[90] Morris Joseph (1848–1930), who succeeded David Woolf Marks as minister of the West London Synagogue in 1893, was a moderate easily acceptable to the congregation's conservative lay leadership. Joseph termed his views an "intermediate position." He differed from Marks mainly in not distinguishing as sharply between the authority of the Written and Oral Law. While recognizing the validity of biblical criticism, he stressed its tentativeness and believed the subject should not be discussed from the pulpit. And having abandoned fundamentalism with regard to Scripture, he balanced that departure with greater veneration for postbiblical Jewish literature and an advocacy of modified traditional observance. Joseph was at his most radical in no longer ascribing absolute authority to any sacred text and in placing the burden of religious decision upon the individual. But few practical conclusions emerged from such a potentially explosive idea. They were muted in what had become the West London Synagogue's own traditional atmosphere.[91]

If the new immigrants found Reform Judaism unattractive because of its formality, some of the most acculturated English Jews were repelled by its closeness to Orthodoxy. Educated in non-Jewish schools, their world was English; they knew English literature well, but possessed little knowledge of Judaism. What they did know of it they found intellectually or morally repugnant: the anthropomorphic God, the supernatural revelation at Sinai, the idea of chosenness represented by the primitive rite of circumcision, the flawed virtues of biblical characters.[92] The Talmud was no longer the issue, as it had been two generations earlier. It was now the Bible and the prayerbook—indeed, Judaism as such—that were problematic. Nothing distinctively Jewish seemed worth preserving, and its universal elements could be found elsewhere as well. Such alienated English Jews favored mixed marriages and found a new spiritual home for themselves outside Judaism. By the end of the nineteenth century some were joining the Unitarian church, others a new movement called Theism. Unitarianism, which arose in England a hundred years earlier, maintained the centrality of the New Testament, with which well-educated English Jews were increasingly familiar, but divested itself of all Christian dogmas. The Theistic church, founded in London in 1871, was equally rationalistic but at the same time more fully universalistic, welcoming former Jews along with former Christians. Jewish adherents of both churches could pray in English on Sundays, knowing that the service would reflect their own views far better than any Jewish worship, Orthodox or Reform.[93] But most of the very Anglicized British Jews remained nominally within Judaism. They were basically secularists who drifted about the periphery, without crossing over into any other affiliation. The new Liberal movement which arose in English Jewry at the end of the nineteenth century was especially intended to address the religious situation of these peripheral Jews.

The spiritual progenitor of what became "Liberal" Judaism in England was Claude Goldsmid Montefiore (1858–1938).[94] On his father's side a grandnephew of the staunchly Orthodox Moses Montefiore, he was on his mother's a grandson of Isaac Lyon Goldsmid, who had been instrumental in creating the English Reform movement. Montefiore grew up within the West London Synagogue and always retained an emotional attachment to it, though his university years removed him from it intellectually. At Oxford, where he was one of the first Jews to matriculate, Montefiore came under the profound and enduring influence of Benjamin Jowett, the Master of Balliol College.[95] Known especially as the translator of Plato's dialogues, Jowett was also a theologically trained liberal religious thinker. He took Montefiore under his wing and invited him regularly, along with other favored students, to his country retreat. In Jowett, Montefiore found a Christian who combined common sense and healthy skepticism with a deep religious faith, a model for his own religious development. Importantly for Montefiore, Jowett did not deride either the Old Testament or postbiblical Judaism. "The language of the prophets," he wrote, "has a much nearer relation to our feelings than the language of St. Paul, and infinitely nearer than the language of dogmatic theology." And to Montefiore personally he suggested that neither Christianity nor Judaism should see itself as the only legitimate faith: "Each religion has its function and truth, and the one may be a complement for the other." After Jowett had asked Montefiore to deliver the prestigious Hibbert Lectures for 1892 on the faith of ancient Israel, he suggested that the presentation should "make the Hebrew religion more intelligible, more connected to us, to contain more of the principles in which a good man lives; to make it less a source of religious enmity among mankind." In Germany the very extension of such an academic honor to a Jew would have been regarded as highly inappropriate, the notion that Christians had something to learn about ancient Israel from a Jewish perspective almost unimaginable. As we have seen, exclusivistic German theologians like Harnack provoked polemical responses intended to protect the honor of Judaism. Oxford liberalism had a very different effect on the young Montefiore. He became convinced that Jowett's teaching "can be translated, and it needs to be translated, into Jewish." What that meant to Montefiore was above all to universalize Judaism fully, removing those narrower elements which militated against appreciation of truths outside it. Those truths might be found in biblical criticism or even in the New Testament. Jowett suggested to Montefiore that he devote himself "to the Jewish race as the task of your life," and his disciple readily took up the challenge.[96]

While still at Oxford, Montefiore steeped himself in the writings of the German Reformers. He regretted that their efforts to transform Judaism from a tribal into a "catholic" religion had found so little echo in England. He derided the inconsistencies of the Breslau Seminary and associated himself especially with Geiger, whose greater regard for historical continuity in Judaism made him more appealing than Holdheim.[97] The Liberal Judaism which Montefiore himself set forth in subsequent writings mostly resembled the German variety which he had discovered. He, too, put ethical monotheism at the center, saw ritual commands as only instrumental, stressed the mission of Israel, and rejected Jewish nationalism. Where Montefiore's thought differed, the variation was mainly due to the more tolerant—while also critical—religious thought he encountered in England and the possibility for freer expression of ideas within the British Jewish community.

Whereas in Germany the need to preserve unity within the collective *Gemeinde* inhibited outspoken advocacy of radical ideas by community rabbis, English Jewry lacked an equivalent all-encompassing structure. The West London Synagogue had existed independently for two generations, and there was no practical reason why a new, less compromising movement should not come into existence alongside it. Such a movement, as Montefiore early envisaged it, would differ especially in its unequivocal acceptance of biblical criticism. It would show that the critical spirit need not vitiate the true values of religion. For if one believed that final religious authority lay within each individual, not in the text, then it did not matter that the Pentateuch was composed of diverse sources, that Moses was not its author. Nor did it matter that certain biblical customs were repugnant or the conduct of some biblical characters was less than exemplary. The Bible's shortcomings were attributable to its human aspect. Indeed, belief in the unmediated divinity of the biblical text was detrimental to religion, for "if the Bible were perfect, God would have revealed Himself all at once, and

Claude G. Montefiore.

progress in religion would have been neither possible nor desirable." The Bible, in Montefiore's view, was indeed a record of highest inspiration, but it was not in its totality a mandate for all times. "The book is not good because it is from God; it is from God so far as it is good. . . . The final authority is within."[98]

Among the books of the Bible, Montefiore found more to affirm in the prophetic literature than in the Pentateuch. Biblical criticism had created a mist around the figure of Moses; tradition associated him with outdated ritual commands as well as moral ones. But if Moses was unquestionably the founder of Israel's religion, the Prophets could be seen as its "second founders," their doctrines encompassing the very essence of modern Judaism. So persuaded was Montefiore of the greater contemporary relevance of the Prophets that he seriously suggested giving symbolic expression to the shift in importance. Were a Liberal Jew to build a synagogue without reference to past custom, he declared, that Jew "would not put scrolls of the Law into an ark and make that ark the most sacred part of the building. If he had such an ark, he would put in it the prophecies of Amos, Hosea and Isaiah, rather than the Pentateuch, for the Prophets are more primary and more essential than the Law."[99]

Montefiore's Prophetic Judaism extended beyond the boundary of the Hebrew Bible into the New Testament. While he did not advocate that Jews regard the Gospels as Scripture, he did argue that Jesus, as a Jew in the prophetic tradition, deserved Jewish appreciation. Paul too, he believed, possessed a profound religious genius, and his epistles included noble elements worthy of Jewish adoption. To be sure, the New Testament also contained a great deal Jews could not accept—particularly Jesus' purported special relationship with God. To a Jew, Jesus could only be *a* Master, not *the* Master—as he was even for Unitarians. But then the Liberal Jew was no less required to pick and choose from his own Hebrew Bible. "If we can exercise a careful eclecticism in Deuteronomy and Isaiah, we can also exercise it in the Epistles to the Romans and the Corinthians."[100] Opening the borders of Judaism to take in what was compatible with it in Christianity was for Montefiore not only a response to Jowett, it was also Montefiore's way of neutralizing the attraction for Jews of Unitarianism and Theism. One could remain a Jew and still accept basic teachings from Christianity. The New Testament would simply "complement" or "supplement" Judaism.

Montefiore's suggestion that Jews look favorably upon Christian teaching was the most controversial of his ideas. For if the essence of Judaism lay in its universal doctrines and it could legitimately draw even the founder of Christianity into its circle, then what was left to set Judaism apart? Why not, after all, become a Theist or a Unitarian? Why not intermarry? Montefiore's frequently reiterated reply focused on two basic points, relating respectively to past and future. Judaism, he stressed repeatedly, was a "historical religion." Its basic doctrines were indeed universal, but they had been formulated, preserved, and developed by Jews. Jews had given their lives for them and Jewish memory sustained loyalty to them. Judaism, for Montefiore, was a "religious home" or, in another metaphor, a particular "channel" in which the waters of universal faith flowed with greater momentum.[101] Judaism also possessed "one narrower dogma"—the election and mission of Israel. Like the German Reformers, Montefiore fervently believed that Israel was divinely chosen to carry a universal message to humanity. Jews might accept or reject the inherited burden, but they could not deny it without rejecting their spiritual identity. For Montefiore personally, the idea was crucial. "Till the earth is filled with the knowledge of the One God—the God of Israel—the Jews will be his witnesses," he wrote in a letter. "I should collapse morally and *spiritually* if I did not believe that."[102] That divinely ordained mission, in Montefiore's thought, was the one specifically Jewish commandment. It provided an enduring "ought" for remaining Jewish where Halakhah and sacred texts had lost intrinsic authority.

Montefiore defined the Jews as a "religious brotherhood." He would not call them a nationality or, in the present, a people. Proudly he declared himself "an Englishman of the Jewish persuasion."[103] When the British government consulted him on the Balfour Declaration, he spoke against its adoption, and before it was promulgated, he joined in a letter of protest to *The Times* of London. Though his anti-Zionism was widely shared by English Jews across the religious spectrum, Jewish nationalism was especially repugnant to Montefiore because it denied the Jewish mission. Only occasionally in his writings and speeches does one hear a more conciliatory note. Once he pondered the possibility that a new generation of Jews growing up in Palestine might combine Jewish nationality with the universal faith of Liberal Judaism. And in an address to American Reform rabbis in 1910 he pointed out that it was possible to be a Zionist and still a good Liberal Jew if one believed, for example, that antisemitism would endure and that the Sabbath could be properly celebrated only in the Jews' own land. But personally Montefiore never did reconcile himself to Zionism, even in the 1930s. Admitting the diminishing support for his position, he called himself a "diehard."[104]

Undoubtedly Montefiore's strong identification as an Englishman was an important factor in his anti-Zionism. But it would be an error to discount his religious argument against Jewish nationalism as mere rationalization. For Montefiore, like Jowett, was, despite all of his rationalism and devotion to historical criticism, a fervent believer. At the heart of his universal faith was a theism that affirmed the dominion of God over nature and history. God was "a person, but not like ourselves." He believed that "man and God communicate with each other" and that God hears prayer. The worship service presented an opportunity to feel that God was near and to accept God's will into one's own life. The link was "mysterious," he admitted, but nonetheless real.[105] That so many of the Zionist leaders did not share his own religiosity helped to make the movement odious in his eyes.

Montefiore's personal religious and moral ideal was saintliness—and sympathetic contemporaries did indeed consider him a saint.[106] Though born to wealth and status, he was exceptional within the closely knit Jewish aristocracy, or "cousinhood," as it has been called. He neither smoked nor drank, was usually serious if not solemn, paid little attention to external appearance, and sought few worldly pleasures. He was an intellectual among financiers, a philanthropist who believed good works were required by his religion, not merely by his status. Unlike many of the German Reformers, Montefiore never underwent a sharp break with Orthodoxy and his life ran its course untroubled by the inner turmoil and ambivalence which characterized theirs. His Liberal Judaism emerged less out of a rejection of tradition than an attraction to broader horizons. Within a regular circle of Christian clergymen he could frankly discuss the religious issues of the day, feeling fully at home in their midst. Among fellow Jews he sought a liberalization of outlook, which he believed would make Judaism more appropriate to the intellectual and religious climate in which they lived. He was not, however, a man who easily took organizational initiatives. Montefiore outlined a program for Liberal Judaism in England and he remained its mentor, but he did not bring it into institutional existence.

That honor belongs to Lily Montagu (1873–1963), the first significant woman in the history of the Reform movement.[107] Unlike Montefiore, Montagu grew up in a strictly Orthodox home. Her father, a newcomer to wealth, was among the founders of the affluent but wholly traditional New West End Synagogue. As a child she was tutored in religion by the synagogue's minister, Simeon Singer, later the compiler of the standard Orthodox prayerbook. Her prominent origins endowed her with a status that would be most helpful in her work, but her traditional background proved an enduring pain, as her father, to whom she was closely attached, utterly rejected her liberal vocation. Early drawn to personal faith when childhood fears were calmed by reassurance that God was near, Lily Montagu had already in adolescence fused religion with social amelioration, beginning a long career of work for and among underprivileged Jewish girls. But she could not find inspiration in the Orthodox synagogue. Her personal religious consciousness initially owed more to Victorian writers than to Jewish texts or ceremonies. Indeed, had she lived in Germany during the Romantic age, she might well, like the "salon Jewesses" of a hundred years earlier, have sought religious fulfillment outside of Judaism.[108] That she was able to be religious within the Jewish community was due mainly to her acquaintance with Montefiore's early writings.

Not only did Montagu adopt Montefiore's still inchoate Liberal Judaism, she also felt a kinship with him that was grounded in a similar sense of religious vocation. Fifteen years younger than he, she always regarded Montefiore as her intellectual guide and model. Her own writings and sermons echoed his universalism, his view of the Bible, his anti-Zionism, and his intolerance of mixed marriage. Still, her particular religiosity possessed a slightly different impulse. Even more than Montefiore she dwelt upon religion as personal experience. She spoke frequently of the external God who cares for and loves each person as well as of the "God within." A Jew who did not pray to God was, in her eyes, not a Jew "in the real sense of the word." She was personally observant both of the Sabbath and the dietary laws. Keeping the latter, she argued, could "only strengthen our conception of the innumerable sacrifices which Judaism demands in the cause of truth and righteousness."[109] Montagu also expressed the conviction that Liberal Judaism was especially suited to what she regarded as the particular spiritual characteristics of women. Just as women were oriented inward, so did Liberal Judaism place ultimate authority for belief and practice within the individual soul; in demanding reverence for all of life, it accorded with the synthetic unifying conceptualization, as opposed to scientific analysis, which distinguished the female intellect from the male.[110] Finally, Montagu's style was different. Montefiore's was theological, expository, scholarly, often over the heads of his hearers when he turned essays into sermons. Montagu invariably wrote and spoke as a preacher. She exhorted and remonstrated, almost always choosing the first person plural. Theory was less her concern than practical commitment and action.

Once Montagu had come to the conclusion that genuine religiosity was possible within Judaism as well as outside it, she determined to create an association that would give it expression. In 1899 she outlined plans for drawing together a "band of worshippers" attached to one another by common piety and moral commitment. They would seek to "revive Judaism, and having reconciled its dogma with our highest conception of truth and beauty, allow it again to bind us to the God who cares for us."[111] Two years later, Montagu wrote a letter to friends and relatives urging them to participate in a collective effort that would "strengthen the religious life in our midst."[112] The letter was not a manifesto of religious reform. It said nothing directly critical of Orthodoxy or religiously radical. The new association, as she envisaged it, would simply extend into religion the social obligations to fellow Jews felt by members of her class. The blessing of religion was to be restored to those who had lost it.

Positive response to the letter came from traditionalists no less than from liberals. That the organizer was a woman made little difference in the British context, where women were already playing an active role in Christian religious life.[113] Moreover, as the daughter of a respected Orthodox family, Miss Montagu deserved a hearing. What was not realized at first was the inherent contradiction present in Lily Montagu's idea. The new association was to be acceptable to all serious Jews since it intended to bring the religiously wayward back to Judaism. But the character of the Judaism which it would foster—as soon became apparent—lay well beyond what most English Jews were ready to accept as their own.

The Jewish Religious Union was formed at a series of meetings held during the fall and winter of 1901/1902.[114] Pressured by Lily Montagu, Montefiore agreed to serve as president. Montagu herself became one of three vice presidents, along with the Orthodox minister and family friend Simeon Singer, and Albert Jessel, a prominent laymen in the United Synagogue. Two other Orthodox ministers, more liberal than their colleagues, joined the JRU's twelve-person organizing committee, as did other leading Orthodox laymen and Morris Joseph, the minister of the West London Synagogue. This broad spectrum of English Jewry could unite on the new Union's expressed aim: "To provide means for deepening the religious spirit among those members of the Jewish Community who are not in sympathy with the present Synagogue Services, or who are unable to attend them." That aspiration would be implemented by establishing religious services supplementary to those of existing synagogues, by holding public lectures, and by issuing publications.[115]

The JRU was greatly strengthened in this formative period by the active participation on its organizing committee of Israel Abrahams (1858–1924), the best-known Jewish scholar in England.[116] Abrahams' father had been the principal of Jews' College, the Orthodox institution which trained Jewish ministers, and he himself taught homiletics there. In 1902 Abrahams was appointed Reader in Talmudic and Rabbinic Literature at Cambridge University. At the time that he joined the JRU his *Jewish Life in the Middle Ages* (1896) was on its way to becoming a classic and his column on Jewish books appeared regularly in the *Jewish Chronicle.* Together with his close friend and agemate Claude Montefiore, Abrahams edited the *Jewish Quarterly Review,* a journal devoted both to scholarship and to the liberalization of Judaism. Montefiore and Abrahams agreed on basic issues: on political Zionism, biblical criticism, and openness to Christianity. They differed in that Abrahams possessed a deeper feeling of worldwide Jewish cultural unity and a greater appreciation for Jewish ritual. Though opposed to Herzlian Zionism, Abrahams was a proponent of modern spoken Hebrew and later advocated the early establishment of a center for Jewish learning at the new university in Jerusalem.[117] While intellectually no less a liberal than Montefiore, Abrahams spoke readily of Liberal Jews' "emotional agreement" with their traditional coreligionists and of the close bond among all Jews resulting from common religious symbols and holiday celebration.[118] Even opponents of Liberal Judaism admired Abrahams, tried to minimize his Liberal affiliation, and declared that he was really beyond parties, a reconciler rather than a rebel. But Montefiore eulogized him as "our Rabbi" and fully recognized the value of having so widely respected a scholar in the Liberal camp.[119] When Liberal Judaism was accused of lacking depth or Jewish loyalty, the common response was: "But what about Abrahams?" It was Abrahams, later the annotator of Simeon Singer's standard Orthodox prayerbook, who helped create the liturgy for the JRU services and who defended its historical authenticity when Chief Rabbi Hermann Adler condemned it as un-Jewish.[120]

Before the establishment of the JRU there had been some earlier liturgical experiments. In 1890, before he became minister of the West London Synagogue, Morris Joseph had conducted ideologically modified Sabbath afternoon services in the West Hampstead Town Hall, and in 1899 two efforts were made to establish Sunday services.[121] But none of these ventures was able to survive organizational weakness and Orthodox opposition. The Jewish Religious Union, by contrast, with its broadly based, respected, and devoted leadership, augured for better success. After careful deliberation, its Committee decided to hold services at 3:30 on Saturday afternoons, when those Jews who worked in the morning would be free to attend and when they would not compete with the congregational worship. The possibility of Sunday worship was rejected as undermining the historical Jewish Sabbath.

On October 18, 1902, the JRU held its first service in a rented hall at the Hotel Great Central in West London.[122] Reverend Simeon Singer read the liturgy; Claude Montefiore gave the sermon. Men and women sat together, with hats optional for the men, but mostly worn. A mixed choir sang to the accompaniment of a harmonium. There was no Torah scroll from which to read, and with a few exceptions the liturgy was in English. Each participant was handed an "Order of Service" which indicated the particular prayers, readings, and hymns for the day. The texts, based on the tra-

ditional liturgy but freely departing from it, avoided reference to reinstitution of sacrifices, return to Zion, and resurrection. The mission of Israel took its place in the
provisional prayerbook and the Ten Commandments were recited in unison while the
participants stood.[123] English hymns, some of them composed by non-Jews, were sung
by the congregation. The freely chosen scriptural text for the day was Ezekiel's vision
of the dry bones, apparently representing for the JRU those skeletal Jews whose religious faith it hoped to revive. Three hundred to four hundred men and women
attended that first service, which lasted a little over an hour.

In succeeding weeks ten different preachers spoke, among them Abrahams, Joseph,
the Orthodox ministers Singer and Wolf, and the Zionist Harry S. Lewis. Justifiably,
the JRU prided itself on its free pulpit, where laymen as well as ministers were at
liberty to express conflicting views. Abrahams could also note that there was a remarkable spirit of volunteer effort and participation. The readers, who similarly changed
from week to week, were genuine *shelihe tsibur,* he said, representatives of the congregation rather than professionals; the volunteer choir was composed almost entirely
of members.[124] A year later the initial success of the West End services prompted the
establishment of an East End branch, which lasted until 1911. Intended to appeal to
the children of Russian Jewish immigrants who could not share their parents' religious
views, it differed from the West End services only in the absence of a musical instrument. Between 150 and 200 mostly younger people attended the first of these services.
The Union itself grew to 300 members in the first year, at which point membership
stabilized.[125]

Recognizing that both wider credibility and a more conducive atmosphere for
prayer could be gained only if services were held in the sanctuary of an existing synagogue, the JRU first approached the Chief Rabbi and then, following his refusal, the
West London Synagogue in quest of a suitable arrangement. But even the Reform
congregation could not sanction the mixed seating or liturgical freedom on which the
JRU, at Montagu's urging, decided to insist. As a result of this refusal to compromise,
the new organization suffered renewed attack and one by one the more traditional
clergymen in its leadership felt compelled to resign. In the last sermon of the first year,
Abrahams could still say: "Our Union stands in no hostility to the current Judaism.
It seeks not to oppose or even change it, but to supplement it."[126] Yet already a few
months later, the complexion of the JRU had changed from a broadly based venture
to bring back the "drifters" into an ideologically committed Liberal movement. The
internal contradiction was now clearly apparent. Enthusiasm flagged outside the inner
circle and attendance at services declined. For another six years the JRU held back
from creating a third denomination in English Jewry. But by 1909 the majority of the
JRU Committee was convinced their venture would succeed only if it left behind all
pretense of being inclusive and merely supplementary to existing institutions. That
year the Committee changed the name of its organization to the "Jewish Religious
Union for the Advancement of Liberal Judaism" and proceeded to form a synagogue
that would provide a full congregational life for Liberal Jews. Two years later services
were held in a disused chapel now renamed the "Liberal Jewish Synagogue," and in
1912 Rabbi Israel Mattuck (1883–1954), a Lithuanian-born ordinee of the Hebrew
Union College in Cincinnati, was installed as its first minister. The JRU continued as
a support group for the new synagogue, as the publisher of occasional papers on various aspects of Liberal Judaism, and as the initiator of branch services elsewhere in
London.

Under Mattuck's guidance the Liberal Jewish Synagogue grew to 416 members by 1915. Shortly after it built a handsome building in St. Johns Wood in 1925, its numbers reached nearly 1,500, by now exceeding the West London Reform Synagogue. Sunday services were added in the twenties and a new attempt by Basil Henriques to conduct Friday evening services of a Liberal kind in the East End drew 400 to 500 regularly.[127] From the start, Mattuck set a clearly radical course for the synagogue. His inaugural sermon stressed that Liberalism meant complete freedom of thought and practice. There was actual harm, he believed, in maintaining any doctrine or practice of ancient Judaism which modern Jews could no longer intellectually accept. Not Jews alone, he argued, but all men were potentially "God's faithful people."[128] Mattuck's prayerbooks, issued beginning in 1912, not only altered the liturgy, but abandoned the traditional sequence of the prayers, so that London's Liberal Jewish service bore little resemblance even to Liberal worship in other communities.[129] Radical too was the decision to open the pulpit to occasional sermons by Lily Montagu, beginning in 1918, and allowing her to read the service for the first time in 1920.[130] All in all, by the mid-twenties, English Liberal Judaism most resembled the contemporary Reform Judaism of America in which Mattuck had been trained. It had no parallel in Europe except for Berlin's long-established *Reformgemeinde* and a small congregation that had arisen in France.

At the turn of the century French Jewry, now concentrated in Paris and numbering about 80,000, found itself newly divided and spiritually weak. The Dreyfus Affair, beginning with the arrest of Captain Alfred Dreyfus for alleged treason in 1894 and serving to sustain antisemitic agitation for more than a decade, made all French Jews less secure and drew a few of them to Zionism. While the earlier inner rift between Ashkenazim and Sephardim had long ceased to matter, a growing influx of east European Jews sowed fresh division, this time between newcomers and native-born. Official French Judaism, with its centrally organized consistory system, was scarcely able to slow the ongoing process of religious neglect. Despite the veneer of Catholic externals, it was no more capable of resisting secularization than French Catholicism itself. All but a very few French Jews worked and sent their children to school on Saturdays; synagogue seats remained mostly empty. Only a tiny minority of the native French Jews observed the dietary laws. Jewish intellectuals, like their French counterparts, were drawn to free thought rather than religious philosophy. Under Chief Rabbi Zadoc Kahn a new effort at religious accommodation was undertaken with the institution of sermon-centered Saturday afternoon services (especially for women) and Sunday lectures on biblical subjects. But most French Jews remained indifferent to such efforts, and for a few they seemed insufficient.[131]

During the mid-nineties a small circle had begun to form in Paris which, after a decade, would emerge as an independent Liberal synagogue.[132] We can trace its intellectual roots to the thinking of a recently deceased French Jewish orientalist, James Darmesteter (1849–1894). A disciple of the leading nineteenth-century French scholar Ernest Renan, Darmesteter enjoyed great prestige as a professor at the Collège de France and as a pioneer in the study of Zoroastrianism. Although he early forsook Orthodox Judaism, this energetic young man continued to find great value in the prophetic literature of the Hebrew Bible. He came to believe that, while neither traditional Judaism nor Christianity could maintain itself against the claims of scientific thought, what he called "prophetism" could. Far from conflicting with science, prophetic thought supplied humanity with a moral impetus that science itself could not produce. The religion of the twentieth century, he claimed, would arise out of the "fusion of prophetism with science." Moreover, since it preceded both historical Judaism and Christianity, the prophetic literature could provide a bridge between them. Shedding its pagan accretions, Christianity could "retrace its steps to the mountain, and pass back from Golgotha to Zion." In so doing, it would learn to strive for progress in this world, rather than salvation in the world-to-come. At the same time Jews too could rid themselves of all the elements of their tradition that conflicted with modernity by focusing simply on the divine unity and messianism taught by their own prophets.[133] Theodore Reinach, who was likewise an orientalist as well as a leading member of the Paris Liberal circle, called Darmesteter himself "the last and not least eloquent of our prophets."[134] More than anyone else, it was Darmesteter who was the spiritual progenitor of French Liberal Judaism.

Among French Christians, too, voices were then being raised which called for a liberalization of religious dogma and a return to the prophetic tradition. Charles Loyson, known as Père Hyacinthe, was toward the end of the century one of the most influential Catholic preachers and theologians in France. Rejecting both papal infallibility and the divinity of Jesus, Hyacinthe, like Darmesteter, sought a reconciliation between religion and science and also a common ground for Judaism and Christianity. He took part in the Paris Jewish Liberals' discussions, counseling them in their effort to create a new religious movement among French Jews.[135] Also part of the Liberal circle was a Protestant minister, Pastor Charles Wagner, who at a congress of liberal Christians held in Geneva in 1905 called upon his coreligionists to show greater respect for Israel as the people of the ancient Prophets.[136]

That same Geneva congress also heard the young rabbi of Dijon, Louis-Germain Lévy (1870–1946), deliver an address on the fundamental principles of Judaism. Lévy, who was unique among French rabbis in having also earned the Docteur ès lettres, praised Protestantism for its devotion to human progress, but also stressed the rootedness of "pure Christianity" in the Hebrew Prophets. There were likewise Jews, he told his Christian listeners, who were striving to turn Judaism back to its prophetic heritage: "You and we are going back [to the Prophets] by two different paths, but which converge in a like harmony of conceptions and sentiments."[137] The previous year Lévy had published his views more fully in a book entitled *Une religion rationnelle et laïque.*[138] Here he called for a rational Judaism which, like liberal Protestantism, would be a religion of the laity and hence free from hierarchical authority. For Lévy, as for other French religious thinkers of the day, natural science and positivist philosophy represented religion's chief antagonists, and his book was chiefly devoted to showing that liberal religion, and Judaism in particular, could be compatible with both. Drawing on a variety of Jewish and non-Jewish thinkers, Lévy argued that Judaism was not bound by religious dogmas in conflict with scientific inquiry. It was "essentially a practical morality for life." Even Comtean positivism was not a problem for Judaism, since it was bound by no elaborate metaphysics. Judaism went beyond secular thought only in that its morality culminated in the religious idea of holiness and rose to a cosmic point of view. God was the supreme unifying principle, the "conscience of consciences," and the moving spirit behind biological evolution. Judaism thus understood, Lévy concluded in this essentially apologetic work, could stand proudly before the bar of modern thought. Not surprisingly, it was Lévy, the intellectual among French rabbis, whom the Paris liberal circle chose as its spiritual leader.

By 1900 the Paris group had begun to call itself the Union Libérale Israélite, and that year it formally set forth a program which was to remain essentially unchanged.[139] The Union wanted a religious service which would eliminate the prayers that did not express their sentiments, such as those regarding sacrifices and return to Jerusalem. They wanted worship to be shorter, mostly in French, and take place on Sunday as well as the Sabbath. They also wanted religious instruction "in keeping with our modern aspirations," a more meaningful Bar Mitzvah ceremony, and adult education. In seeking consistorial sanction, they pointed to the existence of special services for the most orthodox Paris Jews and to the precedent for Reform services outside of France. However, repeated efforts by the Union to gain official approval and the use of a hall or synagogue from the Paris consistory proved futile. It was not until after the separation of church and state in France in 1905 that the group felt free to establish a religious institution on its own.[140] The first service, held in rented quarters on the rue Copernic near the Étoile, took place on a Sunday morning in 1907 during the week of Hanukah.

The hundred or so families that joined the Union were predominantly drawn from the *beau monde* of Paris Jewry, those who lived in the fashionable sixteenth arondissement near the Bois de Boulogne. But none of the founders were Rothschilds. Most of the early members were merchants, some intellectuals.[141] Within the inner circle a significant founding role was played by a group of enthusiastic women. One of them, Marguerite Brandon-Salvadore, had published an anthology which collected passages from Bible, Talmud, and medieval Jewish literature, dividing them according to themes for each day of the year.[142] Apparently close to Pastor Wagner, she complained in a published letter that Catholicism and Judaism alike lagged behind Protestantism in the liberation from clericalism and in dealing with the contemporary crisis of antireligiosity.[143] Indeed, so great was the influence of women in the early Union that the editor of the *Archives Israélites* thought he could discredit the new movement on their account. Since "in women imagination usually supplants judgment," he noted, one needed to beware of this "well intentioned feminine clan, animated by the most sentimentally religious dispositions," which was participating so actively in the new subversive movement. Women's religious and education role, he concluded, was best exercised in the home.[144]

At the first service, Lévy chose to speak, as he had in his book, of the compatibility of Judaism with rational thought and natural science. Clearly that issue was paramount for him, and perhaps also for most of his listeners. Like the earlier German Reformers, Lévy here argued that Judaism, as a religion of spirit, did and always would advance with the progressive revelation of truth.[145] His sermon was set within a service similar to that of the Reform Congregation of Berlin (which Lévy by one account had visited) and of the Jewish Religious Union of London. Women sat with men, the latter with heads uncovered. The liturgy was much abbreviated and mostly in the vernacular. Lévy himself read the service facing the congregation. Sabbath prayers were not used, these being reserved for the Friday night and Saturday morning services, which, since they were apparently intended for the more traditional members, also included a larger measure of Hebrew.[146]

By 1912 the Union had doubled in size, conducted religious instruction for young people, and held occasional lectures for adults. Although its opponents branded the Union schismatic and revolutionary, its leadership defended it as a movement of Jewish spiritual renewal.[147] Of course it was not Zionist, holding with Darmesteter that since the emancipation of 1791, "there is no longer a history of the Jews in France; there is only a history of French Judaism."[148] Moreover, the Union celebrated Jewish holidays almost exclusively for their universal meaning, so that even the eminently national festival of Purim was transformed into "the holiday of feminine grace."[149] Yet at least one Zionist observer agreed with its members that the Union's existence served to strengthen Jewish identity. Lévy's sermons, he noted, were not concerned to diminish traditional attachments, of which his hearers possessed very few, but to exalt Judaism in modern form before alienated Jews who had dissociated themselves from it almost entirely. "Who knows," he wrote, "perhaps what seems destructive and even absurd to east European Jews, who still remember Judaism as it was, may be useful and important for the Jews of France, who have almost nothing further to lose and can only gain."[150]

Like the Jewish Religious Union in London, the Union Libérale Israélite long remained a religious pariah within Paris Jewry. Here as there the wealthiest and most influential Jews stayed within the Establishment—which in France meant the consistorial system and its synagogues. Just as Orthodoxy across the channel had modeled itself on the Church of England, so consistorial Judaism had adapted externally to the dominant French Catholicism. But the Union Libérale, with its Protestant leanings—ever and again pointed out by its opponents—had allied itself with a minority.[151] Thus it had little attraction for those who sought merely a form of worship conducive to the French milieu. Its members were those Jews who were geniunely concerned with the conflict of science and religion or who were dissatisfied with the lengthy and almost exclusively Hebraic services of the consistorial synagogues. It also attracted the most universalistic French Jews and those who wanted to worship on Sunday. In succeeding years the Union remained small, reaching about 400 members in the mid-twenties. In its isolation, it looked enviously upon the much greater success of its counterparts elsewhere, especially across the ocean.

6

America:
The Reform Movement's
Land of Promise

By the eve of World War I, a moderate Liberal Judaism had for some time been numerically dominant in Germany and a similarly restrained Neology claimed the allegiance of most Hungarian Jews. Limited, largely nonideological innovations were also to be found in English Reform, in the French consistorial synagogues, in Austria, and in some synagogues further to the east. But radical reform in Europe remained confined to the Reform Congregation of Berlin and the Liberal synagogues in France and England. Only in the United States had a thoroughgoing Reform Judaism won large-scale adherence. Intellectually dependent on Europe for its religious ideology and until the last decades of the nineteenth century for most of its leadership, American Reform soon became the most successful in implementing the Reform program. Born in Europe, the Reform movement thrived fully, and almost easily, in America. The United States lacked the obstacles that had lain in the path of European Reform while providing an environment which could scarcely have been more conducive.

As we have seen, the Reform movement in Europe suffered repeatedly from government intervention in Jewish religious affairs. Whether such interference was intended to stifle reform or to sustain it with the heavy hand of external authority, it served to hinder the movement's free development, either holding it back or giving it an odious name. The assumed link between emancipation and religious change, though explicitly rejected by the Reform leadership when put in terms of precondition, served nonetheless to introduce motives that were not purely religious. European governments, for reasons of control, were also interested in maintaining a united Jewish community and Jews themselves saw value in the embracing nature of the German *Gemeinde* or the French *consistoire*. Would-be reformers had to exist within the limitations imposed on them as a single faction within such larger entities, and few chose to assume the financial burden and religious isolation of departing from them. Reform in Europe also appeared as a rebellion against long-established traditions and against an entrenched rabbinical leadership that fought against it with every available weapon. To reform there meant, at least initially, to overturn a structure of authority and a way of life that had reigned for centuries. It meant also to do constant battle with European intellectual tendencies which did not favor it. In Germany, Christian exclusivism among progressive intellects from Hegel and Schleiermacher to Wellhausen and Harnack put Reformers on the defensive, while conservative Protestant tendencies distinctly favored Jewish traditionalists. In Russia the Orthodox church provided no model of reform, nor did Catholicism in east central Europe and in France. In Great Britain the example of the Church of England served to encourage a similarly traditional Jewish religious establishment.

These European barriers to Reform were mostly absent in the United States. True, individually and collectively, Americans were not entirely free of prejudice, but in the United States there was no government control over religion, no conservative established church to set the pattern of religious life. A multitude of denominations and sects competed for adherents in a free market of religions, and even a heresy such as deism, sanctioned by some of the Founding Fathers, enjoyed a measure of respect. Until 1840 there was no ordained rabbi in America to lend the weight of his authority to traditional practice. Laymen, usually with limited knowledge, assumed the roles of cantor, teacher, and ritual slaughterer. There were no officially recognized communities, no effective means for enforcing religious conformity. Among the early Jewish settlers in America disregard for Jewish observance was rampant and mixed marriage not infrequent. One was not born into a Jewish community, as in Europe, but affiliated—or not—with a particular synagogue. Religion was less a heritage carried with little reflection from generation to generation than a conscious voluntary choice. Because America was so different from Europe, it often seemed that the inherited traditional Judaism was an Old World phenomenon, and out of place in the New.

Although the classical Reform ideology in America was almost fully developed in Europe and merely transplanted to the United States, it found an intellectual climate in America which was far more hospitable than in Germany, the land of its origin. Abroad autocratic government had lent weight to similar authoritarianism in religion; individual freedom was circumscribed by laws and institutions which perpetuated traditional sources of power and influence. Personal interests were placed after those of state and church. But individual authority in religious matters was the very hallmark of Reform, an ideal that could not flourish where it was thought suspect, if not dangerous. By contrast, individualism by the middle of the nineteenth century had become a fundamental component of Americanism. As propagated by Ralph Waldo Emerson, the doctrine meant a willingness to break sharply with the past, to rely on the sovereign self and almost never on tradition. The sublime, Emerson held, lay not in ritual, but in the moral nature of humanity; redemption not in the church but in the individual soul. In his famous Divinity School Address of 1838 he noted: "The stationariness of religion; the assumption that the age of inspiration is past, that the Bible is closed . . . indicate with sufficient clearness the falsehood of our theology. It is the office of a true teacher to show that God is, not was; that He speaketh, not spake."[1] For Emerson, as for the Jewish Reformers, revelation was not limited to the past. America would be different from Europe because it would reach forward not back. America, Emerson said, "has no past: all has an onward and prospective look."[2] Not only the Transcendentalists of Emerson's stripe, but most Americans possessed an inveterate optimism which held that their country would succeed where Europe had failed. Its new institutions would make possible the realization of human potential, which the Old World, trapped under the burden of its past, could never hope to achieve. Religion would of course play a role in that progress, but it would have to be the free man's faith, not imposed but self-chosen, more the product of individual experience than of inherited law and tenet.

True, the United States to which German Jewish immigrants acculturated in mid-nineteenth century was by no means uniformly set upon the path of such religious liberalism. The Puritan tradition, the ecstatic revivals, the persistence of orthodox theology were all characteristic. But Unitarianism was enjoying an influence far beyond its numbers and radical writers like Theodore Parker, who believed in separating religion's permanent elements from its transient, time-bound forms, had become vocal advocates of historical criticism. The Catholic church in the United States was stretched between its own authoritarianism (especially papal infallibility after 1870) and the countervailing values of democracy. Finding themselves in the unaccustomed position of a religious minority, American Catholics were forced to incorporate at least some elements of Americanism that were strange to their own tradition. Liberals emerged in their midst who recognized the religious merits of non-Catholics, made peace with a secular, democratic state, and worked toward an American Catholicism quite different from its European counterpart.[3] Protestants and Catholics alike recognized that the religious coloring of the United States had not been finally determined. Each denomination—and so too the Reform Jews—could believe that it offered precisely what the new country needed.

We have seen that the Reform movement in Europe was deeply enamored of the notion that modern Israel possessed a special mission among the nations. There, however, the idea of religious vocation seemed fatuous to many in view of the fact that Jews were persistently regarded as outsiders, neither rooted in medieval European institutions nor able to transform such institutions gradually into modern ones. German Jews could never really feel they were partners in shaping the destiny of the nation with which they so much identified. The United States was different in this regard as well. Like the major European nations it had its own profound sense of mission, but that mission rested upon a destiny not only unfulfilled but not even wholly determined. In America Reform Jews could feel that their own concept of mission might be woven into a larger still inchoate national purpose. Americans did not intend to pass on an endemic heritage, but to instruct the world in new lessons gained during their country's short historical experience. Puritans, Transcendentalists, Evangelicals, Liberals—all clothed American destiny in religious terms, linking it to their own particular beliefs. All of them perceived God's hand in the shaping of America.[4] So too Isaac Mayer Wise, the most influential of nineteenth-century American Jewish Reformers, could believe that George Washington and his compatriots were "chosen instruments in the hands of Providence," that in its unique environment of liberty the American people would "work out a new and peculiar destiny."[5] Judaism, Wise believed, would help shape that destiny—the people chosen of old would play their role as part of a people chosen of new. Imbued with typically American optimism, Wise could even believe that Reform Judaism, as a progressive, universal, and non-authoritarian religion, would become the common faith of America.

Charleston, South Carolina—Cradle of American Reform

Jews had lived in North America for at least 170 years, from 1654 to 1824, before we hear of the first organized effort at religious reform. During that time their numbers had grown from a mere handful to perhaps 5,000. Some had fought in the War of Independence, others had helped pay for it. By the 1820s a few had grandparents or even great-grandparents who were born in America and the majority spoke English as their native tongue. They had established congregations in Newport, New York, Philadelphia, Charleston, and Savannah, all of them following the Sephardi rite. But while their synagogues remained traditional, individual religious behavior in many instances did not. As early as 1777, a Christian observer from Germany noted: "The Jews [in America] cannot . . . be told, like those in our country, by their beards and costume, but are dressed like all other citizens, shave regularly, and also eat pork . . . moreover do not hesitate to intermarry."[6] Jewish education was limited at best and any significant knowledge of Hebrew was a rarity. Constituting only a tiny fraction of the population—about one-tenth of one percent—the early American Jews were all but engulfed by their environment.[7]

In the first decades of the nineteenth century the largest Jewish community in the United States was Charleston, South Carolina, with about 600 souls. Its particular environment was one of the most dynamic cities of the new republic: a flourishing center of ocean trade which had long combined broad commercial interests with broad-minded acceptance of religious diversity. Jews had voted in local elections there since long before the Revolution; they held a variety of public offices. An 1811 source suggests that by that year they were "chiefly Carolinians, the descendants of German, English, and Portuguese emigrants." Frequently they were affluent, even ostentatious. Some gave their children a classical education and saw them grow up to be lawyers, teachers, writers, and government officials—as well as businessmen. Charleston Jews interacted with Gentiles socially as well as commercially, playing a disproportionate role in Masonic activities. In 1750 they had formed Kaal Kodesh Beth Elohim, the fifth American Jewish congregation, and by 1794 had constructed an elegant synagogue. They observed a special relationship with the Spanish–Portuguese synagogue of London, Bevis Marks, which at least once sent them a minister. Although English sermons had been given on special occasions as early as 1791, the service continued to follow the traditional Sephardi rite as required by its constitution.[8]

By 1824 a considerable proportion of Beth Elohim's membership was sufficiently dissatisfied with the essentially unchanged, imported ritual to attend a meeting on November 21 of that year and to sign a petition requesting certain moderate reforms. The demands of the forty-seven signatories were all of a formal nature. After first protesting their continuing belief in Judaism as the "true faith" and in Israel as "God's chosen people," they asked that the *ḥazan* (the cantor and reader) repeat some of the Hebrew prayers in English so at least the most important portions of the service would command more attention and respect. They also desired a weekly English "discourse" expounding the basic texts and principles of Judaism, a more abbreviated service, and elimination of the disruptive and unseemly tendering of honors (conducted in broken Spanish) in exchange for contributions. This "holy work of reformation," they hoped, would bring back those fellow Jews who "are wandering gradually from the true God, and daily losing those strong ties which bind every pious man to the faith of his fathers." Other denominations, the petitioners noted, were sending missionaries all over the globe to increase their numbers, while Jews were failing to retain even their own. They also explicitly rejected the possibility of abolishing "such ceremonies as are considered land-marks to distinguish the Jew from the Gentile." Aware of reform efforts along the same lines "even amidst the intolerance of Europe," they called for a similar Jewish "reformation" among "the free citizens of America." Written in a tone of respect and conciliation, the petition was an attempt to bring about reform from within.

Their efforts, however, were treated with disdain. On constitutional grounds the proposals were judged to have insufficient support for official deliberation. It was only once they had been rebuffed that about a dozen men, in January 1825, decided to form an independent Reformed Society of Israelites. The following month forty-three individuals accepted a constitution that declared far more radically than the petition that "the great cause of many of the calamities with which mankind have been so often visited resulted from a blind observance of the ceremonial law, to the neglect of the essential spirit of revealed religion contained in the Law and the Prophets."[9] The group also adopted a ten-point creed, based on Maimonides' Thirteen Articles of Faith, but differing from it on four salient points: for the resurrection of the dead it substituted immortality of the soul and for the revelatory status of the entire Torah that of the Ten Commandments alone; it introduced the novel tenet of "good faith towards all mankind"; and it replaced the traditional belief in a personal messiah with a statement that was at the same time a rejection of Christianity: "I believe with a perfect faith, that the Creator (blessed be His name!) is the only true Redeemer of all His children, and that He will spread the worship of His name over the whole earth."[10] Probably to give ceremonial status to their creed, the Society obtained two Hebrew paraphrases of the English, one by a Jew, the other by a Gentile.

The group chose to call itself a society rather than a congregation, perhaps to indicate its broader scope. It sought not merely to create another opportunity for collective worship but to propagate common principles and aspirations different from those of their fellow Jews. Many of its members had not belonged to Beth Elohim. Quarterly they held plenary meetings and yearly listened to orators from their midst expound the purposes of the society. Some of the members were well off, others, including the chief ideologues, were men of very modest means. They were intellectuals and professionals, merchants and civil servants. At least nineteen of the forty-three who signed the constitution were active in civic or political affairs. Twenty-three out of an identifiable thirty-three were native-born Americans, thirteen of them Charlestonians. Twenty-one out of thirty-three, whose dates of birth are known, were born after 1790 and hence were relatively young men when they joined the Society. Having gained about fifty members by 1826, some two hundred with their families, the Society was at least two-thirds the size of the Synagogue. Other native-born Jews, they claimed, mostly agreed with their thinking on the subject of worship but did not join on account of a "tender regard for the opinions and feelings of their parents."[11]

The outstanding intellectual of the Society was Isaac Harby (1788–1828), a native-born Charlestonian of Sephardi ancestry who had achieved some prominence as a playwright, literary and political essayist, educator, and editor. His Jewish orientation is already apparent from a letter of protest that he wrote to Secretary of State James Monroe when the latter, acting partly on religious grounds, dismissed Mordecai Manual Noah from his position as United States consul in Tunis. Harby reminded Monroe in 1816 that in America Jews were not, as in Europe, a tolerated sect, but rather "a portion of the people" and that it was on the basis of equal, inalienable constitutional rights that Jews were appointed and elected to office. Of course religious ties continued to exist in America but they were less important than the political ones which united everyone: "I am not only Mr. Noah's *co-religionaire,*" he wrote. "I am his *fellow-citizen.* The latter relation is, in my mind, infinitely stronger than the former." However, should religious distinctions regrettably come to prevail in America, then Jews would "prove too weak for the numerous disciples of other doctrines." In order to preserve their own pride they would then have to abandon America forever and "seek asylum on some foreign shore, among rocks and deserts if *liberty there* holds her residence." In short, it was Harby's early belief that if, contrary to all expectations, the United States would not be true to its own principles, the Jew in turn would have no choice but to seek that same liberty in the desolate land of Israel.[12]

Monroe's act of intolerance was not isolated. In nearby Maryland a "Jew Bill," which would finally remove Jewish disability to hold elective office in the state, suffered a series of defeats, beginning in 1818, and a version finally secured passage and ratification in both houses of the legislature only in 1825 and 1826.[13] Such prejudice contravened Harby's conception of the American ideal. Perhaps it also persuaded him that equality in fact depended on a blurring of externally apparent religious distinctions. A Christian contemporary wrote of him at the time: "He is a firm 'Jew inwardly,' but is willing to accommodate the 'Jew outwardly' to the conciliatory, compensating and sacrificing spirit of the age."[14] Yet more than disappointment it was hope or expectation that nourished Harby's reformist purpose.

At the first anniversary meeting of the Society, in November 1825, Harby delivered a memorable oration.[15] In large measure his words were an apotheosis of America, which on account of its natural and political blessings was nothing less than "the land of promise spoken of in our ancient scriptures." Therefore, when America lived up to its ideals, Jews required neither "some stony desert" (again the land of Israel) nor a "marshy island" (the Jewish colony which Mordecai Manuel Noah was just then founding on Grand Island in New York).[16] They required only "this happy land" in which they already dwelled.

Yet a residue of bigotry remained on American shores, among Christians and among Jews. The purpose of the new society, as Harby saw it, was therefore to encourage Jews to shake off their own religious prejudice along with all those elements of their religion that contravened rational thought or offended aesthetic sensibility. What may have been appropriate or at least inoffensive in Europe was not necessarily appealing to Jews imbued with American values and more cultivated tastes. Neither Harby nor any of the other exponents of the Society's ideology had any conception of a progressive or historically evolving Judaism. In 1825 that notion had not yet appeared even among European Reformers. Their objective was rather to restore the pristine, classical Judaism, stripping its present-day variety of "foreign and unseemly ceremonies; divesting it of rubbish, and beautifying that simple Doric column, that primeval order of architecture, which raises its plain but massy head amid the ruins of time and the desolation of empires."

That classical faith, to Harby's mind, was biblical Judaism, which alone could be adapted to the spirit of the modern age. By contrast, he and the other ideologues of the Society were persistently virulent in their denunciation of rabbinism. Even the relatively moderate petition of 1824 had already noted that the signers wished to worship God in an enlightened fashion, not as "slaves of bigotry and priestcraft." Harby and his compatriots equated talmudic rabbis with the medieval monks and priests whose power and prejudice had held back the progress of civilization. Not only had the Rabbis made false claims to the authority of revelation, they had plunged Israel into a "bondage of the mind deeper than Egyptian darkness." European Judaism still cowered beneath rabbinic authority and European Jewish immigrants unfortunately brought that subservience with them to America where it was completely out of place. But in an enlightened, free environment it was destined to dissolve. Harby's antirabbinism was no doubt influenced by the works of eighteenth-century deists, some of whose writings we know were in his library, and specifically by the prejudices of the French Protestant scholar Jacques Basnage, whose *History of the Jews* served as a resource for Harby's oratory.[17] It may also be that some echoes of the longstanding controversy over the Oral Law in the Marrano community and particularly among the Sephardim in England reached Harby and his associates. However, what seems most basic is that rabbinic Judaism came to symbolize for the Charleston Reformers that medieval, European, unfree Judaism which, like its Christian counterparts, was inherently unsuited to building religious pluralism in the new, free nation.

In the two succeeding years, orators before the Society added one important—and very American—element to Harby's views: social pragmatism. "We look not to the antiquity of rites and ceremonies as a just criterion for their observance by us," said Abraham Moise in 1826, "but to their propriety, their general utility, their peculiar applicability to the age and country in which we live, to the feelings, sentiments and opinions of Americans." A year later Isaac N. Cardozo echoed the thought: "As all civil institutions are here founded on rational and equal principles, and look chiefly to the public benefit, those of a religious nature should partake of the same simplicity, and possess the same direct and positive good in their effects on society."[18] Thus the elements in Judaism that were worthy and capable of survival would be decided, neither by Halakhah nor by historical significance, but by the group's determination of what was relevant and useful to them as individuals and to the society in which they lived.

Of the Society's religious services we know that they were conducted in a Masonic hall, that there was a choir and instrumental music, and that men sat with their heads uncovered.[19] Probably they began sometime in 1825. The liturgy, which drew upon Sephardi tradition, was compiled by Harby, Moise, and David Nunes Carvalho. The last, who knew more Hebrew than the others, served as volunteer reader. Until 1830 there was no printed prayerbook, only slightly variant handwritten versions prepared by or for individual members.[20] The Society's manuscript prayerbook represents the first radical liturgy produced in the Reform movement anywhere, preceding by twenty years the 1845 prayerbook of the Berlin Reform Congregation, the earliest European liturgy to which it can be compared. Much of the service was in English, though basic prayers and a few hymns remained in Hebrew. In some instances the service followed · the original intention of the earlier petition, with prayers said first in Hebrew and then repeated in the vernacular. The compilers apparently felt free to rearrange passages arbitrarily and even to leave out such basic prayers as the *avot*, which inaugurates the petitionary section. Although resurrection remained, references to animal sacrifices, return to Zion, and the anticipated advent of the messiah were all excised; the additional service for the Sabbath was eliminated and the worship was reduced to a fraction of its normal length. On Friday evenings a prophetic reading was introduced, on

Saturday mornings an English sermon on the Torah portion of the week. Carvalho composed some English hymns based on Hebrew texts; others came from non-Jewish sources. Although there were prayers for the three Pilgrimage Festivals and the High Holidays, the prayerbook had none for the postbiblical holidays of Hanukah and Purim.

The Society's philosophy regarding ritual appears most clearly in a holiday prayer, which begins by recounting the "splendid ceremonial" at the ancient Temple in Jerusalem, only to continue:

> But at present there is allotted to the Children of Israel another age and another destiny. *Forms* are less necessary where the mind is more enlightened. Customs and ceremonies are changed and only the word of Jehovah remains immutable. We render to God not the fat of lambs, but the offerings of our lips—*uneshalmah farim sefatenu* [Hosea 14:3]. For God will receive that which we offer in sincerity of heart. Instead of sacrifice we shall present our temperance, our fortitude, and our continence. Instead of rich gifts we shall offer our humble merits, our good deeds, our charitable acts to the Throne of grace.[21]

The Society's prayerbook also contained an individual confirmation ritual which included recitation of the Society's version of the Maimonidean creed, a marriage ceremony in which the bride was allowed to respond "I accept this ring in token of the bond of marriage," and also prayers for circumcision, burial, the house of mourning, and various private occasions. If these liturgies were all used—and specific evidence is lacking—then the Society had become fully a congregation, in fact if not in name, for at least some of its members.

Beginning in 1826 the Society sought to raise money for its own building. But the effort proved insufficient so that in 1833 the funds gathered had to be returned to their donors with interest. In that year also the Society seems to have ceased formal existence—we know of no officers after 1833. With diminished ranks and on an informal basis, however, it may well have continued for some years longer.[22]

Neither the rise of the Society nor its collapse can be attributed to any one cause. This earliest instance of Reform in America was only slightly influenced by the German model. Although the Charleston Reformers were aware of the Reform movement in Europe, reference to events abroad was made only to bolster their case.[23] Similarly, opposition to the Oral Law among some Jews in England during the eighteenth century, though never mentioned explicitly, may have played a secondary role. So too may more immediate influences, such as the presence in Charleston of a broadminded Unitarian minister who was close to Harby and perhaps to some of the others.[24] One must also recall the political aspirations and the contemporary setbacks. But at bottom it was the sentiment, easily arrived at on their own, that America was different from Europe which best explains the movement. That notion permeates the writings of these Reformers. Rabbinism, they were ready to believe, meant European medievalism, a foreign and injurious authoritarianism; classical, biblical Judaism alone was suited for Jewish life in America. As free men they felt no compunctions about rearranging and altering the service in accordance with their own beliefs. Relying on their own reason and their own feelings, they would make American Judaism no less liberal than the country in which they lived.

The high hopes entertained by the Society did not come to practical fruition. Their synagogue was never built; a majority of the community did not join them. The general economic situation in South Carolina soon worsened, no doubt inhibiting contributions. In 1828 two of their most important leaders, Harby and Carvalho, left Charleston to make a living elsewhere, one in New York and the other in Baltimore. Lacking professional leadership and deprived of two of its most talented and necessary volunteers, the Society foundered. Moise tried to hold it together, but the élan had dissipated. Personal conflict apparently also split the group and caused defections.[25] Gradually some members dissociated themselves entirely from Jewish matters. Others, in some instances drawn by family ties, drifted back to Beth Elohim, which in 1836 was showing new signs of life.

Indeed, it was to be in the old congregation that remnants of the Society would again play the role of Reformers. They now helped to transform Beth Elohim into the first regular American congregation with an organ and a variety of synagogue reforms.

A decade after the formation of the Reformed Society of Israelites, Beth Elohim continued to be in the control of avowed traditionalists. In 1836 its leadership sought and found a new *hazan* whom they fully expected would support and strengthen the practice of Orthodox Judaism. But Gustavus Poznanski (c. 1805–1879) was to disappoint the traditionalists bitterly, soon turning from a man noted for his meticulous observance of the ceremonial law into a proponent of Reform ideas and practices.[26] Poznanski, who was born in a small town in Prussian-controlled Poland, had spent some time in Hamburg and Bremen before coming to the United States. He was serving as a *shohet* (ritual slaughterer) and assistant *hazan* for Shearith Israel congregation in New York when he was elected to the position in Charleston. At first Poznanski gave no indication of incipient heresy and received hearty support from the traditionalists. He married into a wealthy Charleston family, laying the basis for lifelong financial independence. So well was he regarded that already in 1838 the congregation granted him life tenure. At this time Poznanski's reforming was limited to the introduction of greater decorum and reverence—improvements to which none could seriously object. Yet during those first years in Charleston his views were changing. Perhaps memories of the Hamburg Temple were rekindled as he encountered remnants of the Reformed Society of Israelites; or perhaps he had some ambivalent reformist feelings all along; or the Charleston environment made some specific impact. Whatever his motivation, we know that already in 1839, Poznanski, in a private conversation with the traditionalist president of Beth Elohim, suggested the introduction of organ music.[27] A year earlier the synagogue had burned to the ground and, as was so often the case in Europe later during the nineteenth century, the construction of a new building raised the question of installing an organ. Poznanski apparently also had a personal interest in this particular reform. He was known to be a talented musician and the musical quality of worship was probably for this reason a matter of special concern. Whether upon Poznanski's urging or in an independent initiative, thirty-eight members of the congregation one year later signed a petition requesting that an organ be placed in the new building. Despite opposition from the synagogue trustees, a membership meeting, at which Poznanski lent sanction to the proposal, gave its approval by a vote of forty-six to forty. As a result, some of the traditionalists broke off to form their own congregation, Shearith Israel, while former members of the Reformed Society and some Jews who had belonged to neither camp now joined Beth Elohim.[28]

On March 19, 1841 the elegant new structure with its then fashionable Doric columns was solemnly dedicated. A member of the congregation played the new organ and a well-trained choir sang. Poznanski gave an address which the *Charleston Courier* said was chiefly devoted to vindicating the introduction of instrumental music by reference to both Scripture and reason. Poznanski also defended "the reformed practice of conducting certain portions of the service in the vernacular language of the people, instead of in a tongue unintelligible to most of them." He used the occasion, as well, to mention the Damascus blood libel of the previous year, praising the intervention of Moses Montefiore on behalf of the oppressed and persecuted Jews of Syria. It was apparently in contrasting the liberty and equality enjoyed by American Jews with the unfortunate lot of their coreligionists in Damascus that Poznanski "kindled with a noble and generous enthusiasm" and spoke the often cited words: "This synagogue is our temple, this city our Jerusalem, this happy land our Palestine, and as our fathers defended with their lives that temple, that city and that land, so will their sons defend this temple, this city, and this land."[29] His statement was thus as much an enthusiastic affirmation of America as differing from other Jewish diasporas as it was a denial of traditional Jewish messianism. Just as for Harby fifteen years earlier, so too for Poznanski, the United States was the modern Jews' promised land.

At first the worship service in the new synagogue remained almost entirely in Hebrew and quite traditional, with only the organ music setting it apart.[30] However, Poznanski's reform impulse soon manifested itself again, this time affecting both theory and practice. He formulated a new English version of the Maimonidean creed, which was inscribed in golden letters on white tablets and permanently displayed in the synagogue. The twelfth principle was changed to read: "We believe that the Messiah announced by the Prophets is *not* come, the Prophecies in relation to his coming not being fulfilled." Essentially a denial of Christian claims, the tenet was heterodox only in not directly affirming Jewish messianism. The thirteenth principle, however, clearly substituted immortality of the soul for resurrection of the body, and Poznanski's creed was soon condemned as leading astray from orthodoxy.[31]

When Poznanski, on the first day of Passover in 1843, suggested to the congregation that it discontinue observing the second days of festivals he caused a new division and precipitated a long court case that was finally resolved in favor of the Reformers in 1846. Meanwhile a series of ritual reforms was gradually implemented including more use of English, abolition of the second days, a three-year Torah reading cycle, elimination of the Haftarah reading, and recital of only a single *kaddish* in memory of the dead.[32]

With Beth Elohim in the hands of the Reformers and Shearith Israel serving the religious needs of the Orthodox since 1841, Charleston Jewry was now denominationally split into two regular congregations, the first American community to be thus divided rather than between Sephardim and Ashkenazim. Abraham Moise, one-time president of the Reformed Society of Israelites, had returned to serve as a trustee of Beth Elohim. When Isaac Leeser, the Philadelphia traditionalist leader, called for a convention to create a union of all American congregations in 1841, Moise wrote a resolution, almost unanimously approved by Beth Elohim's membership, refusing to participate. The members rejected submission to what they regarded as an ecclesiastical authority "alien to the spirit and genius of the age in which we live, and wholly inconsistent with the principle of American liberty." Such an organization, moreover, would doubtless prove "hostile to the march of improvement or the progress of enlightened and rational reform."[33] In a personal letter to Leeser, Moise added that it did not make sense for Beth Elohim to send delegates "when it is well known that we are at present the only open and avowed reformers in the United States."[34] In 1841 Beth Elohim did indeed stand alone, as had the Society of Reformed Israelites before it. But the isolation was just then about to end.

The Americanization of Reform—Isaac Mayer Wise

At the time of the Charleston organ controversy the most prominent Jewish religious leader in America was Isaac Leeser (1806–1868).[35] Leeser had come to the United States from Germany at the age of eighteen with only a limited knowledge of Jewish and secular subjects. But he read widely on his own, proved himself articulate, and within five years was chosen the *ḥazan* of the influential Sephardi Mikveh Israel congregation in Philadelphia. His *Occident,* begun in 1843, became the first American Jewish periodical of significance and it spread his name widely among the various communities. Later he translated the Bible and prayerbook into English, published a shelf of textbooks, and established a short-lived rabbinical school. He perpetually sought to achieve unity among American Jews. Leeser was an Orthodox Jew, but not of the old type. He pioneered the regular English sermon in his congregation, railed against mystical currents in east European Judaism, and favored eliminating those elements in the synagogue that detracted from its sanctity. He enthusiastically joined Rebecca Gratz in establishing the first Sunday school for Jewish children, though it admittedly followed the Christian model. But Leeser was also a halakhic Jew who insisted that change could be justified only in accordance with Jewish legal tradition. Historical development, either in modes of thinking or in the Jews' circumstances, was not to his mind sufficient grounds for religious reform. He vigorously defended those beliefs that Reform rejected: the personal messiah, the divinity of the Oral Law, bodily resurrection, the divinely initiated return to Palestine, and the reinstitution of animal sacrifices. Leeser advocated a purely formal accommodation to America, an enlightened orthodoxy of belief and practice which would adopt American dress without inner transformation. Like Samson Raphael Hirsch in Germany, the European religious leader whom he resembles most closely, Leeser favored a linguistic, cultural, and patriotic adaptation. But Judaism itself, because divine, was necessarily eternal. For some Reformers Leeser became at times a compatriot in the common effort to unify and strengthen Jewish life in America. But more often, and for all of them, he was the antagonist, rooted in America yet strident in his anti-Reform polemics, the symbol of an integration which they regarded as shallow or incomplete.

During the first years of Leeser's career there was little or no Reform with which to do battle, only the widespread lack of observance to be deplored and the need to defend against the persistent importunities of Christian missionaries. But by the decade of the 1840s the impulse for religious reform began to spread in America. It arose within existing congregations and it brought together new circles devoted to its principles from the start. By 1855 there were congregations with varying degrees of reformed ritual in Charleston, Baltimore, New York, Albany, and Cincinnati. In succeeding years the number and size of Reform congregations would increase at a rapid pace and reforms would become more radical.

The rise of the Reform movement in America after the initial Charleston episode must be attributed to both Germanizing and Americanizing trends.[36] Neither trend alone will explain it. Of the immigrants who swelled the Jewish population from about 5,000 in 1825 to about 250,000 in 1875 the vast majority came from German-speaking lands. At first they were almost exclusively rural Jews, many of them from the small towns and villages of southern Germany. They possessed little secular education. They came to America in flight from restrictive legislation and in quest of economic betterment. Whether or not they were observant in their new homes often depended on the opportunities available where they settled, in American towns or along the advancing frontier. Only in the forties and fifties did a significant number of relatively more educated and affluent Jews make their way to the United States. Some of them had gained acquaintance in Germany with at least a moderate reform—a more decorous synagogue, vernacular sermons, and a slightly abbreviated ritual. This second generation of German immigrants sought in America the same kind of ritual with which they were familiar in Germany, even as the earlier generation had sought to replicate their particular minhagim, whether of southern or northern Germany, in the United States. The desire of the later immigrants for modifications in the traditional service now encountered similar wishes on the part of those earlier settlers who had taken root in America and looked to reforms as a channel of religious Americanization. When religious leaders, familiar with the theory as well as the practice of the Reform movement in Germany, came to America they found a lay impetus for religious reform already present. The task the laymen assigned them—and they to themselves—was to give it an intellectual foundation and to direct its course.

In April 1842 a group of laymen in Baltimore formed the Har Sinai Verein, a society of German Jews dedicated from the start to creating a Reform congregation.[37] One of the founders was an immigrant from Hamburg who was commissioned by his associates to familiarize them with the Hamburg Temple prayerbook, which was then adopted for the religious service. The Hamburg Temple just at that time had attracted fresh attention on account of the new building and revised prayerbook which, as we have seen, provoked a lively and bitter controversy. No doubt the victory of the Hamburg Reformers was a topic of conversation among Baltimore Jews and brought the Hamburg Temple into active consideration as a possible model for their own worship. Another factor seems to have been the arrival in Baltimore in 1840 of Abraham Rice, the first ordained rabbi to settle in America and a staunch champion of orthodoxy. Rice became rabbi of the *Stadt Schule* (Baltimore Hebrew Congregation) and apparently drove away some of the men who could not accept his views and authority.

The Har Sinai Verein held its first lay-led service at the High Holidays in the fall of 1842. We know that the congregation sang hymns from the Hamburg Temple hymnbook accompanied by a parlor organ. As in Hamburg, the men wore hats and sat apart from the women; the liturgy was mainly in Hebrew. After twelve years a more radical group broke off briefly in 1854 and for the first time in America held its weekly service on Sunday. But soon it rejoined Har Sinai, which then invited David Einhorn to become its rabbi.

Three years after the formation of Har Sinai, in 1845, Congregation Emanu-El was officially organized in New York.[38] It emerged from a *Cultus-Verein* (worship association), similar to the Verein in Baltimore, whose purpose was to create a new congregation with a reformed ritual. The founders of Emanu-El were principally men who had arrived in America with some general intellectual background and liberal views. As in Baltimore, they were relatively young and were dissatisfied with the traditional German rite services in their city. They too did not initially tamper with head coverings or separate seating but immediately introduced German hymns, and once they had a proper building, installed an organ. Although for the first decade Emanu-El used the traditional prayerbook, it soon had a triennial reading of the Torah, confirmations, and a briefer service. It eliminated honors and blessings for individual congregants and by the fall of 1855 had instituted family pews and a mixed choir, and abolished the *talit* as well as observance of the second days of festivals. The congregation sponsored an elementary day school until 1854, then a religious school on Sabbaths and Sundays. Its synagogue in 1855 seated more than 1,000, and its attendance of about 300 on a Saturday morning was thought better than the average among other congregations in the city. Within the largest Jewish community in America, Emanu-El, after a decade, was already drawing the most successful and financially well-established Jews in the city.

Emanu-El differed from Har Sinai in that it was able from the beginning to employ a spiritual leader of some knowledge and ability. Leo Merzbacher (1809 or 1810–1856), a Bavarian Jew, came to America in the early 1840s with the *morenu* degree of talmudic competence from the great traditionalist scholar and champion of antimodernist Orthodoxy, Moses Sofer. He had also studied at the universities of Erlangen and Munich. In New York, Merzbacher served two existing congregations, but they soon broke with him, at least partly because he openly advocated some mild reforms. His availability was a major factor in the organization of Congregation Emanu-El, where he was employed as rabbi and lecturer until his untimely death in 1856.[39]

In 1849 the Emanu-El board directed Merzbacher to prepare a ritual especially for the congregation. When it finally appeared in 1855 as *Seder Tefilah: The Order of Prayer for Divine Service,* handsomely printed and bound in two volumes, it was the first American Reform liturgy compiled by a rabbi. It is striking that although Merzbacher preached exclusively in German, the literal prayerbook translation and its preface were in English.[40] One can only speculate that the use of English may have been a concession to Americanization and perhaps also for non-Jewish visitors. In any case the service was conducted almost exclusively in Hebrew supplemented by German hymns from the Hamburg *Gesangbuch.*

In some respects Merzbacher's prayerbook was traditional. It opened from right to left and retained references to resurrection and the restoration of the Temple. But it radically abbreviated the service, omitting not only repetitions but a large portion of the less central elements in the liturgy.[41] The Additional Service *(musaf)* was retained only on Yom Kippur. Angelology was excised as were references to the sacrifices, vengeance, and the exaltation of Israel above other peoples. There was no *kol nidre* for the eve of Atonement. While prayers for the messianic return to Zion were generally eliminated, Merzbacher somewhat inconsistently retained the formula translated as: "But because of our sins we have been carried captive from our land, and removed from our country." From the Hamburg prayerbook he took over the Aramaic addition to the *kaddish* which makes specific reference to the dead, and when Merzbacher's successor, Samuel Adler, revised the prayerbook in 1860, he introduced a novel Hebrew prayer for the comfort of mourners into the weekday petition when recited in a house of mourning.[42] Merzbacher's liturgical work caused a bit of a stir. Bernard Illowy, an Orthodox rabbi then serving in St. Louis, when approached by several laymen who favored its adoption, replied it was not a Jewish prayerbook and that anyone using it was "entirely excluded from all religious communion."[43] *Seder Tefilah* also had some influence on later American Reform Jewish liturgy. But perhaps because its author died a few months after publication and so could not tout its virtues, his prayer-book was soon eclipsed by those of David Einhorn and Isaac Mayer Wise. Only at Temple Emanu-El and a very few other synagogues, such as Anshe Mayriv in Chicago, did "Merzbacher–Adler" remain the standard liturgy until near the end of the century.

Of frail health, lacking dynamism, and very much dependent upon the will of Emanu-El's lay leadership, Merzbacher was not able to spread his reformist ideas widely. In Charleston, Gustavus Poznanski was seeking to withdraw from profes-sional religious leadership. Nor during his New York period was Max Lilienthal (1815–1882), later a leading reformer, ready to play an active role. Lilienthal had arrived in America in 1845 at the age of thirty, having already achieved some noto-riety. Armed with rabbinical ordination and a doctorate from the University of Munich, he had traveled to Russia in 1839 to become teacher and preacher of the Jewish community in Riga, which possessed a strongly German orientation. There he had introduced both regular sermons and the confirmation ceremony for girls. Later, at the behest of the Russian Minister of Education, he had undertaken a well-publi-cized venture to persuade Jews in the Tsarist Empire of the benefits they would derive from educational reform. Disillusioned by what he came to recognize as the govern-ment's bad faith, he left for the freer climate of America. But once in the United States Lilienthal did not immediately act the reformer. The terms of his position as rabbi of three German congregations in New York made him entirely subject to the will of traditionalist lay leaders. He could only introduce confirmation and rules of decorum. When the union of congregations dissolved in 1847, Lilienthal opened a private Jew-ish school and in 1854 began urging moderate reform guided by Jewish law. In the press he defended the Talmud as "not a system of immovable stability, but of progress and development."[44] However, only after he came to Cincinnati in 1855 did Lilienthal become a Reform activist.

Thus the American Reform movement in the 1840s still lacked a leader who pos-sessed the same influence as Isaac Leeser. Moderate reforms had begun in a few con-gregations; a growing number of laymen were seeking a religious expression of Juda-ism more in keeping with their heightened sense of being Americans. But there was no one as yet to transform individual local initiatives into a common cause.

It was Isaac Mayer Wise (1819–1900) who, more than anyone else, succeeded in stimulating, unifying, and giving direction to American Reform.[45] Though not an out-standing intellectual or an original thinker, Wise was an uncommon man. Initially plagued by recurrent severe depressions, hypochondria, and the wish for death, he was able to overcome his debilitating self-doubts and assume a supreme, manic self-con-fidence that enabled him to face enemies and personal defeats with near equanimity, always certain that eventually he would succeed. In time, two thoughts fixed them-selves firmly in his mind: "that I had a talent for all things, and that I was a child of destiny."[46]

Wise's talents were indeed extraordinary. He could express himself easily, dra-matically, and effectively in writing, lectures, and sermons. Though not a scholar by temperament, with a few weeks of reading he could present competent popular dis-cussions on an astounding variety of topics, always supplying his own critical opin-ions. His memory was prodigious; he was acquainted with all the details of Jewish life in America and abroad. His knowledge of Jewish sources was sufficient to confront scholars greater than he when the need arose. He had read the basic works of German *Wissenschaft des Judentums* and kept up with the progress of Jewish scholarship. Wise also knew well how to deal with people, to win friends and supporters for his projects. He conducted polemics effectively, often simply overwhelming opponents with his outpourings of rhetoric or confusing the issue until they gave up in despair. Controversy did not discourage him; he thrived on it. A good fight stimulated interest, and it made Jews think. Above all, Wise reaped the advantage of a psyche that endowed him with boundless energy: he edited and did much of the writing for two weekly newspapers, led a large congregation, and traveled around the country dedicating synagogues, giving guest sermons, and gaining supporters for old and new projects. He wrote historical novels and histories of ancient Israel. And in addition to his other tasks, he eventually founded and became president and professor of theology at the first successful American rabbinical school. Wise was known everywhere in American Jewry, a powerful force that moved sometimes in this direction, sometimes in that, but was always driving toward some goal.

Wise was born in the Bohemian village of Steingrub, the son of a poor Jewish schoolmaster. He studied in a yeshivah near Prague and may have attended some university courses in Prague and Vienna. But Wise's formal education was meager. He did not learn Greek or Latin, did not earn a doctorate, and may not even have received a regular rabbinical degree. Yet his training was sufficient to qualify him as a schoolmaster, like his father, in the Bohemian village of Radnitz. There he remained for three years from 1843 to 1846. But apparently Wise soon became restless. Larger horizons had opened before him during his studies. In Vienna he had spent time in the homes of the preacher Isaac Noah Mannheimer and the cantor Solomon Sulzer. In 1845 he was a spectator at the Frankfurt Rabbinical Conference; he read the political writings of the German Jewish liberal Gabriel Riesser and the religious philosophy of Samuel Hirsch. Teaching children and giving German sermons in the Radnitz synagogue proved not very rewarding tasks and the prospects for a better position in Europe seemed bleak. Very likely Wise had also developed, as he later claimed, an intense desire for the freer atmosphere which America could offer him. In any case, with wife and child, he left Europe behind in 1846 and never looked back with any regret. Later he would insist that he was an American in spirit even while still in Bohemia.

In the United States Wise found an environment perfectly attuned to his own values and instincts. America, he quickly realized, was a land unburdened by hampering, hobbling traditions. It was a place where individuals could freely elaborate their own ideas and seek to convince others of their validity. Very little was fixed; most everything was still being shaped. Religion was untrammeled by state control and no one faith was favored above others. Here American Judaism could compete equally with other denominations and prove its worth. It was only necessary to show that the ancestral faith was well suited to American values.

Wise became a persistent enthusiast of America, seldom its critic. For Jews caught up in the process of Americanization, his reformist ideas answered their question as to if and how Judaism could be related to the American milieu. Ancient Israel, he suggested to them, was the prototype of American democracy; loyalty to Judaism was therefore very good Americanism. In introducing his first book, *History of the Israelitish Nation,* Wise noted that Moses had already "promulgated the unsophisticated principles of democratic liberty and of stern justice in an age of general despotism and arbitrary rule. . . . Moses formed one pole and the American revolution the other, of an axis around which revolved the history of thirty-three centuries." Later Wise determined that "theocracy is identical with democracy," for in Ancient Israel, as in America, no earthly monarch stood between the individual and the word of God. Only if America should depart from its ideals and enact laws contrary to his personal religious conviction, then "I am an Israelite first and would treat my country as being in a state of rebellion against me. . . . First my God and then my country is as good a motto as any."[47] Though sometimes forced to compromise, Wise opposed the desire of Jewish immigrants from Germany to perpetuate the German language in sermons, prayer, and Jewish education. While he recognized that Reform owed much to its European progenitors, he was convinced that only in America could it succeed fully. Here its ideas would necessarily gain ever greater acclaim, for here alone Judaism could participate fully in a national destiny.

Wise has generally been regarded as a moderate Reformer, though he has also been deemed a closet radical.[48] There is some truth to each conception. Wise was not beyond dissembling traditionalism on some issues even as he remained genuinely conservative on others. But it must be emphasized that the precise ultimate course of Reform, whether moderate or radical, was not really Wise's basic concern. He was determined above all else to establish a strong and united Judaism in America, and he was quite ready to be flexible in utilizing whatever organizational means or unifying philosophy could most effectively achieve that end at any particular time. Of course there were limits. Wise never accepted the divinity of the Oral Law or even of the Torah in its totality. Nor could he, on the other hand, espouse a Judaism devoid of divine revelation, providence, and the traditional Sabbath. But within those boundaries he was ready to maneuver and to accept ambiguous formulations. Consistency, moreover, was simply not his highest value.

Some of Wise's vacillation was certainly self-serving. He possessed a strain of opportunism along with a penchant for self-aggrandizement. Unity would have to be achieved under his aegis. But some of Wise's inconsistency was also due to honest reconsideration, to varying polemical contexts, or simply to the use of a phrase for the sake of effect. Wise, for example, would at times stress that he was above all a Reformer, writing on one occasion with typical hyperbole: "The reforming spirit was innate in me; it was my foremost characteristic." Yet at other times he would call himself and his associates Orthodox Jews, by which he really meant that Reform Judaism was not an aberration or even merely a branch on Judaism's tree; it was the trunk itself.[49] If Wise's expressed views, with regard to talmudic authority, for example, grew more radical in the course of time, it is less likely that he harbored such views secretly and consistently from the start than that his personal ideas on the subject became less conservative or that, in the absence of a firm conviction to the contrary, he was ready to shift his views forward toward the center of a progressively more radical movement.

Yet in one most important point of belief Wise remained consistent. He always maintained that God had directly revealed His will to Moses and that Moses himself, not later writers, had composed virtually all of the Pentateuch. To be sure, Wise was a rationalist. He did not believe in miracles that violated the laws of nature. The Red Sea, he argued, parted on account of natural causes; incredible myths made their way into the biblical text. But Sinai was a real event, "a direct revelation from on high" during which God literally transmitted the Ten Commandments, the "laws of the covenant," to Moses and to Israel. The truth of that event was sufficiently attested by the Bible itself, the entire people of Israel which witnessed it, and the faithful, uninterrupted tradition that preserved the memory. True, Wise did not call the event super-natural, but he rejected the notion of mere inspiration or of a revelation that came only from within. Unlike more radical Reformers, he did not believe in a "progressive revelation." Sinai was unique and unrepeatable. Its revelation was not the product of evolution; it had burst into existence suddenly. Development and practical applica-tion, but not a new or higher religious truth, followed after it: "The truth established on Mount Sinai remains truth forever." The laws of Moses, apart from the Decalogue, represent the first expansion and application of the Sinaitic principles. The Talmud and later rabbinic literature continued that process. All laws and interpretations that came after Sinai were subject to change. In their time they had made unavoidable, though limited concessions to their age, in the case of the Bible to slavery, bigamy, blood vengeance, primitive modes of worship involving sacrifices, and a hereditary priesthood. But the Sinaitic revelation itself remained immutable, rooted in the divine. For all of his reformist stance, there was an undeniable strain of fundamen-talism in Wise. Without the rockbed of Sinai as the firm ground of faith Judaism would fall victim to relativism and to dismemberment by biblical critics. For the indi-vidual too revelation provided the certainty that protected against "pessimism, mis-anthropism, despair and suicide." If the Pentateuch were, as some biblical critics claimed, a patchwork, stitched together by deceitful priests, then "whence do I know that there is an only, unique, and eternal God, who is merciful, just, loving and true?" The prophetic books were relatively less important to Wise. While other Reformers began speaking frequently of Prophetic Judaism, Wise continued to anchor his faith in Sinai.[50]

Postbiblical Jewish history, for Wise, was a heroic tale: a glorious struggle for inde-pendence waged by the Maccabees, a desperate defiance of Rome, an unparalleled perseverance and a remarkable creativity in the Diaspora. The rabbinic literature, Wise recognized, was the bulk of Israel's productivity in the Diaspora and he paid it full tribute, but he linked modern Judaism especially to the medieval philosophical tradition. Beginning with Saadia in the tenth century, according to Wise, rabbinic her-meneutics ceased to be the sole authority for the exposition of Scripture. Philology and philosophy became "the final arbiters of scriptural teachings." According to Wise, "it may be truly maintained that the school now called Reform had its origin then and there." The trend continued via Maimonides—but not via the uncritical com-mentaries of Rashi—on to Mendelssohn and *Wissenschaft des Judentums,* wherever reason was the guiding light of exegesis.[51] Wise gave relatively less credit to the Ger-man Reformers of the nineteenth century, for the future of the movement by then, he believed, lay in America. A new stage in Jewish history had begun on this side of the ocean. Late in life he wrote: "American Judaism, i.e., Judaism reformed and recon-structed by the beneficent influence of political liberty and progressive enlightenment, is the youngest offspring of the ancient and venerable faith of Israel. . . . It is the Amer-ican phase of Judaism."[52]

Wise had arrived in New York in the summer of 1846 at the age of twenty-seven. Thanks to the recommendation of Max Lilienthal, he was very soon elected rabbi of Beth El in Albany, founded in 1838. There he remained for four turbulent years. Sup-ported by a faction of the congregation, Wise was able to introduce a mixed choir, confirmation, German and English hymns, and to eliminate *piyutim* and the sale of honors. But another faction opposed him. He aroused ire when he warned an officer of the congregation that unless he closed his business on the Sabbath, he must, according to a rule of the congregation, resign his position of leadership. Further antagonism resulted from a personal dispute with a kosher butcher, who also served as cantor of the congregation. Wise had dared to declare his meat unfit because he was an alleged gambler and frequenter of saloons. By 1850 Wise's opponents could also declare him an avowed heretic, since on a trip to Charleston he had denied belief in resurrection and a personal messiah.[53]

Amid charges and countercharges Wise was dismissed from his position, but nonetheless appeared in clerical garb for the New Year service and insisted on performing his ceremonial tasks. Later he recalled what happened:

> Everything was quiet as the grave. Finally the choir sings Sulzer's great *En Komokho*. At the conclusion of the song I step before the ark in order to take out the scrolls of the law as usual, and to offer prayer. Spanier [the president] steps in my way, and, without saying a word, smites me with his fist so that my cap falls from my head. This was the terrible signal for an uproar the like of which I have never experienced.[54]

The melee that followed was quelled only by a sheriff's posse that hurried to the scene. The faction favoring Wise now split off and formed a new congregation, Anshe Emeth, while the traditionalists remaining at Beth El speedily undid Wise's reforms.

Anshe Emeth, which soon numbered about eighty families, was thus a Reform congregation from the start. Here Wise's innovations found ready support. Here too he introduced an organ and, in 1851, for the first time anywhere in a synagogue, the family pew. Mixed seating, which took root in European Reform only much later, was to spread very broadly in the United States. Its adoption by the American Reform movement, and later by Conservative Judaism as well, reflected the practice of most American churches where it symbolized not only a higher degree of women's equality but also a link between religion and the values of family life.[55]

During the Albany years, from 1846 to 1854, Wise frequently expressed views that were his heritage from German Reform. "Judaism acknowledges and permits rational progress," he wrote in 1849, "a development and interpretation of the given up to its highest potential." He forthrightly stated his belief that much of the ceremonial law had breathed its last, leaving behind lifeless rote observance. Only those rituals that could instill love of God and moral truth belonged to "the essence of Judaism." Ceremonials were means, not ends, and hence could be judged by their adequacy. Moreover, not all Jews required them to the same degree. Yet Wise was also defining himself quite conservatively: "I am a reformer, as much so as our age requires; because I am convinced that none can stop the stream of time, none can check the swift wheels of the age; but I have always the *Halacha* for my basis; I never sanction a reform against the *Din* [Jewish law]."[56] Wise was clearly determined from the start to create a transformed Judaism, but he recognized that it could be successful only if built on the still widely accepted foundation of rabbinic authority.

In 1854 Wise left Albany to become the rabbi of Bene Yeshurun in Cincinnati, a traditional congregation in which a reformist party was on the ascendant. Cincinnati was then the largest metropolis west of the Alleghenies, a bustling commercial entrepôt on the Ohio River. Its Jewish community had reached 2,500 by 1854 and would more than double in the next decade. Its Jews were well established, though they would not be affluent until after the Civil War. Bene Yeshurun, organized in 1840, was composed mainly of Bavarian Jews; it differed in composition and rite from the older "English congregation," Bene Israel. In Cincinnati, where he remained the rest of his life, Wise could flourish in an atmosphere still redolent with the pioneering spirit that so well matched his own view of life. Here he could unleash his full energies and hope to find a sympathetic, even enthusiastic response. He insisted upon and received a life contract. But perhaps chastened by his experience in Albany, he was careful not to cause antagonism. Under his influence the congregation adopted reforms gradually and grew to 220 members by 1859, making it, after Emanu-El in New York, the second largest congregation in the United States. When Max Lilienthal came to Cincinnati as rabbi of Bene Israel in 1855, Wise gained a colleague and supporter. Bene Israel then began the introduction of its own synagogue reforms, so that the two largest of the four Cincinnati congregations were embarked on a similar course.[57]

Wise was now ready to assume the role of national Jewish leadership to which he aspired. Only three months after taking over his new position in Cincinnati he founded the *Israelite,* a weekly Jewish newspaper that soon challenged Leeser's *Occident* in Philadelphia and Robert Lyon's *Asmonean* in New York as the chief sounding board for American Jewish opinion. To his readers Wise announced with typical bombast that he had put depression behind him: "The powerful impulse of the heart triumphed victoriously over fear and melancholy thought; and we re-appear before our friends as cheerful as ever, with an unchanged and immutable confidence in our cause, and with the firm determination to defend it at any and every risk." He was now intent on using all his energies for the sake of "our aged and venerable mother, Judaism," preparing the ancestral faith for its destined role as "*the religion* emphatically of the civilized world." Pretentiously but confidently, he applied Isaiah's words to himself: "And I heard the voice of the Lord saying: whom shall I send and who shall go for us? And I said: behold here I am, send me."[58]

Early in 1855 Wise began agitating in the *Israelite* for a conference to unite American Jewry. His knowledge that earlier attempts to convene such a meeting, by Leeser in 1841 and by Wise himself in 1848, had failed to win support could not quell his ardor. He recognized, however, that only if Orthodox as well as Reform congregations could be induced to participate would such a gathering succeed. By August he had prepared the official call for a conference in Cleveland that October and he had gathered endorsements, not only from like-minded rabbis, but from traditionalist colleagues as well. All in all, nine rabbis signed the proposal, which called for deliberation on union, a regular synod, a common liturgy referred to as *Minhag America,* and a plan for Jewish education.[59]

Although three of the Orthodox signatories did not attend the Cleveland conference, Isaac Leeser did, and there were other Orthodox delegates among the rabbinical and lay representatives from eight cities. Consequently, however, the chances of agreement seemed slim. The parties sat apart and glowered at each other with a suspicion unrelieved when Wise was elected president. Once it became apparent that the alternatives were forced compromise or failure, Wise chose the former, disarming Leeser by proposing that the conference agree on the divinity of the Bible and the obligatory authority of the Talmud. Merzbacher, Wise, and Leeser then discussed Wise's proposal through much of the night. The following day the conference adopted a call for a congregational synod that would be guided by common belief in the Bible as "of immediate divine origin" and the Talmud as containing "the traditional, legal, and logical exposition of the biblical laws which must be expounded and practiced accord-

Isaac Mayer Wise.

David Einhorn.

ing to the comments of the Talmud."[60] Though he later defended the platform vigorously, this was probably a more traditional position than Wise's own, even at that time. But he recognized the value of committing the Orthodox to a common program with the Reformers, and he believed that within the projected synod the Reform faction would succeed in achieving its goals. Overcome with "glowing enthusiasm," Wise composed triumphal hymns. An "American Judaism, free, progressive, enlightened, united and respected," seemed within grasp.[61]

Radical Reform in America—David Einhorn

Wise's hopes were speedily dashed. Upon his return to Philadelphia, Isaac Leeser was pressed to defend making common cause with avowed Reformers.[62] It was not long until Leeser realized that Wise and his associates were proceeding to introduce liturgical and other innovations heedless of the conservatism he thought implied by the Cleveland principles. The union of moderate Reform and modernist Orthodoxy, represented by the presence of Wise and Leeser together at Cleveland, was crumbling on the right.

However, the fiercest opposition to the Cleveland platform did not come from Orthodoxy. It arose within that faction of the American Reform movement that was unwilling to give even lip service to talmudic authority for the sake of religious unity. Har Sinai in Baltimore and Emanu-El in New York formally dissociated themselves from the platform. Almost immediately there was criticism, as well, from the European Reformers Leopold Stein and Ludwig Philippson.[63] Wise's compromise was seen as a betrayal of Reform ideology, an inconsistent and unconscionable step backwards.

Thus Wise not only failed permanently to win over Orthodox moderates; in the attempt he seriously alienated the small but growing party of thoroughgoing Reformers in America and their sympathizers abroad.

By chance it was only a few weeks before the Cleveland conference that the first ideologue of European radical Reform Judaism arrived in America. David Einhorn (1809–1879) was already forty-six years old when he accepted the invitation of Har Sinai in Baltimore to become its rabbi; his Reform philosophy had crystallized abroad and would not change substantially in America.[64] Einhorn almost immediately became Wise's severest critic, not only on account of his colleague's views, but also because of Wise's style of popular leadership. Einhorn was a very different sort of personality from Wise. While the Cincinnati rabbi was affable, dynamic, often careless in expression, Einhorn was reserved, scholarly, intensely serious, and careful to formulate his views in well qualified, often intricate German sentences. He attracted respect, not enthusiasm; he possessed the gifts of an intellectual, not of a popular leader. Einhorn's circle of influence would always remain limited to the few who could understand and appreciate his message. Yet it was Einhorn's uncompromising radicalism, rather than Wise's accommodating moderation, which by the end of the century would characterize American Reform.

David Einhorn was born in the Bavarian village of Dispeck near Fürth. A talmudic prodigy at the Fürth yeshivah, he received a rabbinical diploma there at the age of seventeen. But his studies at the universities of Würzburg, Munich, and Erlangen soon robbed him of his orthodoxy, so that as a dreaded "neologue" he could find no rabbinical employment in Bavaria. Finally, in 1842, he was able to gain the rabbinate of Birkenfeld in the Grand Duchy of Oldenburg. After five years there, he assumed Holdheim's old position in Mecklenburg–Schwerin, and for a few months in 1852 he served as rabbi of the radical Reform congregation in Pest before the government closed it down. While in Birkenfeld, Einhorn had been among the European rabbis who defended Abraham Geiger's right to combine free scholarly inquiry with the rabbinical office in Breslau. In an erudite responsum he had expressed the view that while the Talmud was "a channel of the divine," it was not divine in and of itself. On the other hand, he had also joined rabbinical colleagues in condemning the radical Frankfurt *Reformfreunde* for failing to recognize the divinity of Mosaism and the progressive role played by the Talmud in its time. In 1845 and 1846 Einhorn participated actively in the rabbinical conferences at Frankfurt and Breslau. Here he was among the radicals. He wanted services conducted mostly in German, the "mother tongue" of German Jews, which alone could express their ideas and feelings. While recognizing that the Frankfurt conference quite properly stood on talmudic grounds, he insisted that the gathered rabbis were by no means bound to follow every talmudic dictate. At Breslau he agreed with Samuel Holdheim that Sabbath *rest* was merely symbolic and hence flexible to a point, though Sabbath *sanctification* was absolute. In his later years he would favor a supplementary Sunday service, but he would always insist on preserving the historical Saturday Sabbath.[65]

Shortly before he left Europe, Einhorn published the first installment of what was intended to be a multivolume theoretical elaboration of Mosaism. Here he embarked on the task of explaining Mosaic laws in order to determine their essence, to trace them back to a single principle which he defined as a delicate balance of unity and individuality. Like his philosophical colleagues Steinheim, Formstecher, and Samuel Hirsch, Einhorn went on to set Judaism sharply apart from pagan Greek philosophy.

Against Mendelssohn and in keeping with Reform ideology, Einhorn here maintained that Judaism did indeed have dogmas and implied that these, rather than the laws, were Judaism's basic characteristics. What especially set Einhorn's work apart from other Reform writings was its focus on symbolism, its attempt to disclose the religious reality beneath ritual acts, especially the sacrificial service of the Temple. Einhorn noted that the synagogue quite rightly "always *felt* the importance of sacrifices, but without *comprehending* that importance, without grasping the eternally true idea on which the sacrifices were based and distinguishing the idea from the symbolic and hence transitory shell."[66] Later he would name his prayerbook *Olat Tamid,* recalling the ancient perpetual offering.

Perhaps as early as his university years, and under the influence of the German philosopher Friedrich Schelling, Einhorn adopted the notion of a prebiblical, primordial monotheism that was the common possession of all humans.[67] It was an idea that would persistently play a central role in Einhorn's religious thought. In 1857 he wrote that the "real shibboleth" of Reform Judaism was this:

> Judaism in its essence is older than the Israelites; as pure humanity, as the emanation of the inborn divine spirit, it is as old as the human race. The origin and development of the human spirit are also its own origin and its own development. It is rooted in Adam and culminates in a messianically perfected humanity. It was not a religion, but a religious people, that was *newly* created at Sinai, a priest people called upon, first of all, to impress the ancient divine teaching more deeply upon itself and then to bring it to universal dominion.[68]

Here indeed was the essence of Einhorn's Reform Judaism, the nucleus of ideas which he chose especially to stress. Judaism, as Einhorn conceived it, begins and ends in universalism. Revelation is inherent in the human spirit from the beginning of universal, not Jewish history. It is never external, although the Bible pictures it that way at Sinai. God does not speak to human beings from outside themselves, but only from within to those who possess special gifts. Even Moses perceived God only in his spirit. The divine spirit brings light to its human counterpart; it mediates between God and man. While for Christianity the word becomes flesh, for Judaism it becomes spirit, a gift to all ages and all peoples. Thus Sinai revealed nothing new; it "simply disclosed to human nature its dearest and sweetest secrets." Revelation, understood in this way, is more process than event, more rediscovery and increased awareness than transmission. Within the Bible, Einhorn traced the advance of revelation from Noah to Abraham and Moses. But spiritual apprehension of the divine does not stop there. The basic religious and moral truths of the Torah do indeed remain immutable but the divine influence in the human spirit continues. There are "further revelations" which make the biblical doctrines more definite or clearer and the moral laws stricter.[69] Revelation, then, is progressive, or put differently, the human spirit in its historical progress opens itself to God ever anew. Einhorn expressed this idea enthusiastically in relation to scientific achievement at the time the transatlantic cable was completed in 1866:

> Ceaselessly the word of God reveals itself in the advancing knowledge of His works, in the shaping of history! Never, never does the divine spring of revelation run dry among the children of man. And a time like the present, in which human research has given birth to a giant straddling the ocean, is not merely as filled, but in an incomparably greater degree more filled with God than was gray antiquity.[70]

The most significant and novel element of the Sinaitic revelation was therefore neither theological nor moral. With regard to a conception of God, Sinai only elevated earlier notions of the unique Creator who is exalted above all creatures, purely spiritual, yet personal and always present. But at Sinai for the first time Israel accepted its moral responsibility as the chosen people of that God. Despite his universalism, Einhorn did not reject the controversial idea of the election of Israel. Already at the Frankfurt conference he had noted its practical value in the European context where it created "a beneficial self-esteem over against the reigning church." And at least as early as 1844, Einhorn had associated chosenness with the priesthood of the entire Jewish people in accordance with the biblical verse "You shall be to Me a kingdom of priests and a holy nation" (Exod. 19:6). The features of Jewish particularism—its ceremonials and its separation from the other religions of the world—were to Einhorn the Jews' priestly garb, which they were not free to remove until messianic times.[71]

No one stressed more than Einhorn the mission of this priest people to the nations of the world. The destruction of its ancient temple and political institutions became the starting point of a universal and still unfinished task. Hence the events which had evoked mourning for nearly 2,000 years were in fact providential, not a punishment for sin but a necessary condition for universal priestly activity. The Ninth of Av, commemorating the destruction of both temples, became in Einhorn's prayerbook a day of joy as well as sadness. Einhorn's liturgy did not pass over the tragedy, but pointed beyond it to new light: "Not like an outcast son did Your firstborn go forth into the strange world, but as Your messenger for all the families of the earth." As once the Aaronide priests offered sacrifices in the ancient Temple, so the priesthood of all Israel was thenceforth required to present different sacrifices, more acceptable to God: love of God and humans, pure and holy conduct. Thus "the day of sorrow and fasting has become a day of gladness" and a time of rededication to building the "new Jerusalem" that will embrace all humanity. Einhorn did not believe in a personal messiah. All of Israel collectively was the messianic people. The phrase in the *ya'aleh ve-yavo* prayer for the festivals which speaks of "the remembrance of the messiah the son of David Your servant" in Einhorn's version became "the remembrance of all Your people the house of Israel, Your messiah."[72]

On account of its mission, Israel was required to maintain its separate identity, however universal its religious faith. Einhorn usually spoke of the Jews as a *Stamm,* something more than a religious community, a group of common ancestry, to which he ascribed a common historical purpose. It was on account of his fervent belief in the Jewish mission that Einhorn was a lifelong opponent of mixed marriages and refused to officiate at such ceremonies even when pressed to do so. On one occasion he called mixed marriages "the nail in the coffin of the small Jewish race."[73]

That Einhorn personally took the moral mission of Israel seriously is clear from his stand on slavery. Already in Germany he had castigated what he regarded as the enslavement of the Jews by a government that treated them like stepchildren.[74] He had called, as well, for the religious emancipation of women.[75] In America, within months of his arrival, he branded black slavery "the cancer of the Union." Applying his Reformer's distinction between principles and laws, he argued that while the Bible's laws tolerate slavery, its principle that all humanity is created in the image of the divine boldly militates against it. When Morris Raphall, the Orthodox rabbi of B'nai Jeshurun in New York, defended Negro slavery on the basis of the Bible in 1861, Einhorn was aroused to write a lengthy critique. Urged to keep politics from the pulpit, he asked rhetorically: "Is not the question of slavery above all a purely religious issue?" It was his outspoken stand on slavery that forced Einhorn to flee Baltimore for his life in April 1861. Later he claimed that it was also on account of his unwillingness to remain silent that *Sinai,* the German-language monthly he had founded shortly after his arrival in America, lost half its subscribers and died after seven volumes in January 1863.[76]

Einhorn's feelings about the United States were highly ambivalent. On the one hand it represented to him the environment of freedom which Judaism required in order to flourish. Therefore it was the land of Judaism's future. He developed the highest regard for its statesmen: Washington, Jefferson, Lincoln. But he would not subvert religion to patriotism, and he was as often America's critic as its admirer. Despite the constitution, there was a significant trend to foist Christianity on everyone, both in the schools and in public life. Americans neglected the education of their youth and worshiped the almighty dollar. They severely punished a poor man for stealing a crust of bread but allowed wealthy capitalists to steal millions. Einhorn detested American ostentatiousness, violence, and admiration for deeds rather than ideas. In nineteenth-century America success meant being a good showman, and a showman Einhorn was neither able nor willing to be. His favorite word for American popular culture was "humbug." To be called "reverend" in the United States, he once noted, often all you needed was a lot of impudence, a white neckerchief, a robe, and anyone's printed collection of sermons.[77]

Unlike Wise, Einhorn looked to Germany and to German Reform Judaism for inspiration. He felt more comfortable with the greater value Germans placed on serious intellectual endeavor in religion as opposed to practical activity. The German language always remained for Einhorn the "language of our spirit and our heart . . . the language that brought the Reform idea to life and continued to bear it." For the foreseeable future German would have to remain the vehicle for liturgy and sermons. Einhorn personally used it without exception in his writings and from the pulpit. And in his final sermon he said of himself:

> Germany is my home. I am an *ivri,* a wanderer, and I journeyed with thousands of my brethren from there to this God blessed republic! As proud as I am of my adopted citizenship . . . I will never forget that the old home is the land of thinkers, presently the foremost land of culture, and above all the land of Mendelssohn, the birthplace of Reform Judaism. . . . If you sever from Reform the German spirit or—what amounts to the same thing—the German language, you will have torn it from its native soil and the lovely flower must wilt.[78]

Einhorn was never fully at home in America. Despite his veneration for American ideals and his defense of its highest principles, he remained a stranger to the rough-and-tumble of its daily life. He really was, as he defined himself, a wandering Hebrew, justifying his own alienation by the Jewish mission still unfulfilled.

Not surprisingly, Einhorn had little regard for Isaac Mayer Wise. While in print he tried to ignore the popular Cincinnati rabbi, his letters abound in expressions like *shafel* (toady), "chief humbugger," and "Jewish pope."[79] When Wise published his prayerbook, *Minhag America,* in 1857 and sent a copy off to Baltimore, Einhorn could not bear to even open it. Rather than ignore the prayerbook entirely, *Sinai* carried a critical review by Wise's more radical successor in Albany, Elkan Cohen. From the time of his arrival in America Einhorn sought to differentiate his brand of Reform from Wise's. He urged his congregants not to fear the specific designation "radical Reform." "Radical Reform," he told them, "wants a Judaism that bears the royal messianic mantle; moderate Reform—a Judaism swathed in Orthodox and reformist rags." Radical Reform was by nature uncompromising. Its motto was "first truth, then peace." For the radical Reformer "truth, which means peace with God, must stand higher than peace with humans and a stormy turbulent sea must be more precious than the calm of a stagnant swamp that exudes only polluting vapors."[80] By nature radical Reform was decisive, unyielding, revolutionary. But, at the beginning in America, it was also rather lonely.

Einhorn's direct influence was very limited. Har Sinai, with seventy families, was not large, nor was Keneseth Israel in Philadelphia during the years Einhorn served it from 1861 to 1866. While at Har Sinai, Einhorn complained that although educated German Jews were coming to America in ever larger numbers, very few of them were settling in Baltimore. From time to time Einhorn was asked to speak in like-minded congregations: at Temple Emanu-El in New York and at Keneseth Israel in Philadelphia before he became its rabbi. But his carefully prepared German presentations were far less in demand than Wise's flamboyant addresses in English. *Sinai,* Einhorn's ponderous monthly, maintained itself precariously and was received by far fewer readers than those who every week read Wise's lively *Israelite.*[81] During the fifties Einhorn had only two intellectually significant sympathizers. When Samuel Adler arrived in New York to assume the rabbinate of Temple Emanu-El in 1857, Einhorn welcomed the presence of a veteran, similarly inclined colleague. Likewise in Bernhard Felsenthal, who became preacher and teacher of Temple Sinai in Chicago, Einhorn discovered a talented and deep-thinking supporter and confidant.[82] But there were few others. For at least a decade after his arrival, Einhorn's radical Reform remained a fringe phenomenon.

Einhorn had arrived in Baltimore virtually on the eve of the Cleveland conference. Though invited to attend, he stayed away, claiming the need to get settled. Yet the gathering had barely dispersed when Einhorn launched his *Sinai* with blasts at the conference's position on the Talmud. True, Einhorn held, the Talmud was one of the most significant phases in Judaism's development, had enriched it manifoldly, "reformed" Mosaic law, and introduced the welcome novel concept of the immortality of the soul. But it was also obsolete, morally narrow, and focused on the letter rather than the spirit of biblical Judaism. It misinterpreted biblical texts and had encumbered Judaism with a stifling array of petty religious regulations. Where the Talmud had made religious advances it had happened without conscious intent. Only when life wrested change did the Rabbis force new interpretations into the letter of the law.[83]

But it was not only the Cleveland conference's acceptance of talmudic authority that irritated Einhorn. It was the very notion of religious authority, as much the proposed permanent synod as the imposition of rabbinic Judaism. Freedom, religious not less than political, was among Einhorn's most cherished values. He called Judaism "the religion of freedom" and remained ever suspicious of any attempt to infringe congregational autonomy or individual conscience. Any manner of hierarchy was anathema. Though later he favored the radicals formulating their own collective statement, Einhorn never himself put forward a plan for a general rabbinical synod or even for congregational union. One of the things he appreciated most about America was that, unlike in Germany, radical rabbis did not need to be hypocrites; they did not have to play at being Orthodox to avoid offending conservatives within a religious community seeking to serve all.[84]

The men of Cleveland, he thought, had negotiated a "foul peace." Not only would the dead hand of the past choke the living spirit, but a collective will would impose itself on individual religious reflection. "Let the free American Israel be on its guard against such hierarchical strivings," Einhorn warned. At Cleveland, he asserted, the participants had constructed a "Tower of Babel" intended to serve as a pedestal for Wise's various initiatives, his Zion College in Cincinnati and his projected prayer-book. Einhorn was certain that their tower would never reach the heavens, that God had confounded their speech.[85] As it turned out, on that point Einhorn proved correct: the tower was indeed a failure. But Wise was not dismayed. Undaunted, he simply picked up the bricks and kept on building elsewhere.

Rivalry and Rift

Not long after the furor over the Cleveland conference died down, the attention of American Jews was drawn to a larger rift that was tearing into the fabric of America. Slavery was a divisive issue for Jews no less than for Gentiles. The Orthodox rabbis Morris Raphall and Bernard Illowy defended it from Scripture; Einhorn, as we have seen, vigorously denounced it. So did the Reformers Bernhard Felsenthal and Lieb-mann Adler in Chicago. But Isaac Mayer Wise was among those who argued for states' rights. Cincinnati lay just north of the Mason–Dixon line. It was a station on the Underground Railroad, but its trade was largely with the South, where Wise's congre-gants had business associates and friends. Half of the subscribers to Wise's *Israelite* were Southerners at the time, and he had traveled extensively in the region. Wise did oppose slavery, but on this moral issue, as earlier and later on specific Jewish matters of belief and practice, he preferred unity—in this case of the American Union—over the provocation of separation for the sake of principle. Thus he remained silent or neutral as the Civil War raged about him. Not until well into the conflict did Wise come to venerate Abraham Lincoln, a man he had earlier despised along with aboli-tionists in general. Like his more conservative colleague Benjamin Szold in Baltimore, Wise deplored radical solutions.[86]

The years immediately following the Civil War brought unparalleled prosperity to the United States and to American Jewry. Some Jews, indeed, had already managed to increase their wealth substantially during the war years. In one community after another they were soon ready to express their newfound status by constructing opu-lent, monumental synagogues. Wise's congregation in Cincinnati, with 220 families the second largest in America in 1859, undertook to build a grand structure as early as 1863, still in the midst of the war. Completed in 1866 at a cost of more than a quarter million dollars, it was modeled to a degree on the Moorish synagogues then fashionable in Germany. Two slender, minaretlike towers ascended from its multi-domed roof, while, somewhat later, the interior was lavishly decorated with Hebrew verses and geometrical designs. Similar grand structures were built at the same time or shortly thereafter in San Francisco, New York, Philadelphia, and other communi-ties. While in 1860 there were, by one estimate, only 77 synagogues in the United States with a capacity of 34,412, by 1870 their number and capacity had more than doubled to 152 edifices capable of seating 73,265. The value of synagogue property

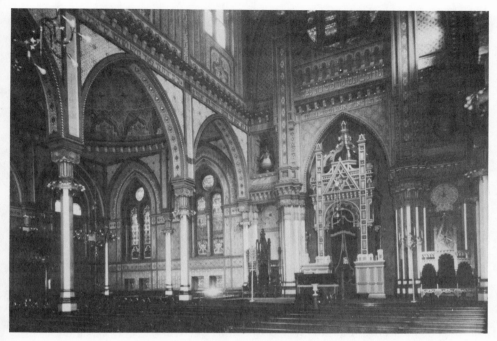

Interior of Bene Yeshurun (Isaac Mayer Wise) Temple, Cincinnati, completed in 1866.

had increased even more dramatically, by 354 percent. To help pay for the new structures pews were sold at public auction, the most desirable one at Temple Emanu-El in New York bringing \$9,300.[87]

With the construction of new synagogues or the renovation of old ones came a quickening pace of religious reform.[88] The lavish buildings were thought incomplete without a magnificent organ. In 1860 Wise could claim only a dozen "organ congregations"; eight years later there were more than thirty. Temple Emanu-El in New York could now boast an instrument said to be the largest in the country except for Music Hall in Boston, while that of Bene Yeshurun in Cincinnati was acclaimed as the "best in the West." Even synagogues that were relatively traditional at the time, like Rodeph Shalom in Philadelphia and Baltimore Hebrew Congregation, adopted the organ in the early seventies. Less frequent as yet was the employment of non-Jewish choristers to assist, and sometimes to replace, the cantor and volunteer Jewish choir.

Mixed seating too became commonplace, as did the abolition of the second days of holidays. Many synagogues abbreviated the Torah reading by introduction of the triennial cycle and by the 1870s began to reduce it further, for example by reading only selected verses from the weekly portion and forgoing a complete reading entirely. Orthodox prayerbooks were increasingly put aside in favor of unorthodox. Relatively traditional synagogues chose the conservative prayerbook edited by Benjamin Szold and revised by Marcus Jastrow, middle-of-the-road ones Wise's *Minhag America,* and those drawn to radical Reform picked Einhorn's *Olat Tamid.* Use of vernacular in the liturgy became accepted practice, the relative proportion of Hebrew varying among the congregations. Gradually the explicitly Reform congregations also discarded the prayer shawl and then the headcovering for men. In some instances congregational boards allowed a period of choice before making bareheadedness mandatory. While the confirmation ceremony was very common by the late seventies, only a few congregations—Emanu-El in New York and Har Sinai in Baltimore, for example—had as yet gone so far as to prohibit the traditional Bar Mitzvah. In some instances it was a lay faction, eager for a style of worship appropriate to the congregants' rising status, that pressed for change; in other places rabbis sought the reforms for reasons of principle.

American Jewry was rapidly becoming both affluent and increasingly Reform. Wise could wax exultant: "Everywhere the temples of Israel, the monuments of progressive Judaism, as though touched by a magic wand, rise in proud magnificence, and proclaim with a thundering voice [against the opponents of Reform], we are right and you are wrong." Only "a small minority of our coreligionists still preserve some of the antiquated forms and overcome notions, but they are harmless remnants of bygone days." To Wise's mind, therefore, the struggle with Orthodoxy was over. It was dying a natural death. Against the radical Reformers he insisted that "Reform is no question any longer, and it is useless to harp away continually the outworn theme. With a very few and unimportant exceptions in the Atlantic cities, the American Hebrew community is decidedly progressive and in full sympathy with the best ideas of the age." Others shared Wise's conclusion. A New York correspondent for the German *Israelitische Wochenschrift* wrote in a similar vein: "Here in America attacks [upon talmudic Judaism, thought necessary in Germany] have become wholly superfluous. The meager residues of Orthodoxy which one still finds in this land are insignificant."[89] For Wise and his supporters the really important objectives—now more clearly than ever—were Americanization and union.

Neither of these two goals could be easily attained. Americanization, so obvious an ideal for Wise, had its severest critics not in the traditionalist camp, but among the radicals. While Isaac Leeser and Wise fervently propagated it, opposition came from David Einhorn, from those rabbis associated with him, and from a portion of the Reform laity.[90]

In the first half of the nineteenth century most German Jews who migrated to America had been only superficially Germanized. They had not gone to a German University; they spoke Judeo-German. Americanization was their first experience with integration into the modern world. It was otherwise with many of those who came later, from the forties until the Civil War. To a greater or lesser degree they carried German cultural baggage with them on the migration to America. In the United States they found a large non-Jewish community of German speakers, organized into a variety of social and fraternal societies. Jews could join such groups easily—indeed more easily than their prototypes in the old country. Often German Jews looked back with nostalgia to the physical and cultural landscape of their youth and they sought to preserve something of those memories in their new homeland. During the fifties, sixties, and even into the seventies German was frequently the language of Jewish schools, synagogue minutes, liturgy, and sermons. Even as late as 1874 it was estimated that the German language predominated in the majority of the Jewish congregations in the United States.

To the minds of many of the later immigrants Reform Judaism was an integral part of their German heritage. They had been confirmed by German liberal rabbis;

they were accustomed to a reformed liturgy, to the newer German synagogue melodies, and to the Reform ideas expounded from liberal German pulpits. While by necessity they learned to use English in business and on the street, they chose to preserve German in the home and, no less than Hebrew, as the sacred language of the synagogue. As we have seen, Einhorn's position on the religious necessity of maintaining German was clearcut. But he was not alone. Other radical Reformers, like Samuel Adler in New York and Bernhard Felsenthal and Isaac Löb Chronik in Chicago, shared his view that American Jewry was still not ready to strike out on its own, that its future, religiously and culturally, depended on the ability to transmit the heritage of German Jewry's religious values and the achievements of its Jewish scholarship. Every aspect of the way it was done in Germany remained important. At Har Sinai in Baltimore, a pioneer congregation of radical Reform, men and women continued to sit separately until 1873, simply because that was the custom in Germany. Only at the end of the sixties and thereafter did the most loyal Germanizers begin to waver. Their American-born children preferred to speak English and some of the children could not understand the German sermons. Moreover, the rabbis noted that German Reform, bound by the constraints of the local united community, had stagnated into conservatism. By the eighties they could also see more clearly how endemic anti-semitism still was in German society while appreciating more fully how a freer American climate had enabled its Jews to rise socially and economically, to build their magnificent religious and philanthropic institutions. Although German consciousness would linger among Reform Jews for another generation and more, it was later increasingly defined as the special German identity of *American* Jews who had wrested religious hegemony from their brethren abroad. As Rabbi Adolf Moses of Mobile, Alabama put it—in German—in 1882: "From America salvation will go forth; in this land [and not in Germany] will the religion of Israel celebrate its greatest triumphs."

Germanization versus Americanization was one of the major issues that separated the Einhorn and Wise factions. Another, as much a matter of personal prestige as differing ideology, was the question of whose prayerbook would serve American Reform congregations. As early as 1847 Wise had prepared the outline for a "Minhag America," an American rite which would displace the rituals that Jewish immigrants brought with them from their various places of origin. But the short-lived New York Rabbinical Court in whose commission he had prepared the outline disbanded before the project could be completed. Wise revived it at the Cleveland conference, which appointed a committee to produce such a unifying liturgy. In frequent sessions, held mainly during the winter of 1856/57, Wise met with the two other members of the committee, who happened at the time to hold pulpits in Cincinnati. Although Wise alone presented the proposed material piecemeal while his colleagues simply played the role of critics, the committee adopted the principle that "no one man is authorized to make a prayer-book for the congregations."[91] That statement was likely intended not simply as a representation of their own position, but as a direct attack on David Einhorn, who had not only expressed himself against the principles adopted in Cleveland, but in 1856, within months of the conference, had already published the first part of his own liturgy entitled, in German, *Prayerbook for Israelite Reform Congregations.*[92] To Einhorn's mind there could not, and should not, be a single ritual for all

American synagogues. Reform congregations should be able to worship from a liturgy that did not dilute their principles. A Reform prayerbook, he believed, could fulfill its purpose only if it was "of a single cast."[93]

In 1858 Einhorn's prayerbook, now given the added Hebrew title *Olat Tamid,* appeared in complete form for the entire liturgical year. Begun in Europe, it bears some structural resemblance to both the Hamburg Temple prayerbook and the liturgy of the Reform Congregation in Berlin; it also draws upon the scientific research of Leopold Zunz.[94] But *Olat Tamid* is no merely eclectic work. It consistently expresses the religious ideology of its editor. Einhorn modified the Hebrew text, provided his own—sometimes nonliteral—translations, and composed a number of well-crafted original German prayers. Repeatedly he voiced his commitment to Israel's priestly and messianic role among the nations. And he transformed the concept of resurrection ("who revives the dead") into immortality of the soul ("who plants within us eternal life"). Moreover, *Olat Tamid* did not provide for alternatives. The worshiper opened it—from left to right—and followed along a liturgy that contained some prayers in Hebrew, others in German, but did not allow for altering the given language of a particular text. Symbols like the *etrog* and *lulav* (citron and palm frond) for the holiday of Sukkot were eliminated because Einhorn believed they had lost their religious significance.[95]

Yet Einhorn's prayerbook lacked neither tradition nor spirituality. Though much abbreviated, it retained the basic sequence of prayers, and about half the liturgy remained in Hebrew. "Reform ritual," Einhorn wrote to Felsenthal, "must under no circumstances remove any traditional religious element that can be made fruitful for the present day." He criticized the Berlin Reform prayerbook because it appealed only to the worshiper's reason.[96] Because he found little value in physical rituals, Einhorn sought to make the prayers inspirational. Worship, as he conceived it, was to be a geniuine *olat tamid,* the perpetual offering through which the Jewish people renewed its priestly relationship to God.

When *Minhag America* appeared in 1857, between the partial and complete versions of Einhorn's liturgy, it was similar to *Olat Tamid* on most points of ideology. Wise's prayerbook too eliminated references to the messianic return to Zion and restoration of the sacrificial cult; it too abbreviated the service, though less radically. But *Minhag America* differed fundamentally in the breadth of its appeal; it was intended not as a Reform, but as an American *sidur.* Thus Wise's prayerbook did not present an integral Hebrew-vernacular liturgy with texts predetermined to be in one language or the other. Opened from the right, it presented a totally Hebrew text, with even the prayer rubrics and instructions in (unvocalized!) Hebrew. A congregation could easily use *Minhag America* for an exclusively Hebrew liturgy. In fact, Wise's own Bene Yeshurun, for a surprisingly long time, continued to use virtually this text alone. But opened from the other side, there was a complete translation of the Hebrew texts. German-speaking congregations could acquire the prayerbook with the German vernacular, Americanized ones with Wise's—rather wooden—English version. By shuttling back and forth between Hebrew and translation each congregation could create its own preferred mixture.[97] Should a traditionalist male worshiper desire to pray wearing *talit* (prayer shawl) and *tefilin* (phylacteries), he would find the appropriate Hebrew prayers on the included "List of Blessings." Although like Einhorn Wise did not believe in bodily resurrection, *Minhag America* sidestepped that controversial issue by leaving the Hebrew text intact, altering only the vernacular renditions. Consistency and uniformity of ideology were clearly less important than devising a prayer-book that could gain entry into the largest number of congregations. Moreover, a sin-gle prayerbook, even if used differentially, might provide the basis for congregational, as well as liturgical unity.

In the competition that now began between the Einhorn and Wise prayerbooks, it was *Minhag America* that proved more successful. Einhorn's partisans felt pressed to attack it. Felsenthal deemed Wise's liturgy a bowdlerized, rather poor imitation of Merzbacher's Emanu-El prayerbook and nitpicked at its errors of translation. His own Chicago Sinai Congregation, chartered in 1861 as a distinctly Reform synagogue, was the first in the West to adopt *Olat Tamid*.[98] When Felsenthal moved to the new Zion congregation in 1864, it too adopted Einhorn's prayerbook. So did the congregation of another radical, Solomon Sonneschein, in St. Louis, as well as synagogues in Phil-adelphia, Pittsburgh, Rochester, Kansas City, and, with Einhorn's move there, also New York. *Olat Tamid* had gone through three printings when Einhorn issued an English–Hebrew version in 1872 for "the edification of my English-speaking brethren in faith." His prayerbook was thus not without influence. But Wise's liturgy was clearly the more popular. It spread to the small towns where there was only a single congregation and where a compromise liturgy was just what was needed. As he trav-eled about the country Wise persuasively touted the virtues of his prayerbook. At Oheb Shalom in Baltimore and Beth El in Detroit it was adopted immediately after his visits. *Minhag America* soon became the dominant liturgy of congregations in the Midwest and South where Wise's influence was the greatest. By 1870 he could boast that more than fifty congregations had adopted it; four years later he claimed one hundred, making his prayerbook perhaps the most widely used in America during the seventies.[99] Tenuously linked to the Cleveland conference, whose authorization was prominently displayed on the title pages, it was that meeting's only tangible outcome.

As Wise's Americanizing and latitudinarian efforts bore fruit, the radical Reform-ers, who were predominantly but not exclusively concentrated in the East, sought to regroup their forces. Since the demise of Einhorn's *Sinai* in January 1863, they had lacked an organ of their own which would set forth their views and counteract the movement for a unity of compromise which Wise propagated so vociferously and effectively in his newspapers and on his congregational visits. Finally, in 1869, they succeeded in creating a weekly newspaper entitled *Jewish Times*. Published in New York and edited by Moritz Ellinger, an acid and able layman, it attempted to appeal broadly to the radical faction by including both English and German sections. Einhorn himself, now serving as a rabbi in New York, was among the contributors, as were Rabbis Samuel Adler of Temple Emanu-El, Bernhard Felsenthal in Chicago, and the recently arrived Samuel Hirsch in Philadelphia. It was in an early issue of the *Jewish Times* that Adler and Einhorn together published their call for a rabbinical conference that would be wholly unlike its Cleveland predecessor. Deliberately they invited only "their theologically educated colleagues, who favor decided religious progress." Such like-minded men, they trusted, would be able to concur on basic principles that would set Reform clearly apart from Orthodoxy. The assembled rabbis would also deal with various practical issues, especially marital questions, which, they noted, were still unfortunately decided in accordance with the *Shulhan Arukh* rather than the princi-ples of Reform.[100]

The proposed conference met unostentatiously at the home of Samuel Hirsch in

Philadelphia. For four days, in November 1869, the rabbis deliberated in the familiar German language. Thirteen men attended, nearly all belonging to the radical faction. Six were from New York and Chicago; only one was from a small town, Selma, Alabama. Unwilling to risk exclusion from this circle, Wise came too, though he arrived a day late. As the host, Hirsch was selected president, but it was Einhorn who was clearly in charge. His proposals, printed in advance, became the basis for discussion, while all other suggestions were deferred to future meetings. Although there were occasional tensions, disagreements, and a couple of close votes, the conference on the whole went forward harmoniously and, at least on the surface, in a spirit of collegiality.[101]

The seven principles adopted by the conference were intended to distinguish Reform Judaism as much by it rejections as its affirmations. Each of them asserted a nay along with its yea. The messianic goal of Israel was not restoration but the union of all humanity; the fall of the second Jewish commonwealth was not punishment for Israel's sins but the beginning of Israel's priestly mission; inner devotion and sanctification, not the sacrificial cult, constituted the only sacrifices pleasing to the All-Holy; distinctions between Aaronide and non-Aaronide, once valid, were so no longer; Israel's chosenness should continue to receive emphasis but only with equal stress on its universal aims and on the equal love of God for all His children; the belief in bodily resurrection must give way entirely to the idea of spiritual immortality; and finally, although the cultivation of Hebrew should remain a sacred obligation, Hebrew must make way for the vernacular, which alone is understood by the overwhelming majority of Jewish congregants.

Only a few substantive issues were raised during the discussion of Einhorn's principles. Adler and Felsenthal wanted to include a specific condemnation of the agitation begun in Europe for the possible establishment of a "pseudo-state" *(Scheinstaat)* in Palestine. But their suggestion was turned down, perhaps because the group did not want to make specific mention of such proto-Zionism. Kaufmann Kohler, who had just come from the Leipzig Synod and was serving Beth El in Detroit, joined Adler and Hirsch in pleading for a formulation that was more favorable to Hebrew than Einhorn's original suggestion. They did succeed in forcing Einhorn to modify a clause which could be misinterpreted to mean that Hebrew would at some time give way entirely to the vernacular. But the emphasis, even in Einhorn's new version, remained on intelligibility.

The second set of agenda concerned matters of marriage, divorce, and circumcision. Here too the members of the conference were for the most part ready to accept Einhorn's proposed drafts, simply abbreviating them and making minor revisions. They agreed that in the wedding ceremony the bride would no longer play merely a passive role. Not only would she give the groom a ring in exchange for the one he offered her, she would speak the same Hebrew formula beginning "Be thou consecrated unto me with this ring." But the Philadelphia rabbis markedly differed on the final words of the spoken formula. Traditionally, it read "according to the law of Moses and Israel." Einhorn rejected that formulation because Mosaic and rabbinic law did not provide for mutual espousal, nor did it prohibit polygamy. He wanted the words "according to the law of God." But Hirsch thought that any reference to law, even to the rather nebulous idea of the "law of God," was inappropriate in Reform Judaism. He therefore proposed "according to the teaching of God and the custom of

Israel." But Solomon Deutsch, then the rabbi of Har Sinai in Baltimore, found that Hirsch's formulation would exclude mixed marriages, which he at any rate was not ready to rule out. With Einhorn's formulation linked to tradition by retaining the word "law" and Hirsch's by maintaining the particularity of Israel, the assembly split closely. Einhorn's version barely passed.

The rabbis also expressed their opposition to polygamy (practiced by Mormons and by Jews in the Orient), extramarital relations (seemingly prevalent among some Jewish men as among non-Jews), levirate marriages, and marriage restrictions upon Jews of priestly lineage. They also voted to accept civil divorce and abandon use of the Jewish *get,* although two participants, Solomon Sonneschein of St. Louis and Moses Mielziner of New York, favored its retention in modified form. Yet the majority were not ready to accept a civil divorce in every instance. Some states, and especially U.S. territories, allowed the dissolution of marriages on what the rabbis regarded as rather flimsy grounds. Although Hirsch argued that here too the law of the land must be accepted without question, the majority insisted on the right of the rabbi to examine the legal basis for a divorce and possibly refuse to officiate at the remarriage of one of the partners if he found it morally inadequate. In contrast, out of concern for the sad lot of the *agunah* (straw widow) under Jewish law, the rabbis were in every instance willing to accept the state's declaration that a disappeared husband was presumed dead after a time and that the wife was then free to remarry.

Wise's participation in the conference remained insignificant until the presentation of Einhorn's last proposal, which dealt with circumcision. Without in any way opposing the rite, the rabbis declared that a son born of a Jewish mother, no less than a daughter, should be regarded as Jewish whether or not he had in fact been circumcised. With this position, supported by Jewish law, Wise did not openly disagree. Rather he sought to go further and declare that male proselytes to Judaism did not need to undergo the operation. This suggestion produced the only confrontation at Philadelphia between Wise and Einhorn. It involved a basic principle. For all of his universalism, Einhorn was a Jewish elitist who opposed the prospect of massive proselytization for the same reason that he abhorred mixed marriage. As he put it here: "The acceptance of proselytes, through which Judaism acquires many impure elements, must be made more difficult and it is precisely circumcision which can form a barrier against the influx of such elements." Wise's view was just the opposite: "Let us open the gates so that 'On that day the Lord shall be one' will become a reality." Though it was briefly debated, Wise's proposal was laid aside for the next conference along with all the other suggestions that had not originated with Einhorn.

The rabbis now selected four commissions to deal with the remaining resolutions and determined that they would meet again the following year in Cincinnati. Wise and Lilienthal were selected to make the arrangements. However, Wise's suggestion that a *Gemeindetag,* an assembly of the congregations, take place at the same time was turned down. In Einhorn's view, the congregations were "not yet ready to raise themselves onto the high plane of Judaism." Einhorn also noted that such a lay gathering might well demand the introduction of a single prayerbook, using a compromise liturgy, that would impose "retrogression" on the most advanced congregations. This rejection of the congregational meeting meant a severe blow to the project that Wise regarded as more important than any rabbinical deliberations. Of course he was also aware that his own influence was most limited among these theologically educated,

Germanizing rabbis, in whose midst he would always remain a poorly trained upstart. His true following was among the masses, among the laity which cared more for charisma than formal intellect, more for inherited tradition than consistent principle.

By attending the Philadelphia conference Wise had proven visibly that he too belonged to the rabbinical elite. But as traditionalists began to attack the Philadelphia resolutions, he distanced himself from them. While Einhorn delivered and published lectures in defense and explanation of the Philadelphia conference, Wise complained that the meeting had had to be "eminently Einhornian or nothing" and that the principles, adopted before he arrived, should have been expressed more positively.[102] Negatives could only antagonize. It was, for example, possible to express belief in the immortality of the soul without explicitly rejecting resurrection. The conference had foolishly ignored the fact that, while most congregations were in favor of progress, they abhorred radicalism. Einhorn was right about the gap between the Philadelphia rabbis and the laity, but in their unwillingness to compromise they were weakening, not strengthening, American Jewry. Wise was therefore ready to abandon the radicals. During the following months he involved himself in a separate initiative, one that would rapidly outflank his rivals and leave the Philadelphia gathering an isolated incident.

As early as the following summer an assembly of thirteen rabbis representing ten cities and towns, most of them in the Midwest, met in Cleveland. Only two of the participants, Wise and Solomon Sonneschein, had been present in Philadelphia.[103] They were gathered for one principal purpose: to revise and thus to gain an even greater following for Wise's *Minhag America.* Yet, surprisingly, the idea for the conference had not emanated from Wise; it had come from Adolph Hübsch, a rabbi in New York. Hübsch (1830–1884) had arrived in America in 1866 from Prague as the first rabbi of Ahavath Chesed, then a relatively small congregation consisting mostly of Bohemian Jews, few of them wealthy. Although Hübsch possessed a doctorate, his colleagues in New York looked down on the conservatively inclined "Bohemian rabbi" and treated him with mild contempt. But Wise immediately wrote a letter of welcome to his fellow Bohemian, and assured him that "America is larger than New York." Hübsch had not gone to Philadelphia and had even been among those publicly protesting its resolutions. However, with the projected construction of a new building for his congregation, he was in search of an appropriate non-Orthodox ritual. Since *Minhag America* in its existing form did not please him, he pressed for the collective creation of a new common prayerbook. At first Wise was hesitant. But once he persuaded Hübsch to make *Minhag America* the basis for the new liturgy, he worked with him to convene the meeting.[104] Although little more than initial liturgical revisions were made during a few sweltering summer days, the Einhorn party immediately launched a vicious attack on this act of apparent perfidy. Ellinger, in the *Jewish Times,* spared no epithets. He declared Wise "the Barnum of the Jewish pulpit," a "man who had studied to cover up his ignorance and magnify his superficiality," who "arrogates to himself the role of dictator." Wise's prayerbook was "an abortion" without the virtue of either the old or the new.[105] His Eastern colleagues now wanted no more to do with Wise, certainly not to accept his welcome to the Midwest. Accusing Wise of creating a schism by acting independently for the benefit of his own *Minhag America,* nine of the rabbis who had been present in Philadelphia publicly declared their unwillingness to attend the projected second meeting in Cincinnati.[106]

Perhaps Wise was hoping for just such an outcome. In any case it left his field entirely open. That fall the group which had met in Cleveland reconvened in New York City—on enemy territory—under the aegis of Adolph Hübsch's congregation. Though a perfunctory effort was made to seek reconciliation with Rabbis Einhorn and Adler, it proved fruitless. Prayer by prayer the assembled rabbis went over the Hebrew text of *Minhag America,* making mostly minor revisions. But they also went beyond liturgy. As a rabbinical assembly they were willing to rule on other matters, to declare, for example, that celebration of the second day of the New Year had no biblical basis and that there was no prohibition against men praying with uncovered heads. Radical a decade earlier, these ideas had gained broader appeal by 1870. Since after six days in New York the liturgical revision was still incomplete, the conference decided to reconvene once more the following year, in the summer of 1871, in Cincinnati.[107]

The third gathering was considerably larger than its predecessors, in part because Wise opened it to men of limited rabbinical training. Twenty-seven "reverends," only twelve of whom bore the rabbinical title, were present, nearly half of them from Ohio and almost all from the Midwest. Hübsch, the only New Yorker, presided. The Cincinnati conference officially discussed and approved the project for which Wise had so long privately agitated in the *Israelite:* a rabbinical seminary in Cincinnati and a union of congregations to support it. A committee produced the outline for a rabbinical curriculum and the entire assembly voted to create a "Union of Israelite Congregations of America" along with an authoritative synod as soon as twenty congregations with 2,000 paying members were ready to join. The conference also completed work on the revised prayerbook, which Wise declared was now ready to go to the printer.[108]

However, all did not go smoothly in Cincinnati. The assembly decided that the new prayerbook would have its own title, not "Minhag America"; Hübsch's congregation soon decreed that its rabbi should, after all, produce his own prayerbook.[109] But the greatest damage to Wise's hopes came in debate over a theological issue. During the last session Jacob Mayer of Cleveland had said: "I believe not in a personal God, neither do I address my prayer to a personal God." Thereupon Wise "proposed for debate" that the biblical God be understood—in Spinozist fashion—as "the substance, unlimited, eternal and infinite." He had indeed come to the conclusion that the personal God was not Jewish, but "a philosophical fiction to explain the [Christian] incarnation." Moreover, at the conference Wise had expressed doubt as to whether God actively forgives the sinner on the Day of Atonement, inducing his colleagues immediately and unanimously to repudiate his view.[110] Wise's frank, unconsidered remarks, clearly revealing the unorthodox side of his own theology, gave his enemies an opportunity they could not afford to miss. For all of his radicalism, Einhorn had always held fast to the belief in a personal God who related inwardly to each individual. So did Kohler and Hirsch, who now both contributed articles on the subject to the *Jewish Times.* Moreover, this was an issue where radicals to Wise's left and traditionalists to his right could join hands to strike out against him. Fourteen rabbis, ranging from Einhorn and Adler to the conservative Benjamin Szold of Baltimore, signed a protest against the "flagrant blasphemies" uttered in Cincinnati and in defense of belief in a personal God. In Philadelphia Samuel Hirsch and Marcus Jastrow, despite their differences, joined in a separate denunciation. Although Max Lilienthal, Wise's colleague in Cincinnati, bravely attempted to mediate, his effort was without success.[111] The most prestigious liberal rabbis had now declared themselves openly against Wise and they scared off their colleagues. Thus the Einhorn faction was able to abort Wise's rabbinical conferences as he had put an end to their effort begun in Philadelphia. Indeed, Wise's grand schemes for congregational union and a seminary would have been brought fully to a halt had they not just then received decisive support from the only constituency which still remained sympathetic, the lay leaders of midwestern congregations.

An Ephemeral Broad Unity

Lay sentiment in favor of union was building up rapidly in congregations west of the Alleghenies. The realization was taking hold that Jewish religious life in America could not be sustained by individual synagogues alone. Rabbinical leadership was scarce everywhere, but especially in the West. Lacking almost entirely were native-born preachers and teachers who could transmit the message of Judaism easily and effectively in English. The Sabbath schools were without appropriate teaching materials. Under these circumstances European-born parents perceived the danger that their inheritance could evaporate in the liberal, seductive atmosphere of America. Wise's repeated calls for a domestic institution to train American rabbis therefore fell on receptive ears. The lay leaders had built synagogues, orphanages, and hospitals. Some were now ready to unite for the purpose of giving at least a portion of their charitable funds for a rabbinical seminary. Wise sensed the mounting appeal of his project to the laity and set his plans accordingly. He could no longer "covenant" with the rabbis, he wrote to Hübsch, for they were too often motivated by timidity, ambition, or a sense of their own importance. But he had a fresh plan: to allow the laity to act on their own. Hübsch might laugh all he liked; the new strategy would work.[112]

Though Wise had urged congregational union since 1848, and almost succeeded in pulling together a congregational convention early in 1869, the lay initiative which now emerged in Wise's own congregation put their rabbi on the sidelines. Moritz Loth, the president of Bene Yeshurun, was not only a man of wealth and business acumen, but somewhat of an intellectual and the author of novels. He was also a Jew of distinctly conservative convictions, at least with regard to observance, and highly suspicious of radical Reform. Perhaps because he recognized that Wise had become too controversial a figure, or perhaps simply because he intended to do things his own way, Loth did not involve his rabbi in the process that led to the founding of a congregational union. On October 10, 1872, Loth proposed to a general meeting of the congregation that it join with the four other Cincinnati synagogues in calling a congregational convention. The purpose of the meeting would be to form a union having a threefold aim: to establish a rabbinical seminary, to publish proper books for religious schools, and "to adopt a code of laws which are not to be invaded under the plausible phrase of reform; namely that *Milah* [circumcision] shall never be abolished, that the Sabbath shall be observed on Saturday and never be changed to any other day, that *Shechitah* [ritual slaughter] and the dietary laws shall not be disregarded, but commended as preserving health and prolonging life." On this basis even the two Orthodox congregations in Cincinnati were brought into the process. The "call for a convention" went out from a united Cincinnati Jewry to every known congregation in the West and South. It spoke not of reforms but of the obligation "to preserve the Jewish identity" in America, an objective which could be reached only if "some of our youth, conversant with the language of the land, should be educated for the Jewish ministry, and as teachers and expounders of our sacred principles."[113]

The convention, which established the Union of American Hebrew Congregations, met in Cincinnati on July 8–10, 1873.[114] Thirty-four congregations from thirteen states were accredited. Together they possessed close to 2,000 members. The largest were Bene Yeshurun of Cincinnati and Adas Israel of Louisville, each with 200 families. Most of the delegates were from smaller towns: Portsmouth and Youngstown, Ohio; Quincy and Peoria, Illinois; Natchez and Vicksburg, Mississippi. Only one Chicago congregation, Anshe Mayriv, was represented.[115] Cincinnati dominated the proceedings. Moritz Loth was elected president and Julius Freiberg, the president of the other large Reform congregation, Bene Israel, became vice-president. Eleven of the twenty members chosen for the Executive Board were Cincinnatians. However, having once launched the project and taken control of it, the delegates from the West and South resolved that henceforth the Union would be a national organization, open to congregations anywhere in the country. Wise's dream of Jewish religious unity was thus at last reaching fulfillment. Nothing less dramatic than the words of Isaiah (9:5) could express his exuberance: "For a child was born unto us; a son was given unto us, and the dominion shall be upon his shoulder."[116]

In fact, with Loth's devoted parenting, the newborn child grew healthily during its early years. By the first regular meeting of the UAHC Council, held the following year in Cleveland, the number of congregations had increased to fifty-five; in 1875 the Union had more than doubled in size, boasting seventy-two congregations with about 4,000 members. To be sure, there were—again in Wise's words—vile and violent attempts "to strangle the infant in its cradle." But while such attacks succeeded in deflecting donations from wealthy Jews in the East, they were unable to hinder the new Union from increasingly gaining strength. Once it became apparent that the UAHC and its seminary were indeed viable, eastern congregations, grudgingly to be sure, also joined.[117]

Most of the East Coast congregations joined as the result of a successfully negotiated deal. As long ago as 1859, in the wake of the Mortara Case, an egregious instance of the surreptitious conversion and abduction of a Jewish child in Italy, representatives from twenty-four American congregations, almost all from the East, had met to create the Board of Delegates of American Israelites. Its principal purpose was to act collectively in defense and support of Jewish rights and interests anywhere in the world. Although Isaac Leeser wanted the Board to adopt a broad religious program as well, the majority opposed the introduction of potentially divisive issues. While Reformers had been initially suspicious of its traditionalist founders, by 1873 even Emanu-El of New York was brought in when the agenda was definitively limited to Jewish defense. Here then was a congregational union with a different geographical basis and a different purpose. As the UAHC grew, it became increasingly logical and desirable for the Board to merge with it on a mutually acceptable basis. A single nationwide organization could more easily attain both educational and political aims. By 1876 merger explorations were under way and two years later unification could officially take place. Under the agreement the Board of Delegates became a standing committee of the UAHC, continuing to pursue its political purposes from New York. In return, the Union constitution was amended to expand its aims and to give Easterners half of the thirty seats on the UAHC Executive Board. As a result, by 1879 the Union could boast 118 congregations, more than half of the known congregations in the United States.[118] Among them were large, decisively Reform synagogues such as Emanu-El and Beth El in New York, as well as some quite traditional ones. It seemed as if the broadly based UAHC, though still representing not more than a fifth of the total Jewish population, was on its way to becoming the dominant religious organization in American Jewry.

During its first years the propagation of Reform Judaism was neither an overt nor a covert purpose of the UAHC. Not only would the discussion of doctrinal and ritual issues have threatened to break up the still fragile union, but it appeared that with greater or lesser rapidity nearly all of American Jewry was in any case moving at least toward a moderate Reform. Conservative congregations were adopting *Avodat Yisrael,* the Szold–Jastrow prayerbook, which on doctrinal points, like exile as punishment and reinstitution of the sacrificial service, was hardly more traditional than *Minhag America.* To be sure, there were still enclaves of Orthodoxy, especially in the East, but it was felt that they could not long resist. Scientific achievements—the steam engine and electricity—were breaking down all barriers, ushering in an age of cosmopolitanism and a "broad spirit of catholicity."[119] In fact the problem now was the disappearance of Judaism. There were thousands of Jews, born in the United States, for whom its ritual traditions were "as strange as the customs of the Mohammedans or the Parsees."[120] Only a small minority of children received any formal Jewish education. In a Jewish population of about a quarter of a million, secular Jewish associations attracted about 40,000, synagogue membership less than a third that number.[121] The fear was rife that mixed marriage would soon produce considerable losses to the Jewish community. Only a native religious leadership, it was felt, could stem the tide that was flowing on to complete assimilation. For the founders of the Union, teaching Judaism, not its reform, was the issue.

Although the UAHC expended about 10 percent of its funds for its Board of Delegates, for assistance to Sabbath schools, and for publication of an inexpensive version of Leeser's Bible translation, its principal activity throughout the early years was support of its rabbinical seminary, the Hebrew Union College.[122] The first Jewish seminary to be successful in America, HUC was launched with great éclat but under the most humble of circumstances. Following a grand opening ceremony, Isaac Mayer Wise began his duties as but the volunteer and part-time head of a faculty which at first could boast only a single paid instructor. Potential students were hard to find. Wise relates that "Jewish literature had become so despicable and superfluous a branch of learning and education in the estimation of the rich, and the position of the rabbis so mean and undesirable for the sons of wealthy people, that no family of means would think of having a son educated for the Jewish pulpit."[123] When classes began, in the fall of 1875, there were only nine pupils, aged thirteen to seventeen, mostly indigent and supported by the College. They were starting out on an eight-year program in Jewish studies simultaneously with attendance at high school and then university. The demands were ambitious: students were expected to read widely in the classical texts of Judaism—Babylonian and Palestinian Talmud, Midrash and Codes, no less than the Bible. However, they were not expected to be familiar with much contemporary Jewish scholarship and no attention was given to biblical criticism. Doctrinal issues were purposely avoided. Wise did not want the College branded as Reform or radical in any respect. By concentrating on the classical heritage, the curriculum would prepare a rabbinate most broadly acceptable to American congregations.

Gradually the College grew and attained stature. In 1879 Moses Mielziner, the ablest modern scholar of rabbinics in America at that time, joined its faculty as professor of Talmud. Other scholars followed. Regularly panels of outside examiners measured the students' progress and were generally pleased. Radicals and conservatives served together on these panels and as delegates to the councils of the Union. David Einhorn and Samuel Hirsch participated in the work of the Union and College alongside Sabato Morais, Frederick de Sola Mendes, Benjamin Szold, and Marcus Jastrow—men who would soon become pillars of American Conservative Judaism. As the president of the seminary's faculty, however modest, Wise had become nothing less than the titular spiritual head of all non-Orthodox American Jewry. His long-standing opponent, Bernhard Felsenthal, felt compelled to note Wise's accomplishment:

> Dr. Wise *is* now at the head of the College not only, but of all Israel in the United States. It is *he* who educates the rabbis for America. It is *he* who defines the course in which Judaism in this country has to run. It is *he* who gives shape and color and character to our Jewish affairs. *He* is the central sun, around which the planets and trabants are moving, some near to him, some more distant. That is all right, and we submit to the hard facts. He has succeeded, and "nothing is so successful as the success."[124]

When the College ordained its first four students in 1883, representatives from more than a hundred UAHC congregations gathered to celebrate the occasion. Resounding music and festive oratory flowed over the throng that filled the massive, ornate Bene Yeshurun temple. The men and women assembled there were witnessing a first-ever event in American Jewish history. Yet that very ordination ceremony, it is clear in retrospect, marked the high point of Jewish religious unity in America. So wide a spectrum could not be contained under any organizational aegis for very long. Differences became visible that very evening when a lavish dinner, carelessly ordered by Cincinnati laymen from a local Jewish caterer, turned out to feature a variety of shellfish. Yet this scandalizing "Trefa Banquet" was only symbolic of fundamental tensions already apparent. Regional, religious, ethnic, and social differences would make this newborn unity ephemeral. The conservatives soon went their own way, while Reform Judaism in America, for the next generation, became preeminently radical.

7

"Classical"
Reform Judaism

The last decades of the nineteenth century and the first years of the twentieth witnessed the widest swing of the Reform pendulum away from traditional Jewish belief and practice. During this time the American movement gained a clearer sense of its own identity, as it distinguished itself more sharply from Orthodoxy and from an emergent Conservatism. Reform Judaism now came to represent the particular religious affiliation of American Jews of German descent, whether of the first, second, or third generation. Reform temples served as citadels of an Americanized Judaism, practiced by men and women whose socioeconomic status and German cultural heritage set them apart from the multitude of their coreligionists arriving from eastern Europe.

In its drift to radicalism, the Reform of this period tested the outer limits of Jewish identity. Its leaders were forced to explain where it differed from the Ethical Culture movement and from Unitarian Christianity. They experimented with Sunday morning services and debated the issue of rabbinical sanction for mixed marriage. The great questions of the day drew their attention. Rabbis sought to instruct their members not on Judaism alone, but on Darwinism, biblical criticism, and the latest findings of natural science. Increasingly, social justice became one of the movement's major concerns, serving as a practical application of the moral principles which at this time greatly overshadowed ritual as the basis of Reform religious expression. Education was oriented to Jewish ethics far more than to learning Jewish customs and ceremonies. And the first common liturgy of the movement reflected the dominant universalism.

This generation also witnessed the flourishing of two remarkable rabbis, each an influential scholar and intellectual. Though Kaufmann Kohler and Emil G. Hirsch were neither bitter rivals nor advocates of fundamentally antagonistic religious goals—as Isaac Mayer Wise and David Einhorn had been—their narrower differences were nonetheless significant in setting out the theological and practical perimeters of Reform in this era.

Much of the religious debate during these years—as also thereafter—took place within the newly founded Central Conference of American Rabbis, whose yearly conventions became a weathervane for shifting rabbinical views. The laity, still exclusively male in the composition of its leadership, usually followed the rabbis, but some found them too radical or individualistic, while others went even beyond the most radical rabbis in casting off traditions.

At a later time, this period in the history of Reform Judaism became known as its "classical" phase, to distinguish it from the "neo-Reform" which arose in reaction to it. Yet, as we shall see, the border dividing the two periods is not clearly marked. Even during the classical years, signs of rebellion were abundantly visible. Well before World War I, some of the movement's most prominent leaders had become Zionists and rabbinical calls for the recovery of tradition were already heard.

Although American Reform Judaism had been moving in the direction of radicalism since the end of the Civil War, and a circle of its leading rabbis had declared doctrinal independence from Orthodoxy as early as the Philadelphia conference of 1869, the clear and decisive commitment to the classical position came only in 1885. With the adoption that year of the influential Pittsburgh Platform, whose principles, though often assailed, remained the guide of the movement for half a century, the conservatives within Reform either veered toward radicalism or departed. The movement was left less divided internally but also further from Jews outside it.

The Pittsburgh Platform

The gathering of nineteen rabbis in Pittsburgh in November 1885 must be understood as an attempt to lay down a set of defining and definitive principles which would distinguish Reform Judaism from a wholly nonsectarian universalism on the one hand and from more traditional expressions of Judaism on the other.

The major universalist challenge to Reform Judaism had arisen a decade earlier, but continued to be felt. Felix Adler, son of the rabbi of Temple Emanu-El in New York, Samuel Adler, had planned to follow in his father's footsteps. However, upon his return from rabbinical studies at the liberal seminary in Berlin, he admitted he could not subscribe to the gradualism of religious evolution espoused by his teacher, Abraham Geiger. The young Adler was able to accept neither a theistic God concept nor the notion that Israel was God's chosen people, destined to remain separate for the sake of a priestly mission. He could see no need for continued Jewish separation. If the goal was universal, might it not best be achieved by dropping all particularism, even in the present, and proceeding to establish a more moral world on the basis of an eclecticism that drew from multiple religious traditions? In 1876/77 Felix Adler founded the New York Society for Ethical Culture, which later established branches elsewhere as well. A brilliant thinker and effective orator, he drew enormous crowds to his weekly Sunday morning lectures. Prominent among those attracted to Adler were Reform Jews whose specifically Jewish identity had become marginal and who found in Ethical Culture a substitute religion that was intellectually respectable, ritually undifferentiating, and morally earnest.[1]

Adler did not hesitate to attack Reform Judaism as a kind of halfway house between an untenable orthodoxy and a complete liberation from religious authority. His critique was the more painful because Adler himself had emerged from the inner circle of Reform Judaism and because when he spoke of Judaism, or of Reform Judaism, it was with appreciation for his heritage, not with rancor. He was no angry rebel—who might more easily have been dismissed—but a reflective thinker of prophetic moral commitment who simply declared that even Reform Judaism, still tied to the authority of its tradition, was inadequate to the intellectual and ethical challenges of the day. Adler would not recognize the validity of Jewish religious change from within. Measuring Judaism by the standards of an inflexible orthodoxy, he found that Reform Jews were in fact scarcely any longer Jews at all. They simply refused to recognize that fact and take the final step beyond all particularism.[2]

Although Ethical Culture's tangible attraction for Reform Jews was mainly limited to New York, its arguments were a challenge to Reform Judaism everywhere. Its leaders could not afford to see their movement as erecting a catapult that would propel its adherents beyond the Jewish pale. And they had to attack the idea of an ethics which could exist without the divine authority underlying Jewish texts. In Chicago, Emil G. Hirsch preached that Judaism was itself an ethical culture movement, but one that was planted on firm historical foundations. When Adler visited Cincinnati, Isaac Mayer Wise commented that "the Professor" preached on the basis "There is no God and Felix Adler is his prophet." And Wise sought to stigmatize Adler by equating the Jewish freethinker with his counterpart of Christian origins, Col. Robert Ingersoll, whose popular preachment of agnosticism had long been a public scandal.[3]

The most agitated response came from Kaufmann Kohler, who in the late seventies served as the rabbi of Temple Sinai in Chicago. The Sinai Literary Association, a group of young men whom Kohler had hoped to influence religiously, invited Adler to be their guest speaker. But Kohler would have none of it. He denounced the founder of Ethical Culture as "a man who has deserted the Jewish flag, and openly professes his disbelief in God and immortality." He would not allow his temple to be disgraced by "one who blasphemes God and Judaism." Disagreeing with his Chicago colleagues Liebmann Adler and Bernhard Felsenthal, who were more tolerant, Kohler clearly drew the line: "No rabbi in or outside America dares consider himself a Jewish minister while approving the ideas and expressions with which the Standard Hall lecturer in New York most irreverently and insultingly assailed the Jewish religion." Kohler admitted that he had been asked whether his own radical views did not lead in the same direction. But he insisted they did not. Whatever his heterodoxy, he had remained a theist and a believer in revelation.[4] Yet Kohler could not easily put Adler's challenge out of mind, especially after 1879, when he took over David Einhorn's last pulpit, Temple Beth El in New York.

For all the attention Adler received, however, his voice spoke for only a minute fraction of American Jews, those ready to step beyond Judaism's outermost periphery. What Kohler encountered in New York during the early 1880s was not only its Ethical Culture Society, but also a large body of religious conservatives and a growing multitude of east European immigrants. Beginning in 1879, the *American Hebrew* provided a local sounding board for the traditional point of view. Some of the conservatives, in New York and elsewhere, had been drawn to Reform Judaism as representing a wide consensus and the best organizational basis for congregational union and the training of rabbinical leadership. Although some had begun to have second thoughts following the Trefa Banquet of 1883, they lacked a clear formulation of where they differed and a rallying point for their discontent. Both were provided in 1885 when Alexander Kohut, a Hungarian-born rabbi of impressive scholarly credentials, arrived in New York and very soon began a popular series of German-language lectures on the talmudic tractate *Ethics of the Fathers.* In elaborating his text, Kohut clearly established an intermediate position between Reform and Orthodoxy.

Ahavath Chesed, the congregation which invited Kohut, was part of the Reform movement, though on its more conservative wing. It belonged to the UAHC; it had introduced mixed seating, instrumental music, and other ritual reforms; and its rabbi, Adolph Hübsch, had been a close associate of Isaac Mayer Wise. But when Hübsch died in 1884, the board decided to invite Kohut, certain that his stature and moderation would attract new members and that he would continue the established practices of the congregation. Kohut was indeed and self-admittedly the exponent of "a Judaism of the healthy golden mean." But it quickly became apparent that the mean, in his view, did not run through the Reform movement.[5]

Kohut's lectures echoed Reform themes. He averred that the principles of the American Declaration of Independence "are pure biblical thoughts"; he equated the strengthening of Judaism in America with the establishment of a new Jerusalem and a new Zion. Echoing Einhorn, he spoke of the Jews' "priestly vocation." But he set his own modernized Judaism, unambiguously on the old foundation. Law, not spirit, was its unalterable basis. His declared standpoint was Mosaic–rabbinic Judaism which, since it embodied the word of God, could not be subject to massive change. Only forms might be altered as a concession to the times. Kohut was willing to excuse the Jew who was less than fully observant provided he recognized the binding nature of the law that he transgressed. But he branded the Reformer, who rejected the law's divinity in principle, as not a Jew at all, as one who "has banished himself from the camp of Israel." In a frequently cited passage he declared: "Such a reform which seeks to progress without the Mosaic–rabbinical tradition, such a Reform is a Deformity: is a skeleton of Judaism without flesh and sinew, without spirit and heart."[6] In declaring Reform Jews essentially non-Jews, Kohut was pressing from the other side a similar case to that which Felix Adler was making from the vantage point of Ethical Culture: Reform, without realizing or admitting it, had crossed the boundary of historical Judaism.

Again it was Kohler who jumped into the breach. In his own series of lectures during that same summer of 1885, the Beth El rabbi launched into a spirited defense of the Reform Judaism that Kohut had so tellingly attacked. Mosaism and rabbinic Judaism were appropriate for earlier ages, he argued. But the age of man's maturity called for freedom from the letter, from blind authority, "from all restrictions which curb the minds and encroach upon the hearts." The contemporary Jew had "outgrown the guiding strings and swaddling-clothes of infancy"; he was ready to walk on his own. What he required was not law, but a "living Judaism," both enlightened and pious, appealing to reason and emotion.[7]

The Kohut–Kohler debate attracted wide attention. Each man's synagogue was crowded to overflowing as their principled dispute drove away indifference and aroused new interest in religious issues. But the debate also sharpened the division between conservatives and radicals, creating the outlines of two emerging camps.[8] It thus became clear, at least to Kohler, that bringing conservatives gradually into line with the Einhorn tradition of Reform was no longer a realistic possibility. The time was past when the borders could be left unmarked. Reform Judaism was neither a portal to Ethical Culture nor merely a few formal concessions to modernity. A clear, succinct, and positive self-definition had become a necessity.

After consulting with Isaac Mayer Wise in Cincinnati and Samuel Hirsch in Philadelphia, Kohler invited to a conference "all such American rabbis as advocate reform and progress and are in favor of united action in all matters pertaining to the welfare of American Judaism."[9] Those who came to Pittsburgh, or sent their regrets, were mostly rabbis from the Midwest. Though the initiative was not his own, Wise too chose to attend. As the head of the Hebrew Union College, he could not afford to be left out, though he must have realized that his presence in a gathering likely to reach radical conclusions might well jeopardize the continued participation of more traditional congregations in the UAHC.

The conference paid Wise the honor of electing him president, but it was Kohler who dominated the proceedings. He read a prepared paper which deplored the fact that Reform was popularly perceived as essentially a liberation from old forms, not a positive program. It was therefore necessary to formulate a set of principles that would be broad-minded enough to accept the results of modern research in comparative religion, ethnology, and biblical criticism while at the same time "positive enough to dispel suspicion and reproach of agnostic tendencies or of discontinuing the historical thread of the past." Kohler called for a wide range of constructive efforts which would refute the notion that Reformers were simply "rebels and traitors" against the law. His list included caring for poorer Jews and bringing them into the synagogue, publishing pamphlets and tracts on Judaism, producing a uniform system of religious instruction and a common liturgy, and the encouragement of more household observance and festivity. But all of this was only leading up to his proposed platform, which would serve as the theoretical basis for any practical program. That platform was referred to a committee, shortened, altered, and added to. But as it emerged from debate, the eight-paragraph statement remained basically Kohler's document. And the conference accepted it unanimously.

Unlike the Philadelphia principles of 1869, the Pittsburgh Platform is not in essence a document of rejection.[10] Its main purpose is not to declare where Reform departs from Orthodoxy (though that is not entirely lacking), but what it seeks to affirm. Beginning with the recognition that consciousness of God pervades other religions as well, the platform immediately takes a position that cuts off the Ethical Culture perspective: "Judaism presents the highest conception of the God-idea as taught in our Holy Scriptures and developed and spiritualized by the Jewish teachers in accordance with the moral and philosophical progress of their respective ages." The following paragraphs then set forth the specifically Reform view of Jewish tradition over against Orthodoxy. The Bible receives recognition, not as revelation (though Kohler originally insisted on the use of that term in a spiritualized sense), but as "the record of the consecration of the Jewish people to its mission as priest of the One God." The Bible is admittedly primitive in some respects, the Mosaic legislation merely a means for the Jews' early education to their religious task. But even in the present, the moral laws remain binding and those ceremonies that serve "to elevate and sanctify our lives" receive affirmation. Only in its fourth paragraph does the tone become stridently critical: laws regarding diet, priestly purity, and dress, it maintains, are "apt rather to obstruct than to further modern spiritual elevation."

It has often and correctly been observed that the Pittsburgh Platform gushes with the optimism of its setting and age. Like other Americans, the rabbis were caught up in the resurgence of hopefulness that swept across the United States after the tragedy of the Civil War and remained into the twentieth century. Where they differed was to link the glorious future of humanity with their own religious messianism. What the rabbis at Pittsburgh called the "modern era of universal culture of heart and intellect" was for them but Israel's age-old hope divested of its particularistic elements. As a religious community, Jews would preserve their historical identity, they noted, but through their ever-progressing religion they would participate actively in the universal task of ushering in the better age. The immortal human soul, rooted in the divine, would—almost necessarily it seems—find its bliss in righteousness. Only the last paragraph, added by Emil G. Hirsch, tacitly recognized that much misery yet remained in the premessianic world. It was therefore a Jewish obligation "to participate in the great task of modern times, to solve on the basis of justice and righteousness the problems presented by the contrasts and evils of the present organization of society."

The Pittsburgh Platform accomplished its intended purpose. While it did not set forth any new doctrine, except perhaps in the explicit commitment to economic justice, it did put together concisely for the new English-speaking generation that heritage of Reform Jewish ideas developed over nearly a century by individual thinkers in Europe and America. Within its particular polemical context it unabashedly asserted Jewish religious supremacy and the continuing need for separate Jewish existence. At the same time it established Reform Judaism, not on the basis of biblical or rabbinic law, but on a conception of God and morality anchored in, but also departing from, the texts which first reflected it. Wise called it a "Declaration of Independence"— which was correct in more than one respect. Not only was Reform Judaism now clearly an entity unto itself. Its spiritual leaders had also set down for all to see those principles which most of them had long perceived to be self-evident, but which they had not previously formulated into an authoritative text.

Promulgation, interpretation, and denunciation followed. Secular and Jewish newspapers in America and Europe printed the platform and commented on it. A Southern rabbinical conference, composed mainly of Reformers, unanimously endorsed it. So did other rabbis, like Bernhard Felsenthal and Samuel Hirsch, who had not been present. In Cleveland it was supposedly "received with joy and admiration." Wise regularly reprinted the text in his *American Israelite.* For the Cincinnati rabbi the conference finally healed his rift with the radicals and assured their continuing support for his institution. Within a few weeks Kohler himself, together with Rabbis Emil G. Hirsch of Chicago and Adolph Moses of Louisville, founded a new periodical in English and German entitled the *Jewish Reformer,* which printed the full proceedings of the Pittsburgh conference in six installments along with appropriate interpretation. This new weekly, which received impetus from the Pittsburgh gathering, was the first Reform newspaper in the East since the demise of the *Jewish Times* in 1879. Three portraits adorned its masthead, as if to assert a pedigree: Moses Mendelssohn (who made Reform possible), Abraham Geiger (who established its ideology in Europe), and David Einhorn (who brought it uncompromised to America). Like the Pittsburgh Platform itself, the newspaper—though short-lived—was intended to produce the inner consolidation of Reform Judaism which Kohler considered necessary.[11]

It was, however, the negative reaction provoked by the Pittsburgh conference which, ironically, proved to have the most unifying effect. Felix Adler used the occasion to condemn the "race pride" that even Reformers evidently possessed and their failure to recognize that in some moral matters Jews could and should learn from Christians. He also reaffirmed that Judaism was not susceptible to fundamental change without ceasing to be itself.[12] More troublesome was the effect of Pittsburgh on the conservatives, especially those who had had a share in the work of the UAHC and the Hebrew Union College. Rabbi Benjamin Szold of Baltimore, once a supporter of Reform institutions, denounced the platform and unsuccessfully demanded that his congregation withdraw from the Union. Other rabbis of the conservative wing joined in casting the odium of Pittsburgh upon Cincinnati. When the UAHC met in 1886, it adopted a resolution declaring that it was responsible only for its own acts; and the head of the College's Board of Governors was forced to stress that no tenets of any platform were taught at HUC, only "Judaism pure and simple."[13] But there was no containing the damage. Wise, the rabbinical head of the Hebrew Union College, had presided at Pittsburgh and afterward had defended its proceedings. The thought of establishing a rival, more traditional seminary in the East—bruited about even before the Pittsburgh conference—was now transformed into a concerted plan.[14] Regularly the conservative weekly, the *American Hebrew,* agitated for its realization. Funds were gathered, an association formed, and by 1887 the first classes were held at the new Jewish Theological Seminary in New York. Just as the issue of Hebrew had led to the departure of Zacharias Frankel from the Frankfurt rabbinical conference in 1845 and the consequent division of German Reform, so did the Pittsburgh conference, a generation later, irreparably divide the Reform movement in America. A new Jewish entity now emerged on the right, which, as one of its principal founders, Sabato Morais, admitted to Kaufmann Kohler, drew a line between their (liberal, pluralistic) theory and their (traditional, conformist) practice.[15]

At the end of 1885 the secessionists were sometimes described as Conservatives (with a capital "C"). The one-time faction had become fully a party and was beginning to take shape as a denomination.[16] Wise's often frustrated dream of a unified liberal Judaism in America once again—and finally—lay in shambles. "We Reformers know we are in the minority," wrote Emil G. Hirsch a few weeks after Pittsburgh.[17] Henceforth it would be as only one of the "branches" of American Judaism that Reform would shape its narrower destiny.

Ideologists: Kaufmann Kohler and Emil G. Hirsch

As Reform Judaism in America assumed a separate organizational identity, it also developed the distinct corpus of beliefs and attitudes that marked its classical period. Two brothers-in-law, each married to a daughter of David Einhorn, became the chief architects of that generation's religious ideology. Kaufmann Kohler (1843–1926) and Emil G. Hirsch (1851–1923), as we shall see, differed in temperament and degree of radicality, but in matters of principle they were not far apart. For decades their thinking, expressed especially in sermons, articles, and lectures, was reflected with minor variations by lesser lights in pulpits throughout the United States.[18] In their day, Kohler and Hirsch were the giants.

Kaufmann Kohler was a lifelong religious zealot.[19] Though he passed from the strict orthodoxy of his youth to the radical theology of classical Reform, he never became a liberal. Fervently and intolerantly, he fought what he loved to call "the battles of the Lord," assailing those forces which he believed stood in the way of an occidentalized and universalized, but firmly theistic modern Judaism. Kohler spent the first twenty-six years of his life in Germany, and for all his devotion to America, remained very much a European. It was the European yeshivah and university that shaped his thinking, European formality and earnestness that determined his personal style. Born in Fürth, in Bavaria, he grew up in the world of Jewish tradition and studied with the most important Orthodox rabbis, including Samson Raphael Hirsch. But he also engaged in higher secular studies, and the conflict between the two worlds became unbearable for a mind unable to tolerate contradiction. At length he came under the influence of Abraham Geiger's theology and the ethnic psychology of Moritz Lazarus and Heymann Steinthal.

When at the age of twenty-four Kohler published his doctoral dissertation on Jacob's blessing, he noted that gaining personal freedom of thought, within the context of Jewish faith and the Jewish community, had been a slow process and that he had purchased it at a high price.[20] The dissertation, however, indicated just how far he had come. Its introduction reflected the ideas of the German Reformers: Judaism was not to be understood as law, but as the "eternal moral idea"; revelation was internal rather than external, not dependent on the verity of a revealed biblical text. Its topic indicated that Kohler had chosen to begin his scholarly career at the most radical point of Jewish *Wissenschaft,* textual criticism of the Pentateuch itself. The dissertation concluded that Jacob's blessing of his sons reflected not the patriarchal period, but the time of tribal separation after the conquest of Canaan. The blessing was simply "put into the mouth of Jacob." Yet there was also a Jewish touch that set Kohler's work apart from contemporary Protestant Old Testament criticism. Calling upon his erudition in rabbinic sources, Kohler was able to embellish his study with references to midrashim and medieval Jewish commentaries. It was not just the text, but how Jews understood it, that was important to the young scholar.

Jacob's Blessing made Kohler too radical for any German Jewish community. He came to America where he served briefly at Temple Beth El in Detroit, then for longer periods at Temple Sinai in Chicago, and after 1879, as David Einhorn's successor at Temple Beth El in New York. Three years after the death of Isaac Mayer Wise, in 1903, he became president of the Hebrew Union College, occupying that influential position, along with the College's chair of Jewish theology, until 1921. In the last decades of the nineteenth century and the first of the twentieth, it was especially Kaufmann Kohler who spoke for American Reform Judaism.

Unlike Kohler, Emil G. Hirsch was born into Reform.[21] His father, Samuel Hirsch, we have seen was one of the significant systematic theologians during the period that German Judaism first encountered German philosophy. Though Emil, too, was born in Europe—in Luxembourg where his father then served—he was only fifteen when his family moved to Philadelphia, and soon thereafter he attended the University of Pennsylvania. Although he did return to Berlin for his rabbinical and advanced secular studies, in style and substance Hirsch was more Americanized than Kohler and his influence was more concentrated on one particular city. For many years he was

Kaufmann Kohler.

Emil G. Hirsch.

Professor of Rabbinic Literature and Philosophy at the University of Chicago; and he regularly took stands and participated in projects with local non-Jewish social and economic reformers. He spent nearly his entire rabbinical career at Temple Sinai in Chicago, a congregation that prided itself on being among the most influential and radical in America. His extraordinary oratorical talent regularly filled its immense sanctuary with 2,000 listeners. For thirty years, beginning in 1891, Hirsch edited the *Reform Advocate,* the flagship journal of radical Reform. Like Kohler, Hirsch was an intellectual and a scholar, like his brother-in-law also an editor and major contributor to the *Jewish Encyclopedia.* But unlike him, he was noted for his biting sarcasm, a tool of discourse Kohler eschewed. On the scale of religious radicalism Hirsch stood to the left of his brother-in-law, differing especially on whether there was continuing value in Jewish ceremonies.

Neither Kohler nor Hirsch was an original Jewish thinker. Self-admittedly, they were both heirs of the Europeans. What they did accomplish—more effectively than Einhorn—was to translate the ideas of Geiger and the other Germans into the popular thought of American Reform. For the second and third generations of German Jews in America they provided reasons for not being Orthodox on the one hand and not ignoring or leaving Judaism on the other. Mostly their justifications were the old ones, sometimes expressed with new eloquence: the prophetic heritage, the mission of Israel, the universal messianic goal. Their thought is interesting, however, because of its new foci. European Reform ideologues had been forced especially to confront those Christian theologies and secular philosophies that portrayed Judaism as an outdated form of religion. In late nineteenth-century America the intellectual challenges were new ones, affecting Christianity no less than Judaism. Higher biblical criticism, comparative religion, Darwinism, and social relevance stood at the top of the list.[22] Not philosophy but science, not theoretical ethics but applied morality were the criteria that now measured the legitimacy and value of modern religion.

Kohler and Hirsch were both uncompromising biblical critics. Although Kohler did not consider biblical criticism an appropriate topic for the pulpit, he introduced it into the curriculum of the Hebrew Union College for the first time as soon as he became its president. For Hirsch, biblical criticism sounded the death knell of Orthodoxy even as it supported Reform's claim that rituals were not the essence of Judaism:

> Modern scholarship has spoken and its voice cannot be hushed. It has shown that Moses is not the author of the Pentateuch; that Sinai is not the cradle of what is highest and best in Biblical Judaism . . . that the whole apparatus of priestly institutionalism is of non-Hebraic origin: the veritable "laws of the Gentiles." The Abrahamitic rite, the dietary and levitical laws, sacrificial ritualism, the festal cycle, and the like, are not indigenous to the Jewish soil.[23]

By the beginning of the twentieth century it was not so much the already established documentary hypothesis, revealing various sources for the text of the Pentateuch, that disturbed observant Jews. It was the emerging disciplines of comparative religion and folklore. To the dismay of traditional Judaism, their practitioners analyzed biblical commandments in terms of the cultic practices associated with neighboring primitive religions. But here too science seemed to validate the position of classical Reform. "The dietary laws are a survival of a species of totemism," Hirsch wrote, and added that the research of W. Robertson Smith had made that quite plain. Circumcision was originally a ceremony of initiation into the tribe or clan. Kohler described the later *tefilin* (phylacteries) and *mezuzah* (biblical inscriptions on the doorpost) as "talismans" whose origin was in primitive blood daubing and called the wearing of the *talit* (prayer shawl) "fetishism." Such laws, spurned by Reform Jews in practice, seemed totally discredited by discovery of their parallels elsewhere in the ancient Near East.[24]

What remained uniquely Jewish was the religion of the Prophets, and that for Hirsch was the basis of Reform Judaism. Unlike Orthodoxy, Reform had nothing to fear from biblical criticism because its truth did not depend on the origin of sacred texts. What did matter was the intrinsic value of the sources, their religious meaning—and herein the Bible was richer and nobler than any other literary work. As Kohler sermonically put it: "The Bible is holy *not because it is inspired, but because and insofar as it does still, inspire.* It is not true because God has spoken the word, but because in the truth, the comfort, the hope, the final victory of justice which it holds out, you hear God speak to you in soul stirring strains."[25] Viewed as a human document, the Bible itself became an instrument that conveyed—in some of its parts—an indispensable religious and moral message. Dividing its wheat from its chaff was not only the task of biblical criticism but also of conscience. Authority lay not in the text but within the reader—or, more precisely, in the reflection of divine moral law within the soul of every believing Jew.

Darwinism represented a broader challenge. Not only did it undermine the biblical conception of human creation, it substituted a mechanical process of human descent that seemed to leave no room for divine guidance. Beginning in the 1870s, the impact of Darwin in America was immense. Churchmen were forced either to reject the doctrine or find a way to harmonize it with religion. Christians who chose the latter path could soon look to John Fiske, a brilliant New England intellectual who showed how biological evolution might itself be understood as the plan of a providential deity that moved all of creation toward a higher goal.[26] Evolutionary biology, in other words, did not necessarily exclude teleology. By following the thought of Fiske and others, it was therefore possible both to be a Darwinist and to remain a theist.

Among earlier American Reform Jews, Darwinism was treated with contempt.[27] As a form of "materialism," it was thought hostile to all religion. Einhorn had dismissed theories that made for the "brutalization of our species"; Wise decried Darwinian theory for robbing humans of their preeminence and making all of nature a battleground. But by the 1880s, Jews who wanted to seem modern felt they had to believe in Darwin even if they hadn't read him.[28] Kohler, Hirsch, and the younger generation of Reform rabbis had no choice but to take Darwinism seriously. Fortunately, the model of Christian colleagues and their own progressive understanding of Judaism made the task relatively easy.

As early as 1874, Kohler had recognized that Darwinism was "the cornerstone and the capstone of the modern view of nature."[29] But he also noted that biological evolution was only the first stage of human development: once the organism was externally complete, it could then develop its inward spiritual powers. In fact, spiritual evolution, in its subjective impact, was a moral imperative to overcome what remained of the animal. Its message was: "Strive upward, forward to victory over the lower world of your origins!" Spiritual progress, moreover, had almost from the first been the key to the Reformers' understanding of Judaism itself and its role in the world. To complete the evolution of man was simply another way of stating the mission of Israel. "Reform Judaism," according to Kohler, was "the necessary outcome of the age of evolution." Not surprisingly, spiritual evolution became Kohler's most frequent theme.[30] Though he never gave up belief in revelation, that traditional concept was transformed into the divine perspective on evolution.[31] Hirsch's views were similar: "Our cosmogony . . . is that of evolution," he declared in 1883. In application, Hirsch even went into Darwinian specifics. "The morally stronger," he believed, "alone triumphs." What was Israel's historical survival, therefore, if not a sign of its moral "fitness" and the objective excellence of its religion? Since the Jews were chosen by God, just as nature chooses, what was the election of Israel if not a form of "selection"?[32]

Darwinism also shielded classical Reform Judaism from biblicism. True, Reformers continued to describe their faith as Prophetism, but evolutionary thought in biology, like earlier evolutionary philosophy, militated against fixing upon any particular phase of Jewish religion. For Kohler, the evolution of Judaism resulted from continuous interaction with the environment. The sacrificial cult which characterized Mosaism was assimilated from ancient Israel's neighbors. So too the next stage of Israel's worship, prayer, was the result of Persian influence. Since the synagogue represented a religious advance over the Temple, rabbinic Judaism was a higher evolutionary form than Mosaism. Thus only with the Rabbis did the old sacerdotal distinctions become virtually meaningless and all Israel embark on its mission as a "kingdom of priests." Yet what one generation assimilated, another felt compelled to purify or cast out. Rabbinic Judaism had also absorbed customs and practices whose superstitious character rendered them inappropriate for modern Jews. In recent generations the evolutionary process had therefore gone beyond Rabbinism to the multifaceted modern faith of Reform Judaism, itself once again the product of interaction with the environment. In each instance Judaism had absorbed new ideas and shaped them "in consonance with its own genius."[33]

Despite their fundamental agreements, Kohler and Hirsch were not fully alike. Kohler is best understood as a progressive, Hirsch as an unswerving radical. As Geiger in Europe had increasingly emphasized the importance of historical continuity along with religious progress, while Holdheim had ever pointed to the sharp break represented by modernity, so did these two men disagree along similar lines. As he overcame the lingering effects of his rebellion against Orthodoxy, Kohler's religious trajectory reversed course. Increasingly during the last decades of his life he thought of Reform not so much as a break with tradition as a closely linked step ahead. Kohler could even speak of Conservatism as differing from Reform only in degree, but not in principle. Hirsch, unlike Kohler, occasionally preferred the designation "Reform*ed* Judaism," thereby implying a separated, new form that would never reach back to reabsorb what it had given up. Their differences were most apparent in the realm of religious practice. Kohler believed in the efficacy of prayer, that while God would not interfere in the natural order, He would grant new spiritual power to the one who prays. Hirsch preferred to define prayer in purely human terms as "the attempt to bring home to man from the emotional side of his nature, and to sharpen within him, the sense of duty and responsibility." Kohler was a Reform pietist. Frequent and strident were his tirades against atheism. As president of the Hebrew Union College he insisted on a religious atmosphere: that students regularly attend services and that reverence pervade the mode of instruction. Hirsch, on the other hand, was proud of the fact that at Temple Sinai prayer played a very secondary role to the sermon. Liturgical celebration, to his mind, was considerably less important than aiding the sick and motherless.[34]

Kohler was a man of sentiment who, for all of his criticism of Orthodox practice, never lost appreciation for the emotional side of religion and increasingly stressed the importance of symbol and ceremony.[35] Earlier Reformers had spoken repeatedly of the need to separate the kernel of faith from the husk of forms in which it was wrapped. Kohler began to reverse the thrust: "We must never forget that nothing grows on the tree or in the soil without the shielding leaf and husk." Of course rabbinic ceremonialism, for the most part, would no longer do. What was needed, therefore, was to sift old customs and to create new ones that would give poetic expression to the universal truths which Reform had chosen to stress. Kohler particularly wanted more attention to ceremonies in the home on Sabbaths and festivals.[36] But for Hirsch, the unrepentant radical, ceremonials represented an earlier evolutionary stage in Judaism's history; currently the ethical deed was quite properly driving out the symbolic act. As a rationalist, Hirsch had little regard for sentiment, which he depicted as feminine; as a religious moralist, he regretted that symbolism distracted Jews from religion's principal object. His opposition to Halakhah was absolute. Judaism, as he affirmed it, lived under the *moral* law alone. Repeatedly Hirsch defined his God in the words of the English poet and literary critic Matthew Arnold as "that Power, not ourselves, which makes for righteousness," a force independent of humanity but working through it. The Jew lived his "moral theism" preeminently by works in the world. Social justice—a minor theme in Kohler's writing and practical work—was for Hirsch of the essence.[37]

It is symptomatic of their differences that Hirsch's best known work should be entitled *My Religion,* whereas Kohler's was called *Jewish Theology.* Hirsch did not attempt to derive his own faith directly from traditional Judaism. It was, of course, composed predominantly of Jewish elements, especially Prophetism, but it also embraced ideas from outside the tradition. Over the years, Hirsch had weighed, refined, and reshaped his collective heritage into a personal mold which was better termed the carefully reasoned religion of Emil G. Hirsch than historical Judaism.[38] Kohler's major creative venture was of a very different kind. Marshalling his immense erudition in Jewish texts, he produced a historical and systematic theology of Judaism tracing the development of Jewish religious thought, concept by concept, from biblical to modern times. He devoted close to half his volume to the Jewish idea of God, the rest to Judaism's conception of man, Israel, and the messianic hope. In his work, Kohler sought to be both historical scholar and Reformer, the one in documenting textually the development of Jewish beliefs, the other in exposing them to modern criticism and sensibility. His *Jewish Theology* is not itself an original work of Jewish thought, but a summing up and defense of nineteenth-century Reform Judaism viewed through the history of its component elements.[39] It is more prosaic than poetic, descriptive than evocative, carefully formulated rational reflection rather than existential effusion. Yet it became influential precisely because it was not simply Kohler's personal religion. It was the credo of classical Reform Judaism, seen as the newest emergent of an evolving faith.

The Organized Movement

Although Kohler and Hirsch were the most significant figures during American Reform's classical phase, they did not play a leading role in the organized activity of its rabbis. Neither served as president of the Central Conference of American Rabbis (CCAR), and Hirsch rarely attended its conventions. Despite their general influence, Hirsch, and also Kohler (until he became president of HUC in 1903), remained to a degree outsiders because they were Einhorn's sons-in-law and because they had not studied in Cincinnati. The CCAR, like the UAHC, was an institution that lay in Isaac Mayer Wise's orbit, and upon his death it passed on to his disciples.

Created in 1889, the Central Conference of American Rabbis was the last national institution of American Reform Judaism to make its appearance. Wise purposely founded it only after the Hebrew Union College had ordained some twenty rabbis "who could be relied upon to rally to his standard when it was raised." Of course Wise was immediately elected president "in spite of his strenuous protests," and he continued to serve in that capacity for eleven years. Upon his death in 1900, his students began to serve two-year terms.[40] The word "Central" was used in the association's title since there were already regional rabbinical organizations in the East and South, and indeed the first members were preponderantly from the Midwest. However, Wise's Conference very soon took on a national character, displacing its predecessors.

At first the CCAR grew rapidly. Beginning with thirty members, it had ninety within a year, all of them serving congregations. A plateau of about 135 was reached in 1895 and thereafter growth depended largely on how many men the Hebrew Union College ordained each year. On the eve of World War I, there were about 200 Reform rabbis in America.

Unlike the UAHC and HUC, the CCAR was a Reform institution from the start. In its first *Yearbook* it printed the resolutions passed by the German rabbinical conferences and synods as well as those adopted by the American Reformers in Philadelphia and Pittsburgh. Wise made it clear that within the CCAR all would have to give

Gathering of the Central Conference of American Rabbis,
celebrating Isaac Mayer Wise's eightieth birthday, March 14, 1899.

due consideration to the "just demands of time and place and the circumstances they produce." The organization, he said, would be composed of *Gesinnungsgenossen,* of partisans.[41]

At its yearly meetings, held sometimes in cities and sometimes in summer resorts, the CCAR dealt with professional concerns, listened to academic lectures, and addressed issues. As a professional body, it raised funds for "indigent ministers" and fought what it considered the pernicious—but widespread—practice requiring that rabbis aspiring to a pulpit give a "trial sermon." As a learned society, it commissioned scholarly presentations from its best qualified members, nearly always preceding discussion of a practical issue with a survey of its historical and halakhic background. At least twice there were lectures in Hebrew, and annually Professor Gotthard Deutsch, the HUC historian, presented a survey of the year's events in the Jewish world. In 1916 the program also included, for the first time, an old-fashioned *shi'ur,* the rabbis gathering on Saturday afternoon to study a rabbinic text in the traditional manner. Until the creation of the *Hebrew Union College Annual* in 1924, the CCAR's *Yearbook* served the HUC faculty and other rabbis as an outlet for lengthy scholarly articles and even book reviews. It was likewise as a scholarly body that the CCAR designated three of its most learned members to join with three Conservative scholars in a Board of Editors which, under the leadership of Max Margolis, produced the standard Jewish Publication Society translation of the Bible in 1917.

In the same capacity, the CCAR assumed responsibility for presenting the history and beliefs of Judaism at the World's Parliament of Religions held in Chicago in 1893.[42] During three evening sessions of the general body as well as at a preceding denominational congress, CCAR members made almost three quarters of the forty-two presentations on Judaism. H. Pereira Mendes, by designation, represented the traditionalists. Alexander Kohut's appearance was prevented by illness; his two papers were printed in the proceedings. In Chicago the leading Reformers—Wise, Kohler, Hirsch, Gustav Gottheil of Temple Emanu-El in New York—as well as a number of younger men had an unusual opportunity to speak publicly for what one Christian called "the mother church from which all the Christian denominations trace their lineage." Although Mendes delivered a paper on "Orthodox or Historical Judaism," there was none specifically on Reform Judaism—perhaps because that was not necessary. As preponderantly represented by the CCAR, Judaism itself was displayed as normatively Reform. In 1893 there was still no American equivalent body of Conservative or Orthodox rabbis to challenge the CCAR's prerogative.

It was, however, far easier to present Judaism for Gentiles than to reach internal agreement on how to preserve, strengthen, and help it progress. During the first two decades of its existence no issue so evenly divided the CCAR as the related matters of creed and synod. Each was a different form of the question of authority—the one with regard to belief, the other with regard to practice. It was Max Margolis, the biblical scholar not yet finally turned Zionist, who in a learned paper vigorously urged the CCAR to adopt a creed that would clearly define what "Reformed" Jews believe in. His principal opponent turned out to be Kaufmann Kohler, who argued against such a statement on two grounds: it would lend finality where Reform Judaism needed to remain fluid and it would tend to create a schism. By 1905, when the issue of creed came to a head, Kohler—one-time author of the Pittsburgh Platform—was more interested in keeping the Reform movement within Judaism than in laying down distinctive and comprehensive principles of belief. Most Reform rabbis agreed with him. Neither then nor later did the CCAR adopt a formal creed.[43]

The proposed synod was an even more divisive issue. Wise himself had favored such a representative assembly of rabbis and laymen, which would enjoy a broader authority than either the CCAR or the UAHC possessed on its own. His disciples began to urge it earnestly shortly after Wise's death. They argued that an end must be brought to the prevalent anarchy in matters of religious practice, that only rabbis and laymen together could establish binding norms for such matters as conversions and burials. But the underlying motive for urging the synod seems not to have been the need for decision making at all. The project in its essence was a counterthrust to Zionism. The synod was to be a representative assembly of Jews who believed that their ties were religious, not national; though limited to America, it was intended to rival the yearly international congresses that the Zionists had begun to convene in 1897. Hyman Enelow, chairman of the CCAR Committee on Synod, put it candidly when he reported in 1904: "The Jew needs a central institution. If Israel is a Nation, it must be Zion. If Israel is a Church, it must be a Synod." However, many rabbis opposed the project—less for Zionist reasons than because they feared for their religious independence. They did not welcome the prospect of a stronger central authority than that already presented by the CCAR. Hirsch and Kohler were both against the idea, as was the fiercely independent Bernhard Felsenthal. In addition, it was soon discovered that influential members of the Reform laity lacked enthusiasm for the idea. After a vote at the CCAR meeting in 1904 produced a deadlock, the scheme was allowed to die a slow death.[44] Clergy and laity remained organizationally separate, with no single Reform institution able to speak for the American movement as a whole.

In view of Isaac Mayer Wise's persistent but unsuccessful efforts to gain the adoption of a single unifying liturgy for American Jews, it is not surprising that the CCAR should turn almost immediately to the compilation of a prayerbook—one which would serve, if not all of American Jewry, at least those synagogues belonging to the UAHC. By 1890 Reform congregations were worshiping not only from versions of Wise's *Minhag America* and Einhorn's *Olat Tamid,* but from a variety of prayerbooks compiled by individual rabbis for their own use. While a generation earlier Wise's conservative liturgy had enjoyed the greatest popularity, by the last decade of the century most UAHC congregations were estranged from its traditional format. Einhorn's prayerbook better fit the mood and theology of Reform Judaism in its classical phase. Yet for the CCAR simply to adopt *Olat Tamid* would have been too painful an affront to its own president. The solution reached was to create something new: a *Union Prayer Book* (*UPB*; in Hebrew: *Seder Tefilot Yisrael*), which drew especially on Einhorn's work but mixed in elements from other American liturgies.[45]

The earliest version of the *UPB,* Volume One (for Sabbaths, festivals, and weekdays) was compiled for the CCAR by Rabbi Isaac Moses of Chicago and printed in 1892 with its copyright. But then the Conference decided to reconsider. Hirsch and Kohler had publicly derided Moses' work as a dilution of Einhorn's prayerbook that lacked the unity and force of the original. Together they had announced a new English translation of *Olat Tamid,* which Hirsch in fact later carried out for his congregation and for those others that continued "to love *their* Einhorn."[46] In view of the criticism, the CCAR appointed a committee to work anew on the Moses prayerbook, successfully drew Kohler into the enterprise, and finally published acceptable prayerbooks both for the High Holidays (1894) and for the remainder of the year (1895).

This first collectively produced liturgy of American Reform Judaism created a model that was slightly reshaped from time to time, but not fundamentally altered for eighty years. Its two volumes opened from left to right as befitted a prayerbook that was preponderantly in English. Its theology was basically Einhorn's, the style of the translations elevated, sometimes even poetic. Responsive readings were introduced to increase congregational participation. Appended for Sabbath use were brief readings in English from the Pentateuch and the Prophets or Writings. In keeping with the importance classical Reform attributed to content, these readings did not correspond to the weekly portions assigned by tradition. It mattered more that the selection read should convey a meaningful religious or moral message than that it match what was read that particular Sabbath—about animal sacrifices and leprosy, for example—in non-Reform synagogues.[47] Necessarily, the prayerbook also reflected the optimistic mood of late nineteenth-century America. "We rejoice that after the long, dreary night a new morn is dawning," the worshipers were asked to enthuse. "The truths revealed to Israel are becoming the possession of an ever greater number of men."[48] Such sentiments, the possibility of using more or less Hebrew by reading either the left-hand page or the right (for those prayers provided in both languages), and the stamp of approval granted it by the CCAR—these enabled the *Union Prayer Book* rapidly to displace its predecessors in Reform congregations. Although there were a few major synagogues that rejected the *UPB* because it was too traditional or because they continued to prefer their own liturgy, twenty years after its publication this standard liturgy of Reform was being used in over 300 congregations (even some that were not UAHC affiliated), and the more than 100,000 copies sold had contributed appreciably to the finances of the CCAR.[49]

During its first decades the Central Conference went on to produce other liturgical works as well. Together with the Society of American Cantors it published a *Union Hymnal* in 1897. That work consisted mostly of English hymns on universal themes, a few "lifted bodily" from the hymnal of the Episcopalians.[50] In 1907 the *Union Haggadah* appeared, providing a Passover eve home ritual that eliminated all passages which expressed cruelty or vengeance (the Ten Plagues, the petition that God spill out His wrath on the Gentiles who did not know Him), or which indulged in a fanciful exegesis that violated sober rationality. Nevertheless, the *Union Haggadah* called for the traditional symbols of the ceremony, reproduced a number of the familiar Passover songs, and even added a new Hebrew *piyut*. Indeed, by the first decade of the twentieth century Reform Judaism was giving more attention to home observance. Its Haggadah, as well as a special prayerbook containing Sabbath and festival rituals for the home (1911), attested to this new interest.

Yet, on the whole, classical Reform clearly intended to minimize the role of symbol and ritual. While in the vast majority of Reform synagogues the rabbi still read from the Torah scroll, in some it was merely shown to the congregation, and Emil G. Hirsch's Sinai in Chicago went so far as to remove both scroll and ark from the synagogue.[51] Numerous Reform congregations replaced the raucous sound of the *shofar* on the High Holidays with the more controlled tones of a trumpet. Or they mimicked its blast on an organ, whose prominent pipes towered over the pulpit in many a contemporary synagogue. Nor did Hebrew survive because of its symbolic value. While most Reform synagogues retained at least some passages in the ancient tongue, a census of 1906 revealed that more than a hundred had eliminated Hebrew passages altogether.[52] Although classical Reform rabbis might exhort their congregants to fast on the Day of Atonement, neither they nor their flock kept the dietary laws. Emil G. Hirsch wrote contemptuously of "kitchen Judaism" with its emphasis on "trivialities," and it was not unusual for shellfish to be served at congregational dinners.[53] The prevalent view was that ceremonialism amounted to Orientalism and that casting off ceremonies better revealed the purer Judaism of faith in God and love of man that lay beneath it.

Halakhic issues were settled by giving precedence to personal meaningfulness and individual sensibility. Thus the CCAR resolved in 1893 that converts could be accepted into the covenant of Israel "without any initiatory rite, ceremony or observance whatever." Neither circumcision nor immersion was required, only knowledge and commitment. David Philipson's view was typical: "Let a young man receive a thorough course of instruction in the religion, let him promise to live as a Jew and raise his children as Jews and surely we can ask no more."[54] Similar considerations, it was felt, obtained for children of a mixed marriage. According to Kaufmann Kohler, such offspring should no longer be viewed exclusively "by the primitive national standard which determines the racial character of the child only by the blood of its mother." The Jewishness of the father and the influence of religious training should also be taken into account.[55] The burial rite too was severed from the binding force of Jewish custom when the CCAR permitted cremation, then a widespread practice among non-Jews.[56]

In their congregations classical Reform rabbis were first and foremost preachers. Ability on the pulpit was invariably the criterion of success or failure.[57] More often than not, sermons were topical and unrelated to a scriptural text. While some rabbis

Contemporary sketch entitled
"Yom Kippur Worship (Reform)," 1895.

chose inspirational themes, others presented popular academic lectures that were more informative than uplifting. The most eminent preachers combined great oratorical skill with broad knowledge of contemporary intellectual issues. A successful sermon educated listeners on the questions they had read about in the newspapers and presented an answer that was linked in some way to Jewish values. Gustav Gottheil expressed the common view of his contemporaries:

> The Reformed Rabbi of to-day is a public teacher; he instructs at all services; the Temple is his academy. . . . [Preaching] does not confine itself to religious topics, strictly speaking, but draws into the sphere of its discussions every vital topic that occupies the public mind.[58]

Leading rabbis preferred to be called Doctor, or even Mister, rather than Rabbi, accentuating their general learning rather than their denominational capacity. Of Hirsch an admirer wrote that "he was spared the petty annoyances of later day communal activities, such as pastoral calls, personal visitation on insignificant as well as noteworthy events among the members of his congregation."[59] Although by the end of the century there was a tendency to criticize academics in the pulpit and to lay greater stress on the performance of pastoral functions, the most prominent rabbis long continued to be those who combined consummate oratorical skill with the intellectual capacity to shed light on current issues.

Successful rabbis were admired—even venerated—by the laity. Some received munificent salaries and exercised the dominant influence in their congregations. Often the life of a temple revolved about the personality of its rabbi. However, where lesser men occupied the pulpit—and especially in smaller towns—rabbis were frequently treated as mere employees whom the Board of Trustees could hire or fire at will.[60] Seeing themselves as prophetic spokesmen for Judaism, rabbis felt they deserved the respect and honor of the laity. The leading laymen, however, were usually business-men whose pride in acquired wealth reflected an American social context that deemed acquisition of riches a mark of superior achievement and the necessary prerogative for exercising power. The Reform laity's acceptance of rabbinical authority, therefore, was no foregone conclusion.

In some instances, laymen urged their rabbis to undertake even more radical reforms than they themselves desired. Hirsch balked—and was sustained—when the president of his congregation suggested that the Jewish High Holidays be celebrated on the nearest Sunday.[61] One observer believed that radicalism, and intellectualism generally, characterized the Reform laity of the North, whereas those in the South, responding to their environment, laid more stress on piety and visible forms.[62] Indeed, there were also conservative laymen in Reform synagogues who were troubled about the arbitrary prerogatives exercised by individual rabbis. At the 1894 council of the UAHC, Leo N. Levi, a prominent Jewish lawyer from Texas, castigated the Reform rabbinate for its failure to respect the authority of the Pentateuch, its penchant for novelty, and its reliance on reason. He called for a rabbinate which subordinated indi-vidual views to "a perfect faith in God's law written in the Torah." Reform, in his view, should rid Judaism of trivial ceremonies but not effect a revolution in doctrine and principles. Levi's remarks must have struck a responsive chord with many fellow laymen, for when he finished, "the hall rang with applause and cheers." A group was formed that arranged for circulation of 10,000 copies of his speech gratis. Wise, how-ever, immediately "thundered his indignation at this unworthy attack on the rabbis," winning back most loyalties, and that evening the officers of the CCAR drew up a formal protest in which they suggested that Levi could learn much from the more sophisticated view of Judaism that had recently been presented at the World's Parlia-ment of Religions. Later Kohler wrote his own detailed response to Levi in which he admitted the prevalence of a regrettable arbitrariness and anarchy in Reform Judaism but rejected the Texas layman's fundamentalist theology and his call for religious uniformity.[63]

Collectively, however, the Reform laity did not dictate religion to its rabbinate. The UAHC was content to gather funds for the Hebrew Union College and to support those few other activities that were best carried on by a congregational union. Within a few years the UAHC had been able to recover from the rash of attacks and resig-nations that followed the Trefa Banquet and the Pittsburgh conference. It would not again reach its 1883 membership of 102 congregations until after the turn of the cen-tury, but since congregations were growing in size, the loss in individual membership was made up as early as 1890. At the beginning of the twentieth century, membership grew rapidly, doubling to 200 congregations with over 23,000 members in 1917. Although the percentage of eastern congregations increased slightly, to 27 percent dur-ing World War I, the UAHC's center of gravity remained very much in the Midwest. While some of the largest individual contributors were members of the New York and Chicago German Jewish aristocracy, the greatest number of donations came from closer to home, a large percentage from Cincinnati itself. Not surprisingly, it was Cin-cinnati Jewry that furnished the presidents of the UAHC and its inner circle of leadership. These men saw to it that the organization's principal objective remained the rabbinical seminary which graced their community and lent it national prominence. Well into the twentieth century, by far the largest share of the UAHC budget went to support the College.[64]

Three years after the death of Wise in 1900, the presidency of HUC was offered to Kaufmann Kohler, thereby ending once and for all the old factionalism in the Reform rabbinate.[65] The new president immediately brought the College into line with his conception of Judaism. Biblical criticism now entered the curriculum, Midrash came to overshadow Talmud, head coverings were not tolerated in the chapel. Advocacy of Jewish nationalism was barred from the classroom, as was the expression of any agnostic tendency, which, Kohler argued, often went along with Zionism. In Kohler's view, the Hebrew Union College was unlike a university where all points of view must be tolerated. It was rather dedicated to the purpose of training rabbis whose theology would correspond to the tenets of Reform Judaism and whose personal piety could serve as a model for their congregants. As the College expanded, it moved from its small downtown quarters to a spacious new campus in the hills above the city. Its library attained research status and its faculty grew in size and scholarly achievement. HUC graduates soon occupied nearly all of the Reform pulpits. Since their institutions served different constituencies, harmonious relations, as well as genuine mutual respect, prevailed between Kohler and Solomon Schechter, his contemporary as president of the Conservative Jewish Theological Seminary.[66]

The Union's remaining functions were located in its Department of Synagogue and School Extension and in its Board of Delegates on Civil Rights. The former published religious school texts and helped organize new congregations. It shipped educational materials to Jewish families on farms who had no access to a religious school. It sent rabbis or printed sermons to small Jewish communities without rabbinical leadership; it organized a student congregation at the University of Michigan and provided religious services at summer resorts. In the Bronx it subsidized a new synagogue until it could be self-supporting. Generally, the Department did the "missionary" (or outreach) work of the UAHC, building support in those areas where there were no Reform institutions and endeavoring to reach the younger generation with more systematic educational material. The Board of Delegates, on the other hand, worked to protect the general interests of American Jews. Centered in Washington, it fought antisemitism, laws prohibiting work on Sundays, Bible reading in public schools, and restrictions on free immigration. It also championed the rights of Jews in eastern Europe.[67]

Although a rival Orthodox Jewish Congregational Union was formed in New York in 1898, it was not perceived as a serious threat to the UAHC. Far more troublesome was the creation of the American Jewish Committee in 1906. Though not a congregational body, the Committee drew its support largely from the same lay constituency. In its defense of Jewish rights, it duplicated the work of the Board of Delegates. Its very existence implied that the leadership of American Jewry should emanate from an organization that was not tied to the synagogue and which made religion appear a less important criterion of Jewishness than ethnic solidarity. The Jewish lodge and club—especially B'nai B'rith—had long been rivals of the synagogue and the UAHC; the American Jewish Committee, emerging out of the German elite of New York to speak for American Jewry, was perceived as a revolt from within. At the twentieth

Main building of Hebrew Union College in Cincinnati, completed in 1912.

council of the UAHC in 1907, Rabbi Henry Berkowitz reminded the delegates that it was, after all, the bond of religion, represented by their Union, which united the Jews. Rabbi Moses Gries of Cleveland put it to them even more directly:

> Have we not now an American Jewish Committee? It is self-created—it is self-appointed—it has no right to exist. . . . The historic right to leadership is with this Union and the duty of leadership is still upon us. . . . [The Union's] life springs from the synagogue and the temple, the very heart of Jewish life and power.[68]

Despite such anxiety, however, the UAHC survived the creation of the American Jewish Committee and soon even cooperated with it. Other national organizations, like the American Jewish Congress, came upon the scene during World War I and thereafter, further reducing the central position briefly enjoyed by the UAHC. The congregational framework of American Jewish life, which Wise had always held up as the basis for Jewish unity, was increasingly becoming but one organizational model among others.

Within the UAHC and in the leadership of local congregations Jewish women long played a subordinate role. Both men and women in the Reform movement shared the prevalent notion that the woman's primary role was to be her husband's helpmate and the mother of their children. Twice the CCAR turned down resolutions in support of women's suffrage, before it finally passed one in 1917—only three years before adoption of the constitutional amendment.[69] Rabbis were highly ambivalent about the penetration of women into spheres other than the domestic. Emil G. Hirsch, for example, denied that men and women were equal in natural competencies, but as a political liberal, he favored women's suffrage and could not deny the platform of Sinai Congregation to Jane Addams, the Chicago social reformer. Kaufmann Kohler held up an ideal of gentle femininity and doubted that it was woman's vocation "to become a man." But he decried the discrimination against women in traditional Judaism and early declared that the synagogues, too long dominated by the petty commercialism of the men, required the idealism of women's spirit. He even added: "Yes, we need Reform Jewish leaders from the feminine sex."[70] In actual fact, women's rise to positions of leadership in the Reform movement was a slow process. It began with the extension of congregational membership to widows and unmarried women; then came synagogue voting rights for all women. By the second decade of the twentieth century, women were gaining access to religious school committees and in some instances to synagogue boards.[71] Women began to serve as delegates to the biennial councils of the Union as early as 1896, though during the first years they were exclusively the wives of rabbis or lay delegates, who were in any case accompanying their husbands.

Reform did pride itself that within the synagogue the greater equality of women was visible in both the family pew and the ceremony of confirmation. During the latter it could occur that a female confirmand would read the Ten Commandments from the Torah scroll. While the ordination of women as yet received no serious consideration, a remarkable Californian, Ray (Rachel) Frank, achieved celebrity status on the West Coast when, during the 1890s, she preached to Reform and Orthodox congregations, gave brilliant lectures to Jews and Gentiles, and on more than one occasion officiated at High Holiday services.[72]

In 1893 American Jewish women organized nationally for the first time when a group at the World's Parliament of Religions conducted their own Jewish Women's Congress and thereupon formed the National Council of Jewish Women.[73] Two decades later, Reform Jewish women created a national organization, which differed by its focus on the synagogue and the Reform movement rather than on communal social work. The National Federation of Temple Sisterhoods (NFTS) was formed in 1913 at the festive UAHC biennial council that dedicated the new buildings of HUC. It drew together local groups that had come into existence earlier and included among its projects raising scholarship funds for the College, establishing a museum of ceremonial objects at HUC, and publishing an art calendar depicting the great women of Israel. Within a year, eighty-eight sisterhoods had joined the federation. The progenitor and first president of NFTS was Carrie Simon, the wife of a prominent Reform rabbi in Washington, D.C. In 1915 she was invited to address the council of the UAHC on "Woman's Influence in the Development of American Judaism." Her speech was articulate, forceful, and Jewishly knowledgeable. Hardly a radical feminist, Simon believed that her sex's first duty was to the home and childbearing. But she told the delegates that women's emancipation was no longer to be argued. It was to be reckoned with. And the synagogue would do well to take best advantage of women's talents.[74]

In their individual synagogues, sisterhood members were most active in the sphere of Jewish education. They raised money for the religious school, often taught the children, and increasingly helped to run the schools as well. The Reform religious school—or "Sabbath school," as it was then usually called—had become the prevalent form when better public education and the desire for social integration induced parents to withdraw their children from the day schools which, in the 1850s, were the pride of larger Reform congregations. By the 1870s, rabbis were expressing the strong opposition to "sectarian schools" that would characterize the Reform movement for nearly a century. Limited to a few hours a week, the religious school was unable to undertake the intensive curriculum which had been taught in the day schools. Most met as few as two hours per week. Hebrew especially suffered, students but rarely achieving any real competence in the language. While in the majority of schools some Hebrew was taught, it was often optional and in quite a few not taught at all. Children who behaved well in public school resented the additional burden of weekend classes. As one observer noted, comparing the two: "*There* attention and quiet, *here* indifference, often wild noise; *there* decent respectful behavior toward the teacher, *here* only the opposite." Under these circumstances it seemed impossible to convey more than basic familiarity with the Bible and the beliefs of Judaism. Jewish doctrines were initially taught with the aid of a catechism, and answers learned by rote were reproduced at the confirmation ceremony.[75]

The improvement of Reform religious education became an ongoing and expanding project of the UAHC.[76] Beginning in 1886, its Sabbath-School Union, and later its Department of Synagogue and School Extension, first published selections from the Bible and from rabbinic and medieval literature that conveyed a moral lesson. Then came curricula, a few graded textbooks, and in 1907, *Young Israel,* a rather stilted periodical for Jewish religious schools. Adult education was the domain of a Jewish Chautauqua Society, founded by a Reform rabbi, Henry Berkowitz, in 1893 and modeled on the Christian Chautauqua movement. The Society organized study circles and held yearly assemblies that proved especially valuable for religious school teachers. Eventually the UAHC took more direct responsibility for pedagogic competence, establishing a small Teachers' Institute at HUC in 1909. Still, Reform Jewish education on the eve of World War I remained much thinner than in the earlier day school or in succeeding decades when its focus broadened and it received more time. But, then, learning the basic tenets of monotheism and morality—with some help from Jewish sources—did not require more than one morning a week. And that universal educational goal fit well with American Reform Judaism in its classical phase.

From Prophetic Idealism to Applied Social Justice

A Reform Judaism in which moral action took precedence over religious observance could evoke commitment only if it presented its adherents with specific moral objectives that would be as Jewishly significant for them as ceremonials were for traditionalists. One of the weaknesses of European Liberal Judaism was that it failed to develop a program of applied social justice. In the United States, however, a favorable political climate and a parallel development in Christianity made possible a redirection of religious energies toward ameliorating inequities and cruelties in American society.[77]

One looks in vain for social criticism in Jewish sermons delivered during the twenty years after the American Civil War. It was then the common belief, of rabbis no less than Christian clergymen, that an unbridled capitalism would eventually bring prosperity to all. Had Emil G. Hirsch not insisted at Pittsburgh that his colleagues take note of contemporary social injustice, it is unlikely they would have done so. And in fact it took another two decades until issues of industrial abuse assumed a position of importance on the Reform agenda. As late as the 1890s, the prevalent social optimism, fed by a Darwinian certainty that the future would necessarily be better than the past, militated against severe critique. If American society had its problems, they lay not in the system itself, but in individual lack of character. Rabbis preached personal morality rather than public action, social service rather than social justice. Where they did deal with issues, they were meliorists who expressed more fear at the prospect of socialism than horror at the excesses of capitalism. Rabbi Henry Berkowitz, for example, took pains to tell his congregation that the situation of working people was not worse than at earlier times in human history. Radical solutions bred of despair, he warned, were no answer at all. And socialism, moreover, was antithetical to Judaism: it "sees nothing healthful, nothing encouraging, nothing reassuring; while, on the other hand, Judaism is wreathed in a halo of light, and sends out warming rays of hope and good cheer and trust into every heart." Berkowitz did recognize the need for "constructive solutions," such as arbitration and profit-sharing, to improve the lot of the worker, but what he preached was less a call to social action than a moral exhortation to both sides: let the workers "vanquish sloth" and the employers check their greed. A higher level of individual conduct would then dissolve class enmity.[78] Emil G. Hirsch was exceptional when, as early as the late eighties and nineties, in the wake of increasingly violent strikes and riots, he spoke out forcefully against laissez-faire capitalism. Hirsch condemned the sweatshops and argued in favor of the six-day work week, unemployment insurance, and provisions for workers' old age.[79]

For the Reform rabbinate as a whole, the transition from a prophetic Judaism that spoke only of individual conduct to one that addressed specific social issues is ascribable to two outside influences: the American Progressive movement and the Christian Social Gospel. The Progressives, whose influence swept America in the years before World War I, added a new social activism to the established current of optimism. They rejected the pessimism and radicalism of the socialists, but they espoused political intervention into a hitherto unregulated capitalist system. The Reform rabbinate wholeheartedly endorsed the social program of President Theodore Roosevelt, which he—and they—justified in moral terms. The very word "progress" echoed Reform's cherished principle of structured evolution and development, now applied to society.[80]

The Christian counterpart of Progressivism was the Social Gospel movement, which entered liberal churches during the same years. Its chief exponents, men like Washington Gladden and Walter Rauschenbusch, insisted that moral conduct—not dogma or ceremony—was "the supreme and sufficient religious act." As religion required a social purpose, so did social movements require religious enthusiasm as well as the precedents offered by Jewish and Christian tradition. Rauschenbusch saw Israel's Prophets as "the revolutionists of their age. They were the dreamers of Utopias. They pictured an ideal state of society in which the poor should be judged with equity and the cry of the oppressed should no longer be heard." While preachers of the Social Gospel held up Jesus as their principal model of social reformer and were not always friendly to the Jews, their attention to the message of Amos, Micah, and Isaiah made Jewish Reformers feel that liberal Christianity and Reform Judaism were now drawing on common values for a common American cause. In their eyes the Social Gospel was not something they were importing from Christianity. The contrary was true. As one rabbi put it, Christianity "is forsaking her historical position and enlisting under the banner of prophetic Judaism."[81]

It was the Reform rabbinate, not the laity, which agitated for the transition to social activism. Perhaps, like Protestant ministers, the rabbis were attempting to put forward the social relevance of the pulpit at a time when increasingly secular congregants were less affected by narrower religious subjects. Perhaps also the prophetic role was the rabbi's endeavor to forcefully reassert his own status against the wealthy businessmen who dominated his congregation and whose values reflected the capitalist ethos.[82] In any case, during the early years, it was the Central Conference of American Rabbis that presented the Reform position on matters of social justice.[83]

In 1908 the CCAR first lent its official support to the campaign against child labor. At its convention the following year it heard a paper by Solomon Foster entitled "The Workingman and the Synagogue," which, though socially progressive in tone, saw the rabbi as mediator, not partisan, in the conflict between capital and labor. The paper provoked the anger of Stephen Wise, who had already successfully intervened for Jewish bakers against their employers in New York. Some rabbis, especially the younger men, now pressed the CCAR to put its moral weight behind a complete agenda of social measures. For a decade, the development of such a comprehensive program preoccupied the Conference. While earlier conventions had focused on liturgy and religious practice, the rabbis now discussed white slavery, venereal disease, working conditions, and juvenile delinquency. Finally, in 1918, the CCAR adopted a Declaration of Principles, the first social justice platform of Reform Judaism. It called for a more equitable distribution of the profits of industry, a minimum wage, an eight-hour day, a safe and sanitary working environment with particular reference to the special needs of women, abolition of child labor, adequate workmen's compensation, health insurance, proper housing for workers, and mothers' pensions. It insisted on the right of labor to organize and bargain collectively and favored mediation and arbitration in industrial disputes. "The ideal of social justice," it declared, "has always been an integral part of Judaism."[84]

The CCAR's 1918 statement was neither an isolated venture in its American context nor far ahead of its time. A similar platform had been issued by the Protestant Federal Council of Churches in 1912, and the Catholic Bishops were to issue their own program the following year. Some of the recommendations had already been embodied in state or local laws. But on certain points the program went beyond Protestants and Catholics, and it presented specific imperatives which American society in 1918 had not yet fully accepted. It was, in other words, sufficiently in advance of reality to be meaningful and close enough to it not to be utopian.[85]

The conscience of the CCAR did not confine itself to American social inequities. There were some injustices in its own house. Jewish congregations sold the most desirable pews to families willing and able to pay the most and set minimum dues that were beyond the reach of the poor. Not everyone had a vote in the congregational meeting. The CCAR began to urge democratization of the synagogue in 1911, by which time only four or five congregations, in various parts of the country, had introduced the unrestricted minimum in dues, the unassigned pew, and the universal ballot.[86] Six years later, in formulating a model synagogue constitution, it called upon synagogues to institute all three provisions. But in some congregations inequality continued to exist for years thereafter. Indeed, despite the efforts of the rabbis, to working people the established synagogue in the first decades of the century often looked more like a "rich man's institution," allied with oppressive capital, than one where they felt at home. Only over a longer period of time did the Reform temple lose its class character.[87]

Reaching the Boundary, Reversing the Thrust

As Reform rabbis shared the rising concern of Christian colleagues with American industrial evils, so too did they identify broadly with liberal ministers whose religious philosophy closely approximated their own. They were especially drawn to the Unitarians, that Christian denomination in America which combined a high level of rationality with an encompassing tolerance. Reform rabbis found that the Unitarians possessed a readily acceptable conception of Jesus as prophet rather than redeemer, though as Jews they collectively and unanimously declared that he played no role in their religion.[88] From time to time, Reform rabbis and Unitarian (or other liberal Protestant) ministers exchanged pulpits, or their congregations worshiped together. Already in the late sixties and seventies, Isaac Mayer Wise and some of his colleagues had actively participated in Octavius B. Frothingham's interdenominational Free Religious Association. Given their similarity of religious philosophy and social relations, it is not surprising that some Jews and non-Jews proposed Reform Judaism and Unitarianism unite. One Reform rabbi, Solomon Sonneschein of St. Louis, went so far as to consider employment as a Unitarian minister. In Boston, Rabbi Solomon Schindler, who introduced Reform to New England, enjoyed an intimate relationship with Minot J. Savage, a prominent Unitarian clergyman and intellectual. Schindler admired the Unitarians for doing in Christianity just what the Reformers were doing in Judaism. He preached rationalism and biblical criticism, decried ceremonialism, and declared that the core of Judaism was "the religion of humanity." Eventually, he moved not only beyond Judaism, but beyond all religion, professing himself a socialist and an agnostic. His successor, Charles Fleischer, likewise left his ancestral faith for a socially progressive nondenominationalism.[89]

For most Reform rabbis, however, Unitarianism was as much a threat as it was a welcome companion on the path of religious liberalism. Like Ethical Culture, Unitarianism implied that Judaism possessed no ongoing mission. Indeed, even the most enlightened Christian clergymen insisted that Christianity had superseded its mother faith. Jesus was its last and most perfect flower. Most Reformers therefore echoed Isaac Mayer Wise, who repeatedly declared the opposite: Judaism was inherently superior to Christianity and hence it—and not the offspring—would be the religion of the future. Or, if uncomfortable with Wise's triumphalism, they adopted Emil G. Hirsch's boast that, while Unitarians had had to innovate in substituting deed for dogma, Jews needed only to revert to the Prophets.[90] Except for a few at the extreme, classical Reform rabbis sought to balance their tolerance and appreciation for other faiths with emphasis on both the historical priority and the teleological primacy of Judaism.

As a result, the great majority of classical Reform rabbis opposed mixed marriages.[91] Kohler, following Einhorn, repeatedly warned of their danger. A CCAR survey taken in 1912 revealed that only seven of more than a hundred respondents had officiated at mixed weddings. Wise's congregation as late as 1892 constitutionally barred from membership anyone married to a non-Jew. However, the CCAR balked when Samuel Schulman of Beth El in New York and William Rosenau of Oheb Shalom in Baltimore in 1909 presented a resolution declaring "that a rabbi ought not to officiate" at a mixed marriage as such marriages were prohibited by the Jewish religion. Like creed and synod a few years earlier, the proposed resolution became for some a matter of collective authority impinging on individual conscience. It had to give way before a consensus statement that simply stated: "The Central Conference of American Rabbis declares that mixed marriages are contrary to the tradition of the Jewish religion and should therefore be discouraged by the American Rabbinate."[92]

The inner conflict between the desire to remain securely within the Jewish fold and the pressure of circumstances to depart from tradition—even toward Christian practice—came to focus on the issue of Sunday services. In Germany only the independent Reform Congregation in Berlin worshiped exclusively on the Christian Sabbath. In America the Sunday movement spread at one time or another to about three dozen synagogues, including some of the largest, and it continued to win new adherents even after World War I.[93]

Rarely did proponents of Sunday services justify them by any felt desire to bring Jewish Sabbath observance into line with Christian. The argument was nearly always based on necessity: with Jews unwilling or unable to absent themselves from work on Saturday, services were sparsely attended, for the most part only by women, children, and the retired. Only Sinai Congregation in Chicago and one or two others went so far as actually to abandon the Saturday morning service in favor of Sunday. And even Hirsch claimed to have transferred nothing, adding: "I am ready today, tomorrow, as I always have been, to preach on Saturday, but not to vacant pews, and not as a vicarious Scapegoat in a wilderness of empty space."[94] Neither Sinai, nor apparently any other congregation, used a Sunday liturgy that included any traditional prayers making specific reference to the Sabbath. Congregations with Sunday services severely limited the Sunday liturgy, giving prominence to a lengthy sermon or lecture and lending the occasion an ambience that was more homiletical or academic than celebratory. The frequent presence of large numbers of non-Jews provided an additional rationale for reducing denominational features. The success or failure of the Sunday service depended on the oratorical skill of the rabbi. Where he was a talented speaker—like Hirsch, Joseph Krauskopf in Philadelphia, and later Stephen Wise in New York—the congregation could regularly exceed a thousand. Where he possessed less ability, the service sometimes failed and was abandoned.

Kaufmann Kohler began the trend to Sunday services in the United States when he initiated them at Sinai in 1874. By the time of the Pittsburgh Conference in 1885 they had spread to only a very few other places, but the movement possessed enough perceived momentum that the rabbis at Pittsburgh felt they had to deal with the issue.

They declared unanimously that although they fully recognized the importance of maintaining the historical Sabbath "as a bond with our great past and the symbol of the unity of Judaism the world over . . . there is nothing in the spirit of Judaism, or its laws, to prevent the introduction of Sunday services in localities where the necessity for such services appears, or is felt."[95] Following Pittsburgh, the incidence of Sunday services grew, spurred sometimes by lay pressures, sometimes by rabbinical initiative. In some places they were only a brief experiment, in others they lasted for decades. A 1905 estimate notes "about thirteen," one in 1906 "about twenty," and still in 1914 the number was perceived to be growing steadily.[96] By then Sunday services were being held in all the major Jewish communities. Rabbis Joseph Krauskopf in Philadelphia and J. Leonard Levy in Pittsburgh published collections of Sunday liturgies with a different brief service for each of the thirty occasions on which such services were held during the year. The CCAR itself, in 1907, provisionally issued a special prayerbook of six "Morning Services" which included a rubric for the reading of Scripture, but no specific Sabbath references. It was used by about half a dozen congregations.[97]

The great majority of American Reform congregations did not conduct Sunday services despite all of the pressure to do so. Wise had opposed the practice from the start and continued to exercise his influence against it. In smaller cities, like Peoria and Fort Wayne, Reform congregants overwhelmingly favored keeping the principal service on the traditional Jewish Sabbath.[98] The more typical solution to the Saturday problem was the one Wise himself had introduced in his congregation as early as 1869: the late Friday evening service, held at a fixed hour each week and enhanced by a sermon or lecture.[99] The practice spread rapidly, to Conservative congregations no less than Reform. But during the first decade of the twentieth century there were enough influential congregations that had instituted some form of Sunday service that it was not possible to condemn the practice without splitting the movement. For three consecutive years, beginning in 1902, the CCAR discussed the Sabbath issue. Finally, it simply reaffirmed the balanced position adopted nineteen years earlier in Pittsburgh.[100]

By the time the CCAR dealt with the Sunday service issue, one of its chief proponents had changed his mind. Early in his career, during the mid-seventies, Kaufmann Kohler had gone so far as to hope for an eventual common Sabbath observance that would religiously unite all humanity. By 1879, however, he was favoring Sunday services only as an expedient—and necessarily as a weekday ritual.[101] A decade after that, in 1891, he was ready to confess that, in any form, the innovation was a fundamental error. Now he argued there was "something in the very air of the Sunday service that chills the heart. Reason alone, cold, proud reason dictates the words. The soul is not there." And there was another motive for reconsideration as well: "the changed attitude of the world towards the Jew and the principles he represents." The resurgence of antisemitism in Europe and its appearance as a new exclusivism in America had destroyed the sanguine hopes that once generated Reform's willingness to depart from distinctive ways. That optimism had been premature:

> How rudely have we all been roused from our dream! How shockingly were all the illusions of the beginning of the nineteenth century destroyed by the facts developed at its close! What a mockery has this so-called Christian civilization turned out to be! What a shame and a fraud has this era of tolerance and enlightenment become! . . . Dare we, in the face of such great disappointments, recognize the pre-

dominance of Christian culture, by accepting the Christian Sunday as our day of rest, in place of the ancient Sabbath? . . . Our duty today is to maintain our Jewish identity and to preserve our Jewish institutions without faltering, without yielding. We must, *with united forces, rally around our sacred Sabbath.*[102]

By the end of the century Kohler had become more interested in keeping Reform within Judaism than in reaching outward beyond it.

The heyday of classical Reform Judaism was also the period of massive immigration by east European Jews. Their arrival speedily reduced the relative proportion of German Jews in America and, since Reform congregations remained almost exclusively German Jewish in those years, likewise diminished the relative influence of Reform institutions. At the turn of the century, when the UAHC could claim to represent no more than 40,000 individuals, there were already over a million Jews in the United States. Half the Jewish population was living in New York City, which had only five Reform congregations. Of an estimated 1,700 synagogues in the United States in 1907, less than 10 percent belonged to the UAHC. Even in midwestern communities Reform Jews soon found themselves a minority.[103] The German Jews (and therefore the Reform Jews) were losing their hegemony—first demographically, then in community leadership—to the east Europeans.

The large immigration of Jews so different from themselves created a profound ambivalence in their coreligionists of German Jewish lineage. The east Europeans were a hodgepodge of atheists and socialists, Zionists and resolutely Orthodox. They spoke Yiddish and persisted in their own subculture, negating the Reform principle that Jews were different only in religion. One reaction of German Jews in the United States was to make their Reform synagogues bastions of Americanism, setting themselves apart from the uncouth, un-Americanized greenhorns regularly disgorged from the steerage of ships reaching New York. Isaac Mayer Wise branded the east Europeans' ideologies "the idiosyncrasies of those late immigrants." David Philipson was appalled that "in this age of bath-rooms public and private" the growing Orthodox element in Cincinnati was soliciting funds for a ritual bath. "Oh! the shame of it," he shuddered. Later, more optimistically, he ventured that "ghettoism and reactionism are merely passing phases in the Americanization of our most recently arrived brethren."[104]

But if east European Jews were to Americanize, was it not the responsibility of German Jews to speed them along the way? Accepting that task was not only a way to protect their own image in the eyes of Gentiles, but also a genuine expression of concern for less fortunate brothers and sisters. For all the repulsion that the ideas, manners, and customs of the east Europeans aroused in some German Jews, Reform institutions consistently fought against immigration quotas and restrictions, and even radical Reform rabbis like Joseph Krauskopf praised the mettle of the new immigrants.[105] The UAHC's Board of Delegates took measures both to assist persecuted Jews abroad and to combat any discrimination against those who reached America. When the CCAR met in New York City in 1909, the delegates visited Ellis Island, touring the facilities that greeted the newcomers. Imbued with a sense of *noblesse oblige,* Reform Jews, individually and collectively, contributed to the charities active on New York's Lower East Side. Leading members of Temple Emanu-El made possible the reorganization and regeneration of the Jewish Theological Seminary in New

York, enabling it to appeal effectively to east European Jews seeking an Americanized Jewish leadership, but one more traditional than Reform.[106]

There were even early efforts to bring east European Jews directly into Reform Judaism, a kind of intra-Jewish missionary endeavor. In 1904, apparently following the example of an ecumenical "People's Church" organized that year in New York, the movement set out to establish and support a "People's Reform Synagogue" in the Orthodox section of Philadelphia. Begun by Rabbi George Zepin of the UAHC staff, it was turned over to Rabbi Max Raisin, a graduate of HUC who was of Russian Jewish origin and a Zionist. Although a huge crowd appeared for Raisin's first service, attendance dropped rapidly thereafter and the venture failed. Organ, choir, and a modernized liturgy could arouse the curiosity of the new immigrants but could not create a lasting attachment.[107] Reform possessed little appeal for the first, and only occasionally for the second generation of east Europeans. The descendants of the immigrants entered the movement in larger numbers only after World War I.

Still, individual Reform congregations increasingly went out of their way to make east European Jews feel welcome. Rabbi Horace J. Wolf was not alone in deploring the fact that the Reform temple had become "a class institution" and suggesting that its motto should rather be "Here let no Jew feel himself strange." By 1904 Rabbi William Rosenau was even willing to look at the other side of the influence equation, telling his colleagues "what the immigrant Jew can give to us."[108]

A formidable barrier separating Americanized German Reform Jews from a good many of the east Europeans was the issue of Zionism. Reform Judaism and Jewish nationalism seemed to many in both camps to be simply incompatible. The mission of Israel demanded a providential Diaspora that would never end, and America was the land in which that religious and moral mission could be best carried out. Reform Jews placed American flags in their synagogues, put "America the Beautiful" into their hymnal, and dwelt on similarities between Judaism and the republican form of government. They defined themselves as Jews by belief alone, and they were determined to build their spiritual Zion in America.[109] Zionism, they argued, frequently went along with atheism, and one could not be a proper Jew without a belief in God. Or Zionism followed from Orthodoxy: "If Judaism is to be a religion essentially ceremonial and unprogressive, it must live alone."[110] To Reform Jews, Zionism was a counsel of defeat, a surrender to the forces of antisemitism rather than the valiant fight to defeat them. It was retreat substituted for advance, a fantastic nightmare for the beautiful American dream.

Institutionally, classical Reform Judaism put itself on record as fundamentally opposed to political Zionism.[111] At its convention in 1897, just a few weeks before the First Zionist Congress in Basle, the CCAR declared unanimously: "We totally disapprove of any attempt for the establishment of a Jewish state. Such attempts show a misunderstanding of Israel's mission." A year later, the UAHC followed suit. Its resolution said: "We are unalterably opposed to political Zionism. The Jews are not a nation, but a religious community. . . . America is our Zion. Here, in the home of religious liberty, we have aided in founding this new Zion, the fruition of the beginning laid in the old." The promulgation of the Balfour Declaration in 1917, giving British legal sanction to a Jewish national home in Palestine, provoked a new series of resolutions. This time the rabbis spoke less stridently. They expressed grateful appreciation for the document "as an evidence of good-will toward the Jews" and indicated their support for the immigration of persecuted Jews to Palestine. But they could not subscribe to the idea that Palestine was the national home of the Jewish people. The UAHC delegates, for their part, simply reasserted that "Israel is at home in every free country and should be at home in all lands."[112] Such sentiments would remain characteristic for most Reform Jews well into the period after World War I.

Yet it is of interest that, even in its classical phase, American Reform Judaism was by no means uniformly anti-Zionist.[113] As early as the turn of the century, a few leading Reform rabbis had become Zionists. The senior among them was Bernhard Felsenthal, at one time a militant radical, an admirer of David Einhorn, and an officer of the Free Religious Association. In the 1890s Felsenthal turned toward Zion, perhaps because he realized that the loose bond of individualistic religion required the firmer tie of ethnic attachment. In 1896 he helped to found the Chicago Zionist Organization and would have attended the First Zionist Congress had he been younger. Shortly thereafter, he confessed his belief that the Zionist movement was "the most significant and profound Jewish endeavor of the present century."[114] Gradually other Reform Jews joined him. By 1918 some members of the UAHC Executive Board were described as "ardent Zionists."[115] And before 1920 well over a dozen American Reform rabbis were active supporters of the Zionist movement. Their number included men associated with influential congregations: in New York Gustav Gottheil and Judah Magnes of Temple Emanu-El and Stephen Wise of the Free Synagogue, in Philadelphia Joseph Krauskopf of Keneseth Israel.[116] In 1909 the CCAR elected an officer of the Federation of American Zionists, Rabbi Max Heller of New Orleans, to its presidency. Four other members of the CCAR who were already Zionists in 1920 went on to become presidents of the Conference.

Zionization of Reform Judaism required the formulation of an ideological rapprochement. The easiest Zionist plank to accept was advocacy of Jewish colonization in Palestine. Isaac Mayer Wise had favored it, and so did most of his disciples. From there the path to political Zionism of the American variety was not all that long. To be sure, political Zionism did raise the question of long-term loyalty to the United States, but American Zionists, after all, did not take Herzl seriously when he claimed that Jews had no more secure a future in America than they did in Europe. American Zionism, as Justice Louis Brandeis formulated it, was more philanthropic than ideological, mostly an extension of the colonization idea. Moreover, by the first years of the twentieth century, even a Reform anti-Zionist like Kohler was calling the Jews "a religious nation," and noting that "religion and peoplehood in Judaism constitute an indissoluble entity." What especially bothered Kohler—and others—was that most Zionists tended to neglect the religious element in favor of the national.

Some Reform Jews found it easier to be cultural Zionists than political ones, though here too there were some problems. Reform Judaism was committed to the belief that Jewish spiritual creativity on a high level was possible in the Diaspora and not—as Ahad Ha-Am claimed—only in a Palestinian spiritual center. However, Felsenthal early argued that Ahad Ha-Am's spiritual center could be understood as a beacon for the Jewish mission of bringing light to the nations. Prophetic Judaism—the very essence of Reform—could emanate from a model Jewish state. That too was the view of Emil G. Hirsch.[117] Moreover, as Stephen Wise added, for the foreseeable future at least, Diaspora Jews could continue to play their own role in that mission.

Increasingly, the Zionists in Reform ranks distinguished between "official Reform Judaism" and Reform Judaism as it was in essence. The former was only "a particular school of Reform Judaism"; the latter could easily encompass Zionism. The basic principle of Reform, they argued, was religious development, and that set it in opposition to Orthodoxy, not to Zionism. When Rabbi Martin Meyer of San Francisco identified himself as a "Reform Jewish Zionist" in 1917, he was affirming a composite Jewish identity that incorporated both elements without conflict. Toward the end of his life, in 1919, even Kaufmann Kohler—never a Zionist—could declare:

> Let Palestine, our ancient home, under the protection of the great nations, or under the specific British suzerainty, again become a center of Jewish culture and a safe refuge for the homeless. We shall all welcome it and aid in the promotion of its work. Let the million or more of Jewish citizens dwelling there . . . be empowered and encouraged to build up a commonwealth broad and liberal in spirit to serve as a school for international and interdenominational humanity. We shall all hail the undertaking and pray for its prosperity.[118]

He insisted only that there also be a place and a task for Jews in America.

By the 1920s it was becoming no harder ideologically for Reform Jews to be Zionists than for any other Jews in America. Most Reform rabbis and laypeople remained in opposition. But here too a shift in direction was under way.

At the beginning of American Reform Jewry's classical phase, its proponents had clamored for ever more progress, for "developing Judaism further into the all-encompassing religion of humanity."[119] They had exalted reason and denigrated ritual, identified most strongly with the larger community of humankind, and pressed toward the boundary of Jewish identity. But by the end of the period very different ideas were being expressed, though not yet consistently and still without collective force.

In retrospect one can see signs of the new trend, to look inward and backward as much as forward, scattered across the landscape of later classical Reform. As early as 1905, Rabbi Max Heller expressed his feeling that the Pittsburgh Platform represented "in more than one way an obsolete standpoint."[120] A CCAR Responsa Committee, established in 1907 to answer ritual questions, began to deal with such matters as wedding and mourning practices, tracing their historical development in text and practice. Successful efforts were made to revive the neglected harvest festival of Sukkot by actively involving children in bringing fruits to the pulpit or putting on an appropriate pageant for their parents. More than one rabbi called for a new emphasis on what Rabbi Louis Wolsey called "the specially Jewish aspect of our religion."[121] Jacob Schiff, one of the most affluent and influential Reform laymen, explaining to a UAHC convention why he also supported the Jewish Theological Seminary, noted: "There can be no healthy Reform that has not its origin in Orthodoxy"; without the continuance of Orthodoxy, Reform would be in danger of disappearing.[122] Rabbi Louis Grossman of Isaac Mayer Wise's temple in Cincinnati even suggested that Reform itself needed to recapture the orthodox spirit, if not the orthodox manner.[123] And Kohler too lost his denominational zeal. "Today not Reform, but *Judaism,* must be the sole object of our solicitude," he told the CCAR in 1898.[124] At the turn of the century such sentiments were just beginning to take hold. A generation later Reform Judaism's new thrust would become dominant.

8

Reorientation

The years between the world wars were not an exciting time for American religion. Automobiles, radio, the movies—not church or synagogue—captured popular attention. Few attended services; fewer gave their children a serious religious education. America was more openly secular than ever before. Fundamentalist Protestantism attracted widespread ridicule when it fought the teaching of evolution in the Scopes trial of 1925; Prohibition soon became a pious hypocrisy. Those with wealth supported organized religion largely because it provided transcendent justification for an ethics of acquisition, while the poor, for their part, associated it with capitalist exploitation. Though the two decades were markedly different—the twenties a period of buoyant optimism and hedonistic indulgence, the thirties a sobering reminder of human finitude—neither the Jazz Age nor the Great Depression evoked much religious zeal.[1]

Not surprisingly, the same was true for American Jewry. The prevalent lassitude with regard to observance and education, the conception of religion as an ornament of bourgeois culture—these prevailed to a similar degree among Jews. The second generation of east Europeans mostly abandoned religious Judaism entirely, only a minority affiliating with Conservative or Reform congregations. One study, made in 1929, showed that in New York City more than three-quarters of Jewish schoolchildren did not know the Hebrew alphabet and had received no instruction in the Jewish religion.[2] Under the assimilatory pressure of new places of residence and attendance at institutions of higher education, the Yiddish language and culture succumbed rapidly. In the universities, which increasingly attracted young Jews, atheism—or at least agnosticism—was deemed the only intelligent viewpoint on religion. For some Jews political radicalism became the basis of a broader, trans-Jewish identity.

Reform Judaism, in this situation, had great difficulty fostering enthusiasm for its cause. For all of its rabbis' efforts to be relevant, for all their pronouncements on social justice, it could not—and some of its adherents *would* not—shake its image as a genteel upper-class institution that demanded little from its affiliates. Taking the wind out of a favorite Reform sail, a college professor told the CCAR in 1922: "I do not meet Jews who make me feel that we are a people with a mission." The vigorous battle over ritual reform, which had earlier raised the salience of religious interest in Reform congregations, was now mostly a thing of the past. The tide had turned away from radical innovation. The major conflict over Zionism usually flared up in the national, rather than the congregational arena. Rabbis spoke repeatedly of anemia, indifference, paralyzing apathy. And except for the most talented among them, they often spoke to half-empty synagogues.[3]

If nonetheless Jewish awareness was not entirely dormant during the twenties, that was due mostly to unpleasant stimulation from the outside. "We laymen do not take our Judaism seriously except when a persecuting Gentile world forces us to do so," said the college professor. With the conclusion of the world war, the United States not only turned from international responsibility to narrow self-interest; it also virtually shut its gates to immigrants and became obsessed with the alleged dangers of foreign influence. The great Jewish floodtide from eastern Europe now washed up against the barrier of stingy immigration quotas first imposed in 1921 and made more severe in 1924. America was to be for the Americans alone, and not everyone even agreed that Jews already on its shores qualified fully. During the Red Scare just after the war, American xenophobes associated the Jews with Bolshevism. In the early twenties Henry Ford propagated the libel of an international cabal called the "Elders of Zion." A revived Ku Klux Klan attracted millions to its gospel of hatred against Catholics, Negroes, and Jews. Christian missionaries redoubled their approaches to lapsed Jews, believing that Christianization and Americanization were one. In Washington, the Department of the Interior appointed a "Special Collaborator and Racial Advisor on Americans of Jewish Origin," whose tasks included the inculcation of American ideals, traditions, and standards.[4]

Both the end of the mass migration and the questioning of Jewish Americanism lay behind a program for Reform Judaism set forth in the early twenties. Its chief progenitor and publicist was the new president of the Hebrew Union College, Julian Morgenstern (1881–1976). An American-born graduate of HUC and a critical Bible scholar of some note, Morgenstern sought, like Kohler, to play an intellectual role in the movement. Although not a theologian, he did possess the insight of a historian, and it was his perception of the contemporary historical situation of American Jews which prompted him to plot out a new direction for Reform. Morgenstern's argument—which he repeated often—went like this. A period of American Jewish history has ended. While the east European immigrants were arriving in large numbers, American Jewry necessarily possessed a dominantly foreign complexion. German Jews busied themselves with philanthropic activities to ease the immigrants' lot and speed their cultural integration. The community was necessarily split between those already at home in America and those not yet familiar with its ways. Absorbed with helping and being helped, neither group was able to give religion its due. But now the possibility of religious revival in modern garb had appeared. Ethnic differences among Jews would disappear, revealing anew Isaac Mayer Wise's vision of a united American Judaism. The significance of their German origins would increasingly diminish among

Reform Jews even as awareness of their east European background declined among descendants of the newer immigrants. Reform congregations would give up their Teutonic coldness and the excess of rationalism they had imported from Germany while the Russians and Poles would cast off their inappropriate vestigial orthodoxy. Just as society in general was drawing together, so would the Jewish community: "If America represents a large melting-pot," Morgenstern told his rabbinical colleagues, then "Jewry in America represents a smaller melting-pot into which are cast Jews and Judaism from various lands." Though American Reform Jews, like their non-Reform coreligionists, had fought against immigration quotas, the new limitation provided an "opportunity to develop a unified American Judaism." That Judaism, Morgenstern argued, could not be Conservatism, which he accused of focusing only on externals. As self-confidently as Isaac Mayer Wise two generations earlier, he set forth his conviction that there would soon be only "Foreign Judaism and American Judaism"— with the latter approximating Reform.[5]

Morgenstern's triumphalism was intended to inspire his listeners. In reality, Reform did not immediately gain ground within the Jewish community; proportionately it declined as Conservatism made rapid gains.[6] But the interwar period did witness a progressive diminution of differences between Reform Jews and their coreligionists. The rapprochement appeared most clearly in the broadening conception of Jewish identity, the progressive reappropriation of traditions, and the turn toward Zion.

A Revolution in Reform Jewish Education

A survey of 125 Reform religious schools, taken in 1924, reflects the persistence of classical Reform values after World War I. In most of the schools children were receiving only one and a half hours of actual instruction, with another half hour for assembly. With few exceptions, there was additional weekday instruction only for the confirmation class. Pupils mainly studied Bible and Jewish history in order to derive morals for daily life. Two-thirds of the schools taught Hebrew (twenty-eight having introduced it after 1916), but only half required its study, so that only 27.7 percent of the students were actually taking the subject. Less than 10 percent of congregational budgets went directly for the school.[7]

Twenty-four years later, in 1948, much had changed.[8] A new survey revealed that while 85 percent of the schools still met only once a week, they now held class for about two hours, and in the larger schools for two and a half. While Hebrew remained optional in about half the schools, nearly all of them offered it and the proportion of students taking it had nearly doubled.[9] The age of confirmation was steadily rising from thirteen or fourteen to fifteen or sixteen. In fact, children remained in Reform religious schools much longer than in the weekday schools sponsored by the Orthodox and Conservatives. There were adult study programs in about half the synagogues, not including those sponsored by sisterhoods and brotherhoods. But the most remarkable educational development in the interwar period was the enrichment and refocus of the curriculum. In scarcely more than two decades the Union of American Hebrew Congregations had published over 300 textbooks, adult education volumes, plays, teachers' guides, resources for youth groups, and similar literature. The educational

Emanuel Gamoran.

goal, moreover, was no longer simply to make Jewish young people into better human beings, but to make them also into dedicated members of the Jewish people.

There are many factors that contributed to this new departure in Reform Jewish education: the influx of east European Jews into Reform congregations, the Nazi threat, the spread of Zionism. But it is unlikely that this educational shift, so fundamental for the reorientation of the American Reform movement as a whole, would have occurred as it did were it not for the key role played by a remarkable layman, an outsider–insider in Reform ranks who in 1923 took charge of its educational program and dominated it for thirty-five years.

Emanuel Gamoran (1895–1962) was a small man with a large fund of energy and an imperious will.[10] He was "a regular little Napoleon," one secretary recalled, who always had his mind made up and possessed little tolerance for disagreement. Although neither of German Jewish ancestry nor a Reform rabbi, Gamoran was able to exercise inordinate influence on the Reform movement precisely because he was "tough," knew his mind well, and displayed unquestionable competence.

Born into a family with hasidic antecedents, Gamoran came to New York from Bessarabia at the age of twelve. To train himself as an educator, he attended Teachers College of Columbia University, where he studied especially with John Dewey's disciple William Heard Kilpatrick. At the same time he enriched his Jewish knowledge at the Teachers Institute of the Jewish Theological Seminary, coming under the influence of its dean, Mordecai Kaplan. At Columbia Gamoran learned the new activist and functionalist approach to education: children should not just listen but do; activities and projects were as important as absorbing subject matter; education was socialization and preparation for life in a democratic society. From Mordecai Kaplan he learned to regard Judaism more broadly than as a religion. Although when Gamoran studied with him Kaplan had not yet published his highly influential *Judaism as a Civilization* (1934), the founder of Reconstructionism had already elaborated his view of Jewish life as embracing music, art, and literature. Gamoran fully accepted Kaplan's broader conception as well as his naturalist theology that made God an impersonal moral force and Jewish observances folkways rather than divine commands. While still in New York, Gamoran was also close to Samson Benderly, a physician who headed the Jewish community's Bureau of Jewish Education and introduced the concept of intensive Jewish education supplementary to the public school. As one of the "Benderly boys," Gamoran began to work for the improvement of Jewish education in New York. He scarcely thought of Reform Judaism or of Cincinnati.

The UAHC, however, still lacked a professional in the field of education and, under pressure from the Reform rabbis, was determined to get the best educator available.[11] Its Secretary, Rabbi George Zepin, consulted Dewey and Kilpatrick, approached Gamoran, and would not let him refuse. Gamoran finally agreed, provided his employers were fully appreciative of his Zionist commitment and would at least listen seriously to his opinions. Once in Cincinnati, the new educational director of the Reform movement set up a kosher household, though—in good Kaplanian fashion—with the intention that all Jews should be able to eat there rather than out of any belief that dietary laws were mitzvot. Following a nine-month trip to Palestine in 1924, the Gamorans began to speak Hebrew in their home, and yearly they erected a *sukah* on the porch. The Orthodox called the family Reform, and Reform Jews called them Orthodox. By preference Gamoran was a Jew "without a label"; yet his arena of activity was now Reform Judaism, and he rapidly set about reforming it in his own way.

In his doctoral dissertation at Columbia Gamoran had argued that Jewish education must fit its environment.[12] What had been appropriate in Russia and Poland was not appropriate and could not work in America. Jewish education in the United States should foster humanistic, democratic values and correspond to the modern *Zeitgeist* with its scientific orientation. On these points Reform Jews could easily agree. But Gamoran went further: in addition to ethical values, the religious school must also stress "survival values," those particularistic ideas and observances that would preserve the Jewish people. They included furthering the establishment of a normal and complete Jewish life in Palestine and developing a broadly based Jewish culture in the Diaspora.

On the UAHC staff in the early twenties Gamoran was the only avowed Zionist. He reported to the joint UAHC–CCAR Commission on Jewish Education headed by the implacable anti-Zionist rabbi of Cincinnati, David Philipson. In an unguarded moment, Gamoran once admitted that he liked it best when the Commission did not meet. In fact, though there were disagreements over the injection of Zionist motifs into the educational literature, they usually resulted in compromise or a Gamoran victory. The Commission members agreed with the educational director on the need for intensifying Jewish education (including additional weekday sessions), and they respected Gamoran's energy and ability to get things done.[13] Though the Hebrew Union College never invited him to give a course, the CCAR repeatedly called on Gamoran to speak at its conventions and eventually changed its constitution so he could be a member. Gamoran told the rabbis that the whole approach to Reform Jewish education, based on teaching Judaism as a religion, was misconceived and did not work: "If we are going to teach theology to little tots of seven or eight, we are going to fail." Religion could be taught effectively only within a larger context. Religious and ethical values would emerge naturally in the course of developing a broader loyalty to the living, changing Jewish people. Specifically, there should be less doctrine and "moralizing"—less of what he branded "the Sunday School atmosphere"—and more attention to customs and ceremonies, to modern Hebrew, and to current events in the Jewish world. The children would undertake "projects" enabling them to experience the substance of Jewish life rather than merely learning the principles of Jewish belief and conduct.[14]

One reason that Gamoran was accepted and his ideas carried through was that, unlike many other Zionists, he was not a secularist. Though influenced by the cultural Zionism of Ahad Ha-Am, Gamoran leaned more to the views of the biblical scholar and modern Jewish thinker Yehezkel Kaufmann, who regarded religion as the chief and indispensable cause for Jewish survival. Gamoran himself stressed that while the Jewish religion could not in the long run exist without its firm basis in Jewish people-hood, neither could the Jewish people exist without its religion. He was critical of Kaufmann only on Reform Jewish terms: Kaufmann had overlooked modernism in Jewish religion and given insufficient credit to Jewish life in the Diaspora.[15] In this centrality which Gamoran ascribed to religion in Judaism Gamoran was closer to the Reformers than to his mentor Kaplan, who only later designated Judaism a *religious* civilization.

Gamoran was tireless. He commissioned and edited new textbooks, worked out a religious school curriculum, and was co-author of a series of primers in modern Hebrew. He founded and edited a quarterly magazine called *The Jewish Teacher;* he traveled about the country visiting schools and trying to raise their level. The textbooks were unquestionably his greatest achievement. Series appeared on holidays, heroes, history, literature, and the Jewish community. The UAHC published books for adults, written by Hebrew Union College professors, as well as for children. Illustrations, attractive typography, and good paper made religious school books no longer seem a generation behind their public school equivalents. In the interwar period the UAHC was the only national organization printing such texts. By 1930 they were finding their way into Conservative and Orthodox as well as Reform schools. Even during the Depression new texts continued to appear.[16] Because its literature was no longer narrowly doctrinal the Reform movement had become a powerful force in American Jewish education.

Gamoran's pedagogy, based on cultural pluralism, did not vitiate Morgenstern's conception of an inner-Jewish melting pot. The new textbooks helped bridge the gap between German and east European Jews; they foresook the older classical Reform while educating to the spirit of modern America. Yet Morgenstern remained in that tradition which regarded Judaism as above all a religion of prophetic morality, while Gamoran's efforts were directed to broadening the scope of Reform Jewish identification. Among rabbis and laity it was Gamoran's views that became increasingly influential.

Reform rabbinical education in the interwar years reflected the tension between the competing conceptions of Jewish identity.[17] At Hebrew Union College in Cincinnati, Prophetic Judaism continued to loom large in the curriculum. Moses Buttenwieser taught the prophetic literature with critical competence and great enthusiasm for the subject. After the appointment of Abraham Cronbach to a newly created chair of Jewish social studies, students had the opportunity not only to study the Prophets but to consider ways of applying prophetic morality to current social problems. Cronbach, like Buttenwieser—and like the professor of homiletics and Midrash Israel Bettan—was a universalist in the classical Reform mold. He believed that religion was essentially reverence for human personality, that it should be concerned more with high aims and noble purposes than with dogma or ritual. As a religious humanist, Cronbach exercised considerable influence on students who were themselves intellectually uncomfortable with theism; as an uncompromising pacifist, he set an example for those who were leaning in that direction. Only in the late thirties, when Cronbach remained loyal to his undiluted universalism and absolute pacifism despite the Nazi threat, did his popularity rapidly wane.

In the Morgenstern years (1922–1947) Jewish scholarship flourished at the Hebrew Union College. In 1924 the first volume of the *Hebrew Union College Annual* appeared. At a time when there was only one other Jewish scholarly periodical published in the United States, the *Jewish Quarterly Review, HUCA* was able rapidly to establish an excellent reputation, especially in the areas of Bible and rabbinics. The College's expanded faculty included outstanding, seasoned scholars in Talmud (Jacob Z. Lauterbach) and medieval Jewish history (Jacob Mann), as well as promising younger men in a number of areas. Its new theologian, Samuel S. Cohon, would in the thirties play a role among the rabbis similar to Gamoran's in the Union.

HUC students in the interwar period were mostly the American-born sons of poor east European families. Their years at the College were not alone scholarly and practical preparation for the rabbinical role. They were also an introduction to the values and ambience of Reform Judaism, with its still pervasive German Jewish atmosphere, especially in the older congregations. In Cincinnati students could take pride in their new dormitory and gymnasium and, beginning in 1931, make use of a modern, well-equipped library. In the Morgenstern years, unlike the period of Kohler's presidency, both students and faculty enjoyed complete freedom of expression. They could be Zionists, socialists, and even severe critics of the College. In fact, a 1930 survey of student opinion showed that 69 percent were favorable to some form of Zionism, 22 percent were neutral, and only 9 percent were opposed. But during this time—and especially in the twenties—the Hebrew Union College still lay in the shadow of the older, classical Reform Judaism. Tucked away from the teeming mass of New York Jewry, it could indulge a slower pace in meeting the new realities of American Jewish life.

Hebrew Union College seemed especially anachronistic to one of Reform Judaism's most aggressive rebels. Stephen Samuel Wise (1874–1949) was born in Budapest and grew up in New York City.[18] He did not attend HUC but studied independently and received private ordination. Yet in some ways he was a classical Reform Jew. His theology was far from orthodox; he did not put much store by ritual; he conducted services and gave sermons for crowds of Jews and Christians on Sunday mornings in Carnegie Hall. Even Reform rabbis could not forgive him when he announced in one sermon that Jews should reclaim Jesus as their own. And Wise took second place to no Reform rabbi in his active advocacy of social justice, especially taking the side of workers against their exploitative employers. But Wise was an early and militant Zionist, part of that small but influential band of Reform rabbis who had joined Zionist ranks long before the majority of their colleagues. Wise did not get on well with many of the CCAR's leaders and only rarely attended the conventions. He greatly admired Emil G. Hirsch, not only for his commitment to social causes, but also as a fellow despiser of the rabbinical mass.

Stephen Wise was not an actor to perform in another's play. He wrote his own scripts and cast himself in the leading role. His self-confidence, combined with the gifts of an impressive appearance, a magnetic personality, thunderous, eloquent speech, and a remarkable intelligence, gave him the daring to strike out repeatedly on his own. Denied exclusive rabbinical authority and complete freedom from board domination at Temple Emanu-El in New York, Wise founded his own Free Synagogue in which no one could contest his right to speak and act as he chose. Dissatisfied with the patrician-dominated American Jewish Committee, he created a rival American Jewish Congress. So, too, he conceived the idea of a second Reform seminary—though it would not carry that denominational label and would in principle serve the entire American Jewish community. In 1922 Wise opened the Jewish Institute of Religion in the heart of Manhattan. Though lacking a congregational body from which to draw financial support, he courageously set out to challenge Hebrew Union College. Cincinnati, he argued, was training Reform rabbis in a narrow Reform spirit. In New York he would educate more broadly oriented spiritual leaders: "liberal" rabbis for *kelal yisrael,* the totality of the Jewish people.

Unlike Hebrew Union College, the Jewish Institute of Religion was not able to attract leading scholars permanently to its faculty. They came to the JIR from Europe as visitors, or like Harry Wolfson, Shalom Spiegel, and Salo Baron, remained only until they received better academic employment elsewhere. The permanent faculty consisted mostly of talented pedagogues or of noncritical scholars like the talmudist Chaim Tchernowitz. The students came because of Wise himself. He was their mentor, model, and inspiration. To a man they shared his Zionist passion and his conviction that the rabbi's task was to serve all Jews. Its focus on Wise himself and its almost sole dependence on his abilities as a fund-raiser proved, however, to be the principal weakness of the JIR. In the thirties and forties it suffered substantially as income dried up during the Depression and Wise became ever more preoccupied with fund-raising for the United Palestine Appeal, organizing a World Jewish Congress, and alerting America to Nazi atrocity. Following World War II, with Wise aging and no longer in good health, negotiations went forward to merge Hebrew Union College with the Jewish Institute of Religion. By that time, however, the orientation of the Cincinnati institution was no longer so different from its rival in New York. The Jewish people centered philosophy that Gamoran applied to the education of Jewish children and Stephen Wise to the training of rabbis had become dominant in the American Reform movement.

The American Reform Synagogue Between the Wars

Throughout the interwar period the Reform synagogue was on the defensive. Morgenstern's prediction that an age devoted to Jewish philanthropic endeavors would be followed by one devoted to religion did not at all come true. On the contrary, Jews continued to organize as much for self-defense, to aid their fellow Jews, and simply to engage in social activities as they did for any religious purpose. Jewish community centers proliferated, and in city after city Jewish Federations came into existence, organizing charitable activities and providing prestigious opportunities for local Jewish leadership.[19] The persistent question addressed by rabbis and laity in this period was therefore how to stem the synagogue's continuing drift toward the periphery.

An early solution was to bring nonreligious activities under its own umbrella. New synagogues frequently boasted a social hall for dancing and entertainment and a kitchen to prepare food for celebrations. The first congregation to build its own gymnasium was The Temple in Cleveland, which did so in response to a petition by its young people as early as 1901. Later Temple Sinai in Chicago built the Emil G. Hirsch Center, complete with both a gymnasium and a swimming pool. So successful was that project that as many as 10,000 persons made use of the center or temple each week. In the twenties dramatic groups were all the rage, and synagogues prided themselves on sponsoring one or more.[20] Although the trend toward such "synagogue centers" began in the Reform movement before the rise of Mordecai Kaplan's Reconstructionism, Kaplan's idea of Judaism as a civilization spurred their proliferation in Reform, as it did in Conservative Judaism. The people-centered conception of Jewish identity that Kaplan fostered and elaborated served as the theoretical basis for such expanded functions of the synagogue. However, not all Reform Jews favored the trend. Some felt that since the temple existed preeminently for worship and education, the introduction of extraneous activities could only divert its energies from more fundamental purposes. Not surprisingly, it was the remaining champions of classical Reform who especially opposed the synagogue center concept. But others, as well, assailed Kaplan for failing to accord religion sufficient prominence in his philosophy of Jewish life. Moreover, his denial of Jewish chosenness undermined what rabbis continued to preach regularly from Reform pulpits: the doctrine of the priest people's mission, which underlay the universalist teleology of Reform Judaism.[21]

On the national level major decisions affecting American Jewry lay in the hands of the American Jewish Committee, the American Jewish Congress, and the Anti-Defamation League of B'nai B'rith. For nearly half a century the UAHC had maintained its own organization dealing with Jewish defense. But in 1925 it adopted the recommendation of a special committee to abolish the Board of Delegates on Civil Rights. Henceforth it would "concentrate its efforts upon its religious purposes and abandon every other activity which tends to dissipate its energy." The work that had been done by the Board of Delegates, the committee concluded, was being adequately performed by other agencies.[22]

The Reform movement could compensate for this withdrawal from secular Jewish affairs only by attempting to expand the national influence of Judaism as a religion. Rabbi Abram Simon of Washington, D.C., then president of the CCAR, proposed in 1924 that Reform Jews could best accomplish that end collectively with the other Jewish denominations. He suggested that American Jewry, already united for philanthropy and defense, should unite its synagogues as well. Following up on his idea, Simon was able to stimulate creation of the Synagogue Council of America in 1926, bringing together the rabbinical and lay bodies of Reform, Conservative, and Orthodox Judaism. The SCA became a permanent fixture of American Jewish life and did succeed in raising the profile of the American synagogue. It supported cultural activities of a national scope and represented the Jewish religion to Christian groups. But it did not fulfill the hope of regaining centrality for the synagogue in American Jewish life. It was not even able to deal with most specifically religious issues, since these necessarily divided the constituents. CCAR delegates to the SCA in 1931 vetoed a resolution urging that all Jewish community dinners observe the dietary laws. Yet three years later they reversed their position, in accordance with the majority sentiment of their colleagues.[23]

Among Reform laymen the most persistent advocate of restoring the synagogue's centrality was Judge Horace Stern (1879–1969), a prominent jurist in Philadelphia and a leading figure in many American Jewish causes. At the 1923 Council of the Union, Stern indicted the contemporary synagogue for rapidly becoming "a mere theological shell." His solution at that time was both enhancement of its spiritual atmosphere and adoption of the synagogue center idea. In 1931 he proposed a specific plan. The synagogue should be reorganized, he suggested, bringing into it all the activities now located outside its walls. Each member would join at least one synagogue group devoted to local and national charitable work, foreign relief, Palestine, the protection of Jewish rights, or Jewish education. Thus the synagogue would not be merely one Jewish institution among others but would contain the activities of all others within it. The CCAR gave its endorsement to this "Stern Plan" and the UAHC appointed a committee to consider it. But when the CCAR asked Mordecai Kaplan to discuss Stern's idea at its convention in 1932, he told them it was "sheer quixotism to try to restore the wholeness of Jewish life by demanding for the synagogue the position of centrality and primacy." And indeed nothing came of the project. Like it or not, synagogue leadership—whether Reform, Conservative, or Orthodox—had to accept the fact that the amorphous broader community, and not the house of worship, lay at the center of organized Jewish life.[24]

While even Kaplan's Reconstructionism remained at least partially on religious ground, other Jewish ideologies in the 1920s did not. There were, of course, the secular Zionists and the Jewish socialists. In addition, a circle of Jewish intellectuals had gathered around the *Menorah Journal,* a periodical representing the Menorah movement, organized among Jewish students at Harvard in 1906. In 1925 and 1926 its editor, Henry Hurwitz, published a number of articles highly critical of organized Jewish religion. The talented young writer Elliot E. Cohen launched a devastating attack on the modern synagogue and rabbinate, which he called "The Age of Brass." Jewish religious leadership, Cohen argued, was like a brass band trumpeting its own praise; it was strong on rhetoric, but weak on knowledge. Endlessly it pounded the drum of the Jewish mission, trying to compensate for lack of inner strength. Cohen called for critical self-examination and better Jewish education, but not for religious renewal. That same year Horace Kallen (1882–1974), already well known as a philosopher, Zionist ideologue, and proponent of cultural pluralism, sounded a similar pointedly anticlerical note. Eschewing religious Judaism, Kallen had earlier argued for a broader "Hebraism" to replace the religion-focused "Judaism." He now advocated making rabbis into glorified social workers and leaving Jewish knowledge to professional scholars. Finally, Hurwitz himself wrote a piece implying that the salvation of American Jewry would come not from the synagogue, but from the Menorah movement.[25]

Rabbi Abba Hillel Silver of Cleveland responded angrily to the *Menorah Journal* articles with a piece entitled "Why Do the Heathen Rage?" Hurwitz had originally requested Silver's article for the *Menorah Journal* itself. But he suppressed it and the essay had to be printed elsewhere. As a scholarly Zionist rabbi, Silver was in a particularly strong position to defend the modern rabbinate and synagogue against the Jewish intellectuals. Upbraiding Cohen, Kallen, and Hurwitz for their prejudice, Silver eloquently upheld both the mission idea as an ideal that prompts Jews to noble action and the essential survival value of the Jewish religion. Neither Zionism nor Jewish culture alone would preserve the Jews. The Jewish religion, which Kallen had termed "a small part of the total fullness of the life of the Jewish people," was for Silver "its very heart and life blood."[26]

Though Silver's response could not persuade the intellectuals, other Jews were drawn to Reform. In spite of the frustration incurred by efforts to broaden the synagogue's influence and the persistent carping of outsiders, the movement grew during the 1920s. Congregational membership, which stood at less than 23,000 units in 1917, reached over 60,000 in 1930. The number of UAHC congregations in the same period climbed from 200 to 285, the latter representing about two-fifths of the congregations belonging to all three nationally organized Jewish denominations. In an American Jewish population more than 80 percent east European, few of the new members were of German-Jewish lineage. At Cincinnati's Rockdale Temple most children entering the religious school in 1927 came from families until recently Orthodox. A survey of Reform congregations in the large cities, conducted in 1931, showed that German and east European parentage were already represented in equal proportions and that the percentage of the latter was rising rapidly. Seventy percent of the members were now over forty and almost all were financially well off. Belonging to a Reform temple continued to convey prestige and to symbolize a higher degree of Americanization. Affiliation was a mark of achieved status, and during the prosperous twenties affording membership was not difficult for families rising on the economic scale.[27]

Those members who wanted to play an active role in their Reform congregations had more opportunity than ever to do so. Aside from the religious services in the sanctuary and the recreational activities of the synagogue center, there were the temple auxiliaries, which expanded in the interwar years. Just about every Reform congregation now had a Sisterhood, its members continuing to play a significant role in the temple's educational program. Nationally, the NFTS still focused on the Hebrew Union College, raising the funds for its dormitory, completed in 1925, but now also becoming a major support of the Jewish Braille Institute.[28] In 1923 the National Federation of Temple Brotherhoods was formed with the intention of giving men a more active role in synagogue life. Before there were Brotherhoods, Abba Hillel Silver noted in 1926, the "essential work of the liberal synagogue was largely in the hands of women and ecclesiastics," giving the program an air of "isolation and irrelevance." The men would simply attend services from time to time and a few of them manage the temple's financial affairs. The Brotherhoods were created to change that. By the late twenties they had undertaken programs in adult education, social projects, an annual Brotherhood Sabbath, and ushering at religious services. Nationally, they took over support of the Jewish Chautauqua Society, which was now redirected to dispelling prejudice by educating Gentile university students about Judaism. The most remarkable Brotherhood project was holding large-scale Hanukah celebrations in major cities, thereby helping to revive a holiday heretofore quite neglected in Reform circles. Nonetheless, within the Reform synagogue men remained scarcer than women. Not only did women predominate at services, but nationally Sisterhoods outnumbered Brotherhoods in chapters and individual membership by more than three to one.[29]

The last temple auxiliary to develop a national organization was the youth group. Local associations of religious school alumni had met occasionally for social activities and sometimes for study in a number of Reform congregations as early as the twenties.

Temple Sisterhoods had played a major role in organizing them. But the UAHC did not provide any national guidance until the early thirties when it appointed its first Director of Youth Activities, began to supply program materials, and started to publish a periodical called *The Youth Leader*. By the late thirties there were a few score clubs in local congregations and some regional activity. As similar youth groups, both non-Jewish and Jewish, had begun to hold national conventions, the UAHC called one for its own young people in 1939. The result was the National Federation of Temple Youth, at first composed largely of men and women in their early twenties, with the age level dropping to the teens after World War II. NFTY soon prospered and grew rapidly.[30]

The UAHC was less successful with what it called "university welfare work," its effort to bring Reform Judaism to the college campus. Although the Union had budgeted funds enabling rabbis to conduct services and lectures for Jewish students since 1906, the effect of such rabbinical visits was severely limited. In 1923, when there were about 20,000 Jewish men and women studying in colleges, universities, and professional schools, the UAHC was supporting twenty student congregations, but they languished for lack of resident professional guidance. Only at the University of Illinois did a Reform rabbi serve in a full-time capacity. With the UAHC concentrating its energy on raising a multimillion dollar endowment for Hebrew Union College, B'nai B'rith increasingly entered the Jewish college scene, and its Hillel Foundations soon drove the sporadic Reform endeavors to the sidelines.[31]

If during the twenties leaders of Reform temples often complained that the synagogue failed to attract many of the unaffiliated and lacked eminence in the larger Jewish community, they were at least able to carry on and even to expand its activities. During the Great Depression they were fortunate if they could manage at all. Congregational membership dropped as one family after another found itself unable to afford temple dues. At Temple Emanu-El in New York membership dropped 44 percent, from 1,652 families and individuals in 1930 to 874 in 1942, and it did not return to the 1930 level until five years after World War II. The UAHC supplied synagogue presidents with sample letters that urged and exhorted members to reconsider resignation. While Emanu-El refused to waive dues for those unable to pay, other congregations carried newly impecunious members on their books, expecting they would make good their debt when times improved. Boards of Trustees had no choice but to curtail temple programs. Paid choirs and paid religious school teachers were now judged unaffordable luxuries that could be replaced by volunteers; synagogue bulletins became less elaborate and appeared less frequently. Congregations that had afforded guest speakers were forced instead to rely exclusively on the local talent of their own rabbi and members. In the small congregations decisions were agonizing. Some had to let their rabbi go, creating a pool of anxious unemployed; others voted themselves out of existence. Most HUC students in the worst Depression years reached ordination with little prospect for a congregation. The CCAR president spoke of "an unholy scramble for pulpits." In more than one synagogue the rabbi's sermons began to focus on the personal problems of daily life, seeking to provide consolation and hope.[32]

Except for the Hebrew Union College, whose newly raised 3.2 million dollar endowment had been conservatively invested, the national institutions of the Reform movement suffered as well. The CCAR saw its investments shrink by about a fifth; a quarter of its members stopped paying dues. Scores of congregations dropped out of the UAHC or refused to send contributions. From a high point of 61,609 families and individuals in 1930, membership dropped to 52,294 in 1934. The number of congregational units did not descend equally only because synagogues not paying dues (95 in 1933) were kept on the rolls.[33]

By 1935 the Union's financial situation began to improve, but the malaise of "bad times" continued to hang over it like a heavy fog inhibiting movement. In the late thirties dissatisfaction with the Union's lack of initiative was widespread, especially among rabbis. Critics held the UAHC responsible for the decline of passion and sense of mission that had earlier characterized Reform. Its lay leaders, business or professional men, could give only part-time attention to the cause. The highest paid official, Rabbi George Zepin, was a hard-working, modest man who lacked charisma and drive.[34] It seemed as if the Reform movement was running out of steam, letting opportunities slip by, and falling into a secure but troubling stagnation.

As part of a self-evaluation which the Union leadership finally felt necessary in 1941, it invited Rabbi Louis Mann of Temple Sinai in Chicago to address that year's Council on "The Failures of the Union and Where Do We Go from Here." Mann pulled no punches. If the Reform movement had not grown in proportion to the Jewish population it was largely the Union's fault for refusing to accept challenges. Since it did little, it failed to attract funds, which in turn served as the excuse for doing even less. It was a vicious circle. Paraphrasing the title of Winston Churchill's recent book, Mann reminded the delegates that much had happened in American Jewish life "while the Union slept." Jewish young people were increasingly attending universities—but the UAHC had abandoned that fruitful domain to B'nai B'rith's Hillel. Similarly, it had given up antidefamation, closing down its Board of Delegates in 1925. A year later it had allowed the Hebrew Union College to be independently incorporated for the purpose of directly attracting funds, thus depriving itself of a most valuable asset. What remained was the production of worthwhile material for education and guidance, but that made the Union little more than a "religious mail-order business," busy mimeographing and addressographing, but providing no active and visible leadership for a religious movement. Reform Judaism lacked a proper journal and a national radio program. Sending its regional rabbis to organize small-town congregations of twenty or so families, it had failed to expand the movement in the larger cities with their massive Jewish populations. Detroit and Pittsburgh still had only one Reform congregation. There were hardly more than 6,500 Reform-affiliated families in the entire city of New York. In short, the Union—and therefore the Reform movement—was plagued by a torpor that was depriving it of eminence among American Jews.[35]

Mann's words—and those of others who echoed him—were taken very seriously. The Union retired George Zepin, replacing him first with the dynamic and beloved Rabbi Edward Israel of Baltimore; then, following Israel's sudden death, with Professor Nelson Glueck of Hebrew Union College, and afterwards with the ambitious and energetic Rabbi Maurice Eisendrath. The UAHC tripled congregational dues from one dollar per congregational family to three and set out to reverse the vicious circle by embarking on new activities. Now it also devoted more effort to creating new Reform congregations in the large cities. A New York Federation of Reform Synagogues came into existence in 1942 and started drawing larger numbers to organized Reform from the largest reservoir of the American Jewish population.[36]

Beginning in 1943, the Union finally published a monthly illustrated magazine. For two decades it had issued newsletters that did little more than recite the Union's achievements, print the names of donors, and provide practical advice for synagogue administration. *Liberal Judaism* was very different. Its focus was not just the Reform movement, but world Jewry. The very title, avoiding the word "Reform," suggested less denominationalism and broader scope. Suddenly Reform Judaism was no longer presenting itself as an encapsulated denomination. The adult movement was finally catching up with its religious schools, defining itself in relation to the Jewish people instead of in purely religious terms. For the first time also east European Jewish culture received its due within the national Reform movement. *Liberal Judaism* printed a translated article by the prominent Yiddish writer Joseph Opatoshu; it celebrated the sixtieth birthday of the Yiddish literary critic S. Niger with a full-page photo. There was an article on the Russian maskil and onetime proponent of religious reform Moshe Leib Lilienblum, and even a photo of Chaim Zhitlowsky, the revolutionary socialist and leading advocate of Yiddishism who had just died. Nor did the magazine neglect the Hebrew renaissance. There were appreciative articles on its poets, Hayyim Nahman Bialik, Saul Tchernichowsky, and I. L. Peretz. East European Jews in Reform ranks could now feel that their traditions were not strange to Reform Judaism, that they were being incorporated alongside the legacy of Zunz, Chorin, and Einhorn, who received attention in a series called "Reform's Founding Fathers." Zionism too entered its pages. The first issue carried an illustrated interview with Moshe Shertok (later Sharett), head of the Jewish Agency's political department, entitled "The Yishuv's Army of Freedom." Later there were photo portraits of Theodor Herzl, David Ben-Gurion, and Chaim Weizmann. *Liberal Judaism* also served as a vehicle for adult education, publishing translated excerpts from classical sources and historical pieces by the popular Jewish scholar Cecil Roth.

Strikingly absent in the early issues of *Liberal Judaism* was the theme of social justice. Apparently it was pushed aside by Reform Judaism's new celebration of Jewish peoplehood and the particular concerns forced on all Jews during the war. That, however, was quite a change from the preceding decades when it had been one of American Reform Judaism's most conspicuous—and controversial—endeavors.

Social Justice Approaching Socialism

In the twenties and thirties, more than ever before, American Reform Judaism applied its prophetic ethics directly and radically to social issues. Just what degree of social change the biblical imperative "to do justly" required became a point of dispute among rabbis, and especially between rabbis and laity. The CCAR Commission on Social Justice, particularly during the years it was headed by the energetic and capable Edward Israel, succeeded in gaining public attention for rabbinical resolutions and, for the first time, played a tangible role in labor disputes and in the legislative process.[37]

The CCAR's social justice platforms were widely distributed. That of 1918 was printed as a full-page advertisement in major journals of American public opinion; the 1928 program appeared in a Yiddish version.[38] During the twenties the Commission did most of its important practical work together with the major Protestant and Catholic organizations. Social action was an arena in which the Reform rabbinate could act (self-appointedly to be sure) as the representative of all American Jewry. In 1922, in the first such cooperative venture with non-Jews, the Commission participated in a joint letter to President Harding requesting government intervention in the coal strike. It called particular attention to the plight of miners and their families, and it stressed the unbearable situation of the poor, who were unable to heat their homes as the price of ever scarcer coal rose beyond their reach. Later the Commission joined in an investigation of steel and railroad strikes that to some extent played a role in the settlement. In the thirties, Rabbi Israel testified frequently before congressional committees considering social legislation. One presidential candidate in 1932 (the source does not give a name) even cited the CCAR's most recent social justice platform.[39]

That platform had appeared in a new version in 1928. Although in general it echoed its predecessor of a decade earlier, the later statement was broader and in some respects more radical. It extended moral responsibility for an enterprise from the employer to the investor, declaring that he too "has the moral duty to know the ethics of the business from which he derives his dividends and to take a definite stand regarding its moral administration." The platform did not explicitly favor socialism but came very close to espousing it. Though conceived before the Depression, it already exhorted that "inequalities of wealth can find no moral justification in a society where poverty and want, due to exploitation, exist." And it declared that "unrestrained and unlimited exercise of the right of private ownership without regard for social results is morally untenable." Specifically, it called for such measures as a living wage sufficient to provide for sickness and old age, public works in time of unemployment, an eight-hour day, a five-day week—and for women in industry: "equal pay with men for equal work."[40]

The platform mentioned race only in its condemnation of lynching. Five years later the Commission did single out the plight of Negroes, denouncing the "conditions existing in several sections of our land which seem to offer evidence of the inability of the Negro to secure economic or civil justice." But it made no specific recommendations. Only during World War II, when racial discrimination was flagrant and highly visible in the armed services and defense industries, did the Commission call for removal of racial bars in trade unions, the admission of the Negro on equal terms to all branches of the army and navy, and elimination of the poll tax used to disenfranchise Negro voters in the South.[41]

During the depression years, as unemployment rose from 3 million in 1930 to 12 million in 1933, the Conference position on social issues slipped further to the left. In 1932 it directly attacked the capitalist system. After excoriating contemporary capitalism for failing to achieve a satisfactory sense of social responsibility and for placing "the safeguarding of investments above the safeguarding of human life," the resolution continued:

> Any system which can be so characterized is neither economically sound nor can it be sanctioned morally. We therefore advocate immediate legislative action in the direction of changes whereby social control will place the instruments of production and distribution as well as the system of profits increasingly within the powers of society as a whole. We feel that by this means alone can there be achieved an adequate distribution of worldly goods and an introduction of a system whereby the working hours in a machine age can be so adjusted in terms of time and pay as to make us feel that we are following our ancient prophetic mandate concerning man's stewardship of the earth for the benefit of all humanity.[42]

The Reform rabbinate was not alone among American religious bodies in expressing such radical views. Some Protestant denominations had also—in their terms—chosen Christ over capitalism. Among Conservative colleagues, as well, these ideas were gaining adherents. The Rabbinical Assembly did not establish its Committee on Social Justice until 1931, twenty-one years after the CCAR created a Committee on Synagogue and Labor. However, in their first major statement, adopted in 1934, the Conservative rabbis denounced the economic individualism that "created prosperity for a few and destitution for the multitude." They favored the creation of a "cooperative economy," looked to the ultimate elimination of the profit system, and advocated a socially controlled industry and agriculture. Specifically their pronouncement called for public ownership of banking and credit, transportation and communications, and all sources of power, including coal and oil.[43]

Nonetheless, not all Reform rabbis could accept their Commission's 1932 statement. The resolution passed in the CCAR convention by a vote of fifty-nine to sixteen, with mostly the older men voicing opposition. These rabbis feared the reaction of the laity. Samuel Schulman, then of Emanu-El in New York, publicly criticized the Commission's "socialistic" views, claiming that the rabbis had made themselves "a kite tail to the kite of the Socialist Party." David Philipson agreed with Schulman in deploring the younger, radical elements that had gained a majority in the CCAR. He noted hearing the cry: "If the Hebrew Union College is graduating socialists, let the socialists support the College!"[44]

The lay leaders were indeed embarrassed, if not outraged, by the rabbis' radicalism. Ludwig Vogelstein, the UAHC chairman, defended the right of individual rabbis to speak freely in their pulpits, but in making their collective statement they had courted the danger of throwing "discredit" on their constituents. "The recent manifesto shows immaturity," he censured, and called it "a parrot-like adoption" of radical positions. Even the liberal Robert P. Goldman, who would succeed Vogelstein as head of the UAHC, found it foolish for the CCAR to expect laymen to go along with its principles. When a year later the Conference publicly singled out Jewish sweatshop owners as an element unworthy of the household of Israel, it must have both angered the guilty and created widespread unease about furnishing ammunition to antisemites.[45]

The lay position on social justice was distinctly ambivalent. On the one hand, laypeople could not deny their own commitment to the implications of Prophetic Judaism. But on the other, they were unwilling to endorse specific political proposals that were unpopular in their business and social circles and with which they did not personally agree. Prominent on the Union's Executive Board were conservative, older men of German-Jewish lineage, whose background and social views clashed sharply with those of the younger, radical, and mostly east European rabbis. In 1925, after a lively discussion, the broader Union Council did endorse the current CCAR social justice platform by a vote of ninety-four to fifty-eight and it created its own commission on social justice. But few within the Union leadership agreed with the young Marcus Lester Aaron of Pittsburgh, who told the 1927 Council that his generation of Reform laymen wanted to define social justice, not in the abstract, but "with reference to specific facts and situations." In 1928 the Union gave up its commission only to have it reappear a few months later with distinctly prescribed limitations. The UAHC Commission now existed "not for the solution of specific factional controversies, but for the pronouncement and preservation of the traditionally sympathetic attitude of

Judaism toward those who are struggling for more equitable and just conditions of life." In other words, it would educate and declare principles, but not take positions.[46]

The Union implemented this limited commitment by joining the CCAR in sponsoring conferences on industrial relations addressed by business and union leaders as well as rabbis. It began to urge the formation of social action committees in local synagogues, though with meager results. Relations with the rabbis remained tense, with the Union in 1935 dissociating itself from "any declaration on controversial, economic, financial or political questions that do not involve basic ethical or religious principles." Rather than put a conservative anchor on its activity, the CCAR a year later turned down a UAHC proposal to merge their two commissions.[47]

Individual rabbis and congregations applied the prophetic teachings in various ways and to different degrees. One rabbi sallied forth to fight the corrupt government of the Pendergast machine in Kansas City; another fought discrimination against Negroes in the South. Among congregations, the Free Synagogue of New York was unquestionably the leader. It possessed a very active Social Service Division, headed by Rabbi Sidney Goldstein, which educated congregants to specific social problems and involved them actively in volunteer projects assisting the sick and needy. The suffering caused by the Depression stimulated other congregations to similar activities. In Cincinnati some 200 homeless and indigent men slept every night in the basement of Plum Street Temple.[48]

One reason for widespread poverty and suffering was, of course, unwanted children whom parents could not afford to raise. The controversial issue of birth control came before the CCAR for the first time in 1926. The National Catholic Welfare Conference had asked the rabbis to join in opposing revision of the federal law prohibiting the dissemination of contraception information through the mail. In response the CCAR Social Action Commission, then headed by Rabbi Ephraim Frisch, produced a resolution that was a strange mixture of progressive and reactionary elements. On the one hand, it urged that the pulpit, the press, and the public forum discuss birth control more energetically and courageously than heretofore. It favored changing the current law that classified birth control information as "obscene matter" and the removal of state laws that inhibited physicians from giving such information to their patients. It even called for social workers to distribute contraception literature to the very poor at state expense. But it did not favor legislation legalizing mail distribution, for that would "encourage immoral practices." Most remarkable was the resort to eugenics. Birth control, it judged, was especially important for the lower classes of society for "there is a growing and justified widespread opinion that the citizenship material ought to be more carefully and eugenically selected." Conversely, it was "requisite to urge parents possessed of high-grade physical, mental and moral qualities and adequate economic resources to beget more children than those types of families at present have."[49] After a confused debate, which showed the rabbis had not yet thought much about this subject, the CCAR decided to postpone the matter.[50] The following year Professor Jacob Lauterbach delivered a paper on the complex talmudic–rabbinic view of birth control in which he surveyed the halakhic history of the subject and argued there was room for liberal interpretation. Reweighing its fear of marital infidelity against its concern for the poor, the Conference in 1929 finally adopted a very general resolution that simply urged the recognition of planned parenthood as "one of the methods of coping with social problems." Yet even in 1929 the CCAR was still the first national religious body in America to adopt a stance favorable to birth control. Three large Protestant denominations followed closely behind.[51]

Social justice was not the only prophetic message that American Reform Jews took seriously. There was also Isaiah and Micah's vision of world peace. While Reform Jews cherished that beautiful ideal, they did not always agree on its implications. During World War I the CCAR voted to override the views of an anguished minority when it refused to endorse Jewish belief as grounds for conscientious objection.[52] In those years it seemed important to prove that the Jews were as patriotic as anyone else. But after the horrors of the war became known, sentiment in the Reform movement—as in Christian religious groups—veered sharply toward pacifism. In 1925 the laity passed a resolution favoring the "outlawry" of war, and even a decade later they still supported international disarmament and avoidance of American embroilment in war should one break out.[53] Sentiment among the rabbis ran even stronger. In 1932 Stephen Wise thoroughly regretted his earlier pro-war position and vowed he would never bless or support any war again. Many rabbis were now absolute pacifists, adhering to the doctrine of nonresistance and wanting the CCAR to urge all Jews never to bear arms. Others espoused pacifism, but claimed the right of self-defense in the event of an invasion. Nearly all agreed on opposition to compulsory military training in American educational institutions and on the need to declare war an illegal tool of national policy. A majority now favored support of conscientious objection on Jewish religious grounds.[54]

It was only on the eve of World War II that the rabbis' collective position began to change. At its 1939 convention, the CCAR resolved to support revision of the Neutrality Act, which kept the United States uninvolved in Europe, and declared it was henceforth necessary to make a policy distinction between innocent and aggressor nations. A year later Rabbi Abram Vossen Goodman noted typically: "As a former pacifist, I have changed my point of view with a great many others." The Conference that year refused to join the Conservative Rabbinical Assembly in keeping a roll of conscientious objectors, for that would encourage men to become COs. It agreed only to unpublicized assistance. Finally, once the United States entered the world conflict, the CCAR—with a very few dissenting voices—expressed "complete support for our country in its present war."[55]

In the late thirties American domestic issues were less on the Reform conscience than specifically Jewish ones. As members of a movement deeply rooted in Germany, Reform Jews were especially stricken by the plight of their coreligionists in Germany. They joined the rest of the American Jewish community in condemning Nazism, in aiding its Jewish victims, and in helping them emigrate. Both the CCAR and the UAHC petitioned the American and British governments to admit more refugees to the United States and to Palestine. The Conference also sent financial aid to rabbis in Europe and subsidized small congregations so they could bring men from abroad to be their rabbis. In the year 1940/41, thirty European rabbis were able to find permanent places in American Reform congregations; others got temporary positions.[56] The Hebrew Union College did its share as well. Refugees from the Liberal seminary in Berlin joined the student body, making up 12 percent of its ranks. After a frustrating and wearisome struggle against restrictionism and blatant antisemitism in the U.S. State Department, the College was also able to obtain visas for eight European scholars. Morgenstern saved their lives and gave them classes to teach—even though HUC scarcely needed to expand its faculty. In fact the College was the only American rabbinical seminary to undertake such an effort.[57] For Reform Jews in World Jewry's darkest hour, justice for all—at least for the present—had to recede behind life for endangered Jews.

Psychology, Theology, and Ceremonies

Reform Judaism's social justice agenda turned its adherents outward, impelling them to judge American society and international relations by prophetic values. Yet even as it made collective pronouncements and activity for social improvement basic to religious commitment, it found that some Reform Jews were seeking more attention for personal religion. As Reform Judaism addressed economic oppression and world peace, it was forced also to consider the effect of prayer and newly emergent challenges to religious beliefs.

Classical Reform Judaism had not been coldly rationalist. Even its most intellectual exponents recognized the role of emotion in religion and that meaningful prayer had to be more than a collective rededication to moral principles. With all of their heresies in theology and liturgy, men like Geiger and Einhorn did not eliminate or even alter prayerbook passages that spoke of God's might, healing power, and salvation. But it was only later, in America of the twentieth century, that some Reform Jews sought to concentrate their faith on God's response to individual needs.

Already before World War I, Christian Science, like Ethical Culture a generation earlier, was drawing Jews away from Judaism. Mary Baker Eddy had founded the Church of Christ, Scientist in 1879, reintroducing into Christianity the tradition of religious healing associated with Jesus. Despite its clearly Christian character, Christian Science attracted Jews to its religious therapy, making them feel their affiliation with it did not remove them from Judaism. The number of Jewish adherents—estimated at first in the hundreds—was sufficiently large that the CCAR felt compelled to take a stand on the issue. In 1912 its convention heard a paper stressing the Christian character of Christian Science. Thereupon it declared Christian Science in fundamental contradiction with Judaism and that it was impossible for a Jew to accept Christian Science without at the same time denying Judaism. Nonetheless, the flow of troubled Jews into Christian Science continued.[58] In order to steal its attraction, three Reform rabbis at different times began to propagate a "Jewish Science." They drew upon models of religious healing from the Bible down to the hasidic masters and made their religious services more personal, consoling, and hopeful. They attracted a few hundred Jews who had withdrawn from Jewish religious life. But Jewish Science, though it lasted into the period after World War II, remained a fringe phenomenon.[59]

More significant was the influence of a moderated personalist impulse on larger circles within Reform Judaism. By the mid-twenties many Reform rabbis thought their movement needed to respond to the desire of some congregants that the synagogue better address their individual religious needs. In 1925, when the number of Jews in Christian Science in New York alone was believed to have exceeded 50,000, Rabbi Louis Witt told the CCAR that what was good in Christian Science was very Jewish and that it only needed to be recovered. A contemporary survey showed that laypeople were less interested in the intellectual issues of religion than in what it could offer them emotionally. Some were even looking for mystical experience. The Conference created a special committee on the Relation of Synagogue to Mental and Physical Healing, which in 1927 recommended that the CCAR declare spiritual healing in keeping with the principles and traditions of Judaism, that it publish booklets on prayer and consolation for synagogues, and that the Hebrew Union College establish a course on religiotherapy or spiritual healing. Rabbi Morris Lichtenstein, one of the founders of Jewish Science, reported that his members—to his own surprise—had actually been healed from many forms of ailment, especially nervous exhaustion. The majority of rabbis, however, was not sympathetic. Felix Levy opposed "stressing the neurotic element in religion" and catering to the abnormal. That year the Conference did not accept the committee's recommendations.[60]

A year later, however, a modified resolution did win adoption. It affirmed that the synagogue could heal ailments of the spirit, and indirectly, through the effect of thoughts of cheer, calm, and courage, help or heal those of the body as well. Of course, it added the qualifications that medical science was of importance for healing both mind and body, and religion was not just a matter of therapy. In succeeding years there continued to be rabbis and laypeople who remained hostile to Jewish healing while others gave it limited approval. Witt's pamphlet on the subject was held up for years, before finally appearing, in the joint UAHC–CCAR tract series in 1947. More universal was the feeling among Reform rabbis that they needed to address themselves effectively to the emotional needs of their congregants. Some formed personal religion groups in their congregations; others began to add a psychological dimension to their counseling work. In 1937 the Hebrew Union College for the first time offered an elective course in pastoral psychology. Indeed, during the late twenties and the thirties psychology was increasingly on the minds of thoughtful Reform Jews, both for what it had to offer religion and also on account of its intellectual challenge.[61]

By the twenties Reform Judaism had fully integrated both Darwinism and biblical criticism. The physical sciences, shaken by the implications of quantum mechanics, seemed, if anything, more favorable to religion than in the nineteenth century. Like Christian theologians, Rabbi Felix Levy could conclude that by demolishing the barrier between matter and energy, quantum theory had left more room for freedom and spirit than had Newtonian physics. Religion, rather than conflicting with physical science, supplied values and purpose to a universe that without religious concepts would lack them. There were even leading natural scientists, including Einstein, who affirmed at least the presence of design in the universe.[62]

It was biological, or human science that presented the real problems. In 1925 John Watson had published *Behaviorism,* in which he defined human beings as machines operating in response to external stimuli and lacking any real thought, consciousness, will, or personality. Unlike quantum theory, behaviorism was a fully deterministic system that left no room for free will. In substituting "conditioning" for moral instruction, it also did away with traditional moral injunction. And of course it left no room for faith in God. Behaviorism gained dominance in American psychology in the twenties and Watson's writings remained the subject of public discussion for years. Just as inhospitable to religion was Freudian psychology, which broadened in the twenties from a form of therapy into a worldview. Complementing his work on dreams and neurosis, Sigmund Freud published *The Future of an Illusion* (1927; English edition, 1928). Here he left no doubt that to his mind science and religion were beyond reconciliation. Religious doctrines were illusions, if not delusions, that had no basis in any reality but the psyche of the believer. Religion, he noted in a line that became classic, was "the universal obsessional neurosis of humanity." In other words, religion was symptomatic of mental disease, the pathological consequence of repression. Freud continued to identify as a Jew, allowing fellow Jews to take pride in his great achievements. But for religious Jews, his reductionism—just because it came from a Jew of such extraordinary brilliance—represented an even more severe threat than Watson's behaviorism.

Yet few rabbis directly addressed these challenges.[63] One who did was James Heller of Cincinnati, who took on both Watson and Freud before the UAHC Biennial Council in 1929. Heller recognized that it was not the scientific view of nature but of human beings that required refutation. Watson had made them into animals; Freud too had deprived them of transcendence. But Heller's response was weak. He simply claimed that, as determinists, Watson and Freud were still living in the Newtonian universe which science itself had declared obsolete. Life, moreover, could not be contained in scientific categories. Introspection would reveal a rich interior world not subject to "illusory and ephemeral theories that lead only to despair."[64]

Far more successful than Heller's attempt to refute psychological theory was Joshua Loth Liebman's effort to integrate it with Judaism. Liebman (1907–1948) was one of the brightest and most creative among the Reform rabbis. In a brief life that ended in his forty-second year, Liebman attained specialized competence in both philosophy and psychology. While serving as a rabbi in Chicago he underwent psychoanalysis and thereafter became the pioneer exponent of psychological awareness in Reform Judaism. From 1939 he occupied the prestigious pulpit of Temple Israel in Boston and reached a wide audience through his fortnightly national radio broadcasts. In 1941 Liebman was the first rabbi to address his colleagues on the new insights they could glean from Freud and his disciples. Liebman was here less interested in confronting Freud's theological challenge—he was himself a religious naturalist—than in expounding psychology's potential for human welfare. More neo-Freudian than Freudian, he saw reason for optimism in psychological theory. Disagreeing with the neo-orthodox Christian theologian Reinhold Niebuhr, he said he did not believe Freudian psychology justified pessimism about human nature. While Niebuhr found in Freudian doctrine confirmation of the traditional Christian view of human sinfulness, Liebman found in psychoanalytic theory a human nature—and hence a society—that was malleable for the good.[65]

In 1946 Liebman published his *Peace of Mind,* a brief volume of psychological insight, religious reflection, and practical advice, which sold well over a million copies. Here he addressed himself to the individual whose personal grief and anxiety, unassuageable by social betterment alone, required an inner peace that psychology and religion, working together, could provide. In *Peace of Mind* Freud appears as the healer, not the iconoclast. Psychiatry has become the ally of religion, "the *key* to the temple, not the temple itself." It serves religion by removing obsessive guilt, irrational fear, and suppressed emotion. Far from implying atheism, it clears the way for religious affirmation. Turning Freud upside down, Liebman as much as declared atheism a neurosis and faith the response of a healthy soul. The God-ideas which psychoanalysis brands illusions, he maintained, are only those that are childish or sick. "Healthy mature religion" remains untouched by its critique.

For Liebman that healthy religion, made possible by psychoanalytic insight and not subject to its critique, was best represented by a Reform Judaism that had abandoned the traditional idea of divine omnipotence. With Emil G. Hirsch, Mordecai Kaplan, and certain liberal Christian thinkers, Liebman spoke of an impersonal natural God, "the power of love and creation, the source of human fulfillment and salvation." Liebman's book was avidly read by many thousand Christians, but his examples were all drawn from Judaism. Judaism's ancient insights, he believed, blended best with the new wisdom of psychology.

In forsaking traditional theism for religious naturalism, Liebman was not alone among Reform rabbis. Beginning in the late twenties, religious humanism's challenge to theism became a bitter, divisive issue. To a limited extent, the more thoughtful laymen ranged themselves on both sides of the debate, but mainly it was a conflict among rabbis, one reflective of trends among liberal Christians. At the one extreme in American thought stood H. L. Mencken, the acerbic apostle of atheism, professional iconoclast, and—by chance—a special foe of the Jews. No rabbi or other religious Jew could adopt Mencken's ideas, but neither could they ignore his deft attacks on religion. Religious humanism among Christians and Jews was in part an attempt to avoid the atheists' knife by conceding some of the argument. Unlike secularists, the religious humanists sought to preserve religion, but they dwelt on its human rather than its divine dimension. For the transcendent, omnipotent, and providential God of theism, religious humanism substituted a finite deity battling for humanity from within the natural world.

The doctrine had its advocates in both the Conservative and Reform movements, creating a severe theological rift in each of them. The religious humanists among the rabbis were usually younger men, those most open to contemporary trends. If for a faction in the CCAR it had become important to stress the healing power of God, for the humanists in its midst prayer had become little more than poetry. Barnett R. Brickner of Cleveland, the leading spokesman for religious humanism in the Conference during the thirties, virtually identified God with human goodness and declared that prayer for him was not petition, but "meditation upon the best we know." Or differently put, "We look upon worship, not theologically, but psychologically."[66]

In Reform Judaism religious humanism remained confined to a vocal minority. At the Hebrew Union College it was represented only by Abraham Cronbach. In both the College and the Conference theism remained the dominant form of belief. At that time its most prominent exponent was Samuel S. Cohon (1888–1959), for thirty-three years Professor of Jewish Theology at HUC.[67] Like his predecessor as theologian of American Reform, Kaufmann Kohler, Cohon displayed erudition, personal piety, and steadfast belief in a transcendent, personal God. Unlike Kohler, however, he was Russian-born, a lover of modern Hebrew language and literature, and open to postrational theological trends; he advocated the revival of Jewish ritual and a more sympathetic attitude to mysticism. As a theologian, Cohon was eclectic rather than original, more the expositor of Jewish sources than the progenitor of new ideas. Yet as an interpreter of the tradition, Cohon provided his own nuances, reshaping Reform theology to better fit contemporary thought and attuning it to his own spirit.

Cohon's theology begins not with general principles, but with the religious consciousness of the individual, specifically with personal experience of the sacred. Following Rudolf Otto, whose *The Idea of the Holy* (1920; English edition, 1923) seems to have profoundly impressed him, Cohon chose to rest Judaism on the universal encounter with the numinous that gave rise to all religion. Judaism, like other faiths, cast the primal religious experience into its own forms, symbols, and values. It made *kedushah* (holiness) into *kidush ha-ḥayim* (the sanctification of life) through observance of moral and ritual commandments. Cohon criticized classical Reform Judaism for stressing only the ethical imperatives, neglecting the mystical element and ceremonial law. In the thirties he became one of the chief proponents of Reform's religious reorientation. Like Gamoran in the textbook literature, Cohon in the seminary classroom and the CCAR propagated a greater appreciation for the complete Jewish legacy and identification with the totality of the Jewish people. Where earlier Reform had stressed individual conscience as the final authority for religious decisions, the thrust of Cohon's thought was toward a revaluation of collective authority within a liberal framework, a serious consideration of what Reform Judaism required not in belief alone but also in practice. Reform Judaism, Cohon declared recalling Bialik's famous essay, needed to restore the balance between Halakhah—Jewish observance—and Agadah—Jewish thought and faith. Like the humanists, Cohon spoke of the psychological value of prayer, but for him it remained basically petition addressed to a personal God. Beyond petition lay what he called "mystical prayer," in which there was "direct experience and realization of the Divine."

In the mid-thirties the majority of Reform rabbis shared all or most of Cohon's views. They too felt that Reform Judaism had changed significantly since the Pittsburgh Platform carved its principles in stone fifty years earlier. And some of them wanted a new general statement. At the CCAR convention in 1935 David Philipson, who was one of two survivors from the Pittsburgh conference, delivered a historical lecture on it and declared that for him the platform had not lost its appeal. But even he recognized that it no longer represented the views of most Reform rabbis. That year the incoming Conference president, Felix Levy of Chicago, appointed a commission to draft a new platform that would reflect the changes Reform ideology had undergone during half a century. The construction of that new platform, however, proved to be far more difficult than anticipated—and for a while collapse seemed imminent.

As its chairman, the commission selected the venerable Samuel Schulman (1864–1955), who had just retired as rabbi of Temple Emanu-El in New York. Schulman was one of the best intellects in the Reform rabbinate, with an excellent command of Jewish sources and broad philosophical interests. But he was a classical Reformer, a non-Zionist who believed fervently in the Diaspora Jewish mission and who placed Jewish religion far above Jewish peoplehood. A past president of the CCAR, Schulman enjoyed the respect of his colleagues; a powerful personality, he was a man who fought for his convictions and his honor. At the first meeting of the commission Schulman accepted the task of drawing up an initial draft. But to everyone's chagrin, his work turned out to be a lengthy, highly theological, and ponderous document that was more argument and exhortation than collective statement. It specified no religious observances and left open the question of whether the Jews were only a religious community or also a nation.

Meanwhile, Cohon—a member of the commission—had prepared his own draft, sent it to Schulman, and written him that he reserved the right to present it independently later. He also sent copies to other members of the commission, which included classical Reformers like Samuel Goldenson and David Philipson, but had a preponderance of revisionists, among whom were Abba Hillel Silver, Stephen Wise, James

Heller, and Barnett Brickner. When Schulman became ill and could not attend the commission's second meeting, Levy decided that Cohon's statement, not Schulman's, would henceforth be the one under discussion. After the offended Schulman resigned from the commission, he made Cohon its chairman. At the 1936 convention, in Schulman's absence and with objections raised to various points in the draft, the best Cohon could secure was a resolution to postpone decision. He then proceeded to solicit suggestions from all members of the Conference, thereby disarming much anticipated future criticism.

A year later Cohon had a newly revised draft and the support of all the remaining members of the commission, including even David Philipson. But Schulman would not give up. He now circulated his version to the entire CCAR, marshalled personal support, and made his appearance at the 1937 Columbus convention ready to confront Cohon head on. Those in attendance therefore found themselves having to choose, not only between two platforms, but between two determined and angry personalities. Opponents of particular points in Cohon's version or of the idea of an authoritative platform as such joined with friends and admirers of Schulman in supporting a resolution against the adoption of any platform at all. That motion succeeded in deadlocking the convention eighty-one to eighty-one. Discussion continued only after Levy, as president, cast the deciding negative vote. Schulman thereupon launched into an attack on Cohon's version, branding it simplistic: "a sort of catechism—a series of definitions, quick to the point and short, that anybody can see." What was required instead, he thought, was "a ringing challenging statement on the living issues of the day." Cohon, in turn, belittled Schulman's text as "a long polemical sermon." But once Levy had broken the crucial tie vote, adoption of the Cohon version became a foregone conclusion. David Philipson, "for the sake of historical continuity," made the final motion to adopt, and only eight of those present asked that their votes be recorded in the negative.[68]

The Columbus Platform—or Guiding Principles of Reform Judaism, as it was officially called—represents a sharp departure from its Pittsburgh predecessor.[69] It is less a declaration of specific Reform tenets than a comprehensive but concise liberal interpretation of religious Judaism. It uses traditional categories—God, Torah, Israel—and clearly reflects the new Reform commitment to observance and Jewish peoplehood. At the same time it is a carefully crafted piece, which selects language inclusive of the widest range of positions, and it is a polemical document that subtly rejects even as it affirms.

Theologically, the platform is indisputably theist, in line with Cohon's conviction that God "rules the world." Yet Cohon removed references in his earlier draft to "the Holy One, unique and mysterious" and to "our personal God," apparently as a gesture to the religious rationalists and humanists. Similarly, prayer becomes, not as originally "the mystic ladder on which the devout soul mounts to the throne of God," but only "the voice of religion," which "directs man's heart and mind God-ward." The platform's section on Torah is indebted to Geiger and the German Reformers for its conception of progressive revelation and of the responsive "genius of Judaism." It reflects the American scene in its paragraph on social justice, which puts the right of all to an adequate standard of living prior to the rights of property; but it is not as radical as the earlier pronouncements of the Conference Commission on Social Justice. In contrast to Pittsburgh, the platform goes beyond individual and social ethics to religious practice in home and synagogue. The Sabbath, the holidays, "such customs, symbols and ceremonies as possess inspirational value," along with the use of Hebrew, appear as requisite for maintaining Judaism as a way of life.

Beneath the surface of the platform one can detect both the influence of Mordecai Kaplan's Reconstructionism and a polemic against it. The broader conception of Jewish identity, the reference to cultivating distinctive forms of religious art and music, and the absence of Israel's chosenness reflect Kaplan's views. But the platform also asserts that the synagogue is "the prime communal agency," that God transcends time and space, and at the very outset it defines Judaism as specifically the *religious* experience of the Jewish people.

Most striking is the paragraph on Israel. While the platform reaffirms the Jewish mission and Reform's inveterate universalism, it also broadly endorses both political and cultural Zionism. In language approximating the Balfour Declaration it affirms the obligation of all Jewry to aid in upbuilding Palestine as a Jewish homeland, and in Ahad Ha-Am's terms it calls for making Palestine not only a haven of refuge—as Herzl insisted—but also a center of Jewish culture and spiritual life.

A reoriented Reform Judaism required not only a new platform but also a new liturgy. Here too Cohon played a role when in 1928 he delivered a severe indictment of the *Union Prayer Book*. By that time the Reform liturgy had already undergone one revision. A new edition of the volume for Sabbaths, festivals, and weekdays had appeared in 1918, for High Holidays in 1920. But this *UPB* was only slightly different from its predecessor. It used the new Jewish Publication Society Bible translation for biblical passages; it added some congregational participation and a bit more Hebrew. But there were no striking changes. Within a decade many rabbis and laypeople—for a variety of reasons—found the liturgy unsatisfactory. When Cohon was asked to give his view of the *UPB*'s theology, he turned his lecture into a merciless critique. "The *Union Prayer Book* unconsciously reflects the present apathy and scepticism toward prayer," he charged. "Therein lies its chief distinction from the traditional Book of Prayer." Cohon found the Reform prayerbook hobbled by its nineteenth-century rationalism; it toned down petitionary prayers to avoid intellectual embarrassment. Its liturgy was not "a cry for health, for sustenance and for relief from pain, sorrow and distress," but only "a vague meditation on an ethical theme." More often than not, the prayers exhorted the self to perform moral acts rather than appealing fervently for divine assistance; they were more soliloquy or autosuggestion than "communion between finite man and the infinite God." Cohon had come to a rather jaundiced conclusion: "The *Union Prayer Book* conveys the impression that it was especially written for a people composed of retired philanthropists and amateur social workers."[70] He wanted a new edition of the *UPB* that would be more distinctly theistic, appealing to the omniscient, all-pervading, all-sustaining providential God. He wanted mystery in prayer, not common sense. All this required a thoroughgoing liturgical reform, and he ambitiously intended to produce a new prayerbook for the Conference in his own name.[71]

But Cohon failed to consider that much of the dissatisfaction with the *UPB* was motivated by concerns directly opposed to his own. Ferdinand Isserman spoke for a number of rabbis when he immediately replied to Cohon: "So far as I am concerned, I cannot offer prayers of petition." And earlier, Ephraim Frisch had complained: "We are constantly speaking to God instead of about Him."[72] While for Cohon the *UPB* insufficiently addressed the personal God, for the religious humanists in the Conference it did so far too much. One of their number, Joseph Baron of Milwaukee, caused consternation when he submitted a humanistic service to the CCAR Committee on Liturgical Literature that was charged with the process of revision. Baron felt at least one of the planned five services for weekdays should represent the point of view of those rabbis and laymen who came to temple not to petition God, but "for the purpose of strengthening themselves in the spiritual and moral ideals of our people." Baron's proposed service systematically excluded the name of God from the English text, retaining it only in the Hebrew. The committee, however, did not accept Baron's submission.[73]

Ranged against the humanists were those rabbis who were serving more conservative congregations. They wanted a prayerbook that opened with a fully traditional service, followed by the liberal liturgy. A third faction, the most active Zionists, wanted above all to restore Zion to the religious service.[74] With these tugs in various directions, the chairman of the committee, Solomon Freehof of Pittsburgh, despaired of producing a prayerbook that would be consistent in theology and yet meet the variety of viewpoints then being expressed in American Reform Judaism. He suggested the *UPB* be supplemented by the publication of a Union Prayer Anthology reflecting diverse theologies. Others wanted to incorporate theological variety into the prayerbook itself, prompting David Zielonka of Tampa to remark that then "our prayerbook will become so large it will be a burden to handle."[75]

All of this held up the work of liturgical revision. A particularly divisive issue arose at the 1930 CCAR convention when someone suggested from the floor that the *Union Hymnal,* then also under review, include a Hebrew version of the *kol nidre* for the eve of Yom Kippur. That liturgical piece, it will be recalled, had been problematic even for the modern Orthodox Samson Raphael Hirsch because antisemites had long claimed it attested to the Jews' duplicity in making promises. The German Reformers had rewritten the text or substituted a vernacular hymn while the *UPB* had done the latter. Yet in many Reform congregations cantor or choir sang the original Aramaic text. The plea for absolution from enforced vows, born of Jewish persecution, continued to move worshipers with its strange words and haunting melody. But the rabbis could not agree here either. Some wanted to continue with an English hymn sung to the *kol nidre* melody, others wanted an acceptable Hebrew text, and still others wanted a reversion to the Aramaic original. In deference to all and to none, the Conference decided that the new hymnal would contain only the melody of the *kol nidre*— with no words at all. More notable about that revised hymnal, however, was that it surpassed its predecessors in compositions of Jewish origin. Deleting 177 hymns by non-Jews, it introduced 200 written by Jewish poets and set to music by Jewish composers.[76]

The newly revised prayerbooks did not make their appearance until 1940 (for Sabbaths, festivals, and weekdays) and 1945 (for the High Holidays). The five complete Friday evening services, while all basically theist, included one version (number 3) that would appeal to the humanists and those who believed prayers must above all strengthen moral commitment. That service contained words of thanks to the coal miners who "dig far away from the sun that we may be warm"; sought divine assistance "to be among those who are willing to sacrifice that others may not hunger"; and perceived God's presence in human acts of righteousness. The fifth Friday evening service was intended especially for the Zionists. It invoked God to "uphold also the hands of our brothers who toil to rebuild Zion" and added the petition: "Grant us strength that with Thy help we may bring a new light to shine upon Zion. Imbue us who live in lands of freedom with a sense of Israel's spiritual unity that we may share joyously in the work of redemption so that from Zion shall go forth the law and the word of God from Jerusalem."

Over all, the new volumes represent clear evidence of return to tradition.[77] The High Holiday volume introduces poetic passages from the Ashkenazi and Sephardi Middle Ages, and the amount of Hebrew is further increased. The most striking innovations, however, deal not with prayer but with ritual. A passage in the morning service for Sukkot makes clear reference to the presence of the symbolic *etrog* and *lulav;* the New Year service includes the blessings preceding the sounding of the *shofar.* The Friday evening service opens with the ritual for lighting Sabbath candles and includes the *kiddush,* blessing God for the fruit of the vine. Previously these last two rituals had appeared only at the end of the prayerbook in a section called "Services in the Home." Now they were made part of public worship in the apparent hope that individuals would learn—or relearn—them by experiencing them in the synagogue. All of this reflected the new appreciation of ceremony and tradition that had been gaining momentum in Reform Judaism for some time. Fewer Reform Jews—mainly those of long Reform lineage and recent rebels against Orthodoxy—still saw Judaism "as an embattled arena, wherein great truths and obsolete observances struggle for mastery."[78]

Surveys taken in 1928 and 1930 give a rough idea of the nature and extent of Jewish practice among Reform Jews in those years.[79] They reveal that about an eighth to a quarter of Reform Jews lit Sabbath candles in their homes on Friday evenings and recited the *kiddush.* The Passover *seder* was celebrated in a third of the Reform homes and the Hanukah lights kindled in 40 percent. About half fasted on Yom Kippur. While only a small percentage said grace at meals, close to half had instituted bedtime prayers for their children. The surveys did not inquire about dietary laws, which were observed rarely by the laity and by only few Reform rabbis. Regrettably, we possess no survey for the state of Reform observance a decade or two later. But judging from the role that symbol and ceremony began to play in the thinking of both laity and rabbis in the thirties and forties, one must conclude that, at least for the leadership, they were assuming much greater importance than in the classical past.

Already in 1926, rabbis who were polled on the subject attested to the appearance of hitherto neglected customs and ceremonies both in their synagogues and in the homes of their congregants. Lee K. Frankel, a well-known pioneer in social and health insurance and a prominent Reform lay leader, told the UAHC Biennial Council in 1927: "If we are to make progress, we must do so by retracing our steps. Progress, in our case, means not only discovering something new, but refinding something we have lost. I refer, in particular, to the home and the religious atmosphere which formerly surrounded it."[80] However, it was not until the late thirties that renewed interest in the ritual ambience of religion entered the institutional agenda. In 1935 the National Federation of Temple Brotherhoods requested the CCAR to work for the reintroduction of ceremonials into Jewish life. Two years later the Union Biennial gave sympathetic consideration to a resolution calling for the reintroduction of "traditional symbols, ceremonies, and customs" into Reform Sabbath services. Some temples now did introduce more traditional services. These were especially the newer congregations, those with a large number of east European Jews, or those with a sizable contingent of more traditionally oriented Liberal Jews fleeing from Germany. Other Reform temples—Emanu-El of New York, Sinai of Chicago, and B'nai Jehudah of Kansas City, for example—remained steadfastly classical. Reform Jews unhappy with the new trend began to level the criticism that Reform was becoming indistinguishable from Conservatism.[81]

In 1938 the Conference and the Union created a joint Committee on Ceremonies with its stated purpose to revive old rituals, introduce new ones, and experiment with original ceremonial materials. In the next few years the committee created unusual ceremonial objects and published leaflets to complement the liturgy then in use. As a result of the committee's efforts, Reform rabbis choosing to abandon the striped pants attire of the classical period could henceforth adorn their "rabbinical gown" with an *"atarah,"* a *talit*-like stole designed especially for their use. By 1945, ninety-one rabbis had chosen to do so. By then there were also 140 congregations that had purchased the committee's most remarkable creation: a *shofar* with a trumpeter's mouthpiece that made it easier to acquire a lost skill. Some congregations instituted the lighting of Hanukah candles in the temple using a large bronze *menorah* crafted for the committee. The largest number of synagogues purchased an abridged and illuminated Purim *megilah* that was written in English on genuine parchment. Reading the scroll of Esther had until then been rare in American Reform congregations, perhaps on account of discomfort with the vengefulness it contains. In the early forties, however, with Hitler a new Haman and Father Charles Coughlin preaching an antisemitic message in America, the Purim story no longer seemed inappropriate. Of the new leaflets, too, the most popular was one for the Purim service that especially emphasized Jewish survival. There were also pamphlets for such occasions as gathering in the synagogue *sukah,* special Sabbaths, and the installation of rabbis and congregational officers. For use outside the temple the committee offered ceremonials to accompany opening the door for the Prophet Elijah at the Passover meal and for the consecration of a new home.[82]

In the late thirties the Reform movement began to educate its laity in ritual observance. A decade earlier Abraham Z. Idelsohn, Professor of Jewish Music and Liturgy at Hebrew Union College, had written a popular, informative series of illustrated articles for the Brotherhoods describing the practices of traditional Jews. The articles seem clearly intended for a generation unfamiliar with orthodoxy: second or third generation Reform Jews and those with east European roots whose parents or even grandparents were already no longer observant. Idelsohn did not scoff even at superstitious customs, but neither did he recommend any practices to his readers. His articles were written to satisfy curiosity, not to present a model.[83] Very different in motivation and content was a book the UAHC published in 1937. Written by a member of its staff, Jacob D. Schwarz, and entitled *Ceremonies in Modern Jewish Life,* it was not a peek at the esoteric world of Orthodoxy, but a factual description of both traditional and "modern" observance. Schwarz, whose travels as the Union's Director of Synagogue Activities instructed him on the innovations of Reform temples around the country, here suggested to the leaders of other synagogues how they too could enrich the religious life of their congregations. In his popular *Leading a Jewish Life in the Modern World,* published in 1942, Rabbi Samuel H. Markowitz went yet a step further. His volume was a practical guide for individual Reform Jews who wanted to enrich their Jewish lives, a kind of how-to book for adults who had forgotten or had never learned. It contained, for example, a Hebrew grace at mealtimes, recipes for holiday dishes, sample place cards and directions for preparing the festive table. Dietary laws and the head covering for men at prayer were not recommended, but they received sympathetic treatment—in Reconstructionist terms—as Jewish folkways.

In the CCAR, reappropriation of tradition raised the possibility of a code for Reform Jewish practice. Felix Levy first suggested one in his president's message of 1937. To close what he considered the yawning gap between Reform and the Jewish masses, Levy proposed a Reform set of rules that would do nothing less than "re-enthrone the Halakhah as central to Jewish life."[84] But Levy's views were not shared by most of his colleagues. Some were utterly opposed to a code just as an earlier generation had been to the proposed authority of a creed or a synod. Others were sympathetic to giving Halakhah renewed attention but opposed binding formulas.

The leading personality in the large middle group was Solomon B. Freehof (born in 1892), one of the finest halakhic scholars in the Reform movement, and through his pulpit in Pittsburgh and his scholarly and popular writings, for many years among the most influential Reform rabbis. A talented mediator, it was also he who guided the revision of the *Union Prayer Book*.[85] Freehof thought there were dangers in a Reform code of practice: it would create a class of violators; it would give customs the status of divine law. If guidance was needed, it would be better for individual rabbis to write codes on their own (as had always been the case in Jewish history) rather than for the movement to do so collectively. But Freehof did favor expanding Reform practice and rooting it in Jewish tradition.[86] In 1944 he put forward a conception of the relation between belief and observance that for Reform Judaism was nothing less than revolutionary. From its earliest history in Europe, the movement had consistently declared that the ethical monotheistic faith was primary in Jewish religion, while ceremonies served only as means to enhance and preserve it. The Reformers' image repeatedly was the kernel and the shell. Freehof now reversed the relationship. In his book *Reform Jewish Practice and Its Rabbinic Background,* he argued that "the foundation of Jewish religious life is Jewish practice upon which are built habits of mind and attitudes toward the universe. . . . First we obey God's commandments and then we learn to understand God's nature. We do not begin with theology, we *arrive* at theology." That was a very traditional notion, but a heretical one in Reform. Where it led Freehof, though, was not to the primacy of Halakhah (law) in Reform but of Minhag (custom). He believed that in the twentieth century Halakhah was too inflexible to respond adequately to new challenges. Only Minhag, traditionally the creation of the masses, "the raw material which the law took up and shifted, rearranged, justified and embodied as the legal practice"—that alone could serve as the vehicle for the creative adaptation of tradition to modern life.[87] Reform, he argued, had developed its own Minhag, for example confirmation, the late Friday evening service, and men and women sitting together at worship. Following the paradigm of Minhag, it could, in a sense, now continue to build Reform Judaism from the bottom up. Freehof embarked on what became a decades-long endeavor to link actual Reform practice with traditional customs, providing it with historical roots, pointing out similarities and differences, encouraging experimentation. With Freehof's work, practice ceased

Solomon B. Freehof.

to be the clothing for ideas—as it was still in Kohler's theology—and entered the substance of Reform Judaism.

Just how seriously some of the younger Reform rabbis regarded Jewish observance became apparent in an extraordinary paper that William G. Braude (born 1907) of Providence, Rhode Island delivered at the CCAR convention in 1942.[88] Braude called on his colleagues to observe the dietary laws at least in part, to avoid riding on the Sabbath except to synagogue or to visit the sick, and to start each day with modified traditional worship. Scattering Hebrew words and phrases, Braude irreverently slaughtered everyone's sacred cow: the Jewish nationalism that had become worship of the nation, the social justice program that imitated Walter Rauschenbusch, and the questionable theories of biblical criticism that were regularly "served up as great delicacies in works bearing the imprimatur of the Hebrew Union College." Since at HUC *Wissenschaft des Judentums* had displaced *talmud torah* (traditional Jewish learning), he thought that perhaps rabbinical students would do well to spend a year at a yeshivah.

The Lithuanian-born, scholarly Braude was a different kind of Reform rabbi, one that was still a tiny minority. Citing Yehezkel Kaufmann and Hayyim Nahman Bialik, along with the German Jewish thinker Franz Rosenzweig, whose work was still little known in America, Braude put forward a traditionalism that would gain adherents only after the war. In the early forties most of his listeners swept aside his (exaggerated) criticisms and seemingly outlandish proposals. Reform rabbis and their congregants at the time were still too occupied disputing the great question that had occupied them for decades: Were the Jews only a religious community or also a people with national aspirations?

The Explosive Issue of Zionism

Despite the presence of active Zionists both in its lay leadership and among its most influential rabbis, the Reform movement in the years following World War I remained predominantly opposed to political Zionism.[89] Biennial councils of the Union and yearly conventions of the CCAR ended with everyone singing "En Kelohenu," the most widely known Jewish hymn, along with "America," emblematic of loyalty and love for the United States. But beginning in the early thirties, collective sentiment began to shift away from this clear dichotomy. Not only did the Reform Zionists become ever bolder, but those who opposed them willingly or unwillingly accepted one compromise after another. Finally, during World War II, the "non-Zionists," as the opponents of political Zionism then preferred to call themselves, felt they had become strangers in their own house. Some of them created a new organization, the American Council for Judaism. Yet after only a short time, nearly all of the rabbinical members abandoned this "last stand." Once there was a state of Israel, virtually every Reform Jew—if not a Zionist in the fullest sense—at least became its friend and supporter.

When Great Britain received the mandate for Palestine in 1920, the CCAR reiterated its earlier rejection of the Balfour formula declaring Palestine a national home for the Jewish people. It reemphasized that, in the Conference's view, Israel remained a religious community, not a nation. But its resolution also stated that the Reform rabbis rejoiced in the decision, recognizing that it would afford an opportunity for those Jews who wished to "live full, free, and happy lives" in Palestine. And it expressed readiness to assist in Palestine's reconstruction. Samuel Schulman, who chaired the Resolutions Committee that year, pointed out that, while certainly no endorsement of Zionism, it was not "the old aggressive anti-Zionism" either.[90] If the great majority of Reform rabbis during the twenties remained leery of Zionist political activity, that was not alone on account of the perceived ideological conflict between fulfillment of a worldwide mission and demographic national concentration or because they feared charges of disloyalty. It was also because they saw Zionism as a rival focus of Jewish identity. In their eyes Jewishness meant either first and foremost religion—which certainly included the obligation of helping one's fellow Jews in Palestine—or it meant a national identity that might or might not include affiliation with a synagogue. A universal faith and national aspirations, they believed, could not both be the essence of Jewishness. Most Reform rabbis who could not accept Zionism were fearful of subordinating their own Jewish sphere—religion—to a transreligious peoplehood. Hence they remained very touchy about working directly with the Zionist Organization of America even as—along with the laity—they supported the Palestine Emergency Fund, cooperated with the practically oriented Palestine Development Council, and played important roles in the Jewish Agency once it was expanded to include non-Zionists.[91]

But the line of demarcation between Judaism as a universal religion and Americanism as national loyalty was becoming less distinct as Reform Jews increasingly broadened their conception of Jewishness. The resulting confusion is well illustrated by an issue that came before the CCAR in 1930. While the rabbis were discussing revision of the *Union Hymnal,* Stephen Wise rose from his seat and inquired with mock innocence whether the words and music of "Hatikvah," the anthem of the Zionist movement, had been purposely omitted from the proposed volume. He immediately received the reply that only "devotional music" would be included. That quieted Wise until overnight he and his partisans discovered that the new hymnal would have room for "America" and "The Star-Spangled Banner." Caught in a contradiction, the opposition was no longer able to respond effectively. The next day, with support from graduates of the Jewish Institute of Religion—who formed a solid phalanx of young Zionists around Wise—a motion to include "Hatikvah" narrowly won adoption. The following year, in Wise's absence, a new resolution even mandated the inclusion of all five verses! When the revised *Union Hymnal* appeared in 1932, it included "Hatikvah" in a section called "The Nation" immediately following "The Star-Spangled Banner." Although the Conference could have put "Hatikvah" into a strictly religious category (and Wise himself had expounded on its *religious* message), it chose instead to recognize it as the national anthem of the Jewish people. At the time David Philipson wrote in his diary: "Had anyone told me twenty years ago that nationalism would make such inroads as to succeed in having the Zionist National hymn 'Hatikvah' incorporated into the hymnal published by the conference, I would have thought him ready for the lunatic asylum."[92]

However, by earlier resolutions, Reform Judaism remained officially opposed to political Zionism. It was not until the mid-thirties that the Zionists in the Conference felt they had sufficient strength to overturn that position among the rabbis. In 1933 the CCAR elected Felix Levy, an avowed Zionist, as vice president, and therefore to succeed as president in 1935. Only once earlier had the CCAR been headed by a Zionist, when Max Heller was its president from 1909 to 1911. By the time Levy took over the Conference presidency it appears that about half of the Reform rabbis were Zionists to some degree.[93] A few months earlier Rabbi Edward Israel had circulated a resolution to all his colleagues that would commit them to the program and prophetic ideals of the Palestine Labor movement. Out of 401 CCAR members at the time, 241 signed the resolution.[94] With the general impression abroad that the Zionist rabbis were rapidly gaining a majority, their opponents tried to "hold down the lid." One of them was ready to introduce a resolution in 1935 that would reaffirm the old anti-Zionism. But the anti-Zionists—as a few like Louis Wolsey of Philadelphia still called themselves—were no longer strong enough to reassert their position. They had to swallow a compromise that shifted the Conference position from opposition to neutrality. In a resolution that the 1935 convention adopted by a vote of eighty-one to twenty-five, the Reform rabbis declared that "acceptance or rejection of the Zionist program should be left to the determination of the individual members of the Conference themselves" and that the CCAR "takes no official stand on the subject of Zionism."[95] Just as the major Zionist organizations were neutral on religion in order to prevent division, so the Reform rabbis had now reached the point where only neutrality on Zionism could preserve harmony.

At the 1935 convention the CCAR listened to two papers on the subject of "Israel" as background for formulating a new plank on the subject in the proposed platform. The two men chosen to write the papers were the outstanding champions of the old classical Reform on the one hand and of the new Zionist variety on the other: Samuel Schulman of Temple Emanu-El, then aged seventy-one, and Abba Hillel Silver of The Temple in Cleveland, then a man of forty-two.[96]

In his paper Schulman recognized as much as anyone that in 1935 the roseate vision of a united humanity which had inspired the earlier Reform universalism had been severely blackened. Liberty and democracy were on the defensive all over the world; aggressive nationalism reigned in central Europe. But as Schulman saw it, that deplorable situation could not change the essential character of Israel. It was still a universally oriented religious community, or in the Hebrew designation that Schulman preferred, *Keneset Yisrael*. That meant Jewish secularists were only "potential Jews," who had not taken up their birthright. If Israel was immortal, Schulman noted, echoing Nachman Krochmal, that was only because it had staked its existence on "the inexhaustible God." Not Reform Judaism, but Jewish nationalism, represented the crucial break in Jewish historical continuity, for in its secularism it enthroned Israel in the place of God. Yet Schulman argued along with many younger men that Reform Judaism had swung too far away from Jewish distinctiveness. He heartily favored the reintroduction of elements from the particularizing ceremonial law. And near the end of his paper he introduced what, in a sense, was a Zionist note:

> Let us send a half a dozen young men or more to Palestine to bring the message of Progressive Judaism. . . . Perhaps just as the Babylonian Hillel taught something worthwhile to the Palestinians of his time, so we may have something worthwhile to teach the self-sufficient nationalists in Palestine of our time. Not to stand aloof is our aim, but recognizing the value of Palestine for hundreds of thousands of our brethren in Israel, let us help increase the settlement and, at the same time, let us bravely uphold the truth that Israel is not a *Goy* like other *Goyim*, but it always was, it is now, and if it is to live at all, will always be, a witness to God.[97]

In short, Schulman was ready to turn the Jewish mission at least partly inward: to infuse practical Zionist endeavor with the spirit of Reform.

The man chosen to present an opposing view, Abba Hillel Silver (1893–1963), was a remarkable combination of equally committed Reform rabbi and militant Zionist.[98] Born in Lithuania, Silver was one of the poor east European boys who traveled to Cincinnati for secular education at its university and ordination at Hebrew Union College. Only two years after completing HUC, Silver became the rabbi of The Temple in Cleveland, one of the leading Reform congregations. A man of commanding presence and authority, he was the undisputed leader of his congregation. The laity looked up to him and basked in his glory. A formal, dignified, and self-demanding man, Silver kept his distance from congregants; few knew him well. Like Solomon Freehof, Silver did not—especially in his busiest years—devote large amounts of time to pastoral duties. Yet he was almost always present to preach and to teach. His Sunday morning services (additional to those on the Sabbath) regularly drew over a thousand Jews and non-Jews. Religion remained for this third-generation rabbi—not less than for Schulman—the focus of Jewish identity. He was "first and foremost *Rabbi* Silver."

But Abba Hillel Silver was also a Zionist—from the time when, at age eleven, he and his brother founded the Dr. Herzl Zion Club in New York City. He grew up with Hebrew and Yiddish, and before he was thirty had established a name for himself as a Zionist orator. Silver was also a militant. With the rise of Hitler, he helped organize a controversial boycott of Nazi goods in the United States. Later—as one of the principal leaders of American Zionism—he condemned as illusory both the faith that Stephen S. Wise placed in President Roosevelt and the trust Chaim Weizmann had

Abba Hillel Silver.

Stephen S. Wise.

reposed in Britain's good intentions. Silver firmly believed that Jews had to wield their own political power or Zionism's enemies would trample it underfoot.

Silver's 1935 paper was a scholarly attack on the Pittsburgh Platform and on classical Reform Judaism in general. The Diaspora, as the Prophets understood it, was not a blessing but a tragedy; the mission of Israel not a higher stage of spiritual development but only "a noble compensatory ideal." Reform universalism, in its aspiration to convert the world, was more Pauline than prophetic. While Silver fully rejected neither the mission idea nor the universal messianic ideal, he refused to see either as a substitute for Jewish nationalism. At length he concluded: "It is the *total* program of Jewish life and destiny which the religious leaders of our people should stress today—the religious and moral values, the universal concepts, the mandate of mission, as well as the *Jewish people itself,* and all its national aspirations."[99] Their religion, as Silver saw it, remained the Jews' "crowning achievement," but to strip away the formative matrix would leave both Jews and Judaism with little prospect of survival. Two years later, in the Israel plank of the Columbus Platform, the CCAR moved in Silver's direction, affirming in general terms the aspirations of Jewish nationalism.

The Reform laity too was changing its position. Thousands of them belonged to congregations headed by nationally prominent Zionist rabbis. In 1930 one family out of five in the large cities already had a member who belonged to the Zionist Organization of America or to Hadassah.[100] Although the canard of dual loyalty doubtlessly bothered some, for others by the mid-thirties the looming Nazi menace was overwhelming such fears. Those of German Jewish background recognized the need to find refuge for German Jews in Palestine at a time when the United States would admit so few. For Reform Jews of east European origin, entering the movement in the twenties and thirties, the strict definition of Judaism as a religion, formulated in the nineteenth century, was a Reform element they did not absorb. In 1927 David Philipson could note that while all the other congregational rabbis in Cincinnati were nationalists, "the great bulk of the people among the Reformers are still with me." But in 1931 Ludwig Vogelstein told the Union's Biennial Council that the UAHC was now seriously divided on the matter of Zionism. He pleaded that delegates not bring up Zionist issues lest it create dissension detrimental to carrying out the Union's religious and educational program.[101]

However, like the Conference, the Union too still had the earlier hostile resolutions on its books. It was thus not possible to avoid the issue entirely without reinforcing the impression that the Reform laity was still committed to anti-Zionism. Even before the CCAR adopted the Columbus Platform, a UAHC Biennial Council, meeting in the winter of 1937, was presented with a pro-Zionist resolution that stopped short only of calling for a Jewish state. It read in part:

> We see the hand of Providence in the opening of the Gates of Palestine for the Jewish people at a time when a large portion of Jewry is so desperately in need of a friendly shelter and a home where a spiritual, cultural center may be developed in accordance with Jewish ideals. The time has now come for all Jews, irrespective of ideological differences, to unite in the activities leading to the establishment of a Jewish homeland in Palestine, and we urge our constituency to give their financial and moral support to the work of rebuilding Palestine.[102]

The resolution was adopted without discussion and with no recorded vote. That same year Robert P. Goldman, a Cincinnati attorney, became the first active Zionist to head the UAHC.

By the late thirties rabbinical opponents of Zionism felt pushed aside. Some of the older men even stopped attending CCAR conventions.[103] Nonetheless, an uneasy truce still prevailed. Neither the Union nor the Conference had come out in favor of a Jewish state, and therefore they had not endorsed the most controversial point on the political Zionists' agenda. On that issue the Union had not changed its earlier position and the CCAR had declared for neutrality. But then James Heller, a fervent Zionist, assumed the presidency of the CCAR in 1941 apparently determined to put the Conference solidly behind Zionist objectives. At the same time militant Zionists had begun clamoring for an independent fighting unit of Palestinian Jews that would serve under Allied command.

The Heller presidency and the Jewish armed force agitation provide the background for the 1942 CCAR debate that forced the non-Zionists to take drastic action. Thirty-three Zionist rabbis sponsored a resolution demanding that the Jewish population of Palestine "be given the privilege of establishing a military force which will fight under its own banner." The Committee on Resolutions recommended a substitute which spoke only of "the opportunity to fight in defense of their homeland." Passage of the original resolution meant favoring a proposal that would give Palestinian Jewry one of the accoutrements of political sovereignty—its own recognized military force flying its own flag—and an important bargaining chip following the war. The substitute resolution was essentially meaningless since it said nothing about a Jewish unit, and some 15,000 Palestinian Jews were in any case fighting as individuals in the British army.

Thus the postponed battle over political Zionism in the CCAR was finally joined. Although adoption of the original resolution amounted to rescinding the neutrality agreement of 1935, Heller, saying times had changed, would not rule it out of order for that reason. During the discussion, opponents of the original resolution pointed out that many laymen would have no sympathy for the proposed CCAR action: it would "deeply wound some of the finest religious spirits in our congregations." Solomon Freehof, ever the mediator, wanted the entire matter expunged from the proceedings. But when it came to a vote, the original resolution passed sixty-four to thirty-eight.[104] For the first time the Conference therefore put itself on the side of political Zionism's maximal ambitions. Those who remained unalterably opposed to a Jewish state now saw no alternative but public dissociation.

Some Reform laymen too were outraged by the CCAR resolution. One of them, Lewis L. Straus of Temple Emanu-El in New York, persuaded his senior rabbi, Samuel Goldenson, to take action. Goldenson, an ex-president of the CCAR, then met with Rabbis Louis Wolsey (also a former Conference president) of Rodef Shalom in Philadelphia and William H. Fineshriber of Keneseth Israel in the same city.[105] Together with twenty colleagues, they issued a call to those 160 rabbis they thought most sympathetic to join them in Atlantic City for "a meeting of non-Zionist Reform rabbis to discuss the problems that confront Judaism and Jews in the world emergency."[106] Learning of their intention, James Heller did everything he could to keep the meeting from taking place. He wrote letters to the CCAR membership justifying his action at the convention and raising the dire prospect of schism; together with the CCAR vice president, Solomon Freehof, he met with Wolsey and Goldenson to negotiate a settlement. If the rebellious rabbis would cancel their meeting, he proposed, then he would recommend a bylaw making neutrality on the Zionist issue a permanent rule and even admit that adoption of the Jewish army resolution had been a mistake. But since he refused to recommend that the army resolution be expunged from the minutes, his compromise was rejected.

Meanwhile, in May 1942, two months after the CCAR convention, the leading Zionists of the world gathered at the Biltmore Hotel in New York City. There they adopted a program which once and for all committed the movement (even Zionists had been divided on the issue!) to the tranformation of Palestine into a "Jewish commonwealth"—a less provocative term for a "Jewish state." By the time the non-Zionist rabbis met at the beginning of June, the Biltmore Program was on everyone's mind.

Zionism now meant nothing less than Jewish sovereignty, a position not favored by the American government and one which some non-Jews thought raised questions about Jewish loyalty to the United States.

The Atlantic City meeting took place with thirty-five men in attendance. It formulated a statement which, in a later revised form, gained the signatures of ninety Reform rabbis, about one-fifth of the Conference. The statement expressed readiness "to render unstinted aid to our brethren in their economic, cultural and spiritual endeavors" in Palestine. But it dissociated the signatories from "the political emphasis now paramount in the Zionistic program," and it added, "We cannot but believe that Jewish nationalism tends to confuse our fellow men about our place and function in society and also diverts our own attention from our historic role to live as a religious community wherever we may dwell." Julian Morgenstern, one of the signers, was so pleased with the statement that he sent it to the regular members of the Hebrew Union College faculty along with his suggestion that—of their own accord—they too might desire to sign it.[107]

Despite the statement's moderation, it aroused great ire. More than 700 rabbis of all three denominations, including James Heller as CCAR president, signed a resolution denouncing it. As laymen began to join the rebellious rabbis, a permanent organization came into being called the American Council for Judaism. But now increasingly the rabbinical founders withdrew as they became convinced that the more fervent lay supporters were more concerned with demonstrating Americanism than with upholding religious ideals. Nonetheless, for a time the ACJ was in a position to challenge Reform institutions. Its rabbinical members withheld support from the CCAR; those lay members who had been major contributors to the UAHC channeled their donations to the ACJ instead. Reform congregations in a number of places split into bitterly antagonistic Zionist and ACJ factions, with the rabbi sometimes a partisan of one side, sometimes trying to act as mediator. The Council was especially strong in the South and West, achieving its greatest success in Texas and California.[108] Its leadership claimed that the ACJ represented "the dominant convictions of the vast majority of Reform Jews in the United States." Although, in fact, the Council never realized large numbers, during the first few years of its existence it represented a formidable threat to Reform unity.

By the time the CCAR convened in June 1943, the lines were clearly drawn. Heller's presidential address was militantly pro-Zionist, unlike any previously delivered before the Conference. He accused the ACJ rabbis of harking back to Reform ideology as it was at the turn of the century and of muddying the waters at a desperate time. While reaffirming the neutrality resolution of 1935, the Conference then explicitly rejected the ACJ contention that Reform Judaism and Zionism were essentially incompatible and called upon colleagues in the Council, which "has already endangered the unity of the Conference," to terminate its existence.[109]

The Union of American Hebrew Congregations had passed no resolution on a Jewish army. But in 1943 it did join the American Jewish Conference, a representative assembly organized to deal with the problems of European Jewry and Palestine. When, after the persuasive oratory of Abba Hillel Silver, that conference passed a resolution calling for establishment of a Jewish commonwealth, the non-Zionist American Jewish Committee (composed predominantly of Reform Jews) withdrew its affiliation. The CCAR delegates supported the Palestine resolution, while the

UAHC representatives abstained since they required an Executive Board decision. Despite mounting pressures for the UAHC to withdraw like the American Jewish Committee, it chose to remain, ratifying most of the Conference statements but, for the sake of unity, taking no action on the Palestine resolution. That compromise angered individual supporters and entire congregations who now protested that by not severing its ties with the American Jewish Conference the Union was tacitly, if not explicitly, endorsing the Zionist position. The Baton Rouge, Louisiana temple even threatened to establish a new league of Reform congregations based on the Pittsburgh Platform of 1885. But the Union, now led by Rabbi Maurice Eisendrath, was unwilling to cut itself off from what was then the major decision-making body in American Jewry. Renewed isolation would have run counter to the current thrust of Reform Judaism.[110]

The closest lay equivalent to the rabbis' revolt occurred within Hebrew Congregation Beth Israel of Houston, Texas. A large and venerable congregation led by prominent German Jews, it had, as the only Reform temple in the city, recently absorbed a growing number of east European Jews who inclined more toward Zionism and traditional practice. The leadership became fearful that this new element might one day be in a position to outvote them and alter the fundamental character of the synagogue. To ward off such a possibility, on November 23, 1943 a special congregational meeting passed a resolution creating two classes of membership. New members seeking to vote would henceforth have to sign a set of principles committing them to classical Reform. Its text read in part:

> We consider ourselves no longer a nation. We are a religious community, and neither pray for nor anticipate a return to Palestine nor a restoration of any of the laws concerning the Jewish state. . . . We accept as binding only the moral laws of Mosaic legislation and Prophetic teaching. . . . We shall maintain and use in connection with our religious services only such ritual and ceremonies as may be approved by the Congregation from time to time and which may symbolize, in effective and beautiful form, the principles of our faith, and which are adapted to the progressive and liberal spirit of our times.

The leaders of the congregation also rejected Reform Judaism's commitment to racial justice and told their associate rabbi, Robert Kahn, he should not criticize the American Red Cross for separating the blood of whites and Negroes. Shortly thereafter they found themselves a new senior rabbi who would vigorously espouse their general point of view. Not satisfied to remain an isolated phenomenon, Beth Israel encouraged other congregations to adopt similar principles. In a widely circulated protest, its leaders argued that the Reform movement had betrayed the heritage of Geiger and Holdheim, of Einhorn and Wise. They attacked the UAHC for remaining in the American Jewish Conference and publishing Gamoran's nationalistic textbooks; the CCAR for its Jewish army resolution and the Zionistic service in its newly revised prayerbook; and the Hebrew Union College for requiring too much Hebrew from entering students and not providing enough Reform history and ideology in the curriculum.[111]

Solomon Freehof, now president of the CCAR, tried to persuade the Beth Israel people that they misunderstood the nature of Reform Judaism. The UAHC, for its part, sent a reply defending its activities. But these responses were relatively mild. Much harsher, but not atypical, was Stephen Wise's editorial, "The Shame of Houston," which spoke of the "Jewish Grand Inquisition," an "almost psychopathic local phenomenon," and a "loathsome brand of cowardly anti-Jewishness."[112] Both the Houston congregation and the American Council for Judaism aroused fierce anger, not so much because they espoused an outworn ideology but because they were perceived as saboteurs, as a serious danger to the Jewish people.[113] American Jewish leadership in 1944 was in the depths of despair. Millions of Jews were being annihilated in Europe and the gates of Palestine remained virtually closed. Despite their best efforts, American Jewish leaders were powerless to save their brothers and sisters. When the American Council for Judaism testified against Zionism before congressional committees and published its views in the press, when the Houston congregation announced to the world that the true Judaism excluded nationalism—they injured the prospect of realizing a safe refuge for at least those Jews who would survive Hitler. But they also aroused an overreaction born of frustration. Freehof believed that desperation was present on both sides. He told the CCAR in 1944:

> We knew that millions were going to their death and we were powerless to aid. We have failed our brothers at the time of their greatest need. All this induced in us a profound sense of frustration which has embittered us more than we can ever realize and is perhaps the cause, certainly it is the spur of our own wild fury at each other. We lash out against each other in the helpless rage typical of those who must admit their futility.[114]

The climactic battle between Zionists and non-Zionists in Reform Judaism bore much of this displaced anger.

When after the war recriminations gave way to sadness at the irreparable loss, and the establishment of the state of Israel, recognized by the United States, settled the basic Zionist issue, the American Council dwindled into insignificance and the Houston congregation forgot its principles. It became apparent that both represented the last major assertion of that classical Reform Judaism whose strength had been waning for many years. The Reform movement, as it emerged from World War II, was fundamentally different from what it had been after World War I. Its best-known rabbis were among the foremost leaders of American Jewry; step by step it was reintegrating traditions it had once cast aside; and it was educating its young people to see themselves as part of an entire people. But in numbers the American Reform movement remained relatively small. Only following the war, especially in the suburbs, and in response to the American religious revival, did the Reform movement enter its period of greatest expansion.

9

An International
Movement

The World Union for Progressive Judaism

In the two decades preceding World War I the European Reform movement had shown new life. The German Liberals had organized nationally, and in men like Hermann Cohen, Leo Baeck, and Max Wiener they enjoyed a new intellectual leadership of a caliber unmatched since the first half of the nineteenth century. In both England and France, Liberal congregations had emerged that adopted a more consistent and thoroughgoing program of religious change than either the West London Synagogue of British Reform or the aesthetically assimilated synagogues of the French consistories. The time now seemed ripe to unite the movement internationally, bringing together its various representatives in Europe and America. Not only would such a union strengthen Reform by creating a broader solidarity; it would also provide an instrument for spreading its message to those countries where it did not yet exist.

Just before the war, the German Liberals invited their counterparts in France, England, and America to send representatives to their regular conference in the fall of 1914 so that together they might take the first steps toward "a permanent union of all Liberal Jews."[1] But the war and residual tensions following it prevented that union from coming about for another dozen years. It was not until 1926 that the English Liberals—with Montefiore, Montagu, and Mattuck in the lead—were able to arrange a conference in London that began to weld Reform into an organizationally united world movement.

The first gathering, like those that would follow, was intended to be a religious and intellectual experience for its participants. The most thoughtful of the leaders delivered lectures and responded to critiques on the tenets of Liberal Judaism, its relation to modern thought and life, and its religious significance for the individual. Large and impressive delegations represented the British Liberals (the British Reform movement joined only later), the German Liberals, and the American Reformers, with a few individuals coming from other places. They gave reports on the history and state of the movement in their respective countries and pledged their support for what Lily Montagu called the fight against Jewish materialism and apathy. Their exhilaration and high anticipation, derived from a sense of common purpose, was spoiled only for a few minutes at one session when the predictably divisive issue of Zionism made an appearance. Before the conference Rabbi Stephen S. Wise had written to Lily Montagu warning her that there must be no attacks on Zionism at the conference.[2] When it opened, Claude Montefiore earnestly suggested that delegates steer entirely clear of that controversial subject, and for the most part they did. However, the sole British Liberal minister who was an active Zionist, Maurice L. Perlzweig, nonetheless insisted on raising the issue, claiming that an anti-Zionist movement could never hope to have influence in eastern Europe. Wise himself then eloquently pleaded for a declaration that Liberal Judaism and Zionism were not incompatible. But the chairman, Rabbi Israel Mattuck, replied with a ruling that the conference would steer entirely clear of that minefield by taking no official stance on Zionism whatever, and he begged Zionists and non-Zionists alike "for heaven's sake not to wreck this first International Conference by beginning to discuss these issues."[3] Though some were unhappy with the ruling, Zionism henceforth remained a bracketed question. Until the establishment of Israel, the world movement's neutrality was broken only by a resolution in 1937 recognizing the value of Palestine as a home for the large number of German Jews then fleeing Nazi oppression. As Montefiore and Montagu, two genuinely pious individuals, envisaged them, the purposes of the world movement were to become and to remain purely religious.

The most significant achievement of the 1926 conference was organizational. As in the case of the Jewish Religious Union two decades earlier, it was Lily Montagu who pressed the practical program: a permanent union that would serve the movement where it already existed and spread it to those places where it had not yet taken root. After a lively discussion on the differing meanings of the terms "Reform" and "Liberal" in various countries and languages, the delegates voted to call their new organization the World Union for Progressive Judaism (WUPJ). Claude Montefiore became its first president, Lily Montagu its honorary secretary and chief organizer.

Two years after the initial meeting in London, in 1928, the World Union held its first official conference in Berlin. In retrospect, it stands out as the high point in the World Union's early history. Attired in formal dress, the delegates gathered for their opening session in the ornate chamber of the one-time Prussian *Herrenhaus* (House of Lords). They worshiped together in the grand old *Neue Synagoge* and saw Lily Montagu ascend the pulpit of the Berlin Reform Congregation to deliver the first sermon ever given by a woman in a German synagogue. The highlight of the conference was the remarkable lecture by Leo Baeck entitled "The Message of Liberal Judaism for Today's Jew."[4] That message, Baeck told the delegates, lay not in any sermon but in the person; not in trying to keep Judaism current with the times, but in setting it *against* the times so as to help order the world for the Kingdom of God. In the nineteenth century Judaism had been too concerned with conformity, with how it appeared to others rather than with what it really was. Now the time had come to

Israel Mattuck, Lily Montagu, and Leo Baeck.

throw away the mirror and to look inside. True Liberalism was an intensive Judaism, a religion of piety that took itself seriously. Such a religion would always have to set the messianic against the existent, the future against the present, great unrealized ideas against the ways of the world. "Begin to create the future," he urged the delegates, and they long remembered his words.

Only a short time after the Berlin conference came the worldwide economic depression followed by the rise of Nazism. While still emerging from its nascent stage, the World Union found itself starved for funds and increasingly deprived of full support from its besieged German constituent. One quarter of its early budget came as a private donation from Montefiore, half from the American UAHC and CCAR. Altogether it amounted to less than £1,400. From the first, the WUPJ was a shoestring operation, a "pygmy" organization, as one of its later presidents said, with high aims but meager means. What funds it did have went mostly into exploring the possibility of spreading Progressive Judaism into those countries where it had not taken firm hold but where some interest had been shown. When the prospects looked good, the World Union sent representatives who helped organize the local Reformers and provided initial funding for a permanent spiritual leader. Such "proselytizing" at first aroused bitter criticism not only among the Orthodox, who apparently felt threatened, but also among some Reform Jews who thought it damaging to relations with traditional Jewry. The WUPJ leadership therefore took pains to respond only to requests made by groups already existing or in the process of formation.[5] It directed its efforts specifically to Jews who were not yet actively affiliated.

While for American Reform Judaism the World Union represented a distant entity of which most congregants remained unaware, in Germany, France, and England it served as an important link connecting the relatively weaker forces of the European Liberals and imbuing them with a sense of common purpose. German Jewish Liberalism especially required such a larger, strictly religious framework. It emerged from World War I having lost the momentum generated in the prewar decades. Antisemitism had reared its head in 1916 when Jews were suspected of not participating equally on the front lines and again later when they became scapegoats for the German defeat. Thus the struggle against discrimination and defamation remained foremost in succeeding years, although the Weimar Republic allowed Jews far wider opportunities for participation in public life. In this ongoing defense effort, Liberal Jews depicted Zionists as undermining the cause. Their national organization, with thirty-seven local political blocs, was determined first and foremost to uproot Zionism; very secondarily did it also advance liberal religion. Its weekly newspaper, the *Jüdisch-Liberale Zeitung,* reflected that sense of priorities. Most voluntary contributions went to the *Central-Verein,* the Jewish defense organization. Unlike their counterparts in the United States, who belonged to independent Reform congregations, Liberal Jews in Germany were part of a community in which the Liberals were simply a faction. Their specific identity emerged only at times of community elections; their affiliation inspired no encompassing or enduring loyalty. Only a few individuals among the Liberals, the rabbis and a small number of laity, were willing to make sacrifices of time and money for the religious values of Liberal Judaism. Bound to fellow Jews by vaguely articulated ethnic ties, having learned only a smattering of Judaism from religion classes held in the German schools, Liberal Jews were religiously apathetic. Their synagogues remained nearly empty most of the year. Mixed marriages grew rapidly to proportions that endangered group survival.[6]

While the Hamburg Temple's liturgy had become increasingly traditional and Hebraic, so that for all practical purposes it was now simply another Liberal synagogue, the Berlin Reform Congregation, out of pious regard for its founders, remained rigid in its radicalism. Its 500 or so members continued to worship on Sunday mornings (though also on Friday evenings) using a liturgy studded with a grand total of thirty-nine Hebrew words. Its prayerbook for the entire year consisted of only sixty-three pages.[7] For their part, the Liberal synagogues continued to use a variety of prayerbooks until 1929 when a common liturgy (the so-called *Einheitsgebetbuch*)— still traditional by American standards—made its appearance.[8] By the end of the twenties, the late Friday evening service had been introduced in Berlin and a few other cities. But still in the 1930s German Liberal Judaism counted only a single synagogue in Berlin where men and women sat together.[9]

With the Depression came the economic collapse of the "good old Jewish middle class," which had been the chief support of Liberal Judaism. Facing a much more severe antisemitism, Liberals now gave even less attention to religion and ever more to Jewish defense.[10] But the Hitler years—ironically—had an opposite effect. The Liberals' political program was now self-admittedly bankrupt. No longer recognized as Germans, most Liberal Jews began to intensify their Jewishness. The longest to hold out in its earlier ideology was the Berlin Reform Congregation. Its preachers continued to insist that nothing had changed and that "patriotism is religion." They still opposed Zionism, closing their eyes as long as possible to the transformed situation of German Jewry and continuing to hope for a Jewish future in the Fatherland. The Liberal Jews, however, rapidly reversed course. Their principal leader, Leo Baeck, assumed the agonizing task of directing a united organization that represented all German Jews to the Nazi government. Their seminary in Berlin became the center for an unprecedented program of adult education. The most important Liberal lay leader, Heinrich Stern, now called for more rigorous religious practice, reconciliation with Zionism, and expanded knowledge of Hebrew.[11] Once virtually abandoned Liberal synagogues began to fill up regularly as persecuted Jews chose them as places to "huddle" securely and reaffirm their own worth. Talented younger rabbis—themselves Zionists—preached dramatically on Israel's survival in spite of its enemies, disguising Nazi foes under the rubric of Pharaohs or Philistines—though that hardly fooled the Gestapo agents who were regularly present. Public Passover *sedarim* and Purim celebrations assumed undreamed of significance and attracted more Jews than could find seats. When the cantor chanted the name of Haman from the Scroll of Esther everyone heard "Hitler" and the noise was deafening.[12] But on the Night of Broken Glass *(Kristallnacht),* November 9–10, 1938, nearly all the synagogues in Germany went up in flames. German Judaism was approaching its end. The country that had been the matrix of the Reform movement now spewed forth destruction. In its own land German Liberal Judaism perished, and only among refugees from the conflagration would it live on a while longer.

In France and England Progressive Judaism made only slight progress during the interwar years. The Union Libérale Israélite, still led by Rabbi Louis-Germain Lévy, grew slightly, incorporating some Russian, Polish, and Oriental Jews. It expanded its synagogue to 450 seats and created a small youth movement. But in France, as elsewhere in Europe and in America during the twenties and thirties, religious apathy reigned supreme.[13] Across the channel, in Great Britain, Liberal Judaism had grown considerably in London (its main synagogue was now the largest in the British Isles), but until 1928 it remained unable to spread outside the English capital. British Reform Judaism was more successful in that regard, having earlier established itself in Bradford and Manchester, but in London it was now the smaller of the two movements. In 1930 the London male membership of both groups stood at about 750 for Reform and 1,250 for the Liberals. Together they made up about one-sixth of the affiliated Jews. Both movements, but especially Reform, received renewed impetus when Liberal rabbis and laity from Germany began to immigrate in sizable numbers during the late thirties, in some instances creating their own congregations. By 1940 total family membership of the two movements had risen to 6,000. Once the Reform movement introduced mixed seating in 1923, and in 1928 began to make ideologically more radical revisions in its liturgy, the gap between Reform and Liberal Judaism in England narrowed, making possible British Reform's 1930 entry into the World Union.[14]

Potentially the largest field for Reform expansion lay to the east, among the Jewish masses of Russia and Poland. As noted earlier, some Russian maskilim of the mid-nineteenth century argued vigorously for changes in Jewish law and a few congregations in various cities modified their religious services, yet ideological reform did not take hold. By the end of the century eastern Jewish communities were divided among competing factions of Orthodox, nationalists, and socialists. The larger cities of interwar Poland did have modernized synagogues that were called "progressive" or "German." Services there were decorous and featured an edifying sermon in Polish or German. In Lvov (Lemberg) one of the synagogues even used an organ, confirmed girls, and abbreviated the service. And Liberal tendencies also persisted among those German Jews who remained in the parts of Poland ceded by Germany after World War I. But the largely wealthy and assimilated Polish Progressives possessed little sense of belonging to a world movement.[15]

Soon after the World Union was formed, it decided to launch a survey of religious conditions among the Jews of Poland, and at its Berlin conference delegates listened to a Polish visitor plead: "We need a real mission; we need people who will bring us Liberalism from the outside." In 1929 the WUPJ sent Meir Lasker, a young Reform rabbi who was fluent in Hebrew and Yiddish, to spend a few months in the larger cities and build up interest. Though Lasker's visit consumed a third of the World Union's budget that year, it was not successful. The most serious of the enlightened Jews were interested in Jewish culture and modern Jewish studies, but not in a Jewish identity that was essentially religious. Reluctantly, the World Union abandoned its efforts. The prospects were not sufficiently hopeful to warrant further expenditures of its limited funds.[16] Moreover, opportunities in other lands looked much more promising.

Among European countries which possessed no Reform movement, Holland seemed to offer the best chance of success. Here the Union had found a few interested individuals who invited Lily Montagu to lecture in January 1930. Later that year Rabbi Lasker settled in the Hague and began to conduct regular services. Although Lasker remained only a few months; Dutch Progressives, despite bitter opposition from the Orthodox, successfully founded a union of "Liberal Religious Jews in Holland" in 1931, and by 1932 there were regular services both in the Hague and in Amsterdam. Among the 136 members at that time were a number of Zionists, one of them the editor of the Dutch Zionist newspaper—and the Hague congregation even used the "Palestinian" pronunciation of Hebrew. Beginning in 1933, the influx of German Jewish refugees to Holland strengthened—and overwhelmed—the congregations. In Amsterdam by the late thirties only 20 percent of the 175 affiliated families were of native Dutch origin. The congregations grew with sufficient rapidity so that in 1937 the World Union could hold its conference in Amsterdam, dramatizing its first—and only—successful interwar venture to spread Progressive Judaism in Europe.[17]

In one other European country—but before the founding of the World Union—had Progressive Judaism succeeded in establishing itself. Religious reform had come to the Jews of Sweden as early as the nineteenth century as an import from Germany. Beginning in the 1850s, the leading Jewish community of Gothenburg introduced an organ and a liturgy based on various German Liberal prayerbooks. Reform ritual reached other Swedish cities as well, in each instance becoming the norm for an entire community. However, just because these communities had to represent all Jews, Swedish Liberalism remained formally outside the World Union and was connected with it only through the reports on its status delivered by an avid proponent at the early WUPJ conferences.[18]

New Plantings Abroad

Unquestionably the most extraordinary participant in the 1926 founding conference of the World Union was Miss Leah Jhirad, who spoke to the gathering on "Liberal Judaism in India." She told of the establishment of a Liberal circle in Bombay the previous year. Modeled on the British Liberal prototype, it had taken the same name: Jewish Religious Union. The Bombay Union had also adopted the British Liberal prayerbook, held regular Sabbath services, and listened to lay sermons in English or Maratti. Women, some dressed in white saris, sat with men and joined in singing melodies, a few of which were unknown outside of India. The group studied together and held Hebrew and religion classes for the children. At that time the congregation consisted of about forty members belonging to seventeen families, most of them young professionals of European origin. Some adherents, especially later, were also educated members of the ancient Bene Israel group. From the first, the Bombay JRU became a regular constituent of the WUPJ, managing as best it could with no rabbinical leadership except for a few years in the late fifties and early sixties when it built Temple Rodef Shalom and enjoyed a short period of efflorescence and growth. In the late sixties the congregation declined as its members began to emigrate to Canada, Australia, and Israel.[19]

It soon became apparent to the leadership of the World Union that the brightest prospects for expanding Progressive Judaism lay in other parts of the British Empire—in South Africa and in Australia. Neither had a Progressive movement, both had a growing Jewish population. South African interest in Progressive Judaism began in 1929 when the Professor of Music at Hebrew Union College, Abraham Z. Idelsohn, used the occasion of a visit to his brother in Johannesburg to deliver a lecture on Reform Judaism. A provisional committee was formed and sought help from the World Union, which in 1933 sent a young HUC graduate, Rabbi Moses Cyrus Weiler, to the South African capital. Weiler fortuitously possessed precisely the qualifications needed for success in the face of severe Orthodox hostility. He combined a forceful personality with oratorical talent and a flair for organization. Most important in a community that prided itself on Zionism and conservatism, Weiler possessed impeccable Zionist credentials and the wisdom to realize that radical reform simply would not fit the local environment. While South African Progressive Judaism drew on the liturgy and educational materials of American Reform, it was always Zionist and more traditional. From the beginning, men and women sat together in unassigned seats, but the men (and women) were required to wear hats, and on Saturday morning most men wore a *talit*. Services soon took place daily. The Progressive *Guide of Practice* prescribed that no forbidden foods could be served at congregational functions and that rabbis might not smoke publicly on the Sabbath. Conversions were actively discouraged lest, in multiplying and creating a majority of converts, they become "the surest way of sounding the death knell of the Reform movement in South Africa." Children of mixed marriages, educated in Judaism, required conversion, either through Bar or Bat Mitzvah (the latter introduced as early as 1938), or by certification if they were older, even if their mother was Jewish and therefore in terms of Halakhah they were Jewish by birth. The religious traditionalism of Progressive Judaism in South Africa and the readiness of the Orthodox to make some changes best explain why Conservative Judaism did not develop there.[20]

The passion for social justice, nurtured especially by American Reform Judaism, proved frustratingly problematic in an environment of severe racial segregation. Weiler softened the contradiction for his congregation in 1945 by urging it to found and support a school for native children in the poverty-stricken Alexandra township of Johannesburg. Such welfare work, and joint statements together with Christians condemning specific acts, were as far as the Jewish community and its rabbi were willing—or able—to go. When another Progressive rabbi, in 1955, openly and alone condemned government policy, his position in South Africa became rapidly untenable.[21]

By 1946 the Progressive congregation in Johannesburg could boast 3,000 members. Twenty years later, the South African Union for Progressive Judaism had synagogues in twelve cities throughout southern Africa. Its roughly 8,000 member families in 1955 constituted 15 to 20 percent of the affiliated Jews. That the percentage did not rise higher was apparently the result of a situation similar to that in Great Britain where the established Orthodoxy, with its Chief Rabbi, provided social prestige without requiring Orthodox practice. With Weiler's departure for Israel in 1956, increasing tensions between whites and blacks, consequent Jewish emigration, and increasing difficulty in securing rabbis who would settle permanently, the Progressive community began to decline. By the mid-seventies, its long-term future had become uncertain.[22]

In a number of respects the history of Progressive Judaism in Australia parallels its development in South Africa. Here too it was the World Union that responded to the first stirrings of local interest, and by securing effective rabbinical leadership, stimulated a movement that was able to take root. In Australia too one of the keys to Progressive Judaism's success was its relative conservatism. Its beginnings are linked with the name of Ada Phillips, a young Australian woman who met Mattuck and Montagu when she visited London in 1928. Back in Australia she aroused interest in Melbourne, and the World Union responded by providing the initial salary for an American rabbi. But that first rabbi was inclined to radicalism and most of the Liberal nucleus in Melbourne was not eager to depart sharply from tradition. Not until the World Union sent Herman Sanger, a German Liberal rabbi who had come as a refugee to London in 1936, did Reform begin to make real progress. Like Weiler, Sanger was a charismatic leader. He possessed excellent scholarly credentials, spoke well from the pulpit, was a Zionist, and, above all, he was quite willing that the visible externals of practice remain traditional—as they had in German Liberalism. With the influx of other refugees from Germany, his constituency grew. Melbourne's Temple Beth Israel introduced mixed seating and the *Union Prayer Book,* but as in South Africa, *kipah* (head covering) and *talit* were the custom. Many congregants avoided eating the biblically prohibited foods. Australian Progressive Judaism differed, however, in its policy toward converts. While here too—as in England and South Africa—Orthodoxy actively discouraged conversion, and in accordance with Halakhah ruled it out absolutely when marriage was a motive, the Australian Progressives welcomed converts, although experience proved that they but rarely became active members of the community. Progressive rabbis did not officiate at mixed marriages, but they accepted the children of such unions as Jews, even when the non-Jew was the mother, provided they had received a Jewish education. Relations between Progressives and Orthodox remained tolerable during the thirties and forties but deteriorated in the fifties when a new extremism pushed aside the more compromising ways of the earlier Anglo-Orthodoxy and traditionalist rabbis ceased to appear on the same platform with Progressives. At the same time the Progressives, having grown in number and proportion, were pressing for greater civic recognition.

From Melbourne Progressive Judaism in Australia spread to Sydney (1938), whose Temple Emanuel soon equalled the Melbourne synagogue in membership. Following World War II, both congregations established religion schools and branches in the suburbs, areas that were neglected by the Orthodox. Congregations now also came into existence in Perth and Adelaide. Across the Tasman Sea, in New Zealand, local Progressives established synagogues in Auckland and Wellington, the former including an especially large number of converts. As the two congregations together had only about 200 families, neither was able to secure the services of a full-time rabbi. By the eighties, the Australian and New Zealand Union for Progressive Judaism numbered eleven congregations with about 8,000 individual members. It accounted for about 20 percent of affiliated Jews in a total Jewish population of 74,000. Two Progressive day schools, in Melbourne and Sydney, were providing some 750 pupils with an intensive Jewish education and the Reform Zionist youth movement, NETZER *(Noar Tziyoni Reformi)*, was the largest Jewish youth movement in Australia. Though assimilation and apathy of course remained major concerns, no South African storm clouds hovered over Progressive Judaism in Australia.[23]

Of all the new Progressive Jewish communities none owed more to the Nazi-instigated German Jewish diaspora than those established in South America.[24] About 50,000 refugees made their way across the ocean to Argentina, Brazil, and the other countries of the continent. Many of them had been professionals in Germany; now they became businessmen, by necessity learning Spanish or Portuguese while German remained their mother tongue and the language with which they were most comfortable. A large percentage had worshiped in Liberal synagogues and longed for their familiar sounds when Jewish holidays approached. Among the refugees were a few Liberal rabbis who were encouraged to transplant the accustomed ritual onto foreign soil. For decades the sermons and congregational bulletins of the South American Progressive congregations remained mostly in German and their services attracted mainly immigrant families. The liturgy came from the *Einheitsgebetbuch* or other German rites; men and women sat apart—as had been customary in the old country. Only very gradually, with the coming of age of the second, native-born generation, did a more indigenous Progressive Judaism emerge in South America.

The first congregation to be established was the Congregação Israelita Paulista (CIP), founded in São Paulo, Brazil in 1936. It coalesced around Rabbi Fritz (Frederico) Pinkuss, an ordinee of the Liberal seminary in Berlin. Like a German unified community *(Einheitsgemeinde)*, it included a Conservative as well as a Liberal sector, each with its own religious services, but the latter by far the larger. Since it was not wholly Liberal in composition—and also because of obstacles in Brazilian law—the CIP did not associate itself directly with the World Union, though Pinkuss personally was a member. The WUPJ played a much larger role in establishing a Liberal congregation to the north, in Rio de Janeiro. Lily Montagu had been able to secure Rabbi Heinrich (Henrique) Lemle's release from a German concentration camp, and with the help of a Joint Distribution Committee grant, made possible his immigration to Brazil. There he established the Associação Religiosa Israelita (ARI) in 1942. Like Pinkuss, Lemle was a Hochschule ordinee, who sought to create an *Einheitsgemeinde,* but he was less traditional in his own practice and more eager to link himself and his congregation with the world movement. After the war, Pinkuss and Lemle compiled a Portuguese and Hebrew Liberal liturgy for the Brazilian congregations. Yet the persistently traditional and German atmosphere in both synagogues resulted, in the sixties, in the formation of a small breakaway congregation in São Paulo that called itself Comunidade Shalom, introduced mixed seating and more Portuguese into the service, and affiliated directly with the WUPJ.

To the southwest, in Argentina, German Jewish immigrants founded the Culto Israelita de Belgrano (CIB) in Buenos Aires in 1939. As in Brazil, they clustered around a German Liberal rabbi who reproduced the service with which they were familiar. After the war, a second congregation, Lamroth Hakol, sprang up in a northern suburb. It drew in some non-German families and departed from the CIB mainly by introducing mixed seating. A strictly indigenous Reform congregation appeared only with the establishment of Congregación Emanu-El in 1964. It produced its own liturgy in Hebrew and Spanish and addressed its appeal to Argentinian Jews of diverse backgrounds. Though Emanu-El was larger than Comunidade Shalom in São Paulo, which it most closely resembled, both of these newer congregations, with about 300 families between them, were overshadowed by the much bigger and more traditional Liberal synagogues. The existence of a Conservative seminary in Buenos Aires also turned the attention of religious Jews more toward a moderate traditionalism. Not conducive to Progressive Judaism at all was the atmosphere created by Latin American Catholicism, which until recently remained an unbreached bastion of authoritarianism and conservatism that induced a polarization between rigid, politically reactionary religion and rebellious atheism. Nonetheless, by the mid-seventies the Progressive movement in South America consisted of six congregations in Brazil and Argentina that were bound to the World Union with closer or looser ties. Together they comprised some 5,000 families, a not inconsiderable representation within communities largely indifferent to religious Judaism.

Progressive Judaism was evident in other Latin American countries as well, with circles emerging in Santiago, Chile, and Montevideo, Uruguay. To the north, Kol Shearith Israel in Panama translated prayers from the American *Union Songster* into Spanish in order to attract young people to its basically English-speaking congregation. In Guatemala a succession of Spanish-speaking rabbis, who had obtained NFTS-funded World Union scholarships to HUC, tried to maintain interest in Reform Judaism with a modicum of success during the 1960s. The venerable Sephardi congregation of Curaçao, merged with Reform Temple Emanuel dating back to 1864, was also served in those years by a Reform rabbi. In Cuba an English-speaking Reform congregation, founded in 1904, for half a century dominated an active Jewish community until the Castro revolution virtually put an end to all Jewish life in 1959.[25]

A final example of the transplantation of German Liberal Judaism is presented by the earliest Reform congregations in the land of Israel.[26] Despite the World Union's official neutrality on Zionism, in 1934 it created an advisory committee for Palestine with the understanding that its objectives would be "of a definitely and exclusively religious character." By then German Liberal Jews had begun emigrating to the land of Israel in increasing numbers, and their Liberal rabbis, as well, were contemplating *aliyah*. A year later, Max (Meir) Elk, who had been a Liberal rabbi in Stettin, settled in Haifa and founded Bet Yisrael, a congregation composed of German immigrants. Similar congregations arose shortly thereafter in Jerusalem (Emet Ve-Emunah) and Tel-Aviv (also Bet Yisrael). Their religious services displayed the accustomed decorum and the congregants sang the familiar Lewandowski melodies. Sermons were partly in German, partly in Hebrew. As in Germany, men and women sat apart, without a partition between them. Unlike the German Liberal congregations, however, the Palestinian ones used a traditional prayerbook (with omissions) and dispensed with all musical instruments. Their three rabbis hoped to win the right to perform marriages from the Orthodox authorities. And in fact Rabbi Kurt (David) Wilhelm in Jerusalem succeeded in that quest after he assured the Chief Rabbi of Palestine, Abraham Isaac Kook, that his congregation did not have mixed seating, an organ, or a revised prayerbook. In Haifa, Rabbi Elk for a time possessed the same privilege until he refused to sign a statement that his wedding ceremonies would always conform strictly to prescribed ritual. In Tel-Aviv, Rabbi Manfred (Meir) Rosenberg had no success with the local chief rabbi at all. Despite such difficulties, the congregations drew a large attendance on the holidays, together attracting more than 2,000 worshipers on Yom Kippur eve in 1938. Their rabbis persuaded the World Union to send them regular support from its small budget and from special contributions, but a persistent effort to gain funding from the Zionist movement was unsuccessful.

Each of the congregations sought to extend its influence. Emet Ve-Emunah instituted a cultural program that featured lectures by leading scholars of the Hebrew University. Bet Yisrael in Haifa started a library and a youth group. The rabbis of all three congregations spoke on Liberal Judaism outside their immediate circle, venturing even to the secular agricultural settlements, which in that period were ideologically hostile to religion. But the congregations remained essentially *Landsmannschaften,* ethnically based societies of German Jews. And even their Liberal heritage was soon forgotten as, after the war, some members and their children drifted off into the dominantly secular environment, while those that remained turned ever more toward tradition. The Tel-Aviv congregation soon sputtered out of existence; the Haifa synagogue became Orthodox. And the Jerusalem congregation, under Wilhelm's successor, withdrew from the World Union after it ceased to supply further funds; it then joined the newly formed Conservative World Council of Synagogues. Progressive Judaism's first attempt to establish itself in Palestine through congregations thus proved a failure. It succeeded only in providing a religious home for Liberal German refugees who sought a familiar milieu during their first difficult years in the country. World Union funds helped the congregations survive for a time, but eventually the pressures of a secular society and a hostile, favored Orthodoxy squeezed out the middle they sought to establish. After twenty years, Progressive Judaism in what was now the state of Israel almost had to start anew.

Almost—because it had succeeded in creating one lasting institution. Rabbi Elk realized soon after his arrival in Palestine that Progressive Judaism could not succeed in a Jewish society if it established synagogues alone. It would have to address a challenge of which Diaspora Reformers had spoken frequently but which, because they lived in a non-Jewish majority, they could never meet—the task of fully integrating religion with modern life. In Palestine, Elk argued, that challenge could be met only through education. Only if the Progressive movement were to organize its own schools could it hope to influence a younger generation that might be able to create an appropriate synthesis for Jews living in their own land. In secular schools Jewish religious sources were taught simply as history and literature, in Orthodox ones as the unmediated word of God. Progressive Judaism would have to raise up a generation that gravitated to neither extreme. At first Elk was able merely to bring together a few children from his congregation during two afternoons a week. But by 1939 he had succeeded in creating the beginnings of a school that eventually bore the name of Leo Baeck. By 1961 that school had 1,000 pupils from diverse economic and ethnic backgrounds. Half its curriculum was devoted to a Progressive interpretation of Jewish sources; its classes related Judaism to social ethics and modern science. All pupils studied Arabic language and culture in the hope that such knowledge would better relations between Jews and Arabs in a city with a large Arab population. It was the Leo Baeck school that would produce some of the first native-born candidates for the Israeli Progressive rabbinate.[27]

In the Postwar World

During the years immediately following World War II, the World Union was as concerned with rebuilding Progressive Judaism in Europe as with establishing it in the land of Israel. In 1938 Leo Baeck had become its second president, following the death of Claude Montefiore. But during the next seven years Baeck was scarcely able to lead. His activities on behalf of German Jewry fully occupied him until 1943, when he was deported to the concentration camp at Theresienstadt. Only after the war, when following his miraculous survival he lived mostly in England, was Baeck able to assume real leadership. At the World Union's second postwar conference, in 1949, Baeck introduced a metaphor for the new situation of world Jewry that many would repeat thereafter. Jewish life, Baeck noted, had seldom been a circle. Usually it had been an ellipse, possessing two foci. That had been true for Babylonia and the land of Israel in ancient times. It was also true in the medieval period; and at present once again there were two foci: the new state of Israel and the larger mass of Jews in the Diaspora. The former was necessarily national in character, the latter international in its aims. The task of the World Union, Baeck believed, should be to direct its energies to both.[28] The international role that Baeck envisaged found expression soon thereafter when the WUPJ gained consultative status as a nongovernmental organization with the United Nations Economic and Social Council, UNESCO, and UNICEF. It was even able to exercise occasional influence, as on the freedom of religion clause in the international Declaration on Human Rights.[29] But the WUPJ's main non-Palestine objective in the first postwar years was to rebuild Progressive Judaism in Europe.

The demise of German Jewry had meant that the World Union was now bereft of what had been one of its three major constituents. For a time it sought to retrieve the loss by devoting a large portion of its energy and funds to the difficult project of reviving Liberal Judaism in postwar Germany. It sent a succession of German-born American rabbis to Berlin and fostered the reemergence of a Liberal bloc there. But for decades it was unable to persuade any Progressive rabbi to remain in the one German city that did have a sizable number of surviving and returning Liberal Jews. Only one synagogue in Berlin held Liberal services, and they were conducted very much in the old manner: organ and decorum, men and women sitting apart.[30]

More successful than the German effort was the World Union's revival of Progressive Judaism in Holland. Both of its prewar rabbis had been murdered in the Holocaust. Yet by 1949 there was again a Liberal congregation in Amsterdam with a new rabbi of Dutch origin. By the mid-fifties it was sufficiently vibrant that the World Union could again hold its conference there in 1957, appropriately choosing to make Amsterdam's native son Baruch Spinoza the major subject of discussion. Smaller congregations followed in the Hague, Rotterdam, and Arnhem.[31] In Sweden, too, Progressive Judaism reemerged after the war, especially following Rabbi Kurt Wilhelm's move from Jerusalem to Stockholm. As in Germany, the Swedish Liberals remained part of an *Einheitsgemeinde*. After a time they created a Liberal Forum to discuss and propagate Progressive Judaism.[32]

To a limited extent Progressive Judaism now also gained a foothold in three European countries which it had barely touched before the war. In Switzerland Progressive Jews in 1957 founded a national organization that joined the World Union, held regular assemblies, published a journal, and by the seventies were holding religious services in a number of Swiss cities.[33] In 1965 a few dozen Jews in Belgium, some of them English speaking, formed the Union Israélite Libérale de Belgique and held High Holiday services for the first time that year.[34] Even in Italy a few very interested individuals formed an Unione Italiana per l'Ebraismo Progressivo. Its activities, which did not include religious services, consisted mainly of publishing the quarterly *La Voce—Ha-Kol* and holding conferences to discuss religious issues.[35]

The World Union undertook its most ambitious European project in France. Rabbi Louis-Germain Lévy had emerged from hiding in Lyons and, as a man now in his seventies, returned to Paris in 1945 to rebuild the severely damaged synagogue on rue Copernic. Under his successor, André Zaoui, the congregation prospered. By 1948 it numbered about 300 members, by the early sixties 600. It drew in a number of French intellectuals, including the well-known writer Edmond Fleg, and created a Hillel Center for Jewish university students in the Latin Quarter. It abandoned Sunday services, allowed the liturgy to become more traditional, and included more Hebrew.[36] In 1955 the World Union met in Paris to launch a project that Zaoui had urged upon it: the establishment of a new Liberal seminary in Europe to replace those the Nazis had destroyed. With no longer any rabbi to support in Berlin and the Israeli movement temporarily in eclipse, the World Union decided to focus its attention and funding on this promising possibility. Under Zaoui's leadership and the World Union's aegis, the Institut International d'Études Hébraïques opened in Paris in October 1955 with seven students who intended to become rabbis or teachers. Support came from the World Union, the Joint Distribution Committee, German reparations funds, and individual donors. It soon employed a permanent faculty of five plus visiting professors who were among the best known Israeli scholars. It even succeeded in publishing two volumes of a scholarly journal. The first ordination took place in 1960 following an oral examination by Progressive rabbis from abroad. Although a few more ordinations followed, during the late sixties and early seventies the school dwindled, eventually becoming solely an institution for adult and teacher education.[37] Its French-language instruction had attracted only a very limited number of rabbinical students, mostly of North African origin; funding from reparations had dried up; and Zaoui himself had gone on *aliyah* to Israel. But most importantly, far more Progressive Jews spoke English than French. In succeeding years French Progressive Judaism did establish a second synagogue in Paris, and small Liberal circles arose in Nice and Marseilles, but the fulcrum of Progressive Judaism in Europe—after the war as before it— lay in England.[38]

Both Liberal and Reform Judaism in Great Britain grew impressively during the postwar years. From a combined total of six congregations in 1940 they had together reached nearly fifty by 1977 with membership well over 30,000. Though spread from Bournemouth in the south to Glasgow, Scotland and Dublin, Ireland, Progressive Judaism in the British Isles proved especially attractive to families freshly settled in the outer suburbs of London, where new affiliations frequently went to Progressive synagogues. Progressive Judaism also received an impetus from English Orthodoxy, which was becoming more restrictive in thought and practice, thus losing much of its earlier broad appeal.[39] Both Progressive movements produced new liturgies. The Liberal *Service of the Heart* (1967) and its High Holiday *Gate of Repentance* (1973) were more traditional than their predecessors, especially in the greatly increased proportion of Hebrew and heightened particularism, but also very modern in format and English usage. Both volumes directly influenced Reform liturgy in America. British Reform's

Forms of Prayer (1977) was less of a change, but it too sought to reflect the new period of Jewish history when Jews lived in awareness of the Holocaust and in relationship to a Jewish state. In 1956 the English Reform movement established Leo Baeck College in London, a venture in which the Liberals joined them eight years later. Unlike the Paris Liberal seminary, Leo Baeck College did succeed over the long run. Despite severe economic difficulties, it became both a growing rabbinical seminary and a spiritual center for European Progressive Judaism. Its students participated regularly in dialogues with Christians and Muslims; their teachers—though mostly part-time—included outstanding scholars representing a wide range of theological opinion. By the eighties, the College's ordinees, both men and women, were serving most of the Progressive congregations in Europe.[40]

Until 1960 England also remained the nerve center of the WUPJ. There its office was located in Lily Montagu's home; there nearly all its conferences were held. When Baeck became too frail to continue as its president, leadership, in 1955, passed to Lily Montagu. But she was better suited for the role of secretary and organizer than that of president. In fact, she readily admitted she was holding the position only until the right person came along to replace her. By now she was also over eighty and her remarkable capacity for work had begun to wane. But no one appropriate for the presidency could be found in Europe. After much soul searching, the London inner circle decided that World Union leadership would have to pass to the United States. Not only had American Reform Judaism, almost from the beginning, underwritten about 90 percent of the WUPJ budget, but in Rabbi Solomon Freehof it offered a scholar and experienced leader who most closely approached the stature of Montefiore and Baeck. In 1959 Freehof became president of the World Union and the following year its headquarters were transferred to New York.[41] The English were left with a WUPJ European Board whose most important activity was publication of a valuable periodical entitled *European Judaism.*[42]

The Israeli Focus

The United States remained the administrative center of the WUPJ for only thirteen years. As the world movement became ever more Zionist, the Israeli focus of Baeck's ellipse seemed the more natural location for its principal offices. Moreover, with the trauma and exhilaration of the Six-Day War in 1967, consciousness of Israel had risen to a high level throughout the Jewish world. In 1968, for the first time, the World Union held its biennial conference in Jerusalem. Five years later, in 1973, the central administration was transferred to Israel, and two years after that the WUPJ formally affiliated with the World Zionist Organization. The international Reform movement, so long neutral on Zionism, had thus placed itself under the Zionist institutional umbrella.

The move and the affiliation not only explicitly recognized the central role played by Israel in world Jewry; they were also motivated by the desire more effectively to assist new Israeli congregations that were then attempting to advance Progressive Judaism in—ironically perhaps—its least hospitable environment. As early as 1953, Rabbi Maurice Eisendrath, president of the UAHC, had urged a fresh start in Israel by creating a movement that would be indigenous and truly liberal. Five years later, the first congregation was formed in Jerusalem. A small group, consisting largely of intellectuals, began it as a circle "for the renewal of religious life." Its members developed their own Hebrew liturgy, drawing much from the Reconstructionist prayerbook. They omitted such elements as the ancient sacrifices, emphasized the Jewish nation, and incorporated modern Hebrew poetry. Men and women sat together and women were called to the Torah; men covered their heads. Yom Kippur services that first year attracted more than 200. The most active of the congregation's founders was Shalom Ben-Chorin, a journalist of German-Jewish origin described by a contemporary as a "short, sandy-haired man with a large mustache and an impish smile." Ben-Chorin was deeply committed to the Jerusalem circle and sought to create similar groups in other cities. Gradually such circles were formed; first in Upper Nazareth, and Herzliyah, then in Kefar Shemaryahu, Ramat Gan, Tel-Aviv, Nahariyah, and Haifa.[43] Some of the early congregations flourished, others did not; new ones continued to emerge. In 1983 there were fifteen that held services for the High Holidays.[44] Most remained small, total membership reaching about 800 families.

A survey conducted in 1978 reveals the demographic profile of the Israeli congregations in that year. Older men and women represented a higher proportion of members than was characteristic of the general population. Nearly half were immigrants from central and western Europe with only 11 percent native-born and a minute fraction of Sephardi origin. The members were better educated than the average Israeli and over half were professionals. Compared to Israelis generally, they were less scrupulous about the dietary laws and avoiding all travel on the Sabbath. But they were more observant by such standards as refraining from bread on Passover, fasting on Yom Kippur, and performing Sabbath rituals. Compared to average American Reform Jews, their level of observance (e.g., 72 percent lighted candles each Sabbath eve) was high indeed. And the proportion that attended Sabbath services every week significantly exceeded even that of Conservative Jews in Israel.[45]

Rabbinical leadership at first came from the Diaspora, especially the United States. However, in the course of time that began to change. After bitter Orthodox opposition, the Hebrew Union College in 1963 had been able to dedicate its new campus in Jerusalem, complete with a synagogue that employed its own Hebrew Progressive ritual. Prominently located on King David Street in Jerusalem, it created a visible presence in the Israeli capital. In Cincinnati the College had educated a few Israelis for the rabbinate; now the possibility arose of training rabbis for the Israeli Progressive rabbinate in Israel. In the seventies a handful of young men undertook to prepare for that arduous task, and the first of them was ordained in 1980. The Israeli congregations joined in a national organization that became known as the Tenuah Le-Yahadut Mitkademet Be-Yisrael (The Movement for Progressive Judaism in Israel). At its conferences, beginning in 1965, rabbis and laity discussed theological and practical issues, sometimes with lively disagreement. In 1977 they adopted a platform which stressed that Progressive Judaism's particular message lay not only in its historical understanding of Judaism, but also in its conviction that Jewish religion, not exclusively defined by the ritual commandments, must also encompass social ethics. And in various ways the Israeli movement did address itself to the problems of Israeli society. It not only passed resolutions but conducted summer camps for disadvantaged children and camps that brought together children from Arab and Jewish families; individual congregations undertook social work projects. But while the commitment to social justice was universally agreed upon, the role of mitzvot proved a divisive topic. A portion of the Israeli movement's leadership took Halakhah very seriously and sought to develop a Progressive Judaism possessing clear and authoritative norms. But another segment, especially among the laity, opposed such intrusion on individual freedom, and a small but vocal faction among the laity argued for humanism rather than theism. The difference of opinion in part reflected the uncertainty of the Israeli movement as to whether it should seek to attract men and women already inclined to religious observance but unable to be Orthodox or to appeal to secularists seeking some religious association but unwilling to consider even a liberalized Halakhah. The platform, though a compromise document, represents a victory for the more traditional point of view.[46]

In 1982, after much controversy between theological conservatives and radicals within its ranks, the Israeli Council of Progressive Rabbis (MaRaM) produced a unified liturgy for the movement called *Ha-Avodah She-Ba-Lev* (The Service of the Heart). It followed Reform practice in its excision of prayers for the rebuilding of the Temple, for the resurrection of the dead, and for the reestablishment of the House of David. It also shortened the prayers so they could be spoken or sung with full concentration. But it added passages and entire services that called attention to "the two central events that affected our people in the twentieth century: the Holocaust and the Return to Zion." Its compilers envisaged that the liturgy would become a source for the study of Jewish prayer and therefore maximally preserved its traditional structure, calling attention to liturgical development by noting the biblical and later sources. Open to the continuing development of Jewish liturgy, they included selections by contemporary Jewish thinkers and poets.[47]

From the beginning, the Israeli Progressive movement encountered the bitter opposition of an entrenched Orthodoxy. Orthodox rabbis and politicians used every opportunity to delegitimize and harass Progressive Judaism. In language reminiscent of nineteenth-century Germany, Israel's chief rabbis warned faithful Jews not to attend Reform or Conservative services.[48] Progressive synagogues had difficulty renting premises; services were disturbed by intruders; funds requested from the Ministry of Religions were seldom forthcoming. Progressive rabbis could not serve as army chaplains; they could not legally officiate at marriages; their conversions, though done in accordance with the Halakhah, remained unrecognized by the Chief Rabbinate. Leading Israeli politicians, while appearing occasionally at the Jerusalem Hebrew Union College or before conferences of the World Union held in Israel, remained well aware of the need to avoid offending coalition partners from the Orthodox political parties.[49] Although the secular media frequently showed sympathy for the Progressive movement as a victim of religious discrimination, few secular Israelis possessed much understanding of its ideology or aims. Israeli schools and textbooks portrayed the Reform movement in stereotypic fashion as inherently assimilationist and anti-Zionist.[50] Most Israelis came from families originating in eastern Europe or Afro-Asia, where Reform had had little or no impact, and few had any direct knowledge of the small Israeli movement. Yet by the late seventies the Israeli "religion gap" between Orthodox and secularists had begun to trouble some of the more thoughtful intellectuals. The prominent Hebrew writer A. B. Yehoshua even suggested that Prime Minister Ben-Gurion and the Labor movement should have given Israeli Progressive Judaism legitimacy by publicly associating themselves with it.[51]

By the seventies it had become apparent to leaders of the Israeli movement that congregations might not be the best vehicle for transmitting its message. Membership was not noticeably growing, the congregational youth groups remained small. Progressive synagogues resembled enclaves of the faithful which exercised little direct

Dedication of Kibbutz Yahel, 1976.
Alfred Gottschalk, president of HUC–JIR, is in the white hat under canopy at left;
Alexander Schindler, president of the UAHC, is carrying the Torah.

impact on Israeli life.[52] The movement's leaders therefore decided to reach out to the collective agricultural settlements, the kibbutzim. In 1970 representatives from the two movements met formally for the first time at the kibbutz seminar center in Oranim. Out of that meeting came the impetus to establish a Reform kibbutz and thus to imbue a natively Israeli institution with the ideology of Progressive Judaism. Six years later, Kibbutz Yahel arose in the Aravah desert north of Eilat, and in 1983 Kibbutz Lotan was established a few kilometers to its south. The young people who first settled at Yahel were two-thirds Israelis, one-third Americans. They successfully established a way of life that mingled agricultural labor and socialist idealism with

Sabbath services, a kosher kitchen, study of Jewish sources, and projects for disadvantaged Jewish children in Eilat.[53] Yahel and Lotan drew their Israeli pioneers largely
from a promising national youth movement that was now more closely linked to the
Israeli scouting movement than to individual congregations.

In the late seventies the Israeli movement still lacked an effective native-born
leader, a central personality possessing the stature and dynamism of a Geiger or a
Wise. Much of its attention remained concentrated on the struggle for religious equality, in which it was sometimes joined by the equally besieged Israeli Conservative
movement. Its leaders frequently wondered if Progressive Judaism, even should it
succeed in gaining equality, would then be able to take firmer root in a soil where
Jewish identification required no synagogues. Yet they realized, as well, that only if it
did eventually flourish there would Israel become—in fact, and not just as symbol—
a genuine focus of the world Progressive movement.

10

The New American Reform Judaism

The generation after World War II witnessed American Reform Judaism's greatest expansion in numbers and in program. It saw new theological ferment within its ranks, unprecedented social activism, a yet fuller appreciation of tradition, and the first appearance of women in positions of spiritual leadership. But there were also some years of nagging self-doubt and the emergence of new rifts every bit as severe as the earlier conflict over Zionism. Beset by unrelenting forces that sapped its vitality and threatened to rip it apart, Reform Judaism passed into the late seventies seeking to throw off its malaise, heal internal division, and regain its earlier confidence.

A Time of Stunning Growth

During World War II American religion liberated itself from the apathy that had plagued it for more than two decades. Following Pearl Harbor, a religious revival began as men in foxholes turned to their chaplains for solace; and it continued when the war was over with Americans priding themselves that their belief in God set them apart from atheistic communism. Growing numbers joined churches and attended regularly. With the end of the Depression, delayed programs to build new religious structures could at last be launched. Even college students, long alienated from religion, showed renewed interest in their faith. During the Eisenhower years, the American Congress added "under God" to the Pledge of Allegiance and made "In God We Trust" the official motto of the United States. Belonging to a church and believing in God became hallmarks of Americanism.[1]

This favorable atmosphere was a major factor in prompting the Jewish religious revival during and following the war. There were, of course, specifically Jewish reasons as well. The Holocaust, though its theological ramifications were little discussed until the sixties, raised Jewish consciousness and created a sense of American Jewry's special responsibility to sustain Jewish survival. The struggle to establish the state of Israel drew in Jews who had been on the periphery but who now identified actively and contributed to the ever vaster sums required to settle the refugees. By the early fifties, however, Holocaust awareness declined. Once the Jewish state had become a viable reality, Israel consciousness, too, receded and membership in Zionist organizations fell off. Likewise diminished was the earlier need to fight antisemitism as exclusionary practices began gradually to give way. What stood firm in the 1950s was religion. While Jewish identity had been steadily moving away from religious expressions toward ethnic ones, that process now reversed itself. "Our rabbis have begun to speak more fervently of a God-centered, rather than of a people-centered, religion and culture," one CCAR member noted to his colleagues. Jews now popularly thought of themselves—and were seen by others—as occupying one-third of a "triple melting pot" consisting of Protestant–Catholic–Jew, in which they were distinguished from Christian counterparts by criteria of religious faith and practice. Religious institutions, which had been fighting a losing battle against the growing influence of community federations, during the 1950s found themselves once more in a position of strength. The synagogue, and not the federation, represented Judaism as Jews and non-Jews then understood it.[2]

The synagogue's new frontier was the suburb. When following the war newly affluent Jews flocked to developing areas outside the great cities, the first institution they created was usually the synagogue. In the city, the Jewish ambience of ethnic neighborhoods had sustained particular identity and obviated the necessity of explaining religious neglect to one's self or to others. In the suburbs good citizenship and proper respectability required that Jews belong to their own local house of worship as Christians were affiliated with neighborhood churches. But conformity was not the only impulse for newly settled Jewish families to join a synagogue. Most of the migrants were young married couples who sought a Jewish education for their children. In the absence of community-wide educational institutions, they turned to the synagogue, which, in addition, offered them personal ceremonies for life-cycle events. The new congregations were almost invariably child-centered as religious schools burgeoned with the effects of the postwar "baby boom." In the absence of competing institutions, the new synagogues also drew philanthropic and social activities under their umbrella, becoming encompassing centers of Jewish life.[3]

Both Conservative and Reform congregations reaped institutional benefits from the migration to suburbia; Orthodoxy fared less well, at least at first. Jews who moved out of the old neighborhoods were those willing to forgo the ready availability of kosher butchers and a synagogue within walking distance of their homes. When new suburban congregations were formed, the decision for Conservative or Reform often depended on local circumstances rather than movement ideology. Conservatism was most frequently victorious, for the image of Reform still bore traces of its classical past, while Conservative Judaism offered a comfortable centrism, explicit ethnic consciousness, and a closer attachment to ceremonial forms still held dear.

Yet the Reform congregations that were established differed less from Conservative counterparts than ever before. Like the Conservative synagogues, they were founded by east European Jews. Although average per capita income continued to be higher among Reform congregants, the differential was declining, and a wide range of economic status could be found in either camp. Internal economic heterogeneity and intermovement homogeneity were gradually becoming the norm.[4] The new Reform synagogues also lacked a controlling leadership of German lineage that espoused classical Reform. In suburbia Reform was preeminently the creation of hitherto unaffiliated second- or third-generation American Jews largely oblivious to the long history of the Reform movement. What they created was less a revision of classical Reform than something without movement continuity, a style of belief and practice with little reference to past ideology. For both Reform and Conservative Jews in the suburbs holidays assumed importance but not dietary laws; rites of passage but not strict adherence to Halakhah. Indeed, it was not unusual for synagogue attendance to be higher among Reform Jews than among Conservative.[5]

What was true of the suburbs was increasingly characteristic for American Reform Judaism as a whole. Of course, some more or less classical congregations remained, especially in the large cities. But as Solomon Freehof observed, the new expansion was transforming Reform Judaism from a movement dominated by second- and third-generation Reform Jews into a body composed mainly of new adherents whose parents or grandparents were Orthodox or who had at least grown up in observant homes.[6] Reform's link with traditional Judaism was once again biological, as it had always been at its points of origin and growth.

Given the inherent advantages of Conservative Judaism, it is unlikely that Reform would have done as well as it did in exploiting the newly propitious circumstances were it not for an aggressive leadership. When Rabbi Maurice Eisendrath (1902–1973) became executive director of the Union of American Hebrew Congregations in 1943, he took charge of an underfunded, scarcely visible organization lodged in a warren of office cubbyholes in downtown Cincinnati. Institutionally, it was overshadowed by Hebrew Union College; laymen who could give it only part-time attention were its leaders. The most significant religious authorities of the Reform movement had been the best known congregational rabbis, especially men who had gained fame, as well, through Zionist activities. Reform Jews could point to no one person who, over a longer period of time, "spoke for Reform Judaism." From the first, Eisendrath was determined to change that. He would raise the Union's institutional profile and secure its primacy within the movement. Making himself its top leader, he would become the spokesman of Reform Judaism to Jew and Gentile alike.[7]

Before he came to the UAHC, Eisendrath had made a name for himself as a congregational rabbi in Toronto. There he gained a reputation as dynamic, articulate, and provocative. Never one to avoid a controversy, Eisendrath advocated absolute pacifism, a binational state in Palestine, and a greater Jewish appreciation of Jesus. Beginning as a classical Reformer, he shifted his positions along with the movement: from anti-Zionism to Zionism, from antiritual to a limited fondness for custom and ceremony. But his religion remained prophetic Judaism, his chief concerns social justice and world peace. For Eisendrath, a Judaism turned mainly inward was simply disloyal to its mission.

Chastened by Rabbi Louis Mann's critique of 1941, the Union was ready to cast its lot with a forceful leader who could bring it out of the doldrums. Without hesitation, Eisendrath set out two objectives. The first was fulfilled when, upon the death of

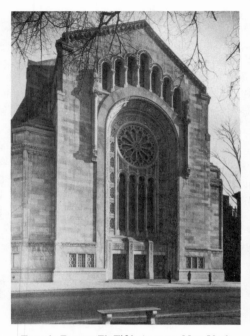

Temple Emanu-El, Fifth Avenue, New York.   UAHC "House of Living Judaism," across
                                                   65th Street from Temple Emanu-El.

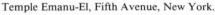

the Union's lay president in 1946, he was elevated to the presidency, which was then made a salaried position and for the first time placed in the hands of a rabbi. Although laymen would hereafter continue to chair its board, the Union was now no longer strictly a lay organization; its highest leadership was henceforth rabbinical. Moreover, its new president was in a position to make the Union—for the first time—clearly the most important of the three national institutions of American Reform Judaism. During the quarter century of Eisendrath's presidency, neither the Hebrew Union College, with its academic and professional focus, nor the CCAR, with its frequently changing leadership, could hope to attain equal status.

Eisendrath's second objective aroused open controversy. He was determined to move the UAHC from Cincinnati to New York, the largest center of Jewish population, where almost all the other major Jewish and Christian organizations had their headquarters. In the florid prose which typified his rhetoric, Eisendrath exhorted the Union's executive board that "we must come out of our provincial shell and accept this challenge rather than to leave these masses, by our default, to others who do dwell closer to them. We need also, in this dynamic day, the momentum which comes from being in close proximity with these vibrant multitudes of our people."[8]

But there soon arose a groundswell of opposition to this scheme that would bring Reform Judaism closer to "masses" and "multitudes." Preceding the UAHC Biennial Assembly of 1948, which was to make the final decision, a Cincinnati-based committee tried to impress on delegates that it would be far less expensive to build a new headquarters in Cincinnati. In truth, their fundamental objection ran deeper than money. Cincinnati had come to symbolize classical Reform Judaism: the German lineage, the Americanism, the minimum of ritual. Cincinnati Reform was rooted in Mid-

Maurice N. Eisendrath.

Nelson Glueck.

America, free from the "contamination" of an eastern metropolis. Its adherents were genteel, middle-class, proper. Once centered in New York, they feared, Reform Judaism would ever more rapidly lose the distinguishing features which second- and third-generation Reform Jews held dear. Opponents of the move were willing to forgo opportunities for greater expansion if such growth meant paying the price of further traditionalization. Not surprisingly, the 1948 Assembly was one of the stormiest in UAHC history. After a discussion which featured selected Cincinnatians speaking in favor of New York and Isaac Mayer Wise's granddaughter, a New Yorker, bearing the torch for Cincinnati, the final vote was a close one, perhaps as little as three to two in favor of the move. But the die was cast. Thanks mostly to Sisterhood fund-raising, an impressive seven-story "House of Living Judaism" arose on Fifth Avenue and 65th Street in New York. Reform Judaism was moving yet closer to the mainstream of American Jewish life.[9]

What remained in Cincinnati was the Hebrew Union College, now drawing a sizable portion of its support from just those elements of the movement that were unhappy with the Union's move and who became increasingly displeased with Eisendrath's very liberal political pronouncements. Its lay supporters likewise cast about for a man who possessed the capacity for dynamic leadership, who would be able to expand the influence of the College in step with the advance of the Union. They found their man in Rabbi Nelson Glueck (1900–1971), a biblical archaeologist on the faculty of HUC. By the time he replaced Morgenstern as president of the College in 1947, Glueck had gained an international reputation for his exploration of ancient sites in eastern Palestine and succeeded in bringing his findings to wider attention through popular books. An east European Jew of humble origins, but linked by marriage to

Cincinnati's leading German Jewish families, Glueck possessed the scholarly stature, connections, personal charisma, and charm which made him an ideal choice for the position. Like Eisendrath, Glueck was essentially a shy, withdrawn person, whom almost no one knew well; like him also, he was a man of towering ambition. As Eisendrath sought to expand the Union, so did Glueck intend to create a larger College. In succeeding years their ambitions would frequently clash as each sought a bigger share of Reform revenues for his own institution. Yet despite the sometimes demoralizing effect of their rivalry, the combined dynamism of the two men did enable the Reform movement to become a far more powerful force than it had been at the end of the war.

According to Eisendrath, the movement's failure to grow in the 1930s had been at least partly its own fault. Reform Judaism had remained aloof from broader Jewish life; its congregations lacked emotional warmth and fervor, they demanded membership fees that made them into class institutions. Reform had been especially myopic in discouraging its own proliferation: "We far preferred the establishment of an Orthodox shul or even a Conservative synagogue directly across the street from our stately Reform temples to welcoming another Reform congregation even a mile or two away."[10] In 1946 the UAHC Biennial Assembly resolved that the Union would itself intervene. Henceforth it would take the initiative in founding new congregations that could draw in the masses of unaffiliated Jews. It would use its own funds to help new synagogues get started and weather the difficult first years; a growing network of regional offices would encourage and assist the local founders. To stir broader interest in Reform Judaism the Union launched what it dubbed "The American Jewish Cavalcade." On a given weekend one or more well-known rabbis would travel to a community and lecture inspiringly on Reform Judaism, usually to large crowds. Leo Baeck was the most valued participant in these Jewish "revival" meetings that multiplied from 1946 to 1951. The Cavalcade brought fresh personalities to Reform pulpits in nearly every city and drew in new members. It also created a deeper sense of belonging to a national movement, thus heightening awareness of the UAHC.[11]

The conducive social situation and religious atmosphere of the late forties and fifties, together with Eisendrath's energy and effective organizational technique, yielded rich results. In twenty-one years, from 1943 to 1964, the Union more than doubled the number of its congregations, from 300 to 656, and more than tripled its family membership from 60,000 to about 200,000. Enrollment in Reform religious schools in the same period grew even faster, exceeding 150,000 in the early sixties. By then, the rolls of NFTY, too, had burgeoned to some 35,500 teenagers throughout the country.[12]

Not surprisingly, the Union's budget, too, advanced dramatically. From $250,000 in 1943/44, it nearly tripled within a decade and continued to soar. To support higher expenditures the UAHC succeeded first in doubling per capita dues from three to six dollars in 1953 and then, only a few years later, in introducing a proportional system that brought 10 percent of congregational dues to the Union. In addition, it enjoyed much larger receipts from the annual voluntary Combined Campaign for the Union and College. When even this total income proved insufficient to pay for the Union's expanding program, it began borrowing money from banks. Yet no one as yet considered this a cause for alarm. Continued congregational growth was assumed, and campaign chairmen were well aware that debt and deficit financing, when held within bounds, spurred supporters to increase their donations.[13]

Hebrew Union College found itself hard pressed to keep up with the demand for rabbis. It responded as best it could, especially by introducing a more active program of recruitment. When in Stephen Wise's declining years the Jewish Institute of Religion seemed no longer able to maintain itself, an agreement was formulated that made Nelson Glueck the head of both HUC and JIR and in 1950 led to their full merger as Hebrew Union College–Jewish Institute of Religion, with campuses in Cincinnati and New York. Four years later HUC–JIR established a branch in Los Angeles principally to draw in potential students from Southern California.[14] Likewise in 1954, the CCAR for the first time appointed a paid executive vice president, who established permanent headquarters in New York City.[15] From less than 500 rabbis in 1943, its membership rose to 850 in 1964 and grew even more rapidly thereafter.

As older Reform congregations experienced a new spurt of growth and new ones came into existence, synagogue construction became a high priority. By 1947 fully one in two Reform congregations was contemplating or already engaged in a major building project. The Union responded with the innovative idea of conferences on synagogue architecture held in New York and Chicago. It brought Jewish architects, such as Percival Goodman, and artists, such as Marc Chagall and Jacques Lipchitz, together with Reform rabbis and lay leaders to talk about synagogue design. The participants agreed that the age of Colonial pillars, Byzantine domes, and Moorish minarets had passed. The new era demanded a modern functional architecture. Postwar Reform synagogues were often built "along accordion lines," with sanctuaries that expanded to take in the social hall for large High Holiday crowds and contracted for greater intimacy among the smaller group of Sabbath worshipers. In the suburbs they were set back from the street and surrounded by trees and shrubbery with windows to let in the landscape. Schoolrooms, formerly relegated to basements, arose as prominent wings of the new synagogue structures, reflecting the new emphasis on Jewish education.[16]

The expansion of Reform Judaism in two regions during this period deserves special attention. In Canada the movement had hitherto enjoyed very limited success. Although a Reform congregation had been established in Montreal as early as 1882, many of its founders had come from the United States and it had aroused bitter local opposition. Established congregations in Hamilton and Toronto did introduce some reforms but, on the whole, at a much slower pace than below the border. Canadian Jewry had not received a large migration from Germany in the nineteenth century, and its east European Jews clung tenaciously to an ethnic identity the more acceptable in the context of multicultural Canada. Reform Judaism remained a small minority with only three UAHC congregations in all of Canada at the end of World War II. In the late fifties, however, Canadian Reform began to proliferate as moves to suburbia became common there as well. Though its share of congregational membership would not grow beyond 15 percent, it did now expand rapidly to more than a dozen congregations with over 5,000 member families.[17]

The most promising frontier was Southern California. After the war it yearly drew thousands of Jewish families westward to its hospitable climate and inviting economic opportunities. Most of those who streamed to Los Angeles and its environs lacked the sense of rootedness which characterized Jewish congregants in the eastern cities. But as they settled down and sought Jewish schools for their children, they linked themselves to existing congregations or established new ones. The Reform movement in Southern California had grown slowly from a single congregation at the beginning of the century to five by the end of the war. Then the pace increased with remarkable rapidity during the late forties and fifties. By 1961 the Southwest Council of the UAHC embraced forty-five congregations scattered throughout dozens of suburbs. There were now more Reform rabbis in Los Angeles than anywhere outside New York. Southern California congregations ranged in character from the nearly classical, well-established, and immense Wilshire Boulevard Temple, a "cathedral synagogue" that drew members from all over the Los Angeles area, to the newer, much smaller neighborhood congregations that were often far more traditional. It was not unusual for the latter to consist mostly of members who had no previous family contact with Reform Judaism and who knew little of its background. More obviously than elsewhere, the Reform Judaism of Southern California sprouted like a new plant whose seeds were imported from outside its own borders.[18]

Covenant Theology

Christian and Jewish critics questioned the depth of the religious revival. The larger numbers who joined churches and synagogues—and even attended more frequently—were, they thought, prompted mainly by social or other extrinsic motives rather than by purely religious ones. Yet without question there was a nucleus within each faith community that was spurred to greater religious seriousness and to asking old questions anew. Among Reform Jews the most important development in religious thought was a new theology characterized especially by its attention to the biblical concept of "covenant."

World War II, even more than World War I, had undermined the optimism characteristic of liberal religion in the nineteenth century. In Protestant circles, the neo-orthodoxy of Karl Barth, which set an unknown supernatural God clearly apart from human strivings, gained a larger following. Especially influential was the Christian existentialism of Reinhold Niebuhr, who taught at Union Theological Seminary in New York. No one more effectively than he punctured the pretensions of utopian striving for social perfection. History, he believed, had demonstrated the pervasiveness of human sinfulness and the inability of human beings to achieve moral progress on their own.

Jews, having experienced their own special tragedy, emerged from World War II "filled with a mood of defeat rather than of victory."[19] Not only had the atomic destruction of Hiroshima and Nagasaki raised immense anxieties about the human future, but the death of their own 6 million and the plight of Jewish refugees barred from entry into Palestine cast a pall of deep despair. By the early fifties some Reform rabbis were seriously examining the somber theologies of religious existentialism. A layman not associated with Reform, Will Herberg, elaborated Niebuhr's dark view of human potential in the absence of transcendent faith. Man's existential predicament, he maintained, required a "leap of faith."[20] Few Jewish thinkers, however, were ready to adopt the Paulinian deprecation of human reason that had become popular among some Christian theologians.[21] Much discussed and widely criticized as un-Jewish, Herberg's work represented an extreme reaction.

At the other end of the theological spectrum stood those liberal theologians whose optimism remained unshaken. Their most important representative was Levi A. Olan

(1903–1984), a Reform rabbi of broad secular culture whose pulpit was in Dallas, Texas. Repeatedly, Olan branded the revolt from reason a "failure of nerve." Christian existentialism had drawn "injudiciously" from Freud's complex psychology to support its attack on humanity's capacity to solve its problems rationally. It had allowed an apocalyptic sense of crisis to overwhelm prophetic hope. Olan was willing to admit that the old optimism needed tempering with greater realism, but he was still convinced that intelligence and imagination were adequate to their postwar tasks. Far from diminished, man now possessed "increasing powers to control the world around him, the animal kingdom, and himself." Faith in God, as Olan understood it, lay in the conviction that the universe could respond to human moral effort. The very hopefulness of the vision and the impetus to strive for its realization were sustained by what he termed "the guiding hand of the creative spirit of the universe."[22]

The liberal impulse represented by Olan continued to be influential among Reform Jews throughout the postwar generation. Indeed, his greater emphasis on human beings than on God, his conception of an impersonal deity, and his hopefulness for the future were widely represented, especially among the laity. In the sixties, other theological positions, even more distant from tradition, attracted support. Prompted especially by the challenge of natural science and Freudian psychology, they brought into the Reform orbit variations of naturalism and divine finitism. Only a new God-denying humanism, emerging from within Reform, moved rapidly beyond its periphery.[23]

Among an increasing number of Reform rabbis, however, the postwar years witnessed a marked theological reorientation in the direction of more traditional views. The influence of Kohler and Cohon waned before that of two major figures who had emerged within German Judaism a generation earlier. Though each a man of unorthodox Jewish faith, neither Martin Buber (1878–1965) nor Franz Rosenzweig (1886–1929) can be classified as a Reform Jew, the one because he rejected all organized religion, the other because of the high level of personal observance which he eventually adopted. Nor was their influence limited to Reform Judaism. But Buber and Rosenzweig opened the eyes of a growing circle of younger Reform rabbis to a viable alternative that could displace the older liberalism which they believed had failed.

Buber's fundamental conception of God as "Eternal Thou," apprehended in dialogue through a form of knowing totally different from that used in the sciences, gave intellectual respectability once more to the personal God revealed in Jewish history and individual experience. Buber and Rosenzweig were especially attractive to Reform Jewish thinkers, for they shared the view that no sacred text could fully reflect the divine revelation; texts were invariably human responses after the fact. Where Buber and Rosenzweig differed was simply on whether the revelation should be understood to impose any ritual obligation at all. Buber rejected that view as infringing upon the spontaneity of divine–human dialogue; Rosenzweig, though initially insisting that the only divine command is to reciprocate God's love, came increasingly to believe in and practice a life of mitzvot, accepting those ritual commandments which addressed his own person.

For long mostly untranslated into English, Buber and Rosenzweig were scarcely known in America until the 1950s. But then their existential theologies, devoid both of liberal essentialist idealism and of the antirationalist tendency of Christian existentialism, rapidly gained attention.[24] To many they seemed to offer an indigenous Jewish way to regain a connection with the ancient sources after biblical criticism had demolished fundamentalism and to reaffirm personal religious encounter after psychology had destroyed earlier notions of religious experience.

By the mid-fifties a circle of at least a dozen Reform rabbis had coalesced around the common goal of creating a new theology for Reform Judaism. For a time some of them met regularly for discussion at a summer camp in Wisconsin, together with a few sympathetic Conservative and Orthodox colleagues.[25] They were united in their rejection of earlier Reform theology, which they found superficial, removed from the classical sources, and deaf to the voice of a personal God. Under the influence of Christian existentialism, they rediscovered more somber assessments of human nature within Jewish tradition and were willing to dwell on concepts like sin and the fear of God that liberal Jewish theology had relegated mostly to the Day of Atonement. From Buber and Rosenzweig they adopted a concept of revelation which substituted divine–human meeting for mere inspiration or human striving to attain a divinely sanctioned moral ideal. Along with Rosenzweig, they also began to take Halakhah seriously, not alone as custom and ceremony, but as divinely ordained commandment. A contemporary observer noted that their focus was on God, not man. They were concerned with the authoritative claims made upon them by traditional texts and traditional observance.[26]

Yet these neo-traditionalists were orthodox neither in belief nor in practice. Some of them were "rediscovering" Judaism, having grown up in classical Reform homes. They were eager to experience its message from within; directly from the sources rather than through externally imposed philosophical categories. But while they approached Bible and rabbinic literature with new seriousness, they did not perceive them as the literal word of God. While they were committed to doing God's will, they did not accept as mitzvot all those commandments enshrined in the tradition. Rather precariously, they balanced their desire to be more faithful to the revealed God with their liberal awareness that sacred texts might not fully—or not at all—convey God's word.[27]

One traditional concept, they soon realized, better represented their position than any other. *Berit,* covenant, is one of the most crucial ideas in the Bible. It is particular to Israel, though ultimately universal; it reflects mutuality in the relationship between God and Israel; and it both sets the Jewish people apart and binds it together as a "covenant community." For Reform Jews *berit* was a far more conducive concept than *matan torah,* the giving of the law or teaching on Mount Sinai. The latter implied receipt rather than partnership, unquestioning obligation, and a fixed tradition. But covenant could be understood as an ongoing relationship. It was not limited to the single generation that might or might not have literally stood at Sinai. Every Jew in every age was obligated to renew and to uphold the covenant. As liberals, Jews were also free—on the basis of their own serious confrontation with the texts—to renegotiate its terms. The covenant, in short, was the basis for the historical but also open-ended dialogue between God and Israel.[28]

Covenant theology was not without its problems, the most basic of which was ultimate authority. The new theologians had rebelled against the liberal, and ultimately humanist, notion that the individual selects from the tradition those elements he or she finds personally meaningful, precluding the possibility that individual views or sensitivity might be overridden by divine imperatives. They were therefore determined not to subordinate their own faith to any external principle or personal predilection. Judaism was not merely to supply proof texts for secularly liberal ideas or feelings. It was to be primary, not secondary, in their structure of belief and action. Yet as liberals themselves, they could not accept its crystallized form absolutely. They required the right to "dissent" from tradition, not *a priori* but after extended confrontation with the sources.[29] What remained unclear—and perhaps unresolvable—was the basis for such dissent. Though the tradition was now put first, it was not necessarily also last. Liberal Jews, collectively or individually, were still forced—perhaps through reformulations of covenant—to draw selectively from their past.

Covenant theology continued to have a major influence on Reform Judaism during the sixties and seventies. But now new challenges and issues came to the fore. Some were easily disposed of. The contemporary "Death-of-God" school in American Protestantism never made a broad impact on Reform Jews, in part because they did not require liberation from an oppressive Father–God, in part because the school's immanentism bordered on paganism and evoked hostility to Old Testament belief. No more impressive for Reform Jews was "Situation Ethics" with its love panacea that undermined the independence of justice as a moral category. At most it may have inspired the new attention now paid to the Jewish ethical tradition, just as the more permissive morality of the sixties prompted the formulation of religiously based sexual guidelines for Jewish youth.[30] In fact the most important later elements in postwar Jewish theology were not the result of external intellectual influences at all. They were related instead to contemporary Jewish history. With the Eichmann trial of 1961 and the Six-Day War of 1967, historical acts undertaken against and by Jews in the recent past began to cry out for theological explanation.

There had been some limited attention to the religious significance of the Holocaust in the immediate postwar years. As early as 1946 Rabbi David Polish of Evanston, Illinois had urged that Reform Judaism revive observance of the fast day of Tish'ah Be-Av, on which both ancient temples were destroyed, adapting it to commemorate "our twentieth-century disaster."[31] It was also Polish who told his colleagues in 1953:

> If our sensitivity to revelation were not blunted (and perhaps it will be restored in the souls of our descendants), then a revelation, the full impact of which must yet be made manifest to us, occurred at the Iriya [municipal council chamber] of Tel-Aviv on the fifth of Iyar 1948 [when the independence of the state of Israel was declared] and, yes, in Treblinka, even as Pitom and Raamses were intimations of Sinai.[32]

But neither Polish's liturgical suggestion nor his striking theological statement found an echo in the 1950s. It was only in the following decades that failure to deal explicitly with the Holocaust came to be regarded as a critical theological omission. In 1967 the UAHC prominently featured a symposium on the Holocaust's implications in its popular magazine and commissioned an anthology of Holocaust writings, including contributions on its theological impact.[33] Emil L. Fackenheim, a Liberal rabbi from Germany teaching philosophy at the University of Toronto, now began to deal at length with the seeming eclipse of divine presence at a time when 6 million of God's chosen people went to their death. Unwilling to consider the alternatives of God's death, powerlessness, or total unfathomability, Fackenheim chose to believe that God had spoken to Israel out of the midst of the slaughter. "Whereas no redeeming voice is heard at Auschwitz, a commanding voice is heard, and it is being heard with greater clarity.

Jews are not permitted to hand Hitler posthumous victories." That meant Jews were mandated to survive as Jews, to remember the victims, and to resist despair of God or of the world. Adding one to the traditional list of Jewish imperatives, Fackenheim called this the 614th commandment.[34]

Though Reform theologians drew no causal connection between the Holocaust and the establishment of the Jewish state, in the wake of a seemingly miraculous salvation in the Six-Day War, they did note a prevalent sense of renewed divine presence: God had not after all, it seemed, forsaken Israel.[35] Some in the Reform movement felt great hesitation to accept any bald ascription of revelatory and salvific significance to contemporary events; some came to believe that "Holocaust theology" was one-sided. But few still believed that Auschwitz and Jerusalem could remain outside any persuasive Jewish theology. All in all, Jewish theologians in the seventies had become relatively less concerned with the dialogue between God and Israel in ancient times and more intent on understanding its presence—or absence—in their own age.

Civil Liberties, Civil Rights, and Vietnam

As the forties, with their intense focus on the fate of the Jewish people, drew to a close, the Reform movement began once more to look outward at American society. In 1948 the Union and the CCAR created a joint Social Action Commission. When, after a brief period of dormancy the Commission received a paid staff, Reform Judaism for the first time possessed the capacity to expand social action well beyond the mere adoption of resolutions at UAHC and CCAR conventions. In fact, with the creation of a Union staff for the Commission, leadership in social action passed from the orbit of the Conference to that of the UAHC, which now began a vigorous program to deepen social consciousness on the congregational level. A majority of Reform synagogues soon established social action committees that studied the major issues, formulated statements, and engaged in local projects. A UAHC volume, *Justice and Judaism,* was twice reprinted within a year and went into many thousands of Reform homes; congregational social action committees used it as a topical guide for their work.[36] An observer noted at the time that "the long-bemoaned gap between the rabbis and the lay people on social issues" was neither so vast nor so deep as to be unbridgeable.[37] Quite possibly the new lay activism on social issues was in part yet another reflection of the east European influx into Reform Judaism—in this instance an importation of more liberal social views. Possibly also the German Jews in the movement, who could scarcely ignore long-time Reform preachments about prophetic Judaism, found it easier to support a program that paid relatively less attention to economic issues and focused more on civil liberties, on civil rights, and on international peace.

Soon after the end of the war, Reform Jews began to express concern at the growing infringement of free speech in the United States. In 1947 a rabbi noted that "the word 'Communist' is used as an epithet to destroy the reputations of liberal-minded men and women"—just as "atheist" had been in Jefferson's day. The following year the CCAR adopted a resolution condemning the widespread imputation of guilt by association and the ever more common branding of individuals and organizations as subversive without any clear basis for the charge. While recognizing that there was indeed a Communist danger, the Reform movement in the 1950s condemned the prevalent practice of exacting loyalty oaths and the technique of character assassination that was stock in trade for the House Un-American Activities Committee and for the investigations of Senator Joseph McCarthy. Similarly of concern during the fifties were encroachments on the separation of church and state. Reform laity and rabbis condemned government aid to parochial schools, the intrusion of religion into public education, and religious services conducted in municipal parks. They were grateful for the Supreme Court decision of 1962 which explicitly forbade prayer in public schools.[38]

What most occupied the social conscience of Reform Jews during the fifties and well into the sixties, however, was the struggle for Black civil rights. As early as 1946, the CCAR issued a comprehensive statement entitled "Judaism and Race Relations," which called for an end to the Negroes' inferior economic conditions, to the persisting bane of lynchings, segregation in the armed forces, and discrimination in the professions. In declaring an "incessant war upon all manifestations of injustice to the Negroes," it called for the establishment of a Fair Employment Practices Commission and open housing, for outlawing the poll tax, and the abolition of segregation in public facilities.[39] But the civil rights "take-off point" for Reform Jews, as for Americans generally, came in the wake of the Supreme Court decision of 1954 outlawing segregation in public education. It soon divided the country—and occupied the Reform movement for over a decade.

Within a few months of the Supreme Court decision in *Brown* v. *Board of Education,* the UAHC Biennial General Assembly had voted overwhelmingly to urge its speedy implementation throughout the land.[40] In succeeding years, rabbis, rabbinical students, and laity together participated actively in the increasingly bitter campaign for racial equality. They joined the Freedom Riders in the South and the Mississippi Summer Project to help register Black voters. They marched with Martin Luther King, Jr. in Selma and Montgomery, Alabama. Seventy Reform rabbis participated in the great Washington march of August 1963, while in St. Augustine, Florida a group of them was arrested and spent time together in prison. One Reform rabbi, Arthur Lelyveld of Cleveland, was severely bloodied when two white ruffians in Hattiesburg, Mississippi, set upon him with an iron bar.[41]

But the forays of northern Reform Jews into Alabama, Mississippi, and other segregationist states were always followed by retreat to safer environs. For those Jews living in the South, the Black civil rights struggle was a recurrent nightmare. Day by day they lived in an atmosphere of apprehension and sometimes fear. There were those Reform laypeople (and at least one Reform rabbi) in the Deep South who would not raise a hand to help the Blacks. They believed—with some justification—that if they took a liberal position in word or deed, White Citizens Councils, Klansmen, or simply unsympathetic neighbors might boycott their businesses or even threaten their persons. Morally, they argued that concern for their own safety had to take precedence.[42] Others were willing to do what they could where Christian groups would join them, and they lent their support to statements made by the national Reform movement.[43] But when the UAHC invited Martin Luther King to be its General Assembly banquet speaker in 1963, the Reform rabbis of Mississippi protested that its national lay organization had in this instance displayed no regard at all for their safety. By inviting King it was embarking on "a brinksmanship unworthy of a Jewish doctrine of responsibility toward Jews also!"[44] By then it was clear that such fears were not unfounded. In 1958 an epidemic of synagogue bombings had begun to spread across the South—from Miami and Jacksonville to Nashville, Atlanta, and later to Meridian and Jackson, Mississippi. Violent threats were made against southern rabbis who dared to be in the vanguard. Nonetheless, some Reform rabbis in the South helped to create interracial councils of clergy, kindergartens, and choirs, and invited Black speakers to express their views from temple pulpits. They played tangible, if not central roles in establishing the mechanisms of local desegregation. Almost without exception, more traditional rabbis did less.[45]

Meanwhile, Maurice Eisendrath was determined to increase the impact of Reform social action by establishing a presence in Washington, D.C. The objective of the proposed center would be twofold: first and foremost, to influence Congress directly on those moral issues where the national bodies of Reform Judaism had taken a stand; second, through research, publications, conferences, and internships, to educate rabbis, rabbinical students, and laity to the questions then under public discussion. Christian denominations had established similar centers. With a large grant promised by Kivie Kaplan, a prominent Reform Jewish civil rights leader, Eisendrath persuaded the 1959 UAHC Biennial Assembly to approve the plan, and the Union proceeded to purchase a stately structure that had earlier been the Ecuadorian Embassy. As in the case of the move to New York, however, this project, too, provoked vociferous denunciation. Now it came mainly from two of the largest and most influential congregations in the Reform movement: Temple Emanu-El of New York and Washington Hebrew Congregation. The leadership of the former had long resented the visible presence of the Union directly across 65th Street and even more its president's claim to speak for all Reform Jews; the Washington congregation also feared it would be overshadowed, in this case by a Union presence in the nation's capital. In a vigorous campaign these two congregations drew a few others to their side, especially some in the South which did not want Reform Judaism's position on civil rights to receive greater national attention. Not surprisingly, their concerns were clothed in lofty principle: the proper sphere of religion, the opponents contended, was belief, precept, and individual conscience, not collective political action. They marshalled sufficient strength to force a new vote on the issue. But in a dramatic confrontation at the General Assembly of 1961, the proponents of what was now called the Religious Action Center won by a proportion of at least four to one.[46]

By the mid-sixties a new issue, the war in Vietnam, was beginning to overshadow civil rights.[47] Among all major American Jewish organizations, those of the Reform movement were the first and most outspoken in opposing United States military action in Southeast Asia. As early as 1964, before Vietnam had become a prominent issue, the CCAR called for a negotiated settlement of the conflict. As the war escalated the following year, the Conference expressed its conviction that "there can be no 'military solution' to the fundamental social and economic problems of the Vietnamese." In the Union, it was Eisendrath who led the drive against the war. In November 1965 he told the UAHC General Assembly: "We transgress every tenet of our faith when we fight on another's soil, scorch the earth of another's beloved homeland, slay multitudes of innocent villagers." The Assembly responded with a resolution calling for a cease fire and negotiated peace. This Reform position on Vietnam in 1965 represented a minority view both within American public opinion and among Jews. It was not echoed by other major Jewish organizations. The Jewish War Veterans were the most vociferous defenders of U.S. policy. But the Orthodox laity and rabbinate likewise supported the American "determination to resist Communist aggression," while the Conservative rabbinate collectively remained silent until 1966, although Rabbi Abraham Joshua Heschel spoke out eloquently.

In 1967 the Reform movement's official opposition to the Vietnam war ran into two difficulties. The first was a small internal revolt led, as earlier on the issue of the Religious Action Center, by Temple Emanu-El of New York. That congregation now chose to withdraw from the Union, principally on account of the UAHC president's statements on Vietnam, which were widely believed to represent the views of all Reform Jews. Late in 1966 Eisendrath had gone so far as to publish an open letter to Lyndon Johnson in which—at Hanukah time—he compared the American President to the tyrant Antiochus Epiphanes.[48] That ruler more than two millennia earlier, he argued, had also been singularly intolerant of views differing from his own, though he too may have had the active support of a tiny Jewish splinter group, the "Veterans of Syrian Wars." Twenty-five Reform congregations (about 4 percent) soon gave their support to Emanu-El, which stayed out of the Union for over a year. Moreover, the reluctance of some congregants around the country to go along with critique of the American role forced the CCAR to strengthen the hand of those rabbis whose antiwar statements were endangering the freedom of their pulpits.[49]

The second difficulty was raised by the Six-Day War. "We must not be embarrassed by the charge that we are doves on Vietnam and hawks on Israel," said Rabbi Jacob Weinstein, then president of the CCAR.[50] But it became yet more delicate to maintain that composite visage once the Israelis expressed their full support of American policy in Vietnam.

Securing a sufficient number of Reform chaplains likewise became a severe problem as the American presence in Vietnam grew. Once the CCAR—on a rather close vote—had decided to support selective conscientious objection to the general draft in 1967, it could not easily thereafter deny the same privilege to rabbis with regard to the chaplaincy. Although ever more Jewish chaplains were needed, the Orthodox and Conservative movements had shifted to a voluntary chaplaincy. The Reform movement, however, still maintained a self-imposed quota system dating back to the Korean War. While some rabbis continued to urge the overriding moral necessity of serving Jewish soldiers in the armed forces, and for a time considered requiring chaplaincy or alternative service for all new rabbinical graduates, the Reform rabbinate, too, finally settled on a purely voluntary chaplaincy in 1969.[51]

In the final stages of the war Reform rabbis and laity participated in demonstrations and protests against the renewed bombing. A few were arrested for trespassing on federal property. One young Reform rabbi from the Boston area reflected that since his arrest congregants were taking his views more seriously: "My actions, more than all the sermons I had preached, got my point across." Generally, he felt, the readiness to apply principles had given new authority to his rabbinate. When the end of the conflict finally came, the CCAR urged unconditional amnesty for all those whose consciences had prevented them from participating in the war.[52]

By that time, however, Reform Jews, like American Jewry generally, had begun once more to turn their attention inward. In part the shift was due to specifically Jewish concerns that returned to the forefront or that appeared prominently for the first time. In the months of anxiety during the spring of 1967, as the future of the severely endangered state of Israel lay in the hands of fickle or hostile world powers, American Jews felt a renewed sense of obligation to their own. When the Israelis won the Six-Day War in June, the intense identification born of fear turned into a shared sense of relief and joy that lasted for years. At about the same time the plight of Soviet Jewry, which worsened after 1967, called forth new feelings of Jewish responsibility.[53]

But it was not alone the causes of Jews in Israel and the Soviet Union that by the late sixties overshadowed Reform Jewry's broader program of social action. There were also severe disappointments with Christian religious leaders and with Blacks. During World War II, the Reform movement had launched a successful program of institutes for Christian clergy. In 1948 there were ninety such lectures and discussions held around the country. Invited scholars spoke on a variety of Jewish subjects under the auspices of a local Reform congregation. They brought knowledge of Judaism to influential non-Jews and helped dispel prejudice.[54] In the early sixties, with a Catholic president in the White House and a new spirit of ecumenism introduced by the Second Vatican Council, the interfaith movement rose yet higher on the Reform agenda.[55] Reform Jews worked closely with Christians for nuclear disarmament, for adoption of the genocide treaty, and for an end to the Vietnam War. But when Christian leadership remained silent in the face of Israel's perilous situation in May 1967, a wave of disappointment swept across the American Jewish community. After that, it was more difficult to arouse enthusiasm for ecumenical endeavors.

At about the same time that relations between Jews and Christians were worsening, the Black–Jewish partnership was falling apart. As the Blacks' struggle for civil rights turned to economic issues and often became violent, it unleashed antisemitism directed not only at Jewish slumlords but at Jews as such. Black militantism and separatism now frustrated the continuing desire of Jewish liberals to support the Black cause as if it were their own. Some Reform leaders, like Maurice Eisendrath, nonetheless urged acceptance of the new leadership's demand for "reparations," even though Jews, as a group, were not responsible for Black deprivation. A resolution of the UAHC General Assembly in 1969 reaffirmed that "Jewish imperatives require that we be ever sensitive to the aspirations and just demands of our country's minorities." But the Assembly refused to support Eisendrath's proposal that the Jewish community mount a major campaign, similar to the United Jewish Appeal, in order to pay its share of reparations due American Blacks.[56] It would not recognize any specific Jewish guilt or debt. On the new issues, such as busing and affirmative action, the Reform movement took a liberal stance in the face of a mounting Jewish backlash, but the sense that the Black cause was vital to its own moral integrity continued to wane.[57]

The entire concept of the mission of Israel—so long cherished by Reform Jews—now came under attack. Not all Reform Jews any longer agreed that the Jewish goal was to enlighten and aid non-Jews. The value of Judaism should instead be measured by what it gave to the individual Jew. As one rabbi argued, "A meaningful philosophy of Jewish existence must validate Jewish existence in personal terms. 'What will it mean in my life if I identify myself with Judaism?'"[58] Even those Reform Jews who continued to occupy themselves with social action looked harder for peculiarly Jewish foundations and refocused their agenda to embrace oppressed Jews in the Soviet Union, Syria, and elsewhere in addition to impoverished agricultural workers, others deprived throughout the world, and the continuing threat of nuclear weapons.[59]

Malaise

In the late 1960s severe self-doubt and anxiety about the future displaced the ebullience that had characterized American Reform Judaism since the war. Divided and uncertain of its course, it long remained in a state of crisis.

In the flush of the American religious revival and the quest for religious identity in suburbia, the remarkable growth of the American Reform movement had continued for about two decades. In 1969 its leadership could lay claim to a million adherents. But by the end of the sixties, stagnation was settling in. Only a handful of new congregations joined each year; membership lists in existing congregations either remained static or slightly declined; a few temples had no choice but to merge in order to remain viable.[60] Religious schools now shrank in size as the "baby-boom" generation passed on to college. Temple youth groups likewise suffered from the demographic decline, as well as from the rebelliousness and pervasive sense of a "generation gap" that made teenagers want to distance themselves from institutions associated with their parents.

Assuming ongoing growth, the Union had continued to borrow from the banks. When expansion ceased, the debt became burdensome. By 1975, when its accumulated liability reached a million dollars, congregational leaders responded by demanding a balanced budget and an orderly program of debt reduction even if that meant some curtailment of program. The number of rabbinical positions was now insufficient for the supply of Reform rabbis, inducing a few to enter Conservative pulpits and the College–Institute to reduce the size of its entering classes.[61]

A major factor in the demographic stagnation of the synagogues, which affected Conservative no less than Reform congregations, was the renewed efflorescence of the Jewish federations. The Six-Day War, along with a greater acceptance of cultural—and not just religious—pluralism in the United States, produced a resurgence of ethnic identification that was largely expressed through more active participation in community- and Israel-oriented organizations. As federations began to undertake educational and cultural activities in addition to their philanthropic campaigns, they increasingly impinged on the sphere of the synagogue. Congregational life, which had regained a measure of centrality during the fifties, was once again relegated to the periphery. American Jews identified increasingly with the Jewish people as a whole rather than with a particular religious current. Federations, not synagogues, received their more basic and inclusive loyalty.[62]

Moreover, it now appeared that Reform Judaism in America would be second to its Conservative rival and unable to reach the unaffiliated majority. In the mid-fifties, Reform Judaism was still the larger in both congregations and congregants. But a national Jewish population study completed in 1972 revealed that by then Conservative Judaism could claim 23 percent of American Jews, whereas only 14 percent were affiliated with Reform congregations. Nine percent were Orthodox; and no less than 53 percent held no congregational membership, a marked increase in unaffiliated Jews from about 40 percent a decade earlier. Local surveys that asked about identification rather than affiliation confirmed the primacy of Conservative Judaism by use of a broader measure.[63]

The malaise afflicting Reform Judaism in the late sixties and early seventies was most painful for its rabbinate. During at least two decades the rabbinical role had been in a process of transformation. Once preaching ability had been the chief criterion of rabbinical success or failure. Meticulously prepared sermons had frequently lasted a half hour or more and been preserved for posterity in temple bulletins and local community newspapers. Now sermons became briefer and their subject matter shifted from larger issues to narrower themes often touching on some aspect of interpersonal relationships. Temple boards had learned to attribute greater value to pastoral, counseling, and administrative skills. They no longer expected that their rabbi would regularly fill the synagogue; they seldom came to hear him themselves. While the fifties had witnessed a rise in attendance at services, by the late sixties there was a perceived decline. College-educated congregants did not look to their rabbi for worldly wisdom, and with the proliferation of academic Jewish studies in the 1970s, few rabbis could claim the highest level of expertise even in their own domain. As Jewish leadership passed to the federations, the rabbis' influence in community matters diminished as well. And with the exclusion of Whites from the Blacks' ongoing struggles and the end of the Vietnam War, the visible public role that some Reform rabbis had assumed in American life during the sixties likewise melted away. Individual rabbis still exercised national leadership, especially in Zionist affairs, but most of their colleagues found aspirations for a prophetic role mostly giving way before the performance of priestly and pastoral functions for individual congregants. Success in the new rabbinate required a sometimes difficult contraction of ego, an ability and a willingness to lead from within.[64]

In 1965 a special CCAR committee on rabbinical status confirmed the existence of a state of crisis long in the making. Predominantly it saw the crisis as one of waning rabbinical authority. Reform rabbis no longer felt they were effective leaders. Lacking the authority of revealed texts to which more traditional colleagues could appeal, they found that respect for their position and person did not prevent the encroachments of temple officers and boards. Lay leaders had begun to regard rabbis as corporate executives who were expected to perform in accordance with their desires and expectations. One prominent rabbi felt "demeaned, browbeaten, and crushed." By the late sixties, a sizable minority of Reform ordinees was choosing to work in noncongregational positions, with Jewish organizations and with Hillel Foundations, or deciding to leave the rabbinate entirely. Uncertain of the extent and precise nature of rabbinical discontent, the CCAR commissioned a comprehensive survey that would include the views of rabbis, rabbinical students, and a sample of the laity. When completed, it substantiated the leadership's anxiety. Two out of five rabbis thought the rabbinate was indeed in crisis. Seventy-one percent perceived a "Jewish distance" between themselves and the congregation. And only a bare majority of the respondents affirmed that they would choose the rabbinate if they could start their careers over. Especially rabbis with the least traditional theologies expressed dissatisfaction with their vocational choice, as theological and professional doubt apparently went hand in hand. The survey also revealed that nearly two-thirds of the respondents were eager to move closer to Conservative Judaism, but almost the entire remainder, 29 percent, hoped for a thrust in the opposite direction, toward religious humanism. Clearly the Reform rabbinate was discontented and severely at odds.[65]

The rabbis laid part of the blame for the crisis at the doors of the College–Institute. At a time when theological education in America was coming under general attack for its purported lack of social and practical relevance, many rabbis deemed the HUC-

JIR curriculum, with its concentration on the analytical study of classical texts, largely inadequate to the spiritual and professional needs of congregational rabbis. Students shuffling between the roles of jeans-clad humble learners and rabbinical authorities in biweekly student congregations complained of the severe tension inherent in their status. They grumbled about professors insensitive to their spiritual quest, which for most of them now involved both more traditional practice and more theological doubt. Influenced by the spirit of campus revolt in the sixties and by disgust with an America engaged in the Vietnam War, frustrated by a curriculum which they thought lacked the prized quality of relevance, Reform rabbinical students expressed a degree of discontent and bitterness even exceeding that of the ordained rabbis. After a period of severe turmoil, the College–Institute responded as best it could. Stirred to action by the rabbinate, the students, and the establishment of a new rival rabbinical seminary by the Reconstructionist movement in 1968, HUC–JIR undertook to reform its curriculum. It instituted a first year in Jerusalem, gave students more choice in the selection of courses, began to bring congregational rabbis to the campus, and allowed students a greater role in determining the religious life of the school.[66]

With the approach of its centennial in 1973, the UAHC decided to undertake its own survey during 1970/71. Using a representative sample of adults, college students, and confirmation class pupils from twelve congregations, the survey both confirmed widespread withdrawal from liberal activism and revealed that the younger generation was less particularistic than its elders. On such matters as the relative importance of support for Israel, contribution to Jewish philanthropies, synagogue membership, and marrying within the faith, there was a large differential between parents and children. The most distressing finding was that the majority of the respondents—old and young alike—did not regard their temple as an object of significant emotional investment. The synagogue was not their principal reference group and their loyalty to it was only segmental. They were therefore neither greatly enthusiastic nor greatly disturbed by the current state of Reform Judaism; they were simply indifferent to it. The only hopeful finding was the discovery that within each congregation there were some members who sought to make it into a more embracing community, one that offered opportunities for intensive Jewish experience. But for most, Reform Judaism was peripheral to their lives and they were content to let it remain that way.[67]

This lower intensity of Jewish identity was, of course, not limited to the Reform movement. By the late sixties it had become an important contributing factor to the steeply rising rate of mixed marriage among American Jews in general. In an atmosphere where Christian prejudice against marrying Jews was dying out, where young Jews and Christians formed close relationships on college campuses, and where exclusivism of all sorts was regarded with disdain, mixed marriage entered more and more families from all Jewish backgrounds. Reform rabbis were faced with the question of what sanction or condemnation to invoke upon the phenomenon generally and how to relate to those individuals that came within their own orbit. While virtually all Reform rabbis opposed mixed marriage in principle, they were sharply divided on whether to give their blessing to such unions once the couple had decided for matrimony. At the one extreme was a handful of rabbis that would perform a wedding for any mixed couple with no stipulation whatever. They were responsible for a highly disproportionate number of the mixed ceremonies. Far to the other side was the majority of the Reform rabbinate, which refused to officiate at such occasions under any circumstances. In between lay a large group that was favorably inclined provided certain conditions were met. Their requirements varied from rabbi to rabbi, but usually included the intention to establish a Jewish home and raise the children as Jews, a course of study in Judaism, and synagogue membership.

The opponents of rabbinical officiation argued that to participate in a mixed marriage ceremony was a violation of their integrity as rabbis, would split off the Reform movement from the rest of the Jewish religious community, was often requested simply to placate parents or grandparents, and might discourage conversion to Judaism. Proponents held that refusal served to distance the couple from Judaism, meant losing children who might otherwise be raised as Jews, and showed a callous lack of human sensitivity.[68] The rabbinical survey mentioned earlier showed that 41 percent of Reform pulpit rabbis were performing mixed marriages under some set of conditions. Although a large majority of congregants preferred that their children marry Jews, most now wanted a rabbi who would officiate for mixed couples at least in certain instances. Within the rabbinate, the issue was not generational; nor were the percentages very different from what they had been thirty years earlier. What had changed was the social situation. The sheer number of current requests was now so great that Reform rabbis found themselves repeatedly faced with congregational families begging sanction for a mixed marriage. Some temple boards became reluctant to engage rabbis who adamantly refused.[69]

The mixed marriage issue did not arise at CCAR conventions between 1909 and 1947. In the latter year Solomon Freehof could still claim that Reform officiation at mixed marriages was rare and generally limited to unusual circumstances. Nonetheless, at a time of intense Jewish particularism, between the Holocaust and the establishment of the Jewish state, a considerable number of rabbis wanted to shift from the 1909 position, which simply discouraged mixed marriage, to one that explicitly called upon Reform rabbis not to officiate. The new resolution, however, failed on a close vote of seventy-four to seventy-six, and the old one was then simply reaffirmed. Fifteen years later the matter came up again. This time it was the proponents of liberalization who pressed for a resolution that would tacitly sanction rabbinical officiation—but they too were rebuffed.[70] Then in 1971, in the face of increased congregational pressures on rabbis who refused, the opponents of officiation once again took the initiative. They felt the situation now demanded a stronger statement that would "preserve our self-respect as a rabbinic body." The showdown came two years later, in 1973. After careful preparation of strategy, the Conference's inner circle of leadership pressed its case for a resolution whose operative clause declared CCAR "opposition to participation by its members in any ceremony which solemnizes a mixed marriage." Too long, they argued, had the 1909 statement served as "a screen behind which one could do, and did, as one pleased." Opponents countered that the Conference had "no right to legislate conscience." After a long, passionate, and bitter debate, the first part of the resolution, which opposed rabbinical participation, passed by a vote of 321 to 196, or slightly more than three to two. The losing faction was little appeased by a later sentence explicitly recognizing the fact that Reform rabbis "have held and continue to hold divergent interpretations of Jewish tradition," but which did not exalt such differences. All agreed on a final section urging encouragement of individuals who had already entered into a mixed marriage to identify personally and raise their children as Jews. But the resolution as a whole represented a severe defeat for those universalist rabbis who believed their position Jewishly and humanly correct.[71]

Another major controversy in the early and mid-seventies concerned the proper relationship of Diaspora Jews to the state of Israel. In the flush of the 1967 victory, American Reform Jews had celebrated Israel and given little thought to the still veiled consequences of its territorial gains. The CCAR passed a resolution to "institute Israel Independence Day as a permanent festival to be observed annually on the fifth day of *Iyar* as part of our spiritual history and religious life." It decided to hold some of its annual conventions in Jerusalem. By 1970, however, as Israeli public opinion began to divide sharply on the future of the West Bank and other occupied areas while the official Jewish leadership in America suppressed any Diaspora divergence from Israeli policy, some leaders of the Reform movement began to break ranks. The Reform magazine for laity published a collection of diverse Israeli views, and Eisendrath introduced the symposium by identifying with those Israelis who condemned "ostrich-like denial of the very existence of a Palestinian entity," provocative resettlement of occupied territories, and inadequate initiatives regarding Arab refugees. He called for the same free and open discussion of such issues among American Jews as there was in Israel. During the seventies a growing number of Reform rabbis and laity similarly called for the encouragement of such dissent as was based on loyalty and love. Some joined a controversial organization called Breira, which urged Israel to actively explore all options for peace and negotiate with any group willing to recognize its existence and to foreswear terrorism. Other Reform Jews, however, were leery of such criticism since it might, they thought, be used by Israel's enemies. They found Breira a danger to the state and Reform participation in it an embarrassment. Confrontation between the two factions was sometimes bitter. However, both rabbinate and laity soon adopted a position that called for free discussion of Israeli issues within the American Jewish community. The rabbis, in addition, favored ultimate self-determination for the Palestinian Arabs, while the laity espoused no specific solution to the Arab–Israeli impasse.[72]

Renewal

Although the anxiety born of inner division and uncertain direction was not quickly or easily dissipated, the American Reform movement in the 1970s underwent a period of renewal. Although it continued to have difficulty in reaching out to the periphery, at its center it was creating a new liturgy, a Reform Halakhah, and the opportunity for more intensive Jewish education. It strengthened spiritual leadership by opening its rabbinate to women, restructured congregations to encourage more encompassing participation, moved even further into the mainstream of Jewish life, and adopted a new platform expressive of shared commitments. By the end of the decade, a cautious hopefulness was dispelling the malaise.

In nearly every Reform congregation the trend to greater traditionalism continued. More rabbis and congregants covered their heads at worship, more of the service was in Hebrew—now almost invariably in the Sephardi pronunciation. Hidden choirs gave way to visible cantors, who were increasingly graduates of the movement's School of Sacred Music. The penitential *selihot* service, held late on the Saturday evening before Rosh Hashanah, gained entry into the liturgical cycle. For a while, Bar and Bat Mitzvah rituals were a cause for dispute. As highly personalized ceremonies, opponents argued, they detracted from the congregational nature of the Saturday morning service, and the receptions that followed were often garishly ostentatious. Moreover, they tended to diminish the significance of confirmation and discourage continued Jewish study after the age of thirteen. Yet the emotional need they fulfilled proved irresistible. Bar and Bat Mitzvah quickly became a powerful symbol of the link between three generations, at a time when that link was not always apparent. The occasion also provided an indispensable stimulus to preparatory Hebrew education and it drew large numbers to a Saturday morning service that otherwise gathered only very few. A survey taken in 1960 showed that by then more than 96 percent of Reform congregations had adopted the increasingly popular ceremony.[73]

Jewish liturgical music in the postwar period shifted from operatic tunes to melodies based on internally Jewish modes, especially biblical cantillation. Rhythms now bore a closer relationship to the flow of the Hebrew language. Gradually the hallowed melodies of Sulzer and Lewandowski gave way to new ones by contemporary composers. The Israeli influence was especially apparent in the introduction of popular folk songs and in the greater proportion of congregational hymns sung in Hebrew. In many congregations the organ—once the hallmark of Reform—assumed less musical significance, especially where it had to make room for the more informal style of the guitar. Only on the High Holidays did it remain unchallenged. Hasidic tunes, too, found their way into the much expanded musical repertoire.[74]

For American Reform Judaism the seventies was a period of intense liturgical creativity. The first volume to appear was a new Reform Haggadah for Passover.[75] Larger and more lavishly illustrated than its predecessor, it was both more traditional and more radical. Abandoning the earlier didacticism, it allowed for a richer, multivalent symbolism. Classical elements once abandoned, such as the Ten Plagues, reappeared. Yet the Haggadah departed from accepted practice in restoring the ancient custom of eating the ceremonial foods at the beginning of the recitation instead of directly before the meal. It created immense variety by interspersing optional readings, especially material on the Holocaust and the Jewish national rebirth. With the new Haggadah, the individual Reform *seder* could range from the classical and highly Hebraic to a greatly abridged, mostly vernacular service that was specifically relevant to the contemporary Jewish age.

The creation of new prayerbooks for the American movement proved a difficult task. Although the more active laity was generally satisfied with the *Union Prayer Book,* by the late sixties most rabbis were unhappy with it. Many thought some prayers too theocentric, and others, which stressed God's goodness, blasphemous after the Holocaust. But they could not at all agree on the direction that liturgical revision should take. Some wanted to continue the trend toward a more traditional liturgy; others desired greater room for innovation and for unorthodox theology. Increasingly, individual rabbis were producing their own experimental liturgies, which, occasionally or regularly, they substituted for the *UPB*. The Liturgy Committee of the CCAR soon found it could not achieve the degree of compromise that would allow for uniformity. It chose instead to opt for wide theological and stylistic variety. When *Sha'are Tefilah—Gates of Prayer* for weekdays, Sabbaths, and festivals appeared in 1975, it was nearly 800 pages long and far exceeded its predecessor in all physical dimensions. Rather than an integral prayerbook, it was a compendium of multiple liturgies done by many hands. Traditionalists found it contained the blessings for donning phylacteries and prayer shawl, reintroduction of the Aramaic half-*kaddish* separating elements of the liturgy, and the traditional *alenu* sharply distinguishing Israel's destiny from those of other peoples. In fact in one form or another, in one place or another, the new prayerbook contained nearly every classical theme except for the messianic hope of reestablishing the ancient sacrificial service. But the radically inclined, too, could draw satisfaction. There were some highly innovative liturgies, some that were mostly in English, and a Friday evening alternative that bordered on religious humanism. One critic judged that only the bookbinder's art could press together so much contradiction between the covers of a single volume. Yet the internal dissonance was troublesome only if consistency was judged more valuable than inclusiveness. Because *Gates of Prayer* offered something for everyone and because at least some of the innovation possessed wide appeal, it was able—after some resistance—to win acceptance even in temples where attachment to the earlier Reform prayerbook was profound, especially among older congregants. The new prayerbook represented—and celebrated—the diversity that, for better or worse, characterized the movement.[76]

Gates of Prayer was followed in short succession by a prayerbook for the home, *Gates of the House* (1977), a book of readings on Reform Jewish liturgy, *Gates of Understanding* (1977), and a new High Holiday liturgy, *Gates of Repentance* (1978). Also during the 1970s the first two volumes of the UAHC-sponsored *The Torah: A Modern Commentary* appeared. Completed in 1981, that highly praised work marked the first time the Reform movement anywhere had created its own interpretation of the weekly scriptural readings.

The emergence of a more solid center was most apparent in the area of individual practice. Surveys showed that by the mid-fifties ritual observance among Reform Jews was twice what it had been a generation earlier: 59 versus 26 percent lit Sabbath candles, 26 versus 15 percent recited the Friday evening *kiddush*. Lighting the Hanukah candles and participating in a Passover *seder* went from 40 and 33 percent to 81 and 74 percent. By then close to a quarter of the surveyed Reform Jews also kept some degree of *kashrut,* even if it amounted only to avoiding pork in their homes. During the next twenty years, observance continued to rise for those rituals associated with family-oriented festival celebrations. Hanukah candles and the Passover *seder* became almost universal.[77]

Increasingly, Reform rabbis expressed interest in following Jewish custom on ritual issues that arose in their congregations. They were eager to learn the position of the rabbinic sources. Whereas in earlier years the Responsa Committee of the CCAR had received less than a dozen inquiries a year, in the 1960s more than 200 questions were reaching it annually. Once again, as in the earliest period of its history, the Reform movement was seeking traditional legal precedent for its practice. During the twenty years between 1960 and 1980 the committee's chairman, Solomon Freehof, published seven volumes of responsa, drawn from those opinions which he thought of greatest general interest. The vast majority of the responsa dealt with specific issues that had arisen with regard to life-cycle practices, from circumcision to burial. The remainder included synagogue arrangements, holiday celebrations, medical ethics, and such individual matters as conversion, suicide, and homosexuality. What made Reform responsa different from traditional examples of the genre was the nondeterminative status of the Halakhah. The enterprise was motivated by the desire to know and take seriously the Jewish legal tradition, and to create a greater sense of relationship and continuity with it. But in the Reform perspective Jewish law remained human, if nobly so, authoritative enough to influence but not to wrest the final decision from individual conscience. Reform subjectivism was still dominant, except that the Halakhah had been given greater weight in individual decision making. As Freehof frequently noted, Reform responsa were intended to provide "guidance, not governance."[78]

The responsa provided such guidance only on specific issues. Hence they could not satisfy the more fundamental desire, now increasingly expressed, for a comprehensive guide to Reform practice—for nothing less, in fact, than a Reform Halakhah. In general, those rabbis who were covenant theologians were also the chief advocates of an authoritative guide to what God required of Jews in the area of ritual practice. They wanted to link their conception of a revealing God with ceremonial acts, understood as mitzvot. They also believed that, reciprocally, a regimen of Jewish living would fortify awareness of the covenant relationship.[79] The covenant theologians were joined by others of less traditional views who saw the value of such a guide in making Reform Jews more aware of what the tradition offered them and encouraging them to enrich their religious life, even if observance was not understood as divine command. On the other side of the issue stood those rabbis and laypeople who feared the constricting effect of any Reform code.

As early as 1938, the UAHC Committee on Synagogue and Community had recommended adoption of a "Code of Reform Jewish Ceremonial Observance." Shortly after Eisendrath became Union President, he told the UAHC General Assembly that only a movement which "hews to at least a minimum code of practice, which demands at least a modicum of observance in ceremonial as well as in social and moral conduct, will possess that authority and effectiveness necessary to withstand the spiritual chaos of our time." But while 85 percent of Reform Jews in 1953 favored a guide to help them select practices voluntarily, only about a third of the laypeople and only 28 percent of the rabbis were ready to accept an authoritative code.[80] Despite early efforts by lay and rabbinical committees in the forties and fifties, no collectively endorsed ritual guide would be issued until decades later. What did occur is that individual rabbis composed their own guides, thereby following the traditional precedent that prominent scholars compiled law codes, which then gradually won general acceptance. The first of such Reform works was a simple booklet of suggestions for establishing a Jewish home that one congregational rabbi gave to the couples that he married. The second was similar, but intended to familiarize new congregants with the observances sanctioned by Reform Judaism. Neither could claim to be a code; neither spoke the language of obligation.[81] The third effort, *A Guide for Reform Jews,* by Rabbis Frederic A. Doppelt and David Polish (1957), went much further. That book addressed the Reform Jewish community as a whole, and it spoke the language of mitzvot, understood theologically as reenacting "spiritual moments in Jewish history when the Jewish people came upon God." It also introduced the categories of halakhot, defined as the accepted ways to perform mitzvot in concrete life situations, and minhagim, those folk customs that were subsidiary to mitzvot and did not possess equivalent authority. What gave the Doppelt–Polish guide its distinctly Reform character was the authors' readiness not only to dispense with many of the traditional mitzvot, especially the prohibitions, but boldly to introduce new ones. Thus confirmation became obligatory, as did the observance of a memorial day for the martyrs of Nazism and a religious celebration for Israel Independence Day.[82]

Collectively, the Reform movement first produced a guide limited to Sabbath observance entitled *Tadrikh Le-Shabat—A Shabbat Manual* (1972). Its sometimes tortured language could scarcely conceal the painful compromise which alone had made possible its broad endorsement by the CCAR. Eschewing both belief in God as the One who commands and the notion of mitzvot as mere folkways, the Sabbath guide spoke of a God who "offers an opportunity to introduce an 'ought' into our existence," leaving open the specific role and weight of the divine and the human. It did use the language of mitzvot and it included prohibitions as well as positive imperatives for Sabbath observance. But most of the book was devoted simply to presenting home rituals for the Sabbath, from the lighting of the candles at its beginning to the *havdalah* ceremony at its conclusion. Despite the theological division among Reform Jews, few could doubt the value of teaching those less informed how to enrich their Sabbath experience.

Seven years later the CCAR extended guidance to the Jewish life cycle. Like its predecessor, *Gates of Mitzvah* (1979), too, remained theologically vague, reserving interpretation of the word "mitzvah" to four divergent appended essays. Although for the most part the mitzvot it listed were traditional ones, others, such as a couple being tested for genetic disease before marriage, rested solely on a CCAR resolution. It urged readers to study and consider the value of *kashrut,* but it did not designate dietary laws as mitzvot.

Clearly these guides were a far cry from the Orthodox *Shulḥan Arukh.* Yet they represented an effort unprecedented in American Reform Judaism. Their goal was to delineate Reform practice, not just descriptively as Freehof had already done in 1944, but prescriptively and collectively. To be sure, most Reform Jews did not reach the level of observance mandated for the Sabbath and for life-cycle events. But as they began to circulate within the Reform community, these books did provide evidence that Reform Judaism possessed standards of practice, even though they represented an ideal. Those Reform Jews who wanted to come in from the periphery now had guides to show them the way.[83]

The effort to enrich observance depended in the long run upon the ability to raise a more knowledgeable and committed younger generation. Reform Jewish education in the post-Gamoran era became more professional, diversified, and—for some— intensive. The National Association of Temple Educators, founded in 1954, gave new status to Reform Jewish educators; HUC–JIR now provided professional training for religious school principals and teachers. During the 1950s, the UAHC's most touted educational innovation was its new Audio-Visual Department, which began to produce an array of filmstrips designed to enliven learning in the religious school. The most promising educational advance, however, was the camping program. Following World War II, an increasing number of religious schools began to send their students to newly purchased or rented camp facilities where, during a weekend or vacation period, they could create a more encompassing and conducive educational environment, often teaching more, and with less resistance, in a concentrated camp session than in many weeks of Sunday morning classes. The UAHC began to acquire its own camps, first in Oconomowoc, Wisconsin and Saratoga, California, later in almost every region of the country. Largely through the impact of camping programs, the National Federation of Temple Youth grew into a major youth movement. Its yearly leadership institutes drew the best Reform Jewish youth and prompted some to seek professional careers in the movement. Adopting nomenclature from the Kennedy years, NFTY also launched a Torah Corps for intensive study, an urban Mitzvah Corps for social work in American ghettos, and an overseas Mitzvah Corps to aid disadvantaged families in Israel. For many years its special project was support of the Leo Baeck School in Haifa.[84]

The Reform religious school curriculum continued to shift from instruction in religious and ethical principles to the creation of tangible Jewish experiences. Jewish attitudes, habits, and appreciations, achieved through affective learning, were now as valued as the transmission of factual information. The textbooks of this era focused even more than earlier upon specifically Jewish concerns rather than on a universal message; the educational goal shifted further from a Reform Jewish identity to a more encompassing identification with all Jews, regardless of religious movement. Though theology was not absent, the Reform curriculum of the seventies was much more oriented to sociology—to learning about Jews more than to learning about Judaism. By the late seventies, enrollment in most Reform religious schools had either stabilized or was again rising.[85]

Prompted by Bar and Bat Mitzvah preparation and the influence of Israel, Hebrew instruction continued to expand during the postwar years. The vast majority of children in Reform religious schools now received some exposure to the language.[86] By 1977 nearly all schools had raised the age of confirmation to the tenth grade, the larger ones providing postconfirmation classes as well. Yet the perceived inability of the one or two day a week school to provide more than a smattering of Jewish knowledge prompted some rabbis and congregants in the early 1960s to urge the creation of Reform options for more intensive Jewish education. In the 1940s American Orthodoxy had established a growing network of day schools. A decade later the Conservative movement, after brief internal opposition, began to do the same. For Reform Jews, deeply committed to the public schools, to the separation of church and state, and to educational integration, day schools represented a far more controversial issue. For a long time rabbis and laity remained sharply divided. Opponents argued vehemently that Reform Judaism and the all-day Jewish school were nothing less than incompatible, that they represented a retreat from broader social responsibility. However, in 1968 the UAHC–CCAR Commission on Jewish Education, by a large majority, decided to encourage Reform day schools. A 1969 survey showed that the rabbis, too, were in favor by a proportion of better than four to one. But the broader lay leadership was not yet ready to make the establishment of day schools a UAHC-sponsored project. The initiative therefore passed to local congregations, some of whose members were already sending their children to Conservative or private schools. Under the impetus of the new particularism, and to some extent also negatively motivated by the decline of public education, congregational day schools began to appear in the early 1970s, first in New York and Miami, then in Los Angeles, Phoenix, and Toronto. By 1981 the number of Reform day schools had risen to nine and enrollment seemed destined to increase.[87] Though they represented only a minute share of Reform Jewish education, the day schools were a further indication of resurgent vitality.

For a time the apex of the Reform educational system, Hebrew Union College–Jewish Institute of Religion, remained shaken by rabbinical and lay critique. In the early 1970s, the existence of four campuses—in Cincinnati, New York, Los Angeles, and Jerusalem—seemed to many in the movement both inefficient and unsupportable. Its leadership was forced to seriously consider closing the Cincinnati campus, which had been a product of Isaac Mayer Wise's chance move to that city in 1854, and which now resided in a Jewish community that constituted less than one percent of American Jewry. Only after prolonged deliberation, and mostly on account of the expense and loss of donations that would result from any closing, did a Board of Governors task force recommend maintaining all four campuses. But that task force also recognized that the multiple-campus network had a distinct advantage. It provided the possibility for specialization extending beyond the common and focal rabbinical training program. Cincinnati became the center for graduate studies, New York for sacred music and education, Los Angeles for education, undergraduate studies, and communal service, and Israel for archaeological excavations. Cincinnati also possessed the American Jewish Archives, established by the well-known historian Jacob Rader Marcus in 1947, and it was there that the scholarly *Hebrew Union College Annual* and the books published by Hebrew Union College Press were edited. Following the death of Nelson Glueck in 1971, Rabbi Alfred Gottschalk, who as a child had fled from Nazi Germany, became president of the College–Institute. His remarkable skill as a fund-raiser enabled the school to continue the accelerated expansion of facilities and faculty that his predecessor had begun.

Perhaps the event of most fundamental significance in the history of the College–Institute during these years occurred in 1972, when it became the first seminary anywhere to ordain a woman as rabbi. The issue was first raised forty years earlier when Martha Neumark, the daughter of an HUC professor, unleashed a flurry of debate, halakhic opinion, and simple prejudice with her request to receive ordination. In the end, the CCAR supported her, concluding that women "cannot justly be denied the privilege of ordination," while the HUC faculty decided unanimously that, despite the position of the Halakhah, "in view of the fact that Reform Judaism has in many other instances departed from traditional practice, it cannot logically and consistently refuse the ordination of women." But when the College's Board of Governors received the matter for final disposition, they balked at the prospect, fearing that the synagogue might become yet more "an affair of the women." A majority voted to continue the existing practice of ordaining only males. Thereupon the matter was put to rest for a generation. When it was raised again among Sisterhood leaders in 1958, even they were initially divided. By then, however, one woman, Regina Jonas, had received private ordination upon completing her studies at the Liberal seminary in Berlin, and for a brief time had served as a rabbi before perishing in the Holocaust. Another woman, the widow of a Reform rabbi, had taken over her husband's pulpit in Meridian, Mississippi from 1951 to 1954. And in the mid-fifties mainline American Protestantism had begun breaking with tradition by admitting women to prestigious seminaries and ordaining them as ministers. With these precedents, and also because of the shortage of rabbis during that period of congregational growth, a CCAR committee in the late 1950s once again explored the issue and expressed its support for the ordination of women. However, in the absence of suitable candidates, the matter remained academic until a decade later when Sally Priesand was admitted to HUC–JIR in Cincinnati. Upon ordination, the new rabbi found that some congregations were unwilling to consider her and that uprooting deep-seated attitudes would be a long and difficult struggle. At each stage, first the assistantship to an older male rabbi, then the achievement of independent status, she confronted the difficult task of breaching formidable psychological barriers. Yet with the reemergence of feminism in America, more women candidates for the rabbinate appeared. As the number of women rabbis increased and as American women generally began to play a larger role in all professions, female rabbis ceased to be a curiosity. The movement came to value them as a hitherto untapped source of spiritual leadership.[88]

The increasing influence of women in Reform Judaism was apparent in other areas as well. Between 1956 and 1970 the percentage of congregations that had elected women to their boards rose from 72 to 96 percent. By the 1950s, there were already a few Reform congregations with women presidents; in 1973, when such presidencies were no longer unusual, the UAHC elected its first woman vice chairman. Under the influence of the feminist movement, Reform Judaism supported the Equal Rights Amendment and women's freedom to obtain abortions. Its textbooks began to present female role models other than mothers and teachers and its Sisterhoods adapted their programs to the rising percentage of working women. *Gates of Prayer,* in its English portions, removed male language in reference to the worshipers: "all men" became "all"; "fellowship" became "friendship." One English version of the *avot* prayer made reference to the "God of our mothers" as well as of our fathers. Yet, although there were experimental substitutions of nongender names and pronouns also for God, the standard Reform liturgy in the 1970s continued to refer to deity as "our Father, our King" and as "He" and "Him." Moreover, the Hebrew prayers remained untouched by feminist criticism.[89]

As synagogue leadership diversified with the inclusion of women, congregational membership likewise became more varied as it embraced an ever larger percentage of converts. A 1953 study estimated that in that year about 2,000 American non-Jews converted to Judaism, half of them under Reform auspices. By the late sixties, perhaps as many as 7,000 were converting annually and the number was continuing to rise. More women converted than men, and about nine out of ten did so in connection with marriage to a Jew. In 1947 the CCAR had resolved that sincere candidates were acceptable whether or not their conversion was prompted by impending matrimony. Shortly thereafter, the Conference urged more active efforts to draw in proselytes— along with unaffiliated Jews. The UAHC too, somewhat later, launched a program to find prospective converts among nonpracticing Christians. In the larger cities it sponsored ongoing courses entitled "Introduction to Judaism."[90]

Candidates for Reform conversion were expected to attain a basic knowledge of Jewish beliefs and practices as well as some familiarity with Jewish community institutions. Frequently the prospective Jewish spouse attended the classes as well, with the result that such couples received a higher than average amount of adult Jewish education. The Reform conversion ceremony required proselytes to disavow their former faith, pledge loyalty to Judaism and the Jewish people, establish a Jewish home, participate actively in Jewish life, and rear their children in the Jewish faith. They were not required to undergo ritual immersion in a *mikveh;* male converts did not have to be circumcised or, if already circumcised surgically, to undergo the symbolic drawing of a drop of blood. Reform rabbis felt that these physical acts, though required by Halakhah, vitiated rather than enhanced the spiritual nature of the process. In 1953, when even among Conservative rabbis only a small minority required these practices, Reform rabbis were almost unanimous in disregarding them. But thereafter, in the attempt to build bridges to more traditional Jews and out of deference to the more halakhically oriented Israeli movement, a broadening shift in attitude began to occur. While very few Reform rabbis in the 1970s made *tevilah* (ritual immersion) and *hatafat dam* (drawing a drop of blood) mandatory, an increasing number presented candidates for conversion with the option of following halahkhic procedure.[91]

The influx of new converts profoundly changed the character of Reform congregations. A review of membership records for one large temple revealed that as early as 1964 at least 10 percent of affiliated families included one or more converts, and the proportion was rising. By the seventies, converts were frequently playing important roles in synagogue life. Some were congregational officers or Sisterhood presidents; many taught in religious schools. While not all "Jews by choice" became actively Jewish, those who did often displayed a higher degree of religious commitment than born Jews, in some instances drawing their reluctant spouses into congregational activity as well. Sometimes, too, they were forced to fight tacit rejection, strive mightily to overcome residual elements of their former identity, and adjust to the fact that fellow congregants, unlike themselves, simply took Judaism for granted. Probably on account of the Christian model with which they grew up, converts understood being Jewish in fundamentally religious, rather than ethnic terms. In contrast to born Jews, who in the 1970s looked to the community and to Israel-oriented Jewish organizations as primary, Jews by choice identified far more with the synagogue. As such, they too—along with female leadership—furnished a fresh resource for congregational life.[92]

Within Reform synagogues in the 1970s, Jews by choice mingled with distinctly differing kinds of born Jews. There remained a diminishing sector of German ancestry, mostly third- and fourth-generation Reform Jews, who retained their attachment to classical Reform Judaism. Concentrated in a few large-city congregations, they now made up less than 20 percent of the movement, but in some temples they represented a disproportionate percentage of the wealthier families. Within the Reform laity they were the most ideological and fervent in their commitment to Reform as a separate entity. Directly opposed to the remaining classicists were the advocates of traditionalism. They were mostly the men and women of east European ancestry and were proportionately the less affluent. Many had recently come from Orthodox and Conservative Judaism. They supported the trend toward more elaborate custom and ceremony, though more often for reasons of emotional impact than out of commitment to Halakhah. The synagogue and its rituals were a way for them to express solidarity with the Jewish people and its heritage.[93] Most of the younger rabbis also leaned in the traditionalist direction, in their case often out of theological and halakhic conviction. Unlike earlier generations, the Reform Jews of the 1970s were thus a very diverse group: born Jews and Jews by choice, Jews of German and east European ancestry, wealthy and middle-class, classicist and neo-Reform.

The fragmenting effect of this diversity was exacerbated by the new privatism in synagogue life that became cause for complaint in the 1970s. Many congregants had come to regard the synagogue mostly as a supplier of private needs. They frequently saw it as a service institution, which provided the religious ceremonies associated with birth, puberty, marriage, and death. They valued rabbis according to their ability to enhance individual lives rather than the collective life of the congregation. For most laypeople, the religious philosophy of the movement was far less significant than the synagogues' occasional psychological effect on individual lives. Though not limited to Reform Judaism or even to Jews, this constriction was particularly felt in the Reform synagogue where the attachment of many members tended to be peripheral, and easily diminished to High Holiday observance and emotionally important life-cycle events.[94]

It became apparent that the large synagogue in its totality could rarely attract strong feelings of identification. A growing number of both Conservative and Reform rabbis therefore began to create intermediate groups between congregation and family that could, within the framework of the temple, serve as meaningful communities. These *havurot,* which originated in the contemporary counterculture of Jewish young people outside the synagogue, studied and celebrated together, visited their sick, counseled their troubled, and shared individual joys. They were able to combat alienation more effectively than the large synagogue with its busy rabbinical leadership. In the literature of the Reform movement the idea of creating synagogue *havurot* first occurs in 1966 in connection with Sabbath observance. However, *havurot* did not become a common occurrence in Reform synagogues until a decade later. Contemporary studies showed that members of these semiautonomous subgroups developed a stronger sense of religious community than average congregants. Although the focus of their religious identification was the *havurah,* they tended also to participate more actively in the synagogue as a whole. Though made up of only a small minority within a minority of Reform synagogues, they created a sense of participation that had wider impact. Like *Gates of Mitzvah,* the *havurot* in the 1970s provided a vehicle for those congregants who sought to give Reform Judaism a more central role in their lives.[95]

It now also began to appear that Reform Judaism's demographic stagnation might be coming to an end. A 1973 survey of temple administrators revealed that congregational membership was again rising, with the largest gains coming in Florida, Texas, and California. Religious school enrollments were also expanding once more, and by the late seventies there were again more rabbinical positions available than rabbis to fill them. Statistical evidence revealed that Reform Judaism possessed special appeal for third- and fourth-generation American Jews, leading one sociologist to predict it was "on its way to becoming the largest American Jewish denomination." A Greater Boston survey showed that from 1965 to 1975 relative preference for Reform had increased at the expense of both Orthodox and Conservative Judaism. While children of Conservative Jews frequently favored Reform, the opposite was seldom true. As American Jews migrated from the northeastern cities with relatively low Reform affiliation to middle-sized communities in the South and West, they became more likely to join Reform temples. Population trends among American Jews in the late 1980s were creating a Jewish community that in its majority was ever more closely approximating the social composition and intellectual profile of the Reform synagogue: generally high levels of affluence and secular education, a larger share of mixed couples and converts, a firm belief in gender equality, rootedness in American culture, and a liberal orientation in politics.[96]

One additional reason for Reform's broad attraction was that it continued the move toward full participation in the larger Jewish community. Although on some issues, such as rabbinical officiation at mixed marriage and manner of conversion, the Reform movement was set apart by its own internal division, in most other matters it was more than ever a part of *kelal yisrael.* When Maurice Eisendrath died in 1973, he was replaced by a rabbi associated primarily with the field of education, the UAHC vice president, Alexander Schindler. Unlike his predecessor, Schindler possessed a large measure of *yiddishkeit*—Jewish ethnic feeling. That quality stood him in good stead when, as UAHC president, he became the first Reform religious leader to head the Conference of Presidents of Major American Jewish Organizations, the most representative body of American Jewry. Under Alfred Gottschalk, HUC–JIR likewise attained greater recognition in the general Jewish community, especially through its program for training professional community leadership and its Jewish museum in Los Angeles.

Though still divided on Israeli political issues and increasingly alienated by Israel's treatment of its own Reform Jews, American Reform Judaism in the late 1970s also became more actively Zionist. In 1977, in order both to support Israel with greater vigor and to press its own concerns more effectively, it created the Association of Reform Zionists of America (ARZA). ARZA soon became a constituent of the World Zionist Organization and developed a program calling for liberal Israeli political policies and religious equality for all Israeli Jews. It gave American Reform Judaism its own distinctive voice within the Zionist enterprise, which, more than any other collective endeavor, united world Jewry. Though only a minority of Reform Jews paid the extra membership fee to join ARZA, an increasing number did so. And a few younger American Reform Jews took Zionism seriously enough to settle in Israel, especially on the Reform kibbutzim. In 1976 the UAHC had affirmed its "special duty" to encourage and assist them.[97]

Was the new American Reform Judaism then sufficiently different to warrant a new platform that would replace the one adopted in Columbus in 1937? Given the undeniable diversity, was a common position even possible? Despite widespread disagreement on the answers to both questions, the approach of the UAHC centennial in 1973 and the HUC centennial in 1975 created an impetus at least to attempt a new formulation. Representatives from the HUC–JIR faculty, the congregational rabbinate, and the laity began to meet for that purpose in 1971. They wrote lengthy position papers, fervently discussed the most important questions, but failed to reach agreement on basic issues of theology and Halakhah. After nearly three years, they simply gave up, and the failed effort seemed but one more example of Reform disunity.[98]

Yet even as the official committee was deliberating, an informal alumni seminar at the New York campus of HUC–JIR was composing its own "platform" under the guidance of Professor Eugene Borowitz. Traditionalist both in theology and in its affirmation of Halakhah, the document produced here was not a possible vehicle for consensus. However, when the official venture collapsed, CCAR president Robert Kahn in 1975 turned to Borowitz and to a new committee—this time composed only of Conference members. He charged it with formulating at least a unifying "statement" that would help "heal the wounds in our movement." In about a year the broadly constituted new committee had agreed on a consensus document that was, in fact, a new platform. Adopted readily by the CCAR in 1976, "Reform Judaism: A Centenary Perspective" remarkably well reflected the state of the movement.[99]

In full awareness of American Reform's fragmentation, the new platform began by asserting the unity which it hoped to demonstrate. But before that demonstration, it proceeded to display an unprecedented degree of historical awareness. The platform noted that during a hundred years Reform teachings had spread well beyond Reform Jewry. Most Jews had come to believe that religious tradition must interact with modern culture, religious forms satisfy aesthetic sensibilities, critical scholarship be applied to Jewish sources, and change be recognized as a fundamental reality in Jewish life. On the other hand, Reform itself had learned lessons, and therefore changed: the Holocaust had shattered its earlier optimism, the state of Israel raised its consciousness of the Jews as a people. Whereas earlier platforms had dwelt on religious beliefs and actions, the Centenary Perspective repeatedly spoke the language of "survival," thereby counterbalancing the familiar universalistic aspirations.

To achieve consensus, the platform avoided taking a clear theological position. It affirmed "God's reality" without mentioning covenant, humanity's "share in God's eternality despite the mystery we call death" without specifying individual immortality. It explained Torah as resulting from "the relationship between God and the Jewish people" and Israel as an "uncommon union of faith and peoplehood." Mitzvot became "claims made upon us"—for some made by God, for others by the past or by the self. Beginning with history, the Centenary Perspective also ended with history, affirming that "with God's help people are not powerless to affect their destiny" as they work and wait for the messianic age. Like a traditional text, the new platform left much to individual interpretation.

Yet however vague and equivocal, however precarious its dialectical balance, the 1976 Perspective did give the movement a new sense of oneness. Underlying the obvious differences, it insisted, were some common lessons, teachings, and goals that Reform Jews could collectively articulate and affirm. True, the new American Reform Judaism did not enjoy the fuller ideological unity of the old; in many respects it remained internally divided. But with fresh growth, creativity, and an expression of unity, it completed the 1970s with greater self-confidence and better founded hope.

Epilogue: In Quest
of Continuity

At the end one asks once more: What, after all this history and contemporary divergence, binds the Reform movement together? Where is its diachronic and synchronic continuity? More specifically, what do contemporary Reform Jews in the Americas, Europe, Australia, South Africa, and Israel share with the nineteenth-century founders? The answer must begin: in some respects very little. The early Reformers were rebels against a traditional Judaism then crystallizing into an Orthodoxy that stood in the way of religious change, and that they believed could not meet the challenges of the modern world. Committed to their conception of an evolving Judaism as the only hope for Jewish religious survival at a time when Jews were integrating with their environments, they strove to bring the entire Jewish community into the camp of religious modernity. For Geiger and his contemporaries in Germany, for Wise and his associates in America, the future lay with a purified and progressive Judaism, and they were Reformers in the literal sense, seeking to reshape Jewish belief and practice with an eye to that future.

Present-day Reform Judaism no longer seeks to reform Judaism for all Jews, though many of its ideas and practices have found support beyond its institutional boundaries. Reluctantly it has made its peace with a Jewish world where it occupies one position on the spectrum between a persisting Orthodoxy and a secularism that replaces religion with Jewish national or ethnic identity. Within that spectrum it is pulled by contradictory forces simultaneously toward greater traditionalism and toward greater accommodation with environmental realities over which it has little control. The countervailing forces make it difficult to detect any clear direction of thrust.

What binds today's Reform Jews to the founders and to one another is neither a common theology nor a wholly common regimen of religious life. Some Reform Jews are selectively moving toward more traditional concepts and practices, others are on a personal odyssey away from them, yet others remain indifferent. Some retain an overriding commitment to universalism, others enthusiastically endorse the new particularism. There is less a sense of moving along together than a shared feeling of tension that cannot be fully resolved, even as the contradictory forces and divisive issues which produce it themselves remain beyond final resolution.

The movement today represents that current within religious Judaism that flows precariously in a channel close to its edge. Unlike Conservative Judaism, it does not possess the comfort of being in the center; unlike Orthodoxy, it lacks the security of unshaken faith. Some of its waters are always threatening to spill out and be lost. Yet for well over a million Reform Jews there is no course that better combines universal moral aspiration and intellectual honesty, drawn from inside the Jewish heritage, with Jewish religious faith and ethnic loyalty.

To be a Reform Jew today means to live in a community whose shared affirmations of tenet and intent, formulated and reformulated in books, sermons, and platforms, remain ever in flux, even when the individual seeks to give them permanence through persistent application to daily life. That is a situation common to all religious liberalisms. What endures and binds, however, is not merely the "condition" of being a Reform Jew. There is also an ongoing task. The German Reformers spoke repeatedly of integrating two elements: *Lehre und Leben,* the teaching (Torah) and the life led in the modern world. Individual Reformers and Reform communities have differed— and continue to differ—on the relative weight to be assigned each of these elements. Those closest to tradition have stressed the teaching, those furthest from it have argued for the decisive impact of modern life. Yet the reestablishment of the scale's fulcrum in every generation, in every individual religious conscience, and in the collective life, has been an enduring characteristic of Reform. Perhaps it is the ongoing and common task of creating ever anew that shifting and delicate balance between Torah and modernity—and of relating the two to each other—that in the broadest sense best defines the Reform movement.

Appendix:
Platforms of American
Reform Judaism

1885
1937
1976

The Pittsburgh Platform (1885)

In view of the wide divergence of opinion, of conflicting ideas in Judaism to-day, we, as representatives of Reform Judaism in America, in continuation of the work begun at Philadelphia, in 1869, unite upon the following principles:

First. We recognize in every religion an attempt to grasp the Infinite, and in every mode, source or book of revelation, held sacred in any religious system, the consciousness of the indwelling of God in man. We hold that Judaism presents the highest conception of the God–idea as taught in our Holy Scriptures and developed and spiritualized by the Jewish teachers, in accordance with the moral and philosophical progress of their respective ages. We maintain that Judaism preserved and defended, midst continual struggles and trials and under enforced isolation, this God–idea as the central religious truth for the human race.

Second. We recognize in the Bible the record of the consecration of the Jewish people to its mission as priest of the one God, and value it as the most potent instrument of religious and moral instruction. We hold that the modern discoveries of scientific researches in the domains of nature and history are not antagonistic to the doctrines of Judaism, the Bible reflecting the primitive ideas of its own age, and at times clothing its conception of Divine Providence and justice dealing with man in miraculous narratives.

Third. We recognize in the Mosaic legislation a system of training the Jewish people for its mission during its national life in Palestine, and to-day we accept as binding only the moral laws, and maintain only such ceremonies as elevate and sanctify our lives, but reject all such as are not adapted to the views and habits of modern civilization.

Fourth. We hold that all such Mosaic and rabbinical laws as regulate diet, priestly purity and dress originated in ages and under the influence of ideas altogether foreign to our present mental and spiritual state. They fail to impress the modern Jew with a spirit of priestly holiness; their observance in our days is apt rather to obstruct than to further modern spiritual elevation.

Fifth. We recognize in the modern era of universal culture of heart and intellect the approaching of the realization of Israel's great Messianic hope for the establishment of the kingdom of truth, justice and peace among all men. We consider ourselves no longer a nation, but a religious community, and, therefore, expect neither a return to Palestine, nor a sacrificial worship under the sons of Aaron, nor the restoration of any of the laws concerning the Jewish state.

Sixth. We recognize in Judaism a progressive religion, ever striving to be in accord with the postulates of reason. We are convinced of the utmost necessity of preserving the historical identity with our great past. Christianity and Islam being daughter religions of Judaism, we appreciate their providential mission to aid in the spreading of monotheistic and moral truth. We acknowledge that the spirit of broad humanity of our age is our ally in the fulfilment of our mission, and, therefore, we extend the hand of fellowship to all who cooperate with us in the establishment of the reign of truth and righteousness among men.

Seventh. We reassert the doctrine of Judaism that the soul of man is immortal, grounding this belief on the divine nature of the human spirit, which forever finds bliss in righteousness and misery in wickedness. We reject, as ideas not rooted in Judaism, the beliefs both in bodily resurrection and in Gehenna and Eden (Hell and Paradise) as abodes for everlasting punishment and reward.

Eighth. In full accordance with the spirit of Mosaic legislation, which strives to regulate the relation between the rich and poor, we deem it our duty to participate in the great task of modern times, to solve, on the basis of justice and righteousness, the problems presented by the contrasts and evils of the present organization of society.

The Columbus Platform: "Guiding Principles of Reform Judaism" (1937)

In view of the changes that have taken place in the modern world and the consequent need of stating anew the teachings of Reform Judaism, the Central Conference of American Rabbis makes the following declaration of principles. It presents them not as a fixed creed but as a guide for the progressive elements of Jewry.

A. Judaism and its Foundations

1. Nature of Judaism. Judaism is the historical religious experience of the Jewish people. Though growing out of Jewish life, its message is universal, aiming at the union and perfection of mankind under the sovereignty of God. Reform Judaism recognizes the principle of progressive development in religion and consciously applies this principle to spiritual as well as to cultural and social life.

Judaism welcomes all truth, whether written in the pages of scripture or deciphered from the records of nature. The new discoveries of science, while replacing the older scientific views underlying our sacred literature, do not conflict with the essential spirit of religion as manifested in the consecration of man's will, heart and mind to the service of God and of humanity.

2. God. The heart of Judaism and its chief contribution to religion is the doctrine of the One, living God, who rules the world through law and love. In Him all existence has its creative source and mankind its ideal of conduct. Though transcending time and space, He is the indwelling Presence of the world. We worship Him as the Lord of the universe and as our merciful Father.

3. Man. Judaism affirms that man is created in the Divine image. His spirit is immortal. He is an active co-worker with God. As a child of God, he is endowed with moral freedom and is charged with the responsibility of overcoming evil and striving after ideal ends.

4. Torah. God reveals Himself not only in the majesty, beauty and orderliness of nature, but also in the vision and moral striving of the human spirit. Revelation is a continuous process, confined to no one group and to no one age. Yet the people of Israel, through its prophets and sages, achieved unique insight in the realm of religious truth. The Torah, both written and oral, enshrines Israel's ever-growing consciousness of God and of the moral law. It preserves the historical precedents, sanctions and norms of Jewish life, and seeks to mould it in the patterns of goodness and of holiness. Being products of historical processes, certain of its laws have lost their binding force with the passing of the conditions that called them forth. But as a depository of permanent spiritual ideals, the Torah remains the dynamic source of the life of Israel. Each age has the obligation to adapt the teachings of the Torah to its basic needs in consonance with the genius of Judaism.

5. Israel. Judaism is the soul of which Israel is the body. Living in all parts of the world, Israel has been held together by the ties of a common history, and above all, by the heritage of faith. Though we recognize in the group loyalty of Jews who have become estranged from our religious tradition, a bond which still unites them with us, we maintain that it is by its religion and for its religion that the Jewish people has lived. The non-Jew who accepts our faith is welcomed as a full member of the Jewish community.

In all lands where our people live, they assume and seek to share loyally the full duties and responsibilities of citizenship and to create seats of Jewish knowledge and religion. In the rehabilitation of Palestine, the land hallowed by memories and hopes, we behold the promise of renewed life for many of our brethren. We affirm the obligation of all Jewry to aid in its upbuilding as a Jewish homeland by endeavoring to make it not only a haven of refuge for the oppressed but also a center of Jewish culture and spiritual life.

Throughout the ages it has been Israel's mission to witness to the Divine in the face of every form of paganism and materialism. We regard it as our historic task to cooperate with all men in the establishment of the kingdom of God, of universal brotherhood, justice, truth and peace on earth. This is our Messianic goal.

B. Ethics

6. Ethics and Religion. In Judaism religion and morality blend into an indissoluble unity. Seeking God means to strive after holiness, righteousness and goodness. The love of God is incomplete without the love of one's fellowmen. Judaism emphasizes the kinship of the human race, the sanctity and worth of human life and personality and the right of the individual to freedom and to the pursuit of his chosen vocation. Justice to all, irrespective of race, sect or class, is the inalienable right and the inescapable obligation of all. The state and organized government exist in order to further these ends.

7. Social Justice. Judaism seeks the attainment of a just society by the application of its teachings to the economic order, to industry and commerce, and to national and international affairs. It aims at the elimination of man-made misery and suffering, of poverty and degradation, of tyranny and slavery, of social inequality and prejudice, of ill-will and strife. It advocates the promotion of harmonious relations between warring classes on the basis of equity and justice, and the creation of conditions under which human personality may flourish. It pleads for the safeguarding of childhood against exploitation. It champions the cause of all who work and of their right to an adequate standard of living, as prior to the rights of property. Judaism emphasizes the duty of charity, and strives for a social order which will protect men against the material disabilities of old age, sickness and unemployment.

8. Peace. Judaism, from the days of the prophets, has proclaimed to mankind the ideal of universal peace. The spiritual and physical disarmament of all nations has been one of its essential teachings. It abhors all violence and relies upon moral education, love and sympathy to secure human progress. It regards justice as the foundation of the well-being of nations and the condition of enduring peace. It urges organized international action for disarmament, collective security and world peace.

C. Religious Practice

9. The Religious Life. Jewish life is marked by consecration to these ideals of Judaism. It calls for faithful participation in the life of the Jewish community as it finds expression in home, synagog and school and in all other agencies that enrich Jewish life and promote its welfare.

The Home has been and must continue to be a stronghold of Jewish life, hallowed by the spirit of love and reverence, by moral discipline and religious observance and worship.

The Synagog is the oldest and most democratic institution in Jewish life. It is the prime communal agency by which Judaism is fostered and preserved. It links the Jews of each community and unites them with all Israel.

The perpetuation of Judaism as a living force depends upon religious knowledge and upon the Education of each new generation in our rich cultural and spiritual heritage.

Prayer is the voice of religion, the language of faith and aspiration. It directs man's heart and mind Godward, voices the needs and hopes of the community, and reaches out after goals which invest life with supreme value. To deepen the spiritual life of our people, we must cultivate the traditional habit of communion with God through prayer in both home and synagog.

Judaism as a way of life requires in addition to its moral and spiritual demands, the preservation of the Sabbath, festivals and Holy Days, the retention and development of such customs, symbols and ceremonies as possess inspirational value, the cultivation of distinctive forms of religious art and music and the use of Hebrew, together with the vernacular, in our worship and instruction.

These timeless aims and ideals of our faith we present anew to a confused and troubled world. We call upon our fellow Jews to rededicate themselves to them, and, in harmony with all men, hopefully and courageously to continue Israel's eternal quest after God and His kingdom.

The San Francisco Platform:
"Reform Judaism—A Centenary Perspective" (1976)

The Central Conference of American Rabbis has on special occasions described the spiritual state of Reform Judaism. The centenaries of the founding of the Union of American Hebrew Congregations and the Hebrew Union College–Jewish Institute of Religion seem an appropriate time for another such effort. We therefore record our sense of the unity of our movement today.

One Hundred Years: What We Have Taught

We celebrate the role of Reform Judaism in North America, the growth of our movement on this free ground, the great contributions of our membership to the dreams and achievements of this society. We also feel great satisfaction at how much of our pioneering conception of Judaism has been accepted by the Household of Israel. It now seems self-evident to most Jews: that our tradition should interact with modern culture; that its forms ought to reflect a contemporary esthetic; that its scholarship needs to be conducted by modern, critical methods; and that change has been and must continue to be a fundamental reality in Jewish life. Moreover, though some still disagree, substantial numbers have also accepted our teachings: that the ethics of universalism implicit in traditional Judaism must be an explicit part of our Jewish duty; that women should have full rights to practice Judaism; and that Jewish obligation begins with the informed will of every individual. Most modern Jews, within their various religious movements, are embracing Reform Jewish perspectives. We see this past century as having confirmed the essential wisdom of our movement.

One Hundred Years: What We Have Learned

Obviously, much else has changed in the past century. We continue to probe the extraordinary events of the past generation, seeking to understand their meaning and to incorporate their significance in our lives. The Holocaust shattered our easy optimism about humanity and its inevitable progress. The State of Israel, through its many accomplishments, raised our sense of the Jews as a people to new heights of aspiration and devotion. The widespread threats to freedom, the problems inherent in the explosion of new knowledge and of ever more powerful technologies, and the spiritual emptiness of much of Western culture, have taught us to be less dependent on the values of our society and to reassert what remains perennially valid in Judaism's teaching. We have learned again that the survival of the Jewish people is of highest priority and that in carrying out our Jewish responsibilities we help move humanity toward its messianic fulfillment.

Diversity Within Unity, the Hallmark of Reform

Reform Jews respond to change in various ways according to the Reform principle of the autonomy of the individual. However, Reform Judaism does more than tolerate diversity; it engenders it. In our uncertain historical situation we must expect to have far greater diversity than previous generations knew. How we shall live with diversity without stifling dissent and without paralyzing our ability to take positive action will test our character and our principles. We stand open to any position thoughtfully and conscientiously advocated in the spirit of Reform Jewish beliefs. While we may differ in our interpretation and application of the ideas enunciated here, we accept such differences as precious and see in them Judaism's best hope for confronting whatever the future holds for us. Yet in all our diversity we perceive a certain unity and we shall not allow our differences in some particulars to obscure what binds us together.

I. God

The affirmation of God has always been essential to our people's will to survive. In our struggle through the centuries to preserve our faith we have experienced and conceived of God in many ways. The trials of our own time and the challenges of modern culture have made steady belief and clear understanding difficult for some. Nevertheless, we ground our lives, personally and communally, on God's reality and remain open to new experiences and conceptions of the Divine. Amid the mystery we call life, we affirm that human beings, created in God's image, share in God's eternality despite the mystery we call death.

II. The People Israel

The Jewish people and Judaism defy precise definition because both are in the process of becoming. Jews, by birth or conversion, constitute an uncommon union of faith and peoplehood. Born as Hebrews in the ancient Near East, we are bound together like all ethnic groups by language, land, history, culture and institutions. But the people of Israel is unique because of its involvement with God and its resulting perception of the human condition. Throughout our long history our people has been inseparable from its religion with its messianic hope that humanity will be redeemed.

III. Torah

Torah results from the relationship between God and the Jewish people. The records of our earliest confrontations are uniquely important to us. Lawgivers and prophets, historians and poets gave us a heritage whose study is a religious imperative and whose practice is our chief means to holiness. Rabbis and teachers, philosophers and mystics, gifted Jews in every age amplified the Torah tradition. For millennia, the creation of Torah has not ceased and Jewish creativity in our time is adding to the chain of tradition.

IV. Our Obligations: Religious Practice

Judaism emphasizes action rather than creed as the primary expression of a religious life, the means by which we strive to achieve universal justice and peace. Reform Judaism shares this emphasis on duty and obligation. Our founders stressed that the Jew's ethical responsibilities, personal and social, are enjoined by God. The past century has taught us that the claims made upon us may begin with our ethical obligations but they extend to many other aspects of Jewish living, including: creating a Jewish home centered on family devotion; life-long study; private prayer and public worship; daily religious observance; keeping the Sabbath and the holy days; celebrating the major events of life; involvement with the synagogue and community; and other activities which promote the survival of the Jewish people and enhance its existence. Within each area of Jewish observance Reform Jews are called upon to confront the claims of Jewish tradition, however differently perceived, and to exercise their individual autonomy, choosing and creating on the basis of commitment and knowledge.

V. Our Obligations: The State of Israel and the Diaspora

We are privileged to live in an extraordinary time, one in which a third Jewish commonwealth has been established in our people's ancient homeland. We are bound to that land and to the newly reborn State of Israel by innumerable religious and ethnic ties. We have been enriched by its culture and ennobled by its indomitable spirit. We see it providing unique opportunities for Jewish self-expression. We have both a stake and a responsibility in building the State of Israel, assuring its security and defining its Jewish character. We encourage *aliyah* for those who wish to find maximum personal fulfillment in the cause of Zion. We demand that Reform Judaism be unconditionally legitimized in the State of Israel.

At the same time we consider the State of Israel vital to the welfare of Judaism everywhere, we reaffirm the mandate of our tradition to create strong Jewish communities wherever we live. A genuine Jewish life is possible in any land, each community developing its own particular character and determining its Jewish responsibilities. The foundation of Jewish community life is the synagogue. It leads us beyond itself to cooperate with other Jews, to share their concerns, and to assume leadership in communal affairs. We are therefore committed to the full democratization of the Jewish community and to its hallowing in terms of Jewish values.

The State of Israel and the diaspora, in fruitful dialogue, can show how a people transcends nationalism even as it affirms it, thereby setting an example for humanity which remains largely concerned with dangerously parochial goals.

VI. Our Obligations: Survival and Service

Early Reform Jews, newly admitted to general society and seeing in this the evidence of a growing universalism, regularly spoke of Jewish purpose in terms of Jewry's service to humanity. In recent years we have become freshly conscious of the virtues of pluralism and the values of particularism. The Jewish people in its unique way of life validates its own worth while working toward the fulfillment of its messianic expectations.

Until the recent past our obligations to the Jewish people and to all humanity seemed congruent. At times now these two imperatives appear to conflict. We know of no simple way to resolve such tensions. We must, however, confront them without abandoning either of our commitments. A universal concern for humanity unaccompanied by a devotion to our particular people is self-destructive; a passion for our people without involvement in humankind contradicts what the prophets have meant to us. Judaism calls us simultaneously to universal and particular obligations.

VII. Hope: Our Jewish Obligation

Previous generations of Reform Jews had unbounded confidence in humanity's potential for good. We have lived through terrible tragedy and been compelled to reappropriate our tradition's realism about the human capacity for evil. Yet our people has always refused to despair. The survivors of the Holocaust, on being granted life, seized it, nurtured it, and, rising above catastrophe, showed humankind that the human spirit is indomitable. The State of Israel, established and maintained by the Jewish will to live, demonstrates what a united people can accomplish in history. The existence of the Jew is an argument against despair; Jewish survival is warrant for human hope.

We remain God's witness that history is not meaningless. We affirm that with God's help people are not powerless to affect their destiny. We dedicate ourselves, as did the generations of Jews who went before us, to work and wait for that day when "They shall not hurt or destroy in all My holy mountain for the earth shall be full of the knowledge of the Lord as the waters cover the sea."

Notes

JJGL	*Jahrbuch für Jüdische Geschichte und Literatur*
JNUL	Jewish National and University Library, Jerusalem
JQR	*Jewish Quarterly Review*
JR	*The Jewish Reformer*
JRJ	*Journal of Reform Judaism*
JSS	*Jewish Social Studies*
JT	*Jewish Times*
JZWL	*Jüdische Zeitschrift für Wissenschaft und Leben*
LBIA	Leo Baeck Institute Archives, New York
LBIYB	*Leo Baeck Institute Year Book*
LJ	*Liberales Judentum*
MGWJ	*Monatsschrift für Geschichte und Wissenschaft des Judentums*
PAAJR	*Proceedings of the American Academy for Jewish Research*
PAJHS	*Publications of the American Jewish Historical Society*
PUAHC	*Proceedings of the Union of American Hebrew Congregations*
P.T.	Palestinian Talmud
REJ	*Revue des études juives*
RJ	*Reform Judaism*
RW	*La Régénération—Die Wiedergeburt*
SR	*The Synagogue Review*
TE	*Tradition und Erneuerung*
TJHSE	*Transactions of the Jewish Historical Society of England*
UB	*The Union Bulletin*
UI	*L'Univers Israélite*
VJ	*The Voice of Jacob*
WZJT	*Wissenschaftliche Zeitschrift für jüdische Theologie*
YIVO	*YIVO Annual of Jewish Social Science*
ZGJD	*Zeitschrift für die Geschichte der Juden in Deutschland*
ZJD	*Zur Judenfrage in Deutschland*
ZRG	*Zeitschrift für Religions- und Geistesgeschichte*
ZRIJ	*Zeitschrift für die religiösen Interessen des Judentums*

Prologue

1. Samuel Holdheim, "Rabbi Jochanan ben Sakai, ein Retter und Reformator des Juden-thums," in *Predigten über die jüdische Religion,* 3 (Berlin, 1855): 289–310.

2. *CCARY,* 20 (1910): 197–245. In *The Jewish Spectator,* March 1957, pp. 7–11, Jakob J. Petuchowski once again posed the question: "How old is Reform Judaism?" He answered: "Reform Judaism is as old as Judaism itself!"

3. See Robert Gordis, "A Dynamic Halakhah: Principles and Procedures of Jewish Law," *Judaism,* 28 (1979): 263–82 and the responses in *ibid.,* 29 (1980): 4–109.

4. P. T. *Peah* Ch. 2, Halakhah 4. Cf. B. T. *Megilah* 19b; *Sifra, Behukotai,* 8:13.

5. Menachem Elon, *Ha-mishpat ha-ivri,* 1 (Jerusalem, 1973): 224.

6. See Elliot W. Dorff, "The Interaction of Jewish Law with Morality," *Judaism,* 26 (1977): 455–66.

7. Mishnah *Gitin* 4:2–5, 5:8–9.

8. Mishnah *Sheviit* 10:3.

9. B. T. *Sanhedrin* 71a.

10. B. T. *Menahot* 29b.

11. B. T. *Eruvin* 13b.

12. B. T. *Baba metsia* 59b.

13. Elon, *Ha-mishpat ha-ivri,* 232–36.

14. Yitzhak Baer, *A History of the Jews in Christian Spain,* 1 (Philadelphia, 1961): 241; Shem Tov Falaquera, *Igeret ha-vikuah,* ed. Adolf Jellinek (Vienna, 1875), 19; Gershom Scholem, *Major Trends in Jewish Mysticism* (New York, 1946), 397–98; H. J. Zimmels, *Ashkenazim and Sephardim* (London, 1958), 258.

15. Eliyahu Ashtor, *The Jews of Moslem Spain,* 3 (Philadelphia, 1984): 137–40.

16. Naphtali Wieder, *Hashpa'ot islamiyot al ha-pulhan ha-yehudi* (Oxford, 1947); S. D. Goitein, *Jews and Arabs* (New York, 1955), 182–84.

17. This was for a time the position of the well-known heretic Uriel Acosta. See his "Theses Against the Tradition," in Carl Gebhardt, ed., *Die Schriften des Uriel da Costa* (Amsterdam, 1922), 3–32.

18. Jakob J. Petuchowski, *The Theology of Haham David Nieto* (2d edn., New York, 1970), xiv–xvii.

19. For late medieval times, see Moritz Güdemann, *Geschichte des Erziehungswesens und der Cultur der Juden in Deutschland während des XIV. und XV. Jahrhunderts* (Vienna, 1888), 141–69.

20. Ze'ev W. Falk, *Jewish Matrimonial Law in the Middle Ages* (London, 1966), 1–34; Güdemann, *Geschichte des Erziehungswesens,* 132.

21. Zimmels, *Ashkenazim and Sephardim,* 247; Joseph Gutmann, "Christian Influences on Jewish Customs," in Leon Klenicki and Gabe Huck, eds., *Spirituality and Prayer: Jewish and Christian Understandings* (New York, 1983), 128–38.

22. Richard Krautheimer, *Mittelalterliche Synagogen* (Berlin, 1927), 12, 140–42.

23. Joseph Gutmann, "How Traditional Are Our Traditions?," *CCARJ,* April 1968, p. 59.

24. Herman Pollack, *Jewish Folkways in Germanic Lands, 1648–1806* (Cambridge, Mass., 1971), 154, 317.

25. Solomon Lipschütz, *Te'udat shelomoh* (Offenbach, 1718), 16a–19b.

26. Isaac Rivkind, "A Responsum of Leo da Modena on Uncovering the Head," in *Louis Ginzberg Jubilee Volume,* Hebrew Section (New York, 1946), 416–17.

27. Azariah de' Rossi, *Me'or enayim,* ed. David Cassel (Vilna, 1866), 196. Reference must also be made to a document that was not normative and enjoyed but limited influence among the Reformers once it was published for the first time by Samuel Reggio in *Behinat ha-kabalah* (Gorizia, 1852), pp. 6–65. It is worthy of mention simply because it is so thoroughgoing in its critique of tradition and proposals for reform as to parallel the most radical trends of the nineteenth century. Scholars remain divided on the authorship of the "Kol Sakhal," which bears only a pseudonym but has frequently been attributed to Leon Modena (1571–1648). For conflicting views see Ellis Rivkin, *Leone da Modena and the Kol Sakhal* (Cincinnati, 1952), Isaac E. Barzilay, "Finalizing an Issue: Modena's Authorship of the Qol Sakhal," *Salo Wittmayer Baron Jubilee Volume,* 1 (Jerusalem, 1974): 135–66, and Howard Ernest Adelman, "Success and Failure in the Seventeenth Century Ghetto of Venice: The Life and Thought of Leon Modena, 1571–1648" (Ph.D. dissertation, Brandeis University, 1985), 166–82, 577–98. While the rationalist author accepts the Pentateuch as the literal word of God and insists that its precepts be carried out scrupulously, he regards all later Jewish religious literature, including the Talmud, as only human and hence subject to critique. He dwells in particular on Jewish liturgy, proposing arbitrary changes which radically shorten the traditional texts of the prayers. Since unlike the Torah, the prayerbook does not possess sanctity, its components may be altered at will. Like the later Reformers, the author stresses the importance of concentration in prayer which, to his mind, requires a greatly abbreviated liturgy and silent devotion while the congregation listens to the song of its cantor. The "Kol Sakhal" also opposes the celebration of the second days of holidays since their observance is both an unwarranted appendage to the biblical commandments and imposes a financial hardship on Jews who must on that account spend additional days without productive labor. It further rejects the rabbinic expansion of biblical precepts in such matters as dietary laws, ritual slaughter, and circumcision. The author's critique of ritualism sounds a note often heard two centuries later: "The days between the New Year and the

Day of Atonement are properly a time of repentance in preparation for receiving atonement on the tenth day, and thus [the Rabbis] should have elaborated on the laws of repentance. They should have delivered exhortations with regard to repentance and not dwelt upon whether a *shofar* (ram's horn) that is cracked lengthwise or across is ritually fit. They should have commanded reconciliation with fellow men, return of stolen goods, and giving up prostitutes and forbidden foods. They should have urged people to confess, pray, and perform acts of charity. For these matters most require exhortation ... but they dealt only briefly with what requires elaboration and at length with what does not" (pp. 49–50). The author of the "Kol Sakhal" also gave unusual weight to the opinion of Gentiles. He wrote: "It is appropriate to distinguish one period [of history] from another and to permit [certain deviations from accepted Jewish practice] in order not to create or increase [the Gentiles'] hatred of us, for it is great in the age of our enslavement, and we must attempt to find favor in their eyes as much as we can without violating our religion" (pp. 55–56). By the time the "Kol Sakhal" finally appeared in print, neither its absolute faith in the literal authority of the Pentateuch nor its wholesale polemical derogation of later tradition were characteristic of the Reform movement. Yet its composition does offer further evidence that radical ideas were abroad, at least in small circles, long before the Jewish confrontation with modernity. The radical reformer David Einhorn was sufficiently intrigued by the "Kol Sakhal" to translate it into German and present serial installments in his American periodical *Sinai* (1 [1856] and 2 [1857]).

28. *Lev Tov* was written by Isaac ben Eliakim of Posen and first appeared in 1620 in Prague. The citation is from Jacob Meitlis, "The Bodleian MS. 'Libesbriv,' a Reform Text of the Pre-Haskalah Period" [Yiddish], *Yivo Bleter*, 2 (1931): 326. Cf. *Shulḥan Arukh, Oraḥ Ḥayim* (1:4): "Better few supplications with *kavanah* than many without it." Sentiments anticipating those of the Reformers can also be found in a manuscript composed by Isaac Wetzlar in Northern Germany in 1749. See Morris M. Faierstein, "The Liebes Brief: A Critique of Jewish Society in Germany (1749)," *LBIYB*, 27 (1982): 219–41.

29. Güdemann, *Geschichte des Erziehungswesens*, 225–26; Pollack, *Jewish Folkways*, 162.

30. Cecil Roth, *The Jews in the Renaissance* (Philadelphia, 1959), 32.

31. Shmuel Dothan, "Rabbi Jacob Emden and his Generation," *HUCA*, 47 (1976): Hebrew Section, 121. Cf. Joseph Melkman, *David Franco Mendes* (Jerusalem and Amsterdam, 1951), 109–10. For the view that, with few exceptions, messianic faith remained quite firm until the middle of the eighteenth century, see Barouh Mevorah, "The Messiah Question in the Disputes over Emancipation and Reform, 1781–1819" [Hebrew] (Ph.D. dissertation, Hebrew University, 1966), 21–25.

32. Cited by Dothan, "Rabbi Jacob Emden," *loc. cit.*

Chapter 1

1. See, for example, Gershom Scholem, *Major Trends in Jewish Mysticism* (3d edn., New York, 1954), 304; *idem, The Messianic Idea in Judaism* (New York, 1971), 84, 90, 140, 170.

2. Jacob Katz, "On the Question of the Relation of Sabbatianism to Haskalah and Reform," in Siegfried Stein and Raphael Loewe, eds., *Studies in Jewish Religious and Intellectual History Presented to Alexander Altmann,* Hebrew Section (University, Ala., 1979), 83–100.

3. Rudolf Glanz, *Geschichte des niederen jüdischen Volkes in Deutschland: Eine Studie über historisches Gaunertum, Bettelwesen und Vagantentum* (New York, 1968).

4. Selma Stern, *The Court Jew* (Philadelphia, 1950), 227–46.

5. Azriel Shohet, *Im ḥilufe tekufot: reshit ha-haskalah be-yahadut germaniyah* (Jerusalem, 1960), 49–173; Heinz Moshe Graupe, *The Rise of Modern Judaism,* trans. John Robinson (Huntington, N.Y., 1978), 13–70; I. M. Jost, *Geschichte des Judenthums und seiner Sekten,* 3 (Leipzig, 1859): 295.

6. *Ha-Measef,* 2 (1785): 28.

7. Moses Hirschel, *Kampf der jüdischen Hierarchie mit der Vernunft* (Breslau, 1788), 13, 34.

8. Moritz Kalisch, *Berlins jüdische Reformatoren nach der Thronbesteigung Friedrich Wilhelms III. und IV.* (Berlin, 1845), 65–66, 69. Cf. Gershom Scholem, "Zionism—Dialectic of Continuity and Rebellion," in Ehud ben Ezer, ed., *Unease in Zion* (New York and Jerusalem, 1974), 287.

9. Michael A. Meyer, "The Orthodox and the Enlightened—An Unpublished Contemporary Analysis of Berlin Jewry's Spiritual Condition in the Early Nineteenth Century," *LBIYB*, 25 (1980): 101–30.

10. Elaborated in my *The Origins of the Modern Jew: Jewish Identity and European Culture in Germany, 1749–1824* (Detroit, 1967), 11–28.

11. Moses Mendelssohn, *Jerusalem and Other Jewish Writings*, trans. Alfred Jospe (New York, 1969), 104–105.

12. The sources are given in Israel Zinberg, *A History of Jewish Literature*, trans. Bernard Martin, 8 (Cincinnati, 1976): 84–85. When a physician and student of Kant, Marcus Herz, advocated late burial a decade and a half later, his attitude toward tradition was very different from Mendelssohn's. He urged his case, in part, because in this instance Jews should follow the example of "our cultured and enlightened neighbors *(Mitvölker)*." He rejected Mendelssohn's compromise because the customs of the ancestors in ancient Palestine were for him not relevant to the issue. "Why always this exaggerated attachment to ancient custom," he asked rhetorically, "since it has not the least connection with our spiritual happiness *(Glückseligkeit)*?" Marcus Herz, *Über die frühe Beerdigung der Juden* (Berlin, 1788), 52–53. In 1792 a newly created Jewish fraternal society determined to honor the wish of any sick member who preferred to remain unburied for three days after his death. Ludwig Lesser, *Chronik der Gesellschaft der Freunde in Berlin* (Berlin, 1842), 15.

13. B. T. *Sanhedrin* 46a, based on Deut. 21:23.

14. The primary sources for the incident are in Moses Mendelssohn, *Gesammelte Schriften, Jubiläumsausgabe*, ed. I. Elbogen *et al.*, 16 (Berlin, 1929): 154–68 and in *ZGJD*, n.s., 1 (1929): 284–87. The most complete discussion is in Alexander Altmann, *Moses Mendelssohn: A Biographical Study* (University, Ala., 1973), 288–94.

15. *Shulḥan Arukh, Oraḥ Ḥayim* 690:17.

16. See [Elkan Henle], *Über die Verbesserung des Judenthums* (Frankfurt a/M, 1803), 30 and Altmann, *Moses Mendelssohn*, 292–93.

17. Moses Mendelssohn, *Gesammelte Schriften*, 7 (Berlin, 1930): 9.

18. Mendelssohn, *Jerusalem and Other Jewish Writings*, 34–35, 101–102.

19. *Works of Spinoza*, trans. R. H. M. Elwes, 1 (New York, 1951): 72.

20. For a general treatment see Bernard D. Weinryb, "Enlightenment and German-Jewish Haskalah," *Studies on Voltaire and the Eighteenth Century*, 27 (1963): 1817–47.

21. Christian Wilhelm Dohm, *Über die bürgerliche Verbesserung der Juden* (Berlin and Stettin, 1781), 28, 87, 124–27, 142–44.

22. Immanuel Kant, "Der Streit der Facultäten," in *Sämmtliche Werke*, ed. K. Rosenkranz and F. W. Schubert, 10 (Leipzig, 1838): 307–308.

23. An anonymous writer, who referred to himself as "a cosmopolitan," insisted that if Jews wanted equal rights in the city of Hamburg they would have to undergo a comprehensive "reformation." He noted that "every religious party is cleansing its religion of superstitions and human laws, gradually approaching the religion of nature and reason—but the Jews continue stubbornly to adhere to their ancient ceremonial law . . . and out of pride refuse to change anything." [Julius Friedrich Knüppeln], *Über die politische, religiöse und moralische Verfassung der Juden* (Hamburg, 1798), 30.

24. See my *German Political Pressure and Jewish Religious Response in the Nineteenth Century*, The Leo Baeck Memorial Lecture 25 (New York, 1981).

25. Ernst Troeltsch, "Die Aufklärung," in *Gesammelte Schriften*, 4 (Tübingen, 1925): 371–72.

26. Gotthold Ephraim Lessing, *Die Erziehung des Menschengeschlechts* (Berlin, 1785), 13–53.

27. Hajo Holborn, *A History of Modern Germany 1648–1840* (New York, 1964), 134–35.

28. Johann Gottfried Herder, "Vom Geist der Ebräischen Poesie," in *Sämmtliche Werke,* 11 (Berlin, 1877): 221.

29. Sources are cited by Isaac Eisenstein-Barzilay, "The Treatment of the Jewish Religion in the Literature of the Berlin Haskalah," *PAAJR,* 24 (1955): 39–68.

30. Mendel Bresselau in *Ha-Measef,* 6 (1790): 310. On this summons see Zinberg, *A History of Jewish Literature,* 97–99; Moshe Pelli, "The First Call of a Hebrew *Maskil* to Convene a Rabbinic Assembly for Religious Reforms" [Hebrew], *Tarbiz,* 42 (1973): 484–91.

31. Mordecai Gumpel Schnaber, *Yesod ha-torah* (Hamburg, 1792), 2a–2b, 72a–72b. On Schnaber see Zinberg, *A History of Jewish Literature,* 34–37 and Heinz Mosche Graupe, "Mordechai Gumpel (Levison)," *BLBI,* no. 17 (1962): 1–12. Schnaber's significance for the Reform movement is somewhat exaggerated by Moshe Pelli, *The Age of Haskalah: Studies in Hebrew Literature of the Enlightenment in Germany* (Leiden, 1979), 131–50.

32. Recent evaluations of Saul Berlin differ sharply. See especially Raphael Mahler, *Divre yeme yisrael dorot aḥaronim,* 2 (Merhavya, 1954): 77–79, 336–42; the two Hebrew articles by Moshe Samet in *Kirjath Sepher,* 43 (1968): 429–41 and 48 (1973): 509–23; and the various articles by Moshe Pelli listed in his *The Age of Haskalah,* 171–89.

33. [Saul Berlin], *Ketav yosher* (Berlin, 1794), 3b.

34. Passages cited are from [Saul Berlin], *She'elot u-teshuvot besamim rosh* (Berlin, 1793), 10a–10b, 77a, 108b–109a. A few of the responsa are summarized by Louis Jacobs, *Theology in the Responsa* (London, 1975), 347–52.

35. Salomon Maimon, *Lebensgeschichte,* 2 (Berlin, 1793): 180–84.

36. Lazarus Bendavid, *Etwas zur Charackteristick der Juden* (Leipzig, 1793), 45, 51. Bendavid had gradually given up observance of Jewish law and regular attendance at synagogue. Instead he frequented churches for the sake of the music and the sermons. He finally ceased going to synagogue altogether when, on account of his violation of ritual commandments, he was denied the right to lead the prayers. Jacob Guttmann, "Lazarus Bendavid: Seine Stellung zum Judentum und seine literarische Wirksamkeit," *MGWJ,* 61 (1917): 32–33. A decade later there was still a class of Jews who "based natural religion . . . on the authority of Moses and the Prophets." Aaron Wolfssohn, *Jeschurun, oder unparteyische Beleuchtung der dem Judenthume neuerdings gemachte Vorwürfe* (Breslau, 1804), 114.

37. The earlier literature on Ascher is cited in two recent studies: Walter Grab, "Saul Ascher: Ein jüdisch-deutscher Spätaufklärer zwischen Revolution und Restauration," *Jahrbuch des Instituts für Deutsche Geschichte,* 6 (1977): 131–79; Michael Graetz, "The Formation of the New 'Jewish Consciousness' in the Time of Mendelssohn's Disciples—Saul Ascher" [Hebrew], *Meḥkarim be-toledot am yisrael ve-erets yisrael,* 4 (1978): 219–37.

38. Saul Ascher, *Leviathan oder Über Religion in Rücksicht des Judenthums* (Berlin, 1792). There is a Hebrew translation of Parts Two and Three with an introduction by Michael Graetz (Jerusalem, 1982).

39. *Ibid.,* 237.

40. *Ibid.,* 232.

41. [Sabattia Joseph Wolff], *Freymüthige Gedanken über die vorgeschlagene Verbesserung der Juden in den Preussischen Staaten* (Halle, 1792), 25–33. Jewish educational reform in Germany is treated comprehensively by Mordechai Eliav, *Ha-ḥinukh ha-yehudi be-germaniyah bime ha-haskalah ve-ha-emantsipatsyah* (Jerusalem, 1960).

42. Isaac Abraham Euchel, *Gebete der hochdeutschen und polnischen Juden* (Königsberg, 1786), iv–x. Premodern rabbinic authorities had, of course, also stressed the importance of the subjective state of the worshiper and the need for concentrated devotion (*kavanah*), though the intent of prayer remained the fulfillment of an obligation to God. See, for example, Isaiah Horowitz, *Shene luḥot ha-berit* (Fürth, 1762), 349b–51a. The old viewpoint was later defended

by a traditionalist rabbi opposing the reformers. He wrote a responsum to show that the worshiper who prays in Hebrew, even if he does not understand what he is saying, nonetheless fulfills his religious obligation. Abraham Löwenstamm, *Tseror ha-hayim* (Amsterdam, 1820), 28a–35b.

43. A. A. Wolff, *Die Stimmen der ältesten glaubwürdigsten Rabbinen über die Pijutim* (Leipzig, 1857).

44. Euchel, *Gebete*, 433; *Ha-Measef*, 3 (1786): 205–206.

45. *Ibid.*, 72.

46. Mendel Bresselau in *ibid.*, 6.2 (1790): 313–14; Wolff, *Freymüthige Gedanken*, 8.

47. Joel Loewe in *Ha-Measef*, 3 (1786):139.

48. Euchel's translation has already been noted. Friedländer's was entitled *Gebete der Juden auf das ganze Jahr* (Berlin, 1786).

49. See Benno Gottschalk, "Die Anfänge der deutschen Gebetsübersetzungen," in *Festgabe für Claude G. Montefiore* (Berlin, 1928), 58–64; Ismar Elbogen, "David Friedländers Übersetzung des Gebetbuchs," *ZGJD*, n.s., 6 (1935): 130–33.

50. Euchel, *Gebete*, 420.

51. *Ibid.*, xxii.

52. Cited by Gottschalk, "Die Anfänge der deutschen Gebetsübersetzungen," 62. Friedländer replied with a sarcastic attack on Fleckeles' position, which appeared as a special supplement to *Ha-Measef*, 4 (1788).

53. I have drawn here especially on Mahler, *Divre yeme yisrael*, 1 (Merhavya, 1952): 211–51; D. M. Sluys, "Het reglement van de Adath Jeschurun (de 'Neie Killoh') te Amsterdam," *Nieuw Israëlietisch Weekblad*, June 12 and 19, 1931; S. E. Bloemgarten, "De Amsterdamse Joden gedurende de eerste jaren van de Bataafse Republiek (1795–1798)," *Studia Rosenthaliana*, 1.1 (1967): 66–96, 1.2 (1967): 45–70, 2.1 (1968): 42–65; Dan Michman, "David Friedrichsfeld—A Fighter for Enlightenment and Emancipation of the Jews" [Hebrew], *Mehkarim al toledot yahadut holand*, 1 (1975): 170–73. I also profited from conversations with Dr. Joseph Michman in Israel in 1977 and 1983. See his arguments minimizing the religious reforms of Adath Jeschurun in *Studia Rosenthaliana*, 18 (1984): 149–58; his discussion of reunification in the form of a consistory, *ibid.*, 19 (1985): 127–58; his "The Diskursen of the Neie and the Alte Kille in Amsterdam (1797–1798)" [Hebrew], *Proceedings of the Ninth World Congress of Jewish Studies*, Division B, Vol. 2 (Jerusalem, 1986), 9–16; and his "The Impact of German–Jewish Modernization on Dutch Jewry," in Jacob Katz, ed., *Toward Modernity: The European Jewish Model* (New Brunswick, 1987), 180. For a biased but informative contemporary account, see *Sulamith*, 2.1 (1808): 55–68, 90–97.

54. L. Fuks, "De Zweedse familie Graanboom," *Studia Rosenthaliana*, 1.2 (1967): 85–106.

55. *Hanukat ha-bayit bet ha-keneset adat yeshurun* (Amsterdam, 1797).

56. Israel Graanboom, *Melits yosher* (Amsterdam, 1809). This defense of the customs of the synagogue, by the son of its rabbi, appeared after Izak Graanboom's death and the dissolution of Adath Jeschurun. Yet there continued to be interest in the community's practices. See Jaap Meijer, *Joodse Wetenschap in Nederland: Een referaat buiten-de-orde* (Heemstede, 1982), 16–19. The author himself may have hoped that at least the synagogue—if not the separatist community—would be permitted to continue. See, for example, *Melits yosher*, 8a. A few items from the pamphlet are translated in Jakob J. Petuchowski, *Prayerbook Reform in Europe* (New York, 1968), 48–49. A contemporary refutation was published by Isaac Maarsen in *Otsar Ha-Hayim*, 9 (1933): 110–20.

57. Graetz claims that the prayer directed against the "slanderers" (often mistakenly thought to refer to Christians) was also left out. However, Israel Graanboom makes no mention of such an omission. Heinrich Graetz, *Geschichte der Juden*, 11 (Leipzig, 1870): 232.

58. [Andreas Riem], *Leviathan oder Rabbinen und Juden* (Jerusalem [in fact Leipzig], 1801), vi. Riem makes the Dutch maskilim out to be far more radical in matters of religion than is indicated by the customs of Adath Jeschurun. See pp. 325–36, 446.

59. Recently published archival sources indicate that even before Louis' order some leaders of Adath Jeschurun were ready for reunification. See Meijer, *Joodse Wetenschap,* 17–18.

60. The speeches which they gave at the Sanhedrin and other materials pertinent to the delegation are in *Sulamith,* 1.2 (1807): 15–27, 95–110.

61. Frances Malino, *The Sephardic Jews of Bordeaux* (University, Ala., 1978).

62. *Pétition des Juifs établis en France, adressée à l'Assemblée Nationale* (Paris, 1790), 73–74. This petition may have influenced Saul Ascher's *Leviathan,* published two years later.

63. Zosa Szajkowski, "Jewish Religious Observance During the French Revolution of 1789," *YIVO,* 12 (1958/59): 211–34.

64. Diogene Tama, ed., *Organisation civile et religieuse des Israélites de France et du royaume d'Italie* (Paris, 1808), 146.

65. The best and most comprehensive recent analysis of the Assembly of Notables and the Great Sanhedrin is Simon Schwarzfuchs, *Napoleon, the Jews and the Sanhedrin* (London, 1979). See also the individual contributions in Bernard Blumenkranz and Albert Soboul, eds., *Le Grand Sanhedrin de Napoléon* (Toulouse, 1979), and Gil Graff, *Separation of Church and State: Dina de-Malkhuta Dina in Jewish Law, 1750–1848* (University, Ala., 1985), 71–94.

66. Tama, *Organisation,* 141.

67. Cf. Barouh Mevorah, *Napoleon u-tekufato* (Jerusalem, 1968), 83.

68. *Sulamith,* 3.1 (1810): 348.

69. *Ibid.,* 2.2 (1809): 418–19; 3.1 (1810): 181–82.

70. Cf. Ismar Elbogen, "Die Bezeichnung 'jüdische Nation,'" *MGWJ,* 63 (1919): 200–208.

71. *Sulamith,* 1.2 (1807): 4.

72. Others were disappointed too. See S. Lax, "Reform der jüdischen Nation," *Allgemeiner Anzeiger der Deutschen,* June 29, 1807, pp. 1775–76.

73. *Sulamith,* 1.2 (1807): 8–9.

74. The most comprehensive biographical treatment of Jacobson as a Jew is Jacob R. Marcus, *Israel Jacobson: The Founder of the Reform Movement in Judaism* (Cincinnati, 1972). His economic activities are detailed in Heinrich Schnee, *Die Hoffinanz und der moderne Staat,* 2 (Berlin, 1954): 109–54, while a balanced early evaluation is provided by Isaac Marcus Jost—who knew Jacobson personally—in *IA,* 1 (1839): 225–27, 234–35, 242–44.

75. B. H. Auerbach, *Geschichte der israelitischen Gemeinde Halberstadt* (Halberstadt, 1866), 140.

76. Aside from Jost, see the account of Jacobson's visit to small towns of the Westphalian countryside in Monika Richarz, ed., *Jüdisches Leben in Deutschland: Selbstzeugnisse zur Sozialgeschichte 1780–1871* (Stuttgart, 1976), 73–74. When two years before his death Jacobson heard the Book of Jonah being chanted on the Day of Atonement, he was so overcome that he impetuously rose from his seat and loudly proclaimed the text: "Ivri anokhi ve-et adonay elohe hashamayim ani yare" (Jonah 1:9). Gotthold Salomon, *Der wahrhaft Fromme stirbt nicht* (Altona, 1828), 15.

77. Jacobson's abiding admiration for France prompted Goethe to refer to the Geheime Finanzrat Israel Jacobson as der finanzgeheimrätliche jacobinische Israelssohn! The text is quoted by Schnee, *Die Hoffinanz,* 133.

78. *Ibid.,* 131–32.

79. Israel Jakobsohn, *Unterthänigste Vorstellung an Seine Hoheit den Fürst Primas* (Brunswick, 1808).

80. Herbert A. L. Fisher, *Studies in Napoleonic Statesmanship: Germany* (Oxford, 1903), 224–55. Fisher notes that among the members of Jerome's Council of State was the veteran champion of Jewish emancipation Christian Wilhelm Dohm.

81. The transactions of the deputies and early documents relating to the consistory were published by Jeremiah Heinemann in his *Allgemeines Archiv des Judenthums,* 3 (1843): 1–70, 97–132. Additional documents are contained in the various issues of *Sulamith* and in Ludwig Horwitz, *Die Israeliten unter dem Königreich Westfalen* (Cassel, 1900). The most comprehen-

sive scholarly treatment is Felix Lazarus, *Das königlich westphälische Konsistorium der Israeliten* (Pressburg, 1914). The records of the consistory are in the Staatsarchiv in Magdeburg, East Germany. I have been able to use a small collection of relevant documents in the Arthur Bluhm Collection at the Leo Baeck Institute Archives in New York.

82. In 1808 Schottlaender wrote an open letter to fellow Jews in which he outlined his hopes for the consistory. It may well have been intended to put forward his own candidacy. [Bendet Schottlaender], *Sendschreiben an meine Brüder die Israeliten in Westfalen die Errichtung eines Jüdischen Consistoriums betreffend* (Brunswick, 1808). It was reprinted in Hebrew translation in *Ha-Measef,* 9.1 (1809): 9–21.

83. In 1812 Berlin decided on his own that the Cassel Jewish burial society should honor the will of one of its members which stipulated that he not be buried until the second day after his death. *Sulamith,* 4.2 (1815): 162n.

84. See especially *Allgemeines Archiv des Judenthums,* 119–22, and the items in the Bluhm Collection.

85. It was first published in *Sulamith,* 2.2 (1809): 300–305.

86. Interestingly the text calls the sermons *gottesdienstliche Reden.* Apparently the more common term for a sermon, *Predigt,* was still considered too Christian.

87. For the sermons themselves and their background see Markus Brann, "Zur Centenarfeier der deutschen Predigt in der Synagogue," *Jahr-Buch zur Belehrung und Unterhaltung,* 45 (1897): 89–104.

88. Lazarus, *Das . . . Konsistorium,* 25. Jacobson's German sermon was preceded by a Hebrew one delivered by Rabbi Berlin.

89. The text is in *Sulamith,* 2.1 (1808): 15–30.

90. Phoebus Philippson, *Biographische Skizzen,* 1–2 (Leipzig, 1864): 185. His first sermon is printed in *Sulamith,* 2.1 (1808): 276–85, where the special service for the occasion of the duke's jubilee is also reproduced. When the duke entered the synagogue, the choir sang "Eine feste Burg ist unser Gott."

91. His memorandum of August 30, 1811, printed from the Bluhm Collection in Bernhard Brilling, "Briefe des Königlich Westfälischen Konsistoriums der Israeliten in Kassel an die Rabbiner Abraham Sutro und Marcus Baer Adler (1809–1812)," *Udim,* 4 (1974): 53.

92. The relevant documents are in *Sulamith,* 3.1 (1810): 90–96, 145–48, 294–97 and in part also in Horwitz, *Die Israeliten.* 59–62.

93. *Bekanntmachung wegen besserer Einrichtung des Gottesdienstes in den Synagogen des Königreichs Westphalen* (Kassel, 1810). It was also printed in *Sulamith,* 3.1 (1810): 366–80. Five members of the consistory signed the document, but Jacobson's name is missing, probably because he was away. English translations of excerpts from the text and from later synagogue regulations are presented in the chapter "Order and Decorum" by Petuchowski, *Prayerbook Reform in Europe,* 105–27.

94. *Allgemeines Archiv des Judenthums,* 32.

95. Horwitz, *Die Israeliten,* 68–70; Auerbach, *Geschichte der israelitischen Gemeinde Halberstadt,* 140.

96. The decision is printed in *Sulamith,* 3.1 (1810): 15–17, where it is followed by a similar permission with regard to the use on Passover of sugar refined in Europe. A new controversy over this issue arose in eastern Europe during a famine in 1868. Seymour Siegel, "The War of the *Kitniyot* (Legumes)," in *Perspectives on Jews and Judaism,* ed. Arthur A. Chiel (New York, 1978), 383–93.

97. Auerbach, *Geschichte der israelitischen Gemeinde Halberstadt,* 216–19, 225–26; *Ha-Measef,* 9.2 (1810): 59n.

98. Heinrich Graetz, *Geschichte der Juden,* 309.

99. Menahem Mendel Steinhardt, *Divre menaḥem* (Offenbach, 1804), 4b.

100. Cf. B.T. *Ḥulin* 7a.

101. Mendel Steinhardt, *Divre igeret* (Rödelheim, 1812), 8a.

102. *Ibid.*, 10b. Both in his introduction and in this fifth responsum Steinhardt makes reference also to certain "secret reasons" (*te'amim kemusim*) which he cannot reveal. I am at a loss to explain why he should mention such reasons at all if they were indeed to remain concealed. One can only speculate what they might have been: perhaps pressure put on Steinhardt by Jacobson, perhaps a desire to break the hold of the traditionalists, perhaps even some political motive. However, none of these three possibilities is documented.

103. For example, the *yehi ratson* prayer on the New Year, which was eliminated, mentions the mystical name of God composed of twenty-two letters and makes reference to the "secrets" of the Torah. One of the supplications eliminated from the Monday and Thursday service contains the passage: "Look from heaven and see how we have become a mockery and a derision among the nations. We are considered sheep brought to slaughter—to be slain and destroyed, beaten and shamed."

104. *Sulamith*, 3.1 (1810): 9–10; Lazarus, *Das . . . Konsistorium*, 45–50; Eliav, *Ha-ḥinukh ha-yehudi*, 119–29. At the dedication of new quarters for the school's synagogue a program of German hymns was presented. Tenor, bass, alto, and soprano voices sang solos and a choir also participated. I have found no reference to the identity of the singers. See *Gesänge bey Einweihung der Konsistorial-Schul-Synagoge zu Cassel* (Cassel, 1813). The hymns regularly sung were published with musical notes as *Hebräische und Deutsche Gesänge zur Andacht und Erbauung* (Cassel, 1810).

105. Eger's letter in the original Hebrew and in German translation is in Auerbach, *Geschichte der israelitischen Gemeinde Halberstadt*, 219–22. The Hebrew alone was reprinted by Mevorah, *Napoleon u-tekufato*, 151–54. Steinhardt justifies the use of the vernacular in *Divre igeret*, 9b–10a.

106. Primary sources are *Sulamith*, 3.1 (1810): 383–84, an announcement of October 11, 1810 in the Bluhm Collection, and a memorandum in Horwitz, *Die Israeliten*, 54–56.

107. Leopold Zunz, *Gesammelte Schriften*, 2 (Berlin, 1876): 215; *Sulamith*, 5.2 (1819): 398.

108. *JJGL*, 30 (1937): 138; *Literaturblatt des Orients*, 5 (1844): 121–22.

109. For the development of the confirmation ceremony and the catechism in their educational context see Eliav, *Ha-ḥinukh ha-yehudi*, 257–70. Various catechisms are discussed by Jakob J. Petuchowski, "Manuals and Catechisms of the Jewish Religion in the Early Period of Emancipation," in *Studies in Nineteenth-Century Jewish Intellectual History*, ed. Alexander Altmann (Cambridge, Mass., 1964), 47–64.

110. *Sulamith*, 4.1 (1812): 247–49; *Jedidja*, 2.1 (1818–19): 207–16. Cf. *Sulamith*, 1.2 (1807), 51–52.

111. *Ibid.*, 3.1 (1810): 11–12, 5.2 (1819): 398.

112. The first confirmation of Jewish girls was apparently that conducted by M. H. Bock in 1814 at his private school in Berlin. Eliav, *Ha-ḥinukh ha-yehudi*, 268.

113. *Sulamith*, 4.2 (1815): 399–401; Horwitz, *Die Israeliten*, 62–64.

114. Lazarus, *Das . . . Konsistorium*, 69–71; Gerhard Ballin, *Geschichte der Juden in Seesen* (Seesen, 1979), 36–38.

115. For the history and character of the structure, see *Jüdisches Litteratur-Blatt*, 18 (1889): 183–84; N. Friedland, *Zur Geschichte des Tempels der Jacobsonschule* (Seesen, 1910); Rachel Wischnitzer, *The Architecture of the European Synagogue* (Philadelphia, 1964), 174–76; Ballin, *Geschichte der Juden in Seesen*, 30–31; Harold Hammer-Schenk, *Synagogen in Deutschland* (Hamburg, 1981), 150–52; and Carole Herselle Krinsky, *Synagogues of Europe* (Cambridge, Mass., 1985), 316–18. The only other German synagogue to have a tower containing bells (though many had steeples without them) was that in Buchau, completed in 1839.

116. Paul Christian Kirchner, *Jüdisches Ceremoniel, D.i. Allerhand Jüdische Gebräuche, Welche Die Juden in und ausser dem Tempel . . . pflegen in acht zu nehmen* (Erfurt, 1717). A later edition of the same work, published in Nürnberg in 1724, contains an engraving entitled "Neumonds Gebeth ausser dem Tempel."

117. Mendel Levin Broese [*i.e.,* Mendel Bresselau], *Gebeth der Gesellschaft der Brüder am Einweihungs-Tag des Tempels* (Breslau, 1802).

118. Wischnitzer, *The Architecture of the European Synagogue,* 176; *Sulamith,* 6.1 (1820/ 21): 225.

119. *Sulamith,* 3.1 (1810): 311–12.

120. "His house of God must become for the Israelite that which once the holy temple in Jerusalem was for him." Gotthold Salomon, *Predigten in dem neuen Israelitischen Tempel zu Hamburg,* 1 (Hamburg, 1820): xi.

121. The only extensive primary source for the occasion, which also gives the text of Jacobson's speech, is *Sulamith,* 3.1 (1810): 298–317. Excerpts are given in English translation in W. Gunther Plaut, *The Rise of Reform Judaism* (New York, 1963), 27–31. Following Jacobson, Jeremiah Heinemann gave an address condemning prejudice and praising religious freedom. It was printed as *Rede bei der Einweihung des Jakobs-Tempels zu Seesen* (Cassel, 1810).

122. J. Maenss, "Die Juden im Königreich Westfalen," *Geschichts-Blätter für Stadt und Land Magdeburg,* 42 (1907): 63, 65; Arno Herzig, *Judentum und Emanzipation in Westfalen* (Münster, 1973), 13–14, 44–45; Jost, *Geschichte des Judenthums,* 326n; Jacobson to Abraham Sutro, December 22, 1811, in Brilling, "Briefe des Königlich Westfälischen Konsistoriums," 53.

123. *Sulamith,* 4.2 (1815): 251, 400–401n3. However, Abraham Sutro, who had requested and received a position as rabbinical adjunct under the consistory, became an active opponent of later reforms in Westphalia.

124. On the Berlin Jewish salons, see my *The Origins of the Modern Jew,* 90–114.

125. For the use of this terminology see, for example, I. M. Jost to S. M. Ehrenberg, March 14, 1816, Jost Letters, LBIA, AR 4294; I. N. Mannheimer to L. Zunz, October 6, 1822, *MGWJ,* 61 (1917): 100.

126. On Friedländer see *The Origins of the Modern Jew,* 57–84 and the literature cited there. See also the introduction by Yerachmiel Cohen to a Hebrew translation of Friedländer's letter to Provost Teller: *Igeret lehod ma'alato ha-adon teler* (Jerusalem, 1975), iii–xii.

127. *MGWJ,* 41 (1897): 375–76.

128. [David Friedländer], *Über die, durch die neue Organisation der Judenschaften in den Preussischen Staaten nothwendig gewordene Umbildung 1) ihres Gottesdienstes in den Synagogen, 2) ihrer Unterrichts-Anstalten, und deren Lehrgegenstände, und 3) ihres Erziehungs-Wesens überhaupt* (Berlin, 1812). Excerpts in English translation are in Petuchowski, *Prayerbook Reform in Europe,* 131–33.

129. For the immediate reaction see Moritz Stern, *Beiträge zur Geschichte der jüdischen Gemeinde zu Berlin,* 6 (Berlin, 1934): 18–25.

130. Nahum N. Glatzer, ed., *Leopold Zunz: Jude—Deutscher—Europäer* (Tübingen, 1964), 77–78.

131. Josef Fischer, "Et Rejsebrev fra I. N. Mannheimer," *Tidsskrift for Jødisk Historie og Literatur,* 1 (1917–19): 296–97. I am grateful to Prof. Hans-Georg Richert of the University of Cincinnati for aiding me with the translation of this Danish letter.

132. For this incident and the course of the following political struggle, interpreted from archival sources, see my "The Religious Reform Controversy in the Berlin Jewish Community, 1814–1823," *LBIYB,* 24 (1979): 139–55.

133. *Sulamith,* 4.2 (1815): 66–70; Nahum N. Glatzer, ed., *Leopold and Adelheid Zunz: An Account in Letters, 1815–1885* (London, 1958), 4–5; Jost, *Geschichte des Judenthums,* 332–33; idem, *Geschichte der Israeliten,* 10.3 (Berlin, 1847): 14–16. The three preachers were Isaac Levin Auerbach (1791–1853), Eduard Kley (1789–1867), and Carl Siegfried Günsburg (1784–1860).

134. Hugo Rachel and Paul Wallich, *Berliner Grosskaufleute und Kapitalisten,* 3 (Berlin, 1967): 130–31, 296; Maurice Bloch, "La Mère de Meyerbeer," *UI,* 51 (1896): 507 ff.; Giacomo Meyerbeer, *Briefwechsel und Tagebücher,* ed. Heinz Becker, 1 (Berlin, 1960): 31–45, 62, 280–81, 294–95.

135. Rachel and Wallich, *Berliner Grosskaufleute und Kapitalisten,* 2 (Berlin, 1938): 62–64;

R. S. Gumpertz to L. Zunz, October 5, 1820, Zunz Archives, JNUL; Fischer, "Et Rejsebrev," 294. On Joseph Muhr, who later became a champion of the conservative rabbi Zacharias Frankel, see Markus Brann, "Der älteste jüdische Gemeindeverband in Preussen," in *Beiträge zur Geschichte der deutschen Juden. Festschrift zum siebzigsten Geburtstage Martin Philippsons* (Leipzig, 1916), 344–45.

136. C. S. Günsburg to Aaron Wolfssohn, December 7, 1911, Leopold Stein Collection, LBIA, 3265/12.

137. Fischer, "Et Rejsebrev," 293. The wealthy's support of Jewish university students can be seen as a transmutation of the traditional obligation to maintain young men studying Talmud in a yeshivah.

138. The most recent studies of the *Verein für Cultur und Wissenschaft der Juden,* citing earlier sources, are Hanns Günther Reissner, *Eduard Gans, Ein Leben im Vormärz* (Tübingen, 1965) and Meyer, *The Origins of the Modern Jew,* 162–81.

139. *MGWJ,* 61 (1917): 97–98.

140. Nahum N. Glatzer, "On an Unpublished Letter of Isaak Markus Jost," *LBIYB,* 22 (1977): 129–37.

141. For examples of early sermons see J. Wolf, *Sechs deutsche Reden, gehalten in der Synagoge zu Dessau,* 2 vols. (Dessau, 1812–13); Isaac Levin Auerbach, *Predigt am Freudenfeste der Tora gehalten in einem Privat-Tempel zu Berlin* (Berlin, 1815); Leopold Zunz, *Predigten. Gehalten in der neuen Synagoge zu Berlin* (Berlin, 1823); M. Kayserling, *Bibliothek jüdischer Kanzelredner,* 1 (Berlin, 1870): 1–220. For a detailed analysis of influences see Alexander Altmann, "Zur Frühgeschichte der jüdischen Predigt in Deutschland: Leopold Zunz als Prediger," *LBIYB,* 6 (1961): 3–57 and his "The New Style of Preaching in Nineteenth-Century German Jewry," in *Studies in Nineteenth-Century Jewish Intellectual History,* 65–116.

142. *MGWJ,* 61 (1917): 100–101; Leopold Zunz, *Die gottesdienstlichen Vorträge der Juden* (Berlin, 1832), 458.

143. Moses Lemans, *Imrah tserufah* (Amsterdam, 1808), 3a, 14a; *Ha-Measef,* 8 (1809): 218–30. On the controversy, see Dan Michman, "David Friedrichsfeld," pp. 159–60. Some time earlier the traditional rabbi of Frankfurt, Nathan Adler, had prayed using the Sephardi pronunciation. H. J. Zimmels, *Ashkenazim and Sephardim* (London, 1958), 308–11. Isaac Euchel, in his 1786 translation of the prayerbook, used Sephardi Hebrew in transliterating the captions.

144. Ludwig Geiger, *Geschichte der Juden in Berlin,* 2 vols. (Berlin, 1871), 2: 225; Meyerbeer, *Briefwechsel,* 31–32.

145. The anonymously published prayerbook consists of a number of sections which appeared separately and were then bound together. The first installment was called *Gebete am Sabbath Morgens und an den beiden Neujahrs-Tagen.* There is no indication or hint anywhere of place or date of publication. Apparently only one copy of this prayerbook survived as part of the library of the Berlin Jewish Community. It was seen by Ludwig Geiger when he wrote his history of Berlin Jewry, published in 1871, and it was outlined in some detail, together with the Kley–Günsburg prayerbook, by Simon Bernfeld in an appendix to his *Toledot ha-reformatsyon ha-datit be-yisrael* (Cracow, 1900), 240–47. I was fortunate enough to rediscover it in the Jewish National and University Library in Jerusalem. The prayerbook edited by Kley and Günsburg is called *Die deutsche Synagoge,* 2 vols. (Berlin, 1817–18). The installments of the anonymous prayerbook were probably issued as early as 1815 since Jacobson sent copies of the prayers and hymns used in his home to the Minister of the Interior in December of that year. It also seems to be the earlier of the two because the texts of the German hymns do not appear here. Instead there are references to numbers that correspond to Heinemann's *Religiöse Gesänge für Israeliten,* which was reissued in Cassel in 1816 from a shorter version that appeared as early as 1810. Thus worshipers originally had to use prayerbook and songbook together before the Kley–Günsburg prayerbook incorporated the hymns into its text.

146. It is not certain whether the *musaf,* the additional prayer, was omitted on Sabbaths. It

is missing from Kley–Günsburg, but the anonymous prayerbook mentions that it is recited wholly in Hebrew and then gives the rubrics (p. 30).

147. One of the preachers, Isaac Levin Auerbach, published a defense of their use of the vernacular: *Sind die Israeliten verpflichtet ihre Gebete durchaus in der hebräischen Sprache zu verrichten?* (Berlin, 1818).

148. Glatzer, *Leopold Zunz,* 87–88; Zunz, *Die gottesdienstlichen Vorträge,* 457.

149. Fischer, "Et Rejsebrev," 296.

150. *Ibid.,* 295–96; Glatzer, *Leopold Zunz,* 118; Siegmund Maybaum, *Aus dem Leben von Leopold Zunz* (Berlin, 1894), 8; *Sulamith,* 6.1 (1820/21): 227–30.

151. Though biased, the most accurate source on Liebermann seems to be Yekutiel Greenwald, *Korot ha-torah ve-ha-emunah be-hungaryah* (Budapest, 1921), 41–42. See also the announcement in *Sulamith,* 5.2 (1819): 141. The two volumes were sold as one from the beginning, and all copies I have found have the tracts bound together. It may be that the Italian responsa were requested by the Berlin circle before Liebermann became involved. For a classification of the arguments used, see Moshe Pelli, *The Age of Haskalah,* 91–108. English translations of selected passages from the Hebrew polemics for and against reform are found in Alexander Guttmann, *The Struggle over Reform in Rabbinic Literature During the Last Century and a Half* (New York, 1977).

152. On the remarkable similarity between Liebermann's rhetoric and that of the maskilim in eastern Europe, see Zinberg, *A History of Jewish Literature,* 9: 251.

153. Saul Ascher, *Die Germanomanie* (Berlin, 1815), 61–63; cf. his *Die Wartburgs-Feier* (Leipzig, 1818), 28; I. M. Jost to S. M. Ehrenberg, December 30, 1818, Jost Letters, LBIA, AR 4294; *IA,* 1 (1839): 243; Glatzer, "On an Unpublished Letter," 137; *idem, Leopold and Adelheid Zunz,* 13, 34. Jost claimed Zunz was influenced by "the advice of the young men" (*atsat ha-ne'arim; cf.* I Kings 12). Taking Zunz's side, Eduard Kley wrote to him from Hamburg on August 21, 1822: "Is the preacher the hireling of the congregation or the free servant of the word? Is he the abject flatterer of the mighty ones or the organ of the God of truth? And this already at the beginning, when the office of preacher is just getting started? Do they want again to strangle their priests and prophets?" Zunz Archives, JNUL.

154. Fischer, "Et Rejsebrev," 295.

155. In addition to the sources cited in my "The Religious Reform Controversy," see B. Weinryb, "Zur Geschichte der Aufklärung bei den Juden," *MGWJ,* 76 (1932): 150–52.

156. *Gabriel Riesser's Gesammelte Schriften,* ed. Meyer Isler, 3 (Frankfurt and Leipzig, 1867): 149.

157. Helga Krohn, *Die Juden in Hamburg 1800–1850* (Frankfurt a/M, 1967), 5–35.

158. L. J. Riesser, *Send-Schreiben an meine Glaubens-Genossen in Hamburg, oder eine Abhandlung über den Israelitischen Cultus* (Altona, 1819), 8–9.

159. Eduard Duckesz, *Iwoh Lemoschaw* (Cracow, 1903), xxv–xxvi.

160. Salomon Jacob Cohen, *Historisch-kritische Darstellung des jüdischen Gottesdienstes* (Leipzig, 1819), vii–ix.

161. Protokolle des Vorsteherkollegiums, May 25, 1820, CAHJP, AHW 273a/1; *cf. Die Juden in Hamburg,* 18–19.

162. Glatzer, *Leopold and Adelheid Zunz,* 4–5; *Sulamith,* 5.1 (1817/18): 420–21; Hermann Jonas, *Lebensskizze des Herrn Doctor Eduard Kley* (Hamburg, 1859), 10–13.

163. David Leimdörfer, ed., *Festschrift zum hundertjährigen Bestehen des Israelitischen Tempels in Hamburg 1818–1918* (Hamburg, 1918), 11–17; *Sulamith,* 5.2 (1819): 196–97; Caesar Seligmann, "Zur Entstehungsgeschichte des Hamburger Tempels," *LJ,* 10 (1918): 70–73.

164. Michael A. Meyer, "The Establishment of the Hamburg Temple" [Hebrew], in *Studies in the History of Jewish Society in the Middle Ages and the Modern Period Presented to Professor Jacob Katz* (Jerusalem, 1980), 219–20.

165. *Jeschurun,* 5 (1866): 171–75; Menahem Mibashan, *Kitve menaḥem mibashan,* 1 (1937): 145–58.

166. *AZJ,* 4 (1840): 47–48; *IA,* 2 (1840): 18–19. Bresselau carried on an extended scholarly and personal correspondence with Zunz, some of it in Hebrew characters. However, when Bresselau died, his children had no use for their father's excellent collection of Hebraica. Bresselau's letters are in the Zunz Archives, JNUL.

167. Hammer-Schenk, *Synagogen in Deutschland,* 154 and illustration no. 109; Eduard Kley to Aaron Wolfssohn, March 1, 1819, Leopold Stein Collection, LBIA; *Sulamith,* 5.2 (1819): 402; Fischer, "Et Rejsebrev," 289. However, Heinrich Graetz was aghast on a visit to the temple in 1840 that "ladies sat close beside men." Marcus Brann, "Aus H. Graetzens Lehr- und Wander-jahren," *MGWJ,* 64 (1920): 145.

168. Zunz, *Die gottesdienstlichen Vorträge,* 459; Aaron Chorin, *Ein Wort zu seiner Zeit* (Vienna, 1820), 47; Seckel Isaac Fränkel, *Schutzschrift des zu Hamburg erschienenen Israeli-tischen Gebetbuchs* (Hamburg, 1819), 8–9; Jost, *Geschichte der Israeliten,* 10.3: 12. Although in the Hamburg temple only 43 percent of the seats were for women, this was a much higher per-centage than in traditional synagogues where no room was made for unmarried women. Samuel Echt, *Die Geschichte der Juden in Danzig* (Leer/Ostfriesland, 1972), 45, 49.

169. On Kley see especially Jonas, *Lebensskizze* and David Leimdörfer, "Der Hamburger Tempel und seine ersten Prediger," *LJ,* 10 (1918): 75. See also Kley's *Predigten in dem neuen Israelitischen Tempel zu Hamburg,* 2 vols. (Hamburg, 1819–20).

170. Gotthold Salomon, *Selbst-Biographie* (Leipzig, 1863); Kayserling, *Bibliothek jüdischer Kanzelredner,* 142–55; Phoebus Philippson, *Biographische Skizzen,* 3 (1866). Salomon pub-lished numerous sermons, both individually and in collections.

171. *Ordnung der öffentlichen Andacht für die Sabbath- und Festtage des ganzen Jahres. Nach dem Gebrauche des Neuen-Tempel-Vereins in Hamburg,* ed. S. I. Fränkel and M. I. Bresselau (Hamburg, 5579 [1819]). For an outline of the Sabbath services, comparing them with the tra-ditional liturgy, see Petuchowski, *Prayerbook Reform in Europe,* 49–53. See also Ismar Elbogen, *Der jüdische Gottesdienst in seiner geschichtlichen Entwicklung* (3d edn., Frankfurt a/M, 1931), 402–11.

172. For the first fifteen years the temple used a collection of hymns gathered by Eduard Kley and originally published in 1818. I have seen only the second edition: *Religiöse Lieder und Gesänge für Israeliten zum Gebrauche häuslicher und öffentlicher Gottesverehrung* (Hamburg, 1821). Later the association published its own songbook: *Allgemeines Israelitisches Gesangbuch eingeführt in dem Neuen Israelitischen Tempel zu Hamburg* (Hamburg, 1833). This publication produced a controversy with Kley, which may have been one of the causes for his early retire-ment in 1840 at the age of fifty-one. See the anonymous *Das neue Tempelgesangbuch und Herr Dr. E. Kley* (Leipzig, 1845).

173. Leimdörfer, *Festschrift,* 25, 70. The Sephardi pronunciation of Hebrew was retained by the temple until 1909. At the time when the temple was established, some wealthy Ashkenazi Jews were leaving their own community and joining the Sephardi one. The Hamburg Senate prohibited such transfers in 1821. Hartwig Levy, *Die Entwicklung der Rechtsstellung der Ham-burg Juden* (Hamburg, 1933), 30.

174. Cohen, *Historisch-kritische Darstellung,* xx; Moritz Henle, "Bemerkungen zum Gesang im Hamburger Tempel," *LJ,* 10 (1918): 76–79; A. Z. Idelsohn, *Jewish Music in Its Historical Development* (New York, 1929), 238–42.

175. *Sulamith,* 6.1 (1820/21): 225–27; Glatzer, *Leopold and Adelheid Zunz,* 18–19; *idem, Leopold Zunz,* 113–14.

176. The Baden government had insisted that the place of worship be called neither a syn-agogue nor a temple. The demise of the Karlsruhe group was provoked when, like the reformers in Berlin, it sought joint use of the community synagogue. In response, the government decided not to allow any religious division within the Jewish community. Adolf Lewin, *Geschichte der badischen Juden* (Karlsruhe, 1909), 202–203. See also "Beyspiel eines für Andacht und Unter-richt durch die teutsche Landessprache sich bildenden Mosaischen Tempelvereins zu Carls-ruhe," *Sophronizon,* 2 (1820): 51–67; *Sulamith,* 4.2 (1815): 252; 5.2 (1819): 339–41; *RW,* 1

(1836/37): 101–103; Zunz, *Die gottesdienslichen Vorträge,* 461–68. Kley wrote to Zunz, November 3, 1820 and January 1, 1822, that he hoped the preachers would create regular communication, a degree of spiritual unity, and even liturgical conformity among the various congregations. But that was not acheived. Zunz Archives, JNUL.

177. The course of the political struggle in the community is documented in my "The Establishment of the Hamburg Temple," 220–24.

178. The self-critical and conciliatory tone of Eliezer's second letter (pp. 87–96) contrasts sharply with the vituperation of his earlier contribution to the volune (pp. 22–24).

179. Berlin first published *Kadur katan* (n.p., n.d.) and then made it the introduction to his longer work, *Et ledaber,* published in 1819 in Breslau or Dyhernfurth. On Berlin see Louis Lewin, *Geschichte der Juden in Lissa* (Pinne, 1904), 238–39; Moshe Samet, "The Social and Historical Doctrine of R. Nachman Berlin" [Hebrew], *Ḥevrah ve-historyah* (Jerusalem, 1980): 125–35.

180. *Tseror ha-ḥayim* (Amsterdam, 1820). The author claims that it was completed as early as 1819, before the appearance of *Eleh divre ha-berit.*

181. See Barouh Mevorah, "Messianism as a Factor in the First Reform Controversies" [Hebrew], *Zion,* 34 (1969): 189–218. The historian Isaac Marcus Jost, sometimes considered a radical assimilationist, thought the traditionalists wholly justified in condemning these omissions. Jost, *Geschichte des Judenthums,* 338.

182. Fränkel, *Schutzschrift des zu Hamburg erschienenen Israelitischen Gebetbuchs*; [Meyer Israel Bresselau], *Über die Gebete der Israeliten in der Landessprache* (n.p., 1819).

183. It was published anonymously without indication of place in 1819 and reproduced by Simon Bernfeld as an appendix to his *Toledot ha-reformatsyon ha-datit be-yisrael,* 253–66. An annotated translation into English constitutes the rabbinical thesis of Donald Rossoff (Hebrew Union College–Jewish Institute of Religion, Cincinnati, 1981). Its literary qualities are discussed and an annotated Hebrew text is provided in Yehuda Friedlander, *Be-mistere ha-satirah* (Israel, 1984), 77–142. Another Hebrew defense of the Berlin and Hamburg reformers was published pseudonymously by the Posen maskil David Caro, as Amitai ben Avida Ahitsedek, *Berit emet* (Constantinople [in fact Dessau], 1820). Aaron Chorin's renewed defense of religious reform, *Davar be-ito* (Vienna, 1820), appeared also in German versions in Hebrew and Gothic characters.

184. Bresselau's tract, in turn, provoked a vicious refutation by a Moravian rabbi who pointed out that the nations of the world had nothing to fear at the coming of the messiah. Only those "evil men" of Israel (clearly the reformers) who had rebelled against God's Torah and reviled its students would be destroyed. L. Reinitz, *Lahat ha-ḥerev ha-mithapekhet* (n.p., 1820), 32a.

185. L. J. Riesser, *Send-Schreiben an meine Glaubens-Genossen in Hamburg, oder eine Abhandlung über den Israelitischen Cultus* (Altona, 1819). Riesser's son, Gabriel, joined the Hamburg temple and became one of its directors in 1840.

186. For a detailed discussion of the project see Stephen M. Poppel, "The Politics of Religious Leadership: The Rabbinate in Nineteenth-Century Hamburg," *LBIYB,* 28 (1983): 439–57.

187. Moses Moser to Immanuel Wohlwill, May 3/4, 1824, *LBIYB,* 11 (1966): 296.

188. *Theologisiche Gutachten über das Gebetbuch nach dem Gebrauche des Neuen Israelitischen Tempelvereins in Hamburg* (Hamburg, 1842), 25.

Chapter 2

1. The challenge of Spinoza and his influence on modern Jewish thought is especially stressed by Eliezer Schweid, *Toledot ha-hagut ha-yehudit ba-et ha-ḥadashah* (Jerusalem, 1977).

2. *The Chief Works of Benedict de Spinoza,* trans. R. H. M. Elwes, 1 (New York, 1951): 19, 49, 55–56, 68, 199. See also Paul R. Mendes-Flohr, "Spinoza: Renegade or Meta-Rabbi,"

Forum, 27 (1977): 54–63; Isaac Franck, "Spinoza's Onslaught on Judaism," *Judaism,* 28 (1979): 177–93 and *idem,* "Was Spinoza a 'Jewish' Philosopher?," *ibid.,* 345–52.

3. *The Chief Works of Benedict de Spinoza,* 72, 120–22.

4. *Ibid.,* 165.

5. Gotthold Ephraim Lessing, *Die Erziehung des Menschengeschlechts* (Berlin, 1785). *Cf.* Michael Graetz, "*Die Erziehung des Menschengeschlechts* und jüdisches Selbstbewusstsein im 19. Jahrhundert," *Wolfenbütteler Studien zur Aufklärung,* 4 (1977): 273–95.

6. On Kant's and Hegel's conceptions of Judaism see Nathan Rotenstreich, *The Recurring Pattern: Studies in Anti-Judaism in Modern Thought* (London, 1963), 23–75. A wide range of views is presented in David Charles Smith, "Protestant Attitudes toward Jewish Emancipation in Prussia" (Ph.D. dissertation, Yale University, 1971).

7. Immanuel Kant, *Religion within the Limits of Reason Alone,* trans. Theodore M. Greene and Hoyt H. Hudson (Chicago, 1934), 116–20.

8. *Ibid.,* 115.

9. *Ibid.,* 97.

10. *Ibid.,* 100–114.

11. According to Kant this would be especially true of Judaism. "The pure moral religion," he wrote, "is the euthanasia of Judaism." Immanuel Kant, "Der Streit der Facultäten," in *Sämmtliche Werke,* 10 (Leipzig, 1838): 308.

12. Friedrich Schleiermacher, *On Religion: Speeches to Its Cultured Despisers,* trans. John Oman (New York, 1958), 238. *Cf.* Joseph W. Pickle, "Schleiermacher on Judaism," *The Journal of Religion,* 60 (1980): 115–37.

13. Friedrich Schleiermacher, *The Christian Faith,* trans. H. R. Mackintosh and J. S. Stewart (Edinburgh, 1928), 37–38.

14. *Ibid.,* 44–62.

15. Rotenstreich, *The Recurring Pattern,* 67. See also Hans Liebeschütz, *Das Judentum im deutschen Geschichtsbild von Hegel bis Max Weber* (Tübingen, 1967), 24–42; Emil L. Fackenheim, *Encounters between Judaism and Modern Philosophy* (New York, 1973), 81–134.

16. The general secondary literature on these three thinkers includes the following: Max Wiener, *Jüdische Religion im Zeitalter der Emanzipation* (Berlin, 1933), 120–65; Albert Lewkowitz, *Das Judentum und die geistigen Strömungen des 19. Jahrhunderts* (Breslau, 1935), 385–418; Hans Joachim Schoeps, *Geschichte der jüdischen Religionsphilosophie in der Neuzeit* (Berlin, 1935), 65–132; Julius Guttmann, *Philosophies of Judaism,* trans. David W. Silverman (New York, 1964), 308–21, 344–49; Nathan Rotenstreich, *Jewish Philosophy in Modern Times* (New York, 1968), 106–36, 149–74; Jacob Fleischmann,, *Be'ayat ha-natsrut ba-mahshavah ha-yehudit mi-mendelson ad rosentsveig* (Jerusalem, 1964), 68–105; Schweid, *Toledot ha-hagut ha-yehudit,* 219–63; 281–91; and Heinz Moshe Graupe, *The Rise of Modern Judaism,* trans. John Robinson (Huntington, N.Y., 1978), 224–35. My general interpretation corresponds most closely to that suggested by Moshe Schwarcz, "Religious Currents and General Culture," *LBIYB,* 16 (1971): 9–11.

17. However, there has been a revival of interest. See Hans-Joachim Schoeps *et al.,* eds., *Salomon Ludwig Steinheim zum Gedenken* (Leiden, 1966); *Salomon Ludwig Steinheim, 100. Todestag, Gedenkfeier im Christianeum am 23. Mai 1966* (Hamburg, 1966); Joshua O. Haberman, "Salomon Steinheim's Doctrine of Revelation," *Judaism,* 17 (1968): 22–41; Aharon Shear-Yashuv, *The Theology of Salomon Ludwig Steinheim* (Leiden, 1986); Moshe Schwarcz, *Hagut yehudit nokhah ha-tarbut ha-kelalit* (Jerusalem, 1976), 37–71; Gary Lease, "Salomon Ludwig Steinheim's Influence: Hans Joachim Schoeps, A Case Study," *LBIYB,* 29 (1984): 383–402.

18. S. L. Steinheim, *Die Offenbarung nach dem Lehrbegriffe der Synagoge,* 1 (Frankfurt a/ M, 1835); 2 (Leipzig, 1856); 3 (Leipzig, 1863); 4 (Altona, 1865).

19. *Ibid.,* 1: vii–xii, 5–12, 360–61; Abraham Geiger, "Salomon Ludwig Steinheim," *JZWL,* 10 (1872): 285–92.

20. Steinheim, *Die Offenbarung,* 1: 358–64, 2: 465–66.

21. *Ibid.*, 1: 185–87, 4: 357.

22. Heinz Moshe Graupe, "Steinheim und Kant," *LBIYB*, 5 (1960): 140–75.

23. S. L. Steinheim, *Moses Mendelssohn und seine Schule* (Hamburg, 1840), 37; *idem, Die Offenbarung*, 1: xvii, 2: vii–viii, 3: 318–22; *idem*, "Synagoge und Tempel, ein modernes Schisma," *AZJ*, 6 (1842): 564, 567–68.

24. S. Formstecher, *Die Religion des Geistes, eine wissenschaftliche Darstellung des Judenthums nach seinem Charakter, Entwicklungsgange und Berufe in der Menschheit* (Frankfurt a/M, 1841), v, 4–7. Reprinted: New York, 1980.

25. *Ibid.*, 4, 11, 33.

26. *Ibid.*, 63–72.

27. See Bernard J. Bamberger, "Formstecher's History of Judaism," *HUCA*, 23.2 (1950/51): 1–35.

28. Formstecher, *Die Religion des Geistes, 74–82, 196, 393–95.*

29. *Ibid.*, 358–59; cf. Lewkowitz, *Das Judentum*, 411–12.

30. Formstecher, *Die Religion des Geistes*, 353–57, 413–52.

31. On various phases in the development of Hirsch's thought, see Jacob Katz, "Samuel Hirsch—Rabbi, Philosopher and Freemason," *REJ*, 125 (1966): 113–26; Gershon Greenberg, "Samuel Hirsch: Jewish Hegelian," *REJ*, 129 (1970), 205–15; *idem*, "The Historical Origins of God and Man: Samuel Hirsch's Luxembourg Writings," *LBIYB*, 20 (1975): 129–48 (where reference is made to Greenberg's remaining articles on Hirsch); Michael A. Meyer, "Ob Schrift? Ob Geist? Die Offenbarungsfrage im deutschen Judentum des neunzehnten Jahrhunderts," in Jakob J. Petuchowski and Walter Strolz, eds., *Offenbarung im jüdischen und christlichen Glaubensverständnis* (Freiburg, 1981), 162–79. A bibliography is in *CCARY*, 25 (1915): 184–90.

32. Letter of April 16, 1841, Zunz Archives, JNUL, 40792-g14.

33. Samuel Hirsch, *Die Religionsphilosophie der Juden oder das Prinzip der jüdischen Religionsanschauung und sein Verhältniss zum Heidenthum, Christenthum und zur absoluten Philosophie* (Leipzig, 1842).

34. Greenberg, "The Historical Origins of God and Man," 129–30. The Jewish philologist and philosopher Heymann Steinthal claimed that Hirsch permanently shaped his conception of Judaism and that he provided him, when he was young, with "armor for battle against the opponent whom I would get to know only at the university—Hegel." H. Steinthal, *Über Juden und Judentum* (Berlin, 1910), 197.

35. For Hirsch's defense of rabbinic literature, see Hirsch, *Die Religionsphilosophie der Juden*, 460, 593n.

36. Cf. Eliezer Schweid: Hirsch "succeeded in moving from the measurement of his Judaism by the criterion of his environment to the measurement of his environment by the criterion of his Judaism." Schweid, *Toledot ha-hagut ha-yehudit*, 261.

37. Hirsch, *Die Religionsphilosophie der Juden*, v, ix.

38. Aside from the general histories of Jewish thought, see Emil L. Fackenheim, "Samuel Hirsch and Hegel," in Alexander Altmann, ed., *Studies in Nineteenth-Century Jewish Intellectual History* (Cambridge, Mass., 1964), 171–201. For Hirsch's thought in relation to the left-wing Hegelians, especially Ludwig Feuerbach, see Manfred H. Vogel, "Does Samuel Hirsch Anthropologize Relgion?,"*Modern Judaism*, 1 (1981): 298–322.

39. Hirsch, *Die Religionsphilosophie der Juden*, xxvi, 43–46, 98n, 438, 445.

40. *Ibid.*, xxx, 457–528, 545, 545n.

41. *Ibid.*, 621–839.

42. *Ibid.*, 537–620.

43. *Ibid.*, viii, 868–82. *Cf.* Samuel Hirsch, *Die Messiaslehre der Juden in Kanzelvorträgen* (Leipzig, 1843), 372–93.

44. *Zeitschrift für die Wissenschaft des Judenthums*, 1 (1822/23): 197.

45. On *Wissenschaft des Judentums* see the articles by Ismar Schorsch in *LBIYB*, 22 (1977): 109–28; 25 (1980): 3–19; 28 (1983): 413–37; Paul Mendes-Flohr, *Ḥokhmat yisrael* (Jerusalem,

1979); and of the earlier literature especially Wiener, *Jüdische Religion im Zeitalter der Emanzipation,* 175–257.

46. *Die gottesdienstlichen Vorträge der Juden* (Berlin, 1832), 450.

47. *Ibid.,* 475.

48. *Zeitschrift für die Wissenschaft des Judenthums,* 1 (1822/23): 117–18.

49. Recent general studies of Hirsch, citing the earlier literature, include Noah H. Rosenbloom, *Tradition in an Age of Reform: The Religious Philosophy of Samson Raphael Hirsch* (Philadelphia, 1976); Pinchas E. Rosenblüth, "Samson Raphael Hirsch—Sein Denken und Wirken," in Hans Liebeschütz and Arnold Paucker, eds., *Das Judentum in der Deutschen Umwelt 1800–1850* (Tübingen, 1977), 293–324; Schweid, *Toledot ha-hagut ha-yehudit,* 291–309; and Mordechai Breuer, *Jüdische Orthodoxie im Deutschen Reich 1871–1918* (Frankfurt a/M, 1986), 61–82.

50. Isaac Heinemann, "Studies on R. Samson Raphael Hirsch" [Hebrew], *Sinai,* 12 (1948/ 49): 251.

51. When he first came to Frankfurt, a critical observer described Hirsch as "a handsome man very much resembling Charles V. His delivery is pure and sonorous, though highly affected, his gestures *in the highest degree* theatrical, so that it borders on the unbearable. The content [of the sermon] was the purest morality, full of platitudes, without strict organization; orthodoxy was noticeable only insofar as he symbolized customs. The traditionalists say he satisfies them, the women are enchanted." Isaac Marcus Jost to S. M. Ehrenberg, November 21, 1851, LBIA, AR 4294.

52. Heinemann, "Studies on R. Samson Raphael Hirsch," 252–60; *idem,* "Supplementary Remarks on the Secession from the Frankfurt Jewish Community under Samson Raphael Hirsch," *HJ,* 10 (1948): 126–27.

53. When Moses Mendelsohn (of Hamburg) offered to translate his *Nineteen Letters on Judaism* into Hebrew, Hirsch supposedly objected because "there was no point to it." Eduard Duckesz, *Ḥakhme Ahu* (Hamburg, 1908), 121.

54. Ben Usiel [S. R. Hirsch], *Igrot Tsafon: Neunzehn Briefe über Judenthum* (Altona, 1836), 79.

55. Saemy Japhet, "The Secession from the Frankfurt Jewish Community under Samson Raphael Hirsch," *HJ,* 10 (1948): 106.

56. Rosenbloom, *Tradition in an Age of Reform,* 109–10.

57. For example, *Igrot Tsafon,* 35–36, 41–43, 52, and references in *Zion,* 46 (1981): 57–58.

58. *Igrot Tsafon,* 25; *Ḥorev: Versuche über Jissroels Pflichten in der Zerstreuung* (Altona, 1837), viii, xiv, 28; *Gesammelte Schriften,* 6 vols. (Frankfurt a/M, 1902–12), 1: 84–85, 91, 158, 160–67; 3: 165–66.

59. *Gesammelte Schriften,* 3: 489–504.

60. *Ibid.,* 1: 431; 3: 491; 6: 393.

61. *Ibid.,* 1: 81–85; 5: 318–509; 6: 384–418; *Der Pentateuch, übersetzt und erläutert,* 1 (Frankfurt a/M, 1920): 149; *Naftule Naftali: Erste Mittheilungen aus Naphtali's Briefwechsel* (Altona, 1838), 66.

62. On his identification with the lonely prophet Elijah see Robert Liberles, "Champion of Orthodoxy: The Emergence of Samson Raphael Hirsch as Religious Leader," *AJS Review,* 6 (1981): 43–60.

63. The only full-length biography of Samuel Holdheim is the still valuable book by his disciple Immanuel Heinrich Ritter, *Samuel Holdheim. Sein Leben und seine Werke* (Berlin, 1865).

64. David Einhorn in *Sinai,* 5 (1860): 289–97; Abraham Geiger in *JZWL,* 3 (1864/65): 216–18.

65. Holdheim always insisted upon the title of rabbi as well as preacher, regarding the latter designation as degrading what was essentially a teaching vocation. He also stressed that Judaism, unlike Christianity, lacked the concept of a "spiritual pastorate." Samuel Holdheim, *Ge-*

schichte der Entstehung und Entwickelung der jüdischen Reformgemeinde in Berlin (Berlin, 1857), 173.

66. The enmity is virulent in the treatment accorded Holdheim by the historian Heinrich Graetz, the colleague and disciple of Zacharias Frankel, one of Holdheim's bitterest polemical opponents. Heinrich Graetz, *Geschichte der Juden,* 11 (Leipzig, 1870): 561–67.

67. *Geschichte der . . . Reformgemeinde,* 11n.

68. Immanuel H. Ritter, "Samuel Holdheim: The Jewish Reformer," *JQR,* 1 (1889): 202–15.

69. *Die Religionsprincipien des reformirten Judenthums* (Berlin, 1847), 15–16.

70. The Kantian influence on Holdheim is especially apparent in these sermonic words: "Conscience is that indubitable revelation of religion to which Judaism attaches its teaching. . . . Every revelation must be verified by the inner voice of conscience. Reason not only has a weighty say in [individual] matters of religion, rather it is the most certain touchstone of everything that is taught in the name of religion." *Antrittspredigt bei dessen Einführung in sein Amt als Rabbiner und Prediger der Genossenschaft für Reform im Judenthum zu Berlin* (Berlin, 1847), 8.

71. "Life alone, untroubled by the principle underlying the law, has in fact transformed Jewish marriage into a magnificent tree of life. It has woven everything good and admirable which rabbinic literature says about the marriage relationship into a beautiful garland to adorn the Jewish wife." *Über die Autonomie der Rabbinen und das Princip der jüdischen Ehe* (Schwerin, 1843), 260.

72. *Ibid.,* vii, 14–17.

73. *Das Ceremonialgesetz im Messiasreich* (Schwerin, 1845), 3–8, 40–42, 55, 70.

74. Wiener, *Jüdische Religion im Zeitalter der Emanzipation,* 97.

75. *Gemischte Ehen zwischen Juden und Christen* (Berlin, 1850), 64; *Einsegnung einer gemischten Ehe zwischen einem Juden und einer Christin in Leipzig* (Berlin, 1849), 3.

76. *Das Ceremonialgesetz,* 88; *Die Religionsprincipien,* 23–25.

77. *Die Religionsprincipien,* 27.

78. " . . . the elements and conditions of our age are so utterly different from those of rabbinic Judaism that the Jew has only the alternative either to be a rabbinic Jew and live outside of time or to live in time and cease to be a rabbinic Jew." *Das Ceremonialgesetz,* 122–23.

79. Unlike his colleagues, Holdheim demanded a consistent distinction between religious elements that were worthy of survival (*lebenswürdig*) and those that were merely capable of survival (*lebensfähig*). "Offene Briefe über die dritte Rabbiner-Versammlung," *INJ,* 7 (1846): 363.

80. *Der religiöse Fortschritt im deutschen Judenthume* (Leipzig, 1840), 9.

81. *Das Ceremonialgesetz,* 50.

82. *Vorträge über die mosaische Religion* (Schwerin, 1844), xiv; *Die erste Rabbinerversammlung und Herr Dr. Frankel* (Schwerin, 1845), 18; *Das Ceremonialgesetz,* 135–36n. Holdheim also rejected the idea that Judaism should in any way be altered for the sake of emancipation. He admitted that his own critique of the Talmud could in fact be used by the enemies of Jewish equality, but he would not be deterred by apologetic considerations. *Das Religiöse und Politische im Judenthum* (Schwerin, 1845), iv–viii; *INJ,* 9 (1848): 118.

83. *Über die Autonomie der Rabbinen,* ix; Michael A. Meyer, "German-Jewish Social Thought in the Mid-Nineteenth Century—A Comment," in Werner E. Mosse *et al.,* eds., *Revolution and Evolution: 1848 in German-Jewish History* (Tübingen, 1981), 332–35.

84. *Ma'amar ha-ishut* (Berlin, 1861), 1. Even a hostile writer on Holdheim considered it to possess scholarly merit. Bernfeld, *Toledot ha-reformatsyon,* 181.

85. *Programm zur öffentlichen Prüfung der Zöglinge der Religionsschule* (Berlin, 1860), 9–10. For other examples of this contradictory tendency see Jakob J. Petuchowski, "Abraham Geiger and Samuel Holdheim: Their Differences in Germany and Repercussions in America," *LBIYB,* 22 (1977): 147–49.

86. There is only one full-length biography of Zacharias Frankel and, regrettably, it is wholly uncritical: Saul Phinehas Rabbinowitz, *R. Zechariah Frankel*, 3 vols. (Warsaw, 1898–1902). Briefer biographical studies may be found in *MGWJ*, 25 (1876): 12–26; 45 (1901): 193–278 (which also contains a bibliography of Frankel's writings); and in *The Menorah*, November 1901, pp. 329–66. On Frankel's first steps in the rabbinate see Marcus Brann, *Wie Zacharias Frankel nach Teplitz kam* (Berlin, 1917) and Brann's earlier article in *Jahrbuch zur Belehrung and Unterhaltung*, 46 (1898): 100–26. A selection of Frankel's writings in Hebrew translation is available in Rivka Horwitz, ed., *Zechariah Frankel ve-reshit ha-yahadut ha-pozitivit historit* (Jerusalem, 1984).

87. Frankel to Solomon Herxheimer in Bernburg, June 30, 1836, CAHJP, P46/3.

88. As far as I can determine, only one writer has alluded to the determinative role of faith in Frankel's thought. Ismar Elbogen, "Der Streit um die 'positiv-historische Reform,'"in *Festgabe für Claude G. Montefiore* (Berlin, 1928), 24–29.

89. *Vorstudien zu der Septuaginta* (Leipzig, 1841), xi; *ZRIJ*, Anzeige und Prospectus (1843): 4, 8; 1 (1844): 14–15, 18, 101; 2 (1845): 10, 180; "Über palästinische und alexandrinische Schriftforschung," in *Programm zur Eröffnung des jüdisch-theologischen Seminars zu Breslau* (Breslau, 1854), 42.

90. *ZRIJ*, 2 (1845): 177.

91. *MGWJ*, 4 (1855): 45–55; *ZRIJ*, 1 (1844): 14, 93; 2 (1845): 173. Note, however, that unlike Mendelssohn—and like Steinheim—Frankel attributed also the theological teachings of Judaism to revelation. He regarded monotheism as the essence of Judaism. *Ibid.*, 1 (1844): 7–8. For evidence of the limits Frankel placed on biblical studies see Michael A. Meyer, "Jewish Religious Reform and Wissenschaft des Judentums," *LBIYB*, 16 (1971): 35–37.

92. Frankel to Meir Wiener in Hannover, April 23, 1855, Hebrew Union College Library Archives, Cincinnati; *MGWJ*, 1 (1852): 444; Michael A. Meyer, "A Division of Opinion on the Modern Education of Rabbis in Germany in the Nineteenth Century" [Hebrew], *Proceedings of the Sixth World Congress of Jewish Studies*, 2 (Jerusalem, 1975): 195–200. In speaking to a group of Breslau seminary graduates, Frankel concluded with the hope that their theological society would further "Glauben und Glaubenswissenschaft," perhaps a nineteenth-century analogue of the medieval "faith seeking understanding." Z. Frankel, "Das Talmudstudium," in *Vorträge gehalten im jüdisch-theologischen Verein in Breslau* (Leipzig, 1869), 11.

93. *ZRIJ*, Anzeige und Prospectus (1843): 5.

94. *Ibid.*, 2 (1845): 16–17; cf. 1 (1844): 105, 291, 293; 2 (1845): 174. For an earlier example of associating revealed with positive religion in a Jewish context see Salomon Maimon, *Lebensgeschichte*, 2 (Berlin, 1793): 179.

95. *Der religiöse Fortschritt im deutschen Judenthume* (Leipzig, 1840), 28.

96. *ZRIJ*, 2 (1845): 8–9. In his analysis of key terms in Frankel's thought, Ismar Schorsch has especially stressed Frankel's use of "positive" in a legal sense. See his "Zacharias Frankel and the European Origins of Conservative Judaism," *Judaism*. 30 (1981): 343–54.

97. Since Frankel is less than clear regarding the theological status he ascribes to the Oral Law, scholars have been of different minds with regard to it. While Isaac Heinemann argues that Frankel sees talmudic creativity as directly influenced by the Divine Spirit no less than by the times in which the Sages lived, Ismar Schorsch detects a "radical secularization" inherent in Frankel's enterprise and notes that, for Frankel, "in large measure antiquity had become a surrogate for divinity." See Heinemann, *Ta'ame ha-mitsvot be-sifrut yisrael*, 2 (Jerusalem, 1956): 165, 175–76; Schorsch, "Zacharias Frankel," 352, 354. It is, in fact, hard to imagine that Frankel would have removed the mantle of revelation entirely from the Oral Law. Yet in trying to make the ancient Rabbis models for contemporary halakhic creativity, he did stress the human side of their enterprise. In attempting to close the gap between the Sages and the present, he widened the theological gap between Scripture and Talmud.

98. Yet Frankel's scholarship, limited by his traditionalism, was not very innovative. One historian has noted of Frankel: "His scholarly writings are of significant value, but they can not

at all be called pioneering in the manner of Zunz or Geiger." Simon Bernfeld, *Juden und Judentum im neunzehnten Jahrhundert* (Berlin 1898), 131. Louis Ginzberg (in *The Menorah,* November 1901, p. 363) believed it was difficult to say whether Frankel was more the traditional *lamdan* or the modern scholar. Unlike more radical writers, Frankel consistently favored the Masoretic text of the Bible over the Septuagint. See, for example, *ZRIJ,* 1 (1844): 120–28; *Verhandlungen der ersten Versammlung deutscher und ausländischer Orientalisten in Dresden 1844* (Leipzig, 1845), 10–16; and the comment of L. Treitel in *MGWJ,* 45 (1901): 257. Scholars have devoted much effort to determining external influences on Frankel. Already half a century ago Albert Lewkowitz suggested that Frankel's conception of *Wissenschaft des Judentums* was fully congruent with the approach of the conservative legal scholar Friedrich Karl von Savigny and the German "Historical School," which stressed the organic development of law. Since then, this influence has been emphasized repeatedly, and yet nowhere in his extant writings does Frankel mention Savigny (who was an antisemite), nor do any of his immediate disciples refer to such influence. See Lewkowitz, *Das Judentum und die geistigen Strömungen des 19. Jahrhunderts,* 368, 373–74. The only contemporary reference I have been able to find which may link Frankel to the Historical School is in Samson Raphael Hirsch's attack on Frankel: *Vorläufige Abrechnung* (Frankfurt a/M, 1861), 23. Radical reformers tried to cast aspersions on the Jewishness of Frankel's religious thought—especially his emphasis on the collective will of the people—by suggesting that it came from Christian romantic theology, especially that of Schleiermacher's school. See, for example, *INJ,* December 29, 1844, p. 416; Gotthold Salomon, *Die Rabbiner-Versammlung und ihre Tendenz* (Hamburg, 1845), 80–81. For a positive evaluation: Rivka Horwitz, "The Influence of Romanticism on Jewish Scholarship" [Hebrew], *Proceedings of the Eighth World Congress of Jewish Studies,* Division B (Jerusalem, 1982), 107–14. Frankel must indeed have read the literature of his time, but he wanted to believe that his scholarship, his theology, and his motives for reform were indigenous to Judaism itself. Consequently, he must have tried to avoid reference to non-Jewish influences and to minimize any obvious effect they had on him.

99. *Darkhe ha-mishnah* (Leipzig, 1859), 21. Cf. "Über palästinische und alexandrinische Schriftforschung," 41–42.

100. *Der Orient,* 3 (1842): 54; *ZRIJ,* 1 (1844): 19–22, 92–93, 104; 2 (1845): 15, 180.

101. *Der Orient,* 3 (1842): 56, 64, 72; *ZRIJ,* 1 (1844): 26; *AZJ,* 62 (1898): 607; *Jahrbuch zur Belehrung und Unterhaltung,* 46 (1898), 113; cf. Ismar Schorsch, "The Emergence of the Modern Rabbinate," in Mosse, *Revolution and Evolution,* 231–32. The terms *Gemüt* and *gemütlich* are among Frankel's favorites.

102. *Der Orient,* 3 (1842): 63, 359–60, 362–63; *AZJ,* 62 (1848): 438; *Rede bei der Grundsteinlegung der neuen Syngagoge zu Dresden* (Dresden, 1838). The position that Frankel was in some respects a proto-Zionist was taken again recently in Rivka Horwitz, "Zacharias Frankel's 1842 Idea of Jewish Independence in the land of Israel" [Hebrew], *Kivunim,* 6 (February 1980): 5–25.

103. "Sendschreiben an den ehrwürdigen Ober-Rabbiner Herrn Moses Sopher, zu Pressburg," *AZJ,* 3 (1839): Beilage to no. 96.

104. *Der Orient,* 3 (1842): 384; *ZRIJ,* 2 (1845): 16; *MGWJ,* 12 (1863): 153–55; Leopold Löw, *Gesammelte Schriften,* 5 (Szegedin, 1900): 134. When Frankel became a candidate for the rabbinate in Berlin, a traditionalist falsely charged that he had introduced an organ in Teplitz. S. E. Zeller to Prussian Minister Eichhorn, August 31, 1842, CAHJP, P17/549.

105. *Der Orient,* 3 (1842): 71–72. For the liturgical reforms he actually instituted in Dresden, see the following chapter.

106. Frankel's influence reappeared in the twentieth century as the American Reform movement became more favorably inclined to tradition. Samuel S. Cohon, *Day Book of Service at the Altar* (Los Angeles, 1978), 283.

107. A biography of Geiger by his son, evaluations of his work in various areas, and a bibliography of his writings are contained in Ludwig Geiger, ed., *Abraham Geiger: Leben und*

Lebenswerk (Berlin, 1910). A selection of Geiger's writings in English translation was compiled with a biographical introduction by Max Wiener, *Abraham Geiger and Liberal Judaism: The Challenge of the Nineteenth Century* (Philadelphia, 1962; 2d edn.: Cincinnati, 1981). Selections in Hebrew translation appeared in M. A. Meyer, ed., *Avraham Geiger: mivḥar ketavav al ha-tikunim be-dat* (Jerusalem, 1979). A bibliography of secondary literature on Geiger is contained in Jakob J. Petuchowski, ed., *New Perspectives on Abraham Geiger: An HUC-JIR Symposium* (Cincinnati, 1975), 55–58.

108. For Geiger's early life, see especially the diary entries and first letters in his *Nachgelassene Schriften (NS)*, 5 vols. (Berlin, 1875–78), 5: 3–63. I have dealt with Herder's influence on Geiger in my "Jewish Religious Reform and *Wissenschaft des Judentums,*" *LBIYB*, 16 (1971): 27.

109. The most revealing source for Geiger's feelings during the initial years of his rabbinate are his letters to his close friend Joseph Dérenbourg, published in *AZJ*, 60 (1896): 52ff. On the matter of schism see *NS*, 5: 55, 103, 161, 169, 179.

110. *AZJ*, 60 (1896): 165–66, 283.

111. *NS*, 1: 307; 5: 54, 79, 147; *WZJT*, 1 (1835): 2–3; *AZJ*, 60 (1896): 141, 165, 236.

112. *WZJT*, 4 (1839): 321–33; *NS*, 1: 17–18.

113. *AZJ*, 60 (1896): 189, 321.

114. *NS*, 5: 27; *WZJT*, 2 (1836): 1–21; 4 (1839): 309–12; *JZWL*, 3 (1864/65): 254.

115. *WJZT*, 5 (1844): 21.

116. On Strauss see Horton Harris, *David Friedrich Strauss and His Theology* (Cambridge, 1973). Geiger refers to Strauss in *NS*, 2: 268; 5: 89; *WZJT*, 3 (1837): 295–302. However, a meeting of the two men late in their lives (1868) produced mutual dissatisfaction. See *AZJ*, 60 (1896): 165. Geiger criticized Strauss in an appendix to *Das Judenthum und seine Geschichte* (Breslau, 1864), 159–81. Hans Liebeschütz twice argued for the influence on Geiger of the Tübingen School, with which Strauss was for a time associated. See his *Das Judentum im deutschen Geschichtsbild von Hegel bis Max Weber* (Tübingen, 1967), 123–24, and Liebeschütz and Paucker, eds., *Das Judentum in der Deutschen Umwelt*, 44–49. Certainly Geiger followed the Tübingen School in that, like its founder, Ferdinand Christian Baur, he too came to the conclusion that history determines text. But in *JZWL*, 2 (1863): 232–33, he rejected the School's negative view of Pharisaic Judaism. On Baur and his colleagues see Horton Harris, *The Tübingen School* (Oxford, 1975).

117. *NS*, 1: 302–303. Similarly, when Geiger wrote the prize essay which later earned him a doctorate, *Was hat Mohammed aus dem Judenthume aufgenommen?* (Bonn, 1833), he initially used only the text of the Koran in order not to be influenced by later commentators.

118. *Lehr- und Lesebuch zur Sprache der Mischnah*, 2 vols. (Breslau, 1845).

119. Geiger made his position most explicit in a polemical exchange with Heinrich Graetz. See especially Literatur-Blatt to *INJ*, December 14, 1845, pp. 25–26.

120. *Urschrift und Übersetzungen der Bibel in ihrer Abhängigkeit von der innern Entwickelung des Judenthums* (Breslau, 1857). It was reprinted with a flattering introduction by Paul Kahle (Frankfurt a/M, 1928) and appeared in a Hebrew translation with an introductory essay by Joseph Klausner (Jerusalem, 1949).

121. *NS*, 5: 103, 188; *WZJT*, 6 (1847): 114; *AZJ*, 60 (1896): 165, 188; *JZWL*, 9 (1871): 274; Ludwig Geiger, *Abraham Geiger*, 19. The most recent treatment of Geiger as a biblical scholar is Nahum M. Sarna, "Abraham Geiger and Biblical Scholarship," in Petuchowski, ed., *New Perspectives on Abraham Geiger*, 17–30.

122. *JZWL*, 3 (1864/65): 178–84; 7 (1869): 96–111.

123. *WZJT*, 1 (1835): 11; 4 (1839): 321–22. Cf. my "Abraham Geiger's Historical Judaism," in Petuchowski, ed., *New Perspectives on Abraham Geiger*, 3–16.

124. *WZJT*, 2 (1836): 222–23; 5 (1844): 22; *NS*, 2: 266; Ismar Elbogen, "Abraham Geiger," *JJGL*, 14 (1911): 75.

125. *Nothwendigkeit und Mass einer Reform des jüdischen Gottesdienstes* (Breslau, 1861), 4, 6. Emphasis Geiger's.

126. *WZJT,* 3 (1837): 90; *NS,* 1: 301. Speaking to Christian scholars, Geiger complained of their neglect of rabbinic literature, which contains "the spiritual history of a not insignificant portion of fellow inhabitants of the fatherland." See *Verhandlungen der ersten Versammlung deutscher und ausländischer Orientalisten,* 8–9.

127. Elbogen, "Abraham Geiger," 81.

128. "Proben jüdischer Vertheidigung gegen christliche Angriffe im Mittelalter." The series, in five parts, began in M. Breslauer, ed., *Deutscher Volks-Kalender und Jahrbuch,* 1 (1851): 33–66. The most important study, on Isaac Troki, was included in *NS,* 3: 178–223.

129. "Die nordfranzösische Exegeten-Schule im 12. Jahrhundert," in S. L. Heilberg, ed., *Nit'e na'amanim* (Breslau, 1847), 1–44; *Parschandatha. Die nordfranzösische Exegetenschule* (Leipzig, 1855).

130. *Salomo Gabirol und seine Dichtungen* (Leipzig, 1867); *Jüdische Dichtungen der spanischen und italienischen Schule* (Leipzig, 1856). See especially Geiger's sensitive treatment of the Jewish nationalist poet Judah Halevi, in *NS,* 3: 97–177. For all his identification with the unorthodox Venetian rabbi Leon Modena, Geiger criticized him for lacking the historical consciousness that would enable him to transpose himself into the talmudic age and recognize the value of its statutes for preserving Judaism during medieval oppression. *Leon da Modena, Rabbiner zu Venedig* (Breslau, 1856), 43–44.

131. Ludwig Geiger, *Abraham Geiger,* 15, 28, 115, 225; *NS,* 5: 82; *AZJ,* 60 (1896): 55, 320; Joseph Dérenbourg, *Abraham Geiger. Esquisse de sa vie* (Paris, 1875), 4.

132. *AZJ,* 60 (1896): 79, 80, 91, 104.

133. *NS,* 1: 371.

134. *NS,* 1: 355–69, 434–44.

135. *NS,* 1: 34–37; 5: 180–84, 202–203, 279; *WZJT,* 4 (1839): 10.

136. *NS,* 1: 259–60.

137. *WZJT,* 4 (1839): 161–65.

138. *Der Hamburger Tempelstreit, eine Zeitfrage* (Breslau, 1842), 15–16; *Israelitisches Gebetbuch* (Breslau, 1854); *JZWL,* 6 (1868): 1–21; *Plan zu einem neuen Gebetbuche nebst Begründungen* (Breslau, 1870).

139. *WZJT,* 5 (1844): 385; *NS,* 2: 286–87.

140. *NS,* 1: 210–15; 5: Hebrew Section, iii; *Otsar nehmad,* 1 (1856): 52. For a selection of Geiger's Hebrew writings see Samuel Poznanski, ed., *Kvutsat ma'amarim me'et Avraham Geiger* (Warsaw, 1910).

141. *AZJ,* 60 (1896): 259–60, 284, 319, 346.

142. *JZWL,* 6 (1868): 85.

143. *JZWL,* 8 (1870): 88–89; *NS,* 1: 230–82; *WZJT,* 1 (1835): 290.

144. *WZJT,* 1 (1835): 9–10; 5 (1844): 150; *AZJ,* 60 (1896): 91; *NS,* 1: 306; 5: 89.

145. *WZJT,* 3 (1837): 313–14, 330; *JZWL,* 9 (1871): 273; *NS,* 1: 306.

146. *JZWL,* 1 (1862): 2; 9 (1871): 84, 161; 10 (1872): 1–4; *NS,* 5: 226, 291, 329–30, 333–34, 346–48. *Cf.* my "Universalism and Jewish Unity in the Thought of Abraham Geiger," in Jacob Katz, ed., *The Role of Religion in Modern Jewish History* (Cambridge, Mass., 1975), 91–104.

147. *NS,* 5: 348–49. Emphasis Geiger's.

148. *NS,* 5: 167–70, 229–30; *WZJT,* 2 (1836): 539; 4 (1839): 9–12.

149. *Das Judentum und seine Geschichte* (2d edn., Breslau, 1910), 32–37, 74–76; in the English translation of the first section by Maurice Mayer, *Judaism and Its History* (New York, 1866), 54–64, 134–37. Geiger expressed the kernel of these ideas, but in more humanistic fashion, in 1849 (*NS,* 2: 5–6). See also *JZWL,* 9 (1871): 264 and my "Ob Schrift? Ob Geist?," 175–79.

Chapter 3

1. See the fine study by Ismar Schorsch, "Emancipation and the Crisis of Religious Authority: The Emergence of the Modern Rabbinate," in Werner E. Mosse *et al.,* eds., *Revolution and Evolution: 1848 in German-Jewish History* (Tübingen, 1981), 205–47.

2. *ZJD,* 1 (1843): 213–16.

3. Gotthold Salomon of the Hamburg Temple remained always its "preacher," never aspiring to the title or the functions traditionally associated with the office. Ludwig Philippson, by contrast, served from 1833 to 1840 as preacher of the Magdeburg community, then for two years as "spiritual leader" (*Geistlicher*), and thereafter as rabbi.

4. It was published as the second part of his pseudonymous Amitai Ben Avida Ahitsedek, *Berit emet* (Constantinople [in fact Dessau], 1820). Secondary literature includes Robert L. Katz, "David Caro's Analysis of the Rabbi's Role," *CCARJ,* April 1966, pp. 41–46 and Israel Zinberg, *A History of Jewish Literature,* trans. Bernard Martin, 9 (Cincinnati, 1976): 258–61.

5. The contradictory expectations held by different factions within each community regarding their rabbi created not only impossible intellectual and practical demands but also severe pressure to become a hypocrite, a "chameleon." See the complaint of a rabbinical student in *Sulamith,* 8.2 (1838–43): 303–307.

6. Leopold Zunz, *Die gottesdienstlichen Vorträge der Juden* (Berlin, 1832), 456; Steven M. Lowenstein, "The 1840s and the Creation of the German-Jewish Religious Reform Movement," in Mosse *et al.,* eds., *Revolution and Evolution,* 265–66, 276–83. Among the Orthodox protestors to the conferences the number of doctorates was well below 10 percent, even among those who resided in Germany. *Cf.,* however, Schorsch, "Emancipation and the Crisis of Religious Authority," 214–17, where it is pointed out that a number of more conservative rabbis possessed doctorates as well. Schorsch identifies sixty-seven rabbis and preachers with a university degree in Germany by 1847—though this is still a relatively small percentage of the total. When in 1844 the Crefeld Jewish community sought to replace Rabbi Lion Ullmann, who himself possessed a doctorate, four of the five principal candidates possessed a university degree. The qualifications given were similar to those suggested by Caro a quarter of a century earlier, with the addition: "belief in moderate progress." Moritz Veit Collection, CAHJP, P47/1. Although already in the thirties men with doctorates had a distinct advantage in competing for rabbinical positions in certain states, in some cases the high cost of the diploma itself may have persuaded impoverished rabbinical students to be satisfied with university studies without the doctorate. See the Samuel Adler memoir in Stanley Chyet, *Lives and Voices* (Philadelphia, 1972), 13–14.

7. On Rosenfeld see Adolf Eckstein, "Die Israelitische Kultusgemeinde Bamberg von 1803–1853," in *Festschrift zur Einweihung der neuen Synagoge in Bamberg* (Bamberg, 1910), 61–84; Hilmar Bruce Ehrmann, "The Struggle for Civil and Religious Emancipation in Bavaria in the First Half of the Nineteenth Century, as Reflected in the Writings of Rabbi Samson Wolf Rosenfeld" (Rabbinical thesis, Hebrew Union College, 1948).

8. Samson Wolf Rosenfeld, *Die Israelitische Tempelhalle* (Markt Uhlfeld, 1819), 80–81.

9. On Eger see *Allgemeines Archiv des Judenthums,* 2 (1842): 314–36; *AZJ,* 6 (1842): 405, 411–18, 460–62, 762–64.

10. Adolf Lewin, *Geschichte der badischen Juden seit der Regierung Karl Friedrichs, 1738–1909* (Karlsruhe, 1909), 211–21; Reinhard Rürup, *Emanzipation und Antisemitismus* (Göttingen, 1975), 54.

11. F. F. Mayer, *Sammlung der württembergischen Gesetze in Betreff der Israeliten* (Tübingen, 1847), 105. Cantors had similar prescribed official apparel (*ibid.,* 104–105).

12. *Sulamith,* 8.2 (1838–43): 307; Isaac Marcus Jost, *Geschichte der Israeliten,* 10.3 (Berlin, 1847): 226, 234–35; Eckstein, "Die Israelitische Kultusgemeinde Bamberg," 80.

13. Fritz Fischer, "Der deutsche Protestantismus und die Politik im 19. Jahrhundert," *Historische Zeitschrift,* 171 (1951): 475–76; Robert M. Bigler, "The Social Status and Political Role

of the Protestant Clergy in Pre-March Prussia," in Hans-Ulrich Wehler, ed., *Sozialgeschichte Heute: Festschrift für Hans Rosenberg zum 70. Geburtstag* (Göttingen, 1974), 175–90.

14. Michael A. Meyer, *German Political Pressure and Jewish Religious Response in the Nineteenth Century*, The Leo Baeck Memorial Lecture 25 (New York, 1981). An exception to the rule is Rabbi Joseph Maier of Stuttgart in Württemberg. On one occasion he preached to his congregation that "until our religious matters are set fully in order and our worship takes on a form more appropriate to the times, until we are religiously emancipated, our civil emancipation will to a greater or lesser degree strike upon insuperable obstacles." *Welche Hindernisse haben wir aus dem Wege zu räumen?* (Stuttgart, 1835), 32. In 1838 Maier received a death threat on account of his reform efforts. Jabob Toury, *Der Eintritt der Juden ins deutsche Bürgertum: Eine Dokumentation* (Tel-Aviv, 1972), 325–26.

15. *Sulamith*, 6.2 (1822–25): 363–65; *AZJ*, 1 (1837): 25–27; 17 (1853): 474; Jakob J. Petuchowski, *Prayerbook Reform in Europe* (New York, 1968), 124–27.

16. It is important to remember, however, that not only Jewish population increase was forcibly held in check. Similar measures were applied to other disfavored social elements. See Klaus-Jürgen Matz, *Pauperismus und Bevölkerung: Die gesetzlichen Ehebeschränkungen in den süddeutschen Staaten während des 19. Jahrhunderts* (Stuttgart, 1980).

17. J. B. Graser, *Das Judenthum und seine Reform als Vorbedingung der vollständigen Aufnahme der Nation in den Staats-Verband* (Bayreuth, 1828).

18. See Graser's letter of July 1828 to an unidentified friend in the Leopold Stein Collection, LBIA, 3265/11.

19. Adolf Eckstein, "Die Stellungsnahme der bayerischen Staatsregierung zu den Reformrabbinerversammlungen (1837–1846)," *ZGJD*, n.s., 6 (1935): 51–54; Ehrmann, "The Struggle for Civil and Religious Emancipation in Bavaria," 79.

20. Joseph Aub, *Betrachtungen und Widerlegungen, Erstes Heft: Betrachtungen über den Mosaismus und die Neologie der Rabbinen betreffende Königl. Bayer. Ministerial-Entschliessung* (Nürnberg, 1839).

21. See the comparative chart for thirteen of the regulations in Lowenstein, "The 1840s and the Creation of the German-Jewish Religious Reform Movement," 286–97. A few are partially translated and analyzed in Petuchowski, *Prayerbook Reform in Europe*, 105–27.

22. Following promulgation of the Baden synagogue regulation in 1824, specific exceptions were made in response to local circumstances and desires. Lewin, *Geschichte der badischen Juden*, 216. In Mecklenburg–Schwerin, however, Samuel Holdheim in 1843 introduced a regulation based on that of Württemberg, apparently with little regard for the feelings of the traditionalists. Heinrich Graetz, *Geschichte der Juden*, 11 (Leipzig, 1870): 564–65.

23. *AZJ*, 4 (1840): 376–77, 518–19.

24. *Der Orient*, 4 (1843): 109.

25. For the way this prayer was dealt with in synagogue regulations and later in community prayerbooks, see Petuchowski, *Prayerbook Reform in Europe*, 119, 121, 223–25. Holdheim in the same year as Frankel's emendation went further in his Mecklenburg–Schwerin regulation by changing the opening of the prayer to *ve-la-malshinut*, substituting slander for slanderers. But apparently Frankel wanted to leave at least the first words intact, despite the internal contradiction which he thereby introduced into the text.

26. The most comprehensive study of Ludwig Philippson is Johanna Philippson, "Ludwig Philippson und die Allgemeine Zeitung des Judentums," in Hans Liebeschütz and Arnold Paucker, eds., *Das Judentum in der Deutschen Umwelt, 1800–1850* (Tübingen, 1977), 243–91. See also the tribute by Ismar Elbogen, *Ludwig Philippson: Vortrag gehalten in der Gesellschaft zur Förderung der Wissenschaft des Judentums zu Berlin* (Leipzig, 1912).

27. *IPSM*, 1 (1834): 15.

28. The census figures at the end of 1837 were 102,917 Jews with citizens' rights and 80,662 (especially in the Grand Duchy of Posen) without. *AZJ*, 2 (1838): 407.

29. *AZJ*, 5 (1841): 754; Ludwig von Rönne and Heinrich Simon, *Die früheren und gegen-wärtigen Verhältnisse der Juden in den sämmtlichen Landestheilen des Preussischen Staates* (Breslau, 1843), 83–94; Leopold Auerbach, *Das Judenthum und seine Bekenner in Preussen und in den anderen deutschen Bundesstaaten* (Berlin, 1890), 289.

30. Rönne and Simon, *Verhältnisse der Juden,* 146–49; Schorsch, "Emancipation and the Crisis of Religious Authority," 236–37; Heimann Jolowicz, *Geschichte der Juden in Königsberg i. Pr.* (Posen, 1867), 130–33.

31. Meyer Isler, ed., *Gabriel Riesser's Gesammelte Schriften,* 3 (Frankfurt a/M, 1867): 155–56; Monika Richarz, ed., *Jüdisches Leben in Deutschland: Selbstzeugnisse zur Sozialgeschichte, 1780–1871* (Stuttgart, 1976), 223–26; *Der Orient,* 3 (1842): 322.

32. Phoebus Philippson, *Biographische Skizzen* (Leipzig, 1864), 189n. Confirmation of girls began without objection in Königsberg in 1836. Jolowicz, *Geschichte der Juden in Königsberg,* 139. In Prussian Westphalia, however, confirmation and other reforms were newly prohibited that same year when the central government responded favorably to the complaint of Rabbi Abraham Sutro in Münster. Rönne and Simon, *Verhältnisse der Juden,* 94.

33. Letter to Moritz Veit, February 23, 1841, Moritz Veit Collection, CAHJP, P47. Even in the city of Posen, whose Jews were oriented as much to Poland as to Germany, reform stirrings became evident. In 1843 the community selected Solomon Plessner to be its preacher. However, Plessner was a militant opponent of liturgical reform and in his sermons combined a style mod-eled on Christian homiletics and frequent quotations from Goethe and Schiller with a resolute defense of Orthodoxy. Natan Lippman to Leopold Zunz, April 1, 1841, Zunz Archives, JNUL; *AZJ*, 7 (1843): 406; *Der Orient,* 5 (1844): 266.

34. *Der Orient,* 2 (1841): 230–32.

35. See the advertisement in *AZJ*, 2 (1838): 173.

36. Wilhelm Freund to Solomon Herxheimer, February 23, 1838, Wilhelm Freund Collec-tion, CAHJP, P46/4. Freund (1806–1894), a classical philologist and significant influence in the Breslau community, was an enthusiastic proponent of religious reform and an equally vehement detractor of Tiktin. He was a friend of Geiger and the man who introduced him in Breslau. Though he favored Geiger's candidacy from the beginning, at first Freund did not believe Geiger could win the election. See his letters to Leopold Zunz of November 29, 1836 and May 16, 1838, Zunz Archives, JNUL, and Geiger's letter to an unidentified individual (probably Bernhard Beer), August 10, 1838, Geiger File, JNUL.

37. The Reform view of the conflict appears in Abraham Geiger, *Nachgelassene Schriften* (*NS*) 1 (1875): 1–112; *Bericht des Ober-Vorsteher-Collegii an die Mitglieder der hiesigen Israe-liten-Gemeinde,* 2 vols. (Breslau, 1842). The Orthodox side is presented in S. A. Tictin [*sic*], *Darstellung des Sachverhältnisses in seiner hiesigen Rabbinats-Angelegenheit* (Breslau, 1842); anon., *Entgegnung auf den Bericht des Ober-Vorsteher-Collegiums* (Breslau, 1842).

38. This was Geiger's hope even before he became a candidate for the Breslau position. In 1837 he wrote to his friend Joseph Dérenbourg: "We need a rabbi in a large community who possesses great personal dignity and imposing energy, who will know how to win over the intel-ligent portion of the community and together with them fearlessly overthrow multitudes." *AZJ*, 60 (1896): 214.

39. *AZJ*, 4 (1840): 403. One correspondent wrote of Geiger: "The younger generation clings to him in enthusiastic veneration—especially our daughters upon whom Geiger makes a remarkable impression because he knows how to touch upon aspects of the inner life to which the female sex always inclines." *Der Orient,* 1 (1840): 348. *Cf.* 2 (1841): 149; and for Geiger's first, minor synagogue reforms in Breslau, 3 (1842): 145. Geiger's dangerous influence could not be ignored. Tiktin wrote: "People say to me, what will it hurt you if you ignore everything that is being done against your *principles* as long as it doesn't issue from *you?* My answer is that if my fellow man is in danger of drowning, he will surely drown if I don't jump to his rescue. So I must offer him my aid even if it is not taken up or is even rejected." *Darstellung des Sachver-hältnisses,* 20. Emphasis Tiktin's.

40. See the conflicting accounts in Geiger, *NS,* 1: 72–74; *Entgegnung,* 7; *Der Orient,* 3 (1842): 129–30.

41. Michael A. Meyer, "Rabbi Gedaliah Tiktin and the Orthodox Segment of the Breslau Community, 1845–1854," *Michael,* 2 (1973): 92–107.

42. Isaac B. Lowositz, *Rabbinenwahl* (Breslau, 1839), 13–17; Wolf Davidsohn, *Über die Rabbinenwahl in Breslau* (Goldberg, 1840), 16.

43. Israel Deutsch and David Deutsch, *Rücksprache mit allen Gläubigen des rabbinischen Judenthums* (Breslau, 1843), 14.

44. In the statement by nine rabbis from small communities in Upper Silesia appended to Tictin, *Darstellung,* 30. The other Tiktin supporters whose views appeared here (pp. 25–31) were Solomon Eger (or Eiger), chief rabbi in Posen, and the rabbinate of Lissa.

45. Geiger, *NS,* 1: 14–18, 92–112.

46. *Rabbinische Gutachten über die Verträglichkeit der freien Forschung mit dem Rabbineramte,* 2 vols. (Breslau, 1842–43). One of the original letters of invitation, from the council to Rabbi Solomon Herxheimer dated July 11, 1842, is extant in CAHJP, P46/3. Excerpts from the responsa are presented in David Philipson, *The Reform Movement in Judaism* (3d edn., New York, 1967), 61–72, and in W. Gunther Plaut, *The Rise of Reform Judaism: A Sourcebook of its European Origins* (New York, 1963), 64–70. An additional responsum by Rabbi Hirsch B. Fassel of Prossnitz in Moravia, written from a more conservative point of view but nonetheless favoring free inquiry and religious progress, appeared in *Literaturblatt des Orients,* 4 (1843): nos. 5–8.

47. Schorsch, "Emancipation and the Crisis of Religious Authority," 225. One remarkable exception to the rule was Rabbi Joseph Abraham Friedländer (1753–1852), whose responsum was placed first in the collection. Friedländer, who was almost ninety years old at the time of the controversy, had served as rabbi in the town of Brilon since 1784 and become chief rabbi of Prussian Westphalia in 1832. A nephew of David Friedländer, he was among the most radical of the respondents. Earlier he had written a Hebrew tract arguing against the legal obligation to observe second days of Jewish festivals, and in his responsum he explicitly asserted that Mishnah and Talmud were not revealed to Moses at Sinai. See his *Shoresh yosef* (Hannover, 1834) and on him see *Der Israelitische Volkslehrer,* 2 (1852): 295–300. The struggle over religious reform in Westphalia during this period is detailed and interpreted in Arno Herzig, *Judentum und Emanzipation in Westfalen* (Münster, 1973), 41–52.

48. The most damaging talmudic text to the Reform position was held to be B. T. *Sanhedrin,* 99a. It was specifically referred to in the protest against Geiger by the Upper Silesian rabbis.

49. As the board put it: "Men of genuine discernment have spoken their minds openly and with learning on the most significant vital question in Judaism. We, and the interested public in general, have been agreeably convinced *ki lo alman yisrael* (that Israel is not a widower), that there is a valiant group of rabbis among us who give honor to truth, teach our religion in its purity, and do not shy away from battle when it is necessary to enter the ranks for it." Letter to Solomon Herxheimer, October 28, 1842, Herxheimer Collection, CAHJP, P46/3.

50. *Der Orient,* 3 (1842): 345–46; Bonaventura Mayer, *Die Juden unserer Zeit* (Regensburg, 1842), 79–83; Helga Krohn, *Die Juden in Hamburg 1800–1850* (Hamburg, 1974).

51. *AZJ,* 5 (1841): 668, 733. Kley did not observe dietary or Sabbath restrictions.

52. *AZJ,* 2 (1838): 186–88; 6 (1942): 177–79.

53. *AZJ,* 6 (1842): 232; Gotthold Salomon, *Sendschreiben an den Herrn Dr. Z. Frankel* (Hamburg, 1842), 50. That community prayer seemed the most promising, and perhaps the only focus for religious renewal among the nonobservant is illustrated by Leopold Stein's statement: "The worship service ... is now for so many [temple] members, for whom religious activity generally has almost died away and who have grown ever colder toward it, the sole, but still irresistible means of revival by which to instill new life and new warmth." *Theologische Gutachten über das Gebetbuch nach dem Gebrauche des Neuen Israelitischen Tempelvereins in Hamburg* (Hamburg, 1842), 109. The Christian model of religion was here an evident factor.

54. *AZJ*, 2 (1838): 211; 6 (1842): 48; Gotthold Salomon, *Kurzgefasste Geschichte des Neuen Israelitischen Tempels in Hamburg* (Hamburg, 1844), 26–27. For a detailed description of the actual service, see *AZJ*, 2 (1838): 198–99, 210.

55. The petition is dated March 11, 1840 and is in CAHJP, AHW/571.

56. The temple leadership later openly proclaimed its intent to reach out to the poor. *Theologische Gutachten*, 8. That the Orthodox wanted to see the temple's relative conservatism as a ploy to attract the masses is evident from J. Bonn, *Festhalten am Gesetze, Fortschritt im Geiste* (Hamburg, 1842), 19.

57. *Der Orient*, 3 (1842): 101. The traditionalist opponents of the temple seem to have been supported by a faction of the community which was militantly antireligious but because of personal quarrels with temple members wished it ill. Temple directors to community board, October 22, 1841, CAHJP, AHW/571.

58. The Reformers themselves felt that Judaism in recent centuries had been too much focused on past and future, that they needed to give it back its present. *Theologische Gutachten*, 1–2.

59. Bernays to community board, August 29, 1841, in *Der Orient*, 3 (1842): 102–104. In a letter to the board twelve days earlier the temple directors had tried to persuade it to neutralize Bernays' anticipated written opinion, but to no avail. Directorate to board, August 17, 1841, CAHJP, AHW/571.

60. The structure itself, containing 640 seats, was dedicated in 1844. Women still sat upstairs, but in contrast to the usual arrangement, there was a single entrance for both sexes. Harold Hammer-Schenk, *Synagogen in Deutschland* (Hamburg, 1981), 157 and corresponding illustrations.

61. *Seder ha-avodah. Gebetbuch für die öffentliche und häusliche Andacht, nach dem Gebrauche des Neuen Israelitischen Tempels in Hamburg* (Hamburg, 1841), vi.

62. In fact, the new edition seems to have been adopted only in three small towns near Bonn. Petuchowski, *Prayerbook Reform in Europe*, 356.

63. *Ibid.*, 54–55; Ismar Elbogen, *Der jüdische Gottesdienst in seiner geschichtlichen Entwicklung* (Frankfurt a/M, 1931), 413–14.

64. The three documents are contained in *Theologische Gutachten*, 14–18. The dispute is discussed in Stephen M. Poppel, "The Politics of Religious Leadership: The Rabbinate in Nineteenth-Century Hamburg," *LBIYB*, 28 (1983): 457–61.

65. The Ettlinger statement and a criticism of it are in *AZJ*, 6 (1842): 2–6. For a sympathetic treatment of Ettlinger's career see Judith Bleich, "Jacob Ettlinger, His Life and Works: The Emergence of Modern Orthodoxy in Germany" (Ph.D. dissertation, New York University, 1974).

66. David Leimdörfer, ed., *Festschrift zum hundertjährigen Bestehen des Israelitischen Tempels in Hamburg, 1818–1918* (Hamburg, 1918), 90. Riesser was elected to the temple directorate in 1840.

67. Translated excerpts from the *Theologische Gutachten* are in Plaut, *The Rise of Reform Judaism*, 39–42. A listing of the literature spawned by the controversy appears in *Der Orient*, 3 (1842): 231–32.

68. The conflict also brought to the surface differences among the Orthodox. As during the first dispute the temple's threat had led to appointment of the secularly educated Bernays, this time it motivated the more progressive among the traditionalists to urge reforms in the synagoge. They organized a committee which demanded chorales and a proper preacher who could attract the women and young people who were migrating to the temple. Bernays opposed their requests. *AZJ*, 6 (1842): 139–40; *Der Orient*, 3 (1842): 75, 354; Moses Mendelson, *Die Synagogue zu Hamburg, wie sie war und wie sie sein soll* (Kjöbenhavn, 1842).

69. Frankel's requested responsum was rejected by the editors of the *Theologische Gutachten* because of its "inappropriate literary–critical attack" (p. 18). It appeared in *Der Orient*, 3 (1842): 53–56, 61–64, 71–72.

70. The *Theologische Gutachten* includes a brief responsum by Geiger (pp. 63–65), but his critique appeared separately and was reprinted in his *NS*, 1: 113–96.

71. Cf. Salomon, *Sendschreiben*, 49.

72. *AZJ*, 6 (1842): 232–38. His views were largely shared by Dr. Maimon Fraenkel, who represented the directorate on the editorial committee and wrote an introduction to the *Theologische Gutachten*, where he gave his own lay perspective.

73. *AZJ*, 2 (1838): 347; *Der Orient*, 3 (1842): 6, 36.

74. *WZJT*, 2 (1836): 147–53; *RW*, 1 (1836/37): 107–14; Mayer, *Die Juden unserer Zeit*, 69–70; *JJGL*, 22 (1919): 93; H. Baerwald and S. Adler, "Geschichte der Realschule der israelitischen Gemeinde," in *Festschrift zur Jahrhundertfeier der Realschule der israelitischen Gemeinde (Philanthropin) zu Frankfurt am Main, 1804–1904* (Frankfurt a/M, 1904), 50–54; Hammer-Schenk, *Synagogen in Deutschland*, 58–61 and corresponding illustrations. The sources on the mixed seating are not entirely clear and it is possible that at first all seating was separate and later all mixed. The historian Isaac Marcus Jost, who was a teacher at the school, commented privately on the nature of the service shortly after he arrived in Frankfurt: "Connected with the school is a hall for devotions in which a most cultured public gathers every Saturday from ten to eleven o'clock in order to sing and hear a sermon. Many Christians visit it regularly. . . . The audience sits with uncovered heads; every religiously Jewish coloring has been removed. Since this did not entirely appeal to me, I at least saw to it that the talks will be strictly biblical and closely tied to religious teachings. My colleagues agreed with me and the public is most satisfied." Jost to S. M. Ehrenberg, November 20, 1835, LBIA, AR 4294.

75. A sympathetic but critical biography of Creizenach was published by Jost in *Kalender und Jahrbuch für Israeliten*, 2 (1843/44): 81–111. A list of his mathematical works appears in *MGWJ*, 51 (1907): 230–31.

76. *AZJ*, 2 (1838): 4.

77. M. Creizenach, *Schulchan Aruch, oder encyclopädische Darstellung des Mosaischen Gesetzes, wie es durch die rabbinischen Satzungen sich ausgebildet hat, mit Hinweisung auf die Reformen, welche durch die Zeit nützlich und möglich geworden sind*, 4 vols. (Frankfurt a/M, 1833–40). Each volume was also given its own title in Hebrew and German.

78. See especially the prefaces to the four volumes and 2: 2, 12–15, 68–72, 108–10; 3: 69, 111–21. Three translated excerpts are in Plaut, *The Rise of Reform Judaism*, 117–19, 212–13, 225–27.

79. Although Jost was officially a co-editor of *Tsiyon* (1840–42), he admitted that it was Creizenach's idea and that his colleague had done the editorial work. *Kalender und Jahrbuch*, 107–108. Another teacher at the school, N. Zirndorfer, published an impassioned plea for keeping Hebrew in the liturgy. *Sulamith*, 8.1 (1835–38): 351–55.

80. See also Ludwig Philippson's comment on the agitation to set the Talmud entirely aside. *AZJ*, 2 (1838): 332.

81. *AZJ*, 5 (1841): 47–48.

82. *ZGJD*, o.s., 2 (1888): 67.

83. On Jewish masons in Frankfurt see Jacob Katz, *Jews and Freemasons in Europe, 1723–1939* (Cambridge, Mass., 1970), 54–72, 91–95.

84. Documentation for the presentation of the *Reformfreunde* given here may be found in my detailed article, "Alienated Intellectuals in the Camp of Religious Reform: The Frankfurt Reformfreunde, 1842–1845," *AJS Review*, 6 (1981): 61–86. There is also a full chapter on the group in David Philipson, *The Reform Movement*, 107–39.

85. Ludwig Philippson dubbed their position "a mere non-Christianity." *AZJ*, 7 (1843): 502. One outsider who did express serious interest was the subsequently prominent socialist Ferdinand Lassalle. See Edmund Silberner, "Ferdinand Lassalle: From Maccabeism to Jewish Anti-Semitism," *HUCA*, 24 (1952/53): 160–62.

86. Bar Amithai [Joseph Johlson], *Über die Beschneidung in historischer und dogmatischer Hinsicht* (Frankfurt a/M, 1843). The ritual for the eighth day was given the Hebrew designation

Kedushah leyom [*sic*] *hashemini.* It stressed that Israel was chosen from all peoples and sanctified by God's commandments. Cf. Jost, *Geschichte der Israeliten,* 10.3: 218–25. For the political background of the circumcision controversy see *MGWJ,* 69 (1925): 41–46, and Robert Liberles, *Religious Conflict in Social Context: The Resurgence of Orthodox Judaism in Frankfurt am Main, 1838–1877* (Westport, Conn., 1985), 23–65. The issue became immediate when a local Jewish banker left his son uncircumcized but wanted him registered as a Jew.

87. Salomon Abraham Trier, *Rabbinische Gutachten über die Beschneidung* (Frankfurt a/M, 1844).

88. *Der Orient,* 5 (1844): 321–25; *INJ,* 5 (1844): 275; Jost to S. M. and Ph. Enrenberg, June 2, 1844, LBIA, AR 4294. On Stein's travails as rabbi in Frankfurt see Robert Liberles, "Leopold Stein and the Paradox of Reform Clericalism, 1844–1862," *LBIYB,* 27 (1982): 261–79.

89. On Berlin Jewry in this period see *AZJ,* 2 (1838): 324; 9 (1845): 58–59; *Volks-Kalender für Israeliten,* 3 (1843): 49–64; *ZJD,* 2 (1844): 123–36, 413–34; Ludwig Geiger, *Geschichte der Juden in Berlin,* 2 vols. (Berlin, 1871), 1: 185–93, 2: 259–61; Eugen Wolbe, *Geschichte der Juden in Berlin und in der Mark Brandenburg* (Berlin, 1937), 248–76.

90. *AZJ,* 9 (1845): 634–38, 657–58; Arthur Galliner, *Sigismund Stern: Der Reformator und der Pädagoge* (Frankfurt a/M, 1930), 37–38. For details on the difficult struggles by some traditionalists to introduce decorum and better music into the community synagogue in the late thirties, see the documents in the Moritz Stern Collection, CAHJP, P17/549, and Aron Hirsch Heymann, *Lebenserinnerungen,* ed. Heinrich Loewe (Berlin, 1909), 239–51. Likewise on Sachs's reform endeavors in 1844 and the opposition to them, see the Stern Collection.

91. *Der Orient,* 6 (1845): 142, 305; *INJ,* 6 (1845): 88; *AZJ,* 10 (1846): 637–40; Jost to Ph. Ehrenberg, October 13, 1845, LBIA, AR 4294; M. S. Krüger, *Bedenken gegen die neuesten Reformbestrebungen im Judenthume* (Berlin, 1845), 13–14; Eduard Kley, *Noch ein Wort zur israelitischen Reformfrage* (Hamburg, 1845), 11, 17, 27; *JJGL,* 7 (1904): 179; Heymann, *Lebenserinnerungen,* 280–81; Jost, *Geschichte der Israeliten,* 10.3: 241; Graetz, *Geschichte der Juden,* 11: 567–68; Meyer, "Alienated Intellectuals in the Camp of Religious Reform," 83–86.

92. *INJ,* 6 (1845): 87; *JJGL,* 7 (1904): 178–79; Galliner, *Sigismund Stern,* 1–3, 170–72.

93. "Das Judenthum als Element des Staats-Organismus," *ZJD,* 1 (1843): 125–66; "Die Aufgabe der jüdischen Gemeinde zu Berlin für die Gegenwart," *ZJD,* 2 (1844): 26–41, 123–36, 413–34; *Die Aufgabe des Judenthums und des Juden in der Gegenwart* (Berlin, 1845).

94. *JJGL,* 7 (1904): 166; Governor of Brandenburg Meding to Minister of Spiritual Affairs Eichhorn, July 26, 1846, CAHJP, P17/431. Liberals were no more favorably inclined. A Hegelian opponent, himself an ex-Catholic, wrote at the time: "Mosaism, like Catholicism, whatever one may say, is an antiquated formation . . . which no longer possesses any world historical, any lasting justification." F. W. Carove, *Über Emanzipation der Juden, Philosophie des Judenthums und Jüdische Reformprojekte zu Berlin und Frankfurt a.M.* (Siegen and Wiesbaden, 1845), 160. On him see *JSS,* 25 (1963): 150–51.

95. On Bernstein see *JZWL,* 11 (1869): 223–26; *JJGL,* 7 (1904): 174–77; Julius H. Schoeps, "Aron Bernstein—ein liberaler Volksaufklärer, Schriftsteller und Religionsreformer," *ZRG,* 28 (1976): 223–44; *idem,* "Liberalismus, Emanzipation und jüdische Reform: Aaron Bernstein und die Berliner Reformgemeinde," in J. H. Schoeps, ed., *Religion und Zeitgeist im 19. Jahrhundert* (Stuttgart and Bonn, 1982), 59–80; and Michael A. Meyer, "Aron Bernstein—The Enigma of a Radical Religious Reformer," *Proceedings of the Ninth World Congress of Jewish Studies,* Division B, Vol. 3 (Jerusalem, 1986), 9–16. His nephew was the prominent socialist Eduard Bernstein.

96. A. Bernstein, *Ursprung der Sagen von Abraham, Isaak und Jacob. Kritische Untersuchung* (Berlin, 1871).

97. A. Rebenstein, "Unsere Gegenwart," *ZJD,* 2 (1844): 7–25, 65–108. The cited passage is on p. 25, emphasis Bernstein's.

98. A large segment of the speech, including these passages, is contained in Samuel Hold-

heim, *Geschichte der Entstehung und Entwickelung der jüdischen Reformgemeinde in Berlin* (Berlin, 1857), 31–34. Emphasis in original.

99. "Unsere Gegenwart," 23. Bernstein was not a man to mince his words. Five years earlier he had written to a friend about rabbinical hypocrisy: "In truth I am not a zealot and for that reason won't say it in public. But some time try to corner one of our new rabbis with the question: Do you believe what it says in the Bible? And if he's not a scoundrel he will have to say: no! Ask him if his convictions about God, the world, and life are not completely different from the really Jewish ones, and he will have to say: yes! Still, I'm supposed to see the fellow clasping his hands, rolling his eyes, praying, and invoking as sacred what to him in his heart is profane. For me a truly honest blockhead [*Dummkopf*] is ten times preferable to such a scoundrel. What use is all the glossing over! If we have to choose between two fogs, we might at least pick the harmless one." Letter to Moritz Veit, October 21, 1839, CAHJP, P47.

100. For example, by Gustav Adolph Wislicenus in his lectures of 1844 published as *Ob Schrift? Ob Geist? Verantwortung gegen meine Ankläger* (2d edn., Leipzig, 1845).

101. "Unsere Gegenwart," 98. Samuel Holdheim at the time was not so radical. He wrote in reply to Bernstein that he personally believed in "an unmediated divine revelation of God in the Pentateuch and the Prophets. . . . We cannot give up the supernatural conception of Mosaism and Prophecy." *ZJD*, 2 (1844): 334–35.

102. Holdheim, *Geschichte*, 25–26, 54; Stern, "Die Aufgabe der jüdischen Gemeinde zu Berlin," 130–31; Moritz Kalisch, *Berlins jüdische Reformatoren nach der Thronbesteigung Friedrich Wilhelms III. und IV.* (Berlin, 1845), 151. At a later plenary meeting, on June 4, 1845, eight of the nine speakers were men referred to as "Dr." The ninth was a bookdealer. *AZJ*, 9 (1845): 371–74.

103. *AZJ*, 9 (1845): 234–36. It is reprinted in Holdheim, *Geschichte*, 49–52, and fully translated in Philipson, *The Reform Movement*, 231–34.

104. S. Stern, *Die gegenwärtige Bewegung im Judenthum* (Berlin, 1845), 27, 30–31. Bernstein elaborated on the Appeal in A. Rebenstein, *Prinzipien-Entwurf für die Genossenschaft für Reform im Judenthum* (Berlin, 1847). The third author, Moses Simion, likewise commented in what can only be termed a highly conservative interpretation. In an open letter to Zacharias Frankel as editor of the *Zeitschrift für die religiösen Interessen des Judentums,* he tried to show, by citing numerous passages from Frankel's writings in the *Zeitschrift,* that the Association's position was not so very different from the editor's own. Frankel too, for example, had written in favor of following the collective will and faith of the people. In an attached reply, Frankel said that he recognized in Simion's letter "a glowing love for Judaism," and that if it existed likewise among the Association's founders and adherents, their intentions would "by no means be blameworthy." However, he then went on to criticize a number of points in the Appeal. *ZRIJ*, 2 (1845): 219–32. Simon Bernfeld records an oral tradition that Simion, a bookdealer and prominent Berlin Jew, believed fervently in the projected synod, which he hoped would revise, but not eliminate Jewish laws and customs. Until it would convene, Simion had committed himself to strict observance of Jewish law. *Toledot ha-reformatsyon ha-datit be-yisrael,* 207n.

105. The best primary sources for the first few months of the Association's existence are *Erster Bericht der Genossenschaft für Reform im Judenthum abgestattet von deren Bevollmächtigten* (Berlin, 1845) and the subsequent *Zweiter Bericht . . .* (Berlin, 1846).

106. The eyewitness accounts I have used are those of an anonymous correspondent and of Ludwig Philippson in *AZJ*, 9 (1845): 647–49, 658–59, and two anonymous reports written by the first author, one in *JC*, 2 (1846): 49–51, 70–71, 78–79, the other published as *Der Festgottesdienst bei der Berliner Genossenschaft für Reform im Judenthum und die daselbst gehaltenen Predigten von dem Rabbiner Doctor Philippson in Magdeburg. Beurtheilt von einem der Mitglieder* (Altona, 1846). The thinking of the organizers and their instructions to the congregation are in *Zweiter Bericht,* 9–11. The first of a long series of individual prayerbooks for the various occasions of the Jewish year appeared as *Gebete und Gesänge zu dem von der Genossenschaft*

für Reform im Judenthum eingerichteten Gottesdienst in Berlin, für das Neujahrsfest des Weltjahres 5606 (Berlin, 1845).

107. Even when the congregation built its own temple a few years later, there was still separate seating. One commentator explained: "Family pews for Germany would be a gross anomaly. No one is familiar with them or could be. . . . Division by sex is the common rule. In the construction of the Reform synagogue in Berlin the model was none other than the Christian churches. No one thought of family pews." Samuel Hirsch, *Dr. Jastrow und sein Gebaren in Philadelphia* (Philadelphia, 1868), 9.

108. A couple of years later a radical lay leader in Westphalia, who associated himself with the Berlin Association, published a full-scale defense of bareheadedness in the synagogue. He claimed that covering the head was an Oriental way of showing respect, not a Western or German one. Levi Lazarus Hellwitz, *Das Unbedeckte Haupt. Predigt* (Soest, 1847). On Hellwitz's reforming activity in Westphalia see Herzig, *Judentum und Emanzipation in Westfalen,* 49–51.

109. Philippson's sermons, however, were traditional in both form and substance, with citation of biblical passages in Hebrew and multiple reference to Jewish history. They were published as *Predigten, gehalten bei dem ersten Gottesdienste der Genossenschaft für Reform im Judenthum zu Berlin* (Berlin, 1845). The anonymous author of *Der Festgottesdienst* found the preacher's rabbinic interpretations of biblical texts highly inappropriate (p. 20).

110. The deliberations are summarized in Holdheim, *Geschichte,* 149–55. The anonymous author of *Der Festgottesdienst,* 29–32, was appalled by the decision to hold services on Sunday, which he regarded as "the church day." Believing that observance of the historical Sabbath was worthy of financial sacrifice, he and some other members protested the decision. But to no avail.

111. For the Association's application of its principles to Jewish education, see S. Stern, *Prinzipien zur Abfassung eines Religionslehrbuchs der Genossenschaft für Reform im Judenthum* (Berlin, 1847).

112. *Die Reform im Judenthume. Aufruf an die denkenden Israeliten Königsbergs zum Anschluss an die deutsch-jüdische Kirche* (Königsberg, 1845). For Culm and Posen see *Der Orient,* 6 (1845): 158–59, 164–65. See also the references in Lowenstein, "The 1840s and the Creation of the German-Jewish Reform Movement," 267, note 27.

113. The Breslau declaration appears in *AZJ,* 9 (1845): 237–39, and in *Der Orient,* 6 (1845): 129–30, where it is followed by a Geiger response which, while sympathetic, expresses its author's intent to continue on his own path of "gradual progress." Cf. also Geiger's second response, *ibid.,* 142–43. When Geiger gave a public lecture a year later calling for lay groups to urge speedy adoption of rabbinical conference resolutions, his old friend Wilhelm Freund arose and attacked him virulently. *AZJ,* 10 (1846): 234–37. On the succeeding bitter and enduring dispute between them, see Philipson, *The Reform Movement,* 264–68. Freund had not only been a staunch supporter of Geiger in Breslau (see above, note 36), but also the editor of the periodical in which Stern and Bernstein published their articles. He had even been elected to the first committee of the Berlin Association as he was living in the Prussian capital at the time. However, Freund declined the election and henceforth pursued a more conservative course. Later he helped bring Zacharias Frankel to Breslau as head of the new rabbincial seminary in 1854.

114. Moriz Türk, "Das erste Gemeindestatut und die Genossenschaft für Reform im Judentum," in *Festschrift zum 70. Geburtstage von Moritz Schaefer* (Berlin, 1927), 241–57; Galliner, *Sigismund Stern,* 78–83; and the documents in CAHJP, P17/431.

115. A full account of the meeting is contained in *Berathungen der vom 14. bis 16. April 1846 in Berlin versammelten Deputirten der Genossenschaft für Reform im Judenthum* (Berlin, 1846).

116. *Reform-Zeitung. Organ für den Fortschritt im Judenthum.* Ninety-six folio-sized pages appeared from January through December 1847.

117. That Leopold Zunz would not associate himself with the group was a grave disappointment. Like most of the founders of the Berlin Association, Zunz was a member of the Jewish *Kulturverein* and as early as 1834 had supplied the notes and bibliography for Bernstein's German translation of the Song of Songs. He was one of those invited to the first meeting of the

new group, but he did not even bother to respond. After he attended Stern's first lecture, he praised his beautiful speech and honorable sentiments but expressed anxiety about the suspected tendency of the whole. A month later he received a letter from an ambitious young man in Inowrocław who had somehow heard that Zunz was a supporter of radical reforms. The extreme statement modeled on the *Christkatholiken,* which he presented to Zunz for his approval, must have reinforced the Jewish scholar's fears about where the Berlin movement might lead. Nonetheless, Bernstein kept urging "the silent one" and other Jewish scholars, like Bernhard Beer in Dresden, to support the Association. Nahum N. Glatzer, ed., *Leopold Zunz: Jude—Deutscher— Europäer* (Tübingen, 1964), 232; Dr. F. Hamburger to Zunz, February 23, 1845, Zunz Archives, JNUL, G14 40792; *Reform-Zeitung,* 41–43; A. Rebenstein to Beer, July/August 1847, Rebenstein File, JNUL, ARC. Ms. Var. 236.

118. Documents regarding the negotiations of the Association with Holdheim and his final contract are in the Holdheim Archives, CAHJP, P43.

119. This is the first time that the term Reform is used not generically as in *Genossenschaft für Reform im Judenthum,* but to name an institution, the *Jüdische Reformgemeinde in Berlin.* The Berlin group thus became the first European self-designated Reform congregation and its members in the narrower institutional sense "Reform Jews." As early as 1846 an observer remarked that the Association had "sunk into a *Lokal-Chebrah,"* one of many such in Berlin. *Der Orient,* 7 (1846): 319.

120. Holdheim, *Geschichte,* 251. Cf. A. Menes, "The Conversion Movement in Prussia during the First Half of the 19th Century," *YIVO,* 6 (1951): 187–205.

121. *IPSM,* 2 (1835): 10. Emphasis Philippson's. Cf. Jost, *Geschichte der Israeliten,* 10.3: 17– 19, 162–64; *Literaturblatt des Orients,* 1 (1840): 557.

122. Compare, for example, the pure universalism in Elias Birkenstein, *Rede bey der Confirmation eines jungen Israeliten welcher in der Synagoge zu Battenfeld den 8ten November 1817 sein Glaubensbekenntniss öffentlich abgelegt hat* (Frankfurt and Leipzig, 1818) with Salomon Herxheimer, *Bar mizwa; oder, Confirmations-Feier gehalten in der Synagoge zu Eschwege am Sabbathe der Parascha Kedoschim 5589 (den 9 Mai 1829)* (Eschwege, 1829). See also Herxheimer's article on confirmation in *WZJT,* 1 (1835): 68–96. The general trend by the 1830s to reassert particularism is discussed in relation to similar particularist trends in German Christianity in my "Christian Influence on Early German Reform Judaism," in Charles Berlin, ed., *Studies in Jewish Bibliography, History and Literature in Honor of I. Edward Kiev* (New York, 1971), 289–303.

123. One young preacher tried to tell his congregation to treat him as a man of God who was presenting them with the teachings of divine revelation. Within a few months he had moved to another position. Heimann Jolowicz, *Der segenvolle Beruf israelitischer Geistlichen und die Pflichten der Gemeinden gegen sie. Antrittspredigt* (Marienwerder, 1843). A copy is in the Jolowicz Collection, CAHJP, P-2.

124. A good source for the discussions in Wiesbaden is Joseph Aub's report to the Bavarian government. Those assembled decided that individual rabbis should provide scholarly articles on various reforms for Geiger's journal in order to build support before any collective decisions were reached. The report appears in *ZGJD,* n.s., 6 (1935): 51–52. See also the sources listed by Philipson, *The Reform Movement,* 457, and Geiger's letter of April 30, 1837 in response to confirmation of attendance from Rabbis Gutmann and Stein in the Leopold Stein Collection, LBIA, 3264/9.

125. Aside from the lay challenge and the reforming intent, there was another motive for the rabbinical conferences. One after the other representatives of various professions had begun holding national conferences at which professional concerns were often mingled with the expression of a broad cultural and political liberalism. In the year of the Brunswick conference national meetings were held by lawyers, economists, Christian theologians, and booksellers. Like these other groups, the rabbis wanted to meet one another or renew old acquaintances. But their purpose obviously went beyond camaraderie. *INJ,* 5 (1844): 213.

126. Translated excerpts from the printed protocols are contained in the detailed account of the conference proceedings presented by Philipson, *The Reform Movement*, 143–224 and in Plaut, *The Rise of Reform Judaism, passim*. I have compiled a selection of longer excerpts in Hebrew translation with an introduction similar to the analysis given here. *Ve'idot ha-rabanim be-germaniyah ba-shanim 1844–1846* (Jerusalem, 1984). The complete texts appeared as *Protocolle der ersten Rabbiner-Versammlung abgehalten zu Braunschweig* (Brunswick, 1844); *Protokolle und Aktenstücke der zweiten Rabbiner-Versammlung, abgehalten zu Frankfurt am Main* (Frankfurt a/M, 1845); *Protokolle der dritten Versammlung deutscher Rabbiner, abgehalten zu Breslau* (Breslau, 1847).

127. A table of personal and professional data on the participants is presented in Lowenstein, "The 1840s and the Creation of the German-Jewish Religious Reform Movement," 276–79.

128. *AZJ*, 9 (1845): 450; *Sinai*, 1 (1846): 94.

129. Stein to Zunz, June 22, 1846, Zunz Archives, JNUL, 923-407-92.

130. *AZJ*, 8 (1844): 27.

131. *INJ*, 5 (1844): 289, 338.

132. *Protocolle der ersten Rabbiner-Versammlung*, 73.

133. Joseph Maier, *Die erste Rabbiner-Versammlung und ihre Gegner* (Stuttgart, 1845), 40–45; Gotthold Salomon, *Die Rabbiner-Versammlung und ihre Tendenz* (Hamburg, 1845), 33–38; *AZJ*, 8 (1844): 374; *ZRIJ*, 1 (1844): 307n; *Literaturblatt des Orients*, 6 (1845): 116.

134. On the need to reassert the Orthodox position more aggressively following the Brunswick conference and the manner in which it was done, see Bleich, "Jacob Ettlinger," 186–96.

135. *Torat ha-kena'ot* (Amsterdam, 1845), *Sefer kin'at tsiyon* (Amsterdam, 1846). Tables presenting background information on the German rabbis among the 116 protesters and a comparison of them with the conference participants are in Lowenstein, "The 1840s and the Creation of the German-Jewish Religious Reform Movement," 280–85.

136. R. Bellson, *Blätter für Israels Gegenwart und Zukunft*, 1 (1845): 1–6, 16–20, 261–63, 354; W. B. Fränkel, *Die Rabbiner-Versammlung und der Reform-Verein* (Elberfeld, 1844); *INJ*, 6 (1845): 384.

137. *Tokhahat megulah* (Frankfurt a/M, 1845), 3, 26–27.

138. *ZRIJ*, 1 (1844): 89–106, 289–308.

139. *ZRIJ*, Prospectus (1843): 5.

140. Even before the Frankfurt conference Philippson had argued that the true reformer should not fully avail himself of the Talmud's permission to pray in any language. He should rather bear in mind the emotional and historical reasons which speak in favor of retaining Hebrew. Petuchowski, *Prayerbook Reform in Europe*, 99, based on *AZJ*, 8 (1844): 461–63.

141. Perhaps, as some were convinced, he had planned all along to walk out at some point, or perhaps, as one source suggests, he was persuaded to do so by his host in Frankfurt. *INJ*, 6 (1845): 268–69; Gotthold Salomon to Bernhard Beer, February 18, 1846, Salomon file, JNUL, Arc. Ms. Var. 236; Jost, *Geschichte der Israeliten*, 10.3: 251; *AZJ*, 9 (1845): 519. Frankel was joined in his departure by another conservative, Leopold Schott, rabbi of Randegg in Baden, though it is possible that Schott simply needed to be elsewhere to interview for a new job. *AZJ*, 9 (1845): 518–19. Schott had attended the first conference after going through considerable pains to secure permission from the government, a substitute to take over his duties, and funds for the trip from a better off cousin. Like Herxheimer in Bernburg and Samuel Hirsch in Luxembourg, he made plans to implement in Randegg the abolition of the *kol nidre*, which had been decided. *Der Orient*, 5 (1844): 305, 370. He considered himself a member of the *orthodox reformistische Parthei* and he hoped that the conservative faction would be stronger in Frankfurt than it had been in Brunswick. Frankel's announced attendance must have made him believe that it would be. See the Schott Collection in CAHJP, especially Schott's letter to Philippson of August 14, 1844.

142. *E.g., Der Orient*, 6 (1845): 282–83, 290, 351–52.

143. *Protokolle und Aktenstücke,* 106.

144. For the appearance of the concept among traditionalists, see the citations I gathered in *Zion,* 46 (1981): 57–58, and see Bleich, "Jacob Ettlinger," 259–60. Typical of its use in Reform sermons of the time is H. Jolowicz, *Israel's Beruf* (Cöslin, 1846). The mission idea was also staunchly advocated by the historian Heinrich Graetz in his "The Significance of Judaism for the Present and Future," *JQR,* 1 (1889): 4–13; 2 (1890): 257–69. See also Barouh Mevorah, "The Messiah Question in the Disputes over Emancipation and Reform, 1781–1819" [Hebrew] (Ph.D. dissertation, Hebrew University, 1966), 189–95.

145. *Protocolle der ersten Rabbiner-Versammlung,* 61; *Protokolle und Aktenstücke,* 74.

146. See especially Aira Kemiläinen, *Auffassungen über die Sendung des deutschen Volkes um die Wende des 18. und 19. Jahrhunderts* (Helsinki, 1956); *idem, Die historische Sendung der Deutschen in Leopold von Ranke's Geschichtsdenken* (Helsinki, 1968).

147. [Caro], *Berit emet,* 124.

148. Geiger in *WZJT,* 3 (1837): 1–14; *Protokolle und Aktenstücke,* 334–48; *Protokolle der dritten Versammlung,* 253–66. Adler's attempt to show that the Talmud gave women an exalted status produced a refutation by Samuel Holdheim entitled *Die religiöse Stellung des weiblichen Geschlechts im talmudischen Judenthum* (Schwerin, 1846). On this issue, as on others, Holdheim argued that Reform must not cover up its sharp break with traditional conceptions. See also Wolfgang Hamburger, "Die Stellung des Reformjudentums zur Frau," *Emuna,* 10, Supplementheft 1 (1975): 11–22.

149. *INJ,* 7 (1846): 289, 301; *Der Orient,* 7 (1846): 238, 261–62; 279–81, 312; *Sinai,* 1 (1846): 280–83; Abraham Geiger, *Vorläufiger Bericht über die Thätigkeit der dritten Versammlung deutscher Rabbiner* (Breslau, 1846), 3.

150. *ZRIJ,* 3 (1846): 201–204, 339–40, 387; *Sinai,* 1 (1846): 341–46; *Der Orient,* 8 (1847): 13, 51, 72, 297.

151. *Der Orient,* 8 (1847): 320; *AZJ,* 12 (1848): 470; 48 (1884): 247–48; Jacob Toury, *Soziale und politische Geschichte der Juden in Deutschland 1847–1871* (Düsseldorf, 1977), 245–52. As early as January 19, 1848, Isaac Marcus Jost wrote to his friends the Ehrenbergs: "No one is talking of religious reforms any more. . . . Our rabbi [Leopold Stein] wearies himself with complaints; the empty benches take in his words and make no reply." LBIA, AR 4294.

152. It is of course not possible to measure accurately when the majority of German Jewry came to favor the Reform movement, as very broadly defined, or when most German Jews ceased to be fully observant. (Those in the latter category may, of course, have had no sympathy for religious reform.) What is clear is that by midcentury limited reforms (which some, but by no means all Jews who considered themselves Orthodox also supported) were very widespread. One source reports that "a good German sermon, confirmations, the permissibility of prayer in German, synagogal music, etc. are matters which have already permeated the general consciousness and there is scarcely a city where such reforms have not more or less found entry." *Der Orient,* 7 (1846): 63. Of course the self-designatedly "Reform" Jewish Reform Congregation of Berlin remained permanently a small minority in Germany. It was the intermediate position, more or less represented by the rabbinical conferences, which was rapidly gaining adherents. On the issue of numbers see Jacob Toury, *Die politischen Orientierungen der Juden in Deutschland von Jena bis Weimar* (Tübingen, 1966), 2, and Steven M. Lowenstein, "The Pace of Modernisation of German Jewry in the Nineteenth Century," *LBIYB,* 21 (1976): 42.

Chapter 4

1. A translation of the text is given in Ib Nathan Bamberger, *The Viking Jews: A History of the Jews of Denmark* (New York, 1983), 50–57.

2. For religious reform in Danish Jewry see especially Gotthold Weil, "A Copenhagen Report concerning 'Reform' addressed to Rabbi Meir Simha Weil," *Journal of Jewish Studies,* 8 (1957):

91–101 and Kurt Wilhelm, "The Influence of German Jewry on Jewish Communities in Scandinavia," *LBIYB*, 3 (1958): 313–22.

3. The Orthodox faction also claimed that the name of God was pronounced as it is written. And they asserted that Psalm 147 was abbreviated to leave out verses 2 and 12, which refer to Jerusalem. However, they made no complaint about seating. Weil, "A Copenhagen Report," 98.

4. *AZJ*, 3 (1839): 228–29; *MGWJ*, 20 (1871): 277, 332.

5. Josef Fischer, "Et Rejsebrev fra I. N. Mannheimer," *Tidsskrift for Jødisk Historie og Literatur,* 1 (1917–19) 298n.

6. *IPSM*, 2 (1835): 100–104, 107–15; Abraham Alexander Wolff, *Predigt beim Antritte seines Amtes als Priester der mosaischen Gemeinde zu Kopenhagen* (Kopenhagen, 1829), 7. A similar service had been instituted a few'years earlier in Aarhus in Jütland. There the *av ha-raḥamim* prayer was excised. *Sulamith,* 6.2 (1822–25): 282–83; 7.1 (1826–29): 65–72. Although Mannheimer carried on a friendly correspondence with Wolff, he thought him of insufficient talent and stature for the vacant rabbinate in Berlin. Mannheimer to Moritz Veit, March 11, 1840, Veit Collection, CAHJP, P47.

7. *MGWJ*, 20 (1871): 277, 333; Fischer, "Et Rejsebrev," 292.

8. Moses Rosenmann, *Isak Noa Mannheimer: Sein Leben und Wirken* (Vienna and Berlin, 1922), 44–53; Hilde Spiel, *Fanny Arnstein oder die Emanzipation: Ein Frauenleben an der Zeitenwende, 1758–1818* (Frankfurt a/M, 1962), 89, 179, 272, 435.

9. Sigmund Husserl, *Gründungsgeschichte des Stadt-Tempels der.Israel. Kultusgemeinde Wien* (Vienna and Leipzig, 1906), 62, 77; Rosenmann, *Isak Noa Mannheimer,* 59; *150 Jahre Wiener Stadttempel* (Vienna, 1976), 52.

10. Alfred Francis Pribram, *Urkunden und Akten zur Geschichte der Juden in Wien* (Vienna and Leipzig, 1918), 305–27; Husserl, *Gründungsgeschichte,* 80–115, Gerson Wolf, *Geschichte der israelitischen Cultusgemeinde in Wien (1156–1876)* (Vienna, 1876), 132–34.

11. *Sulamith,* 7.1 (1826–29): 267–76, 290–97; *Menorah,* 4 (1926): 150–57, 165; Nikolaus Vielmetti, "150 Jahre Stadttempel. Bilder und Dokumente," in *Der Wiener Stadttempel 1826–1976* (Eisenstadt, 1978), 92–99; Husserl, *Gründungsgeschichte,* 131–32.

12. *MGWJ*, 20 (1871): 334–35; 61 (1917): 298; *Jeschurun,* 8 (1921): 222–31; *JZWL,* 3 (1864/65): 167–74; *Die ersten Statuten des Bethauses in der inneren Stadt* (Vienna, 1926).

13. Joshua O. Haberman, "Isak Noa Mannheimer as Preacher" (Rabbinical thesis, Hebrew Union College, 1945).

14. *MGWJ*, 20 (1871): 281; Rosenmann, *Isak Noa Mannheimer,* 106–20.

15. *Die Erlösung* (Vienna, 1847), 14.

16. Rosenmann, *Isak Noa Mannheimer,* 77–85, 91 note 3, 137–215.

17. Salomon Sulzer, *Denkschrift an die hochgeehrte Wiener israelitische Cultus-Gemeinde* (Vienna, 1876); Maximilian Steiner, *Salomon Sulzer und die Wiener Judengemeinde* (Vienna, 1904); *CCARY,* 14 (1904): 227–43; Eric Werner, *A Voice Still Heard . . . The Sacred Songs of the Ashkenazic Jews* (University Park, Pa. and London, 1976), 209–19; Hanoch Avenary et al., eds., *Kantor Salomon Sulzer und seine Zeit: Eine Dokumentation* (Sigmaringen, 1985).

18. For Homberg's career and views see especially *Sulamith,* 3.1 (1810): 258–64; Gerson Wolf, *Studien zur Jubelfeier der Wiener Universität* (Vienna, 1865), 111–19; Majer Bałaban, "Herz Homberg in Galizien," *JJGL,* 19 (1916): 189–221; Joseph Walk, "Herz Homberg's Bne-Zion" [Hebrew], *Annual of Bar-Ilan University—Studies in Judaica and the Humanities,* 14/15 (1977): 218–32; Homberg's *Imre shefer* (Vienna, 1808); his *Bne-Zion* (Augsburg, 1812); and his *Rede bey Eröffnung der religiös-moralischen Vorlesungen für Israeliten in Prag* (Prague, 1818).

19. It was thus analogous to the examination in catechism required of all Catholic couples. See Ludwig Singer, "Die Entstehung des Juden-Systempatentes von 1797," *JGGJCR,* 7 (1935): 216.

20. On Beer's life see his own *Lebensgeschichte* (Prague, 1839) and Vladimír Sadek and Jiřina Šedinova, "Peter Beer (1758–1838)—Penseur éclairé de la vieille ville juive de Prague," *Judaica Bohemiae,* 13 (1977): 7–28. For a sympathetic treatment of Homberg and Beer, noting their

favorable views on equality for women, see Wilma Iggers, ed., *Die Juden in Böhmen und Mähren: Ein historisches Lesebuch* (Munich, 1986), 62–69.

21. *Geschichte, Lehren und Meinungen aller bestandenen und noch bestehenden religiösen Sekten der Juden,* 2 vols. (Brünn, 1822–23), 1: 5, 125–27, 375; 2: 412–39.

22. *Kos yeshuot oder Kelch des Heils* (Prague, 1802), 70n.

23. In 1819 Beer proposed synagogue reforms in a memorandum to the emperor, setting off protracted government deliberations. Frankišek Roubík, "Die Verhandlungen über die Revision des jüdischen Systemalpatents vom Jahre 1797," *JGGJCR,* 5 (1933): 316–24.

24. See especially Ruth Kestenberg-Gladstein, *Neuere Geschichte der Juden in den böhmischen Ländern. Erster Teil: Das Zeitalter der Aufklärung, 1780–1830* (Tübingen, 1969). She cites the description of synagogue music on p. 31 note 134. Also A. Z. Idelsohn, *Jewish Music* (New York, 1929), 205.

25. The article is reprinted in Siegmund Maybaum, "Aus dem Leben Leopold Zunz'," *Zwölfter Bericht über die Lehranstalt für die Wissenschaft des Judenthums in Berlin* (Berlin, 1894), 34–36.

26. My account of the Association is based especially on a lengthy unpublished letter Ludwig Pollak wrote to Leopold Zunz, March 10, 1835 (Zunz Archives, JNUL, 40792-g19) and on the letters and other sources printed in Maybaum, "Aus dem Leben Leopold Zunz'," 34–58, and in *MGWJ,* 61 (1917): 309–17. Another primary source is Peter Beer, *Reminiscenzen* (Prague, 1837). See also Wilhelm Klein, *100 Jahre Verein für geregelten Gottesdienst der Israeliten an der Altschule in Prag* (Prague, 1937) and František Roubík, "Von den Anfängen des Vereines für Verbesserung des israelitischen Kultus in Böhmen," *JGGJCR,* 9 (1938): 411–47.

27. Nahum N. Glatzer, ed., *Leopold Zunz: Jude—Deutscher—Europäer* (Tübingen, 1964), 182, 185.

28. Vladimír Sadek, "La synagogue réformée de Prague (la 'Vieille école') et les études juives au cours due 19e siècle," *Judaica Bohemiae,* 16 (1980): 122–23.

29. Among the Bohemian communities which adopted a modified ritual were Gitschin, Teplitz, Brandeis, Neubidschow, Schwarzkosteletz, and Böhmisch-Leipa. *AZJ,* 6 (1842): 637; Roubík, "Von den Anfängen," 445 note 35. In Teplitz the organ was played also on Sabbaths and holidays. It was introduced by Zacharias Frankel's successor, David Pick, the only rabbi from the Austrian Empire to attend any of the German rabbinical conferences. Beer, *Reminiscenzen,* 26; Friedrich Weihs, *Aus Geschichte und Leben der Teplitzer Judengemeinde* (Brünn and Prague, 1932), 36–37. In Moravia there is early evidence for modified ritual in Prossnitz and Lundenburg. Bonaventura Mayer, *Die Juden unserer Zeit* (Regensburg, 1842), 44; *Der Orient,* 5 (1844): 357.

30. *AZJ,* 9 (1845): 103–104; Hillel Kieval, "Caution's Progress: The Modernization of Jewish Life in Prague, 1780–1830," in Jacob Katz, ed., *Toward Modernity: The European Jewish Model* (New Brunswick, N.J., 1987), 71–105.

31. See Simon Rawidowicz, ed., *Kitve rabi Nachman Krochmal* (2d edn., London and Waltham, Mass., 1961). Some translated excerpts appear in my *Ideas of Jewish History* (New York, 1974), 189–214.

32. *Kalender und Jahrbuch für Israeliten,* 5 (1847): 217–27; Isaac Marcus Jost, *Geschichte der Israeliten,* 10.3 (Berlin, 1847), 77–80; Idelsohn, *Jewish Music,* 245. After Perl's death, a new cantor who had studied with Sulzer was appointed and officiated in the clerical garb adopted in Vienna. *Der Orient,* 5 (1841): 210, 213.

33. Eliezer Liebermann, *Or nogah* (Dessau, 1818), 21–22. It was in the *Vorstadt* synagogue that Abraham Kohn preached when he first came to Lemberg in 1844.

34. For the early history of the synagogue and the conflicts surrounding it, I used *Österreichisches Central-Organ für Glaubensfreiheit, Cultur, Geschichte und Literatur der Juden,* 1 (1848): 190, 238, 276, 295–96, 335–36; Gotthilf Kohn, *Abraham Kohn im Lichte der Geschichtsforschung* (Zamarstynow near Lemberg, 1898); M. Weissberg, "Die neuhebräische Aufklärungsliteratur in Galizien," *MGWJ,* 57 (1913): 513–24; Majer Bałaban, *Historia Lwowskiej Synagogi*

Postepowej (Lwow, 1937), 14–61; N. M. Gelber, ed., *Lvov,* volume 4.1 of *Entsiklopedyah shel galuyot* (Jerusalem and Tel-Aviv, 1956), 230–68, 429–37. My thanks to Professor Elizabeth Krukowski, who kindly prepared a summary of the relevant material in the Polish Bałaban volume.

35. Since relatives of Solomon Judah Rapoport were involved, it is not surprising that he supported the group. See Raphael Mahler, *Divre yeme yisrael,* 6 (Tel-Aviv, 1976): 278.

36. [Abraha]m [Koh]n, "Briefe aus Galizien," *Kalender und Jahrbuch für Israeliten,* 5 (1847): 197–202; Israel Zinberg, *A History of Jewish Literature,* trans. Bernard Martin, 10 (Cincinnati, 1977): 101–108.

37. Kohn had rabbinical approbation from the traditionalist Samuel Landau of Prague but also an educator's certificate signed by the radical Herz Homberg. While still in Hohenems, he published in Geiger's *WZJT* two scholarly articles that argued for the abolition of certain mourning customs and of the prohibition against wearing leather shoes on Yom Kippur. Geiger made Kohn a member of the scholarly circle that was associated with him in the publication of his journal.

38. Just a few days earlier Kohn had given a sermon on the subject "Thou Shalt Not Murder." When police questioned him about possible suspects, he supposedly said: "Though I die of poison, no Jew has done it." He was buried next to Jacob Meshullam Ornstein, an insult which the Orthodox party, it was alleged, avenged by unearthing Kohn's remains and reburying them elsewhere in the cemetery.

39. *AZJ,* 10 (1846): 353; Ignaz Reich, *Beth-El. Ehrentempel verdienter ungarischer Israeliten,* 3 vols. (Pest, 1867–82), 2: 258; Wolfgang Häusler, "Assimilation und Emanzipation des ungarischen Judentums um die Mitte des 19. Jahrhunderts," *Studia Judaica Austriaca,* 3 (1976): 38. For the relationship between social and intellectual developments in Hungarian Jewry during this period see Michael Silber, "Shorshe ha-pilug be-yahadut hungaryah" (Ph.D. dissertation, Hebrew University, 1985); and for Hungarian Reform generally, his "The Historical Experience of German Jewry and Its Impact on Haskalah and Reform in Hungary," in Katz, ed., *Toward Modernity,* 117–57.

40. Secondary literature on Aaron Chorin includes Leopold Löw, "Aron Chorin. Eine biographische Skizze," in *Gesammelte Schriften,* 5 vols. (Szegedin, 1889–1900), 2: 251–420; Paul Lazarus, "Aron Chorin," in *Minhat todah Max Dienemann zum 60. Geburtstag gewidmet* (Frankfurt a/M, 1935), 56–65; Moshe Pelli, "The Ideological and Legal Struggle of Rabbi Aaron Chorin for Religious Reform in Judaism" [Hebrew], *HUCA,* 39 (1968): Hebrew Section, 63–79. See Löw and Pelli for complete references to Chorin's published works.

41. The recantation of his Beer Temple responsum was printed in *Eleh divre ha-berit* (Altona, 1819), 98. Carefully read, it hints at a lack of genuine repentance and Chorin's feeling that he was being made a sacrificial victim. In the earlier instance he was threatened with having his beard cut off if he did not condemn his own book.

42. Löw, "Aron Chorin," 388.

43. *Igerreth Elassaph, oder Sendschreiben eines afrikanischen Rabbi an seinen Collegen in Europa,* German Section (Prague, 1826), 76–94.

44. *Ibid.,* Hebrew Section, 32a.

45. Still in 1832 Chorin wrote to Zunz, to whom he gave rabbinical approbation two years later, that it grieved him to find that "sadly we have on the one hand [Jewish] nationality without cosmopolitan sense and culture, on the other considerable mature culture without nationality." Zunz Archives, JNUL, g10 40792-119.

46. *Yeled zekunim, oder Kind des hohen Alters,* Hebrew Section (Vienna, 1839).

47. Löw, "Aron Chorin," 400.

48. *AZJ,* 1 (1837): 240; Reich, *Beth-El,* 1: 46–55, 126–27, 2: 265, 267–68; Leopold Löw, *Zur neueren Geschichte der Juden in Ungarn* (2d edn., Budapest, 1874), 106–11.

49. Leopold Zunz, *Die gottesdienstlichen Vorträge der Juden* (Berlin, 1832), 468; *AZJ,* 6 (1842): 97; Maybaum, "Aus dem Leben Leopold Zunz'," 35.

50. *AZJ,* 1 (1837): 452; 9 (1845): 330; 10 (1846): 589, 617–18; 11 (1847): 347–48; *Der Orient,*

8 (1847): 220–21; Ignaz Einhorn, *Die Revolution und Die Juden in Ungarn* (Leipzig, 1851), 48; Reich, *Beth-El*, 2: 16–18; Secretary of the Papa progressive party to Löw Schwab, October 13, 1845, Leopold Löw Collection, JNUL; *Zulässigkeit und Dringlichkeit der Synagogen-Reformen begutachtet von vorzüglichen in- und ausländischen Rabbinen* (Vienna, 1845).

51. Löw, *Zur neueren Geschichte der Juden in Ungarn*, x–xi. A number of sources, beginning with Einhorn, *Die Revolution und Die Juden in Ungarn*, 136, make him the preacher in Lugos. However, that position appears to have been filled by a man named Kohn. *AZJ*, 11 (1847): 347–48.

52. *Rabinische Ceremonialgebräuche in ihrer Entstehung und geschichtlichen Entwickelung* (Breslau, 1837); *Pharisäische Volkssitten und Ritualien in ihrer Entstehung und geschichtlichen Entwickelung* (Frankfurt a/M, 1840); *Der mosaische Gesetzcodex* (Ofen, 1847); *Reform des Judenthums* (Nagy–Becskerek, 1848).

53. *Ibid.*, 4, emphasis in text. Shortly thereafter Brück became an officer in the Hungarian militia, dying either in battle or of the prevalent cholera.

54. *AZJ*, 11 (1847): 42, 625, 694; *INJ*, 8 (1847): 38, 142. On Einhorn, see Reich, *Beth-El*, 1: 194–203. For Einhorn's remarkable talent as a preacher see the dramatic sermon he delivered in the community synagogue in Ofen on January 22, 1848. Entitled *Zur That!* (Ofen, 1848) and embodying a number of midrashim, it compared contemporary Jews to Israelites emerging from slavery by their own God-aided efforts and contemporary opponents of Jewish emancipation to Egyptian taskmasters.

55. *Der Orient*, 9 (1848): 279, 316; L. Schwab, *Gutachten an den Israelitischen Gemeinde-Vorstand zu Pesth* (Pest, 1848); Einhorn, *Die Revolution und Die Juden in Ungarn*, 107–13. Einhorn presented a sermon at the Berlin Reform Association entitled *Mund und Herz* (Berlin, 1848).

56. Löw, *Gesammelte Schriften*, 5: 127. In 1846 Geiger and Frankel both sought to attract Hungarian moderate reformers to their respective conferences. *Ibid.*, 135–37.

57. *AZJ*, 10 (1846): 352; *Der Orient*, 10 (1849): 167; Salo W. Baron, "The Revolution of 1848 and Jewish Scholarship," *PAAJR*, 20 (1951): 83–100; Istvan Deak, *The Lawful Revolution: Louis Kossuth and the Hungarians, 1848–1849* (New York, 1979), 51, 86, 102, 113–16, 314. The inner conflict produced by sustained hope and repeated disappointment is poignantly expressed in Löw Schwab, *Ein Wort zur Zeit* (Pest, 1848).

58. Deak, *The Lawful Revolution*, 114.

59. Ignaz Einhorn, *Grundprinzipien einer geläuterten Reform im Judenthum* (Pest, 1848), 32, emphasis in text.

60. *Ibid.*, 43.

61. Reich, *Beth-El*, 195–96; *CCARY*, 19 (1909): 241–44. For the final period see Gerson Wolf, *Joseph Wertheimer* (Vienna, 1868), 217–28.

62. Zunz, *Die gottesdienstlichen Vorträge der Juden*, 472–74; Nikolaus Vielmetti, "Die Gründungsgeschichte des Collegio Rabbinico in Padua," *Kairos*, 12 (1970): 1–30; 13 (1971): 38–66.

63. Morris B. Margolies, *Samuel David Luzzatto: Traditionalist Scholar* (New York, 1979). Still, Luzzatto did believe in halakhic fexibility, deploring the fixity brought about by Maimonides' codification. To Meir Wiener he wrote on August 20, 1845: "The Talmud, in contrast [to Maimonides], presents all the modifications which our laws have undergone during various centuries and all the different opinions of the ancient sages. Had we only the code of Maimonides, we sould believe that nearly all the laws were given to Moses at Sinai." European Letters, Archives of the Hebrew Union College Library, Cincinnati.

64. Menachem Emanuele Artom, "On the Reform Movement in Italy: The Dispute over Reduction of the Period of Mourning in 1865" [Hebrew], in *Scritti in memoria di Sally Mayer* (Jerusalem, 1956), 110–14. Exceptional was Marco Mortara (1815–1894), the rabbi of Mantua. Early in his career he pointed out the fluidity of the liturgy in ancient times as a model for the present. Later he advocated certain ritual reforms, but with no practical success. See his "Kri-

tische Studien," *IA,* 2 (1840): 202–203, 209, 216–17, 224–25, 233–34. In 1844, following French Jewish practice, Rabbi Jacob Levi introduced the confirmation ceremony in Reggio in the Duchy of Modena. *AI,* 5 (1844): 343–44.

65. Cecil Roth, *The History of the Jews of Italy* (Philadelphia, 1946), 444–45, 492–93; Yomtov Ludwig Bato, "Italian Jewry," *LBIYB,* 3 (1958): 338; Attilio Milano, *Storia degli ebrei in Italia* (Torino, 1963), 374.

66. Cited in Barrie M. Ratcliffe, "Some Jewish Problems in the Early Careers of Emile and Isaac Pereire," *JSS,* 34 (1972): 196.

67. *WZJT,* 5 (1844): 449.

68. Isidore Loeb, *Biographie d'Albert Cohn* (Paris, 1878), 153; Ismar Schorsch, "Emancipation and the Crisis of Religious Authority: The Emergence of the Modern Rabbinate," in Werner E. Mosse *et al.,* eds., *Revolution and Evolution: 1848 in German-Jewish History* (Tübingen, 1981), 243–44; Samuel Cahen in *AIF,* 3 (1842): 129.

69. Simon Schwarzfuchs, *Napoleon, the Jews and the Sanhedrin* (London, 1979), 134–36, 138, 181, 189.

70. Recently a considerable literature has developed on Jewish religious reform in France. It includes Phyllis Cohen Albert, *The Modernization of French Jewry: Consistory and Community in the Nineteenth Century* (Hanover, 1977); *idem,* "Nonorthodox Attitudes in Nineteenth-Century French Judaism," in Frances Malino and Phyllis Cohen Albert, eds., *Essays in Modern Jewish History: A Tribute to Ben Halpern* (Rutherford, N.J., 1982), 121–41; Patrick Girard, *Les Juifs de France de 1789 à 1860* (Paris, 1976); Jonathan I. Helfand, "French Jewry during the Second Republic and Second Empire (1848–1870)" (Ph.D. dissertation, Yeshiva University, 1979); Sharon Muller, "The Evolution of French Judaism: The Reform–Orthodox Controversy and the Rise of Consistorial Judaism" (M.A. thesis, Columbia University, 1979); and Jay R. Berkovitz, "French Jewry and the Ideology of *Régénération* to 1848" (Ph.D. dissertation, Brandeis University, 1982). Dr. Albert kindly read this section in manuscript.

71. On Terquem see *AIF,* 3 (1842): 56; 23 (1862): 313–17; and Richard Menkis, "Les frères Elie, Olry et Lazare Terquem," *Archives juives,* 15 (1979): 58–61.

72. I am grateful to Professor Simon Schwarzfuchs of Bar Ilan University for sending me a microfilm copy of Tsarphati letters that appeared as "Correspondence israélite," Letters 13–27, in the *Courrier de la Moselle,* published in Metz (issues dated from April 20, 1839 to September 16, 1841). Letters 18 and 19 are signed "A. T., de Metz israélite Français" and may be by another writer. See, for example, the reference in Letter 18 that the author is from a family of laborers. But the sentiments correspond with those of Terquem. See also the listing in Loeb, *Biographie d'Albert Cohn,* 155–56, and Berkovitz, "French Jewry and the Ideology of *Régénération,*" 144–56.

73. Letters 15 and 27; *AIF,* 2 (1841): 235; 5 (1844): 684.

74. See Letters 15, 17, 21, and 23.

75. See esp. Letter 23; also *AIF,* 1 (1840): 275–83, 325–32; *AZJ,* 3 (1839): 261.

76. In Letter 23 he railed against the *panégyristes jurés,* presenting as evidence Adolphe Cremieux's letter in *AIF,* 1 (1840): 165–71.

77. Simon Debré, "The Jews of France," *JQR,* 3 (1891): 387.

78. *AIF,* 23 (1862): 317. Apparently only on one occasion was a letter submitted by Terquem to a periodical refused publication. *RW,* 2 (1837): 89–90. After being shocked by his brother's deathbed conversion to Christianity, Terquem gave explicit instructions that he be buried as a Jew. The grand rabbi of Paris, Lazare Isidore, officiated at his funeral.

79. *AIF,* 1 (1840): 276. See also Samuel Cahen, *Coup d'oeil sur les dernieres lettres tsarphatiques* (Paris, 1839).

80. See, for example, *AIF,* 2 (1841): 715–19; 3 (1842): 128–32; 7 (1846): 273–88.

81. *RW,* 1 (1836/37): 320.

82. *AIF,* 1 (1840): 32, 235, 693–94; 3 (1842): 308–12, 427–36, 453–54; 7 (1846): 461, 537–40. The earlier bilingual *La Régénération—Die Wiedergeburt,* published in Strasbourg for a year

and a half from 1836 to 1837, was filled with articles by German Jews or about German Jewish developments. Michael Creizenach of Frankfurt was among its frequent contributors. See also the recent study by Jonathan I. Helfand, "The Symbiotic Relationship between French and German Jewry in the Age of Emancipation," *LBIYB,* 29 (1984): 331–50.

83. *AIF,* 5 (1844): 231–32.

84. Albert, *The Modernization of French Jewry,* 198; Helfand, "The Symbiotic Relationship," 344.

85. *AIF,* 2 (1841): 468–70, 531–35; 5 (1844): 229–44. However, prayer groups with reformed liturgies were apparently established in Reims (1838) and Nice (1867). Albert, *The Modernization of French Jewry,* 197–98.

86. *Ibid.,* 169–72, 240–59; *AIF,* 7 (1846): 285; 8 (1847): 183.

87. Albert, *The Modernization of French Jewry,* 298–302, 385–86; *idem,* "Nonorthodox Attitudes," 128–32; Jonathan Helfand, "Entre tradition et réforme: Une lettre de Marchand Ennery," *Archives juives,* 16 (1980): 31–35; and Girard, *Les Juifs de France,* 231–36.

88. Lazare Wogue, *L'avenir dans le judaisme* (Paris, 1844), 15; Gerson-Lévy, *Orgue et pioutim* (Paris and Metz, 1859), 121; Cahen in *AIF,* 10 (1849): 11, cited by Helfand, "French Jewry during the Second Republic," 104 (emphases in the original); Michael Graetz, *Ha-Periferyah hayetah le-merkaz: perakim betoledot yahadut tsorfat be-me'ah ha-19* (Jerusalem, 1982), 56–65.

89. Letter to the editor of the *Gazette de France,* August 27, 1838, cited by Georges Rivals, *Notes sur le Judaïsme Libéral* (Paris, 1913), 89–90. For two divergent interpretations of Salvador's ideology, see Paula E. Hyman, "Joseph Salvador: Proto-Zionist or Apologist for Assimilation?," *JSS,* 34 (1972): 1–22, and Michael Graetz, "Joseph Salvador's Place in the Emergence of Jewish Consciousness" [Hebrew], *Zion,* 37 (1972): 41–65.

90. *AIF,* 2 (1841): 666–67, 721; 4 (1843): 407–10; *AZJ,* 5 (1841): 417; 7 (1843): 375; Debré, "The Jews of France," 411–12, 416. Both confirmation and a newborn ceremony had been introduced even before the 1840s in Brussels. *AZJ,* 6 (1842): 765–76; *AIF,* 4 (1843): 324–25.

91. *AZJ,* 2 (1838): 350; *AIF,* 2 (1841): 646–48; 5 (1844): 13, 377–79; Werner, *A Voice Still Heard,* 202.

92. *AZJ,* 7 (1843): 331, 375; *AIF,* 5 (1844): 12.

93. *AIF,* 3 (1842): 132; 4 (1843): 538; *AZJ,* 7 (1843): 345–46, 374; Albert, *The Modernization of French Jewry,* 103, 214.

94. Muller, "The Evolution of French Judaism," 77–79.

95. In part the consistory system was itself to blame. It functioned smoothly but did not instill enthusiasm. In 1858 a Dr. Wessely in Pest wrote to Rabbi Michael Sachs in Berlin: "The centralized system which in France has been applied also to the synagogue . . . makes French Judaism into a machine which moves but lacks inner life." Michael Sachs File, CAHJP, P41.

96. The most recent general discussion is Michael Leigh, "Reform Judaism in Britain (1840–1970)," in Dow Marmur, ed., *Reform Judaism: Essays on Reform Judaism in Britain* (Oxford, 1973), 15–40. Of interest for the political background is Robert Liberles, "The Origins of the Reform Movement in England," *AJS Review,* 1 (1976): 121–50; and for the social background, Stephen Sharot, "Reform and Liberal Judaism in London: 1840–1940," *JSS,* 41 (1979): 211–14. The differences between English and continental Reformers are stressed in Steven Singer, "Orthodox Judaism in Early Victorian London, 1840–1858" (Ph.D. dissertation, Yeshiva University, 1981); *idem,* "Jewish Religious Thought in Early Victorian London," *AJS Review,* 10 (1985): 181–210; and Todd M. Endelman, "The Englishness of Jewish Modernity in England," in Katz, ed., *Toward Modernity,* 225–67.

97. Todd M. Endelman, *The Jews of Georgian England 1740–1830* (Philadelphia, 1979), 132–36, 164; V. D. Lipman, *Social History of the Jews in England 1850–1950* (London, 1954), 36–37.

98. [Isaac D'Israeli], *The Genius of Judaism* (London, 1833), 265–66.

99. See the pamphlets listed in David Philipson, *The Reform Movement in Judaism* (2d edn., New York, 1931), 449–50. The significance of Scripture in British thought and politics is clearly

demonstrated in Barbara Tuchman, *Bible and Sword: England and Palestine from the Bronze Age to Balfour* (New York, 1956). See esp. pp. 52, 85, 95, 116 and on this connection also Singer, "Orthodox Judaism in Early Victorian England," 74–78.

100. Isaac Marcus Jost, *Geschichte der Israeliten.* 10.2 (Berlin, 1847): 70–71; David W. Marks to John Simon, October 29, 1840, published in Leonard G. Montefiore, "Reminiscences of Upper Berkeley Street," *SR,* 34 (1960): 253. See also the anonymous defense of the Oral Law against the attacks of the London Society entitled *A Word in Season from an Israelite to His Brethren* (London, 1839). Jewish criticism of the Oral Law in England, however, goes back generations before the Reform rift. Very likely it first emerged out of the Marrano background of early Sephardim, who had not easily accepted the traditions of rabbinic Judaism. See Jakob J. Petuchowski, *The Theology of Haham David Nieto: An Eighteenth Century Defense of the Jewish Tradition* (New York, 1954), 4–13; and also his "Karaite Tendencies in an Early Reform Haggadah," *HUCA,* 31 (1960): 225.

101. The expressions are from the anonymous *A Peep into the Synagogue or a Letter to the Jews* (London, n.d. but apparently late eighteenth century). Cecil Roth believes that the author is a Jew; I am not so sure. See his "An Early Voice for Synagogue Reform in England," in his *Essays and Portraits in Anglo-Jewish History* (Philadelphia, 1962), 211–18.

102. Cecil Roth, *The Great Synagogue London, 1690–1940* (London, 1950), 250–63; James Picciotto, *Sketches of Anglo-Jewish History* (London, 1875), 367–73; Albert M. Hyamson, *The Sephardim of England* (London, 1951), 269–95.

103. Louis Loewe, ed., *Diaries of Sir Moses and Lady Montefiore,* 1 (London, 1890): 83. For elaboration of the political motive see Israel Finestein, "Anglo-Jewish Opinion During the Struggle for Emancipation (1828–1858), "*TJHSE,* 20 (1964): 137–40, and Liberles, "The Origins of the Reform Movement in England," 124–35.

104. Moses Gaster, *History of the Ancient Synagogue of the Spanish and Portuguese Jews* (London, 1901), 171.

105. Vivian D. Lipman, " The Development of London Jewry," in Salmond S. Levin, ed., *A Century of Anglo-Jewish Life 1870–1970* (London, 1970), 46; Hyamson, *The Sephardim of England,* 280; *AZJ,* 5 (1841): 477. "It must be pointed out that this designation of 'British' had no more significance of 'non-foreign' than it has in the title of the 'Board of Deputies of British Jews.'" Arthur Barnett, *The Western Synagogue Through Two Centuries (1761–1961)* (London, 1961), 179. Cf. D. W. Marks, ed., *Seder Ha-Tefilot—Forms of Prayer Used in the West London Synagogue of British Jews,* 1 (London, 1841): xi–xii.

106. *Der Orient,* 1 (1840): 379; *JC,* Supplement to January 29, 1892, p. 17.

107. *IA,* 2 (1840): 245–46. Jost maintained an active interest in British Jewry. He visited England in 1841 and reported his impressions of the Jewish community. Though he was willing and able to deliver a sermon in English, the chief rabbi withheld confirmation of the invitation extended to him in London. *IA.,* 3 (1841): 281–82, 297–98, 314–15, 331–33.

108. On Marks see Montefiore, "Reminiscences," 251–58, and his "David Woolf Marks (1811–1910): The First English Reform Minister," *SR,* 36 (1961): 67–72. (The correct date for Marks's death is 1909.)

109. Hyman Hurwitz, *Essay on the Still Existing Remains of the Hebrew Sages . . . and on the Character and Merit of the Uninspired Ancient Hebrew Literature Generally* (London, 1826); Siegfried Stein, *The Beginnings of Hebrew Studies at University College* (London, 1952), 8.

110. *AZJ,* 6 (1842): 69–70 itemizes the changes. See also Petuchowski, "Karaite Tendencies," 230–32. The revised Hamburg Temple prayerbook of 1841, while not eliminating rabbinically ordained blessings, printed them in parentheses in smaller type and left them untranslated. See Jakob J. Petuchowski, "Reform Benedictions for Rabbinic Ordinances," *HUCA,* 37 (1966): 177–78.

111. *Seder Ha-Tefilot—Forms of Prayer,* 1: xi.

112. D. W. Marks, *Sermons Preached on Various Occasions at the West London Synagogue of British Jews* (London, 1851), 205.

113. *VJ,* 4 (1844–45): 8.

114. *Discourse Delivered in the West London Synagogue of British Jews . . . on the Day of Its Consecration* (London, 1842), 8.

115. *JC,* 1 (1844–45): 121; Liberles, "The Origins of the Reform Movement in England," 143.

116. The two documents have sometimes been confused in the secondary literature. Both are printed in *JC,* 2 (1845–46): 85–86. A Hebrew version of the Caution appeared in *AZJ,* 6 (1842): 29.

117. *JC,* 2 (1845–46): 82–85; Supplement to January 29, 1892, p. 19.

118. Sharot, "Reform and Liberal Judaism," 213; *JC,* 1 (1844–45): 121.

119. Alan Mocatta, "Frederic David Mocatta, 1828–1905," *TJHSE,* 23 (1971): 2–3; Albert M. Hyamson, "An Anglo-Jewish Family," *TJHSE,* 17 (1953): 8.

120. *JC,* Supplement to January 29, 1892, p. 20; Montefiore, "Reminiscences," 256; Jakob J. Petuchowski, *Prayerbook Reform in Europe* (New York, 1968), 67–68.

121. Stein, *The Beginnings of Hebrew Studies at University College,* 5.

122. Gotthold Salomon, *Twelve Sermons Delivered in the New Temple of the Israelites at Hamburgh,* trans. Anna Maria Goldsmid (London, 1839), iv. After Isaac Noah Mannheimer visited London, Gotthold Salomon, in a letter of September 27, 1854, asked him especially to write about the West London Synagogue, calling it one of "*our* concerns" (emphasis in original). Salomon File, JNUL, Arc. Ms. Var. 236.

123. *JC,* 2 (1845/46): 81.

124. Marks, *Discourse,* 7; Benjamin Elkin in *VJ,* 3 (1843/44): 215; Jost, *Geschichte der Israeliten,* 10.2: 70.

125. A detailed account of religious reform in Manchester is found in Bill Williams, *The Making of Manchester Jewry* (Manchester and New York, 1976), 100–110, 191–204, 240–65.

126. V. D. Lipman, "The Age of Emancipation, 1815–1880," in Lipman, ed., *Three Centuries of Anglo-Jewish History* (Cambridge, 1961), 100.

127. *VJ,* 2 (1842/43): 29; Arthur Barnett, *The Western Synagogue through Two Centuries (1761–1961)* (London, 1961), 176–78, 182–85; Singer, "Orthodox Judaism in Early Victorian England," 128–65.

128. Roth, *The Great Synagogue,* 258–63; Finestein, "Anglo-Jewish Opinion," 124–25; Endelman, *The Jews of Georgian England,* 160.

129. Singer, "Orthodox Judaism in Early Victorian England," 310–12; *VJ,* 2 (1842/43): 68; *JC,* 1 (1844/45): 49.

130. *VJ,* 1 (1841/42): 97; 4 (1844/45): 49; *JC,* 2 (1845/46): 81; *AIF,* 3 (1842): 64–65.

131. Lucien Wolf, *Essays in Jewish History* (London, 1934), 325; Raymond Apple, "United Synagogue: Religious Founders and Leaders," in Levin, ed., *A Century of Anglo-Jewish Life,* 13–16.

132. Wolf, *Essays in Jewish History,* 321–23; Montefiore, "Reminiscences," 256; *JC,* Supplement to January 29, 1892, p. 19.

133. *JC,* 1 (1844/45): 122; 2 (1845/46): 80; Supplement to January 29, 1892, p. 21.

134. For an interesting effort to explain English Reform to German Jews, see *AZJ,* 6 (1842): 675–76. For Geiger's opinion of the West London Synagogue, see *WZJT,* 5 (1844): 450–52.

Chapter 5

1. Hajo Holborn, *A History of Modern Germany 1840–1945* (New York, 1969), 99–130; Robert M. Bigler, *The Politics of German Protestantism* (Berkeley and Los Angeles, 1972), 262–67; Jonathan Sperber, *Popular Catholicism in Nineteenth-Century Germany* (Princeton, N.J., 1984), 91–98, 290.

2. Jacob Toury, *Soziale und politische Geschichte der Juden in Deutschland 1847–1871* (Düsseldorf, 1977), 50–51, 161, 299.

3. *JZWL,* 1 (1862): 1. To his colleague in Frankfurt, Leopold Stein, Geiger had written on October 3, 1861: "The times are *not* favorable to the demands of the rabbi who strives for a rational reform, an honest transition from debased conditions into the stream of history and into the needs of the present. Not Judaism alone has taken ill from these conditions; Evangelical Christianity—to say nothing of Catholicism—is suffering from them as well. And the former will not be healed until the latter also seeks its own cure." Stein Collection, LBIA, 3264/10.

4. *AZJ,* 17 (1853): 306–307; Samuel Holdheim Collection, CAHJP, P43; Leopold Donath, *Geschichte der Juden in Mecklenburg* (Leipzig, 1874), 244–57; Toury, *Soziale und politische Geschichte,* 146–48.

5. Steven M. Lowenstein, "The Rural Community and the Urbanization of German Jewry," *Central European History,* 13 (1980): 218–36.

6. In Berlin, for example, the community election of 1849 produced a distinctly conservative leadership, that of 1854 a mixed result which enabled traditionalists to forestall significant change for an additional nine years. But from the mid-sixties liberals were clearly in control. A. H. Heymann, *Lebenserinnerungen* (Berlin, 1909), 313–14, 329–30, 378.

7. Toury, *Soziale und politische Geschichte,* 151.

8. Harold Hammer-Schenk, *Synagogen in Deutschland,* 2 vols. (Hamburg, 1981), 1: 251–309, 2: 610.

9. An interesting brief was solicited from the Berlin Jewish scholar Moritz Steinschneider. See Ismar Schorsch, "Moritz Steinschneider on Liturgical Reform," *HUCA,* 53 (1982): 241–64.

10. *Todah W'simrah,* 2 (Leipzig, 1882): Vorwort (emphasis in original); A. Z. Idelsohn, *Jewish Music in Its Historical Development* (New York, 1929), 269–84; Eric Werner, *A Voice Still Heard . . . The Sacred Songs of the Ashkenazic Jews* (University Park, Pa. and London, 1976), 225–29.

11. Some of the responsa were published. Others are in CAHJP, KGe2/26.

12. *JZWL,* 1 (1862): 97.

13. Steven M. Lowenstein, "The 1840s and the Creation of the German-Jewish Religious Reform Movement," in Werner E. Mosse *et al.,* eds., *Revolution and Evolution: 1848 in German-Jewish History* (Tübingen, 1981), 270–71; Adolf Berliner, *Zur Lehr' und zur Wehr über und gegen die Orgel im jüdischen Gottesdienste* (Berlin, 1904), iii; Ismar Elbogen, "Von den Anfängen der gottesdienstlichen Reform im deutschen Judentum," in *Minḥat todah Max Dienemann zum 60. Geburtstag gewidmet* (Frankfurt a/M, 1935), 37; David Ellenson, "The Role of Reform in Selected German-Jewish Orthodox Responsa: A Sociological Analysis," *HUCA,* 53 (1982): 368–80.

14. The article, entitled "Vom Kultus," indicated only that its author was from the Saale region. *AZJ,* 13 (1849): 520–22.

15. The prayerbooks I discuss here are all fully listed in the chronological bibliography contained in Jakob J. Petuchowski, *Prayerbook Reform in Europe: The Liturgy of European Liberal and Reform Judaism* (New York, 1968), 3–8. Petuchowski has also discussed the prayerbooks and translated significant portions of the prefaces on pages 141–76.

16. The Brunswick prayerbook *Tefillat Jisrael,* published by Rabbi Levi Herzfeld in 1855, was similar to Maier's. It too was basically in German, opened left to right, and was to be used privately while the service itself was conducted in abbreviated form and with minor textual alterations from a traditional prayerbook. Like Maier, Herzfeld anticipated that some portions would soon be used alongside the old *sidur* in the public service. See his Preface, p. iv. Other examples of the same type are Joseph Saalschütz's German prayerbook for Königsberg, published in 1859, and Ludwig Philippson's, intended for no particular community and published in a special edition by the Institut zur Förderung der israelitischen Literatur in 1864.

17. Jakob J. Petuchowski, "Abraham Geiger the Reform Jewish Liturgist," in Petuchowski, ed., *New Perspectives on Abraham Geiger* (Cincinnati, 1975), 42–54.

18. Robert Liberles, "The Rabbinical Conferences of the 1850's and the Quest for Liturgical Unity," *Modern Judaism,* 3 (1983): 309–17.

19. For example *ve-ishe* ("and the burnt offerings") in parentheses after the new *ve-nidvot* ("and the voluntary gifts") on p. 182, and the longer variant texts on pp. 226 and 228 dealing with return to Zion and reinstitution of the sacrificial service.

20. For example, on p. 244 of the first edition Geiger had still retained the Hebrew prayer which begins "On account of our sins were we exiled from our land." In the second edition, on p. 254, the opening lines of the prayer are eliminated and the text goes on to substitute "Accept with favor the expression of our lips" [rather than the required sacrifices].

21. Adolf Eckstein, "Die Entstehungsgeschichte des Joël'schen Gebetbuchs," *MGWJ,* 63 (1919): 210–26.

22. *JZWL,* 6 (1868): 167.

23. Letter of December 11, 1853 in the Steinschneider Collection at the Jewish Theological Seminary, New York. I am grateful to Professor Ismar Schorsch for calling these letters to my attention.

24. *JZWL,* 3 (1864/65): 141.

25. One Reform leader who felt free to violate such statutes even before midcentury was Gotthold Salomon, the preacher of the Hamburg Temple. See his *Selbst-Biographie* (Leipzig, 1863), 52. Rabbinical officiation at mixed marriages in Germany was rare, limited to two or three of the most radical Reform rabbis. Geiger's position on mixed marriages was equivocal. He respected the desire of the mixed couple for religious sanction and saw no moral objection to a rabbi officiating. But he also noted that since Judaism was an endangered minority religion, one could hardly object that it was reluctant to sanction such unions. He wanted the conversion process made easier. *JZWL,* 8 (1870): 88–89.

26. E.g., *JZWL,* 3 (1864/65): 256–57; 6 (1868): 169; *Ben Chananja,* 10 (1867): 637–39.

27. Emil Lehmann, *Höre Israel! Aufruf an die deutschen Glaubensgenossen,*(Dresden, 1869), 12–13.

28. A detailed account of the discussions held in the synods of Leipzig and Augsburg is contained in David Philipson, *The Reform Movement in Judaism* (3d edn., New York, 1967), 284–328. For an extensive analysis of the background, composition, problematics, and effects of the synods, see my "The Jewish Synods in Germany in the Second Half of the Nineteenth Century" [Hebrew], *Studies in the History of the Jewish People and the Land of Israel,* 3 (1974): 239–74, which cites the relevant primary sources.

29. Jewish lay leaders did everything they could to prevent passage of the law. See, for example, the letters of Moritz Kohner, head of the Deutsch–Israelitischer Gemeindebund, to Ludwig Philippson, November 2, 1873 and March 10, 1874, JNUL, Arc. Ms. Var. 460/20. In Wiesbaden, where a separatist group had been organized, the local rabbi, a Reformer, tried in vain to persuade the separatists that the gap between them and the larger community was not as wide as they supposed. Samuel Süskind, *Ansprache an die Männer und Frauen der isr. Religionsgesellschaft* (Wiesbaden, 1876). For the social history of German Orthodoxy in this period see Mordechai Breuer, *Jüdische Orthodoxie im Deutschen Reich 1871–1918* (Frankfurt a/M, 1986).

30. *JZWL,* 1 (1862): 165–74; Joseph Aub, *Predigt . . . bei der Feier des hundertjährigen Geburtstages Israel Jacobson's* (Berlin, 1868), 7.

31. Robert A. Kann, *A History of the Habsburg Empire 1526–1918* (Berkeley and Los Angeles, 1974), 321–22; Gerson Wolf, *Geschichte der Juden in Wien (1156–1876)* (Vienna, 1876), 164–66, 209; Moses Rosenmann, *Dr. Adolf Jellinek: Sein Leben und Schaffen* (Vienna, 1931), 73–74; N. M. Gelber, *Aus Zwei Jahrhunderten* (Vienna and Leipzig, 1924), 162–69.

32. Wolf, *Geschichte der Juden in Wien,* 226; Hammer-Schenk, *Synagogen in Deutschland,* 1: 302–307.

33. Rosenmann, *Dr. Adolf Jellinek,* 81, 121.

34. Among Jellinek's 200 published sermons, I have here drawn specifically upon *Schir Ha-Schirim* (Vienna, 1861); *Das Judenthum unserer Zeit* (Vienna, 1861); *Predigten* (Vienna, 1863);

Israel's Sprache (Vienna, 1859); *Die hebräische Sprache* (Vienna, 1878); *Die hebräische Sprache: Ein Ehrenzeugnis des jüdischen Geistes* (Vienna, 1881); and also the detailed evaluation of Jellinek as a preacher in Rosenmann, *Dr. Adolf Jellinek,* 196–215.

35. Wolf, *Geschichte der Juden in Wien,* 200–204; Rosenmann, *Dr. Adolf Jellinek,* 124–29; Wolfgang Häusler, "'Orthodoxie' und 'Reform' im Wiener Judentum in der Epoche des Hochliberalismus," in *Der Wiener Stadttempel 1826–1976* (Eisenstadt, 1978), 50–53.

36. Wolf, *Geschichte der israelitischen Cultusgemeinde in Wien (1820–1860)* (Vienna, 1861); *idem, Geschichte der Juden in Wien,* 227; Ismar Schorsch, "Moritz Güdemann: Rabbi, Historian and Apologist," *LBIYB,* 11 (1966): 42–66; Mordechai Eliav, "Herzl und der Zionismus aus der Sicht Moritz Güdemanns," *BLBI,* no. 56/57 (1980): 138.

37. Hugo Stransky, "The Religious Life in the Historic Lands," in *The Jews of Czechoslovakia,* 1 (Philadelphia and New York, 1968): 330–42.

38. For the religious situation of Hungarian Jewry in general during this period see Nathaniel Katzburg, "Assimilation in Hungary During the Nineteenth Century: Orthodox Positions," in Bela Vago, ed., *Jewish Assimilation in Modern Times* (Boulder, Colo., 1981), 49–55.

39. *Ben Chananja,* 8 (1865): 681–88; 9 (1866): 274–75; Yekutiel Greenwald, *Letoledot ha-reformatsyon ha-datit be-germanyah u-ve-ungaryah* (Columbus, Ohio, 1948), 64–80.

40. Harriet Pass Freidenreich, *The Jews of Yugoslavia* (Philadelphia, 1979), 45–46.

41. Greenwald, *Letoledot ha-reformatsyon ha-datit,* 80–86. The complete Hebrew text of the decree appears in Jacob Katz, "Sources of Orthodox Trends," in Jacob Katz, ed., *The Role of Religion in Modern Jewish History* (Cambridge, Mass., 1975), 51–53.

42. Robert A. Kann, "Hungarian Jewry during Austria-Hungary's Constitutional Period (1867–1918)," *JSS,* 7 (1945): 357–86; Jacob Katz, "The Uniqueness of Hungarian Jewry," *Forum,* no. 27 (1977): 47–48; Katzburg, "Assimilation in Hungary," 54.

43. Leo Jeiteles, *Die Emancipation des jüdischen Kultus. Ein dringender Mahnruf an die israelitischen Cultus-Gemeinden Ungarns* (Arad, 1868). The same year a new printing of Abraham Löwenstamm's *Tseror ha-hayim,* originally published in Amsterdam in 1820 and directed against the Hamburg Temple, was issued in the Hungarian town of Ujhely. It contained a foreword describing contemporary Hungarian reformers as extending the ruination inflicted by that earlier generation in Germany.

44. Yekutiel Greenwald, *Liflagot yisrael be-ungaryah* (Deva, Romania, 1929), 63–64.

45. The fullest treatments of the congress are Leopold Löw, *Zur neueren Geschichte der Juden in Ungarn* (2d edn., Budapest, 1874), 274–322; Greenwald, *Liflagot yisrael,* 69–82; Nathaniel Katzburg, "The Jewish Congress of Hungary, 1868–1869," in Randolph L. Braham, ed., *Hungarian-Jewish Studies,* 2 (New York, 1969): 1–33; Thomas Domjan, "Der Kongress der ungarischen Israeliten 1868–1869," *Ungarn-Jahrbuch,* 1 (1969): 139–62. More than 300 primary sources are listed in Nathaniel Katzburg, "The Jewish Congress in Hungary in 1868/69" [Hebrew], *Aresheth,* 4 (1966): 322–67.

46. Schick's report on the congress appears in Katz, "Sources of Orthodox Trends," 59–63.

47. In 1930 the Neologists constituted 65.5 percent of the Jewish population, the Orthodox 29.2 percent. A small number of "status quo ante" communities remained as they had been before the congress, rejecting affiliation with either group. Katzburg, "Hungarian Jewry in Modern Times," 163.

48. See the intimate but rather jaundiced view of Budapest Jewish affairs presented by the secretary of its Neologist community, Ignaz Goldziher, in *Tagebuch,* ed. Alexander Scheiber (Leiden, 1978), esp. 81–86, 163. According to the *Encyclopaedia Judaica,* 12: 765, E. Neumann, who served in Nagykanizsa from 1883 to 1918, was the only Hungarian rabbi to incorporate some of the (presumably ideological) ritual reforms suggested by Abraham Geiger.

49. The most comprehensive treatment of Schorr is the chapter devoted to him in Joseph Klausner, *Historyah shel ha-sifrut ha-ivrit ha-hadashah,* 4 (2d edn., Jerusalem, 1953): 58–77. A selection from his writings was edited with an introduction by Ezra Spicehandler as Joshua He-

schel Schorr, *Ma'amarim* (Jerusalem, 1972). Spicehandler also contributed to the subject in three articles appearing in *HUCA*, 28 (1957): Hebrew Section, 1–26; 31 (1960): 181–222; and 40/41 (1969/70): 503–28.

50. Schorr, *Ma'amarim*, 29.

51. For Abraham Krochmal see especially his *Theologie der Zukunft* (Lemberg, 1872), Part One, 82–83, and the chapter devoted to him in Klausner, *Historyah shel ha-sifrut ha-ivrit*, 78–104. The difference between the Galicians and the Germans is portrayed as even greater in Eliezer Schweid, *Toledot ha-hagut ha-yehudit ba-et ha-ḥadashah* (Jerusalem, 1977), 339–48.

52. For a more detailed and fully documented treatment of both practical and theoretical reform efforts in the Tsarist Empire, see my "The German Model of Religious Reform and Russian Jewry," in Isadore Twersky, ed., *Danzig: Between East and West* (Cambridge, Mass., 1985), 65–91. I have drawn on that essay for much of what follows and added only references not appearing there.

53. M. G. Geshuri, "Synagogues and Cantoral Music" [Hebrew], in Itzhak Gruenbaum, ed., *Warsaw,* volume 1 of *Entsiklopedyah shel galuyot* (Jerusalem and Tel-Aviv, 1953), 309.

54. For Gordon as a religious reformer see especially Klausner, *Historyah shel ha-sifrut ha-ivrit*, 334–49.

55. See especially Uriel Tal, *Christians and Jews in Germany: Religion, Politics, and Ideology in the Second Reich,* trans. Noah Jonathan Jacobs (Ithaca, 1969); also my "Great Debate on Antisemitism—Jewish Reaction to New Hostility in Germany 1879–1881," *LBIYB*, 11 (1966): 137–70. The wide-ranging German philosopher Eduard von Hartmann wrote at the time that since the essence of Judaism was to be a "religion of law," once Jewish Reformers ceased to accept the law in its entirety, they ceased to be Jews. It was illegitimate to accept the moral law alone as divine, and hence their Judaism was a fiction. Moreover, as a religion of law, Judaism was inherently incapable of development. "Every religion of law," he concluded, "is essentially unreformable." See his *Das religiöse Bewusstsein der Menschheit im Stufengang seiner Entwickelung* (Berlin, 1882), 499, 537–41.

56. Julius Wellhausen, *Prolegomena to the History of Ancient Israel* (1883) (New York, 1957), 1, 509, 542–48; *idem,* "Israelitisch-jüdische Religion," in *Die Christliche Religion* (Berlin and Leipzig, 1906), 37–39.

57. Friedrich Delitzsch, *Babel and Bible* (New York, 1903), 149–50.

58. Adolf Harnack, *Das Wesen des Christentums* (Leipzig, 1900); *idem, Die Aufgabe der theologischen Facultäten und die allgemeine Religionsgeschichte* (Berlin, 1901); G. Wayne Glick, *The Reality of Christianity: A Study of Adolf von Harnack as Historian and Theologian* (New York, 1967). The equally important theologian Ernst Troeltsch identified himself with Harnack's basic position. Christianity, he held, must be seen "not only as the high point, but also as the point of convergence of all recognizable directions of development in religion." *Die Absolutheit des Christentums* (1902) (Munich and Hamburg, 1929), 11, 90. On the superiority of Christianity in Troeltsch's writings and his unwillingness to grant Jews "disproportionate influence" see Robert J. Rubanowice, *Crisis in Consciousness: The Thought of Ernst Troeltsch* (Tallahassee, 1982), 31–34, 126. On the entire controversy see Uriel Tal, "Theologische Debatte um das 'Wesen' des Judentums," in Werner E. Mosse, ed., *Juden im Wilhelminischen Deutschland 1890–1914* (Tübingen, 1976), 599–632.

59. On the history of the work see the editorial introduction by Ingrid Belke to *Moritz Lazarus und Heymann Steinthal: Die Begründer der Völkerpsychologie in ihren Briefen,* 1 (Tübingen, 1971): lxxiii–lxxiv. The principles published in 1885 are contained in the first volume: *Die Ethik des Judenthums* (Frankfurt a/M, 1898), 409–12. The second volume appeared posthumously in Frankfurt in 1911.

60. This presentation of Lazarus' position draws on my "Problematics of Jewish Ethics," in Daniel Jeremy Silver, ed., *Judaism and Ethics* (New York, 1970), 111–29.

61. In the second volume Lazarus went so far as to state: "At one time the mitzvot were

cultivated, expanded, made more difficult; now we need them less because we have more direct ethical action" (p. 109). See also his posthumously published *Die Erneuerung des Judentums* (Berlin, 1909).

62. It was one of the early works published by the Jewish Publication Society of America, appearing in two parts in Philadelphia (1900/1901).

63. The literature on Hermann Cohen is vast. I have found especially helpful Franz Rosenzweig's introduction to *Hermann Cohens Jüdische Schriften,* 3 vols. (Berlin, 1924), 1: xiii–lxiv; Steven Schwarzschild, "The Democratic Socialism of Hermann Cohen," *HUCA,* 27 (1956): 417–38; Nathan Rotenstreich, *Jewish Philosophy in Modern Times* (New York, 1968), 52–105; Emil L. Fackenheim, *Hermann Cohen—After Fifty Years,* The Leo Baeck Memorial Lecture 12 (New York, 1969); and Eliezer Schweid, "Foundations of Hermann Cohen's Religious Philosophy" [Hebrew], *Jerusalem Studies in Jewish Thought,* 2 (1982/83): 255–306. Cohen is also discussed, along with Lazarus and Baeck, in Pinchas E. Rosenblüth, "Die geistigen und religiösen Strömungen in der deutschen Judenheit," in Mosse, ed., *Juden im Wilhelminischen Deutschland,* 559–80.

64. Hermann Cohen, *Briefe,* ed. Bertha Strauss and Benno Strauss (Berlin, 1939), 74.

65. *Jüdische Schriften,* 2: 66–94.

66. "Über die literarische Behandlung unserer Gegner," *AZJ,* 66 (1902): 412.

67. There is an English translation of Cohen's *Religion der Vernunft aus den Quellen des Judentums* by Simon Kaplan (New York, 1972). Selections from the three German volumes of his shorter Jewish writings, translated by Eva Jospe, appeared as *Reason and Hope* (New York, 1971).

68. See, for example, *Jüdische Schriften,* 3: 135.

69. *Ibid.,* 1: 8.

70. Schwarzschild, "The Democratic Socialism of Hermann Cohen," 435.

71. *Jüdische Schriften,* 3: 41.

72. *Religion der Vernunft aus den Quellen des Judentums* (2d edn., Frankfurt a/M, 1929), 239, 303; *Jüdische Schriften,* 3: 174.

73. For a biography of Baeck which stresses his intellectual development see Albert H. Friedlander, *Leo Baeck: Teacher of Theresienstadt* (New York, 1968); for one which dwells on his community leadership see Leonard Baker, *Days of Sorrow and Pain: Leo Baeck and the Berlin Jews* (New York, 1978). See also Alexander Altmann, *Leo Baeck and the Jewish Mystical Tradition,* The Leo Baeck Memorial Lecture 17 (New York, 1973).

74. "Harnack's Vorlesungen über das Wesen des Christenthums," *MGWJ,* 45 (1901): 97–120.

75. "Romantic Religion," in *Judaism and Christianity,* ed. Walter Kaufmann (Philadelphia, 1958), 189–292.

76. *This People Israel: The Meaning of Jewish Existence,* trans. Albert H. Friedlander (Philadelphia, 1965), 397.

77. "Lebensgrund und Lebensgehalt," *Der Jude,* 2 (1917/18): 78–86.

78. *Rome and Jerusalem: A Study in Jewish Nationalism,* trans. Meyer Waxman (New York, 1918), 77, 94–105.

79. *JZWL,* 1 (1862): 252; *AZJ,* 26 (1862): 610–11; Leopold Löw, *Gesammelte Schriften,* 1 (Szegedin, 1889): 333–55; Gershon Greenberg, "The Reformers' First Attack upon Hess' Rome and Jerusalem: An Unpublished Manuscript of Samuel Hirsch," *JSS,* 35 (1973): 175–97; Shlomo Na'aman, *Emanzipation und Messianismus: Leben und Werk des Moses Hess* (Frankfurt a/M, 1982), 320–23, 504, 507–508.

80. *AZJ,* 61 (1897): 277.

81. *Ibid.,* 338. Both protests are translated in Paul R. Mendes-Flohr and Jehuda Reinharz, eds., *The Jew in the Modern World* (New York and Oxford, 1980), 427–29.

82. *AZJ,* 62 (1898): 268. One of the two who refused to sign was Leo Baeck. See Hermann

Levin Goldschmidt, "Der junge Leo Baeck," *Tradition und Erneuerung,* no. 14 (December 1962): 202–203. A pro-Zionist position was taken in an exchange with Vogelstein by the New York Reform rabbi Gustav Gottheil. *AZJ,* 61 (1897): 421–23.

83. "Zionismus und Deutschtum," *Die Stimme der Wahrheit,* 1 (1905): 165–69.

84. For a more detailed history of the Union see my "Caesar Seligmann and the Development of Liberal Judaism in Germany at the Beginning of the Twentieth Century," *HUCA,* 40–41 (1969/70): 529–54. I have drawn upon that article for my presentation here. See also Roberto D. Graetz, "The 1912 Richtlinien Historically and Theologically Considered" (Rabbinical thesis, Hebrew Union College–Jewish Institute of Religion, Cincinnati, 1972).

85. At least one member of the governing board of the Union was a woman, Rosa Sachs from Berlin. Dritte Sitzung der 15er Kommission, Braun–Vogelstein Collection, LBIA, AR 7163/V.

86. An English translation is contained in W. Gunther Plaut, ed., *The Growth of Reform Judaism* (New York, 1965), 68–73.

87. In view of the apparent greater fidelity to ritual observance by Jewish women than men, it seems likely that had women been better represented at the conference, opposition would not have been as overwhelming. On Jewish women and religion in this period see Marion Kaplan, *The Jewish Feminist Movement in Germany: The Campaigns of the Jüdischer Frauenbund, 1904–1938* (Westport, Conn., 1979), 19–20.

88. An undated circular soliciting members for the *Jüdisch-liberaler Jugendverein Berlin* states: "We need to restore its good old luster to the much maligned term assimilation. . . . The J.L.J. must bring back the clear recognition that we are Germans, of Jewish religion and Jewish ancestry, but Germans." Berlin Collection, CAHJP, KGe 2/64. See also other material in the same file which stresses the need, above all, to combat the Zionists. Most Berlin Jews who valued assimilation chose not to join the radical Reform Congregation, probably because its members had to pay a special assessment for their congregation in addition to community taxes. Moreover, to join the *Reformgemeinde* meant to associate one's self with a group widely perceived as sectarian. It was easiest simply to remain among the mass of Liberals. See also Seligmann's devastating internal critique of German Liberal Judaism in Plaut, ed., *The Growth of Reform Judaism,* 106–109.

89. See Wiener's articles in *LJ,* 5 (1913): 121–22; 9 (1917): 33–37. On Wiener see Hans Liebeschütz, "Max Wiener's Reinterpretation of Liberal Judaism," *LBIYB,* 5 (1960): 35–57; Yehoshua Amir's introduction to the Hebrew translation of Wiener's most important scholarly work, *Ha-dat ha-yehudit bi-tekufat ha-emantsipatsyah* (Jerusalem, 1974), 7–32; and Ehud Luz, "Max Wiener as a Historian of Jewish Religion in the Emancipation Period," *HUCA,* 56 (1985): Hebrew Section, 29–46.

90. Michael Leigh, "Reform Judaism in Britain (1840–1970)," in Dow Marmur, ed., *Reform Judaism: Essays on Reform Judaism in Britain* (Oxford, 1973), 26, 33–40; Stephen Sharot, "Reform and Liberal Judaism in London: 1840–1940," *JSS,* 41 (1979): 215–18.

91. Morris Joseph, *Judaism as Creed and Life* (London, 1903), viii, 14–36, 184–85; *idem,* "Biblical Criticism and the Pulpit," *JQR,* 18 (1906): 291–301; Michael J. Goulston, "The Theology of Reform Judaism in Great Britain: A Survey," in Marmur, ed., *Reform Judaism,* 62–67.

92. A good example of this attitude is Alfred G. Henriques, "Why I Do Not Go to Synagogue," *JQR,* 13 (1901): 63–85. Others, less concerned with theological and intellectual issues, remained respectably Orthodox. See Todd M. Endelman, "Communal Solidarity among the Jewish Elite of Victorian England," *Victorian Studies,* 28 (1984/85): 491–526.

93. C. G. Montefiore, "Judaism, Unitarianism, and Theism," *Papers for Jewish People,* no. 4 (May 1908).

94. On Montefiore see especially Lucy Cohen, *Some Recollections of Claude Goldsmid Montefiore 1858–1938* (London, 1940), which contains valuable material from letters; also Victor E.

Reichert, "The Contribution of Claude G. Montefiore to the Advancement of Judaism," *CCARY*, 38 (1928): 499–520; Lily H. Montagu, *Notes on the Life and Work of Claude G. Montefiore* (Cincinnati, 1938); Chaim Bermant, *The Cousinhood: The Anglo-Jewish Gentry* (London, 1971), 313–27; and Steven Bayme, "Claude Montefiore, Lily Montagu and the Origins of the Jewish Religious Union," *TJHSE*, 27 (1982): 61–71.

95. This influence is detailed most fully in Frederick C. Schwartz, "Anglo-Jewish Theology at the Turn of the Twentieth Century" (DHL dissertation, Hebrew Union College–Jewish Institute of Religion, Cincinnati, 1959), 23–35.

96. Citations are from C. G. Montefiore, "The Religious Teaching of Jowett," *JQR*, 12 (1900): 320, 374–76; Cohen, *Some Recollections*, 54. An important point of difference between teacher and student was that Jowett favored mixed marriages, whereas Montefiore did not. *Ibid.*, 35–36. Montefiore's Hibbert Lectures were entitled *Lectures on the Origin and Growth of Religion as Illustrated by the Religion of the Ancient Hebrews* (London and Edinburgh, 1892).

97. Claude Montefiore, "Is Judaism a Tribal Religion?," *The Contemporary Review*, September 1882, pp. 9–16. A reference to Solomon Formstecher's *Die Religion des Geistes* occurs in his "A Justification of Judaism," *JC*, September 18, 1885, p. 11. A bit later Montefiore wrote that German radical Reform Judaism was the movement with which he felt "the deepest and closest spiritual kinship." *JQR*, 1 (1889): 278.

98. *JC*, September 25, 1885, p. 3; *The Jewish Religious Union, Its Principles and Its Future* (London, 1909), 14. Cf. "Some Notes on the Effect of Biblical Criticism upon the Jewish Religion," *JQR*, 4 (1892): 293–306. Montefiore applied the same criterion of personal judgment to the rabbinic literature in his introduction to C. G. Montefiore and H. Loewe, *A Rabbinic Anthology* (London, 1938).

99. *Liberal Judaism: An Essay* (London, 1903), 98–99, 125.

100. *Jewish Religious Union Bulletin*, November 1914, p. 5; *Liberal Judaism*, 174, 181. For a more extended treatment of Montefiore's views on Christianity, see Walter Jacob, *Christianity Through Jewish Eyes* (Cincinnati, 1974), 93–110.

101. *Jewish Addresses Delivered at the Services of the Jewish Religious Union during the First Session 1902–3* (London and Edinburgh, 1904), 63–75.

102. *JQR*, 4 (1892): 302; *JC*, September 18, 1885, p. 11; Cohen, *Some Recollections*, 218.

103. "Judaism, Unitarianism, and Theism," 5. Earlier he had already written: "In all tastes, feelings, and ideas—apart from religion—I have far more in common with a Christian Englishman than with a Bulgarian Jew." "Liberal Judaism in England: Its Difficulties and Its Duties," *JQR*, 12 (1900): 643.

104. See his "Nation or Religious Community," *TJHSE*, 4 (1903): 1–15; "Has Judaism a Future?," *Hibbert Journal*, 19 (1920/21): 38–39; "The Liberal Movement in English Jewry," *CCARY*, 20 (1910): 188–90; Cohen, *Some Recollections*, 227. On Montefiore and Zionism generally see Stuart A. Cohen, *English Zionists and British Jews: The Communal Politics of Anglo-Jewry, 1895–1920* (Princeton, N.J., 1982), 163–84.

105. *JQR*, 12 (1900): 632–33; *Liberal Judaism*, 49–50, 84–85; Cohen, *Some Recollections*, 175. It is possible that Montefiore's religious views were influenced by the Catholic mystic Baron von Hügel, whom he greatly admired. *Ibid.*, 118–20.

106. "What Would You Have Us Do?," *Papers for Jewish People*, no. 7 (1913): 14; W. R. Matthews, *Claude Montefiore: The Man and His Thought* (Southampton, 1956), 6–7; Hugh W. Montefiore, *Sir Moses Montefiore and His Great Nephew: A Study in Contrasts* (Southampton, 1979), 9.

107. On Lily H. Montagu see especially Ellen M. Umansky, *Lily Montagu and the Advancement of Liberal Judaism: From Vision to Vocation* (New York, 1983). There is also an autobiography entitled *The Faith of a Jewish Woman* (London, 1943) and a filiopietistic biography by Eric Conrad, *Lily H. Montagu: Prophet of a Living Judaism* (New York, 1953).

108. The suggestion is made by Umansky, *Lily Montagu*, 4–10.

109. See especially her *Thoughts on Judaism* (London, 1904), 40–41, 115; Eric Conrad, ed.,

In Memory of Lily H. Montagu: Some Extracts from Her Letters and Addresses (Amsterdam, 1967); and Lily Montagu, *Sermons, Addresses, Letters and Prayers,* ed. Ellen M. Umansky (New York, 1985).

110. "Liberal Judaism in Its Relation to Women," *Jewish Religious Union Bulletin,* June 1914, p. 5.

111. "Spiritual Possibilities of Judaism To-Day," *JQR,* 11 (1899): 216–31.

112. "Three Major Documents in the History of Liberal Judaism in England," *Liberal Jewish Monthly,* 27 (1956): 4.

113. See Umansky, *Lily Montagu,* 37–40.

114. Details in Ellen H. Umansky, "The Origins of Liberal Judaism in England: The Contribution of Lily H. Montagu," *HUCA,* 45 (1984): 309–22. See also Lily H. Montagu, "The Jewish Religious Union and Its Beginnings," *Papers for Jewish People,* no. 27 (1927).

115. See the announcement in *JC,* October 17, 1902, p. 2.

116. On Abrahams see Albert M. Hyamson, *Israel Abrahams: A Memoir* (London, 1940); Herbert Loewe, *Israel Abrahams: A Biographical Sketch* (Cambridge, 1944); David G. Dalin, "Israel Abrahams: Leader of Liturgical Reform in England," *JRJ,* Winter 1985, pp. 68–83.

117. David Yellin, "Israel Abrahams and the Revival of the Hebrew Language" [Hebrew], *Jewish Institute Quarterly,* November 1925, pp. 17–18. Montefiore, by contrast, regarded Hebrew as a "dead language" which could not effectively be taught to Jewish children. See his *Liberal Judaism,* 144–46.

118. Israel Abrahams, *The Union and the Festivals* (London, 1909).

119. Claude G. Montefiore, "Israel Abrahams and Liberal Judaism," in *Jewish Studies in Memory of Israel Abrahams* (New York, 1927), lxii–lxvi. However, Loewe wrote of Abrahams: "To describe him as a Liberal or as an Orthodox Jew in false: he was both, he was neither. He was, if one may venture to coin the term, a super-Jew." Loewe, *Israel Abrahams,* 65.

120. *JC,* January 9, 1903, pp. 11–12.

121. Details in David Philipson, *The Reform Movement in Judaism,* 403–407.

122. An extensive report is in *JC,* October 24, 1902, pp. 9–12.

123. The initial prayerbook was used for only a year. It was called *A Selection of Prayers, Psalms and Other Scriptural Passages and Hymns for Use at the Services of the Jewish Religious Union, London* (London, 1902). It was followed in 1903 by a volume three times the size of the first bearing the same title. A fuller discussion of the liturgy is in Petuchowski, *Prayerbook Reform in Europe,* 71–72.

124. *Jewish Addresses,* 258–59.

125. Sharot, "Reform and Liberal Judaism," 220–21.

126. *Jewish Addresses,* 251.

127. Sharot, "Reform and Liberal Judaism," 221–22; *Jewish Religious Union Bulletin,* June 1924, p. 6.

128. "Three Major Documents," 6–9.

129. Petuchowski, *Prayerbook Reform in Europe,* 72–75.

130. Montagu, "The Jewish Religious Union," 27. Other women also occupied positions of leadership in British Liberal Judaism.

131. Simon Debré, "The Jews of France," *JQR,* 3 (1891): 390–425; *AIF,* 61 (1900): 889–90; 64 (1903): 3–4; *AH,* 81 (1907): 637; George Rivals, *Notes sur le Judaïsme Libéral* (Paris, 1913), 98. For French Jewry generally during this period, see Michael R. Marrus, *The Politics of Assimilation* (Oxford, 1971) and Paula Hyman, *From Dreyfus to Vichy* (New York, 1979).

132. To the best of my knowledge, there exists no proper history of Liberal Judaism in France. Some information is given in Philipson, *The Reform Movement in Judaism,* 423–28, and in J. Bricout, "Chez les Israélites Français," *Revue du Clergé Français,* 40 (1908): 282–300.

133. See the essays contained in James Darmesteter, *Les Prophètes d'Israël* (Paris, 1892). *Selected Essays of James Darmesteter,* edited by Morris Jastrow, Jr. and translated by Helen B.

Jastrow, appeared in the United States (Boston and New York, 1895) shortly after Darmesteter's death. Citations are from the latter volume, pp. 10, 104.

134. Théodore Reinach, "Ce que nous sommes," *Dixième anniversaire de la fondation de l'Union Libérale Israélite* (Paris, 1917), 8.

135. Aimé Pallière, *The Unknown Sanctuary*, trans. Louise Waterman Wise (New York, 1929), 209–12.

136. *Actes du IIIme Congrès international du Christianisme libérale et progressif, Genève 1905* (Geneva, 1906), 126–27.

137. *Ibid.*, 121. On Lévy see *AH*, 81 (1907): 637; *JC,* November 1, 1907, p. 11.

138. The volume first appeared in Dijon in 1904. I have used the third, augmented edition (Paris, 1908). In addition to Darmesteter, Lévy may also have been influenced by Gabriel Séailles, a professor at the Sorbonne who published *Les Affirmations de la conscience moderne* (Paris, 1903) and later wrote a philosemitic introduction to *La Question Juive en Pologne* (Paris, 1915). Helpful for understanding Lévy's views, in addition to his book, are his essay *La Religion Moderne* (Paris, 1913) and his sermon "Je pense, donc je crois," in *Trois Entretiens* (Paris, 1910). Lévy also wrote on the family in ancient Israel and on Maimonides.

139. *AIF,* 61 (1900): 891–92. A later version, in *UI,* May 24, 1907, pp. 300–301, does add the intention "to leave full liberty to individual conscience regarding observance of practices and ceremonies."

140. Details from consistorial archives are in Paula Hyman, "The Jews in Post-Dreyfus France (1906–1939)" (Ph.D. dissertation, Columbia University, 1975), 51–57.

141. *UI,* November 29, 1907, pp. 325–31; *AH,* 81 (1907): 637.

142. *A travers les Moissons* (Paris, 1903). Later this book was sold by the Union along with its prayerbook, the longer writings of Lévy, and Théodore Reinach's *Histoire des Israélites.* Brandon-Salvadore became one of the Union's two vice presidents.

143. *UI,* April 5, 1907, pp. 83–84.

144. Hippolyte Prague, "Le Feminisme dans la Communauté," *AIF,* 67 (1906): 265–67. Having attacked the Union repeatedly during its formative stages, the French Jewish press, organ of consistorial Judaism, deliberately ignored it once it began to function as a synagogue. When the president, Salvador Levi, complained that the *Univers israélite* did not carry a report on the Union's inaugural service, the editor responded brusquely: "We take note of this complaint and declare the incident closed" (December 13, 1907, p. 407).

145. *Office d'inauguration du Temple de l'Union libérale israélite* (Paris, 1907), 6–22.

146. The prayerbook of the Union, called *Des Ailes à la Terre,* is already mentioned in 1908 by Bricout, "Chez les Israélites Français," 299–300. It existed in two volumes by the time the Union began to publish its periodical, *Le Rayon,* in 1912. The single volume in the Hebrew Union College library is undated. For a discussion of the liturgy see Petuchowski, *Prayerbook Reform in Europe,* 77–80, 236–37.

147. See the Union's statement of purpose on the inside back cover of *Le Rayon,* October 15, 1912.

148. *Selected Essays,* 270. Lévy spoke of the desire to elevate the entire human race to the "dignité de 'Amm qadôsch', de groupement saint." *Trois Entretiens,* 23. Reinach called the Jews "a spiritual community" in his *Race, Nation, Religion?* (Paris, 1925), 6.

149. Louis-Germain Lévy, "La raison de'être de l'Union libérale," *Le Rayon,* January 15, 1913, p. 5. The Union opened its ranks also to non-Jews, the most interesting of whom was Aimé Pallière (1875–1949), a Catholic by birth attracted to Judaism. Under the influence of the Italian rabbi Elijah Benamozegh, he became a "Noahide," actively participating in Jewish affairs while still retaining an attachment to his former faith. Though a Zionist, he served for a time as the Union's adjunct preacher and contributed regularly to *Le Rayon.* Pallière described his spiritual odyssey in *Le sanctuaire inconnu, ma "conversion" au judaïsme* (Paris, 1926), which appeared also in English translation as *The Unknown Sanctuary: A Pilgrimage from Rome to Israel* (New York, 1929).

150. Abraham Eliezer Beresniak (AV"K) in *Ha-Shiloaḥ,* 20 (1909): 80.

151. Lévy himself recognized that the Protestantizing charge hurt the Union. See his report in *First Conference of the World Union for Progressive Judaism* (Berlin, 1928), 40.

Chapter 6

1. Cited from Sydney E. Ahlstrom, ed., *Theology in America* (Indianapolis, 1967), 311–12.

2. Cited from Sydney E. Ahlstrom, *A Religious History of the American People* (New Haven, 1972), 603–604.

3. Robert D. Cross, *The Emergence of Liberal Catholicism in America* (Cambridge, Mass., 1958).

4. Edward McNall Burns, *The American Idea of Mission* (New Brunswick, N.J., 1957); Conrad Cherry, ed., *God's New Israel: Religious Interpretations of American Destiny* (Englewood Cliffs, 1971).

5. From a lecture delivered before the Theological and Religious Library Association in Cincinnati, January 7, 1869, in Cherry, *God's New Israel,* 224, 227.

6. Cited in Leon A. Jick, *The Americanization of the Synagogue 1820–1870* (Hanover, 1976), 7.

7. Lou H. Silberman, *American Impact: Judaism in the United States in the Early Nineteenth Century* (Syracuse, 1964).

8. Hannah Adams, *The History of the Jews from the Destruction of Jerusalem to the Nineteenth Century,* 2 (Boston, 1812): 217; *Sulamith,* 7.2 (1830–33): 360; Maurice Mayer, "Geschichte des religiösen Umschwunges unter den Israeliten Nordamerika's," *Sinai,* 1 (1856): 104; Barnett A. Elzas, *The Jews of South Carolina* (Philadelphia, 1905), 147–51; Charles Reznikoff and Uriah Z. Engelman, *The Jews of Charleston* (Philadelphia, 1950), 124; Allan Tarshish, "The Charleston Organ Case," *AJHQ,* 54 (1965): 412.

9. The complete texts of the petition, called a "memorial," and the constitution are in Barnett A. Elzas, *The Reformed Society of Israelites* (New York, 1916), 31–53 and L. C. Moise, *Biography of Isaac Harby* (Macon, Ga., 1931), 52–72. On June 1, 1825 Jacob Mordecai, a prominent Jew of Richmond, Virginia, sent a fourteen-page letter to the Corresponding Committee of the Society in which he affirmed the need to abolish the honors, require unison in the recitation of prayers, and include some English. But this moderately liberal and relatively knowledgeable Sephardi Jew thought the Society was going too far and would likely cause a regrettable schism. A copy of his unpublished letter, which also suggests the Society would give up reading from the Torah scroll, was kindly furnished to me by Mr. Maxwell Whiteman of Philadelphia. On Mordecai, see especially Caroline Cohen, *Records of the Myers, Hays and Mordecai Families from 1707 to 1913* (Washington, D.C., 1913), 40–41.

10. The complete text of the principles is most easily available in David Philipson, *The Reform Movement in Judaism* (3d edn., New York, 1967), 332.

11. *North American Review,* 23 (1826): 74; *Occident,* 1 (1843): 438; Lee M. Friedman, *Pilgrims in a New Land* (New York, 1958), 156–57; Reznikoff and Engelman, *The Jews of Charleston,* 132; Malcolm Stern, "America's First Reform Jews," *AJHQ,* 63 (1973): 118–19; Robert Liberles, "Conflict over Reforms: The Case of Congregation Beth Elohim, Charleston, South Carolina," in Jack Wertheimer, ed., *The American Synagogue: A Sanctuary Transformed* (Cambridge and New York, 1987), 274–96.

12. The text of the letter was published by Jacob R. Marcus in *AJA,* 7 (1955): 68–72. Although the reference to Palestine is not explicit, my interpretation is reinforced by the similar phrase he later used (as indicated below) when the reference was clearly to the land of Israel.

13. Edward Eiches, "Maryland's 'Jew Bill,'" *AJHQ,* 60 (1970/71): 258–79; Liberles, "Conflict over Reforms."

14. *North American Review,* 23 (1826): 75.

15. It is contained in Henry L. Pinckney and Abraham Moise, eds., *A Selection from the Miscellaneous Writings of the Late Isaac Harby, Esq.* (Charleston, 1829), 57–87 and L. C. Moise, *Biography of Isaac Harby,* 99–121.

16. For Harby's critique of Noah's project and also for Noah's own ambivalence and inconsistency regarding religious reform see Jonathan D. Sarna, *Jacksonian Jew: The Two Worlds of Mordecai Noah* (New York, 1981), 67, 72–73, 137–42.

17. Isaac Harby booklist, AJA, Misc.; Silberman, *American Impact;* Lester A. Segal, "Jacques Basnage de Beauval's *l'Histoire des Juifs,"* HUCA, 54 (1983): 312–16.

18. The addresses of Moise and Cardozo appear in L. C. Moise, *Biography of Isaac Harby,* 122–40.

19. Mayer, "Geschichte," 171–72; Elzas, *The Jews of South Carolina,* 161.

20. The printed version, *The Sabbath Service and Miscellaneous Prayers, Adopted by the Reformed Society of Israelites* (Charleston, 1830), was reprinted with an introduction by Barnett A. Elzas (New York, 1916). It contains no Hebrew type, perhaps because none was readily and cheaply available. A "new and enlarged edition of the whole form of prayer," including Hebrew texts, was contemplated. One version of the earlier manuscript prayerbook, that belonging originally to Caroline de Litchfield Harby, was lithographed from the original and published with a preface by Edward L. Cohn as *The Isaac Harby Prayerbook* (Charleston, 1974). Another manuscript version, that belonging originally to David Nunes Carvalho, is deposited in the American Jewish Archives. There may also be a third handwritten copy. The version cited in Raphael Mahler, *Divre yeme yisrael: dorot aharonim,* 7 (Tel-Aviv, 1980), 203–204 contains defects in one of the Hebrew paraphrases of the creed which do not occur in the Harby and Carvalho texts. Mahler's volume was published posthumously and gives no source for the manuscript. Detailed comparisons of the Harby, Carvalho, and printed prayerbooks are contained in two term papers by Lance J. Sussman deposited in the American Jewish Archives. Items unique to one or another of the versions are mostly supplementary to the main services. For a liturgical analysis of the printed prayerbook see Eric Lewis Friedland, "The Historical and Theological Development of the Non-Orthodox Prayerbooks in the United States" (Ph.D. dissertation, Brandeis University, 1967), 8–18.

21. From the Carvalho version, pp. 112–13.

22. If we subtract those individuals later marked as dead, resigned, or expelled from the list of signatures to the constitution we are left with a membership of eighteen out of the original forty-three. But at least one of these, David Nunez Carvalho, was no longer in Charleston after 1828. *Cf.* Stern, "America's First Reform Jews," 118 note 4.

23. Elzas in his various previously cited works stressed the German influence. More recently the case was made by Bertram Wallace Korn in his *German-Jewish Intellectual Influences on American Jewish Life, 1824–1972* (Syracuse, 1972), 17 note 7.

24. This is the influence especially stressed in Silberman, *American Impact,* and already noted earlier in Friedman, *Pilgrims in a New Land,* 154–55.

25. According to Mayer, "Geschichte," 173, one of the causes was "other circumstances, which are not appropriate for public disclosure."

26. On Poznanski see most recently Solomon Breibart, *The Rev. Mr. Gustavus Poznanski, First American Jewish Reform Minister* (Charleston, 1979).

27. *Occident,* 9 (1852): 212.

28. The most complete study of the conflict is in Tarshish, "The Charleston Organ Case," 420–46.

29. Poznanski's address was not printed. Most of the report in the *Charleston Courier,* March 20, 1841, appears also in *AZJ,* 5 (1841): 307–309. Both Gentiles and Jews in Charleston had held meetings in the summer of 1840 where they condemned the accusations made against the Jews of Damascus and extended their sympathy to the victims. The Jews were especially appreciative of the Christian support they received. See the resolutions and deliberations of the meetings in Joseph L. Blau and Salo W. Baron, *The Jews of the United States 1790–1840, A Docu-*

mentary History, 3 (New York and Philadelphia, 1963): 942–50. See also Jick, *The Americanization of the Synagogue,* 83–84.

30. Moise, *Biography of Isaac Harby,* 89.

31. The creed is contained in Jacob C. Levy, "The Reformed Israelites," *Southern Quarterly Review,* 5 (1844): 348. For the opposition to it see *Occident,* 9 (1852): 214–15.

32. Mayer, "Geschichte," 178; *Orient,* 5 (1844): 174. A closer relationship with European Reform, and especially with the Hamburg Temple, now developed. The English translation of Gotthold Salomon's sermons, which had first appeared in England in 1839, was republished in Charleston in 1841. Some of the Hamburg Temple hymns were adapted for use in Beth Elohim and the Hamburg Temple memorial service was taken over for the eve of Yom Kippur. Word of both the establishment of the West London Synagogue and the second Hamburg Temple dispute reached the Charleston congregation and may have given the Reformers encouragement. Mayer, "Geschichte," 176; Levy, "The Reformed Israelites," 333–34.

33. K. K. Beth Elohim Minutes, August 8 and 10, 1841, AJA.

34. In Moise, *Biography of Isaac Harby,* 84.

35. On Leeser see Henry Englander, "Isaac Leeser," *CCARY,* 28 (1918): 213–52; Maxwell Whiteman, "Isaac Leeser and the Jews of Philadelphia," *PAJHS,* 48 (1958/59): 207–44; Moshe Davis, *The Emergence of Conservative Judaism* (Philadelphia, 1965), *passim;* Bertram W. Korn, "Isaac Leeser: Centennial Reflections," *AJA,* 19 (1967): 127–41; Lawrence Grossman, "Tradition under Fire: Isaac Leeser and Reform," *Gesher,* 8 (1981): 73–89; Naomi W. Cohen, *Encounter with Emancipation: The German Jews in the United States 1830–1914* (Philadelphia, 1984), *passim;* Lance J. Sussman, "Isaac Leeser and the Protestantization of American Judaism," *AJA,* 38 (1986): 1–21; and *idem,* "The Life and Career of Isaac Leeser (1806–1868): A Study of American Judaism in its Formative Period" (Ph.D. dissertation, HUC–JIR, Cincinnati, 1987).

36. Americanization and upward social mobility are repeatedly stressed in Jick, *The Americanization of the Synagogue.* Cohen, in *Encounter with Emancipation,* 164–65, suggests a more balanced view.

37. *Sinai,* 1 (1855/56): 198–201; Isidor Blum, *The Jews of Baltimore* (Baltimore and Washington, 1910), 11–12; Charles A. Rubenstein, *History of Har Sinai Congregation* (Baltimore, 1918), 4–16.

38. *Sinai,* 1 (1855/56): 201–203; *Israelite,* January 5, 1855, p. 206; Myer Stern, *The Rise and Progress of Reform Judaism . . . Temple Emanu-El of New York* (New York, 1895), 13–39; Hyman B. Grinstein, *The Rise of the Jewish Community of New York 1654–1860* (Philadelphia, 1945), 353–63, 501–507.

39. Bernhard N. Cohn, "Leo Merzbacher," *AJA,* 6 (1954): 21–24.

40. Comparison with the earlier Leeser translation reveals occasional identity in English formulation. Compare, for example, the *hashkivenu* prayer in Merzbacher 1:21 with Leeser's *The Book of Daily Prayers* (Philadelphia, 1848), 86.

41. Friedland, "The Historical and Theological Development of the Non-Orthodox Prayerbooks in the United States," 19–39; *idem,* "Hebrew Liturgical Creativity in Nineteenth-Century America," *Modern Judaism,* 1 (1981): 324–25.

42. Adler also made the prayerbook more radical by transforming "revivest the dead" into "vivifiest all things" *(meḥayeh ha-kol)* and the messianic reference to "Redeemer" into the abstract "redemption" *(ge'ulah).* The second change occurs only in Adler's revision of the High Holiday liturgy, which appeared in 1863.

43. *Asmonean,* November 9, 1855, p. 28. Leopold Stein published a sympathetic but not uncritical review in *Der Israelitische Volkslehrer,* 6 (1856): 97–102, 204–208.

44. *Israelite,* September 15, 1854, p. 77. On Lilienthal in New York see Sefton D. Temkin, "Rabbi Max Lilienthal Views American Jewry in 1847," in Bertram Wallace Korn, ed., *A Bicentennial Festscrift for Jacob Rader Marcus* (Waltham, Mass., 1976), 589–608.

45. The most detailed biography remains James G. Heller, *Isaac M. Wise: His Life, Work and Thought* (New York, 1965). See also more recently Sefton Temkin, "Isaac Mayer Wise: A

Biographical Sketch," in Doris C. Sturzenberger, ed., *A Guide to the Writings of Isaac Mayer Wise* (Cincinnati, 1981), 5–53. A full-scale psychobiography would contribute greatly to our knowledge of the man.

46. *Reminiscences* (Cincinnati, 1901), 257.

47. Issac M. Wise, *History of the Israelitish Nation, from Abraham to the Present Time,* 1 (Albany, 1854): iv (only one volume appeared); David Philipson and Louis Grossman, eds., *Selected Writings of Isaac Mayer Wise* (Cincinnati, 1900), 173; Joseph H. Gumbiner, "Lost Leader of a Winning Cause: The Founder of American Reform Judaism Reconsidered," *Judaism,* 1 (1952): 171.

48. Henry Illoway, son of the Orthodox rabbi Bernard Illowy and a younger Cincinnati contemporary, claimed that Wise himself was "far from the radicalism of Einhorn and that of the so-called reformers of this latter day." He believed that Wise became more conservative as he got older; Lilienthal, by contrast, grew more radical. Henry Illoway, ed., *The Controversial Letters and the Casuistic Decisions of the Late Rabbi Bernard Illowy* (Berlin, 1914), 3–5. The notion that Wise's "real views" were radical is the thesis of Aryeh Rubinstein, "Isaac Mayer Wise: A New Appraisal," *JSS,* 39 (1977): 53–74. See also Rubinstein's broader treatment of the entire American Reform movement in this period: "Reshitah shel tenuat ha-reformah be-yahadut artsot ha-berit ve-ha-pulmus sevivah ba-shanim 1840–1869" (Ph.D. dissertation, Hebrew University, 1973).

49. *Reminiscences,* 49; *American Israelite,* December 4, 1885, p. 4.

50. See especially his *History of the Israelitish Nation,* 79; *Selected Writings,* 133–40, 197–220; *Judaism and Christianity: Their Agreements and Disagreements* (Cincinnati, 1883), 33–34, 77–79, 105–106; "The World of My Books," trans. in *AJA,* 6 (1954): 143. Wise seems to have identified strongly with Moses, whose noted attributes well fit his own personality: "passionate, rash and impetuous." Moses' "intense love of liberty and of justice" are clearly projections of Wise's own ideals. Not surprisingly, Wise labels Moses "a reformer." *Selected Writings,* 163–69.

51. *Ibid.,* 265–351.

52. Cited in James G. Heller, *As Yesterday When It Is Past* (Cincinnati, 1942), 3.

53. Naphtali J. Rubinger, "Dismissal in Albany," *AJA,* 24 (1972): 160–83.

54. *Reminiscences,* 165.

55. Wise's initiative should not, however, be exaggerated. The church taken over by Anshe Emeth already had family pews, and Wise's congregation simply retained them. On this subject generally see Jonathan D. Sarna, "The Debate over Mixed Seating in the American Synagogue," in Wertheimer, ed., *The American Synagogue,* 363–94.

56. *Israels Herold,* 1 (1849): 73–74, 91; *Occident,* 6 (1848/49): 616.

57. Heller, *As Yesterday When It Is Past,* 19–96.

58. *Israelite,* July 15, 1854, p. 4.

59. *Ibid.,* August 10, 1855, p. 39.

60. *Ibid.,* October 26, 1855, p. 132; November 9, 1855, p. 148; *Occident,* 13 (1855/56): 407–14; *Reminiscences,* 313. The Wise and Leeser accounts do not exactly match.

61. *Reminiscences,* 316–17.

62. *Occident,* 13 (1855/56): 421–30; 14 (1856/57): 72–81.

63. *Sinai,* 1 (1856/57): 27–29; *Israelitische Volkslehrer,* 5 (1855): 409–19; *AZJ,* 19 (1855): 622–23, 634–35.

64. On Einhorn see especially J. Alexander Patten, *Lives of the Clergy of New York and Brooklyn* (New York, 1874), 168–70; the supplement to the *American Israelite,* November 21, 1879; Kaufmann Kohler, "David Einhorn, the Uncompromising Champion of Reform Judaism," *CCARY,* 19 (1909): 215–67; and more recently Bernhard N. Cohn, "David Einhorn: Some Aspects of His Thinking," in *Essays in American Jewish History to Commemorate the Tenth Anniversary of the Founding of the American Jewish Archives* (Cincinnati, 1958), 315–24; Gershon Greenberg, "The Significance of America in David Einhorn's Conception of History,"

AJHQ, 63 (1973): 160–84; *idem,* "The Messianic Foundations of American Jewish Thought: David Einhorn and Samuel Hirsch," *Proceedings of the Sixth World Congress of Jewish Studies,* 2 (Jerusalem, 1975): 215–26; and *idem,* "Mendelssohn in America: David Einhorn's Radical Reform Judaism," *LBIYB,* 27 (1982): 281–93.

65. *Rabbinische Gutachten über die Verträglichkeit der freien Forschung mit dem Rabbineramte,* 1 (Breslau, 1842): 125–39; *AZJ,* 8 (1844): 87–89; *Protokolle und Aktenstücke der zweiten Rabbiner-Versammlung* (Frankfurt a/M, 1845), 27, 49, 186; *Protokolle der dritten Versammlung deutscher Rabbiner* (Breslau, 1847), 57, 198; *Sinai,* 4 (1859/60): 289; Kaufmann Kohler, ed., *Dr. David Einhorn's Ausgewählte Predigten und Reden* (New York, 1881), 89, 312–13. Despite Einhorn's preference for the vernacular in liturgy, in America he was a proponent of Hebrew study for Jewish children and favored day school Jewish education. *Sinai,* 1 (1856/57): 391; *Predigten und Reden,* 67.

66. *Das Princip des Mosaismus und dessen Verhältniss zum Heidenthum und rabbinischen Judenthum* (Leipzig, 1854), 66. Einhorn's interest in symbolism was stimulated by the influential work of Karl Bähr, *Symbolik des Mosaischen Cultus,* 2 vols. (Heidelberg, 1837–39). While methodologically dependent on Bähr, Einhorn engages in repeated and fundamental criticism of his interpretations.

67. Kohler, "David Einhorn," 219–20, attributes the influence to Schelling.

68. *Sinai,* 2 (1857/58): 539. Einhorn claimed that he was the first to say that "Judaism is as old as humanity." *Sinai,* 3 (1858/59): 1093n. The claim that Christianity was the religion of nature had been made as early as 1730 by the English deist Matthew Tindal in his *Christianity as Old as Creation.*

69. *Ner Tamid: Die Lehre des Judenthums, dargestellt für Schule und Haus* (Philadelphia, 1866), 18, 31; *Sinai,* 2 (1857/58): 401, 410; *Predigten und Reden,* 24.

70. *Ibid.,* 177.

71. *Ner Tamid,* 27, 33–38; *Protokolle und Aktenstücke,* 75; *AZJ,* 8 (1844): 88.

72. *Olat Tamid. Gebetbuch für Israelitische Reform-Gemeinden* (Baltimore, 1858), 61, 396–97.

73. Cited by Kohler, "David Einhorn," 265. See also *Predigten und Reden,* 91; *Ner Tamid,* 51; Einhorn to Kohler, January 7, 1870, AJA, MSS Col. 155.

74. *Das vom Judenthum gebotene Verhalten des Israeliten gegenüber seiner stiefväterlichen Behandlung von Seiten des Vaterlandes* (Schwerin, 1847).

75. At the Frankfurt conference Einhorn argued that it was unfair for men to receive religious preference by being called to the Torah, and he was elected to a commission charged with coming up with proposals for women's religious equality. *Protokolle und Aktenstücke,* 144, 169. At Breslau he presented the commission's report. *Protokolle der dritten Versammlung,* 252–66. In America Einhorn favored family pews (despite his Germanism) and created a wedding ceremony in which bride and groom participated equally. *Sinai,* 3 (1858/59): 1020; 6 (1861/62): 205–207.

76. *Sinai,* 1 (1856/57): 259; 6 (1861/62): 2–22, 45–50, 171; 7 (1862/63): 319.

77. *Predigten und Reden,* 85, 109–12, 169–70; *Sinai,* 2 (1857/58): 604. Einhorn was critical of the contemporary Jewish fancy for elaborate cemetery memorials. Here he preferred traditional Jewish custom which, in death, did not distinguish rich from poor. *Ner Tamid,* 85.

78. *Predigten und Reden,* 65, 90.

79. Einhorn to Bernhard Felsenthal, May 25, 1862, AJA, MSS Col. 155.

80. *Sinai,* 3 (1858/59): 837ff.; *Predigten und Reden,* 17, 70.

81. *Sinai,* 1 (1856/57): 19, 190, 362; 2 (1857/58): 668–69. In a letter to Felsenthal, November 14, 1861, Einhorn complained that *Sinai* had only sixty subscribers in New York. AJA, MSS Col. 155.

82. *Sinai,* 1 (1856/57): 359; 3 (1858/59): 1083.

83. *Predigten und Reden,* 29, 83; *Sinai,* 1 (1856/57): 1–3, 28, 65; 2 (1857/58): 411.

84. *Predigten und Reden,* 41; *Sinai,* 6 (1861/62): 244. Einhorn commiserated with his son-

in-law Kaufmann Kohler that in Kohler's Detroit pulpit he was forced to keep the dietary laws and thus "cannot *live* as you *teach.* America is not Europe; here such coercion is aggravating." Letter of July 4, 1870, AJA, MSS Col. 155. Einhorn's position on *kashrut* was that only the laws concerning the eating of blood and of meat from animals that died a natural death were still valid. The rest belonged to Levitical laws of purity and priestly sacrificial laws. *Sinai,* 4 (1859/60): 193ff.

85. *Israelite,* November 10, 1855, p. 157; *Sinai,* 1 (1856/57): 10, 28.

86. Bertram W. Korn, *American Jewry and the Civil War* (Philadelphia, 1951), 17–27, 40–41; Heller, *Isaac M. Wise,* 321–73; Sefton D. Temkin, "Isaac Mayer Wise and the Civil War," *AJA,* 15 (1963): 12–42; Liebman Adler, *His Life through His Letters,* ed. Joan Weil Saltzstein (n.p., 1975), ix, 108.

87. Heller, *Isaac M. Wise,* 375–83; Malcolm Stern, "National Leaders of Their Time: Philadelphia's Reform Rabbis," in Murray Friedman, ed., *Jewish Life in Philadelphia 1830–1940* (Philadelphia, 1983), 183; Uriah Zvi Engelman, "Jewish Statistics in the U.S. Census of Religious Bodies (1850–1936)," *JSS,* 9 (1947): 130–32; *New Era,* 4 (1874): 131.

88. For the progress of synagogue reforms I have drawn upon a cross section of congregational and community histories. See the extensive list of Reform congregational histories compiled by Malcolm Stern in *AJHQ,* 63 (1973): 126–37.

89. *Israelite,* April 29, 1870, p. 8; July 15, 1870, p. 8; January 13, 1871, p. 8; *JT,* 7 (1875/76): 158. Just how meager or not meager the residue was deserves investigation.

90. For a more extensive treatment of German loyalties among American Jews, as well as references to the primary sources, see my "German-Jewish Identity in Nineteenth-Century America," in Jacob Katz, ed., *Toward Modernity: The European Jewish Model* (New Brunswick, N.J., 1987), 247–67.

91. Wise, *Reminiscences,* 343–46; Heller, *Isaac M. Wise,* 302–305.

92. *Gebetbuch für Israelitische Reform-Gemeinden* (New York, 1856).

93. Einhorn to Felsenthal, June 24, 1870, AJA, MSS Col. 155.

94. Eric L. Friedland, "*Olath Tamid* by David Einhorn," *HUCA,* 45 (1974): 313–18.

95. Einhorn gave the rationale for his liturgy in *Sinai,* 1 (1856/57): 97–100, 129–39.

96. Letter of June 24, 1862, AJA, MSS Col. 155; Kohler, "David Einhorn," 253–54.

97. "We must have a Hebrew prayer book and another in the vernacular, and leave it to the choice of each congregation how much of each is to be chosen. So we do in the *Minhag America.* To prescribe for all congregations, this and so much must be read in this or that worship, is folly and petty despotism. Give them the proper material, and let each congregation choose to suit itself." *Israelite,* April 29, 1870, p. 8. Later editions made such selection smoother as vernacular pages were bound opposite the corresponding Hebrew ones.

98. *JT,* 2 (1870/71): 378; Bernhard Felsenthal, *The Beginnings of Chicago Sinai Congregation* (Chicago, 1898), 35.

99. *Israelite,* July 29, 1870, 8; *Reminiscences,* 346; Heller, *Isaac M. Wise,* 304.

100. *JT,* June 4, 1869, p. 8.

101. *Protokolle der Rabbiner-Conferenz abgehalten zu Philadelphia, vom 3. bis zum 6. November 1869* (New York, 1870). There is a complete annotated translation with introduction: Sefton D. Temkin, *The New World of Reform* (Bridgeport, 1974). For the contextual influence on the decision to abandon the Jewish writ of divorce see Shlomith Yahalom, "Radical Trends in the Reform Movement of the U.S.A.—Philadelphia Conference" [Hebrew], *Proceedings of the Ninth World Congress of Jewish Studies,* Division B, Vol. 2 (Jerusalem, 1986), 35–40.

102. *JT,* December 17, 1869, pp. 11–12; *Israelite,* April 22, 1870, p. 8; April 29, 1870, p. 8; May 6, 1870, pp. 8–9; May 13, 1870, pp. 8–9.

103. *Israelite,* June 17, 1870, p. 8; July 22, 1870, p. 8; July 29, 1870, p. 8. Sonneschein, a radical from St. Louis whose congregation used the Einhorn prayerbook, came simply to meet his western colleagues. *JT,* 2 (1870/71): 358.

104. Julia Hübsch, ed., *Rev. Dr. Adolph Hübsch, Late Rabbi of The Ahawath Chesed Con-*

gregation New York (New York, 1885), viii–ix; *Israelite,* December 23, 1870, p. 8; Wise to Hübsch, November 28, 1866, July 30, 1868, March 4, 1870, March 23, 1870, AJA, Box 2333.

105. *JT,* 2 (1870/71): 408–409. A fusion of existing Reform prayerbooks had been proposed by Sonneschein at the Philadelphia conference and was to be dealt with by one of its appointed committees in advance of the second, Cincinnati meeting. The Cleveland conference was therefore preemptive.

106. *JT,* 2 (1870/71): 521.

107. *Israelite,* November 4, 1870, p. 8; November 11, 1870, p. 8; November 18, 1870, p. 8.

108. *Israelite,* June 9, 1871, pp. 8–9; June 16, 1871, pp. 8–9; June 23, 1871, p. 8. Whether the prayerbook revision was really completed at the Cincinnati conference is, however, questionable. Later Wise claimed it was "not half done." Julia Hübsch, *Rev. Dr. Adolph Hübsch,* ix–x. In any case, Wise republished *Minhag America* in 1872 with "revised in conference" printed on the title page.

109. Wise to Hübsch, July 20, 1873, AJA, Box 2333. Hübsch's prayerbook was called *Seder Tefilah, Gebete für den öffentlichen Gottesdienst der Tempelgemeinde Ahawath Chesed,* 2 vols. (New York, 1872).

110. *Israelite,* July 21, 1871, pp. 8–9; August 4, 1871, pp. 8–9.

111. *JT,* 3 (1871/72): 280–83, 297–99, 309, 393–94. Hirsch found the protest of the fourteen too dogmatic. Hirsch to Adler, June 26, 1871, AJA, Correspondence File.

112. Joseph Krauskopf, "Half a Century of Judaism in the United States," *American Jews' Annual,* 4 (1888): 86; *PUAHC,* 1 (1873–79): 3, 28–29, 119; Wise to Hübsch, July 20, 1873, AJA, Box 2333.

113. *PUAHC,* 1 (1873–79): i–xiii, 3; Sefton D. Temkin, "A Century of Reform Judaism in America," *AJYB,* 74 (1973): 25–28.

114. The detailed published proceedings offer the best primary source for the early history of the Union. See also Steven A. Fox, "On the Road to Unity: The Union of American Hebrew Congregations and American Jewry, 1873–1903," *AJA,* 32 (1980): 145–93.

115. Zion Congregation published its reasons for not sending delegates in *JT,* 5 (1873–84): 309.

116. *Israelite,* July 18, 1873, p. 4.

117. *AI,* August 5, 1887, p. 4; March 27, 1919, p. 16.

118. Allan Tarshish, "The Board of Delegates of American Israelites (1859–1878)," *PAJHS,* 49 (1959/60): 16–32.

119. *JT,* December 31, 1869.

120. Ezra Spicehandler and Theodore Wiener, "Bernhard Felsenthal's Letters to Osias Schorr," *Essays in American Jewish History* (Cincinnati, 1958), 394–96.

121. *Statistics of the Jews of the United States, Compiled under the Authority of the Board of Delegates of American Israelites and the Union of American Hebrew Congregations* (Philadelphia, 1880), 55–56.

122. *PUAHC,* 2 (1879–85): 1456. I have dealt in detail with the history of the Hebrew Union College in my "A Centennial History," in Samuel E. Karff, ed., *Hebrew Union College–Jewish Institute of Religion At One Hundred Years* (Cincinnati, 1976): 3–283.

123. *AI,* August 5, 1887, p. 4.

124. Cited from the *Occident* (Chicago), July 20, 1883, p. 4, in Victor Ludlow, "Bernhard Felsenthal: Quest for Zion" (Ph.D. dissertation, Brandeis University, 1984), 203.

Chapter 7

1. For Adler see especially Benny Kraut, *From Reform Judaism to Ethical Culture: The Religious Evolution of Felix Adler* (Cincinnati, 1979); also Michael A. Meyer, "Beyond Particularism," *Commentary,* March 1971, pp. 71–76.

2. Felix Adler, *Creed and Deed* (New York, 1877), 203, 214, 242; *JC,* February 20, 1903, p. 18.

3. *JR,* January 1, 1886, p. 4; *Zeitgeist,* 1 (1880): 1; *Reform Advocate,* 41 (1911): 451; *AI,* 28 (1881/82): 252.

4. *Reformer and Jewish Times,* March 29, 1878, p. 5.

5. Beryl Harold Levy, *Reform Judaism in America* (New York, 1933), 57–60; Moshe Davis, *The Emergence of Conservative Judaism* (Philadelphia, 1965), 222–25.

6. Alexander Kohut, *The Ethics of the Fathers* (New York, 1885), 11–13, 80–81, 111–13, 164–70.

7. Kaufmann Kohler, *Backwards or Forwards?* (New York, 1885), 10–13.

8. *Österreichische Wochenschrift,* August 14, 1885, pp. 2–3; David Phlipson, "The Pittsburgh Rabbinical Conference," *CCARY,* 45 (1935): 193–96.

9. The protocols, which first appeared in the *Jewish Reformer* in 1886, were issued in pamphlet form by the Central Conference of American Rabbis as *Proceedings of the Pittsburg Rabbinical Conference* (n.p., 1923). They have recently been reprinted, together with explanatory lectures, in Walter Jacob, ed., *The Changing World of Reform Judaism: The Pittsburgh Platform in Retrospect* (Pittsburgh, 1985). See also Sefton D. Temkin, "The Pittsburgh Platform: A Centenary Assessment," *JRJ,* Fall 1985, pp. 1–12, and Jonathan D. Sarna, "New Light on the Pittsburgh Platform of 1885," *AJH,* 76 (1986/87): 358–68.

10. For the complete text see Appendix.

11. See *JR,* January 1, 1886, pp. 4, 9; January 8, 1886, pp. 1, 10; *AI,* November 27, 1885, p. 4.

12. *AH,* 25 (1885/86): 52–54. In responding to Adler, both Wise and Gustav Gottheil, rabbi of Temple Emanu-El in New York, recognized that Adler's view of Judaism as unchanging law was remarkably similar to that of Moses Mendelssohn. *AI,* December 4, 1885, p. 6; *AH,* 25 (1885/86): 195.

13. *AH,* 25 (1885/86): 50, 98; *PUAHC,* 3 (1886–91): 2005–2006.

14. One of the Pittsburgh participants, Samuel Naumberg of Allegheny City, Pennsylvania, wrote to Henry Berkowitz on April 6, 1886: "The intended establishment of a *pious* seminary is the first consequence [of the conference], for which it has provided the desired occasion." AJA, Box 1071.

15. *AH,* 32 (1887): 69.

16. *AH,* 25 (1885/86): 18; *JR,* February 5, 1886, p. 1; March 26, 1886, p. 8; *Neuzeit,* 26 (1886): 207. However, for years afterward, the Jewish Theological Seminary group would also be referred to as Orthodox. It was only after less compromising traditionalists attacked the Seminary that the border between Conservatism and Orthodoxy, as we know it today, became clearly defined.

17. *JR,* January 8, 1886, p. 10.

18. An example is Rabbi Jacob Voorsanger of San Francisco's Temple Emanu-El whose writings serve to typify the period in Marc Lee Raphael, *Profiles in American Judaism* (San Francisco, 1984), 20–32.

19. The most insightful presentation of Kohler's personality is Adolph S. Oko, "Kaufmann Kohler," *Menorah Journal,* 12 (1926): 513–21. To the secondary sources listed at the end of Sefton D. Temkin's article on Kohler in the *Encyclopedia Judaica* should be added Samuel S. Cohon, "Kaufmann Kohler the Reformer," *Mordecai M. Kaplan Jubilee Volume* (New York, 1953), 137–55; the first three articles in the Kohler Festschrift, *Studies in Jewish Literature* (Berlin, 1913), 1–38; and Ellen Messer, "Franz Boas and Kaufmann Kohler: Anthropology and Reform Judaism," *JSS,* 48 (1986): 127–40.

20. *Der Segen Jacobs mit besonderer Berücksichtigung der alten Versionen und des Midrasch* (Berlin, 1867), iv.

21. The most enlightening piece on Hirsch's personal characteristics and position within

Reform Judaism is Kohler's memorial address before the CCAR in 1923, reprinted in Kohler's posthumous *Studies, Addresses, and Personal Papers* (New York, 1931), 544–54. See also the impressions in *JC,* June 3, 1910, p. 14 and *AZJ,* 76 (1912): 538. For biography the most complete sources are David Einhorn Hirsch, *Rabbi Emil G. Hirsch: The Reform Advocate* (Northbrook, Ill., 1968) and Gerson B. Levi's introduction to Emil G. Hirsch, *My Religion* (New York, 1925), 11–23. Bernard Martin published two studies of Hirsch's thought: "The Religious Philosophy of Emil G. Hirsch," *AJA,* 4 (1952): 66–82 and "The Social Philosophy of Emil G. Hirsch," *AJA,* 6 (1954): 151–65.

22. Hirsch, *My Religion,* 131, 225.

23. *JR,* April 9, 1886, p. 9.

24. *CCARY,* 2 (1892): 126–28; 17(1907): 205–29; Kohler, *Hebrew Union College and Other Addresses* (Cincinnati, 1916), 306.

25. *Ibid.,* 179. Emphasis Kohler's.

26. On Fiske see, for example, Vernon Louis Parrington, *Main Currents in American Thought,* 3 (1930): 203–11.

27. The most extensive Reform Jewish response to Darwinism is Joseph Krauskopf, *Evolution and Judaism* (Cincinnati, 1887). Joseph L. Blau presented a detailed analysis of this work in his "An American-Jewish View of the Evolution Controversy," *HUCA,* 20 (1947): 617–34. A more broadly focused study is Naomi W. Cohen, "The Challenges of Darwinism and Biblical Criticism to American Judaism," *Modern Judaism,* 4 (1984): 121–57. I have also had the benefit of a lengthy and probing University of Chicago seminar paper by Marc Swetlitz entitled "Responses to Darwin and Darwinism in the Reform Jewish Community in Nineteenth Century America" (1985).

28. *Der Zeitgeist* (Milwaukee), 1 (1880): 73. Wise had criticized Darwinism at length in his *The Cosmic God* (Cincinnati, 1876).

29. *Das neue Wissen und Der alte Glaube* (Chicago, 1874), 11.

30. Kohler, *Studies,* 327; *Hebrew Union College and Other Addresses,* 19, 25, 178–79; *CCARY,* 17 (1907): 223.

31. Therefore for humans it remained "an impenetrable mystery." Kaufmann Kohler, *A Living Faith,* ed. Samuel S. Cohon (Cincinnati, 1948), 125.

32. *Der Zeitgeist,* 3 (1882): 204; E. G. Hirsch, *Reformed Judaism* (Chicago, 1883), 8; *idem,* "Why I am a Jew?," Part Two, in *Twenty Discourses* (New York, 1906), 10–13; *idem, My Religion,* 243–62.

33. *CCARY,* 17 (1907): 210, 217–18, 223; *JT,* July 9, 1869, p. 12; Kaufmann Kohler, *Jewish Theology Systematically and Historically Considered* (New York, 1918), 12. In tracing the centrality of prayer in rabbinic Judaism to Persian influence, Kohler followed Joshua Heschel Schorr.

34. Oko, "Kaufmann Kohler," 515; *CCARY,* 3 (1893): 104; 15 (1905): 83; Kohler, *Jewish Theology,* 271, 274; *PUAHC,* 6 (1904–1906): 4993; Hirsch, *Reformed Judaism,* 9; *idem, My Religion,* 114–30.

35. See especially his lecture to the CCAR entitled "The Spiritual Forces of Judaism," *CCARY,* 4/5 (1895): 131–45.

36. *CCARY,* 17 (1907): 221–29; Kohler, *A Living Faith,* 40, 72–73, 76.

37. Hirsch, *My Religion,* 176, 262, 273, 334–37; *idem, Reformed Judaism,* 10–11.

38. Though the book version was published after Hirsch's death, it is clear from Gerson B. Levi's preface that Hirsch had already himself called the lecture series "My Religion."

39. It had originally appeared in German as *Grundriss einer systematischen Theologie des Judentums auf geschichtlicher Grundlage* (Leipzig, 1910). The 1918 English translation was reissued with an introduction by Joseph L. Blau in 1968.

40. David Philipson, *My Life as an American Jew* (Cincinnati, 1941), 69; *CCARY,* 1 (1891): 6. The first five presidents succeeding Wise were all men who had studied under him. They

gained the presidency despite their relatively young age, which ranged from thirty-nine to forty-nine when they assumed office. Non-HUC graduates sometimes felt they suffered discrimination in the CCAR. J. Morgenstern to A. P. Drucker, December 4, 1908, CCAR Records 4/9, AJA.

41. *CCARY*, 1 (1891): 16; 2 (1892): 9.

42. The Jewish presentations were published by the UAHC as *Judaism at the World's Parliament of Religions* (Cincinnati, 1894). See also John H. Barrows, ed., *The World's Parliament of Religions*, 2 (Chicago, 1893): 1461–67.

43. *CCARY*, 13 (1903): 185–338; 15 (1905): 83–110.

44. *CCARY*, 14 (1904): 116, 146–61; *Views on the Synod* (Baltimore, 1905); Levy, *Reform Judaism in America*, 109–30.

45. Lou H. Silberman, "The Union Prayer Book: A Study in Liturgical Development," in Bertram W. Korn, ed., *Retrospect and Prospect: Essays in Commemoration of the Seventy-Fifth Anniversary of the Founding of the Central Conference of American Rabbis 1889–1964* (New York, 1965), 46–61; Eric Lewis Friedland, "The Historical and Theological Development of the Non-Orthodox Prayerbooks in the United States" (Ph.D. dissertation, Brandeis University, 1967), 67, 115–24; and for a revisionist view, Lawrence A. Hoffman, "The Language of Survival in American Reform Liturgy," *CCARJ*, Summer 1977, pp. 87–106.

46. *AH*, 52 (1892/93): 649; Emil G. Hirsch, trans., *Dr. David Einhorn's Book of Prayers for Jewish Congregations* (Chicago, 1896), v.

47. Conservative rabbi Marcus Jastrow also made arbitrary selections for the weekly Torah reading, picking out portions that particularly appealed to him. Moshe Davis, *The Emergence of Conservative Judaism* (Philadelphia, 1963), 143. The 1918 revision of the *UPB* eliminated the special readings and provided a schedule of Torah portions corresponding to the traditional yearly cycle.

48. Quoted in Levy, *Reform Judaism in America*, 39. Levy also presents a detailed comparison between the Sabbath morning service in the Orthodox prayerbook and in the *UPB* (pp. 14–37).

49. *CCARY*, 21 (1911): 106; 24 (1914): 186, 217.

50. CCAR Records, 5/8, AJA; Gustav Gottheil, "The Jewish Reformation," *American Journal of Theology*, 6 (1902): 278. Some Reform synagogues in the larger cities continued to have cantors, but they were perceived as auxiliary to the choir, which was often—at least in part—Gentile. In 1910 the CCAR passed a resolution that "if feasible, Jewish singers be employed in choirs." Henry Berkowitz, *Intimate Glimpses of the Rabbi's Career* (Cincinnati, 1921), 100; *CCARY*, 20 (1910): 156.

51. *CCARY*, 6 (1895): 68; Lloyd P. Gartner, *History of the Jews of Cleveland* (Cleveland, 1978), 155; Morris A. Gutstein, *A Priceless Heritage: The Epic Growth of Nineteenth Century Chicago Jewry* (New York, 1953), 163–64.

52. Uriah Zvi Engelman, "Jewish Statistics in the U.S. Census of Religious Bodies (1850–1936)," *JSS*, 9 (1947): 142. Here is one rabbi's private view: "It is utter stupidity to expect a mass of people to be devout when they do not understand one word of what is being said in prayer on the pulpit. The Hebrew language is all right for the student and the scholar who understands its beauties and can appreciate them, but it must go, it must be dispensed with in the service of an English speaking people. A few important phrases might be retained, such as the Borchu, the Sh'ma, and the three sentences of the K'dusha." Philipson Diary, September 15, 1890, AJA.

53. Gotthard Deutsch to Joseph Stolz, December 9, 1906, CCAR Records, 3/10, AJA. See the 1895 menu in Frank J. Adler, *Roots in a Moving Stream* (Kansas City, Mo., 1972), 101.

54. *CCARY*, 3 (1893): 36; Philipson Diary, January 25, 1888. See also the formula for the reception of proselytes in *CCARY*, 6 (1895): 55–58.

55. *Proceedings of the Pittsburg Rabbinical Conference*, 16.

56. *CCARY*, 3 (1893): 41.

57. *UB,* July 1915, p. 5; Clifton Harby Levy, "The American Rabbi as He Is," *Godey's Magazine,* May 1898, pp. 563–66; CCAR, *Sermons by American Rabbis* (Chicago, 1896).

58. *AH,* 25 (1885/86): 182.

59. *Reform Advocate,* 61 (1921): 393.

60. Max Raisin, "Autobiography," 16, AJA, Biographies File; Philipson Diary, November 1, 1891.

61. *AH,* 22 (1885): 132; *AZJ,* 49 (1885): 497–98.

62. *CCARY,* 14 (1904): 214–15.

63. *Leo N. Levi Memorial Volume* (Chicago, 1907), 63–89, 150–58; Philipson, *My Life,* 96–97; UAHC Records 69/5, AJA; *AH,* 56 (1894/95): 271–75.

64. *PUAHC,* 3 (1886–91): 2647; 9 (1916–20): 8335; *UB,* January 1917, p. 9; October 1917, p. 9; Steven A. Fox, "On the Road to Unity: The Union of American Hebrew Congregations and American Jewry, 1873–1903," *AJA,* 32 (1980): 145–93.

65. Joseph Krauskopf to Geroge Zepin, March 21, 1903, UAHC Records 19/9, AJA.

66. Michael A.Meyer, "A Centennial History," in Samuel E. Karff, ed., *Hebrew Union College-Jewish Institute of Religion at One Hundred Years* (Cincinnati, 1976), 49–83.

67. The best resources for tracing all these activities are the *Proceedings* of the Union and, beginning in 1911, the *Union Bulletin.*

68. Henry Berkowitz, *The Primacy of the Congregation* (Atlanta, 1907), 4; Moses J. Gries, *The Union: Its Past and Its Future* (Atlanta, 1907), 8–10.

69. Jacob R. Marcus, *The American Jewish Woman,* 2 vols. (New York, 1981), 2: 389–92.

70. Hirsch, *My Religion,* 179, 359–71; D. E. Hirsch, *Rabbi Emil G. Hirsch,* 23; Kohler Papers 13/5, AJA; *JR,* February 5, 1886, p. 13.

71. *CCARY,* 22 (1912): 99; 24 (1914): 210; Marcus, *The American Jewish Woman,* 2: 295–98.

72. *Ibid.,* 1: 78–79; 2: 293–94, 380–83; Reva Clar and William M. Kramer, "The Girl Rabbi of the Golden West: The Adventurous Life of Ray Frank in Nevada, California and the Northwest," *Western States Jewish History,* 18 (1986): 99–111, 223–36, 336–51.

73. *Papers of the Jewish Women's Congress* (Philadelphia, 1894).

74. *UB,* March 1915, pp. 3–11.

75. *Israelite,* June 9, 1871, p. 8; *Proceedings of the First Conference of the Hebrew Sabbath-School Union* (Cincinnati, 1889), 6; *Zeitgeist,* 1 (1880): 23.

76. On early Reform Jewish education see Max A. Shapiro, "An Historical Analysis and Evaluation of Jewish Religious School Textbooks Published in the United States, 1817–1903" (Ed.D. dissertation, University of Cincinnati, 1960) and Max Newman, "Basic Principles of American Reform Judaism and their Reflection in the Movement's Program of Religious Education from 1848 to the Present" (Ph.D. dissertation, HUC–JIR, 1963), 7–94.

77. See especially Leonard J. Mervis, "The Social Justice Movement and the American Reform Rabbi," *AJA,* 7 (1955): 171–230.

78. Henry Berkowitz, *Judaism on the Social Question* (New York, 1888), 113, 128. See also Kohler's similar position in *JR,* February 19, 1886, pp. 11–13.

79. Hirsch, *My Religion,* 131–49; Mervis, "The Social Justice Movement," 197–202.

80. Jerrold Goldstein, "Reform Rabbis and the Progressive Movement" (M.A. thesis, University of Minnesota, 1967).

81. Sydney E. Ahlstrom, *Theology in America* (Indianapolis, 1967), 531–86; *idem, A Religious History of the American People* (New Haven, 1972), 785–804; Ronald C. White, Jr. and C. Howard Hopkins, *The Social Gospel* (Philadelphia, 1976), 37; Egal Feldman, "The Social Gospel and the Jews," *AJHQ,* 58 (1968/69): 308–22; Rabbi Horace J. Wolf, reviewing Graham Taylor's *Religion in Social Action,* in *CCARY,* 24 (1914): 367.

82. Richard Hofstadter, *The Age of Reform* (New York, 1956), 150–52; Goldstein, "Reform Rabbis and the Progressive Movement," 54–57.

83. This is not suggest that individual congregations did not enter the social arena. In fact Rabbi Sidney Goldstein of the Free Synagogue in New York maintained that "Almost every congregation in the country is doing some form of social work, more or less directly and systematically." *CCARY,* 24 (1914): 364.

84. *CCARY,* 28 (1918): 101–103. The platform is reprinted in W. Gunther Plaut, *The Growth of Reform Judaism* (New York, 1965), 123–24.

85. Mervis, "The Social Justice Movement," 176, 179; Goldstein, "Reform Rabbis and the Progressive Movement," 92–94.

86. *CCARY,* 21 (1911): 113, 115–17, 193–212. Temple Beth El of Detroit, which adopted the unassigned pew in 1904, was apparently the first synagogue to do so. Robert A. Rockaway, "The Progress of Reform Judaism in Late 19th and Early 20th Century Detroit," *Michigan Jewish History,* January 1974, p. 11.

87. *CCARY,* 23 (1913): 104; 27 (1917): 125; *UB,* November 1919, pp. 3, 6.

88. *CCARY,* 11 (1901): 86.

89. Benny Kraut, "The Ambivalent Relations of American Reform Judaism with Unitarianism in the Last Third of the Nineteenth Century," *Journal of Ecumenical Studies,* 23 (1986): 58–68; *idem,* "A Unitarian Rabbi? The Case of Solomon H. Sonneschein," in Todd M. Endelman, ed., *Jewish Apostasy in the Modern World* (New York, 1987), 272–308; Arthur Mann, "Solomon Schindler: Boston Radical," *New England Quarterly,* 23 (1950): 453–76; *idem, Growth and Achievement: Temple Israel, 1854–1954* (Cambridge, Mass., 1954), 45–83; Solomon Schindler, *Messianic Expectations and Modern Judaism* (Boston, 1886). Schindler later repented and presented a syllabus of his errors. *AH,* 88 (1911): 666–67.

90. Benny Kraut, "Francis Abbot: Perceptions of a Nineteenth Century Religious Radical on Jews and Judaism," in Jacob R. Marcus and Abraham J. Peck, eds., *Studies in the American Jewish Experience,* 1 (Cincinnati, 1981): 90–113; *idem,* "Judaism Triumphant: Isaac Mayer Wise on Unitarianism and Liberal Christianity," *AJS Review,* 7/8 (1982/83): 179–230; Emil G. Hirsch, *Reform Judaism and Unitarianism* (n.p., 1905); *idem, My Religion,* 45–46, 63.

91. Among nineteenth-century rabbis known to have conducted mixed marriages in the United States are Samuel Hirsch, Emil G. Hirsch, Isaac S. Moses, Max Landsberg, and Jacob Voorsanger.

92. James G. Heller, *As Yesterday When It Is Past: A History of Isaac M. Wise Temple* (Cincinnati, 1942), 165; *CCARY,* 22 (1912): 98; 19 (1909): 119, 170, 174–84.

93. On the Sunday service issue in Reform Judaism see Sidney L. Regner, "The Rise and Decline of the Sunday Service," *JRJ,* Fall 1980, pp. 30–38, and the articles by Kerry M. Olitzky in *AJA,* 34 (1982): 75–88; *JRJ,* Summer 1984, pp. 66–71; and *AJH,* 74 (1984/85): 356–68.

94. *Reform Advocate,* 41 (1911): 452.

95. *Proceedings of the Pittsburg Rabbinical Conference,* 38.

96. *CCARY,* 15 (1905): 114; 16 (1906): 90; 24 (1914): 88. Even Mordecai Kaplan, professor at the Conservative Jewish Theological Seminary, told a colleague in 1918 that "if Judaism is to survive in the diaspora, it must abandon its uncompromising attitude toward the Sabbath and by an act of will adopt Sunday as the Seventh Day." Cited in Mel Scult, "Halakhah and Authority in the Early Kaplan," in Ronald Brauner, ed., *Jewish Civilization: Essays and Studies,* 2 (Philadelphia, 1981): 105. I have also found an instance of an avowedly Orthodox congregation in a small Ohio town that held its weekly service "on the Christian Sabbath because of business on Saturday." *Daily Signal,* Middletown, Ohio, May 1, 1902.

97. Joseph Krauskopf, *The Service-Ritual* (Philadelphia, 1888); J. Leonard Levy, *A Book of Prayer* (2d edn., Pittsburgh, 1902); *The Union Prayer-Book for Jewish Worship: Morning Services* (New York, 1907). The CCAR version was never fully accepted by the Conference itself. Its six morning services were supposedly one for each of the weekdays. *CCARY,* 16 (1906): 116–22; 23 (1913): 93–94.

98. *CCARY,* 13 (1903): 84, 86.

99. There is some disagreement as to when Wise's congregation first instituted the late Friday

evening service. I have followed Aryeh Rubinstein, "Reshitah shel tenuat ha-reformah be-yahadut artsot ha-berit ve-ha-pulmus sevivah ba-shanim 1840–1869" (Ph.D. dissertation, Hebrew University, 1973), 261–62.

100. *CCARY*, 14 (1904): 119–20. A detailed analysis of the CCAR discussion is in Levy, *Reform Judaism in America*, 92–108.

101. *Studies in Jewish Literature Issued in Honor of Professor Kaufmann Kohler* (Berlin, 1913), 25–26; Kohler, *Studies*, 520–21; *idem, A Living Faith*, 19–30.

102. *Ibid.*, 35–39. Emphasis Kohler's.

103. *PUAHC*, 5 (1898–1903): 4529; 6 (1903–1907): 5833; *AJYB*, 31 (1929): 109; Adler, *Roots in a Moving Stream*, 82, 86.

104. *CCARY*, 8 (1898): xii; 18 (1908): 144; Philipson Diary, January 2, 1888. *Cf.* Rabbi Joseph Silverman in *JC*, February 20, 1903, p. 18.

105. Joseph J. Krauskopf, "Native against Foreigner," Lecture VI in his *10 Lectures* (Cincinnati, 1890).

106. However, Rabbi Joseph Stolz found Reform support of the Seminary scandalous. *CCARY*, 12 (1902): 234.

107. CCAR Records 2/12, AJA; *CCARY*, 14 (1904): 33–34; 15 (1905): 198–99; Max Raisin, "Autobiography," 16.

108. *AH*, 96 (1914/15): 391–92; *CCARY*, 14 (1904): 68.

109. *CCARY*, 2 (1892): 48–56; 12 (1902): 236.

110. Philipson, *My Life*, 123; *CCARY*, 15 (1905): 172.

111. Naomi Wiener Cohen, "The Reaction of Reform Judaism in America to Political Zionism (1897–1922)," *PAJHS*, 40 (1950/51): 361–94; David Polish, *Renew Our Days: The Zionist Issue in Reform Judaism* (Jerusalem, 1976), 48–114.

112. *CCARY*, 8 (1898): xli; 28 (1918): 133–34; *PUAHC*, 5 (1898–1903): 4002; 9 (1916–20): 8520–21.

113. The following is based on my "American Reform Judaism and Zionism: Early Efforts at Ideological Rapproachement," *Studies in Zionism*, 7 (Spring 1983): 49–64. Hebrew version in *Ha-Tsiyonut*, 9 (1984): 95–110. Full documentation is given in that article.

114. *PAJHS*, 45 (1955/56): 122.

115. J. R. Morse to Charles Shohl, December 4, 1918, UAHC Records 43/1, AJA.

116. Martin P. Beifeld, "Joseph Krauskopf and Zionism: Partners in Change," *AJH*, 75 (1985/86): 48–60.

117. Hirsch, *My Religion*, 290.

118. *CCARY*, 29 (1919): 287.

119. *Der Zeitgeist*, 1 (1880): 104.

120. Cited in Levy, *Reform Judaism in America*, 69.

121. Gartner, *The Jews of Cleveland*, 160. *Cf.* Rabbi Samuel Schulman in *CCARY*, 22 (1912): 245.

122. *UB*, January 1917, p. 11.

123. *CCARY*, 7 (1897): 128.

124. Kohler, *A Living Faith*, 16.

Chapter 8

1. Sydney E. Ahlstrom, *A Religious History of the American People* (New Haven, 1972), 895–931; Robert T. Handy, *A History of the Churches in the United States and Canada* (Oxford, 1976), 378–89.

2. Uriah Zevi Engelman, "The Jewish Synagogue in the United States," *The American Journal of Sociology*, 41 (1935/36): 50–51.

3. *CCARY*, 32 (1922): 246; 33 (1923): 103, 286.

4. On Christian missionaries see the correspondence in the CCAR Records 11/21, AJA, and

on the racial advisor I. Spectorsky to Central Conference of American Rabbis, December 16, 1918, *ibid.,* 11/16.

5. *CCARY,* 29 (1919): 224–48; 32 (1922): 178–82; 34 (1924): 308–11; *PUAHC,* 53rd Annual Report (1927): 238. For analogous lay views see *Union Tidings,* November 1924, pp. 6–8.

6. *CCARY,* 52 (1942): 251.

7. Emanuel Gamoran, *A Survey of 125 Religious Schools Affiliated with the Union of American Hebrew Congregations* (Cincinnati, 1925).

8. Richard C. Hertz, *The Education of the Jewish Child: A Study of 200 Reform Jewish Religious Schools* (New York, 1953).

9. Though by no means everywhere implemented, the 1937 UAHC curriculum called for devoting about one-third of class time to Hebrew beginning with the second grade. Emanuel Gamoran, *A Curriculum for the Jewish Religious School* (Cincinnati, 1937). Totally unrealistic was Gamoran's first proposed curriculum, which, on the basis of two sessions per week, called for the translation of selections from Genesis as early as the fourth grade. *CCARY,* 33 (1923): 328–39.

10. On Gamoran see Robert J. Wechman, "Emanuel Gamoran: Pioneer in Jewish Religious Education" (Ph.D. dissertation, Syracuse University, 1970); Samuel Grand and Mamie G. Gamoran, eds., *Emanuel Gamoran: His Life and His Work* (New York, 1979); and Kerry M. Olitzky, "A History of Reform Jewish Education During Emanuel's Gamoran's Tenure as Educational Director of the Commission on Jewish Education of the Union of American Hebrew Congregations 1923–1958" (DHL dissertation, HUC–JIR, 1984).

11. Leon Fram, "The Conference and Jewish Religious Education," in Bertram Wallace Korn, ed., *Retrospect and Prospect: Essays in Commemoration of the Seventy-Fifth Anniversary of the Founding of the Central Conference of American Rabbis 1889–1964* (New York, 1965), 181–85.

12. Emanuel Gamoran, *Changing Conceptions in Jewish Education* (New York, 1924).

13. *Liberal Judaism,* June 1944, p. 38; *Catalog of Pupils' Text Books and Teachers' Manuals* (Cincinnati, 1928), 5.

14. *CCARY,* 33 (1923): 343; 34 (1924): 363–64; 36 (1926): 322–36.

15. Grand and Gamoran, eds., *Emanuel Gamoran,* 98–109.

16. *CCARY,* 40 (1930): 384; *Liberal Judaism,* June 1944, p. 41; July 1944, p. 49; *PUAHC,* 61st Annual Report (1935): 67, 72–74.

17. The following accounts of Hebrew Union College and the Jewish Institute of Religion are drawn from, and documented in, my "A Centennial History," in Samuel E. Karff, ed., *Hebrew Union College–Jewish Institute of Religion at One Hundred Years* (Cincinnati, 1976), 85–169.

18. On Wise see especially Melvin I. Urofsky, *A Voice That Spoke for Justice: The Life and Times of Stephen S. Wise* (Albany, 1982).

19. Jacob D. Schwarz, *The Synagogue in Modern Jewish Life* (Cincinnati, 1939), 10–11, 20–21; *CCARY,* 50 (1940): 319–21.

20. *CCARY,* 30 (1920): 276; 35 (1925): 291–92; Milton Richman, "A Study of Three American Reform Temples Between the Two World Wars" (Rabbinical thesis, HUC–JIR, 1952), 12, 31; Fred Rosenbaum, *Architects of Reform: Congregational and Community Leadership— Emanu-El of San Francisco, 1849–1980* (Berkeley, 1980), 89–101.

21. *CCARY,* 34 (1924): 140; 45 (1935): 135–48, 214, 229, 295–99; 46 (1936): 146–52.

22. *PUAHC,* 10 (1921–25): 9620, 9767–88. In an interview at the time, the newly elected chairman of the Union's Executive Board, Ludwig Vogelstein, said that the UAHC was "a union of religious bodies and that the work of these bodies is for the advancement of the Jewish religion. Just that, and nothing more." *Union Tidings,* March 1925, p. 1.

23. *CCARY,* 34 (1924): 154; 35 (1925): 225–27; 41 (1931): 58–59; 44 (1934): 52.

24. *PUAHC,* 10 (1921–25): 9300–9308; 57th Annual Report (1931): 216; *The Synagogue: Its Relation to Modern Thought and Life. Papers Delivered at the 32nd Council, Union of American*

Hebrew Congregations (Philadelphia, 1931), 72–82; *CCARY,* 42 (1932): 255; 43 (1933): 108. When the national conventions of the Reform and Conservative rabbinical associations met in joint session in 1943, the topic of their discussion, not surprisingly, was "The Centrality of the Synagogue in American Jewish Life and Modes of Cooperation to the Attainment of that End." *CCARY,* 53 (1943): 70.

25. *Menorah Journal,* 11 (1925): 101–13, 425–47, 544–59; 12 (1926): 1–21.

26. Silver's article appeared in four installments in the *Jewish Tribune,* July 23, July 30, August 6, and August 13, 1926. His congregation also printed it as a pamphlet together with a documentation of the history of its publication. Silver had himself been a member of the Board of the Inter-Collegiate Menorah Association, but now he resigned from it.

27. *AJYB,* 31 (1929): 119; *CCARY,* 34 (1924): 275; David Philipson, *My Life as an American Jew* (Cincinnati, 1941), 377–78; *Reform Judaism in the Large Cities: A Survey* (Cincinnati, 1931), 10, 47–48. A convenient table of UAHC membership is contained in Marc Lee Raphael, *Profiles in American Judaism: The Reform, Conservative, Orthodox, and Reconstructionist Traditions in Historical Perspective* (San Francisco, 1984), 197–98. In 1926 the UAHC was larger than the Conservative United Synagogue of America by 280 to 211 congregations. The Union of Orthodox Jewish Congregations claimed 200 affiliates, but that represents only a small percentage of actual Orthodox congregations, many of which were independent, small, and informal. *AJYB,* 29 (1927): 27. In 1940, when the UAHC had 302 congregations on its roster, the United Synagogue had 275, of which 80 were in metropolitan New York City. *CCARY,* 50 (1940): 324–25.

28. Sisterhood activities for the period appear in the *Proceedings of the National Federation of Temple Sisterhoods* and, beginning in September–October 1934, in the newsletter *Topics and Trends.* See also Jenna Weissman Joselitt, "The Special Sphere of the Middle-Class American Jewish Woman: The Synagogue Sisterhood, 1890–1940," in Jack Wertheimer, ed., *The American Synagogue: A Sanctuary Transformed* (Cambridge and New York, 1987), 206–30.

29. Brotherhood activities for the period appear in the *Proceedings of the National Federation of Temple Brotherhoods* and, from November 1926, in *Temple Brotherhood Monthly* (later called *The Jewish Layman*). The Silver citation is in the issue of December 1926. See also *Reform Judaism in the Large Cities,* 48; *The Union of American Hebrew Congregations: What It Is . . . What It Does . . . What It Means to You . . .* (Cincinnati, 1938).

30. UAHC, *Catalog of Publications for Jewish Youth* (Cincinnati, 1937); *PUAHC,* 65th Annual Report (1939): 30–33.

31. UAHC, *Jewish Students: A Survey Dealing with the Religious, Educational, Social and Fraternal Activities among Jewish Students at Universities and Colleges* (Cincinnati, 1915); *UB,* November 1922, pp. 12–13; *CCARY,* 33 (1923): 163–98; 34 (1924): 45, 345–51; 40 (1930): 370–71, 411.

32. Ronald B. Sobel, "A History of New York's Temple Emanu-El: The Second Half Century" (Ph.D. dissertation, New York University, 1980), 385–86, 439; *Synagogue Service Bulletin,* October 1933, pp. 12–14; *CCARY,* 41 (1931): 147, 188–89; Samuel H. Goldenson (CCAR Vice President) to congregational presidents, September 22, 1931, CCAR Records, 14/29, AJA; Richman, "A Study of Three American Reform Temples," 56–57, 76.

33. Meyer, "A Centennial History," 119–20; *CCARY,* 42 (1932): 36–37; 43 (1933): 30–31; *PUAHC,* 61st Annual Report (1935): 18; 65th Annual Report (1939): 84.

34. Robert P. Goldman transcript, Biographies File, AJA.

35. *PUAHC,* 67th Annual Report (1941): 188–202. *Cf.* the earlier critiques by Rabbi Morton Berman and B. Benedict Glazer in *CCARY,* 41 (1931): 404–13; and 50 (1940): 324–30.

36. *PUAHC,* 65th Annual Report (1939): 37–39; 68th–70th Annual Reports (1943): 16–19, 27, 72, 98.

37. Edward Israel, arguably the most active advocate of social justice in American Reform Judaism during the interwar years, belies the simplistic conclusion that social justice work was that Reform activity necessarily chosen by rabbis uncomfortable with theology and unwilling to

espouse Zionism. Israel was both a theist with an appreciation for mysticism and an active Zionist. Leonard J. Mervis, "The Social Justice Movement and the American Reform Rabbi," *AJA,* 7 (1955): 217–20.

38. *CCARY,* 31 (1921): 44; 41 (1931): 87.

39. *CCARY,* 32 (1922): 64–67; 37 (1927): 40–43; 42 (1932): 95–96.

40. *CCARY,* 38 (1928): 81–86.

41. *CCARY,* 43 (1933): 59–60; 52 (1942): 99–101. For an early Reform Jewish condemnation of segregation and a plea for equal access to all educational and economic opportunities see Joseph Krauskopf, "The American Negro," *Our Pulpit,* April 16, 1916, pp. 145–54.

42. *CCARY,* 42 (1932): 97–98.

43. Ahlstrom, *A Religious History,* 922; *Proceedings of the Rabbinical Assembly of America,* 4 (1930–32): 359; 5 (1933–38): 156–64. A 1937 survey showed that Conservative rabbis were significantly more inclined to socialism than were their Reform colleagues while Orthodox rabbis remained staunch defenders of capitalism. See Joseph Zeitlin, *Disciples of the Wise: The Religious and Social Opinions of American Rabbis* (New York, 1945), 107–30.

44. Philipson Diary, November 17, 1932 AJA.

45. Vogelstein to Goldman, December 5, 1932, Goldman to Vogelstein, November 25, 1932, Goldman Papers, 7/4, AJA; News Release, June 30, 1933, *ibid.,* 15/3.

46. *PUAHC,* 10 (1921–25): 9809; *Union Tidings,* February 1925, pp. 4–5; *Conference on Perpetuation of Judaism* [at] *30th Council, Union of American Hebrew Congregations* (Cleveland, 1927), 47; *PUAHC,* 55th Annual Report (1929): 10–11, 19, 171.

47. *Some Aspects of Industrial Relations: Proceedings of a Seminar* (Cincinnati, 1931); CCAR Records, 16/16, 16/18, AJA; *PUAHC,* 62nd Annual Report (1936): 10–11, 17; *CCARY,* 46 (1936): 20, 81–85.

48. Mervis, "The Social Justice Movement," 195–96, 214; Frank J. Adler, *Roots in a Moving Stream* (Kansas City, Mo., 1972), 165–71; Urofsky, *A Voice That Spoke for Justice,* 68–69; James G. Heller, *As Yesterday When It Is Past* (Cincinnati, 1942), 197.

49. *CCARY,* 36 (1926): 102–105.

50. During the debate Frisch argued for dissemination of birth control information through social workers in order to reach "those who are breeding who oughtn't to breed." Transcript of 1926 convention, CCAR Records, 34, AJA.

51. *CCARY,* 37 (1927): 369–84; 39 (1929): 85–86; 40 (1930): 78; Mervis, "The Social Justice Movement," 183.

52. *CCARY,* 27 (1917): 173–76.

53. *PUAHC,* 10 (1921–25): 9816; 61st Annual Report (1935): 124.

54. Mervis, "The Social Justice Movement," 189; *CCARY,* 34 (1924): 91–93; 38 (1928): 85–86; 45 (1935): 60–76; 46 (1936): 62–74.

55. *CCARY,* 49 (1939): 147–54; 50 (1940): 124–33; 51 (1941): 130–32; 52 (1942): 106. The Orthodox position on religiously motivated Jewish conscientious objection, expressed in the Synagogue Council of America, was to repudiate the idea completely. During the war individual Reform rabbis and the CCAR collectively also spoke out on behalf of Japanese-Americans who had been transferred inland to detention camps from the West Coast. Rosenbaum, *Architects of Reform,* 129; *CCARY,* 54 (1944): 96.

56. The CCAR presidential addresses, beginning in 1933, reflect the concern over German Jewry. For Union and Conference actions see *PUAHC,* 59th Annual Report (1933): 143–44; 61st Annual Report (1935): 121–23; 68th–70th Annual Report (1943): 267–68; *CCARY,* 47 (1937): 165–66; 48 (1938): 156–57; 49 (1939): 213–14; 51 (1941): 184–85; 52 (1942): 105; 53 (1943): 54–55, 71–72.

57. Michael A. Meyer, "The Refugee Scholars Project of the Hebrew Union College," in Bertram Wallace Korn, ed., *A Bicentennial Festschrift for Jacob Rader Marcus* (Waltham, Mass., 1976), 359–75.

58. *CCARY,* 22 (1912): 229, 233–36, 253–55, 300–21; 29 (1919): 230.

59. Rebecca Trachtenberg Alpert, "From Jewish Science to Rabbinical Counseling: The Evaluation of the Relationship between Religion and Health by the American Reform Rabbinate, 1916–1954" (Ph.D. dissertation, Temple University, 1978).

60. *CCARY,* 35 (1925): 152, 157–67, 237; 36 (1926): 312–14; 37 (1927): 165–93, 352–68.

61. *CCARY,* 38 (1928): 101–10; Louis Witt, *Judaism and Healing* (Cincinnati, [1947]); Philipson, *My Life,* 342.

62. *CCARY,* 41 (1931): 353–54, 357–60; Samuel S. Cohon, *What We Jews Believe* (Cincinnati, 1931), 142–52; Milford Stern, "Alleged Substitutes for Religion," in *The Synagogue: Its Relation to Modern Thought and Life,* 32–34.

63. Rabbi Louis Newman in San Francisco fulminated against Freud as a source of "moral laxity." Abraham Cronbach knew the psychological literature well but devoted his scholarship to describing and criticizing what it had to say about Jewish texts and rituals. Rosenbaum, *Architects of Reform,* 101; *HUCA,* 8/9 (1931/32): 605–740; 19 (1945/46): 205–73.

64. James G. Heller, "Two Psychologists Versus Religion," in *Judaism and the Modern World: Papers Delivered at the 31st Council, Union of American Hebrew Congregations* (San Francisco, 1929), 62–70.

65. *CCARY,* 51 (1941): 256–74, 283–88; Joshua Loth Liebman, "Morality and Immorality" (Recording of speech delivered at Hebrew Union College in 1948, Hebrew Union College Library). On Liebman see Alpert, "From Jewish Science to Rabbinical Counseling," 118–54; Arthur Mann, *Growth and Achievement: Temple Israel, 1854–1954* (Cambridge, Mass., 1954), 100–14; Donald Meyer, *The Positive Thinkers* (New York, 1965), 327–30.

66. *CCARY,* 35 (1925): 217–18; 40 (1930): 163, 304–57; 41 (1931): 148, 151–60; 42 (1932): 176–78. For the humanist influence on Protestants, see Handy, *A History of the Churches in the United States and Canada,* 382.

67. The following draws upon my documented article, "Samuel S. Cohon: Reformer of Reform Judaism," *Judaism,* 15 (1966): 319–28. On Cohon and on the particular issues of chosenness and mission among Reform rabbis of this period see also Arnold M. Eisen, *The Chosen People in America: A Study of Jewish Religious Ideology* (Bloomington, Ind., 1983), 53–72.

68. The history of the Columbus Platform can be followed in detail in the Samuel S. Cohon Papers, 2/6–2/7, and in the Samuel Schulman Papers 7/9–7/11, AJA. A Schulman letter on the subject was printed in *CCARJ,* Summer 1973, pp. 51–54. The public record is in *CCARY,* 46 (1936): 88–107; 47 (1937): 94–114. A condensed version of the Schulman text, printed only after its author exercised extreme pressure, is in *CCARY,* 47 (1937): 418–26. The ordeal came close to breaking Cohon physically. *Day Book of Service at the Altar* (Los Angeles, 1978), 192–93. Stephen S. Wise had nominated Schulman as chairman, apparently put up to it by Felix Levy in the expectation that, as the author, Schulman would be a less troublesome anti-Zionist than as a critical member of the committee.

69. See text in the Appendix.

70. *CCARY,* 38 (1928): 246–70. Cohon's lecture is reprinted in Joseph L. Blau, ed., *Reform Judaism: A Historical Perspective* (New York, 1973), 257–84.

71. *Day Book of Service,* 154–55.

72. *CCARY,* 38 (1928): 277; 30 (1920): 94.

73. *CCARY,* 43 (1933): 87–88; CCAR Records, 15/4, AJA.

74. *CCARY,* 43 (1933): 89; 44 (1934): 66.

75. *CCARY,* 40 (1930): 251–59; 43 (1933): 92.

76. *CCARY,* 40 (1930): 101–108; 41 (1931): 102; *AJYB,* 33 (1931): 45; *Union Hymnal* (Cincinnati, 1932), 383–88. Later the newly revised *UPB* would simply print the Aramaic words *kol nidre* and in parentheses: "The Kol Nidre Chant."

77. For details see Eric Friedland, "The Historical and Theological Development of the Non-Orthodox Prayerbooks in the United States" (Ph.D. dissertation, Brandeis University, 1967), 127–37.

78. *AJYB,* 44 (1942): 106–107; Louis I. Newman, *A New Reform Judaism and the New Union Prayer Book: A Personal Statement* (n.p., 1943); Israel Bettan's Foreword to Jacob D. Schwarz, *Ceremonies in Modern Jewish Life* (Cincinnati, 1937), v.

79. Arthur L. Reinhart, *The Voice of the Jewish Laity: A Survey of the Jewish Layman's Religious Attitudes and Practices* (Cincinnati, 1928); *Reform Judaism in the Large Cities.* Since respondents to questionnaires tend to be those most interested in the subject, the survey results must be taken as maximal.

80. *CCARY,* 36 (1926): 314; *Conference on Perpetuation of Judaism* [*Held at*] *Thirtieth Council, Union of American Hebrew Congregations* (Cleveland, 1927), 34.

81. *CCARY,* 45 (1935): 23–24; 46 (1936): 163; *PUAHC,* 63rd Annual Report (1937): 153–54.

82. *CCARY,* 49 (1939): 185–89; 55 (1945): 142–47; *The Synagogue,* September 1940, pp. 15, 19.

83. Originally appearing in *Temple Brotherhood Monthly,* 1928–29, Idelsohn's articles were reprinted as *The Ceremonies of Judaism* (Cincinnati, 1929).

84. *CCARY,* 47 (1937): 183–86.

85. On Freehof see the studies of his life and works in Walter Jacob *et al.,* eds., *Essays in Honor of Solomon B. Freehof* (Pittsburgh, 1964).

86. *CCARY,* 51 (1941): 289–98.

87. Citations from pp. 4, 7, emphasis Freehof's. See also *CCARY,* 56 (1946): 276–317.

88. *CCARY,* 52 (1942): 276–96, 312–25. Reprinted in Blau, ed., *Reform Judaism,* 104–25.

89. Published treatments of Reform Judaism and Zionism in the interwar period include Irving Levitas, "Reform Jews and Zionism—1919–1921," *AJA,* 14 (1962): 3–19; Arthur J. Lelyveld, "The Conference View of the Position of the Jew in the Modern World," in Korn, ed., *Retrospect and Prospect,* 139–67; David Polish, *Renew Our Days: The Zionist Issue in Reform Judaism* (Jerusalem, 1976), 115–235; Stuart E. Knee, "From Controversy to Conversion: Liberal Judaism in America and the Zionist Movement, 1917–1941," *YIVO,* 17 (1978): 260–89; Howard R. Greenstein, *Turning Point: Zionism and Reform Judaism* (Chico, Calif., 1981); and Cyrus Arfa, *Reforming Reform Judaism: Zionism and the Reform Rabbinate 1885–1948* (Tel-Aviv, 1985).

90. *CCARY,* 30 (1920): 141–42, 154.

91. *CCARY,* 31 (1921): 85–88; 32 (1922): 70; 34 (1924): 106; 40 (1930): 22–25, 156; 41 (1931): 310.

92. Transcript of 1930 convention, CCAR Records, 36; *CCARY,* 40 (1930): 98, 106; 41 (1931): 102–104; David Philipson, *My Life* (Cincinnati, 1941), 423–24.

93. The Conservative movement, while proportionately more Zionist than Reform, was headed by Cyrus Adler, an opponent of political Zionism. The ultra-Orthodox Agudat Israel was opposed to political Zionism on traditional religious grounds.

94. CCAR Records, 4/7; Greenstein, *Turning Point,* 24–25, 140.

95. Louis Wolsey to Samuel Goldenson, May 31, 1935, CCAR Records, 17/7; *CCARY,* 45 (1935): 102–103, 110–12.

96. The speeches are reprinted in Blau, ed., *Reform Judaism,* 393–436. On account of illness Schulman was unable to be present at the convention and his paper was read for him.

97. *CCARY,* 45 (1935): 310–11. It is ironic that non-Zionists were among the most ardent advocates of establishing Progressive Judaism in Palestine while Zionists like Silver and Wise did not promote it at all.

98. On Silver see especially Harold P. Manson, "Abba Hillel Silver—An Appreciation," in Daniel Jeremy Silver, ed., *In the Time of Harvest: Essays in Honor of Abba Hillel Silver on the Occasion of His 70th Birthday* (New York, 1963), 1–27; Leon I. Feuer, "Abba Hillel Silver: A Personal Memoir," *AJA,* 19 (1967): 107–26; and Solomon B. Freehof, "Recollections of Abba Hillel Silver," in Herbert Weiner, ed., *Therefore Choose Life: Selected Sermons, Addresses, and Writings of Abba Hillel Silver,* 1 (Cleveland, 1967): xi–xix.

99. *CCARY,* 45 (1935): 342.

100. *Reform Judaism in the Large Cities,* 13.

101. Philipson, *My Life,* 361; *PUAHC,* 57th Annual Report (1931): 190–91.

102. *PUAHC,* 63rd Annual Report (1937): 158. This Palestine resolution goes considerably beyond its predecessor of two years earlier: *PUAHC,* 61st Annual Report (1935): 123.

103. Philipson Diary, July 3, 1936.

104. *CCARY,* 52 (1942): 169–82; Samuel S. Cohon to James G. Heller, May 3, 1942, Cohon Papers, 2/3.

105. Elmer Berger, *Memoirs of an Anti-Zionist Jew* (Beirut, 1978), 8.

106. For the formation of the American Council for Judaism I have drawn especially upon the ACJ Records, 2/1, 5/4, the Cohon Papers, 2/3, and the Louis Wolsey Papers, 4/8–4/10, AJA. See also the detailed accounts, drawing in part on the same and in part on different archival collections, in Greenstein, *Turning Point* 33–50; David Polish, "The Changing and the Constant in the Reform Rabbinate," *AJA,* 35 (1983): 286–98; Menahem Kaufman, *Lo-tsiyonim be-amerikah be-ma'avak al ha-medinah* (Jerusalem, 1984), 69–73; and Thomas A. Kolsky, "Jews Against Zionism: The American Council for Judaism, 1942–1948" (Ph.D. dissertation, George Washington University, 1986), 100–226.

107. Only two out of seven did.

108. Berger, *Memoirs,* 15–16; Rosenbaum, *Architects of Reform,* 136–39.

109. *CCARY,* 53 (1943): 91–99; 183–94.

110. *Liberal Judaism,* September 1943, pp. 4–7, 33–43; Adolph Rosenberg *et al., Statement of the Union of American Hebrew Congregations on the American Jewish Conference* (n.p., 1945); *CCARY,* 54 (1944): 145–46; *PUAHC,* 68th–70th Annual Reports (1943): 107–108, 110–11, 116–18; 71st–73rd Annual Reports (1947): 19–20, 26–31, 45–46, 90; Abraham Shusterman to Samuel S. Cohon, November 8 and 17, 1943, Lou H. Silberman to Cohon, December 2, 1943, Cohon Papers, 2/3; Maurice N. Eisendrath, *Can Faith Survive?* (New York, 1964), 276–82; Greenstein, *Turning Point,* 101–25.

111. For the Beth Israel revolt I used the Houston, Texas, Congregation Beth Israel Collection, AJA. See also the more detailed account in Greenstein, *Turning Point,* 51–71.

112. *Liberal Judaism,* April 1944, pp. 20–25, 54–58; *Opinion,* February 1944, p. 5.

113. *Liberal Judaism,* September 1943, p. 38; *Reconstructionist,* October 16, 1942, pp. 9, 15, 17.

114. *CCARY,* 54 (1944): 171. Heller felt similarly. James G. Heller, *Reform Judaism and Zionism* (Cincinnati, 1944), 6–7. The rage Freehof describes was evident at the same CCAR convention when, in the Conference sermon, Jacob J. Weinstein compared anti-Zionism to the biblical rebellion of Korah. *CCARY,* 54 (1944): 174–81.

Chapter 9

1. B. Breslauer *et al.,* to I. Mattuck, June 11, 1914, WUPJ Correspondence File, AJA. For much of the following see also Michael S. Datz, "Poor Cousin or Parent Body? The World Union for Progressive Judaism During Its First 50 Years, 1926–1976" (Rabbinical thesis, HUC–JIR, Cincinnati, 1987).

2. Wise to Montagu, April 2, 1926, Stephen S. Wise Collection, 4/4, AJA.

3. *International Conference of Liberal Jews* (London, 1926), 109.

4. "Die Botschaft des liberalen Judentums an den Juden von Heute," *First Conference of the World Union for Progressive Judaism* (Berlin, 1928), 60–68, 148–50.

5. *CCARY,* 37 (1927): 17–40; *First Conference,* 95; Julian Morgenstern to Solomon B. Freehof, December 10, 1930, AJA, Box 1554, File F.

6. *International Conference,* 43–47; *First Conference,* 21–30; Max Dienemann, *Liberales Judentum* (Berlin, 1935), 39–40; Caesar Seligmann, *Erinnerungen* (Frankfurt a/M, 1975), 159; Max P. Birnbaum, *Staat und Synagoge 1918–1938* (Tübingen, 1981), 124–27, 287.

7. Bruno Italiener, ed., *Festschrift zum hundertzwanzigjährigen Bestehen des Israelitischen*

Tempels in Hamburg 1817–1937 (Hamburg, 1937), 13; *Mitteilungen der Jüdischen Reformgemeinde zu Berlin,* April 1, 1920, January 1, 1921; Wolfgang Hamburger, "Aus alten Blättern der Jüdischen Reformgemeinde zu Berlin," *TE,* 27 (May 1969): 542–51; Gebetbuch [der Jüdischen Reform-Gemeinde zu Berlin] (Berlin, 193?).

8. *Gebetbuch für das ganze Jahr* (Frankfurt a/M, 1929). The preface is translated in Jakob J. Petuchowski, *Prayerbook Reform in Europe* (New York, 1968), 206–13.

9. *First Bulletin of the World Union for Progressive Judaism,* December 1929, pp. 6–7. On women and religious reform in Germany see Marion Kaplan, *The Jewish Feminist Movement in Germany* (Westport, Conn., 1979), 162–64. Mainly on account of their coalition with the Orthodox, the Zionists opposed mixed seating.

10. *Second Conference of the World Union for Progressive Judaism* (London, 1930), 169–73.

11. Wolfgang Hamburger, "The Reactions of Reform Jews to the Nazi Rule," in Herbert A. Strauss and Kurt R. Grossman, eds., *Gegenwart im Rückblick: Festgabe für die Jüdische Gemeinde zu Berlin 25 Jahre nach dem Neubeginn* (Heidelberg, 1970), 150–64; Heinrich Stern, *Ernst Machen! Ein Wort an die religiös-liberalen Juden* (Berlin, 1935).

12. Joachim Prinz, "A Rabbi under the Hitler Regime," and Max Nussbaum, "Ministry under Stress: A Rabbi's Recollections of Nazi Berlin 1935–1940," both in Strauss and Grossmann, eds., *Gegenwart im Rückblick,* 231–47.

13. *First Conference,* 38–41.

14. *International Conference,* 59–65; *First Conference,* 30–37; *Second Conference,* 174–79; Michael Leigh, "Reform Judaism in Britain (1840–1970)," in Dow Marmur, ed., *Reform Judaism: Essays on Reform Judaism in Britain* (Oxford, 1973), 41–43; Stephen Sharot, *Judaism: A Sociology* (New York, 1976), 156, 160; *idem,* "Reform and Liberal Judaism in London: 1840–1940," *JSS,* 46 (1979): 221–23.

15. Celia S. Heller, *On the Edge of Destruction: Jews of Poland between the Two World Wars* (New York, 1977), 234–35; Zevi Karl, "The Religious Life of the Jews of Lvov" [Hebrew], in N. M. Gelber, ed., *Lvov,* volume 4.1 of *Entsiklopedyah shel galuyot* (Jerusalem and Tel-Aviv, 1956), 441–50; *First Conference,* 47–51.

16. *Ibid.,* 103; *Second Conference,* 138, 141, 147; Joseph Regensburg, "On Liberal Judaism and Liberal Nationalism" [Hebrew], *Galim,* March 16, 1930. At various times the World Union also had contact with progressively inclined Jews in other countries in the East. During the thirties and forties visitors from Vienna came to its conferences. Montagu corresponded with interested persons or small groups in Czechoslovakia and Hungary. But no World Union constituent was ever formed in eastern Europe.

17. Dan Michman, "The Beginnings of the Liberal (Reform) Jewish Community in Holland" [Hebrew], *Yahadut Zemanenu,* 3 (1986): 75–91; *idem,* "The Public Furor Surrounding the Beginning of the Liberal Jewish Community in the Netherlands (1929–1931)" [Hebrew], *Proceedings of the Ninth World Congress of Jewish Studies,* Division B, Vol. 2 (Jerusalem, 1986): 41–48; WUPJ, *Report of the Fourth Conference* (Holland, 1937), 25–27.

18. Kurt Wilhelm, "The Influence of German Jewry on Jewish Communities in Scandinavia," *LBIYB,* 3 (1958): 325–31; Petuchowski, *Prayerbook Reform in Europe,* 153–55; *International Conference,* 68–70; *First Conference,* 43–46.

19. *International Conference,* 66–67; *First Conference,* 41–43; Hugo Gryn, "Als Rabbiner in Indien," *TE,* 4 (December 1958): 57–60; *Ammi,* 6 (Shavuot 1977): 3–4.

20. Temple Israel, *Facts and Data Regarding the First Jewish Reform Congregation in South Africa* (Johannesburg, n.d.); Gideon Shimoni, *Jews and Zionism: The South African Experience (1910–1967)* (Cape Town, 1980), 50–51; Jocelyn Hellig, "Religious Expressions," in Marcus Arkin, ed., *South African Jewry: A Contemporary Survey* (Cape Town, 1984), 104–107; David Sherman, *Pioneering for Reform Judaism in South Africa* (n.p., n.d.); South African Union for Progressive Judaism, *The Guide of Practice* (Johannesburg, 1956).

21. Shimoni, *Jews and Zionism,* 278–81.

22. WUPJ, *Report of the Fifth International Conference* (London, 1946), 75–77; *Report of*

the Twelfth International Conference (London, 1961), 116–21; *Annual Report* (1977/78): 3; *Ammi*, 8 (Winter 1978): 8–11; Jocelyn Hellig, "South African Judaism: An Expression of Conservative Traditionalism," *Judaism*, 35 (1986): 233–42.

23. Jerome Mark, "Judaism in Australia," *The Westralian Judean*, April 1, 1932, pp. 4–7, and "Practical Reform in Australia," *ibid.*, June 1, 1932, pp. 5–7; Max Schenk, "Liberal Judaism in Australia," *Liberal Judaism*, June 1943, pp. 48–51; Meir Ydit, "Liberales Judentum in Australien," *TE*, 30 (November 1970): 558–59; Peter Y. Medding, *From Assimilation to Group Survival: A Political and Sociological Study of an Australian Jewish Community* (Melbourne, 1968), 79–92; *idem*, "Orthodoxy, Liberalism and Secularism in Melbourne Jewry," in Peter Y. Medding, ed., *Jews in Australian Society* (Melbourne, 1973), 41–60; Rudolph Brasch, "Letter from Australia," *Pointer*, Winter 1972, pp. 10–11; Richard G. Hirsch, "Letter from Jerusalem," November 13, 1984 (mimeo); and especially Eliot Baskin, "Dinkum Liberal: The Development of Progressive Judaism in Australia" (Rabbinical thesis, HUC–JIR, Cincinnati, 1985). According to A. Isaacs, "Melbourne Reform Judaism in the Nineteenth Century," Small Collections, AJA, some ritual reforms were introduced in the St. Kilda Hebrew Congregation as early as 1871. However, they are not directly connected with the later establishment of Australian Reform Judaism.

24. I have drawn a great deal of the following from Clifford M. Kulwin, "The Emergence of Progressive Judaism in South America" (Rabbinical thesis, HUC–JIR, Cincinnati, 1983). See also WUPJ, *Bulletin*, 15 (December 1943): 9–13; Judith Laikin Elkin, *Jews of the Latin American Republics* (Chapel Hill, N.C., 1980), 165–70; *Ammi*, 18 (Summer 1982).

25. On Panama: Jacobo Sasso to Stanley F. Chyet, October 23, 1964, Misc. File, AJA. On Guatemala: Mordecai Schreiber, *Congregacion Bet-El of Guatemala and the Future of Reform in Latin America* (Guatemala City, 1965); Hanita Schreiber to Anna Klenicki [1965], Correspondence File, AJA. On Curaçao: *PAJHS*, 26 (1918): 239–41. On Cuba: Jeffrey A. Kahn, "The History of the Jewish Colony in Cuba" (Rabbinical thesis, HUC–JIR, Cincinnati, 1981).

26. Interestingly, it was mostly the non-Zionists who pushed for the creation of Reform institutions in Palestine—perhaps thereby compensating for their rejection of Jewish nationalism. Rabbi Louis Wolsey included a proposal to that effect already in his CCAR presidential address in 1926, but nothing came of it. *CCARY*, 36 (1926): 143–44; 37.2 (1927): 74, 157–60.

27. M. Elk, "The Religious Building Up of Palestine" [1936] (mimeo), WUPJ Collection, 7/9, and other items in 7/9 and 7/10, AJA; WUPJ, *Bulletin*, November 1938, pp. 8–11; May 1939, pp. 11–13; November 1940, pp. 11–12; *Report of the Tenth International Conference* (Amsterdam, 1957), 35–37; *Twelfth International Conference*, 157–64; M. Elk, "Liberal Education in Palestine," *Liberal Judaism*, February 1949, pp. 30–37; Ze'ev Harari, "Chapters in the History of the Progressive Jewish Movement in Israel" [Hebrew] (Expanded seminar paper, HUC–JIR, Jerusalem, 1974), 2–5.

28. WUPJ, *Report of the Sixth International Conference* (London, 1949), 26, 74. Baeck elaborated on the metaphor of the ellipse with particular reference to American Jews in his "The State of Israel: The Social Character and the Historical Situation," in *Two Series of Lectures* (New York, [1950]), 43–44.

29. WUPJ, *Report of the Eighth International Conference* (London, 1953), 87–112.

30. *Ibid.*, 12–13, 122; *World Union News*, Fall 1984, p. 4. A similar service existed in Budapest where Neologist Judaism reemerged in the postwar period along with its rabbinical seminary, which became the sole source of spiritual leadership for Jewish communities in eastern Europe. WUPJ, *Bulletin*, January 1948, p. 31; *EJ*, Spring 1978, pp. 28–32.

31. *Tenth International Conference, passim;* WUPJ, *News and Views*, Passover 1967, p. 1.

32. WUPJ, *Bulletin*, July 1949, pp. 23–27; *Report of the Ninth International Conference* (Paris, 1955), 153.

33. *TE*, 1 (September 1957): 3; 6 (1959): 81–82; 38 (November 1974): 18; 43 (September 1977): 17–28. In 1965 the Swiss Progressives published their own Sabbath eve liturgy in German and Hebrew. On it see Petuchowski, *Prayerbook Reform in Europe*, 20, 239.

34. For a few years, beginning in 1965, the Belgian Progressive congregation published a newsletter in French and English called *Shofar.*

35. *La Voce—Ha-Kol,* September–November 1954.

36. WUPJ, *Bulletin,* March 1946, pp. 29–30; April 1947, pp. 46–47; September 1948, pp. 20–21; *Sixth International Conference,* 114; *Report of the Seventh International and Twenty-Fifth Anniversary Conference* (London, 1951), 144; Rabi [Wladimir Rabinovitch], *Anatomie du Judaïsme Français* (Paris, 1962), 158–59.

37. *Tenth International Conference,* 30, 55–59; *Report of the Eleventh International Conference* (London, 1959), 27–28, 32, 39, 58–63; *Twelfth International Conference,* 22, 29, 37, 42–45; *Mélanges de Philosophie et de Littérature Juives,* 1–2 (1957): 9–39; 3–5 (1962): 3–5.

38. WUPJ, *News and Views,* Passover 1967, p. 3; *Annual Report,* 1977–78, p. 2; *Ammi,* Spring 1981, p. 14.

39. Ernst J. Cohn, "Auflösung und Aufbau im englischen Judentum," *TE,* 19 (March 1965): 299–306; Leigh, "Reform Judaism in Britain," 43–49; Sharot, *Judaism,* 156–62.

40. Ellen Littmann, "The First Ten Years of the Leo Baeck College," in Marmur, ed., *Reform Judaism,* 160–78; Jonathan Magonet, "The Empty Pulpit: Rabbinic Needs and Training for European Jewry," *EJ,* Winter 1984/85, pp. 13–22; and various historical articles in *EJ,* Winter 1985/Summer 1986, pp. 2–39.

41. *Ninth International Conference,* 32–33; *Eleventh International Conference,* 185; Jacob K. Shankman, "Dr. Solomon Freehof's Role in the World Union for Progressive Judaism," in Walter Jacob *et al.,* eds., *Essays in Honor of Solomon B. Freehof* (Pittsburgh, 1964), 128–49.

42. England also remained the center for the World Union's Youth Section, established in 1951. The Youth Section linked young Progressive Jews in various lands through a "pen pal" scheme and held regular international summer camps.

43. *Eighth International Conference,* 38–42; Schalom Ben-Chorin, "Die erste progressive Gemeinde in Jerusalem," *TE,* 4 (December 1958): 62–64; WUPJ, *News and Views,* October 1958, p. 4; the interesting eyewitness account in *Maariv,* May 16, 1958, p. 2; and the journalistic essay in *Devar Ha-Shavua,* February 18, 1966, pp. 15ff.

44. *The Movement for Progressive Judaism in Israel* (anonymous pamphlet), Box 582, HUC–JIR Library, Cincinnati; *Haaretz,* August 26, 1983, p. 12.

45. Ephraim Tabori, "Reform and Conservative Judaism in Israel: A Social and Religious Profile," *AJYB,* 83 (1983): 41–61. See also his articles in *JRJ,* Spring 1982, pp. 10–15 and *Midstream,* May 1983, pp. 31–35 as well as the 16 articles by various authors published under the heading "Reform and Conservative Judaism in Israel Today and Tomorrow," in *Judaism,* 31 (1982): 390–458.

46. On the ideological issues, see the journal of the Israeli movement, *Shalhevet,* beginning in 1969; on organizational developments, its newsletter, *Telem,* beginning in 1975. The platform of 1977 is printed in *Telem,* 15 (Tammuz 5737): 1–2.

47. For a detailed analysis, see the review-essay by Eric L. Friedland in *Judaism,* 33 (1984): 114–21.

48. A statement widely circulated in 1984 proclaimed—in Hebrew—that "it is strictly forbidden to pray in Reform or Conservative synagogues in which men and women, boys and girls, pray together using divergent rites. Whoever prays in such a place almost certainly has not fulfilled the obligation of hearing the sound of the *shofar,* or the Torah reading, or prayer."

49. On the political and legal aspects of the Jewish religious situation in Israel see S. Zalman Abramov, *Perpetual Dilemma: Jewish Religion in the Jewish State* (Rutherford, N.J., 1976); on the particular issue of the validity of marriages under Reform auspices see Uri Regev, "Nisuin reformiyim" (Rabbinical thesis, HUC–JIR, Jerusalem, 1984).

50. Bennett H. Greenspon, "The Presentation of Reform Judaism in the Israeli Educational System" (Rabbinical thesis, HUC–JIR, Cincinnati, 1977); Eric H. Yoffie, "Israeli Textbooks on Reform Judaism and Orthodoxy," *JRJ,* Spring 1983, pp. 94–101.

51. "What is needed is a religious reform. . . . Had Ben-Gurion at the height of his power,

intellectual influence, and enormous authority gone to pray on Yom Kippur in an Israeli-style Reform synagogue, instead of shutting himself up in his house for the day to pore over Spinoza or Aristotle, he would have endowed reformist thought with a decisive measure of legitimacy. And reformist thought would of course have undergone a radical process of 'Israelization.' A. B. Yehoshua, "The Golah—As a Neurotic Solution," *Forum on the Jewish People, Zionism, and Israel,* 35 (Spring/Summer 1979): 32.

52. See, for example, Shalom Ben-Chorin, "Progressive Judaism in Israel—A Balance Sheet," *CCARJ,* October 1968, pp. 99–104.

53. On the founding of Yahel see the report in *Davar,* November 13, 1976; for its rationale see Matthew Sperber, "Some Preliminary Thoughts on the Approach to Halacha for the Reform Kibbutz" with comments by Michael Langer" (mimeo), SC Box A-84:90, HUC–JIR Library, Cincinnati. See also the pamphlet containing a dialogue between a portion of the kibbutz movement and the Israeli Progressive movement held at Kibbutz Yahel in April 1978 and published as *Tikun bemasoret yisrael* (n.p., n.d.).

Chapter 10

1. Sydney E. Ahlstrom, *A Religious History of the American People* (New Haven, 1972), 949–63.

2. *CCARY,* 63 (1953): 291; Will Herberg, *Protestant—Catholic—Jew* (New York, 1956), 35, 211; Nathan Glazer, *American Judaism* (Chicago, 1957), 108; Maurice N. Eisendrath, *Can Faith Survive?* (New York, 1964), 256–57; Daniel J. Elazar, *Community and Polity: The Organizational Dynamics of American Jewry* (Philadelphia, 1976), 177–79. For a sampling of Reform rabbis' views and priorities in the late 1940s, see *Reform Judaism: Essays by Hebrew Union College Alumni* (Cincinnati, 1949).

3. *Liberal Judaism,* June–July 1949, pp. 62–65; *CCARJ,* April 1955, pp. 4–7, 47: Jacob Sodden, "The Impact of Suburbanization on the Synagogue" (Ph.D. dissertation, New York University, 1962).

4. Charles Liebman, "Changing Social Characteristics of Orthodox, Conservative and Reform Jews," *Sociological Analysis,* 27 (1966): 210–22.

5. Sodden, "The Impact of Suburbanization on the Synagogue," 295; Marshall Sklare and Joseph Greenblum, *Jewish Identity on the Suburban Frontier* (2d edn., Chicago, 1979), 45–213.

6. *CCARY,* 73 (1963): 165.

7. On Eisendrath see especially Avi M. Schulman, "Visionary and Activist: A Biography of Maurice N. Eisendrath" (Rabbinical thesis, HUC–JIR, Cincinnati, 1984); also *CCARY,* 84 (1974): 205–206; Daniel B. Syme, "Interview with Maurice Eisendrath," May 10, 1972, AJA; and Eisendrath's intellectual autobiography *Can Faith Survive?*

8. *PUAHC,* 71st–73rd Annual Reports (1947): 164; *cf. Liberal Judaism,* April–May 1948, pp. 8–13, 41–44.

9. On the controversy see *AI,* November 11, 1948; its UAHC Biennial Special Edition, November 15, 1948; and November 18, 1948; Morton M. Berman Collection, AJA; *PUAHC,* 74th–76th Annual Reports (1950): 316–21; *Liberal Judaism,* August–September 1948, pp. 42–45; January 1949, pp. 34–36.

10. *Liberal Judaism,* August 1946, pp. 60–62.

11. *Ibid.,* January 1947, pp. 3–7, 32–33; February 1947, pp. 6–9; January 1948, pp. 2–4; March 1948, pp. 16–19; March 1951, pp. 41–42.

12. *AJ,* Spring 1964, p. 12; "UAHC Congregational Surveys" (mimeo), 1958–1962. Although most of the new congregations were in suburban areas, in the late fifties nearly three-quarters of Union membership remained in the central cities, with a declining proportion, which in 1959 reached only one in twenty member families, in isolated smaller towns.

13. *PUAHC,* 71st–73rd Annual Reports (1947): 67; 77th–80th Annual Reports (1955): 355, 378–79, 527.

14. For a detailed history of the College–Institute during the Glueck years see my "A Centennial History," in Samuel E. Karff, ed., *Hebrew Union College–Jewish Institute of Religion At One Hundred Years* (Cincinnati, 1976), 171–243.

15. Sidney L. Regner, "The History of the Conference," in Bertram W. Korn, ed., *Retrospect and Prospect: Essays in Commemoration of the Seventy-Fifth Anniversary of the Founding of the Central Conference of American Rabbis 1889–1964* (New York, 1965), 16.

16. *Liberal Judaism*, August–September 1947, pp. 38–42; November 1947, pp. 49–52; Lance J. Sussman, "The Suburbanization of American Judaism as Reflected in Synagogue Building and Architecture, 1945–1975," *AJH*, 75 (1985/86): 31–47. Solomon Freehof devoted a large portion of his *Reform Jewish Practice*, 2 (Cincinnati, 1952) to halakhic issues in synagogue construction.

17. *Liberal Judaism*, June–July 1947, pp. 8–19; Michael Brown, "The Beginnings of Reform Judaism in Canada," *JSS*, 34 (1972): 322–42; Stuart Schoenfeld, "Canadian Judaism Today," in M. Weinfeld *et al.*, eds., *The Canadian Jewish Mosaic* (Toronto, 1981): 133–34.

18. Max Vorspan and Lloyd P. Gartner, *History of the Jews of Los Angeles* (Philadelphia, 1970), 256–62; Norman T. Mendel, "The Rise and Growth of Reform Judaism in Los Angeles" (Rabbinical thesis, HUC–JIR, Cincinnati, 1968).

19. *CCARY*, 56 (1946): 231.

20. Will Herberg, *Judaism and Modern Man* (New York, 1951).

21. Closest to Herberg's views were the earliest essays of Emil L. Fackenheim. See, for example, his *Quest for Past and Future* (Bloomington, Ind., 1968), 45–47; *AJ*, Chanuko 1953, pp. 4–5. Samuel S. Cohon severely criticized the extreme form of the existentialist trend in *CCARY*, 63 (1953): 348–85.

22. See Olan's essays in *CCARY*, 58 (1948): 255–84; 66 (1956): 197–215; 72 (1962): 226–39; Bernard Martin, ed., *Contemporary Reform Jewish Thought* (Chicago, 1968), 21–38; and Jack Bemporad, ed., *A Rational Faith* (New York, 1977), 185–208. That Olan was not, however, a naturalist is clear from his response to Roland B. Gittelsohn in *CCARY*, 74 (1964): 204–208.

23. See Roland B. Gittelsohn, *Man's Best Hope* (New York, 1961) and his "No Retreat from Reason!" in *CCARY*, 74 (1964): 191–203; Alvin J. Reines, "God and Jewish Theology," in Martin, ed., *Contemporary Reform Jewish Thought*, 62–87; Sherwin T. Wine, *Humanistic Judaism* (New York, 1978); Norman B. Mirsky, *Unorthodox Judaism* (Columbus, 1978), 112–25.

24. For a discussion of their influence see Lou H. Silberman, "Concerning Jewish Theology in North America: Some Notes on a Decade," *AJYB*, 70 (1969): 41–45. Early essays on Buber and Rosenzweig by American Reform rabbis appear in *CCARY*, 44 (1934): 203–219; 62 (1952): 410–434; *Liberal Judaism*, April–May 1948, pp. 45–48, 65.

25. The names are listed in W. Gunther Plaut, *Unfinished Business* (Toronto, 1981), 182.

26. *Judaism*, 12 (1963): 479–86.

27. Arnold Jacob Wolf, "Introduction," in A. J. Wolf, ed., *Rediscovering Judaism: Reflections on a New Theology* (Chicago, 1965), 7–11.

28. *CCARJ*, October 1957, pp. 13–18; June 1966, pp. 12–23; Fackenheim, *Quest for Past and Future*, 8, 131; Eugene B. Borowitz, *A New Jewish Theology in the Making* (Philadelphia, 1968), 63–68; Jakob J. Petuchowski, *Ever Since Sinai* (3d edn., Milwaukee, 1979), 64–65, 123.

29. Borowitz, *A New Theology*, 189–95; *idem*, "Faith and Method in Modern Jewish Theology," in Martin, ed., *Contemporary Reform Jewish Thought*, 3–20; Jakob J. Petuchowski, "The Dialectics of Reason and Revelation," in Wolf, ed., *Rediscovering Judaism*, 29–50; Fackenheim, *Quest for Past and Future*, 146–47.

30. Daniel Jeremy Silver, ed., *Judaism and Ethics* (New York, 1970); Eugene B. Borowitz, *Choosing a Sex Ethic: A Jewish Inquiry* (New York, 1969).

31. *Liberal Judaism*, July 1946, p. 42. An early use of the term "Holocaust" occurs in *ibid.*, June–July 1948, p. 53.

32. *CCARY*, 63 (1953): 429.

33. *Dimension,* Spring 1967, pp. 3–32; Albert H. Friedlander, ed., *Out of the Whirlwind* (New York, 1968).

34. *Judaism,* 16 (1967): 272; Fackenheim, *Quest for Past and Future,* 20; idem, *God's Presence in History* (New York, 1970), 67–104; Silberman, "Concerning Jewish Theology," 56–58; Michael A. Meyer, "Judaism after Auschwitz," *Commentary,* June 1972, pp. 59–61.

35. Eugene B. Borowitz, *The Masks Jews Wear: The Self-Deceptions of American Jewry* (New York, 1973), 204–205.

36. *Justice and Judaism* (New York, 1956) was the work of a layman, Albert Vorspan, then executive secretary of the commission, and Rabbi Eugene J. Lipman, its director.

37. *CCARY,* 67 (1957): 88.

38. *Ibid.,* 57 (1947): 65; 58 (1948): 163–64; 60 (1950): 137–50; 62 (1952): 147–62; 70 (1960): 39–42; *Resolutions of the Central Conference Passed by the Central Conference of American Rabbis, 1889–1974* (rev. edn., New York, 1975), 8–9, 23, 25, 47–48; *Where We Stand: Social Action Resolutions Adopted by the Union of American Hebrew Congregations* (rev. edn., New York, 1980), 33–36, 38–39, 57–59, 64; Fred Rosenbaum, *Architects of Reform* (Berkeley, 1980), 159–61.

39. *CCARY,* 56 (1946): 362–68; 58 (1948): 118–26.

40. *AJ,* Rosh Ha-Shono 1956, p. 20.

41. *CCARY,* 71 (1961): 7; 74 (1964): 5, 86; 75 (1965): 103; *AJ,* Winter 1964/65, p. 25.

42. *CCARY,* 74 (1964): 242–53; *AJ,* Winter 1962/63, pp. 8–9, 51.

43. *CCARY,* June 1956, pp. 1–3.

44. Perry E. Nussbaum to Solomon K. Kaplan, October 28, 1963, Nussbaum Collection, AJA. King nonetheless did speak.

45. *CCARY,* 78 (1968): 138; P. Allen Krause, "Rabbis and Negro Rights in the South, 1954–1967," *AJ,* 21 (1969): 20–47; Janice Rothschild Blumberg, *One Voice: Rabbi Jacob M. Rothschild and the Troubled South* (Atlanta, 1985), 55–96.

46. Emily R. and Kivie Kaplan Religious Action Center Scrapbook, AJA.

47. The following is based largely on Irwin A. Zeplowitz, "Jewish Attitudes Toward the Vietnam War" (Rabbinical thesis, HUC–JIR, Cincinnati, 1984).

48. *AJ,* Winter 1966/67, p. 25.

49. *CCARY,* 76 (1966): 19; 77 (1967): 104.

50. *Ibid.,* 9.

51. *Ibid.,* 76 (1966): 37–41; 77 (1967): 53; 78 (1968): 38–65; 79 (1969): 42–72.

52. *Ibid.,* 82 (1972): 21–24; 83 (1973): 48–49.

53. The Reform rabbis had taken a collective interest in the plight of Soviet Jewry as early as 1956. *Ibid.,* 66 (1956): 138–39.

54. *PUAHC,* 74th–76th Annual Reports (1950): 305.

55. Eugene J. Lipman and Albert Vorspan, eds., *A Tale of Ten Cities: The Triple Ghetto in American Religious Life* (New York, 1962).

56. Leon Fram to Maurice N. Eisendrath, November 11, 1969, Eisendrath Collection, 4/2, AJA.

57. *RJ,* October 1972, pp. 6–7.

58. Daniel Jeremy Silver, "A Lover's Quarrel with the Mission of Israel," *CCARJ,* June 1967, p. 16.

59. Richard G. Hirsch, "Toward a Theology for Social Action," *CCARJ,* January 1968, pp. 67–74; *RJ,* November 1973, p. 9. In the period 1972–1977 about 40 percent of UAHC social action resolutions dealt with specifically Jewish issues. In the preceding fifteen years the percentage had been less than 20. Simeon J. Maslin, "The Language of Survival: Social Action," *CCARJ,* Summer 1977, pp. 20–21.

60. *AJ,* Purim 1960, p. 4; UAHC, *Statistical and Financial Data, 1970/71* (New York, 1971); *CCARJ,* October 1971, p. 28; "Mergers, Congregational" File, AJA; *RJ,* March 1974, p. 4.

61. UAHC, *Statistical and Financial Data, 1975/76* (New York, 1976); *CCARY,* 85 (1975): 47–59.

62. *CCARY,* 79 (1969): 241; 86 (1976): 127–43; Elazar, *Community and Polity* , 341–77; Jonathan S. Woocher, *Sacred Survival: The Civil Religion of American Jews* (Bloomington, Ind., 1986). For a local example, see Rosenbaum, *Architects of Reform,* 188–90.

63. Glazer, *American Judaism,* 108; *AJYB,* 59 (1958): 114–17; 74 (1973): 282; Marshall Sklare, *Conservative Judaism* (aug. ed., New York, 1972), 253–55.

64. Bernard J. Bamberger, "The American Rabbi—His Changing Role," *Judaism,* 3 (1954): 488–97; Walter Jacob, "The Decline of the Sermon," *CCARJ,* January 1964, pp. 48–51; Arthur Hertzberg, "The Changing American Rabbinate," *Midstream,* January 1966, pp. 16–29; Morris Lieberman, "The Role and Functions of the Modern Rabbi," *CCARY,* 79 (1969): 211–24; Eugene B. Borowitz, "Tzimtzum: A Mystic Model for Contemporary Leadership," *Religious Education,* November–December 1974, pp. 687–700; Robert L. Katz, "Changing Self-Concepts of Reform Rabbis: 1976," *CCARJ,* Summer 1976, pp. 51–56.

65. *CCARY,* 75 (1965): 89–92; Theodore I. Lenn and Associates, *Rabbi and Synagogue in Reform Judaism* (West Hartford, Conn., 1972), 75, 91, 102, 138, 187, 195.

66. *CCARY,* 78 (1968): 6–7; *CCARJ,* Winter 1973, pp. 3–21; Meyer, "A Centennial History," 233–35, 242. For a comparative treatment see Charles S. Liebman, "The Training of American Rabbis," *AJYB,* 69 (1968): 3–112.

67. Leonard J. Fein *et al., Reform Is a Verb: Notes on Reform and Reforming Jews* (New York, 1972), 37, 74, 140–52. At just the same time the Conservative movement was undergoing a similar crisis of morale. It was brought about by a resurgence in Orthodoxy on the one hand and the steady erosion of observance among the Conservative laity on the other. In Providence, Rhode Island only 12 percent of Conservative Jews were attending religious services once a week. In the third generation the figure was only 2 percent. Most Conservative Jews did not observe *kashrut.* Only a small minority were living by the halakhic standards of their movement. See Sklare, *Conservative Judaism,* 261–82.

68. Allen S. Maller and Marc Lee Raphael, "The Cost of Mixed Marriages," *CCARJ,* April 1971, pp. 83–85. For a highly polemical but valuable presentation of the case for officiation, see David Max Eichhorn, *Jewish Intermarriages: Fact and Fiction* (Satellite Beach, Fl., 1974). See also Eichhorn's letter to Jacob R. Marcus, November 1, 1972, Miscellaneous Files, AJA. Proponents of rabbinical officiation could point to the relative increase in the number of instances where, when the couple came to a rabbi, the Jewish partner was the woman, and to the statistically proven greater likelihood in such instances that the children would be raised as Jews.

69. Lenn, *Rabbi and Synagogue in Reform Judaism,* 128, 134; Irwin H. Fishbein, "Marrying 'in,' Not 'out,'" *CCARJ,* Spring 1973, pp. 31–34; Allen S. Maller, "Mixed Marriage and Reform Rabbis," *Judaism,* 24 (1975): 39–48. A survey conducted in 1937 had revealed that almost a third of Reform rabbis at that time officiated at mixed marriages: 7 percent with no conditions, 26 percent only with conditions. *CCARY,* 47 (1937): 314–23.

70. *CCARY,* 57 (1947): 158–72; 72 (1962): 94.

71. *CCARY,* 81 (1971): 15–16; 83 (1973): 59–97. All eleven living past presidents of the CCAR signed a statement favoring the resolution against rabbinical officiation. About a hundred Reform rabbis who had opposed the 1973 decision briefly joined in a CCAR caucus called the Association for a Progressive Reform Judaism. They pledged to support greater individual autonomy and giving the laity a larger share in decision making, *RJ,* November 1974, p. 7.

72. *Dimensions in American Judaism,* Fall 1970, pp. 4–16; *CCARY,* 79 (1969): 143; 85 (1975): 61–64; 87 (1977): 92; *Where We Stand,* 120–21.

73. *Liberal Judaism,* May 1946, pp. 90–93; *CCARJ,* October 1953, pp. 19–28; June 1954, pp. 26–27, 46; October 1960, pp. 31–33; *CCARY,* 72 (1962): 157–65. South Shore Temple in Chicago had the Bat Mitzvah ceremony as early as 1931. By 1953, 35 percent of Reform congregations had it, with a much larger percentage having Bar Mitzvah.

74. Abraham W. Binder, "New Trends in Synagogue Music," *CCARJ,* January 1955; Bennett

F. Miller, "A Time to Sing: Reform Synagogue Music Today" (Rabbinical thesis, HUC–JIR, Cincinnati, 1974); *Shirim U-Zemirot—Songs and Hymns, A Musical Supplement to Gates of Prayer* (New York, 1977).

75. *Hagadah Shel Pesah—A Passover Haggadah* (New York, 1974).

76. *CCARJ,* October 1959, pp. 8–21; April 1965, pp. 3–42; October 1967, pp. 11–49; Spring 1973, pp. 73–91; Jakob J. Petuchowski, "Bookbinder to the Rescue!," *Conservative Judaism,* Fall 1975, pp. 7–15. For the theoretical bases of liturgical differences see Jack Bemporad, ed., *The Theological Foundations of Prayer: A Reform Jewish Perspective* (New York, 1967). The new prayerbook could be ordered in versions opening like a Hebrew book or like an English one. At first the latter was the more popular. Later sales of the two versions were roughly equal.

77. *AJ,* Purim 1954, p. 22; Stephen Sharot, *Judaism: A Sociology* (New York, 1976), 165. Since one must assume that the respondents to surveys are the more committed Reform Jews, the percentage figures for observance are maximal.

78. *CCARY,* 73 (1963): 163–64.

79. An important early influence seems to have been a lecture by the Conservative theologian Abraham J. Heschel, "Toward an Understanding of Halacha," *CCARY,* 63 (1953): 386–409. Then see Frederic A. Doppelt, "Criteria for a Guide of Practices in Reform Judaism" and Jakob J. Petuchowski, "Problems of Reform Halakhah," *Judaism,* 4 (1955): 254–62, 339–51; and David Polish, "Opportunities for Reform Judaism," *CCARJ,* October 1957, pp. 13–18.

80. William B. Silverman, "A Code of Practice," *Liberal Judaism,* December 1949, pp. 1–5; Eisendrath in *PUAHC,* 74th–76th Annual Reports (1950): 315; "The Survey of Current Reform Practice" (mimeo), April 21, 1953, Morton M. Berman file, AJA.

81. Jerome D. Folkman, *Design for Jewish Living: A Guide for the Bride and Groom* (New York, 1955); Abraham J. Feldman, *Reform Judaism: A Guide for Reform Jews* (New York, 1956). Later examples are Stanley R. Brav, *A Guide to Religious Practice* (Cincinnati, 1962) and Morrison David Bial, *Liberal Judaism at Home: The Practices of Modern Reform Judaism* (Summit, N.J., 1967).

82. See the review of Conservative rabbi Max Arzt in *Judaism,* 6 (1957): 372–74.

83. During the same period Conservative Judaism was moving in the direction of greater religious reform. In 1950 it allowed riding to synagogue on Sabbaths and festivals, in 1969 made observance of second days of festivals optional, and in 1973 gave equal religious status (but not yet ordination) to women. *Judaism,* 25 (1976): 300n. For a recent history of the Conservative movement down to 1985, see Abraham J. Karp, "A Century of Conservative Judaism in the United States," *AJYB,* 86 (1986): 3–61.

84. *AJ,* Winter 1966/67, pp. 19, 24; *RJ,* November 1973, p. 4.

85. Stuart A. Gertman, "The Language of Survival: Curriculum and Textbook," *CCARJ,* Summer 1977, pp. 37–47; *idem, "And You Shall Teach Them Diligently"—A Study of the Current State of Religious Education in the Reform Movement* (New York, 1977); Jeffrey Schein, "Changes in the Reform Curriculum," *JRJ,* Spring 1982, pp. 58–68.

86. *CCARY,* 86 (1976): 76–91.

87. Sylvan D. Schwartzman, "Who Wants Reform All-Day Schools?" *CCARJ,* April 1964, pp. 3–10, 13; Samuel Glasner and Elliot D. Rosenstock, "The Case For/Against a Reform Jewish Day School," *Dimensions in American Judaism,* Summer 1969, pp. 36–39; Daniel B. Syme, "Reform Judaism and Day Schools: The Great Historical Dilemma," *Religious Education,* 78 (1983): 153–81.

88. *AJ,* January 1958, pp. 20–21; *CCARY,* 65 (1955): 13–14; 66 (1956): 3, 90–93; Meyer, "A Centennial History," 98–99; Ellen M. Umansky, "Women in Judaism: From the Reform Movement to Contemporary Jewish Religious Feminism," in Rosemary Ruether and Eleanor McLaughlin, eds., *Women of Spirit: Female Leadership in the Jewish and Christian Traditions* (New York, 1979), 333–54; Garry Allan Loeb, "The Changing Religious Role of the Reform Jewish Woman" (Rabbinical thesis, HUC–JIR, Cincinnati, 1981); Jacob R. Marcus, *The American Jewish Woman: A Documentary History* (New York, 1981), 739–44, 887–93; Alexander

Guttmann, "The Woman Rabbi: An Historical Perspective," *CCARJ*, Summer 1982, pp. 21–25.

89. UAHC, *Synagogue Research Survey No. 11*, September 1971, pp. 10–11; *CCARY*, 85 (1975): 70–71; *RJ*, November 1976, pp. 5, 7.

90. David Max Eichhorn, "Conversions to Judaism by Reform and Conservative Rabbis," *JSS*, 16 (1954): 299–318; Joseph R. Rosenbloom, "Intermarriage and Conversion in the United States," in Bertram Wallace Korn, ed., *A Bicentennial Festschrift for Jacob Rader Marcus* (Waltham, Mass., 1976), 495–99; Freehof, *Reform Jewish Practice*, 2: 128–29; *AJA*, 25 (1973): 105–108; *CCARY*, 67 (1957): 97–100; *AJ*, Winter 1965/66, p. 9.

91. CCAR, *Rabbi's Manual* (rev. edn., New York, 1961), 17–22, 116–17; Herbert Weiner, "Conversion: Is Reform Judaism So Right?," *Dimensions in American Judaism*, Winter 1971, pp. 4–7. The statistics for ritual conversion requirements by Reform and Conservative rabbis in 1953 are in *JSS*, 16 (1954): 309.

92. Frank J. Adler, *Roots in a Moving Stream* (Kansas City, Mo., 1972), 291; Steven Huberman, *New Jews: The Dynamics of Religious Conversion* (New York, 1979); Lydia Kukoff, *Choosing Judaism* (New York, 1981). Since their conversions were not recognized by Orthodox Jews, the converts were also more likely than born Reform Jews to give greater emphasis to their Reform than to their general Jewish identity.

93. Peter J. Rubinstein and Sheldon Zimmerman, "Congregational Perceptions: The Tale of the Tapes," *CCARJ*, Summer 1977, pp. 3–17.

94. Harold Schulweis, "Changing Models of the Synagogue and the Rabbi's Role," *CCARY*, 85 (1975): 136–43.

95. *CCARY*, 76 (1966): 81–82; *CCARJ*, Winter 1975, pp. 31–40; Spring 1975, pp. 45–55; Bernard Reisman, *The Chavurah: A Contemporary Jewish Experience* (New York, 1977); Gerald B. Bubis *et al.*, *Synagogue Havurot: A Comparative Study* (Washington, D.C., 1983).

96. *RJ*, March 1974, p. 4; November 1975, p. 11; *CCARY*, 87 (1977): 75; Bernard Lazerwitz, "Past and Future Trends in the Size of American Jewish Denominations," *CCARJ*, Summer 1979, pp. 77–82; Floyd J. Fowler, *1975 Community Survey: A Study of the Jewish Population of Greater Boston* (Boston, 1977); Mark L. Winer, "Jewish Demography and the Challenges to Reform Jewry," *CCARJ*, Winter 1984, pp. 1–27. The role of geographical location in the relative size of the movements is apparent from the table in *AJYB*, 85 (1985): 171.

97. *CCARY*, 87 (1977): 20–22; UAHC, *Report of the Ad Hoc Committee on Zionist Affiliation* (mimeo, New York, 1977); *Where We Stand*, 119.

98. CCAR Records, 25/16, 26/1-2, 26/8, 27/2, AJA.

99. *CCARJ*, Summer 1973, pp. 55–62; *CCARY*, 85 (1975): 5–9; Transcript of 1976 CCAR Convention, 143–46, CCAR Records. For the text of the platform see Appendix. A collective commentary constitutes *CCARJ*, Spring 1977. See also Borowitz's own extensive personal interpretation, *Reform Judaism Today*, 3 vols. (New York, 1977–78).

Bibliographical
Essay

The historiography of Reform Judaism goes back to a four-volume work by Immanuel Heinrich Ritter, who served as a preacher for the Reform Congregation in Berlin. Entitled *History of the Jewish Reformation,* it began to appear in 1858.[1] Despite its title and length, it was not a comprehensive history but a biographical treatment of selected figures, followed by a historical monograph on Ritter's own congregation. Moreover, it was severely compromised by the author's personal commitments. As an advocate of radical reform, Ritter had little patience with moderates and even less understanding for the outlook of traditional Judaism. In his ideologically skewed perspective, radical figures, like David Friedländer and Samuel Holdheim, appear as central. Yet Ritter produced a valuable insight in suggesting that the Christian writer Gotthold Ephraim Lessing, who put forward a notion of religious evolution, was more influential in determining the ideology of the Reform movement than his Jewish friend Moses Mendelssohn, who believed that Judaism was founded on eternal verities and fixed revelation.[2]

A work similar to Ritter's in stressing the biographical element appeared in the United States toward the end of the last century.[3] Its author, Emanuel Schreiber, was a Reform rabbi in Spokane, Washington, who had studied with Abraham Geiger in Berlin. Each of the nine chapters of his volume is devoted to a single European reformer who advanced the cause. Written in a polemical tone and little read today, the work did make two important contributions: it brought the first integrated awareness of the movement's history in Europe to English readers and it laid down distinct periods in its early development. Schreiber called these periods the "humanistic," the "aesthetical–homiletical," and the "historical–critical." Though requiring refinement and modification, his periodization in general still possesses considerable validity.

The first attempt at a nonbiographical history of Reform Judaism was undertaken by a prolific scholar outside the movement and highly critical of it. Simon Bernfeld was a Jewish nationalist who saw in the movement for religious reform a threat to the unity of the Jewish people and its national aspirations. His *History of the Religious Reformation in Israel,* which appeared in its first edition in 1900 when Bernfeld was living in Berlin, was written in Hebrew and had little in common with the studies of Ritter or Schreiber, except that the title, like Ritter's, suggested a parallel with the Protestant Reformation.[4] Bernfeld readily admitted that the subject of his study was "odious" in his eyes and that he was more sympathetic to a conservative interpretation of Judaism because it put less strain on the bonds of Jewish national unity. He believed that underlying the Reform movement was the widespread desire to "ease the yoke of religion," for which it provided justification; neglect of Jewish law was not without precedent, but never before had it been made into an ideology. All other attempts at explanation, in Bernfeld's view, were mere rationalization. Conceiving the history of the Reform movement as a series of controversies between reformers and traditionalists, Bernfeld set himself up as the historical judge who determines in retrospect the merit of each side's cause. Yet he frankly admitted that it was beyond his capacity to exercise the role with objectivity. Bernfeld's book was reprinted in 1908; a slightly expanded edition appeared in 1923. Still in the 1980s Israeli readers turned to it as an authoritative study and as the most comprehensive treatment of the subject available in Hebrew.[5]

If Bernfeld's history was the work of an outsider lacking sympathetic understanding, the volume which David Philipson, a Reform rabbi in Cincinnati, Ohio, published in 1907 was the creation of an enthusiastic advocate, one of the central figures within the American movement. His *The Reform Movement in Judaism,* revised in 1931 and reprinted in 1967, remained the standard work on the subject in English eighty years after it first appeared.[6] Nothing written after it had been as comprehensive and detailed. Yet its defects and shortcomings are many. Repeatedly, Philipson inserted himself as an apologist for that universalistic conception of Reform Judaism which was prevalent in America at the turn of the century. Like Bernfeld, he too saw himself as the judge of history, except that his evidence for a favorable decision was precisely what swayed his predecessor to condemnation—radical reform in thought and practice. Philipson dwelled especially on practical activity. He lavished attention on rabbinical conferences, synods, new congregations and associations, and controversies with the Orthodox. He arranged the material chronologically and quoted extensively from the sources, but he failed to probe the causes of the movement's fluctuating fortunes. He was too much of a partisan to appreciate the problematic elements within Reform itself. Employing only printed sources bearing directly on the ideology and activity of the movement, Philipson neglected its social base and its relation to European philosophy and modern Christianity. He also neglected the biographical element almost completely, allowing leading figures to appear merely as spokesmen for particular points of view. We learn very little from him about individual motivation. Modern Jewish theology fell outside Philipson's domain since it produced no immediate practical effects, while eastern Europe was wholly excluded because religious reform there did not result in any "organized effort to break away from the rabbinical interpretation of Judaism." Surprisingly, in view of his belief that the future of the movement lay in America, Philipson devoted only a single chapter to "Reform in the United States." From the perspective of the present, his volume seems narrow, superficial, and misfocused.

The period between the world wars produced only two additional books dealing directly with our subject, both of them in German and concentrating almost exclusively on Germany. Caesar Seligmann, a Liberal rabbi in Frankfurt-on-the-Main, published a brief, readable history of the movement which sought to move away from Ritter's and Schreiber's excessive focus on personalities and Philipson's on events.[7] Instead he tried to discover the gradual, less obvious changes in idea and sentiment, the transitions and the spiritual connections. In 1933, Max Wiener, one of the most important scholars and thinkers of late German Liberal Judaism, published an intellectual history of modern Jewry of which about a quarter dealt directly with the history of the Reform movement.[8] Wiener's treatment of the subject represented an important breakthrough. For the first time, the author's own predisposition was not a significant factor. Wiener did not write as the partisan of any one faction in modern Jewry and therefore was remarkably able to see the strengths and weaknesses of competing positions. He was also the first to appreciate fully the influence of external ideas and circumstances as well as inner continuities.

The postwar years have produced two useful volumes of selected, mostly abbreviated sources edited by W. Gunther Plaut and a valuable history of liturgical change in modern European Jewry by Jakob J. Petuchowski.[9] There has also been a continuation of the popular didactic strain, intended to reinforce Reform Jewish identity.[10] On the other hand the wholly unsympathetic current of historiography, manifest in the general Jewish history of the conservatively religious Jew Heinrich Graetz in the nineteenth century and of the Jewish nationalist and secularist Simon Dubnow in the early twentieth, has received new expression as well. For the first time it appeared in an ideological perspective combining Marxism with Zionism in the modern Jewish history of Raphael Mahler.[11]

One can best follow the current situation of the Israeli movement in its newsletter *Kolot* and in the *ARZA Newsletter,* European developments in *European Judaism.* The contemporary American movement is reflected in *Reform Judaism,* published by the Union of American Hebrew Congregations. The deliberations of the Central Conference of American Rabbis appear in its *Yearbook,* while broader concerns receive attention in the quarterly *Journal for Reform Judaism.*

Notes

1. Immanuel Heinrich Ritter, *Geschichte der jüdischen Reformation,* 4 vols. (Berlin, 1858–1902).

2. The extent of this influence has been traced by Michael Graetz, *"Die Erziehung des Menschengeschlechts* und jüdisches Selbstbewusstsein im 19. Jahrhundert," *Wolfenbütteler Studien zur Aufklärung,* 4 (1977): 273–95.

3. Emanuel Schreiber, *Reformed Judaism and Its Pioneers: A Contribution to Its History* (Spokane, Wash., 1892).

4. Simon Bernfeld, *Toledot ha-reformatsyon ha-datit be-yisrael* (Cracow, 1900).

5. Y. Zvi Zehavi, *Tenuat ha-hitbolelut be-yisrael* (Tel-Aviv, 1943) is less significant and even more tendentious than Bernfeld's volume. Zehavi suggests that the Reform movement's sole purpose was to advance Jewish assimilation. He makes Zionism out to be its "antithesis," which rescued the Jewish people from the "great danger" posed by Reform (pp. 23, 65).

6. The most recent reissue (New York, 1967) contains a brief critical introduction by Solomon B. Freehof. See my review in *AJHQ,* 57 (1968): 439–40. An early comparative critique of Bernfeld and Philipson by David Neumark appeared in *Ha-Shiloah,* 19 (1908): 566–73.

7. Caesar Seligmann, *Geschichte der jüdischen Reformbewegung* (Frankfurt a/M, 1922).

8. Max Wiener, *Jüdische Religion im Zeitalter der Emanzipation* (Berlin, 1933). A Hebrew translation was published in Jerusalem in 1974.

9. W. Gunther Plaut, *The Rise of Reform Judaism: A Sourcebook of Its European Origins* (New York, 1963) and *The Growth of Reform Judaism: American and European Sources until 1948* (New York, 1965); Jakob J. Petuchowski, *Prayerbook Reform in Europe: The Liturgy of European Liberal and Reform Judaism* (New York, 1968).

10. For example, Sylvan D. Schwartzman, *Reform Judaism in the Making* (New York, 1955). See also his textbook on the subject entitled *Reform Judaism Then and Now* (New York, 1971) and the text by Eugene B. Borowitz and Naomi Patz, *Explaining Reform Judaism* (New York, 1985).

11. Raphael Mahler, *Divre yeme yisrael dorot aharonim,* 2 (Merhavya, 1954): 160–71; 7 (Tel-Aviv, 1980): 115–86.

Index